Advanced Textbooks in Economics

Series Editors: C.J. Bliss *and* M.D. Intriligator

Currently Available: for details see http://www.elsevier.nl

Volume 17: *Stochastic Methods in Economics and Finance*
A.G. MALLIARIS and W.A. BROCK

Volume 23: *Public Enterprise Economics* (Second Revised Edition)
D. BÖS

Volume 24: *Optimal Control Theory with Economic Applications*
A. SEIERSTAD and K. SYDSAETER

Volume 25: *Capital Markets and Prices: Valuing Uncertain Income Streams*
C.G. KROUSE

Volume 26: *History of Economic Theory*
T. NEGISHI

Volume 27: *Differential Equations, Stability and Chaos in Dynamic Economics*
W.A. BROCK and A.G. MALLIARIS

Volume 28: *Equilibrium Analysis*
W. HILDENBRAND and A.P. KIRMAN

Volume 29: *Economics of Insurance*
K.H. BORCH†; completed by K.K. AASE and A.SANDMO

Volume 31: *Dynamic Optimization* (Second Revised Edition)
M.I. KAMIEN and N.L. SCHWARTZ†

Volume 34: *Pricing and Price Regulation. An Economic Theory for Public Enterprises and Public Utilities*
D. BÖS

Volume 35: *Macroeconomic Theory. Volume A: Framework, Households and Firms*
E. MALINVAUD
Macroeconomic Theory. Volume B: Economic Growth and Short-Term Equilibrium
E. MALINVAUD
Macroeconomic Theory: Volume C: Inflation, Employment and Business Fluctuations
E. MALINVAUD

Volume 36: *Principles of Macroeconometric Modeling*
L.R. KLEIN, A. WELFE and W.WELFE

MEASUREMENT ERROR AND LATENT VARIABLES IN ECONOMETRICS

ADVANCED TEXTBOOKS IN ECONOMICS

VOLUME 37

ELSEVIER

Amsterdam – London – New York – Oxford – Paris – Shannon – Tokyo

MEASUREMENT ERROR AND LATENT VARIABLES IN ECONOMETRICS

Tom WANSBEEK
Erik MEIJER

F.E.W., Rijksuniversiteit Groningen, Groningen, The Netherlands

N·H

2000

ELSEVIER
Amsterdam – London – New York – Oxford – Paris – Shannon – Tokyo

ELSEVIER SCIENCE B.V.
Sara Burgerhartstraat 25
P.O. Box 211, 1000 AE Amsterdam, The Netherlands

First edition 2000

Library of Congress Cataloging in Publication Data

Measurement error and latent variables in econometrics / Tom Wansbeek, Erik Meijer.
p. cm. -- (Advanced textbooks in economics, ISSN 01695568 ; 37)
Includes bibliographical references and index.
ISBN 0-444-88100-X (hardbound : alk. paper)
1. Econometrics. 2. Latent variables. I. Wansbeek, Tom J. II. Meijer, Erik, 1963- III. Series.

HB139 .M43 2000
330'.01'5195--dc21

00-052123

ISBN: 0-444-88100-X
ISSN: 0169-5568

∞ The paper used in this publication meets the requirements of ANSI/NISO Z39.48-1992 (Permanence of Paper).
Printed in The Netherlands.

INTRODUCTION TO THE SERIES

The aim of the series is to cover topics in economics, mathematical economics and econometrics, at a level suitable for graduate students or final year undergraduates specializing in economics. There is at any time much material that has become well established in journal papers and discussion series which still awaits a clear, self-contained treatment that can easily be mastered by students without considerable preparation or extra reading. Leading specialists will be invited to contribute volumes to fill such gaps. Primary emphasis will be placed on clarity, comprehensive coverage of sensibly defined areas, and insight into fundamentals, but original ideas will not be excluded. Certain volumes will therefore add to existing knowledge, while others will serve as a means of communicating both known and new ideas in a way that will inspire and attract students not already familiar with the subject matter concerned.

The Editors

Acknowledgments

In writing this book, we are greatly indebted to Paul Bekker and Arie Kapteyn. Various parts of the book are based on joint work with Paul and Arie, and other parts benefitted from their advice and suggestions. Bart Boon critically read large parts of the manuscript and made many detailed suggestions for improvements. Hiek van der Scheer provided excellent research assistance. We also gratefully acknowledge helpful discussions with Jos ten Berge, Ruud Koning, Geert Ridder, and Ton Steerneman.

Finally, we would like to thank Mike Intriligator, co-editor of this series, for his steady encouragement and cheerful patience over many years.

Groningen, September 2000

Tom Wansbeek
Erik Meijer

Contents

1. Introduction **1**

1.1 Measurement error and latent variables 1
1.2 About this book 4
1.3 Bibliographical notes 7

2. Regression and measurement error **9**

2.1 The model 10
2.2 Asymptotic properties of the OLS estimators 12
2.3 Attenuation 17
2.4 Errors in a single regressor 22
2.5 Various additional results 25
2.6 Bibliographical notes 30

3. Bounds on the parameters **33**

3.1 Reverse regression 34
3.2 Reverse regression and the analysis of discrimination 36
3.3 Bounds with multiple regression 43
3.4 Bounds on the measurement error 46
3.5 Uncorrelated measurement error 52
3.6 Bibliographical notes 56

4. Identification **59**

4.1 Structural versus functional models 60
4.2 Maximum likelihood estimation in the structural model 65
4.3 Maximum likelihood estimation in the functional model 70
4.4 General identification theory 74
4.5 Identification of the measurement error model under normality 78
4.6 A general identification condition in the structural model 82
4.7 Bibliographical notes 87

5. Consistent adjusted least squares **89**

5.1 The CALS estimator 90
5.2 Measurement error variance known 94
5.3 Weighted regression 101
5.4 Orthogonal regression 104
5.5 Bibliographical notes 107

6. Instrumental variables **109**

6.1 Assumptions and estimation 110
6.2 Application to the measurement error model 114
6.3 Heteroskedasticity 118
6.4 Combining data from various sources 120
6.5 Limited information maximum likelihood 123
6.6 LIML and weak instruments 128
6.7 Grouping 131
6.8 Instrumental variables and nonnormality 135
6.9 Measurement error in panel data 138
6.10 Bibliographical notes 143

7. Factor analysis and related methods **147**

7.1 Towards factor analysis 148
7.2 Estimation in the one-factor FA model 151
7.3 Multiple factor analysis 159
7.4 An example of factor analysis 171
7.5 Principal relations and principal factors 175
7.6 A taxonomy of eigenvalue-based methods 178
7.7 Bibliographical notes 182

8. Structural equation models **185**

8.1 Confirmatory factor analysis 186
8.2 Multiple causes and the MIMIC model 191
8.3 The LISREL model 194
8.4 Other important general parameterizations 202
8.5 Scaling of the variables 207
8.6 Extensions of the model 214
8.7 Equivalent models 218
8.8 Bibliographical notes 222

9. Generalized method of moments **227**

9.1 The method of moments 228
9.2 Definition and notation 232
9.3 Basic properties of GMM estimators 236
9.4 Estimation of the covariance matrix of the sample moments 243
9.5 Covariance structures 252
9.6 Asymptotic efficiency and additional information 257
9.7 Conditional moments 261
9.8 Simulated GMM 262
9.9 The efficiency of GMM and ML 266
9.10 Bibliographical notes 273

10. Model evaluation **279**

10.1 Specification tests 280
10.2 Comparison of the three tests 290
10.3 Test of overidentifying restrictions 296
10.4 Robustness 301
10.5 Model fit and model selection 303
10.6 Bibliographical notes 311

11. Nonlinear latent variable models **317**

11.1 A simple nonlinear model 318
11.2 Polynomial models 319
11.3 Models for qualitative and limited-dependent variables 325
11.4 The LISCOMP model 331
11.5 General parametric nonlinear regression 339
11.6 Bibliographical notes 342

Appendix A. Matrices, statistics, and calculus **349**

A.1 Some results from matrix algebra 349
A.2 Some specific results 353
A.3 Definite matrices 356
A.4 0–1 matrices 361
A.5 On the normal distribution 364
A.6 Slutsky's theorem 369
A.7 The implicit function theorem 371
A.8 Bibliographical notes 373

Appendix B. The chi-square distribution **375**
B.1 Mean and variance 375
B.2 The distribution of quadratic forms in general 376
B.3 The idempotent case 378
B.4 Robustness characterizations 380
B.5 Bibliographical notes 385

References **387**

Author Index **421**

Subject Index **429**

Chapter 1

Introduction

This is a book with a transparent title. It deals with *measurement error* and *latent variables* in *econometrics*. To start with the last notion, econometrics, this means that the linear regression model is the point of departure, and that obtaining consistent estimators of its parameters is the main objective. When one or more of the regressors are not observable or not directly observable, the consistency of the estimators is at risk and hence a major problem arises.

Unobservability of regressors can be due to two possible causes, and this leads to the other two elements in the title. One is the error with which a variable may have been measured. What we need in our analysis is veiled by "noise" of some type. The other possible cause is the potentially conceptual or idealistic character of a variable: nothing in the real world around us directly corresponds to what we deem relevant in our model. In the former case we have a data problem, and in the latter a philosophical problem. Despite these differences, their implied econometric problems are to large extent identical and hence warrant an integrated treatment.

1.1 Measurement error and latent variables

That economic observations are often imprecise is a commonplace observation of long standing. For example, national accounts statistics, in particular GDP data, are constructed by national statistical agencies as the outcome of an elaborate processing of a huge amount of data from many sources. Discrepancies exist between estimates based on income data and those based on expenditure data. In order to remove these discrepancies and to balance the estimates, a number of techniques and procedures have been developed and are employed by the statistical agencies. In this process, prior knowledge of the reliability of the constituent parts of the estimates is often used. However, the outcome of the balancing process inevitably leads to figures that suffer from measurement error. Nevertheless, GDP is among the most frequently used variables in macroeconometric research.

Another area where data are produced with a great potential for errors is that of micro data. Microeconometric analysis is a flourishing branch of economic research, and is usually based on data that are obtained from large-scale sample surveys containing many questions. The road leading from the answers of these questions to the entries in the data matrix used by the econometrician is a long one, and even if the original answers given by a vastly heterogeneous group of respondents in a wide variety of circumstances are not too far off the mark (so there are not too many reporting and interpretation errors), additional errors are likely to be introduced in the various subsequent processing stages like coding and data entry.

An "uneasy alliance" is the characterization that Griliches (1986) gives, in his *Handbook of Econometrics* article on economic data issues, of the relation between econometricians and their data. On the one hand, these data are essential to test theories about economic behavior. On the other hand, this task is hampered by problems caused by these very data. These problems include measurement error but there are many more. At the same time, as Griliches points out, there is an ambiguity attached to this last point, because the legitimacy of econometrics is derived from those data problems: perfect data would leave little room for econometrics as a separate field. In this sense the present book owes its existence to this lack of perfection.

Recently a new dimension has been added to the phenomenon of measurement error in econometrics. Much econometric work is based on data sets, collected by a government agency, containing information on a large number of individuals or households. Each record in such a data set often contains up to a few hundred variables. Therefore, there has been a growing concern about privacy issues when such data are released for public use. One path that has actually been followed in practice is to add noise to the data. When the noise generating mechanism is disclosed, econometric work should not be severely handicapped, because this information can be used to correct the estimators. Although this may offer a practical way out of the privacy problem, it has the melancholic undertone of one group of people adding noise to data and the other one eliminating its consequences.

But the story can be given a positive twist. This happens when the notion of measurement error is extended a few steps further. If some variable is measured with error, this might have been caused by clearly identifiable factors. As soon as we know which ones these are, we may apply a better measurement procedure (or hope for more luck) at a later occasion. However, it may also be the case that no better procedure is conceivable since the variable concerned is a purely mental construct and does not correspond one-to-one to something that can, at least in principle, be observed in practice. In fact, quite often economic theorizing involves such *latent* variables.

Typical examples of latent variables appearing in economic models are the productivity of a worker, permanent income, consumer satisfaction, the financial health of a firm, the weather condition, socio-economic status or the state of the business cycle. Although we call those variables latent, we can, for each of these examples, think of related *observable* variables, so some kind of indirect measurement is possible. In this sense the latency of variables is a generalization of plain measurement error, where the relation between the observed variable and its true or latent counterpart is simply that the observed variable is the sum of the true value and the measurement error. However, the mere expression "measurement error" conveys a negative connotation and a smell of failure whereas the expression "latent variables" has an air of exiting mystery around it. In the words of Arthur S. Goldberger, as cited by Chamberlain (1990): "There is nothing like a latent variable to stimulate the imagination."

This suggests a qualitative difference between the two notions. Yet the difference is more apparent than real, and the distinction becomes even more blurred when we realize that there is a continuous grey area between variables that are measured with error and latent variables that are purely mental constructs. For example, there exist many economic models that incorporate the variable "inflation". At first sight, this variable is easily measured through the changes in prices. However, when it comes to actual quantification, one is faced with a variety of price indicators like consumer price indexes and producer price indexes. Even if these indicators taken separately are correctly measured (which is a strong assumption indeed for, e.g., the consumer price index, which is based on elaborate and complicated surveys and is beset with methodological problems, like the tendency to overstate the true value, whatever that may be), they do not develop in a parallel way, especially when there are vehement economic movements. Yet the idea of calling "inflation" a purely mental construct with no directly observable counterpart in the real world will not appeal to most economists.

As another example of this midfield between extremes, consider "income" as a variable in microeconomic models. Many surveys contain detailed, elaborate sets of questions which make it possible to give a numerical value to an array of sensible variables relating to the notion of income. The differences between the variables involve tax, pensions, mortgages, and so on. Occasionally economic theory is explicit as to which income notion is relevant but in many, if not most cases, the theory is by far not sufficiently rich to give such guidance and to suggest preference of one notion of income over the alternatives. Then none of the available variables is likely to be exactly the "true" one. Again note that this issue is different from the question whether the survey has been answered without error. The problem lies not only with the answers but also with the questions!

The discussion up till now, implying that most variables economists work with are latent, has largely been impressionistic, and at this juncture one might first expect a formal definition of a latent variable. However, we do not adopt a definition here or below. It may seem hard to justify to have a book on an important notion without defining that very notion. We have the following considerations. In the first place it is not clear what a satisfactory definition would be. Picking a definition from the econometrics literature is troublesome, because one is hard put to find one. To mention one typical example, Griliches (1974) stays short of a definition and is restricted to a typology of various kinds of unobservables and adds a footnote referring to the "arbitrary and misleading" character of the distinctions. One definition that has been given in the literature is presented in the form of "an essential characteristic" of a latent variable, which "is revealed by the fact that the system of linear structural equations in which it appears can not be manipulated so as to express the variable as a function of measured variables only" (Bentler, 1982, as quoted by Aigner, Hsiao, Kapteyn, and Wansbeek, 1984).

A second reason for not worrying about a definition is that, whatever it may be, the gains from having one are not clear. Definitions are only useful to the extent that they add order or structure to a discussion of a topic. We rather define the notion of latent variables implicitly through the kind of models that will be dealt with.

1.2 About this book

This book is written as a textbook. It is not a research monograph, compendium, encyclopedia, or book of recipes. Most topics dealt with are not new, although some of the mathematical derivations are. The emphasis is on gaining insight into a wide range of problems and solutions coming from a wide variety of backgrounds. To provide such insight, most results have been presented along with their derivations. The "it can be shown"-format has been employed minimally. A number of auxiliary results have been grouped in an appendix. Due to the many derivations given, the text may look quite technical and mathematically sophisticated. Yet the emphasis has not been on mathematical rigor, and we are occasionally quite liberal in this respect, following the time-tested econometric tradition.

The book presupposes a reasonable amount of knowledge of econometrics, statistics, matrix algebra, and calculus at an intermediate level. When going through the text, a student will be able to employ much of the knowledge gained in earlier courses. In our experience, seeing familiar results put to work is stimulating. Most of the text is self-contained, so that we rarely need references to the relevant literature on the spot. In order to increase readability, we have grouped these references in a separate section at the end of each chapter.

The book is organized as follows. Chapter 2 starts out by concentrating on the question as to what goes wrong when, in the multiple regression model, regressors are measured with error. It appears that this will lead to inconsistency of the usual parameter estimators. The inconsistency is typically towards zero but that is not necessarily the case, as is investigated in some depth in the chapter. The region where estimators may lie given the true parameter values is characterized. In chapter 3, the question is reversed, and the region where the true regression coefficients may lie given the inconsistent estimator is characterized. This issue is posed in two forms, one is when bounds are known on the measurement error process, and the other one is when such information is absent. In this context the measurement of labor market discrimination with imperfect productivity measurement is discussed as an important special case.

Chapter 4 paves the way for a discussion of solutions to the measurement error problem. It is shown that the inconsistency of the usual estimators in the regression model caused by measurement error is not just a consequence of a possibly unfortunate choice of estimator, but that the causes lie deeper. Due to an identification problem, no consistent estimators may exist at all. The boundary between identification and non-identification is indicated in detail. The upshot is that the availability of additional information is desirable to be able to obtain reliable consistent estimators.

Additional information can come in various forms. Still remaining within the context of single-equation estimation, chapters 5 and 6 are devoted to handling such information. Two main types are distinguished. One is when additional exact prior knowledge about functions of the parameters is available in sufficient amount. This leads to the so-called consistent adjusted least-squares estimator, which is the subject of chapter 5. The other type comes in the form of instrumental variables, which is discussed in chapter 6. This chapter starts by reviewing the basic theory of the instrumental variables estimator, followed by extensions to heteroskedasticity, to the combination of data from different sources, to the construction of instruments from the available data, and to the limited information maximum likelihood estimator, which is increasingly recognized as a good estimator when the instruments are only weakly correlated with the regressors.

Chapter 7 extends the discussion of instrumental variables to an embedding of the regression equation with measurement error in a multiple equations setting.

In its simplest form, this yields the factor analysis model with a single factor. This development marks the step from measurement error to latent variables. A subsequent extension yields the general factor analysis model with an arbitrary number of factors. Estimation of these models leads to an eigenvalue problem, and the chapter concludes by a review of methods that involve eigenvalue problems as their common characteristic.

Chapter 8 further extends the class of factor analysis models, first by considering restrictions on the parameters of the factor analysis model, and next by relating the factors to background variables. These models are all members of the class of so-called structural equation models, which is a very general and very important class of models, with a joint background in econometrics and the social sciences. This class encompasses almost all linear equation systems with latent variables. For this class of models, several general and complete specifications are used, some of which are associated with specific software programs in which they are implemented. The chapter discusses the three major specifications and shows the link between them.

Structural equation models impose a structure on the covariance matrix of the observations, and estimation takes place by minimizing the distance between the theoretical structure and the observed covariance matrix in some way. This approach to estimation is a particular instance of the generalized method of moments (GMM), where parameters are estimated by minimizing the length of a vector function in parameters and statistics. Given the importance of GMM in general and in estimating models with latent variables in particular, chapter 9 is devoted to an extensive discussion of various aspects of GMM, including the generality of GMM, simulation estimation, and the link with the method of maximum likelihood. The subsequent chapter 10 discusses many aspects of testing and model evaluation for GMM.

Up till then the models have all been linear. Chapter 11 is devoted to a discussion of nonlinear models. The emphasis is on polynomial models and models that are nonlinear due to a filter on the dependent variables, like discrete choice models or models with ordered categorical variables. Two technical appendixes, one containing some relevant results in matrix algebra and calculus and the other containing some technical aspects of the chi-square distribution mainly serving chapter 10, conclude the text.

A major limitation of the book should be stated here. Dynamic models are largely left out of the discussion, except for a brief treatment of panel data models with relatively few measurements in time for a large number of units. Some of the methods that we deal with can be adapted for dynamic models, but a general treatment would require a different framework and is beyond our scope.

1.3 Bibliographical notes

1.1 There is a vast amount of literature on measurement error and latent variables. Many relevant references have been grouped at the end of the book. Most concern specific topics dealt with in the various subject matter sections and chapters. The list of general survey references is limited. As to books, a first compilation of papers relevant for econometricians can be found in Aigner and Goldberger (1977). General comprehensive texts in statistics are Schneeweiss and Mittag (1986), Fuller (1987), and Cheng and Van Ness (1999). Morgenstern (1963) discussed the quality of economic data, and Biemer, Groves, Lyberg, Mathiowetz, and Sudman (1991) is a book-length treatment of measurement error in survey data. A classical econometric analysis involving latent variables is Friedman (1957), dealing with permanent income, but raising many issues of general importance and insight relating to latent variables. Brown and Fuller (1990) is an edited book discussing many aspects of measurement error models.

There are several extensive book chapters dealing with measurement error and latent variables. Kendall and Stuart (1973) gives a thorough treatment of statistical aspects. Humak (1983) contains a long, detailed, and technical chapter concentrating on statistical issues. Aigner et al. (1984) is a chapter in the *Handbook of Econometrics* containing an extensive survey of models and methods. In another volume of the same *Handbook*, Griliches (1986) contains a discussion of issues relating to economic data. Geraci (1987) gives a brief discussion of errors in variables and has some notes on the history of the topic in econometrics. The early history of measurement error in econometrics is discussed by Hendry and Morgan (1989) in the context of their reassessment of confluence analysis and bunch maps (Frisch, 1934).

Of the various survey papers, we mention the older ones by Durbin (1954), Madansky (1959), Cochran (1968), and Moran (1971). More recent ones are Anderson (1984a), Bekker, Wansbeek, and Kapteyn (1985), and Kmenta (1991). A retrospective essay on the history of the role of errors in variables in econometric modeling is given by Goldberger (1972b). See also Goldberger (1971) for the connected theme of links with psychometrics. Chamberlain (1990) is an excellent introduction to the pioneering work of Arthur S. Goldberger on latent variables in econometrics.

For a description of a case where the measurement error is introduced from privacy considerations, see Hwang (1986).

1.2 The attention given to measurement error and latent variables issues in the standard econometric textbooks is overall meager in relation to their importance and is often limited to the inconsistency of ordinary least squares when there is measurement error. Nearly all econometrics texts discuss instrumental variables but do not always link this topic with the topic of measurement error.

As stated in the main text, dynamic models with measurement error are outside the scope of this book. The interested reader is referred to Deistler and Anderson (1989), the pertaining section in Aigner et al. (1984), and the book-length treatment by Terceiro Lomba (1990). The identification of linear dynamic models with measurement error is treated by Nowak (1993). Singleton (1980), Geweke and Singleton (1981a, 1981b), and Engle, Lilien, and Watson (1985) present economic applications and develop dynamic latent variable models extending the static factor analysis model.

Chapter 2

Regression and measurement error

The linear regression model is still the most frequently chosen context for economic research. The use of the model commonly involves a number of so-called classical assumptions. These include that the regressors are measured without error and are not perfectly correlated. Also, the disturbances are independently identically distributed, possibly normal, and are uncorrelated with the regressors. Of course, any of these assumptions can be relaxed in many ways. In this chapter we relax only one assumption, namely that the regressors are measured without error. The other assumptions are maintained for convenience. As will be seen, relaxing just one assumption already creates many complications but provides also new insights.

Our interest is in the effects of measurement error in the regressors on the statistics commonly used in econometrics. These effects take different forms. After introducing, in section 2.1, the model and some relevant notation, we establish in section 2.2 the inconsistency of the usual estimator of the regression coefficients and of the variance of the disturbance term. In section 2.3 we take a closer look at the inconsistency in estimating the regression coefficients and try to establish whether it is in the direction of zero or away from it. More generally, we characterize the area where the estimator can end up when there is measurement error.

Often, in practice, measurement error issues focus on a single regressor. This special case raises two specific questions, which are addressed in section 2.4. First, to what extent and in what way does the measurement error in one variable affect the estimators of the regression coefficients corresponding to the other, correctly measured regressors? And second, the question arises whether it is not better to drop a mismeasured variable altogether.

Section 2.5 concludes the chapter by grouping a number of more or less unrelated topics. These concern measurement error in the dependent variable, the structure obtained when normality is assumed for all random elements in the model, prediction in a regression model with measurement error, and the so-called Berkson model, where the regressor values diverge from the true values in a way that does not lead to the measurement error model.

2.1 The model

In this section we describe the linear regression model when there is measurement error. We indicate a violation of the classical assumptions of the model in that case, and we introduce the notation that helps us analyze, in section 2.2, the induced problems.

The standard linear multiple regression model can be written as

$$y = \Xi\beta + \varepsilon, \tag{2.1}$$

where y is an observable N-vector and ε an unobservable N-vector of random variables. These are assumed to be independently identically distributed (i.i.d.) with zero expectation and variance σ_ε^2. The g-vector β is fixed but unknown. The $N \times g$ matrix Ξ contains the regressors. The regressors are uncorrelated with ε, i.e., $\mathrm{E}(\varepsilon \mid \Xi) = 0$. We adopt the convention that variables are measured in deviation from their mean. This implies that an intercept is not included in the analysis. (Intercepts only become interesting in a more general setting, which is discussed in section 8.6.) Leaving out an intercept simplifies the analysis at hardly any cost, because we are usually not particularly interested in it. So far for the standard model.

If there are errors of measurement in the regressors, Ξ is not observable. Instead, we observe the matrix X:

$$X = \Xi + V \tag{2.2}$$

where V $(N \times g)$ is a matrix of measurement errors. Its rows are assumed to be i.i.d. with zero expectation and covariance matrix Ω $(g \times g)$ and uncorrelated with Ξ and ε, i.e., $\mathrm{E}(V \mid \Xi) = 0$ and $\mathrm{E}(\varepsilon \mid V) = 0$. Some of the columns of V may be zero (with probability one). This happens when the corresponding regressors are measured without error. In that case, the corresponding rows and columns of Ω are zero. Then Ω is not of full rank. The variables in X that contain measurement error are often called the *proxies* for the corresponding variables in

Ξ. The situation with mismeasured explanatory variables is also frequently called *errors-in-variables*.

What are the consequences of neglecting the measurement error when regressing y on X? Let

$$b \equiv (X'X)^{-1}X'y \tag{2.3}$$

and

$$s_\varepsilon^2 \equiv \frac{1}{N}y'(I_N - X(X'X)^{-1}X')y \tag{2.4}$$

be the ordinary least squares (OLS) estimators of β and σ_ε^2. Because most subsequent analysis is asymptotic, we divide, for the sake of simplicity, by N rather than $N - g$ in (2.4). We investigate the probability limits of the two estimators when there is measurement error present, i.e., when (2.2) holds. Substitution of (2.2) into (2.1) yields

$$\begin{aligned} y &= (X - V)\beta + \varepsilon \\ &= X\beta + (\varepsilon - V\beta) \\ &= X\beta + u, \end{aligned} \tag{2.5}$$

with

$$u \equiv \varepsilon - V\beta. \tag{2.6}$$

This shows that the transformed model (2.5) has a disturbance term (2.6) that shares a stochastic term (V) with the regressor matrix. Thus, u is correlated with X and hence $\mathrm{E}(u \mid X) \neq 0$. This lack of orthogonality means that a crucial assumption underlying the use of OLS is violated. As will be shown in section 2.2, the main consequence is that b and s_ε^2 are no longer consistent estimators of β and σ_ε^2. Because consistency is generally considered to be the minimal quality required of an estimator, we are facing a major problem.

In order to analyze it we employ the following notation. Let the sample covariance matrices of Ξ and X be

$$S_\Xi \equiv \frac{1}{N}\Xi'\Xi \qquad \text{and} \qquad S_X \equiv \frac{1}{N}X'X.$$

Note that S_X is observable but S_Ξ is not. As will be discussed extensively in chapter 4, we can interpret (2.1) in two ways. In unfortunate but conventional phrasing, it is either a *functional* or a *structural* model. Under the functional interpretation, we do not make explicit assumptions regarding the distribution of

Ξ, but consider its elements to be unknown fixed parameters. These parameters are often called the *incidental parameters*. Under the structural interpretation, the elements of Ξ are assumed to be random variables. Until chapter 4, the distinction plays no role and the assumption

$$\operatorname*{plim}_{N\to\infty} S_\Xi = \Sigma_\Xi, \tag{2.7}$$

with Σ_Ξ a positive definite $g \times g$ matrix, covers both cases. As a consequence,

$$\Sigma_X \equiv \operatorname*{plim}_{N\to\infty} \frac{1}{N} X'X = \operatorname*{plim}_{N\to\infty} S_X = \Sigma_\Xi + \Omega.$$

Throughout, we will use the notation $M_1 > M_2$ for symmetric matrices M_1 and M_2 to indicate that $M_1 - M_2$ is positive definite. This means that, taking $M_2 = 0$, the notation $M_1 > 0$ indicates that M_1 is positive definite. Correspondingly, the symbol $\geq$ is used to indicate positive semidefiniteness, see section A.3.

We assume that Ξ is of full column rank. (In the structural case, we should add that we assume that this holds with probability one, but we will usually neglect this.) Hence, $\Sigma_\Xi > 0$. Because Ω is a covariance matrix, it satisfies $\Omega \geq 0$. As a result, $\Sigma_X = \Sigma_\Xi + \Omega > 0$ and $\Sigma_X \geq \Sigma_\Xi$. The matrices Σ_X, Σ_Ξ, and Ω further satisfy

$$\Sigma_\Xi - \Sigma_\Xi \Sigma_X^{-1} \Sigma_\Xi \geq 0 \tag{2.8a}$$

$$\Sigma_\Xi - \Sigma_\Xi \Sigma_X^{-1} \Sigma_\Xi = \Omega - \Omega \Sigma_X^{-1} \Omega, \tag{2.8b}$$

as can be easily verified. These results will prove useful later on.

2.2 Asymptotic properties of the OLS estimators

Given the setup of the measurement error model introduced in section 2.1, we can inspect the asymptotic behavior of the statistics b and s_ε^2. We do so below, and also consider the asymptotic behavior of the other major statistic in the regression context, R^2.

The inconsistency of b

Given the notation, we can derive the probability limit of the OLS estimator b of β. This gives the following result:

$$\begin{aligned}\kappa &\equiv \operatorname*{plim}_{N\to\infty} b \\ &= \operatorname*{plim}_{N\to\infty} \left(\frac{X'X}{N}\right)^{-1} \frac{X'y}{N}\end{aligned}$$

$$= \beta + \operatorname*{plim}_{N\to\infty} \left(\frac{X'X}{N}\right)^{-1} \frac{X'u}{N}$$

$$= \beta + \Sigma_X^{-1} \operatorname*{plim}_{N\to\infty} \frac{(\Xi + V)'(\varepsilon - V\beta)}{N}$$

$$= \beta - \Sigma_X^{-1}\Omega\beta$$

$$= \Sigma_X^{-1}(\Sigma_X - \Omega)\beta, \tag{2.9}$$

or, using $\Sigma_X = \Sigma_\Xi + \Omega$,

$$\kappa = \Sigma_X^{-1}\Sigma_\Xi\beta. \tag{2.10}$$

This result constitutes the first, major result on regression when there are errors of measurement in the regressors. It shows that neglecting measurement error induces inconsistency in the OLS estimator of β. A trivial rearrangement of (2.10) yields an equality that will be frequently used in the sequel,

$$\Sigma_X\kappa = \Sigma_\Xi\beta.$$

It is useful to have separate notation for the inconsistency (or bias, we will use the latter word often when there can be no confusion with small-sample properties) of the OLS estimator of β. This is

$$\omega \equiv \kappa - \beta = -\Sigma_X^{-1}\Omega\beta. \tag{2.11}$$

When there is no measurement error, $\Omega = 0$, which implies that $\omega = 0$ and OLS is consistent. We note that the above derivations hold both for the structural and the functional model.

The matrix expression $\Sigma_X^{-1}\Omega$ in (2.11) can be decomposed into the product of $\Sigma_X^{-1}\Sigma_\Xi$ and $\Sigma_\Xi^{-1}\Omega$. The first factor is known as the *reliability* of X as a measurement of Ξ. It is the ratio, in the matrix sense, of the covariance matrix of the true values of the regressors and the covariance matrix of the observed values of the regressors. The second factor is known as the *noise-to-signal ratio*, because Ω is the variance of the 'noise' in measuring the regressor, whose true version or 'signal' has covariance matrix Σ_Ξ.

Intuitively, the inconsistency can be interpreted as follows, where we consider the case $g = 1$ for simplicity. Under the assumptions of the usual regression model the points in a scatter diagram can be thought to have been generated by random *vertical* displacements of points on the regression line. These displacements are the effect of the disturbance term in the regression equation. When in addition there is measurement error there is a second force in operation to disperse the points from the line. These displacements are in a *horizontal* direction. The points in the scatter diagram that are found at the left-hand side of the point scatter will on average suffer more from negative measurement error than from positive measurement error, and at the right-hand side of the point scatter the situation will be exactly opposite. Hence, the regression line fitted on the observed, mismeasured, point coordinates will be flatter than the regression line fitted on the true, error-free point coordinates, if these were available. This systematic distortion in horizontal direction does not disappear in the limit, which causes the inconsistency.

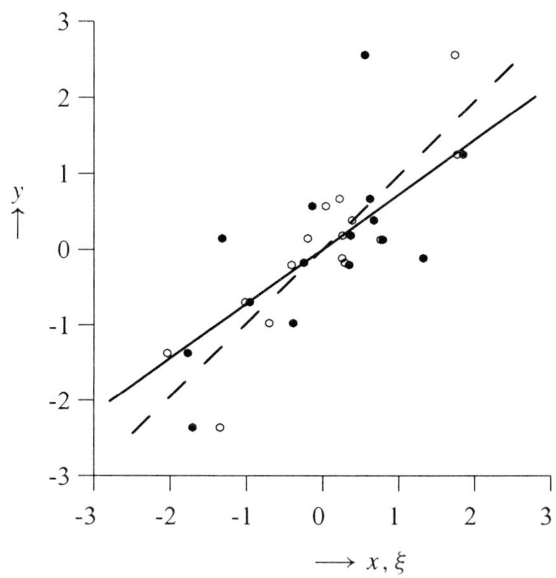

Figure 2.1 *The effect of measurement error: regression line based on data without measurement error (dashed line, open circles) and regression line based on data with measurement error (solid line, filled circles).*

As an illustration, consider figure 2.1, which is based on the following design. We have generated $N = 15$ values ξ_n, ε_n, and v_n, $n = 1, \ldots, 15$, from independent normal distributions with standard deviations 1, 0.5, and 0.5, respectively. The observed variables were subsequently computed as $y_n = \beta\xi_n + \varepsilon_n$, with $\beta = 1$, and $x_n = \xi_n + v_n$. After this, the variables y, x, and ξ were centered. Without measurement error, we would observe ξ directly. The points (y_n, ξ_n) are plotted as open circles. The OLS estimated regression line for these data is the dashed line. The estimated regression coefficient is $\hat{\beta} = 0.974$, which is very close to the true value $\beta = 1$. With measurement error, the points (y_n, x_n) are observed. These points are represented in the figure as filled circles. The regression line for these data is the solid line. The estimated regression coefficient is $\hat{\beta} = 0.720$. Note that $\text{plim}_{N\to\infty} \hat{\beta} = 0.8$ given the parameter values chosen.

The above discussion and the illustration both suggest a bias towards zero in b in the case of a single regressor. This suggestion is correct, but in a multiple regression context things are less clear-cut. We take this up in section 2.3.

The inconsistency of s_ε^2

Now consider the asymptotic behavior of s_ε^2. Elaborating the expression for s_ε^2 using the notation introduced in section 2.1 gives

$$\begin{aligned} s_\varepsilon^2 &= \frac{1}{N} y'(I_N - X(X'X)^{-1}X')y \\ &= \frac{1}{N}(y'y - y'X(X'X)^{-1}X'y) \\ &= \frac{1}{N}(\Xi\beta + \varepsilon)'(\Xi\beta + \varepsilon) - \frac{1}{N} b'X'Xb \\ &= \beta' S_\Xi \beta + \frac{2}{N}\varepsilon'\Xi\beta + \frac{1}{N}\varepsilon'\varepsilon - b' S_X b. \end{aligned}$$

In the limit, we find

$$\begin{aligned} \gamma &\equiv \operatorname*{plim}_{N\to\infty} s_\varepsilon^2 \\ &= \sigma_\varepsilon^2 + \beta'\Sigma_\Xi\beta - \kappa'\Sigma_X\kappa && (2.12a) \\ &= \sigma_\varepsilon^2 + \beta'(\Sigma_\Xi - \Sigma_\Xi\Sigma_X^{-1}\Sigma_\Xi)\beta \\ &= \sigma_\varepsilon^2 + \beta'\Omega\Sigma_X^{-1}\Sigma_\Xi\beta \\ &= \sigma_\varepsilon^2 + \beta'\Omega\kappa && (2.12b) \\ &\geq \sigma_\varepsilon^2. \end{aligned}$$

We conclude that s_ε^2 is inconsistent in the presence of measurement error as well. Unlike the case of b, the effect is unambiguous. The estimator is biased upward in the limit.

The effect on R^2

We now turn to the effect of measurement error on R^2 and on the closely related F-statistic. It should be kept in mind that there is no constant term in the regression and that all variables have been centered beforehand. Premultiplication of inequality (2.8a) by β' and postmultiplication by β, we obtain using (2.10),

$$\beta'\Sigma_{\Xi}\beta \geq \kappa'\Sigma_X\kappa. \tag{2.13}$$

Asymptotically speaking, the left-hand side is the variance of the systematic part of the regression, and the right-hand side is its estimate if measurement error is neglected. Thus, the variance of the systematic part is underestimated.

This also has a direct bearing on the properties of the usual fit measure $R^2 \equiv Nb'S_Xb/y'y$. It converges to

$$\frac{\kappa'\Sigma_X\kappa}{\sigma_\varepsilon^2 + \beta'\Sigma_{\Xi}\beta}.$$

The probability limit of R^2 in the absence of measurement error is

$$\frac{\beta'\Sigma_{\Xi}\beta}{\sigma_\varepsilon^2 + \beta'\Sigma_{\Xi}\beta}.$$

Using (2.13) we find

$$\frac{\kappa'\Sigma_X\kappa}{\sigma_\varepsilon^2 + \beta'\Sigma_{\Xi}\beta} \leq \frac{\beta'\Sigma_{\Xi}\beta}{\sigma_\varepsilon^2 + \beta'\Sigma_{\Xi}\beta}.$$

Thus, when measurement error is neglected, the explanatory power of the model, as measured conventionally by R^2, is underestimated.

When the disturbance term is assumed to be normally distributed, the hypothesis $\beta = 0$ can be tested by means of the commonly employed F-statistic. It has a close relationship with R^2,

$$F = \frac{R^2}{1 - R^2} \cdot \frac{N - g}{g}.$$

In particular, F is a monotonically increasing transformation of R^2 and hence it is also biased towards zero. As a result, the null hypothesis will be accepted too often and hence the hypothesis $\beta = 0$ will not be rejected often enough.

One might wonder whether the bias in the F-statistic for testing $\beta = 0$ could be associated with a similar bias in t-statistics used to test whether one particular element of β is zero. For $g = 1$, this is obviously the case, as the t-test and F-test are then equivalent. The topic of the effect of measurement error on the t-value is further pursued in section 5.2 for the general case where $g > 1$ and where a single variable is mismeasured.

2.3 Attenuation

In this section, we inspect the inconsistency of the OLS estimator more closely. For a start, consider the case in which there is only one regressor (so $g = 1$), which is measured with error. Then $\Sigma_X > \Sigma_\Xi > 0$ are scalars and $\kappa/\beta = \Sigma_X^{-1}\Sigma_\Xi\beta/\beta$ is a number between 0 and 1. So asymptotically the estimator of the regression coefficient is biased towards zero. This phenomenon, that has already been made visible in figure 2.1, is often called *attenuation*. The size of the effect of the regressor on the dependent variable is underestimated. For the case where there is more than one regressor, the characterization of attenuation is more complicated. Not all estimates are necessarily biased towards zero, but there is still an overall attenuation effect.

We now turn to the general multiple regression case. We take β and Σ_Ξ as given and derive a characterization of the set of possible values for κ, with $\kappa = (\Sigma_\Xi + \Omega)^{-1}\Sigma_\Xi\beta$.

Let $c \equiv \Sigma_X\kappa = \Sigma_\Xi\beta$. Note that c can be consistently estimated from the data and hence is known, at least in the limit. Because of (2.8a)

$$\begin{aligned} 0 &\le \beta'(\Sigma_\Xi - \Sigma_\Xi\Sigma_X^{-1}\Sigma_\Xi)\beta \\ &= \beta'\Sigma_\Xi\beta - \kappa'\Sigma_\Xi\beta \\ &= \beta'c - \kappa'c. \end{aligned} \tag{2.14}$$

Taking β as given we find that κ satisfies $\kappa'c \le \beta'c$. The equation $\kappa'c = \beta'c$, or equivalently $(\beta - \kappa)'\Sigma_\Xi\beta = 0$, defines a hyperplane through β perpendicular to the vector c. Because $\beta'c = \beta'\Sigma_\Xi\beta \ge 0$, the set of possible values for κ based on this inequality includes $\kappa = 0$. Hence, the set of possible values for κ is to the left of the hyperplane in the sense that it includes the origin. If $\Omega = 0$, κ coincides with β.

Another linear inequality that should be satisfied is also easily found. From $\Sigma_X \ge 0$, it follows that $\kappa'\Sigma_X\kappa \ge 0$, and as $\Sigma_X\kappa = \Sigma_\Xi\beta$, we have $\kappa'\Sigma_\Xi\beta = \kappa'c \ge 0$. The equation $\kappa'\Sigma_\Xi\beta = \kappa'c = 0$ defines a hyperplane through the origin parallel to the earlier hyperplane $(\beta - \kappa)'\Sigma_\Xi\beta = 0$. Because $\Sigma_\Xi > 0$, the solution $\kappa = \beta$ satisfies the inequality $\kappa'\Sigma_\Xi\beta \ge 0$, and hence this inequality is satisfied by all κ in the half space divided by $\kappa'\Sigma_\Xi\beta = 0$ that includes β.

The complete set of all κ consistent with given β and Σ_Ξ can be derived as follows. Note that $\Sigma_X\kappa = \Sigma_\Xi\beta$ implies that $\kappa'\Sigma_X\kappa = \kappa'\Sigma_\Xi\beta$, or, alternatively, $\kappa'\Sigma_\Xi\kappa \le \kappa'\Sigma_\Xi\beta$, because $\Sigma_X = \Sigma_\Xi + \Omega$ and $\Omega \ge 0$. This is easily seen to be equivalent to

$$(\kappa - \tfrac{1}{2}\beta)'\Sigma_\Xi(\kappa - \tfrac{1}{2}\beta) \le \tfrac{1}{4}\beta'\Sigma_\Xi\beta. \tag{2.15}$$

Consequently, if β and Σ_Ξ are given, κ should be within an ellipsoid with midpoint $\frac{1}{2}\beta$ passing through 0 and β. This ellipsoid is tangent to the hyperplanes $(\beta-\kappa)'\Sigma_\Xi\beta = 0$ in the point β and $\kappa'\Sigma_\Xi\beta = 0$ in the origin. This is depicted in figure 2.2. From the figure it appears that the biases of the elements of the vector of regression coefficients are not necessarily towards zero. It is even possible that all regression coefficients are biased away from zero, as will be shown by an example later on.

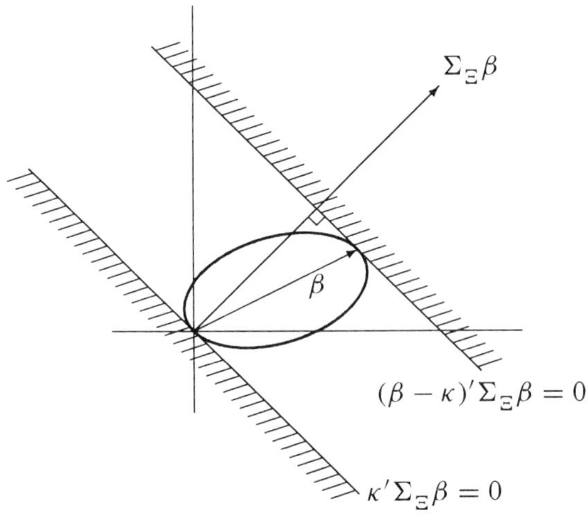

Figure 2.2 *Characterization of the bias in the OLS estimator: the κ's consistent with the given β and Σ_Ξ are within the ellipse shown, or $\kappa = \beta$.*

For every κ strictly within the boundaries of the ellipsoid (2.15), we can construct an Ω that implies this value of κ. A particularly simple way of doing this is, departing from a particular choice of κ, to choose an Ω of rank one. Note that $\kappa'\Sigma_\Xi\kappa \le \kappa'\Sigma_\Xi\beta$ and thus $(\beta-\kappa)'\Sigma_\Xi\kappa \ge 0$ is equivalent to (2.15). Hence, the inequality is strict for all interior points of the ellipsoid. Therefore, the matrix

$$\Omega = \frac{\Sigma_\Xi(\beta-\kappa)(\beta-\kappa)'\Sigma_\Xi}{(\beta-\kappa)'\Sigma_\Xi\kappa} \tag{2.16}$$

is positive semidefinite. With this choice of Ω we immediately find that

$$\Sigma_X\kappa = (\Sigma_\Xi+\Omega)\kappa = \Sigma_\Xi\kappa + \frac{\Sigma_\Xi(\beta-\kappa)(\beta-\kappa)'\Sigma_\Xi\kappa}{(\beta-\kappa)'\Sigma_\Xi\kappa} = \Sigma_\Xi\beta,$$

as required. To check whether the boundary points of the ellipsoid can be attained, observe that any boundary point satisfies the equality $\kappa'\Sigma_\Xi\kappa = \kappa'\Sigma_\Xi\beta$.

If κ is the probability limit of the OLS estimator, then $\Sigma_X \kappa = \Sigma_\Xi \beta$, which now implies $\kappa' \Sigma_\Xi \kappa = \kappa' \Sigma_X \kappa$, or $\kappa'(\Sigma_X - \Sigma_\Xi)\kappa = 0$, or $\kappa' \Omega \kappa = 0$. So, if an Ω exists such that $\Sigma_X \kappa = \Sigma_\Xi \beta$ for a given κ on the boundary of the ellipsoid, then it should be singular and κ should be in its null space. Hence, $\Sigma_X \kappa = (\Sigma_\Xi + \Omega)\kappa = \Sigma_\Xi \kappa$, which leads to $\Sigma_\Xi \beta = \Sigma_\Xi \kappa$ or $\kappa = \beta$, because $\Sigma_X \kappa = \Sigma_\Xi \beta$ and Σ_Ξ is positive definite and hence invertible.

Consequently, the only boundary point of the ellipsoid that can be attained is $\kappa = \beta$. A trivial example is of course $\Omega = 0$, the case without measurement error. Generally, however, it can be any case in which the vector of regression coefficients is in the null space of the covariance matrix of the measurement errors, i.e., $\Omega\beta = 0$. (Of course, one is hard put to find a situation where this occurs.)

Thus, we conclude that a complete characterization of the possible κ's compatible with a particular β and a particular Σ_Ξ that may result from measurement error is given by the set

$$\left\{ \kappa \mid \kappa = \beta \quad \text{or} \quad (\kappa - \tfrac{1}{2}\beta)' \Sigma_\Xi (\kappa - \tfrac{1}{2}\beta) < \tfrac{1}{4}\beta' \Sigma_\Xi \beta \right\}.$$

There is attenuation in a more general (and more ambiguous) sense than in the single-regressor case. The estimates are asymptotically in an ellipsoid through the true value β and the origin.

All biases away from zero

The overall impression from the foregoing will be that measurement error induces coefficients to tend to zero and, if not for all coefficients individually, then at least in some average sense. This was already suggested by the bias term (2.11). However, there exist cases within the confines of the standard measurement error model where all estimators are biased away from zero. In words, all coefficients are overestimated. An example exhibiting this somewhat surprising statement may be in order. Let

$$\beta = \begin{bmatrix} 2 \\ 1 \end{bmatrix} \quad \text{and} \quad \Sigma_\Xi = \begin{bmatrix} 3 & -2 \\ -2 & 3 \end{bmatrix}.$$

It is easily seen that Σ_Ξ is positive definite and hence a possible covariance matrix. Let $\kappa = (2.02, 1.18)'$, so all elements of κ are larger than the corresponding elements of β and have the same signs. It is easily verified that

$$(\kappa - \tfrac{1}{2}\beta)' \Sigma_\Xi (\kappa - \tfrac{1}{2}\beta) = 1.734 < 1.75 = \tfrac{1}{4}\beta' \Sigma_\Xi \beta.$$

Hence, κ is an interior point of the ellipsoid (2.15) and all regression coefficients are biased away from zero. This situation is depicted in figure 2.3, which is similar to figure 2.2. One possible choice for the covariance matrix of the measurement errors Ω that leads to this value of κ is given by

$$\Omega = \frac{1}{0.016}\begin{bmatrix} 0.3 \\ -0.5 \end{bmatrix}\begin{bmatrix} 0.3 \\ -0.5 \end{bmatrix}' = \begin{bmatrix} 5.625 & -9.375 \\ -9.375 & 15.625 \end{bmatrix},$$

as follows by substitution of the parameter values of β and Σ_Ξ in (2.16).

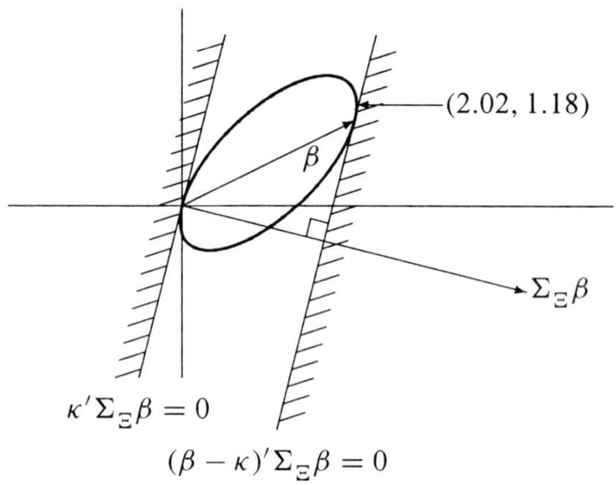

Figure 2.3 *An example in which all regression coefficients may be biased away from zero.*

Admissible values for β

So far, the emphasis has been on 'what goes wrong' if there is measurement error in the regressors. We have basically taken the true β and σ_ε^2 as given and asked the question what happens to the probability limits of their OLS estimators if we vary the measurement error covariance matrix Ω. In the remainder of this section we turn this question around and investigate what we can say about the true values of the parameters given the values of the OLS estimators. To be a bit more precise, we take the values of κ and γ, the probability limits of the OLS estimators b and s_ε^2, as given and try to characterize the set of β's that are compatible with these values. In the following, we also take Σ_X to be given, because it can be consistently estimated by S_X.

The inequality $0 \leq \Omega$ and the equality $\Sigma_X = \Sigma_\Xi + \Omega$ jointly imply that $0 \leq \Sigma_\Xi \leq \Sigma_X$, which is equivalent to $0 \leq \Sigma_X^{-1} \leq \Sigma_\Xi^{-1}$. As $\Sigma_X\kappa = \Sigma_\Xi\beta$,

$\beta = \Sigma_\Xi^{-1}\Sigma_X\kappa$ and hence $(\beta-\kappa)'\Sigma_X\kappa = \kappa'\Sigma_X(\Sigma_\Xi^{-1} - \Sigma_X^{-1})\Sigma_X\kappa$. Combined with the inequality $\Sigma_X^{-1} \le \Sigma_\Xi^{-1}$, this gives

$$(\beta-\kappa)'\Sigma_X\kappa \ge 0. \tag{2.17}$$

Now, assume $(\beta-\kappa)'\Sigma_X\kappa > 0$ and choose $\Sigma_\Xi^{-1} = \Sigma_X^{-1} + \Delta$, with

$$\Delta = \frac{(\beta-\kappa)(\beta-\kappa)'}{(\beta-\kappa)'\Sigma_X\kappa},$$

which is clearly symmetric and positive semidefinite. Hence, Σ_Ξ satisfies the inequalities $0 \le \Sigma_X^{-1} \le \Sigma_\Xi^{-1}$ and $0 \le \Sigma_\Xi \le \Sigma_X$. Note that it follows that

$$\Omega = \frac{\Sigma_X(\beta-\kappa)(\beta-\kappa)'\Sigma_X}{(\beta-\kappa)'\Sigma_X\beta}, \tag{2.18}$$

which is positive semidefinite, because $(\beta-\kappa)'\Sigma_X(\beta-\kappa) \ge 0$ and $(\beta-\kappa)'\Sigma_X\kappa > 0$, so $(\beta-\kappa)'\Sigma_X\beta \ge (\beta-\kappa)'\Sigma_X\kappa > 0$.

Moreover, it is easily seen that $\Sigma_\Xi^{-1}\Sigma_X\kappa = \beta$, so that for any β that satisfies the inequality $(\beta-\kappa)'\Sigma_X\kappa > 0$, a Σ_Ξ has been shown to exist such that the requirements $0 \le \Sigma_\Xi \le \Sigma_X$ and $\Sigma_X\kappa = \Sigma_\Xi\beta$ are met. Consequently, any β that satisfies the inequality $(\beta-\kappa)'\Sigma_X\kappa > 0$ is an admissible value of β. This inequality defines a half-space bounded by the hyperplane $(\beta-\kappa)'\Sigma_X\kappa = 0$.

Let us now study the β's defined by $(\beta-\kappa)'\Sigma_X\kappa = 0$. As we have seen above, this is equivalent to $\kappa'\Sigma_X(\Sigma_\Xi^{-1} - \Sigma_X^{-1})\Sigma_X\kappa = 0$. Evidently, this is only satisfied if $(\Sigma_\Xi^{-1} - \Sigma_X^{-1})\Sigma_X\kappa = 0$, or $\beta - \kappa = 0$. Thus, the only admissible β on the boundary of (2.17) is $\beta = \kappa$.

There is an additional restriction that we have not yet used and that further restricts the set of possible values of β. This is the restriction $\sigma_\varepsilon^2 \ge 0$ or, from (2.12b),

$$\gamma \ge \beta'\Omega\kappa. \tag{2.19}$$

Now, $\Sigma_X = \Sigma_\Xi + \Omega$, so $\Sigma_X\beta = \Sigma_\Xi\beta + \Omega\beta$, or $\Sigma_X\beta = \Sigma_X\kappa + \Omega\beta$. This can be rearranged into $\beta'\Omega = (\beta-\kappa)'\Sigma_X$. Substitution into (2.19) gives

$$\gamma \ge (\beta-\kappa)'\Sigma_X\kappa. \tag{2.20}$$

The equality $(\beta-\kappa)'\Sigma_X\kappa = \gamma$ defines a second hyperplane. This is parallel to the first hyperplane derived above, $(\beta-\kappa)'\Sigma_X\kappa = 0$. These two hyperplanes together bound the set of possible values of β. From the expression for γ as given in (2.12a), it follows immediately that $\sigma_\varepsilon^2 = 0$ in cases where β lies on the second hyperplane, i.e., there is no disturbance term in the regression. This, however, does not restrict the set of admissible β's on the hyperplane $(\beta - \kappa)'\Sigma_X\kappa = \gamma$. With Ω as in (2.18), every β on this hyperplane can be attained.

Thus, we conclude that a complete characterization of the possible β's compatible with a particular value of κ (i.e., the probability limit of the OLS estimator of β) is given by the set

$$\left\{\beta \mid \beta = \kappa \quad \text{or} \quad 0 < (\beta - \kappa)'\Sigma_X\kappa \leq \gamma\right\},$$

where Σ_X is the probability limit of the covariance matrix of the observed regressors, and γ is the probability limit of the estimator of the variance of the disturbances in the equation. This set is illustrated in figure 2.4. It is the set between the two hyperplanes, containing only the boundary point $\beta = \kappa$ of the hyperplane $(\beta - \kappa)'\Sigma_X\kappa = 0$ and containing the entire hyperplane $(\beta - \kappa)'\Sigma_X\kappa = \gamma$.

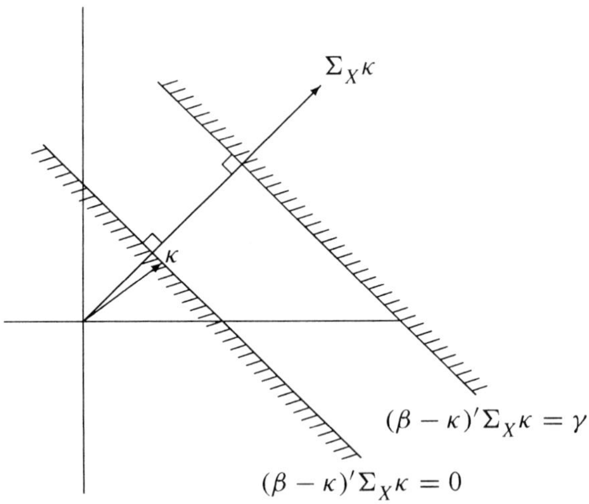

Figure 2.4 *Admissible values of β: β lies between the indicated hyperplanes.*

2.4 Errors in a single regressor

In practice, one often encounters the case where a single regressor is considered poorly measured. This means that Ω, the covariance matrix of the measurement errors, has rank one, because it only has a single nonzero element, in the position on the diagonal corresponding with the poorly measured regressor. The theory developed up till now covers this case, because it is not based on a rank condition for Ω. For this special case, though, a few observations can be made that do not apply in general. We first consider the question what can be said about the signs of the inconsistencies in the OLS estimates. The second issue to be addressed is whether it is worthwhile to omit the single mismeasured variable from the analysis.

The sign of the inconsistencies

Inspection of the expression of the bias of OLS in (2.11) shows that, in a multiple regression setting with only one regressor measured with error, generally all regression coefficient estimators are biased. The problem is not restricted to the coefficient of the single mismeasured variable. However, the signs of the various inconsistencies can be determined in an asymptotic sense. That is, the coefficient of the mismeasured regressor is biased towards zero, and the signs of the biases of the other parameters can be estimated consistently.

This can be shown as follows. Without loss of generality, we may assume that the mismeasured variable is labeled the first variable. Let φ be the measurement error variance. So Ω has a simple structure, $\Omega = \varphi e_1 e_1'$, with e_1 the first unit vector of order g. Substitution of this structure in the expression of the bias in the general case, (2.11), yields for bias vector ω:

$$\omega = -\Sigma_X^{-1}\Omega\beta = -\Sigma_X^{-1}\varphi e_1 e_1'\beta = -\varphi\beta_1 \cdot \Sigma_X^{-1} e_1. \tag{2.21}$$

Hence, on letting $\sigma_X^{i1} \equiv e_i'\Sigma_X^{-1}e_1$, the i-th element of ω is

$$\omega_i = -\varphi\beta_1\sigma_X^{i1}.$$

Apparently, the signs of the elements of ω depend on the signs of the elements of the first column of Σ_X^{-1} and the sign of β_1.

The bias of the first regression coefficient is towards zero, although smaller in absolute size than the true value. This can be seen as follows. Let $\sigma_\Xi^{11} \equiv e_1'\Sigma_\Xi^{-1}e_1$. Then, applying the formula for the inverse of the sum of two matrices (cf. section A.1), we obtain

$$\Sigma_X^{-1} = \Sigma_\Xi^{-1} - \frac{\varphi}{\sigma_\Xi^{11}\varphi + 1}\Sigma_\Xi^{-1}e_1 e_1'\Sigma_\Xi^{-1}.$$

Taking the upper left element of both sides yields

$$\sigma_X^{11} = \sigma_\Xi^{11}\left(1 - \frac{\sigma_\Xi^{11}\varphi}{\sigma_\Xi^{11}\varphi + 1}\right) = \frac{\sigma_\Xi^{11}}{\sigma_\Xi^{11}\varphi + 1} = \frac{1}{\varphi + 1/\sigma_\Xi^{11}} < \frac{1}{\varphi}, \tag{2.22}$$

where we have used $\varphi > 0$. Furthermore, $\sigma_X^{11} > 0$, because Σ_X is a positive definite matrix and hence Σ_X^{-1} is also positive definite. Consequently, $0 < \varphi\sigma_X^{11} < 1$ and hence ω_1 is smaller than β_1 in an absolute sense, with opposite sign. Therefore, the estimate of β_1 is biased towards zero, but the sign of β_1 is estimated consistently.

As a consequence, the signs of the biases of the regression coefficients can be consistently estimated, even when Ω is unknown, because $\varphi > 0$, the sign of β_1 can be consistently estimated, and the signs of the elements of the first column of Σ_X^{-1} can be consistently estimated by the signs of the corresponding elements of S_X^{-1}, because S_X is a consistent estimator of Σ_X.

As a special case, consider the situation in which all off-diagonal elements of Σ_X are negative. Then all elements of Σ_X^{-1} are positive, cf. theorem A.18. In this situation all coefficients are biased towards zero. The argument works the other way around as well. If all elements of Σ_X are positive, all coefficients but the first one are biased away from zero.

In section 5.2, we further discuss the important case of a single mismeasured variable, when we discuss adjustments of inconsistent estimators when additional information is available.

Omitting regressors or using proxies?

When confronted with the fact that measurement error in a single variable contaminates the estimators of all regressors, an alternative approach may be considered. That is, one may just discard the mismeasured regressor and perform regression on the $g - 1$ regressors that do not suffer from measurement error. This will also lead to an inconsistency, which is generally known as the *omitted variables bias*, and this raises the question how this bias compares to the measurement error bias.

First, consider the bias in estimating β when the mismeasured regressor is included. Assume again that this is the first regressor and $\Omega = \varphi e_1 e_1'$. From (2.21), the bias in the second through last elements of b is

$$D'\omega = -\varphi D'\Sigma_X^{-1} e_1 \beta_1, \tag{2.23}$$

with D a $g \times (g - 1)$ matrix obtained from I_g by removing its first column. Consequently, $D'\beta$ equals β without its first element, $D'e_1 = 0$, and

$$I_g = (e_1, D) = e_1 e_1' + DD'.$$

When, on the other hand, we omit the first regressor and perform OLS, we obtain an estimator with probability limit

$$\operatorname*{plim}_{N\to\infty} (D'X'XD)^{-1}D'X'y = (D'\Sigma_X D)^{-1}D'\Sigma_X\beta.$$

The bias $\omega^\dagger$ of this estimator equals

$$\begin{aligned}
\omega^\dagger &= (D'\Sigma_X D)^{-1}D'\Sigma_X\beta - D'\beta \\
&= (D'\Sigma_X D)^{-1}D'\Sigma_X(I_g - DD')\beta \\
&= (D'\Sigma_X D)^{-1}D'\Sigma_X e_1 e_1'\beta \\
&= \frac{1}{\sigma_X^{11}}(D'\Sigma_X D)^{-1}D'\Sigma_X e_1 e_1'\Sigma_X^{-1}e_1 e_1'\beta \\
&= \frac{1}{\sigma_X^{11}}(D'\Sigma_X D)^{-1}D'\Sigma_X(I_g - DD')\Sigma_X^{-1}e_1\beta_1 \\
&= -\frac{1}{\sigma_X^{11}}(D'\Sigma_X D)^{-1}D'\Sigma_X DD'\Sigma_X^{-1}e_1\beta_1 \\
&= -\frac{1}{\sigma_X^{11}}D'\Sigma_X^{-1}e_1\beta_1.
\end{aligned}$$

Apparently, the bias resulting from omitting the 'noisy' regressor is proportional to the bias resulting from using a proxy as given in (2.23). However, the latter bias is smaller in absolute value because, from (2.22), we have $\varphi < 1/\sigma_X^{11}$. Hence, if we are interested in asymptotic bias it is preferable to include a proxy, however imperfect, rather than to exclude it.

2.5 Various additional results

Having established several main results on the effect of measurement error, we now turn to some additional aspects of measurement error, grouped in a single section although they are fairly unrelated. These concern the effect of measurement error in y, the structural model with the additional assumption of normality, prediction in a model with measurement error, and an often encountered situation where the regressor values diverge from the true values but yet no inconsistency arises.

Measurement error in the dependent variable

Up till now, we have considered measurement error in the regressors only and not in the dependent variable y. In order to examine the latter we extend model

(2.1) to a relationship fully between unobservable variables,

$$\eta = \Xi\beta + \varepsilon, \tag{2.24a}$$

related to observable variables through

$$y = \eta + w \tag{2.24b}$$
$$X = \Xi + V. \tag{2.24c}$$

In words, the dependent variable in the regression model is now also unobservable, and y is taken as an imperfect measurement of it. We make the additional assumption that the elements of the N-vector w are i.i.d. independent of the other random variables in the model, and in particular independent of V.

We first consider the case $V = 0$. That is, there is no measurement error in the regressors and only in the dependent variable. The transformed model, in which η and Ξ have been eliminated, is $y = X\beta + u$ with $u = \varepsilon + w$. There is no way to disentangle the role played by the disturbance term ε, which may reflect omitted variables uncorrelated with the regressors, and w, the measurement error in y. Hence, this is a model that satisfies the classical assumptions and OLS is adequate. Of course, the presence of measurement error does have the effect that the sampling variance of the OLS estimator is larger than in the situation without measurement error. Better measurement is preferable in this sense, but imperfect measurement does not lead to incorrectness of the statistical analysis.

Now let $V \neq 0$. By the same argument, we obtain the measurement error model as before as long as w is independent of V. The situation changes when the measurement errors in y and X are correlated, $\mathrm{E}(w(\mathrm{vec}\, V)') = \zeta' \otimes I_N$, say. In that case, (2.1) generalizes to $\operatorname{plim}_{N\to\infty} b = \beta + \Sigma_X^{-1}(\zeta - \Omega\beta)$. Another view of this model is obtained for $\varepsilon = 0$ with probability one. Then the asymmetry between y and X conventionally inherent in the regression model vanishes. Reordering (2.24) gives

$$(\eta, \Xi)\delta = 0$$
$$(y, X) = (\eta, \Xi) + (w, V),$$

with $\delta \equiv (-1, \beta')'$, so a coefficient vector with first element fixed at -1. We have now obtained a very general linear model because any distinction between left-hand side variables and right-hand side variables has vanished. The core of the model is a (single) linear relation between $g + 1$ imperfectly measured variables, with an arbitrary normalization imposed on the parameters of the relation. This general model will be further examined in section 7.5.

Here, we will consider only one particular case of the general model of correlated measurement errors in y and X. This is the case of time series data where the regressors include the lagged dependent variable. When the measurement error in the dependent variable would be uncorrelated over time, the assumptions of the measurement error model as analyzed above still apply. The situation changes when this measurement error is correlated over time.

In order to get a feeling for this model we consider the simplest case of a stationary dynamic model without covariates and with an AR(1) process generating both the observable variable and its measurement error. This gives

$$\begin{aligned} y_t &= \eta_t + w_t \\ \eta_t &= \beta \eta_{t-1} + \varepsilon_t \\ w_t &= \phi w_{t-1} + \zeta_t, \end{aligned}$$

for $t = 1, \ldots, T$, with $|\beta| < 1$, $|\phi| < 1$, and w_t, ε_t, and ζ_t i.i.d. with mean zero and respective variances σ_w^2, σ_ε^2, and σ_ζ^2. The observable variable is a sum of two independent stationary AR(1) processes. When $\hat{\beta}$ is the estimator of β obtained by regressing y on y_{-1}, where y_{-1} is a T-vector with typical element $y_{-1,t} = y_{t-1}$, we have

$$\operatorname*{plim}_{T\to\infty} \hat{\beta} = \frac{\mathrm{E}(y_t y_{t-1})}{\mathrm{E}(y_t^2)} = \frac{\mathrm{E}(\eta_t \eta_{t-1}) + \mathrm{E}(w_t w_{t-1})}{\mathrm{E}(\eta_t^2) + \mathrm{E}(w_t^2)} = \frac{\sigma_\eta^2 \beta + \sigma_w^2 \phi}{\sigma_\eta^2 + \sigma_w^2},$$

with $\sigma_\eta^2 = \sigma_\varepsilon^2/(1-\beta^2)$ and $\sigma_w^2 = \sigma_\zeta^2/(1-\phi^2)$. Clearly, this estimator is inconsistent and its probability limit is the variance-weighted sum of the two AR(1)-coefficients.

Note that in this example, the data are not independent for different observations, which is a second departure from the standard model.

The structural model under normality

The structural measurement error model, i.e., the model where the true values of the regressors are considered random as introduced in section 2.1, allows for some additional insight when the underlying distribution of Ξ is assumed normal. In addition, we assume that the elements of ε and the rows of Ξ and V are independently normally distributed. We now consider this special case.

Under these assumptions, for a typical observation n, $1 \le n \le N$,

$$\begin{bmatrix} y_n \\ x_n \end{bmatrix} \sim \mathcal{N}_{g+1}\left(0, \begin{bmatrix} \sigma_\varepsilon^2 + \beta'\Sigma_\Xi\beta & \beta'\Sigma_\Xi \\ \Sigma_\Xi\beta & \Sigma_X \end{bmatrix}\right),$$

with x_n' the n-th row of X. Using the expression for the conditional normal distribution (see section A.5), we obtain that the distribution of y_n given x_n is

$$\begin{aligned} y_n \mid x_n &\sim \mathcal{N}(x_n'\Sigma_X^{-1}\Sigma_\Xi\beta, \sigma_\varepsilon^2 + \beta'\Sigma_\Xi\beta - \beta'\Sigma_\Xi\Sigma_X^{-1}\Sigma_\Xi\beta) \\ &= \mathcal{N}(x_n'\kappa, \gamma). \end{aligned}$$

For all observations together, this gives $y \mid X \sim \mathcal{N}_N(X\kappa, \gamma I_N)$. In particular, $\mathrm{E}(y \mid X) = X\kappa$ and $\mathrm{Var}(y \mid X) = \gamma I_N$. The model (2.1)–(2.2) can hence be written as $y = X\kappa + \varepsilon^*$, with $\varepsilon^* \equiv y - X\kappa$ distributed independently of X. This formulation sheds light on the measurement error model from a different angle. We now have a regression model that satisfies the maximal set of convenient assumptions that can be formulated for a regression model, but it is couched in terms of the 'wrong' parameters, κ and γ instead of β and σ_ε^2. Hence, OLS provides optimal estimators of these parameters. As a byproduct we obtain the probability limits of these parameters as derived in section 2.1.

In fact, given the very convenient assumptions, we can not only obtain asymptotic results but even small-sample results, without having to condition on X as is commonly done. We have

$$\begin{aligned} \mathrm{E}(b) &= \mathrm{E}_X\big(\mathrm{E}_{\varepsilon^*}(b \mid X)\big) \\ &= \mathrm{E}_X\big((X'X)^{-1}X'\,\mathrm{E}_{\varepsilon^*}(y \mid X)\big) \\ &= \kappa, \\ \mathrm{Var}(b) &= \mathrm{E}_X\big(\mathrm{Var}_{\varepsilon^*}(b \mid X)\big) + \mathrm{Var}_X\big(\mathrm{E}_{\varepsilon^*}(b \mid X)\big) \\ &= \mathrm{E}_X\big((X'X)^{-1}X'\,\mathrm{Var}_{\varepsilon^*}(y \mid X)X(X'X)^{-1}\big) + \mathrm{Var}_X(\kappa) \\ &= \gamma\,\mathrm{E}_X\big((X'X)^{-1}\big) \\ &= \frac{1}{N-g-1}\gamma\Sigma_X^{-1}, \end{aligned}$$

where the last equality is based on an elegant property of the Wishart distribution (see section A.5).

Prediction

Up till now, the general impression left by the measurement error theory is that everything goes wrong with OLS. This is not always the case. Prediction of the value of the dependent variable, at least in the structural model under normality, is not hampered by measurement error.

The objective is to predict y_m, say, using x_m, the corresponding noisy observation. Following standard econometric practice, the formal question is to find an unbiased predictor of $\mathrm{E}(y_m \mid x_m)$. In the structural model under normality, $\mathrm{E}(y_m \mid x_m) = x'_m\kappa$. Hence, an unbiased predictor is given by $x'_m b$, so by combining the noisy value x_m and the biased OLS estimator b.

This possibility of unbiased prediction, in the structural model, by using the biased OLS estimator b does not carry over to the functional model. There we have, still assuming normality,

$$y \mid X, \Xi \sim \mathcal{N}_N(\Xi\beta, \sigma_\varepsilon^2 I_N),$$

so $\mathrm{E}(y_m \mid x_m, \xi_m) = \xi'_m\beta$, which involves both the true regressor values and the parameter vector β. In general, the OLS predictor $x'_m b$ is biased. The essence of problem is that, in the functional case where no distribution underlying Ξ is assumed, Ξ can not be integrated out.

Categorized variables and the Berkson model

A crucial aspect of regression with a mismeasured variable is the induced inconsistency of the regression coefficient estimator. The use of regressor values deviating from the correct ones can be considered the culprit. However, phrased as such this statement is too crude. In a number of econometric models where true and employed regressor values diverge no inconsistency follows.

An important situation where the use of inexact values for a regressor does not automatically lead to an errors-in-variables model is the one where a regressor has been categorized in a number of intervals. This occurs frequently in micro-economic data, where, for example, people were not asked for their exact incomes, but only to which income category (e.g., \$0–10,000, \$10,000–20,000, etc.) they belong. Let z be the categorized variable, with $z_n = j$ if person n falls in income category j, and let ξ_n denote the true, exact, income. Assume that there is no misclassification, i.e., the categories are correct, and assume further that we know the exact income distribution in the population (e.g., from detailed tax records or data from a central statistical agency). From this information, we can compute

$$x_n \equiv \mathrm{E}(\xi_n \mid z_n) = \mathrm{E}(\xi_n \mid \xi_n \in \text{ income class } z_n).$$

Of course, x_n is an imperfectly measured proxy of income. However, note that we can write

$$\xi_n = x_n + v_n, \tag{2.25}$$

with $\mathrm{E}(v_n \mid x_n) = 0$ by construction, and hence $\mathrm{E}(\xi_n \mid x_n) = x_n$, because there is a one-to-one relationship between z_n and x_n. This is different from the usual measurement error situation, in which large values of x may be induced by large values of the measurement error, and hence generally $|\,\mathrm{E}(\xi_n \mid x_n)| < |x_n|$.

The characterization (2.25) leads us to consider the general model, for all observations together,

$$
\begin{aligned}
y &= \Xi\beta + \varepsilon \\
\Xi &= X + V,
\end{aligned}
\tag{2.26}
$$

with $\mathrm{E}(V \mid X) = 0$. This can evidently be rewritten as

$$
\begin{aligned}
y &= X\beta + (V\beta + \varepsilon) \\
&= X\beta + u,
\end{aligned}
\tag{2.27}
$$

with u implicitly defined. Note that, contrary to the usual measurement error model, $\mathrm{E}(u \mid X) = 0$, so that the model satisifes the requirements of the standard linear regression model without measurement error. Thus, the OLS estimator of β is consistent (and unbiased in small samples), and its (asymptotic) covariance matrix is consistently estimated. The estimator of the disturbance variance and the R^2 pertain to the reduced form model (2.27) rather than the structural form model (2.26), however. Whether this is considered a severe problem depends on the application.

The general model discussed here is the so-called *Berkson model*, after Berkson (1950). It has its origin in the natural sciences, where the observed values of the regressor (such as the intended amount of drugs administered to an animal) are often chosen by the researcher, but the actual relevant values are unknown, e.g., because of errors in reading off measurement devices. A similar situation is found in economics when an industrial company wants to model the demand for one of its products as a function of price. The company chooses the price it charges to the retailers, but has no control over the price charged to the customers by the retailers. The company may only know the average price actually charged.

2.6 Bibliographical notes

2.1 An overview article with a striking example of the consequences of measurement error and how to handle it is Cragg (1994).

There are of course many more general measurement error structures conceivable and relevant than the simple white noise considered in section 2.1. A simple extension is to let the error correlate with Ξ. This has been explored by, e.g., Haitovsky (1972) and Bound, Brown, Duncan, and Rodgers (1990). As potential reason for this phenomenon, Haitovsky mentions the case where, in a survey, respondents are likely to understate their true incomes, and the discrepancies between reported and true income increase with income. Buonaccorsi (1989) discusses a model where the true and observed values are linearly related. Bound and Krueger (1991) compare survey data on earnings with tax records and find a negative correlation between measurement error and true earnings, and Bound, Brown, Duncan, and Rodgers (1994) compare survey data on earnings with wage incomes as supplied by the employer. They find that individual reports were fairly accurate, and also that the errors are negatively related to true earnings. Their approach is followed by Albæk, Arai, Asplund, Barth, and Strøjer Madsen (1998) in an analysis of the effects of wages on firm size.

Hwang (1986) analyzed a model where the noise is multiplicative rather than additive.

Incidental parameters, as arising in the functional model, increase in number along with the sample size, which complicates the statistical theory for models with such parameters, like the functional model. This model will be discussed in chapter 4. The "incidental parameters problem" was defined by Neyman and Scott (1948). Lancaster (2000) surveys the history both of the paper and of the problem in the statistics and econometrics literature.

2.2 The impact of measurement error is usually assessed by asymptotic results, and this section is no exception. Another way of analysis is the *perturbation* approach, which is to inspect what happens when (small) disturbances are added to the columns of Ξ. See, e.g., Chatterjee and Hadi (1988).

The term reliability originates in psychological test theory, where the model $X = T + e$ is used, with X the observed test score, T the so-called *true score* (which is the latent variable), and e is the measurement error. The reliability is then defined as the squared correlation between X and T, which is equivalent to $\mathrm{E}(T^2)/\mathrm{E}(X^2)$, which is the scalar equivalent of the expression $\Sigma_X^{-1}\Sigma_\Xi$ used in the main text. The reciprocal of the noise-to-signal ratio is of course the signal-to-noise ratio, which is often used for physical measurements.

2.3 Some results draw on Bekker, Kapteyn, and Wansbeek (1984).

2.4 The results on the consequences of errors in a single regressor are due to Levi (1973). An example of how the formula (2.21) can be used in practice is the study of Kooreman (2000) of the effects of a child benefit system on the expenditure patterns of households. Because he had external information on the size of the measurement error in this type of income data, he was actually able to estimate the size of the biases (see also section 5.2).

The result that, judged by bias, it is better to include than omit a proxy is due to McCallum (1972) and Wickens (1972). The conclusion becomes more complex when second-order considerations are taken into account. When variance rather than bias would be the choice criterion, the conclusion is the other way around. If the two are combined in an MSE criterion, so variance plus squared bias, there are two counteracting forces. For large N, the bias will always dominate the variance, which tends to zero, and the proxy can better be included. For small N the proxy can better be omitted. These results are due to Aigner (1974). For the case of two regressors measured with error, results were given by Garber and Klepper (1980). The general case, with an arbitrary number of regressors, is complicated. Keeping the mismeasured variables in the regression is still better than omitting them, at least in a particular metric, see Bekker and Wansbeek (1996).

On the Berkson model, see e.g., Berkson (1950), Prais and Aitchison (1954), Moran (1971), and Ketellapper (1981).

Chapter 3

Bounds on the parameters

Having looked at the havoc created by measurement error among traditional estimators, one may ask if one can not do better and construct alternative estimators that are consistent. The answer to this question is somewhat subtle. In the generic case, the parameters in the linear regression model are not identified if measurement error is present. This issue is taken up in detail in chapter 4. In this chapter, we address the question to what extent at least something can be inferred about the true parameter values given the values of the (inconsistent) estimators. The kind of results given are in the form of bounds on the parameters that will hold in the limit.

In section 3.1, a first answer to this question is offered in the simple, one-regressor case through a method called reverse regression. It appears that the regression of x on y rather than y on x provides an asymptotic upper bound on the regression coefficient when x is measured with error; it was shown in chapter 2 that the direct regression of y on x provides a lower bound. This result is interesting in itself but has, in a slightly adapted context, found wide applicability in the econometric analysis of wage discrimination in the labor market. This discussion, which is contained in section 3.2, is followed, in section 3.3, by a treatment of reverse regression in a multi-regressor context. There, the situation is more complicated, and the existence of bounds is limited to certain cases.

In some cases, a researcher is willing to specify an upper bound on the measurement error covariance matrix. If so, the scope of obtaining bounds on the parameters widens greatly. The basic theory is presented in section 3.4. It appears that the bounds on the parameters have an ellipsoid character. In section 3.5, the bounds are refined if the additional assumption is made that the measurement errors are uncorrelated across regressors.

3.1 Reverse regression

We consider again the simplest measurement error regression model, that is, the model with a single regressor, and both variables have mean zero. Written in scalar notation, we then have

$$\begin{aligned} y_n &= \beta \xi_n + \varepsilon_n \\ x_n &= \xi_n + v_n. \end{aligned}$$

We call the usual regression of y on x the *direct* regression. It gives

$$\operatorname*{plim}_{N\to\infty} b_{\mathrm{DIR}} = \operatorname*{plim}_{N\to\infty} \frac{x'y}{x'x} = \beta \frac{\sigma_\xi^2}{\sigma_x^2} = \kappa, \tag{3.1}$$

which has the same sign as β, but is smaller in magnitude. This again illustrates the bias towards zero. Another way to obtain information on β from the data is by performing the *reverse* regression, which is the regression of x on y. We then have to invert the result to make it comparable to the result of the direct regression. This yields

$$\operatorname*{plim}_{N\to\infty} b_{\mathrm{REV}} = \operatorname*{plim}_{N\to\infty} \frac{y'y}{x'y} = \beta + \frac{\sigma_\varepsilon^2}{\beta\sigma_\xi^2}, \tag{3.2}$$

which has the same sign as β, but is larger in magnitude. Apparently, reverse regression also gives an inconsistent estimator of β, but now with a bias away from zero. This is illustrated in figure 3.1 for the data of figure 2.1. The estimate of the regression coefficient from the reverse regression is $b_{\mathrm{REV}} = 1.5576$, which is fairly close to its asymptotic value of 1.5.

Thus, the right hand sides of (3.1) and (3.2) bound (in the limit) the true value β from below and above, respectively. Because these bounds can be estimated consistently, by the direct regression and the reverse regression, we can take $(x'x)^{-1}x'y$ and $(x'y)^{-1}y'y$ as bounds between which β should lie (again, in the limit). The bounds are obtained without making assumptions about the size of the measurement error.

From each of the two regressions we can compute the R^2. From the direct regression we have

$$\begin{aligned} R^2_{\mathrm{DIR}} &= 1 - \frac{(y - xb_{\mathrm{DIR}})'(y - xb_{\mathrm{DIR}})}{y'y} \\ &= 1 - \frac{y'\left(I_N - \frac{1}{x'x}xx'\right)y}{y'y} \end{aligned}$$

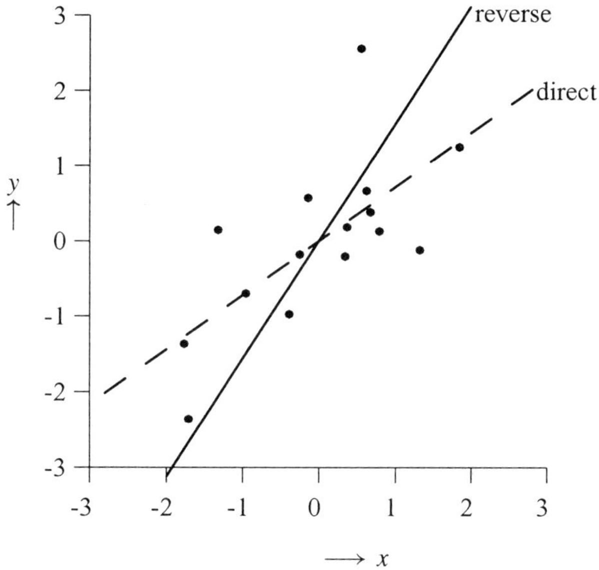

Figure 3.1 *Estimated regression lines of direct regression (y on x) and reverse regression (x on y).*

$$= \frac{(x'y)^2}{(x'x)(y'y)},$$

and from the reverse regression we have

$$\begin{aligned} R^2_{\text{REV}} &= 1 - \frac{(x - y/b_{\text{REV}})'(x - y/b_{\text{REV}})}{x'x} \\ &= 1 - \frac{x'\left(I_N - \dfrac{1}{y'y}yy'\right)x}{x'x} \\ &= \frac{(x'y)^2}{(x'x)(y'y)}. \end{aligned}$$

Of course, both approaches lead to the same result, the squared correlation coefficient between x and y. From the expressions for b_{DIR}, b_{REV}, and R^2, we see that they are related by

$$b_{\text{DIR}} = R^2 b_{\text{REV}}.$$

This leads to the conclusion that the bounds provided by the direct and reverse regressions are tight if R^2 is high.

Another way to look at the same result is obtained by letting

$$\psi \equiv \frac{\sigma_v^2}{\sigma_\varepsilon^2}.$$

When ψ would be known, a consistent estimator of β is given by the root of the equation

$$\psi \hat{\beta}^2 x'y + \hat{\beta}(x'x - \psi y'y) - x'y = 0 \tag{3.3}$$

that has the same sign as $x'y$. This is easily verified by substitution, noting that $x'x/N, x'y/N$, and $y'y/N$ converge to $\sigma_\xi^2 + \sigma_v^2$, $\beta\sigma_\xi^2$ and $\beta^2\sigma_\xi^2 + \sigma_\varepsilon^2$, respectively. When setting $\psi = 0$, OLS is obtained, and letting ψ approach infinity gives the reverse regression. Thus, both regressions form the extreme cases of weighting measurement error in x relative to the error in the equation, or, equivalently, the measurement error in y.

Unfortunately, the results on bounds from direct and reverse regression for the case of a single regressor do not carry over to the multiple regression case in general. As we will see in section 3.3, a generalization is possible under restrictive assumptions only. Before we discuss this generalization we look at a particular case of reverse regression that has attracted much attention in the literature.

3.2 Reverse regression and the analysis of discrimination

There is one particular case where reverse regression has been widely used. This concerns the field of investigation of wage discrimination by gender or race, obviously an issue of great societal relevance. An important econometric research question is whether men are paid more than equally productive women. (Or whites more than equally productive non-whites, but for simplicity we will henceforth only refer to male-female differentials.)

An intuitively appealing approach to this question is to estimate a wage equation by regressing (log-)wages on productivity and possibly other relevant variables and in addition on a dummy variable indicating gender. If the coefficient of the latter shows up significantly it may be interpreted as a signal pointing to discrimination. The unobservability aspect comes in through the productivity variable, which plays a crucial role in the analysis but is at the same time only quantifiable through proxy variables.

Obvious candidates for proxies, often available in datasets, are variables like years of schooling, age, work experience, and job tenure. Still these variables capture only part of someone's productivity and imperfectly measure, for example, firm-specific human capital. When the proxy is a poor one and the measurement error is deemed large relative to the error in the equation, a less biased result may be obtained by running the *reverse* regression of some productivity index on wage and gender. Still a biased result is to be expected, because the income variable, which is now an explanatory variable, is undoubtedly correlated with the disturbance term.

It is possible (and in fact frequently encountered in empirical research) that the two estimates not only differ considerably, but that they are even of opposite sign. In that case, both regressions lead to qualitatively different ideas about the group discriminated against. As an example, consider the following estimated regression equation from Van Schaaijk (1987):

$$\begin{aligned}\log w = 2.78 &+ .29a_2 + .44a_3 + .56a_4 + .63a_5 + .66a_6 \\ &+ .68a_7 + .69a_8 + .60a_9 + .57a_{10} \\ &+ .09e_2 + .29e_3 + .57e_4 + .85e_5 + .15s,\end{aligned}$$

where the symbols have the following meaning: w is wage, the a's are age dummies (21–24, 25–29, 30–34, 35–39, 40-44, 45–49, 50–54, 55–59, 60–64, with 16–20 being the reference group), the e's are (ordered) education dummies, and s is a gender dummy (0 = female, 1 = male). The wages have been computed as average wages based on a sample of 241,000 employees grouped in 2,000 classes. The R^2 is .53.

In particular, this regression gives a coefficient of .15 for the gender dummy, with a t-value of about 7. Because the left-hand side variable is in logarithmic form, this suggests that men are paid 15% more than equally productive women. But, as was argued above, the picture may be biased.

In order to consider the reverse regression we need a scalar measure of productivity. An obvious approach is to use as such the estimated part of the regression without the gender dummy, that is, to use $p \equiv .29a_2 + \cdots + .85e_5$. Then, reverse regression amounts to the regression of p on $\log w$ and the gender dummy. This gives, for the example above,

$$p \equiv (.29a_2 + \cdots + .85e_5) = -1.01 + .45 \log w + .08s.$$

This equation suggests that, controlling for differences in wages, more productivity is required from men than from women, suggesting discrimination against men rather than against women. This impression is reinforced if we rearrange the result in the format of the direct regression:

$$\log w = \frac{1}{.45}(1.01 + p - .08s) = 2.24 + 2.22p - .18s,$$

which confirms that both regressions give contradictory evidence.

A formalization

In order to get an understanding of this phenomenon, we now present a formalization. The direct regression used to assess discrimination is a regression of the logarithm of wage on a number of indicators of productivity like schooling, experience, and job tenure, plus a dummy indicating gender. The coefficient of this dummy can be interpreted as a reflection of discrimination on the market. When the dummy is coded 0 for women and 1 for men, a positive coefficient may indicate discrimination, because it suggests a wage differential between men and women even when accounting for differences in productivity. Empirical findings, like the one discussed above, often point in that direction.

There are, however, various issues that makes such a conclusion debatable. One is economic. A pure discrimination effect would suggest a rent that could be exploited or arbitraged away. In other words, there is 'money lying in the street', which goes against economic rationality. Note, however, that there may be (long-term) productivity differences between men and women that may lead to economically valid wage differentials, but are at the same time socially unacceptable and considered as discrimination. We do not address this issue here, but rather concentrate on an important econometric issue concerning the quality of the estimator of the discrimination coefficient obtained by the direct regression.

The core of the argument is that the indicators that are meant to capture productivity are likely to be only an imperfect reflection of the true productivity. This could bias the estimator of the coefficient. Intuitively, this will arise when, for example, men are more productive than women due to more schooling, on-the-job training, or any other cause imperfectly reflected in the measured variables. Then the latent variable 'productivity' is correlated with the gender dummy and the latter 'picks up' part of the effect of the latent variable, leading to an overestimate of the pure gender effect.

The reverse regression considers the issue from a different angle. It can be used to find another estimate of the coefficient of the gender dummy and, as we will see, this estimator may be an underestimate. Hence, the technique of performing both direct and reverse regression can be jointly employed to bound the true value of the coefficient. If both the lower and the upper bound are of the same sign, this may suggest discrimination even if we do not have a single, consistent, estimator of the coefficient.

To be more specific, the reverse regression is a regression of some productivity index, usually constructed as a linear combination of the productivity indicators weighted with their estimated coefficients from the direct regression, on log wage and the gender dummy. The discrimination issue is now whether men are less productive or qualified than equally paid women. The interpretation of the coefficient of the gender dummy is then the excess productivity or qualification required of men.

In order to have a context to assess the results for the direct and the reverse regression, we need to specify a model relating wages, productivity, and the productivity indicators. The following stylized model captures the essential relevant features of wage formation:

$$y = \tau_y \iota_N + \beta\xi + \alpha z + \varepsilon \tag{3.4a}$$

$$\xi = \mu z + u \tag{3.4b}$$

$$X = \iota_N \tau_X' + \xi\lambda' + V, \tag{3.4c}$$

with the following notation and assumptions. The observables are y $(N \times 1)$ and X $(N \times g)$, denoting log wages and productivity indicators, respectively. The gender dummy is z, with 0 indicating women and 1 indicating men. Because ι_N denotes a vector of N ones, τ_y and τ_X are the intercepts. The disturbance terms are ε $(N \times 1)$, u $(N \times 1)$, and V $(N \times g)$. They are assumed to be i.i.d. with mean zero. Typical elements of ε and u have variances σ_ε^2 and σ_u^2, respectively, and a typical row of V has covariance matrix Ω of order $g \times g$.

According to (3.4b), productivity differs between men and women, reflecting differences in schooling, job tenure, and the like. Because in general the productivity of men is larger, $\mu > 0$. According to equation (3.4a), wages are determined by productivity ($\beta > 0$) and hence, through this variable, indirectly by gender. Gender may also come in directly and α appearing positive may be taken as signaling discrimination against women. Equation (3.4c) states that the various productivity indicators depend on productivity, but also on additional, unobservable factors uncorrelated with productivity.

Asymptotic results

From inspection of (3.4), it is evident that the scale of ξ can be chosen freely. There are no observable implications if we would multiply the latent variable ξ, the unknown coefficient μ, and the unobservable disturbance term u by some constant, c say, when we would divide the unknown coefficients β and λ by c. Therefore, we impose the normalization

$$\sigma_u^{-2} + \lambda'\Omega^{-1}\lambda = 1.$$

Using this normalization, it follows that

$$(\sigma_u^2\lambda\lambda' + \Omega)\sigma_u^{-2}\Omega^{-1}\lambda = \lambda\lambda'\Omega^{-1}\lambda + \sigma_u^{-2}\lambda = \lambda.$$

This evidently implies that

$$(\sigma_u^2\lambda\lambda' + \Omega)^{-1}\lambda = \sigma_u^{-2}\Omega^{-1}\lambda, \tag{3.5}$$

which will prove convenient below.

Before we consider the asymptotic behavior of the estimators in the direct and the reverse regression, we derive a number of probability limits that are helpful in obtaining results. We use the notation M_ι to denote the projection matrix orthogonal to ι_N (i.e., the centering operator of order N) and $M_{z\iota}$ to denote the projection matrix orthogonal to z and ι_N. Furthermore, let

$$\sigma_z^2 \equiv \operatorname*{plim}_{N\to\infty} \frac{1}{N} z' M_\iota z = \pi(1-\pi),$$

where π is the fraction of men in the population where the data can be considered a sample from. Using this notation, we have

$$\begin{aligned}
\operatorname*{plim}_{N\to\infty} \frac{1}{N} X' M_\iota z &= \operatorname*{plim}_{N\to\infty} \frac{1}{N} (\iota_N \tau_X' + \xi\lambda' + V)' M_\iota z \\
&= \lambda \operatorname*{plim}_{N\to\infty} \frac{1}{N} \xi' M_\iota z \\
&= \lambda\mu\sigma_z^2 \\
\operatorname*{plim}_{N\to\infty} \frac{1}{N} y' M_\iota z &= \operatorname*{plim}_{N\to\infty} \frac{1}{N} (\tau_y \iota_N + \beta\xi + \alpha z + \varepsilon)' M_\iota z \\
&= \beta \operatorname*{plim}_{N\to\infty} \frac{1}{N} \xi' M_\iota z + \alpha \operatorname*{plim}_{N\to\infty} \frac{1}{N} z' M_\iota z \\
&= (\alpha + \beta\mu)\sigma_z^2,
\end{aligned}$$

and, because $\operatorname{plim}_{N\to\infty} \xi' M_{z\iota} \xi / N = \sigma_u^2$, we have

$$\begin{aligned}
\operatorname*{plim}_{N\to\infty} \frac{1}{N} X' M_{z\iota} X &= \operatorname*{plim}_{N\to\infty} \frac{1}{N} (\iota_N \tau_X' + \xi\lambda' + V)' M_{z\iota} (\iota_N \tau_X' + \xi\lambda' + V) \\
&= \sigma_u^2 \lambda\lambda' + \Omega \\
\operatorname*{plim}_{N\to\infty} \frac{1}{N} X' M_{z\iota} y &= \operatorname*{plim}_{N\to\infty} \frac{1}{N} (\iota_N \tau_X' + \xi\lambda' + V)' M_{z\iota} (\tau_y \iota_N + \beta\xi + \alpha z + \varepsilon) \\
&= \beta\lambda \operatorname*{plim}_{N\to\infty} \frac{1}{N} \xi' M_{z\iota} \xi \\
&= \beta\lambda\sigma_u^2
\end{aligned}$$

$$\begin{aligned}\operatorname*{plim}_{N\to\infty} \frac{1}{N} y' M_{z\iota} y &= \operatorname*{plim}_{N\to\infty} \frac{1}{N} (\tau_y \iota_N + \beta\xi + \alpha z + \varepsilon)' M_{z\iota} (\tau_y \iota_N + \beta\xi + \alpha z + \varepsilon) \\ &= \operatorname*{plim}_{N\to\infty} \frac{1}{N} (\beta^2 \xi' M_{z\iota} \xi + \varepsilon' M_{z\iota} \varepsilon) \\ &= \beta^2 \sigma_u^2 + \sigma_\varepsilon^2 .\end{aligned}$$

These constitute the auxiliary results. We now turn to the direct and reverse regression in the discrimination model.

First, consider the direct regression by OLS corresponding with (3.4a). Because the single productivity variable ξ is unobservable, it is replaced by a number of indicators contained in X. Therefore, we consider the regression of y on ι_N, X, and z. The coefficient vector with X is denoted by δ. By using the Frisch-Waugh theorem (see section A.1), we find that

$$\begin{aligned}\operatorname*{plim}_{N\to\infty} \hat{\delta} &= \operatorname*{plim}_{N\to\infty} (X' M_{z\iota} X)^{-1} X' M_{z\iota} y \\ &= \beta \sigma_u^2 (\sigma_u^2 \lambda\lambda' + \Omega)^{-1} \lambda \\ &= \Omega^{-1} \lambda \beta ,\end{aligned}$$

where the last step is based on (3.5). Applying the Frisch-Waugh theorem once more gives

$$\begin{aligned}\operatorname*{plim}_{N\to\infty} \hat{\alpha} &= \operatorname*{plim}_{N\to\infty} \frac{z' M_\iota (y - X\hat{\delta})}{z' M_\iota z} \\ &= \frac{1}{\sigma_z^2} \left((\alpha + \beta\mu)\sigma_z^2 - \mu\sigma_z^2 \lambda' \Omega^{-1} \lambda \beta \right) \\ &= \alpha + \beta\mu - \mu(1 - \sigma_u^{-2})\beta \\ &= \alpha + \frac{\beta\mu}{\sigma_u^2} \\ &> \alpha .\end{aligned}$$

This shows the first result. Assuming that the model (3.4) holds, substituting indicators for productivity leads to an overestimate of α, perhaps unduly suggesting wage discrimination in the labor market.

Second, consider reverse regression. That is, we construct the variable $X\hat{\delta}$ and regress it on ι_N, y, and z. Let the coefficient of y in this regression be denoted by γ and the coefficient of z be ρ. Then the estimated reverse regression equation can be written as $X\delta = \tau_{X\delta} \iota_N + \gamma y + \rho z$. Using a derivation that is completely analogous to the derivation of the probability limits of the direct regression, we find that the probability limits of the reverse regression are given by the following expressions:

$$\begin{aligned}
\operatorname*{plim}_{N\to\infty} \hat{\gamma} &= \operatorname*{plim}_{N\to\infty} \frac{y' M_{z\iota} X\hat{\delta}}{y' M_{z\iota} y} \\
&= \frac{\beta^2 \sigma_u^2 \lambda' \Omega^{-1} \lambda}{\beta^2 \sigma_u^2 + \sigma_\varepsilon^2} \\
\operatorname*{plim}_{N\to\infty} \hat{\rho} &= \operatorname*{plim}_{N\to\infty} \frac{z' M_\iota (X\hat{\delta} - y\hat{\gamma})}{z' M_\iota z} \\
&= \frac{1}{\sigma_z^2} \left(\mu \sigma_z^2 \lambda' \Omega^{-1} \lambda \beta - (\alpha + \beta\mu) \sigma_z^2 \frac{\beta^2 \sigma_u^2 \lambda' \Omega^{-1} \lambda}{\beta^2 \sigma_u^2 + \sigma_\varepsilon^2} \right) \\
&= \lambda' \Omega^{-1} \lambda \beta \left(\mu - (\alpha + \beta\mu) \frac{\beta \sigma_u^2}{\beta^2 \sigma_u^2 + \sigma_\varepsilon^2} \right) \\
&= \lambda' \Omega^{-1} \lambda \beta \frac{\mu \sigma_\varepsilon^2 - \alpha \beta \sigma_u^2}{\beta^2 \sigma_u^2 + \sigma_\varepsilon^2}.
\end{aligned}$$

The estimated reverse regression equation becomes in the format of the direct regression $y = (X\delta - \tau_{X\delta}\iota_N - \rho z)/\gamma$. Consequently, the counterpart of α in the reverse regression is $-\rho/\gamma$, and we find

$$\begin{aligned}
\operatorname*{plim}_{N\to\infty} \tilde{\alpha} &= \operatorname*{plim}_{N\to\infty} -\frac{\hat{\rho}}{\hat{\gamma}} \\
&= -\lambda' \Omega^{-1} \lambda \beta \frac{\mu \sigma_\varepsilon^2 - \alpha \beta \sigma_u^2}{\beta^2 \sigma_u^2 \lambda' \Omega^{-1} \lambda} \\
&= \frac{\alpha \beta \sigma_u^2 - \mu \sigma_\varepsilon^2}{\beta \sigma_u^2} \\
&= \alpha - \frac{\mu \sigma_\varepsilon^2}{\beta \sigma_u^2} \\
&< \alpha.
\end{aligned}$$

This shows the second result. Under the assumptions made, reverse regression leads to an underestimate of α.

To summarize the results, we have shown that direct and reverse regression provide us with asymptotic bounds between which the true value of α should lie. If the range of values does not include 0, wage discrimination may have been detected.

3.3 Bounds with multiple regression

We now turn to the problem of finding bounds in the case of multiple regression. For the single regressor case, we saw in section 3.1 that we could bound the true coefficient asymptotically. We may now wonder to what extent we are able to generalize this result to the multiple regression case. The answer is, not very much. The classical result in this area is due to Koopmans (1937). He showed that only under very restrictive conditions such a generalization is possible. We will present his result, albeit in a different formulation, in the form of a theorem, and after that we give an interpretation and a short discussion.

Theorem 3.1 (Koopmans). Let Σ be a symmetric positive definite $m \times m$ matrix and let the elements σ^{ij} of Σ^{-1} be positive. Let Φ be a diagonal $m \times m$ matrix and let the m-vector δ with first element $\delta_1 = 1$ satisfy $(\Sigma - \Phi)\delta = 0$. Then (i) if $0 \leq \Phi \leq \Sigma$, δ can be expressed as a linear combination of the columns of Σ^{-1} with nonnegative weights. Conversely, (ii) for each δ with first element $\delta_1 = 1$ that can be expressed as a linear combination of the columns of Σ^{-1} with nonnegative weights, there exists one and only one diagonal matrix Φ such that $0 \leq \Phi \leq \Sigma$ and $(\Sigma - \Phi)\delta = 0$.

Before proving the theorem, we make a few remarks. Because Σ is nonsingular, any m-vector δ can be written as a linear combination of the columns of Σ^{-1}. The importance lies in the result or requirement that all weights should be nonnegative.

The requirement that $\delta_1 = 1$ is only a convenient, but harmless restriction. Clearly, we can multiply δ with any positive constant without changing the results: if δ is a linear combination of the columns of Σ^{-1} with nonnegative weights, so is $c\delta$ for any $c > 0$. Furthermore, if the first element of δ is negative, the theorem can be modified straightforwardly to yield that δ should now be a linear combination of the columns of Σ^{-1} with nonpositive weights. Finally, if δ is a linear combination of the columns of Σ^{-1} with only nonnegative (or only nonpositive) weights, δ_1 can only be zero in the uninteresting trivial case that all weights are zero, because the elements Σ^{-1} are all assumed to be positive. Note that, similarly, all elements of δ are strictly positive is δ is a linear combination of the columns of Σ^{-1} with nonnegative weights, unless all weights are zero. This will be used in the proof.

In our application of the theorem, we are interested only in situations with $\delta_1 = 1$ and therefore, we use this restriction in the theorem.

Proof. Define $\lambda \equiv \Sigma\delta = \Phi\delta$, $\Lambda \equiv \operatorname{diag}(\lambda)$, and $\Delta \equiv \operatorname{diag}(\delta)$. Let ι_m denote an m-vector of ones. Then, $\lambda = \Lambda\iota_m$, $\delta = \Delta\iota_m$, $\Lambda = \Delta\Phi$, $\Delta = \operatorname{diag}(\Sigma^{-1}\lambda) =$

$\operatorname{diag}(\Sigma^{-1}\Lambda\iota_m)$, and $\Lambda\Delta = \operatorname{diag}(\Lambda\Sigma^{-1}\Lambda\iota_m)$. We first prove (i). According to theorem A.10,

$$0 \le \Phi \le \Sigma \tag{3.6}$$

is equivalent with

$$\Phi \ge \Phi\Sigma^{-1}\Phi. \tag{3.7}$$

This implies

$$\Delta\Phi\Delta \ge \Delta\Phi\Sigma^{-1}\Phi\Delta, \tag{3.8}$$

or $\Lambda\Delta \ge \Lambda\Sigma^{-1}\Lambda$ or $\operatorname{diag}(\Lambda\Sigma^{-1}\Lambda\iota_m) \ge \Lambda\Sigma^{-1}\Lambda$. According to Theorem A.17 this is in its turn equivalent with $\lambda_i\lambda_j \ge 0$ for all $i \ne j$. Hence, either all elements of λ are nonnegative or all are nonpositive. Because $\delta_1 = 1 > 0$ and all elements of Σ^{-1} are positive, all elements of λ must be nonnegative.

To prove (ii), if δ is a linear combination of the columns of Σ^{-1} with non-negative weights and $\delta_1 = 1$, then $\delta_i > 0$ for all i, so Δ is nonsingular and $\Phi = \Lambda\Delta^{-1}$ is unique. Furthermore, if Δ is nonsingular, (3.7) and (3.8) are equivalent and hence, (3.6) follows. □

Before we apply this theorem, we first note that it can be used to derive a complementary result. Let σ^{ij} be a typical element of Σ^{-1}. If $\sigma^{ij} < 0$ for all $i \ne j$ (so that all elements of Σ are positive, cf. Theorem A.18), then using a similar proof as has been given for Theorem A.17, $\lambda_i\lambda_j \ge 0$ for all $i \ne j$ would imply $\operatorname{diag}(\Lambda\Sigma^{-1}\Lambda\iota_m) \le \Lambda\Sigma^{-1}\Lambda$. Because (3.6) implies that $\operatorname{diag}(\Lambda\Sigma^{-1}\Lambda\iota_m) \ge \Lambda\Sigma^{-1}\Lambda$, it can not be true that $\lambda_i\lambda_j \ge 0$ for all $i \ne j$ and $\lambda_i\lambda_j \ne 0$ for some $i \ne j$. In this case, δ is not a linear combination of Σ^{-1} with only nonnegative or only nonpositive weights, unless $\delta = 0$.

Implication of the theorem

The theorem can be brought to bear upon the subject of errors in variables when we make the following choice for Σ, Φ, and δ:

$$\Sigma \equiv \mathrm{E}\,\frac{1}{N}\begin{bmatrix} y'y & y'X \\ X'y & X'X \end{bmatrix} = \begin{bmatrix} \sigma_y^2 & \sigma_{xy}' \\ \sigma_{xy} & \Sigma_X \end{bmatrix}, \tag{3.9a}$$

$$\Phi = \begin{bmatrix} \sigma_\varepsilon^2 & 0 \\ 0 & \Omega \end{bmatrix}, \qquad \text{and} \qquad \delta = \begin{bmatrix} 1 \\ -\beta \end{bmatrix}, \tag{3.9b}$$

where Ω, satisfying $0 \leq \Omega < \Sigma_X$, is a *diagonal* matrix. For this choice of Σ, Φ, and δ, it is easy to check that

$$(\Sigma - \Phi)\delta = 0 \qquad \text{and} \qquad 0 \leq \Phi \leq \Sigma. \tag{3.10}$$

We can now inspect the signs of the elements of Σ^{-1}. If all signs are positive, the theorem is applicable and we can conclude that δ as defined in (3.9) is a linear combination of the columns of Σ^{-1} with nonnegative weights. We will now interpret this result. To that end we use the following equality:

$$\Sigma \begin{bmatrix} 1 \\ -\kappa \end{bmatrix} = \begin{bmatrix} \sigma_y^2 & \sigma'_{xy} \\ \sigma_{xy} & \Sigma_X \end{bmatrix} \begin{bmatrix} 1 \\ -\Sigma_X^{-1}\sigma_{xy} \end{bmatrix} = \gamma e_1,$$

where e_1 is the first unit vector, κ was defined in (2.9), and γ was defined in (2.12a). This result implies that

$$\Sigma^{-1} e_1 = \frac{1}{\gamma} \begin{bmatrix} 1 \\ -\kappa \end{bmatrix}.$$

In words, the first column of Σ^{-1} is proportional to the vector of regression coefficients of y on X or, otherwise stated, is equal to this vector after a normalization. Similarly $\Sigma^{-1}e_2$ is equal to the (normalized) vector of regression coefficients obtained by regressing the second variable on the other variables, including y. Proceeding in this way the columns of Σ^{-1} are seen to be equal to the regression vector of one variable on all other ones. These $g + 1$ regressions are sometimes called the *elementary* regressions. Let the elementary regression vectors be normalized so that their first element equals 1. Then, δ still must be a linear combination of these vectors, with nonnegative weights. However, because the first element of δ is also normalized at 1, it follows that the linear combination must be a convex combination, i.e., the weights are all between 0 and 1 and sum to unity.

This leads to the main result, which is that β lies in the convex hull of the vectors of the (normalized) elementary regressions if all elementary regression vectors are positive. This condition can be formulated slightly more generally by saying that it suffices that all regression vectors are in the same orthant, because by changing signs of variables this can simply be translated into the previous condition. Note, however, that the definition of δ and the elementary regression vectors implies that they are nonnegative if and only if β is nonpositive, i.e., all regression coefficients must be nonpositive. An indication of this can also be found by the requirement that all elements of Σ^{-1} should be positive, which is equivalent to the requirement that all off-diagonal elements of Σ should be negative, i.e., all variables are negatively correlated (again, after a possible sign reversal of some of the variables). Whether this situation is likely to occur in practice must be doubted.

Using the complementary result stated above, it follows that, if all off-diagonal elements of Σ^{-1} are negative (or, equivalently, if all elements of Σ are positive), then β does not lie in the convex hull of the regression vectors of the (normalized) elementary regressions.

3.4 Bounds on the measurement error

In the sections 2.3 and 3.3, we have derived regions where the parameter vector β may lie in the presence of measurement error of unknown magnitude. For general Ω this region was found in section 2.3 to be the region between two parallel hyperplanes. The region characterized in the previous section, based on Ω restricted to be diagonal, can be of practical use but exists only in rather exceptional cases. Much more can be said when further information on the measurement error variances is available. In this section, we explore this situation. As usual, the analysis is asymptotic and we neglect the distinction between finite-sample results and results that hold in the limit. We assume κ and Σ_X to be known, although in practice only their consistent estimators b and S_X, the OLS estimator of β and the sample covariance matrix of the regressors, respectively, are known.

The bounds that we consider in this section are of the form

$$0 \leq \Omega \leq \Omega^* < \Sigma_X, \tag{3.11}$$

with Ω^* given. The motivation behind such a bound is that a researcher who has reason to suppose that measurement error is present may not know the actual size of its variance, but may have an idea of an upper bound to that variance. We will now study to which extent this tightens the bounds on the regression coefficients.

Define

$$\begin{aligned}
\Sigma_\Xi^* &\equiv \Sigma_X - \Omega^* \\
\kappa^* &\equiv (\Sigma_X - \Omega^*)^{-1}\Sigma_\Xi\beta = \Sigma_\Xi^{*\,-1}\Sigma_\Xi\beta = \Sigma_\Xi^{*\,-1}\Sigma_X\kappa.
\end{aligned}$$

The interpretation of κ^* is that it is the probability limit of the estimator of β that would be consistent if the measurement error were maximal, i.e., equal to Ω^*. Further, define

$$\Psi = \Sigma_\Xi^{-1} - \Sigma_X^{-1} \tag{3.12a}$$

$$\Psi^* \equiv \Sigma_\Xi^{*\,-1} - \Sigma_X^{-1}. \tag{3.12b}$$

Note that $\Omega \geq 0$ implies that $\Psi \geq 0$ and $\Psi^* \geq 0$. Because Ψ^* depends on Σ_X, and because Ω^* is a known matrix, we know Ψ^*, again in the asymptotic sense. Further properties involving Ψ and Ψ^* that prove useful later on are

$$\Psi \Sigma_X \kappa = \Psi \Sigma_\Xi \beta = (\Sigma_\Xi^{-1} - \Sigma_X^{-1}) \Sigma_\Xi \beta = \beta - \kappa \tag{3.13a}$$

$$\Psi^* \Sigma_X \kappa = (\Sigma_\Xi^{*-1} - \Sigma_X^{-1}) \Sigma_X \kappa = \kappa^* - \kappa, \tag{3.13b}$$

which, taken together, yield

$$(\Psi - \Psi^*) \Sigma_X \kappa = \beta - \kappa^*. \tag{3.14}$$

We rewrite (3.11) by subtracting its various parts from Σ_X. This gives $\Sigma_X \geq \Sigma_\Xi \geq \Sigma_\Xi^* > 0$, and, consequently, cf. theorem A.12, $0 < \Sigma_X^{-1} \leq \Sigma_\Xi^{-1} \leq \Sigma_\Xi^{*-1}$. Next, subtract Σ_X^{-1} from each part and use (3.12) to obtain

$$-\Sigma_X^{-1} < 0 \leq \Psi \leq \Psi^*. \tag{3.15}$$

We use theorem A.10 to obtain as implications of (3.15)

$$\Psi^* \Psi^{*-} \Psi = \Psi \qquad \text{and} \qquad (\Psi - \Psi^*) \Psi^{*-} \Psi \leq 0, \tag{3.16}$$

where the superscript "–" indicates a generalized inverse, the choice of which is immaterial. This implies

$$\kappa' \Sigma_X (\Psi - \Psi^*) \Psi^{*-} \Psi \Sigma_X \kappa \leq 0 \qquad \text{and} \qquad \Psi^* \Psi^{*-} \Psi \Sigma_X \kappa = \Psi \Sigma_X \kappa,$$

or, using (3.13a) and (3.14),

$$(\beta - \kappa^*)' \Psi^{*-} (\beta - \kappa) \leq 0 \qquad \text{and} \qquad \Psi^* \Psi^{*-} (\beta - \kappa) = \beta - \kappa. \tag{3.17}$$

This constitutes the main result. It characterizes a region where β lies given κ and Ψ^*.

To make it more insightful, this region can alternatively be expressed as

$$\left(\beta - \tfrac{1}{2}(\kappa + \kappa^*)\right)' \Psi^{*-} \left(\beta - \tfrac{1}{2}(\kappa + \kappa^*)\right) \leq \tfrac{1}{4}(\kappa^* - \kappa)' \Psi^{*-} (\kappa^* - \kappa) \tag{3.18a}$$

and

$$\Psi^* \Psi^{*-} \left(\beta - \tfrac{1}{2}(\kappa + \kappa^*)\right) = \beta - \tfrac{1}{2}(\kappa + \kappa^*), \tag{3.18b}$$

where (3.18a) is a direct rearrangement of the first part of (3.17), and (3.18b) follows from (3.13b), because premultiplying both sides by $\Psi^* \Psi^{*-}$ gives $\Psi^* \Psi^{*-} (\kappa^* - \kappa) = \kappa^* - \kappa$. Combining this with (3.17) yields (3.18b). The interpretation of (3.18a) is that it represents a cylinder, which in (3.18b) is projected onto the space spanned by Ψ^*.

The result becomes more insightful when we consider the case where $\Omega > 0$, which implies that there is measurement error in all variables. In that case, Ψ and Ψ^* are nonsingular, so the second part of (3.17) holds trivially and the first part reduces to

$$(\beta - \kappa^*)'\Psi^{*-1}(\beta - \kappa) \leq 0,$$

or, equivalently,

$$\left(\beta - \tfrac{1}{2}(\kappa + \kappa^*)\right)'\Psi^{*-1}\left(\beta - \tfrac{1}{2}(\kappa + \kappa^*)\right) \leq \tfrac{1}{4}(\kappa^* - \kappa)'\Sigma_X\kappa.$$

This is an ellipsoid with midpoint $\frac{1}{2}(\kappa + \kappa^*)$, passing through κ and κ^* and tangent to the hyperplane $(\beta - \kappa)'\Sigma_X\kappa = 0$. An example of such an ellipsoid is depicted in figure 3.2. Without the additional bound (3.11) on the measurement error variance, the admissible region for β would be the area between the two parallel hyperplanes, cf. figure 2.4. By imposing the bound on the measurement error variance, the admissible region for β has been reduced to an ellipsoid. If Ω^* gets arbitrarily close to Σ_X, and hence the additional information provided by the inequality $\Omega \leq \Omega^*$ diminishes, the ellipsoid will expand and the admissible region for β will coincide with the whole area between the two hyperplanes.

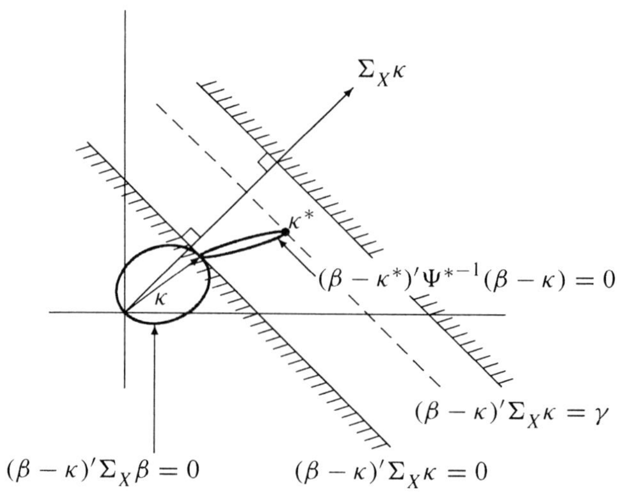

Figure 3.2 *Admissible values of β with bounds on the measurement error: β lies inside or on the ellipse through κ and κ^*.*

The bounds represented by (3.17) are minimal in the sense that for each β satisfying the bound there exists at least one Ω satisfying (3.11) and (3.13a) that rationalizes this β. To see this, choose an arbitrary β satisfying (3.17) and construct a matrix Ψ that satisfies (3.13a) and (3.16). One such Ψ is

$$\tilde{\Psi} = \frac{(\beta - \kappa)(\beta - \kappa)'}{(\beta - \kappa)'\Sigma_X\kappa}$$

if $\beta \neq \kappa$, and $\tilde{\Psi} = 0$ if $\beta = \kappa$. By inspecting figure 3.2, it is easy to see that $\beta'\Sigma_X(\beta - \kappa) > 0$, so $\tilde{\Psi} \geq 0$ if $\beta \neq \kappa$. Clearly, (3.13a) is satisfied for this choice of Ψ. From theorem A.13, it follows that $\tilde{\Psi}$ satisfies (3.16) if

$$(\beta - \kappa)'\Psi^{*-}(\beta - \kappa) \leq (\beta - \kappa)'\Sigma_X\kappa \qquad \text{and} \qquad \Psi^*\Psi^{*-}(\beta - \kappa) = \beta - \kappa.$$

The second part of this expression is just the second part of (3.17). Using this result, the first part can be rewritten as

$$(\beta - \kappa)'\Psi^{*-}\left((\beta - \kappa) - \Psi^*\Sigma_X\kappa\right) \leq 0.$$

This is equivalent with the first part of (3.17), because $\Psi^*\Sigma_X\kappa = \kappa^* - \kappa$.

Bounds on linear combinations of parameters

Using the ellipsoid bounds as derived above will in practice not be straightforward and the concept of an ellipsoid projected onto a space seems unappealing from a practitioner's point of view. However, a researcher is likely to be primarily interested in extreme values of linear combinations of the elements of β, and these can be expressed in a simple way. In particular, bounds on elements of β separately will be of interest among these linear combinations. Using theorem A.13, with $x = \beta - \frac{1}{2}(\kappa + \kappa^*)$ and $C = \frac{1}{4}(\kappa^* - \kappa)'\Sigma_X\kappa \cdot \Psi^*$, it follows that (3.18) implies

$$\left(\beta - \tfrac{1}{2}(\kappa + \kappa^*)\right)\left(\beta - \tfrac{1}{2}(\kappa + \kappa^*)\right)' \leq \tfrac{1}{4}(\kappa^* - \kappa)'\Sigma_X\kappa \cdot \Psi^*.$$

Premultiplying by an arbitrary g-vector λ' and postmultiplying by λ gives

$$\left\{\lambda'\left(\beta - \tfrac{1}{2}(\kappa + \kappa^*)\right)\right\}^2 \leq \tfrac{1}{4}c,$$

with $c \equiv (\kappa^* - \kappa)'\Sigma_X\kappa \cdot \lambda'\Psi^*\lambda$. Hence,

$$\tfrac{1}{2}\lambda'(\kappa + \kappa^*) - \tfrac{1}{2}\sqrt{c} \leq \lambda'\beta \leq \tfrac{1}{2}\lambda'(\kappa + \kappa^*) + \tfrac{1}{2}\sqrt{c}. \tag{3.19}$$

Bounds on separate elements of β are obtained when λ is set equal to any of the g unit vectors. These bounds are easy to compute in practice, by substituting consistent estimators for the various parameters. Of course, these feasible bounds are only approximations and are consistent estimators of the true bounds. Notice that the intervals thus obtained reflect the uncertainty regarding the measurement error and are conceptually completely different from the confidence intervals usually computed, which reflect the uncertainty about the parameters due to sampling variability. Confidence intervals usually converge to a single point, whereas the widths of the intervals (3.19) do not become smaller as sample size increases indefinitely.

An empirical application

To illustrate the theory, we apply it to an empirical analysis performed by Van de Stadt, Kapteyn, and Van de Geer (1985), who constructed and estimated a model of preference formation in consumer behavior. The central relationship in this study is the following model:

$$\mu_n = \beta_0 + \beta_1 \mu_{n,-1} + \beta_2 f_{n,-1} + \beta_3 f_n + \beta_4 y_n + \beta_5 y_n^* + \beta_6 f_n^* + \varepsilon_n. \tag{3.20}$$

The index n refers to the n-th household in the sample, μ_n is a measure of the household's financial needs, f_n is the logarithm of the number of household members, and y_n is the logarithm of after-tax household income. An asterisk attached to a variable indicates the sample mean in the social group to which household n belongs, and the subscript -1 denotes the value one year earlier. Finally, ε_n is a random disturbance term.

The theory underlying (4.19a) allows ε_n to have negative serial correlation. Therefore, $\mu_{n,-1}$ may be negatively correlated with ε_n. This amounts to allowing a measurement error in $\mu_{n,-1}$. The variables y_n^* and f_n^* are proxies for reference group effects and may therefore be expected to suffer from measurement error. Furthermore, f_n and $f_{n,-1}$ are proxies for the effects of family composition on financial needs. Therefore, they are also expected to suffer from measurement error. Finally, y_n may be subject to measurement error as well.

The sample means, variances and covariances of all variables involved are given in table 3.1. A possible specification of Ω^* is given in table 3.2. The column headed '% error' indicates the standard deviations of the measurement errors, i.e., the square roots of the diagonal elements of Ω^*, as percentages of the sample standard deviations of the corresponding observed variables. It should be noted that the off-diagonal elements of Ω^* are *not* upper bounds for the corresponding elements of Ω. In Ω^* the block corresponding to $f_{n,-1}$ and f_n is singular. This implies that in any Ω that satisfies $0 \leq \Omega \leq \Omega^*$, the corresponding block will be singular as well. Thus, this imposes a perfect correlation in measurement error between both variables.

Table 3.1 *Sample means and covariances of the observed variables.*

variable	mean	covariance with						
		μ_n	$\mu_{n,-1}$	$f_{n,-1}$	f_n	y_n	y_n^*	f_n^*
μ_n	10.11	.126						
$\mu_{n,-1}$	10.07	.112	.135					
$f_{n,-1}$	1.01	.088	.092	.270				
f_n	1.00	.089	.089	.260	.275			
y_n	10.31	.124	.121	.088	.092	.178		
y_n^*	10.30	.061	.059	.052	.053	.078	.083	
f_n^*	1.00	.043	.044	.087	.088	.052	.054	.097

Obviously, it is impossible to present the ellipsoid in a six-dimensional space. Therefore, we only present the OLS estimator b, which is a consistent estimator of κ, its standard error se(b), the adjusted OLS estimator b^* that corrects for the maximal amount of measurement error Ω^* and hence is a consistent estimator of κ^*, and the estimates of the extreme values of β from (3.19) by choosing for λ the six unit vectors successively. The results are given in table 3.3.

Comparison of b and b^* shows no sign reversals. Furthermore, the last two columns of table 3.3 show only two sign reversals. These sign reversals pertain to the social group variables y_n^* and f_n^*. Thus, it is possible to vary the assumptions in such a way that the estimates would indicate a negative effect of social group income on the financial needs of the household or a positive influence of the family size in the social group on the financial needs of the household. Note that y_n^* and f_n^* are the variables for which the largest measurement error variances were permitted.

Table 3.2 *Values of* Ω^*.

variable	$\mu_{n,-1}$	$f_{n,-1}$	f_n	y_n	y_n^*	f_n^*	% error
$\mu_{n,-1}$	.0219						40
$f_{n,-1}$		.0061	.0061				15
f_n		.0061	.0061				15
y_n				.0040			15
y_n^*					.013	.010	40
f_n^*					.010	.015	40

Table 3.3 *Extreme values of β.*

	b	se(b)	b^*	lower bound	upper bound
β_1	.509	.026	.950	.491	.968
β_2	$-.013$	.032	$-.123$	$-.132$	$-.004$
β_3	.066	.031	.116	.057	.125
β_4	.298	.031	.044	.010	.331
β_5	.072	.029	.028	$-.098$	.197
β_6	$-.032$	.025	$-.020$	$-.131$	.081

The information conveyed by the extreme values of the estimates is quite different from the story told by the standard errors of the OLS estimates. For example, b_5 is about 2.5 times its standard error and b_3 about 2 times. Still the estimate of β_5 can switch signs by varying Ω within the permissible range, but the estimate of β_3 can not. Combining the information obtained from the standard errors with the results of the sensitivity analysis suggests that β_1, β_3, and, to a lesser extent, β_4 are unambiguously positive. We also see that β_2 does not reverse signs in the sensitivity analysis but the standard error of b_2 suggests that β_2 could be positive. The estimated coefficient b_5 has a relatively small standard error, but this coefficient turns out to be sensitive to the choice of assumptions. Finally, b_6 has a relatively large standard error and this coefficient is also sensitive to the choice of assumptions.

3.5 Uncorrelated measurement error

In the previous section, Ω and Ω^* were allowed to be general positive semidefinite matrices. Frequently, however, it is more natural to assume that the measurement errors are mutually independent, which implies that Ω and Ω^* are diagonal, as in theorem 3.1. In that case, the ellipsoid (3.17) spawned by Ω^* is still an (asymptotic) bound for the solutions β but is no longer a *minimal* bound, because the required diagonality of Ω imposes further restrictions on the set of β's that are admissible.

In this section, we will see how the bounds can be tightened. This will be done in two steps. In the first step, a finite set of admissible vectors β_j is defined and it is shown that these are on the boundary of the ellipsoid (3.17). In the second step, it is shown that any admissible β is expressible as a convex combination of these β_j's and thus the convex hull of these β_j's gives tighter bounds on β.

Let Δ_j be a diagonal $g \times g$ matrix whose diagonal elements are zeros and ones, and let

$$\Omega_j \equiv \Omega^* \Delta_j = \Delta_j \Omega^* = \Delta_j \Omega^* \Delta_j. \tag{3.21}$$

If Ω^* has g_1 nonzero elements then there are $\ell \equiv 2^{g_1}$ different matrices Ω_j that satisfy (3.21). These matrices are the measurement error covariance matrices when some (or no or all) variables are measured without error, so their measurement error variance is zero, and the measurement errors of the remaining variables have maximum variances, that is, equal to the corresponding diagonal elements of Ω^*. Clearly, Ω is (nonuniquely) expressible as a convex combination $\sum_{j=1}^{\ell} \mu_j \Omega_j$, with $\mu_j \geq 0$ for all j and $\sum_{j=1}^{\ell} \mu_j = 1$. Furthermore, let

$$\beta_j \equiv (\Sigma_X - \Omega_j)^{-1} \Sigma_X \kappa = \Sigma_{\Xi,j}^{-1} \Sigma_X \kappa$$

with $\Sigma_{\Xi,j} \equiv \Sigma_X - \Omega_j$. Obviously, the ℓ vectors β_j are admissible solutions and hence they are bounded by the ellipsoid (3.17) spawned by Ω^*.

We first show that all β_j lie on the surface of this ellipsoid. In order to do so, we need some auxiliary results. From (3.21), it follows that

$$\Omega_j = \Omega_j \Omega^{*-} \Omega_j \tag{3.22}$$

and

$$\Omega_j \Omega^{*-} (\Omega^* - \Omega_j) = 0. \tag{3.23}$$

From $\Sigma_{\Xi,j} \equiv \Sigma_X - \Omega_j = \Sigma_\Xi^* + (\Omega^* - \Omega_j)$ we obtain $\Omega^* - \Omega_j = \Sigma_{\Xi,j} - \Sigma_\Xi^*$. Hence (3.23) implies

$$\Omega_j \Omega^{*-} \Sigma_\Xi^* = \Omega_j \Omega^{*-} \Sigma_{\Xi,j}. \tag{3.24}$$

Let

$$\Psi_j \equiv \Sigma_{\Xi,j}^{-1} - \Sigma_X^{-1} = \Sigma_{\Xi,j}^{-1} (\Sigma_X - \Sigma_{\Xi,j}) \Sigma_X^{-1} = \Sigma_{\Xi,j}^{-1} \Omega_j \Sigma_X^{-1}.$$

Analogously, $\Psi^* = \Sigma_\Xi^{*\,-1} \Omega^* \Sigma_X^{-1}$ and $\Psi^{*-} = \Sigma_X \Omega^{*-} \Sigma_\Xi^*$, where Ψ^* was defined in (3.12b). Using (3.22) and (3.24) we obtain

$$\begin{aligned}
\Psi_j \Psi^{*-} \Psi_j &= \left(\Sigma_{\Xi,j}^{-1} \Omega_j \Sigma_X^{-1}\right)\left(\Sigma_X \Omega^{*-} \Sigma_\Xi^*\right)\left(\Sigma_{\Xi,j}^{-1} \Omega_j \Sigma_X^{-1}\right) \\
&= \Sigma_{\Xi,j}^{-1} \Omega_j \Omega^{*-} \Sigma_\Xi^* \Sigma_{\Xi,j}^{-1} \Omega_j \Sigma_X^{-1} \\
&= \Sigma_{\Xi,j}^{-1} \Omega_j \Omega^{*-} \Sigma_{\Xi,j} \Sigma_{\Xi,j}^{-1} \Omega_j \Sigma_X^{-1} \\
&= \Sigma_{\Xi,j}^{-1} \Omega_j \Omega^{*-} \Omega_j \Sigma_X^{-1} \\
&= \Sigma_{\Xi,j}^{-1} \Omega_j \Sigma_X^{-1} \\
&= \Psi_j.
\end{aligned} \tag{3.25}$$

This means that any generalized inverse Ψ^{*-} of Ψ^* is also a generalized inverse of Ψ_j for any j. Furthermore, because $0 \le \Omega_j \le \Omega^* < \Sigma_X$, we have $\Sigma_X \ge \Sigma_{\Xi,j} \ge \Sigma_\Xi^* > 0$, and hence, $0 < \Sigma_X^{-1} \le \Sigma_{\Xi,j}^{-1} \le \Sigma_\Xi^{*-1}$, or $-\Sigma_X^{-1} < 0 \le \Psi_j \le \Psi^*$. Using theorem A.10, this implies

$$\Psi_j = \Psi^* \Psi^{*-} \Psi_j. \tag{3.26}$$

Analogous to (3.13), we have

$$\begin{aligned} \Psi_j \Sigma_X \kappa &= (\Sigma_{\Xi,j}^{-1} - \Sigma_X^{-1}) \Sigma_X \kappa \\ &= \beta_j - \kappa \end{aligned} \tag{3.27a}$$

$$\begin{aligned} (\Psi_\delta^* - \Psi^*) \Sigma_X \kappa &= \left((\Sigma_{\Xi,j}^{-1} - \Sigma_X^{-1}) - (\Sigma_\Xi^{*-1} - \Sigma_X^{-1}) \right) \Sigma_X \kappa \\ &= \beta_j - \kappa^*. \end{aligned} \tag{3.27b}$$

Substitution of (3.27) in (3.17) using (3.25) and (3.26) turns the inequality in (3.17) into an equality when we substitute β_j for β. Therefore, all points β_j lie on the surface of the ellipsoid.

We will now show that β can be written as a convex combination of the β_j. To this end we need to express the matrices Δ_j explicitly. Without loss of generality, we assume that the first $g_1 \le g$ diagonal elements $\omega_1^*, \ldots, \omega_{g_1}^*$ of Ω^* are nonzero, and the remaining $g_2 = g - g_1$ elements are zero. We denote a typical diagonal element of Δ_j by δ_{ij}, $i = 1, \ldots, g$; $j = 1, \ldots, \ell$. Let $\delta_{i1} = 0$ if $i > g_1$ and $\delta_{i1} = 1$ if $i \le g_1$. This determines Δ_1. The other Δ's are constructed as follows. Let $0 \le m \le g_1 - 1$ and $1 \le j \le 2^m$. Then, $\Delta_{j+2^m} = \Delta_j - e_{m+1} e_{m+1}'$, with e_{m+1} the $(m+1)$-th unit vector. This determines the Δ_j's and hence the β_j's. Note that $\beta_1 \equiv \kappa^*$ and $\beta_\ell \equiv \kappa$. As an example, let $g = 4$ and $g_1 = 3$, and thus $\ell = 8$. Then, the columns of the matrix

$$\begin{bmatrix} 1 & 0 & 1 & 0 & 1 & 0 & 1 & 0 \\ 1 & 1 & 0 & 0 & 1 & 1 & 0 & 0 \\ 1 & 1 & 1 & 1 & 0 & 0 & 0 & 0 \\ 0 & 0 & 0 & 0 & 0 & 0 & 0 & 0 \end{bmatrix}$$

contain the diagonals of $\Delta_1, \ldots, \Delta_8$ in that order. Notice that the columns of this matrix are the binary representations of the numbers $0, \ldots, \ell - 1$ in reverse order. Given the definition of the Δ_j, it follows that

$$\Sigma_{\Xi,j} = \Sigma_X - \Omega_j = \Sigma_X - \sum_{i=1}^{g_1} \delta_{ij} \omega_i^* e_i e_i' \tag{3.28}$$

and thus $\Sigma_{\Xi,j+2^m} = \Sigma_{\Xi,j} + \omega^*_{m+1} e_{m+1} e'_{m+1}$. Now, consider $\Sigma_\Xi = \Sigma_X - \Omega$. Given that $0 \leq \Omega \leq \Omega^*$ and that both Ω and Ω^* are diagonal, we can write Σ_Ξ as

$$\Sigma_\Xi = \sum_{j=1}^{\ell} \mu_j \Sigma_{\Xi,j},$$

where $\mu_j \geq 0$ and $\sum_{j=1}^{\ell} \mu_j = 1$. Hence, using $\beta = \Sigma_\Xi^{-1} \Sigma_X \kappa$ and theorem A.8, we have

$$\beta = \Sigma_\Xi^{-1} \Sigma_X \kappa = \left[\sum_{j=1}^{\ell} \mu_j \Sigma_{\Xi,j} \right]^{-1} \Sigma_X \kappa = \sum_{j=1}^{\ell} \lambda_j \Sigma_{\Xi,j}^{-1} \Sigma_X \kappa = \sum_{j=1}^{\ell} \lambda_j \beta_j,$$

with $\lambda_j \geq 0$ and $\sum_{j=1}^{\ell} \lambda_j = 1$. Consequently, β lies in the convex hull of the β_j.

An example of the polyhedral bounds on β is given in figure 3.3. In this figure, the ellipsoid (3.17) is depicted, as well as the vectors β_j, $j = 1, \ldots, 4$, and the polyhedron that bounds the convex hull thereof. From this figure, it is clear that the diagonality of Ω may reduce the region where β may lie when measurement error is present substantially. Moreover, in the example illustrated in the figure, the second regression coefficient is allowed to be zero or negative if only (3.17) is used, wheras it is necessarily positive if the diagonality of Ω is used.

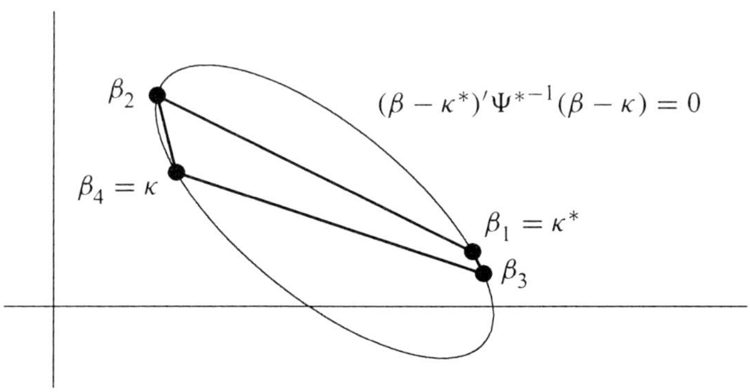

Figure 3.3 *Admissible values of β with bounds on the measurement error and diagonal Ω and Ω^*: β lies inside or on the polyhedron which bounds the convex hull of the vectors β_j, $j = 1, \ldots, 4$.*

In practical applications, the most obvious use of this result is to compute all points β_j and to derive the interval in which each coefficient lies. These intervals will generally be smaller than the ones obtained from the ellipsoid by choosing for λ in (3.19) the g unit vectors successively.

It should be noted that the convex polyhedron spanned by all points β_j need not be a minimal bound, i.e., there may be points in the convex hull of the β_j that are not admissible. However, the bounds for the separate elements of β *are* minimal, but they can generally not be attained jointly for all elements. If the convex polyhedron spanned by all points β_j is not a minimal bound, the set of admissible β's is not convex.

3.6 Bibliographical notes

3.1 The classical result in this section is due to Frisch (1934). An application in financial economics of the bounds in the single regressor case was given by Booth and Smith (1985), where the two variables are return on a securities portfolio and the market rate of return.

Sensitivity for the choice of the ratio of the variances in (3.3) was studied by Lakshminarayanan and Gunst (1984). The case, with a single regressor, where *both* error variances are known, rather than only their ratio, has been discussed by, e.g., Brown (1957), Barnett (1967), and Richardson and Wu (1970). Estimation in this model has been discussed by, e.g., Birch (1964) and Dolby (1976b). Isogawa (1984) gave the exact distribution (and approximations) of this estimator under normality assumptions. Variance estimation and detection of influential observations were discussed by Kelly (1984) using an influence function approach, see also Wong (1989). Prediction in this case was discussed by Lee and Yum (1989). Small-sample confidence intervals were given by Creasy (1956) and amended by Schneeweiss (1982). Ware (1972) extended the model to incorporate the information on the ordering of the true values.

The results of this section have been extended in Levi (1977), where it is shown how reverse regression of the mismeasured variable on the other variables combined with the original regression can be employed to derive consistently estimable bounds on the true values of the regression coefficients.

3.2 The formalization of the discrimination problem is an adaptation of the basic model given in Goldberger (1984b). This paper contains in addition different and more complicated models. The bias in estimating discrimination by regression has also been pointed out by Hashimoto and Kochin (1980). Reverse regression has been proposed by, e.g., Kamalich and Polachek (1982), Kapsalis (1982), and Conway and Roberts (1983), which contains some very simple numerical examples to provide intuition.

Conway and Roberts (1983) showed that usually, the direct regression or the reverse regression or both indicate some form of discrimination. They distinguished between *fairness 1* and *fairness 2*, to indicate that the gender dummy coefficient is zero in the direct and reverse regression, respectively. These can only hold both if the productivity distributions of men and women are equal, irrespective of measurement error. This is highly unlikely, so there always tends to be some form of perceived discrimination, which can not be totally resolved.

Goldberger (1984a) commented on Conway and Roberts (1983). The underestimation of the size of a discrimination effect by reverse regression was also pointed out by Solon (1983). Schafer (1987b) illustrated the effect of varying the assumed size of the measurement error on the discrimination coefficient. A short exposition for a legal audience was given by Fienberg (1988). A more critical treatment has been given in an article by Dempster (1988), which was followed by a number of shorter discussion contributions.

3.3 As to Koopmans' theorem on bounds on regression coefficients when measurement error is present, apart from Koopmans' original proof later proofs have been given by many authors, including Patefield (1981) and Klepper and Leamer (1984). The last reference also gives an empirical example. These authors invoke the Perron-Frobenius theorem. See Takayama (1985, section 4B), for a review of several versions of this theorem. The argument is elegant and is therefore sketched here.

From (3.10) and theorem A.14, it follows that δ is a generalized eigenvector corresponding with the eigenvalue 1, which is the smallest eigenvalue. The eigenvalue equation $(\Sigma - \Phi)\delta = 0$ is equivalent with $(\Phi\Sigma^{-1} - I)\Sigma\delta = 0$, so $\Sigma\gamma$ is the eigenvector corresponding with the *largest* eigenvalue of the matrix $\Phi\Sigma^{-1}$. When $\Phi > 0$, so all its diagonal elements are positive (measurement error in all variables, in addition to the usual error term in the equation), *and* all elements of Σ^{-1} are positive, then all elements of $\Phi\Sigma^{-1}$ are positive. The Perron-Frobenius theorem then implies that the eigenvector corresponding to the largest eigenvalue has only positive elements (or only negative elements, but if the first element is normalized to 1, it has only positive elements). Thus, the vector $\lambda \equiv \Sigma\delta$ is elementwise positive, so $\delta = \Sigma^{-1}\lambda$ is a linear combination of the columns of Σ^{-1} with positive weights.

Note that this is slightly stronger than the result in the main text, where the weights are nonnegative. This means that the boundary of the convex hull is now excluded. This stronger result is obtained from the stronger assumption $\Phi > 0$ instead of $\Phi \geq 0$ as in the main text. It is, however, possible to adapt the proof along the line of the Perron-Frobenius theorem when $\Phi \geq 0$. This then leads again to the result stated in the main text, cf. Kalman (1982). For further results in this context see also Willassen (1987).

3.4 The discussion of much in this section, including the empirical example, is adapted from Bekker et al. (1984). A generalization where the measurement errors in y and X are allowed to be correlated has been given by Bekker, Kapteyn, and Wansbeek (1987). Bekker (1988) considered the case where, in addition to an upper bound Ω^* to the measurement error covariance matrix, a lower bound Ω_* is also assumed.

This type of bounds is due to Klepper and Leamer (1984) and has its origins in the related Bayesian field of finding posterior means in regression where the prior on location is given but where the one on the variance is unknown but bounded; see, e.g, Leamer (1982). For an extension of the results presented here, see, e.g., Klepper (1988b), which is in part devoted to the reverse question as to which bounds on variances lead to certain bounds on coefficients. Leamer (1987) derived bounds through an extension to a multi-equation context.

Iwata (1992) considered bounds in the context of instrumental variables, where the instruments are allowed to have nonzero correlations with the error in the equation and the researcher is willing to impose an upper bound on a function of these correlations. Similar results were obtained by Krasker and Pratt (1986, 1987), who showed that if the measurement errors are correlated with the errors in the equation, then even in the limit we can frequently not be sure of the signs of regression coefficients.

As mentioned in the text, the bounds are asymptotic and should not be interpreted as confidence intervals. How to combine the asymptotic indeterminacy of the bounds with the finite-sample variation in a confidence interval was studied by Willassen (1984).

Notwithstanding this literature on the usefulness of bounds on parameter estimates in nonidentified models, the topic is rather unpopular. To quote Manski (1989, p. 345): "[T]he historical fixation of econometrics on point identification has inhibited appreciation of the potential usefulness of bounds. Econometricians have occasionally reported useful bounds on quantities that are not point-identified [. . .]. But the conventional wisdom has been that bounds are hard to estimate and rarely informative." The theme is extensively treated in the monograph by Manski (1995).

3.5 The results in this section are due to Bekker et al. (1987). Note that, if we take Ω^* to be the diagonal matrix with the same diagonal elements as Σ_X, then we obtain weaker bounds than from Koopmans' theorem, but under weaker assumptions. This can be applied if Σ^{-1} contains both positive and negative off-diagonal elements.

Chapter 4

Identification

As we have discussed in detail chapter 2, the presence of measurement error makes the results of the regression analysis inconsistent. In this chapter we look into the logical follow-up issue, which is to see how deep the problem runs. Is it just a matter of somehow adapting the least squares procedure to take measurement error into account, or are we in a situation where no consistent estimator exists at all and are we unable to get to know the true parameter values in the limit?

These questions are closely related to the question whether the parameters in the measurement error model are identified. In general, identification and the existence of a consistent estimator are two sides of the same coin. So, if we want to know whether we can consistently estimate the measurement error model, checking the identification of this model seems a promising approach.

This is, however, not as straightforward as it seems. There are two versions of the measurement error model, the structural model and the functional model. These models, which were introduced in section 2.1, differ in their underlying assumptions about the process generating the true values of the regressors, the ξ_n. The structural model is based on the assumption that the ξ_n are drawings from some distribution, e.g., the normal distribution. In the functional model on the other hand, $\{\xi_1, \ldots, \xi_N\}$ is taken to be a sequence of unknown constants, the incidental parameters.

Consistency is an asymptotic notion. It is clear that the presence of incidental variables, as in the functional model, may create problems in an asymptotic setting. Such potential problems are absent with the structural model. Hence in discussing the issue of the existence of a consistent estimator in the measurement error model we need to distinguish between the structural and functional model.

This defines the beginning of this chapter. In section 4.1 we first make some general comments on these models relative to each other. We then inspect the various likelihood functions to clarify the relationship between functional and structural models.

In section 4.2, we consider maximum likelihood (ML) estimation in the structural model when the latent variables are assumed normal. We derive the asymptotic distribution of the ML estimators in this normal structural model. As a byproduct we derive the asymptotic distribution of these estimators conditional on the latent variables, i.e., under the conditions of the functional model. In section 4.3, we discuss the likelihood function in the functional model, which is more complicated. The likelihood in that case appears to be unbounded. Nevertheless, the likelihood function has a stationary point, and the properties of the estimators corresponding with that point are investigated.

Having thus considered various aspects of structural and functional models, we turn to the topic of consistent estimation and identification. In section 4.4, we define identification and give the basic theory connected with it. In particular we consider the link between identification and the rank of the information matrix, and derive a general rank condition for identification.

We next apply this theory to the measurement error model, assuming normality. It appears in section 4.5 that the structural model is not identified and that the functional model is identified. This, however, does not imply the existence of a consistent estimator in the functional model. Due to the presence of the incidental parameters, this model represents one of the situations where identification and the existence of a consistent estimator do not coincide.

Normality as an assumption on the distribution of the latent variables appears to play a crucial role in measurement error models. Section 4.6 shows that normality is the least favorable assumption from an identification viewpoint in a structural model. Necessary and sufficient conditions on the distribution of the true value of the regressors are established under which the linear regression model is identified.

4.1 Structural versus functional models

In cross-sectional survey data, one can frequently assume that $\{(y_n, x_n)\}$, $n = 1, \ldots, N$, are i.i.d. random variables. When complex survey sampling, such as stratified sampling, is used to gather the data, which is often the case, this assumption holds only approximatively. Anyhow, we are interested in relations in the population, so the distribution of (y_n, x_n) is relevant. Hence, we estimate this distribution, or, more specifically, some relevant parameters or other characteristics of this distribution, based on sample statistics. The model for the dependencies among the elements of (y_n, x_n) is based on this. This is clearly a case in which a structural model is most relevant.

In experimental data, x_n is chosen by the researcher and is therefore not a random variable. The researcher is interested in the effect different x's have on the responses y. Consequently, the distribution of y_n conditional on x_n, with x_n fixed constants, is relevant. This is clearly a case in which a functional model is most relevant. In the case of measurement errors, however, this leads to the Berkson model and not to the standard functional model.

The standard functional model is appropriate if the observational units are given and interesting in themselves, e.g., when they are given countries. Then, some economically interesting characteristic of these countries (inflation, say) will typically be considered as a given, but imperfectly measured, variable. This leads naturally to the standard functional model.

Frequently, (y_n, x_n) can not be considered i.i.d. random variables. For example, in time series data, the dependencies between x_t and x_u (say) may be very complicated. If we are not so much interested in modeling the time series x, but are mainly interested in the relations between y and x (i.e., the conditional distribution of y_t given x_t), it may be more fruitful to consider a functional model than a complicated non-i.i.d. structural time series model.

An interesting case occurs in quasi-experimental data, where a random sample of individuals is given a certain treatment. For example, a company tries out a specific pricing strategy for a product in one region, but not in another region, which acts as control group. We are now interested in the distribution of y_n conditional on x_n and w_n, where x_n is a fixed constant (the treatment variable) and w_n is a random variable of other (personal) characteristics that are supposedly relevant, but not under the control of the experimenter. This appears to call for a mixed structural-functional model.

Having thus suggested the context for the structural and functional model, we now analyze the link between the two from a statistical point of view. We do so by inspecting their respective likelihoods. We next consider the interrelations between these likelihoods. Throughout this chapter we consider the basic model as given in section 2.1, which for a typical observation is $y_n = \xi_n'\beta + \varepsilon_n$ and $x_n = \xi_n + v_n$, for $n = 1, \ldots, N$, with y_n and x_n $(g \times 1)$ observed and v_n and ε_n i.i.d. normal with mean zero and respective variances Ω and σ_ε^2 and independent of ξ_n. All variables have mean zero. The second-order moments of x_n and ξ_n are S_X and S_Ξ, respectively, in the sample, and Σ_X and Σ_Ξ in the limit or in expectation, with $\Sigma_X = \Sigma_\Xi + \Omega$. The notation for the model for all observations together is $y = \Xi\beta + \varepsilon$ and $X = \Xi + V$.

Until the last section in this chapter, we assume that Ω, the matrix of variances and covariances of the measurement error in the regressors, is positive definite.

This means in particular that all regressors are subject to measurement error. This is of course a strong assumption. The results can, however, be adapted for the case where Ω is of incomplete rank, but this complicates matters without adding insight and is therefore omitted.

The structural model

We first discuss the loglikelihood for the structural case. We assume a normal distribution for the true values of the regressors. Then

$$\begin{bmatrix} y_n \\ x_n \\ \xi_n \end{bmatrix} \sim \mathcal{N}_{2g+1}\left(0, \begin{bmatrix} \sigma_\varepsilon^2 + \beta'\Sigma_\Xi\beta & \beta'\Sigma_\Xi & \beta'\Sigma_\Xi \\ \Sigma_\Xi\beta & \Sigma_\Xi + \Omega & \Sigma_\Xi \\ \Sigma_\Xi\beta & \Sigma_\Xi & \Sigma_\Xi \end{bmatrix}\right)$$
$$\equiv \mathcal{N}_{2g+1}(0, \Sigma^*),$$

where Σ^* is implicitly defined. The corresponding density function is

$$f_{yx\xi}(y_n, x_n, \xi_n) = \frac{1}{(2\pi)^{(2g+1)/2}|\Sigma^*|^{1/2}} \exp\left(-\tfrac{1}{2}\begin{bmatrix} y_n \\ x_n \\ \xi_n \end{bmatrix}' \Sigma^{*-1} \begin{bmatrix} y_n \\ x_n \\ \xi_n \end{bmatrix}\right).$$

If Ξ were observable, the loglikelihood function would be

$$L^*_{\text{struc}} = -\frac{N(2g+1)}{2}\log(2\pi) - \frac{N}{2}\log|\Sigma^*| - \tfrac{1}{2}\operatorname{tr}\left(\Sigma^{*-1}(y, X, \Xi)'(y, X, \Xi)\right).$$

Because Ξ is unobserved, we can not estimate the parameters by maximizing L^*_{struc}. We consider Ξ as a sample from an i.i.d. normal distribution with mean zero and covariance matrix Σ_Ξ. As we only observe y and X, the loglikelihood function is the loglikelihood of the marginal distribution of y and X, that is, the joint distribution of (y, X, Ξ) with Ξ integrated out. This marginal distribution is

$$\begin{bmatrix} y_n \\ x_n \end{bmatrix} \sim \mathcal{N}_{g+1}\left(0, \begin{bmatrix} \sigma_\varepsilon^2 + \beta'\Sigma_\Xi\beta & \beta'\Sigma_\Xi \\ \Sigma_\Xi\beta & \Sigma_\Xi + \Omega \end{bmatrix}\right)$$
$$\equiv \mathcal{N}_{g+1}(0, \Sigma),$$

with Σ implicitly defined. The corresponding density function is

$$f_{yx}(y_n, x_n) = \frac{1}{(2\pi)^{(g+1)/2}|\Sigma|^{1/2}} \exp\left(-\tfrac{1}{2}\begin{bmatrix} y_n \\ x_n \end{bmatrix}' \Sigma^{-1} \begin{bmatrix} y_n \\ x_n \end{bmatrix}\right).$$

Hence, the loglikelihood function is

$$L_{\text{struc}} = -\frac{N(g+1)}{2}\log(2\pi) - \frac{N}{2}\log|\Sigma| - \tfrac{1}{2}\operatorname{tr}\big(\Sigma^{-1}(y, X)'(y, X)\big).$$

We can elaborate this expression in an insightful way. Using $\Sigma_X \equiv \Sigma_\Xi + \Omega$, $\kappa \equiv \Sigma_X^{-1}\Sigma_\Xi\beta$, and $\gamma \equiv \sigma_\varepsilon^2 + \kappa'\Sigma_X\Sigma_\Xi^{-1}\Sigma_X\kappa - \kappa'\Sigma_X\kappa$, we find that

$$\begin{aligned}
\Sigma &= \begin{bmatrix} \sigma_\varepsilon^2 + (\beta'\Sigma_\Xi\Sigma_X^{-1})\Sigma_X\Sigma_\Xi^{-1}\Sigma_X(\Sigma_X^{-1}\Sigma_\Xi\beta) & (\beta'\Sigma_\Xi\Sigma_X^{-1})\Sigma_X \\ \Sigma_X(\Sigma_X^{-1}\Sigma_\Xi\beta) & \Sigma_X \end{bmatrix} \\
&= \begin{bmatrix} \sigma_\varepsilon^2 + \kappa'\Sigma_X\Sigma_\Xi^{-1}\Sigma_X\kappa & \kappa'\Sigma_X \\ \Sigma_X\kappa & \Sigma_X \end{bmatrix} \\
&= \begin{bmatrix} \gamma + \kappa'\Sigma_X\kappa & \kappa'\Sigma_X \\ \Sigma_X\kappa & \Sigma_X \end{bmatrix} \\
&= \begin{bmatrix} 1 & \kappa' \\ 0 & I_g \end{bmatrix} \begin{bmatrix} \gamma & 0 \\ 0 & \Sigma_X \end{bmatrix} \begin{bmatrix} 1 & 0 \\ \kappa & I_g \end{bmatrix}.
\end{aligned}$$

Thus, $|\Sigma| = \gamma|\Sigma_X|$ and

$$\begin{aligned}
\Sigma^{-1} &= \begin{bmatrix} 1 & 0 \\ -\kappa & I_g \end{bmatrix} \begin{bmatrix} \gamma^{-1} & 0 \\ 0 & \Sigma_X^{-1} \end{bmatrix} \begin{bmatrix} 1 & -\kappa' \\ 0 & I_g \end{bmatrix} \\
&= \begin{bmatrix} 0 & 0 \\ 0 & \Sigma_X^{-1} \end{bmatrix} + \gamma^{-1} \begin{bmatrix} 1 \\ -\kappa \end{bmatrix} (1, -\kappa').
\end{aligned}$$

Substitution in the likelihood for the structural model gives

$$\begin{aligned}
L_{\text{struc}} = &-\frac{N(g+1)}{2}\log(2\pi) - \frac{N}{2}\log\gamma - \tfrac{1}{2}\gamma^{-1}(y - X\kappa)'(y - X\kappa) \\
&- \frac{N}{2}\log|\Sigma_X| - \tfrac{1}{2}\operatorname{tr}\big(\Sigma_X^{-1}X'X\big).
\end{aligned}$$

This is the loglikelihood of a linear regression model with random regressors, $y = X\kappa + u$, where the elements of u and the rows of X are i.i.d. $\mathcal{N}(0, \gamma)$ and $\mathcal{N}_g(0, \Sigma_X)$, respectively. The parameter vector of this model is

$$\delta \equiv \begin{bmatrix} \kappa \\ \gamma \\ \sigma_x \end{bmatrix},$$

where $\sigma_x \equiv \operatorname{vec}\Sigma_X$. We encountered this model in section 2.5, where we noted that it is a linear model of the basic form, albeit with different parameters than the original model parameters.

The functional model

To discuss the loglikelihood for the functional model, we need the conditional distribution of (y_n, x_n) given ξ_n. It is given by

$$\begin{bmatrix} y_n \\ x_n \end{bmatrix} \Bigg| \; \xi_n \sim \mathcal{N}_{g+1}\left(\begin{bmatrix} \xi_n'\beta \\ \xi_n \end{bmatrix}, \begin{bmatrix} \sigma_\varepsilon^2 & 0 \\ 0 & \Omega \end{bmatrix} \right),$$

and the corresponding density function is

$$\begin{aligned} f_{yx|\xi}(y_n, x_n \mid \xi_n) &= f_{y|\xi}(y_n \mid \xi_n) f_{x|\xi}(x_n \mid \xi_n) \\ &= \frac{1}{\sqrt{2\pi\sigma_\varepsilon^2}} \exp\left(-\tfrac{1}{2} \frac{(y_n - \xi_n'\beta)^2}{\sigma_\varepsilon^2} \right) \\ &\quad \times \frac{1}{(2\pi)^{g/2}|\Omega|^{1/2}} \exp\big(-\tfrac{1}{2}(x_n - \xi_n)'\Omega^{-1}(x_n - \xi_n)\big). \end{aligned}$$

If Ξ were observable, the loglikelihood function would be

$$\begin{aligned} L_{\text{func}}^* = &-\frac{N(g+1)}{2}\log(2\pi) - \frac{N}{2}\log\sigma_\varepsilon^2 - \tfrac{1}{2}\sigma_\varepsilon^{-2}(y - \Xi\beta)'(y - \Xi\beta) \\ &- \frac{N}{2}\log|\Omega| - \tfrac{1}{2}\operatorname{tr}\big(\Omega^{-1}(X - \Xi)'(X - \Xi)\big). \end{aligned} \tag{4.1}$$

We can not estimate the parameters straightforwardly by maximizing L_{func}^* over β, σ_ε^2, and Ω, because it depends on Ξ, which is unobserved. Because Ξ is a matrix of constants, we must solve this problem by considering Ξ as a matrix of parameters that have to be estimated along the way. Hence, the functional loglikelihood is L_{func}^* with Ξ regarded as parameters:

$$L_{\text{func}}(\beta, \sigma_\varepsilon^2, \Omega, \Xi; y, X) = L_{\text{func}}^*(\beta, \sigma_\varepsilon^2, \Omega; y, X, \Xi), \tag{4.2}$$

in self-evident symbolic notation.

Relationship between the loglikelihoods

There is a relationship between the various loglikelihoods. In order to derive it we first need a closer look at Σ^*. It can be written as

$$\Sigma^* = \begin{bmatrix} 1 & 0 & \beta' \\ 0 & I_g & I_g \\ 0 & 0 & I_g \end{bmatrix} \begin{bmatrix} \sigma_\varepsilon^2 & 0 & 0 \\ 0 & \Omega & 0 \\ 0 & 0 & \Sigma_\Xi \end{bmatrix} \begin{bmatrix} 1 & 0 & 0 \\ 0 & I_g & 0 \\ \beta & I_g & I_g \end{bmatrix}.$$

Hence, $|\Sigma^*| = \sigma_\varepsilon^2 \, |\Omega| \, |\Sigma_\Xi|$ and

$$\Sigma^{*-1} = \begin{bmatrix} 1 & 0 & 0 \\ 0 & I_g & 0 \\ -\beta & -I_g & I_g \end{bmatrix} \begin{bmatrix} \sigma_\varepsilon^{-2} & 0 & 0 \\ 0 & \Omega^{-1} & 0 \\ 0 & 0 & \Sigma_\Xi^{-1} \end{bmatrix} \begin{bmatrix} 1 & 0 & -\beta' \\ 0 & I_g & -I_g \\ 0 & 0 & I_g \end{bmatrix}.$$

Inserting these expressions in L^*_{struc} gives on elaboration

$$\begin{aligned} L^*_{\text{struc}} = & -\frac{N(2g+1)}{2}\log(2\pi) - \frac{N}{2}\log\sigma_\varepsilon^2 - \frac{N}{2}\log|\Omega| - \frac{N}{2}\log|\Sigma_\Xi| \\ & - \tfrac{1}{2}\sigma_\varepsilon^{-2}(y - \Xi\beta)'(y - \Xi\beta) \\ & - \tfrac{1}{2}\operatorname{tr}\bigl(\Omega^{-1}(X - \Xi)'(X - \Xi) + \Sigma_\Xi^{-1}\Xi'\Xi\bigr). \end{aligned}$$

This leads to an interesting interpretation. If Ξ were observable, and we would like to estimate Σ_Ξ from it, the loglikelihood function would be

$$L_\xi = -\frac{Ng}{2}\log(2\pi) - \frac{N}{2}\log|\Sigma_\Xi| - \tfrac{1}{2}\operatorname{tr}(\Sigma_\Xi^{-1}\Xi'\Xi).$$

We conclude that $L_{\text{func}} = L^*_{\text{struc}} - L_\xi$. This means that the loglikelihood of the observable variables in the functional model L_{func} is a conditional loglikelihood. This contrasts with the loglikelihood of the observable variables in the structural model L_{struc}, which is a marginal loglikelihood.

This argument is in fact general and can be simply seen. By the definition of a conditional density, $f_{yx\xi}(y, X, \Xi) = f_{yx|\xi}(y, X \mid \Xi) f_\xi(\Xi)$ and observe that $L^*_{\text{struc}} \equiv \log f_{yx\xi}(y, X, \Xi)$, $L_{\text{func}} \equiv \log f_{yx|\xi}(y, X \mid \Xi)$, and $L_\xi \equiv \log f_\xi(\Xi)$. Notice that this argument does not require normality.

4.2 Maximum likelihood estimation in the structural model

If we restrict attention to the parameter vector δ, deriving the MLE and the information matrix in the structural model is straightforward. Because we will need some of the intermediate results later on, we give the full derivation below. Recall that $S_X \equiv X'X/N$. To obtain properties of the MLE of δ we note (using the results of section A.1) that

$$\begin{aligned} \frac{\partial L_{\text{struc}}}{\partial \kappa} &= -N\gamma^{-1}\left(S_X\kappa - \frac{1}{N}X'y\right) \\ \frac{\partial L_{\text{struc}}}{\partial \gamma} &= -\frac{N}{2}\left(\frac{1}{\gamma} - c\frac{1}{\gamma^2}\right) \\ \frac{\partial L_{\text{struc}}}{\partial \sigma_x} &= -\frac{N}{2}Q_g \operatorname{vec}\bigl(\Sigma_X^{-1} - \Sigma_X^{-1}S_X\Sigma_X^{-1}\bigr), \end{aligned}$$

where $c \equiv (y - X\kappa)'(y - X\kappa)/N$, so that $\operatorname{plim}_{N\to\infty} c = \gamma$, cf. (2.12a). The symmetrization matrix Q_g is defined and discussed in section A.4. Upon differentiating once more we obtain

$$\begin{aligned}
\frac{\partial^2 L_{\text{struc}}}{\partial\kappa\,\partial\kappa'} &= -N\gamma^{-1}S_X \\
\frac{\partial^2 L_{\text{struc}}}{\partial\gamma^2} &= -\frac{N}{2}\left(-\frac{1}{\gamma^2} + \frac{2c}{\gamma^3}\right) \\
\frac{\partial^2 L_{\text{struc}}}{\partial\sigma_x\,\partial\sigma_x'} &= -\frac{N}{2}Q_g\left(-\Sigma_X^{-1}\otimes\Sigma_X^{-1} + \Sigma_X^{-1}S_X\Sigma_X^{-1}\otimes\Sigma_X^{-1}\right. \\
&\qquad \left. + \Sigma_X^{-1}\otimes\Sigma_X^{-1}S_X\Sigma_X^{-1}\right).
\end{aligned}$$

The cross-derivatives are zero. Thus, the MLE of δ is

$$d \equiv \begin{bmatrix} b \\ s_\varepsilon^2 \\ s_X \end{bmatrix} = \begin{bmatrix} (X'X)^{-1}X'y \\ y'M_X y/N \\ \operatorname{vec} X'X/N \end{bmatrix}, \tag{4.3}$$

where $M_X \equiv I_N - X(X'X)^{-1}X'$, and d is asymptotically normally distributed,

$$\sqrt{N}(d-\delta) \xrightarrow{d} \mathcal{N}_{g+1+g^2}\left(0, \mathcal{I}_0^+\right) \tag{4.4}$$

with $\mathcal{I}_0^+$ the Moore-Penrose inverse of $\mathcal{I}_0$, the information matrix in the limit,

$$\begin{aligned}
\mathcal{I}_0 &= -\lim_{N\to\infty} \mathrm{E}\,\frac{1}{N}\frac{\partial^2 L_{\text{struc}}}{\partial\delta\,\partial\delta'} \\
&= \begin{bmatrix} \gamma^{-1}\Sigma_X & 0 & 0 \\ 0 & \frac{1}{2}\gamma^{-2} & 0 \\ 0 & 0 & \frac{1}{2}Q_g(\Sigma_X^{-1}\otimes\Sigma_X^{-1}) \end{bmatrix}.
\end{aligned} \tag{4.5}$$

The reason that we have to use the Moore-Penrose inverse is that $\mathcal{I}_0$ is singular because the $g^2 \times g^2$ matrix Q_g has rank $\frac{1}{2}g(g+1)$. The singularity is due to the symmetry of Σ_X. This leads to the formula

$$\mathcal{I}_0^+ = \begin{bmatrix} \gamma\Sigma_X^{-1} & 0 & 0 \\ 0 & 2\gamma^2 & 0 \\ 0 & 0 & 2Q_g(\Sigma_X\otimes\Sigma_X) \end{bmatrix}$$

for the Moore-Penrose inverse of $\mathcal{I}_0$, which can be verified by straightforward multiplication.

The structural ML estimator under functional assumptions

The functional model was shown to be a conditional model. That means that we can adapt the asymptotic variance for the estimator for the structural model to the asymptotic variance for that estimator under the assumption that the model is functional by conditioning. This result proves useful in the next chapter, where we consider estimators when there is additional information on the parameters, because we can then cover both cases with basically the same methods.

In order to find the asymptotic variance of d under functional assumptions we proceed in three steps. In the first, the joint asymptotic distribution of $\varepsilon'\varepsilon$, $\Xi'\varepsilon$, $V'\varepsilon$, $V'V$, and $\Xi'V$ conditional on Ξ is derived. In the second step, the joint asymptotic distribution of $y'y$, $X'y$, and $X'X$ conditional on Ξ is derived by writing these as functions of the earlier random terms and Ξ. Finally, in the third step, the asymptotic distribution of d conditional on Ξ is derived from this by writing d as a function of these sample covariances.

In the first step, note that $\sqrt{N}(\varepsilon'\varepsilon/N - \sigma_\varepsilon^2)$, $\sqrt{N}(\Xi'\varepsilon/N)$, $\sqrt{N}(V'\varepsilon/N)$, $\sqrt{N}\operatorname{vec}(V'V/N - \Omega)$, and $\sqrt{N}\operatorname{vec}(V'\Xi/N)$ are jointly asymptotically normally distributed conditional on Ξ under fairly general regularity conditions on Ξ by some form of central limit theorem. The according asymptotic variances are

$$\begin{aligned}\operatorname{AVar}\big(\sqrt{N}(\varepsilon'\varepsilon/N - \sigma_\varepsilon^2) \mid \Xi\big) &= 2\sigma_\varepsilon^4 \\ \operatorname{AVar}\big(\sqrt{N}\operatorname{vec}(V'V/N - \Omega) \mid \Xi\big) &= 2Q_g(\Omega \otimes \Omega),\end{aligned}$$

because these do not depend on Ξ, and V and ε are normally distributed, cf. section A.5. Furthermore,

$$\begin{aligned}\operatorname{AVar}\big(\sqrt{N}(\Xi'\varepsilon/N) \mid \Xi\big) &= \lim_{N\to\infty} \operatorname{E}\left(\frac{1}{N}\Xi'\varepsilon\varepsilon'\Xi \mid \Xi\right) \\ &= \sigma_\varepsilon^2 \lim_{N\to\infty}\left(\frac{1}{N}\Xi'\Xi\right) \\ &= \sigma_\varepsilon^2 \Sigma_\Xi.\end{aligned}$$

Analogously, we have

$$\begin{aligned}\operatorname{AVar}\big(\sqrt{N}(V'\varepsilon/N) \mid \Xi\big) &= \lim_{N\to\infty} \operatorname{E}\left(\frac{1}{N}V'\varepsilon\varepsilon'V\right) \\ &= \sigma_\varepsilon^2 \Omega.\end{aligned}$$

Finally, consider $\sqrt{N}\operatorname{vec}(V'\Xi/N)$. Its asymptotic variance is

$$\begin{aligned}&\operatorname{AVar}\big(\sqrt{N}\operatorname{vec}(V'\Xi/N) \mid \Xi\big) \\ &= \lim_{N\to\infty} \operatorname{E}\left(\frac{1}{N}(\Xi' \otimes I_g)(\operatorname{vec} V')(\operatorname{vec} V')'(\Xi \otimes I_g) \,\Big|\, \Xi\right)\end{aligned}$$

$$= \lim_{N\to\infty} \left(\frac{1}{N}(\Xi' \otimes I_g)(I_N \otimes \Omega)(\Xi \otimes I_g) \;\middle|\; \Xi \right)$$
$$= \lim_{N\to\infty} \frac{1}{N} \Xi'\Xi \otimes \Omega$$
$$= \Sigma_\Xi \otimes \Omega.$$

It is easily seen that the conditional asymptotic covariances between the different parts are zero.

Second, write the observable sample covariances as functions of the above random terms and Ξ,

$$\frac{X'y}{N} = S_\Xi \beta + \frac{V'\Xi}{N}\beta + \frac{\Xi'\varepsilon}{N} + \frac{V'\varepsilon}{N}$$
$$\frac{y'y}{N} = \beta' S_\Xi \beta + 2\beta' \frac{\Xi'\varepsilon}{N} + \frac{\varepsilon'\varepsilon}{N}$$
$$\frac{X'X}{N} = S_\Xi + \frac{V'\Xi}{N} + \frac{\Xi'V}{N} + \frac{V'V}{N}.$$

Let $s \equiv \left(y'X/N, y'y/N, (\operatorname{vec} X'X/N)'\right)'$, and let $\sigma_N \equiv \mathrm{E}(s \mid \Xi)$, where we have made the dependence of σ_N on N explicit, because S_Ξ depends on N. It follows from the equations above that $\sqrt{N}(s - \sigma_N)$ is asymptotically normally distributed conditional on Ξ, with mean zero and covariance matrix Ψ, which can be straightforwardly derived from the asymptotic variances of the random terms derived in the first step. Let this covariance matrix be partitioned as

$$\Psi \equiv \mathrm{AVar}\left(\sqrt{N}(s - \sigma) \mid \Xi\right) = \begin{bmatrix} \Psi_{11} & \psi_{12} & \Psi_{31}' \\ \psi_{12}' & \psi_{22} & \psi_{32}' \\ \Psi_{31} & \psi_{32} & \Psi_{33} \end{bmatrix},$$

where the formulas for the submatrices are

$$\Psi_{11} = (\beta' \otimes I_g)(\Sigma_\Xi \otimes \Omega)(\beta \otimes I_g) + \sigma_\varepsilon^2 \Sigma_\Xi + \sigma_\varepsilon^2 \Omega$$
$$= \sigma_y^2 \Sigma_X - (\beta' \Sigma_\Xi \beta) \Sigma_\Xi$$
$$\psi_{12} = 2\sigma_\varepsilon^2 \Sigma_\Xi \beta$$
$$= 2\sigma_y^2 \sigma_{Xy} - 2(\beta' \Sigma_\Xi \beta) \Sigma_\Xi \beta$$
$$\Psi_{31} = P_{g,g}(\Sigma_\Xi \otimes \Omega)(\beta \otimes I_g) + (\Sigma_\Xi \otimes \Omega)(\beta \otimes I_g)$$
$$= 2Q_g(\Sigma_\Xi \beta \otimes \Omega)$$
$$= 2Q_g(\sigma_{Xy} \otimes \Sigma_X) - 2Q_g(\Sigma_\Xi \beta \otimes \Sigma_\Xi)$$

$$\begin{aligned}
\psi_{22} &= 2\sigma_\varepsilon^4 + 4\sigma_\varepsilon^2(\beta'\Sigma_\Xi\beta) \\
&= 2\sigma_y^4 - 2(\beta'\Sigma_\Xi\beta)^2 \\
\psi_{32} &= 0 \\
\Psi_{33} &= 4Q_g(\Sigma_\Xi \otimes \Omega)Q_g + 2Q_g(\Omega \otimes \Omega)Q_g \\
&= 2Q_g(\Sigma_X \otimes \Sigma_X) - 2Q_g(\Sigma_\Xi \otimes \Sigma_\Xi),
\end{aligned}$$

where $P_{g,g}$ is the commutation matrix and Q_g is the symmetrization matrix, see section A.4. Note the special structure of this matrix.

Finally, we note that d is a continuously differentiable function of s, so that we can apply the delta method (see section A.5) to derive its asymptotic distribution from the asymptotic distribution of s. Obviously, d is conditional on Ξ asymptotically normally distributed. The asymptotic mean of d is $\delta_N \equiv (\kappa_N', \gamma_N, \sigma_{XN}')'$, with

$$\begin{aligned}
\kappa_N &\equiv (S_\Xi + \Omega)^{-1}S_\Xi\beta \\
\gamma_N &\equiv \sigma_\varepsilon^2 + \beta'S_\Xi\beta - \beta'S_\Xi(S_\Xi + \Omega)^{-1}S_\Xi\beta \\
\sigma_{XN} &\equiv \operatorname{vec}(S_\Xi + \Omega).
\end{aligned}$$

Given our assumption that $\lim_{N\to\infty} S_\Xi = \Sigma_\Xi$, it follows that $\lim_{N\to\infty} \delta_N = \delta$, but $\sqrt{N}(\delta_N - \delta)$ will typically not converge to zero. (In the structural case, it has a nondegenerate asymptotic distribution.) Hence, the mean of the asymptotic distribution of $\sqrt{N}(d - \delta)$ is not zero. Therefore, we use δ_N instead.

The conditional asymptotic covariance matrix of $\sqrt{N}(d - \delta_N)$ is $H\Psi H'$, where $H \equiv \operatorname{plim}_{N\to\infty} \partial d/\partial s'$. From (4.3), and using the results on matrix differentiation from appendix A, we derive that

$$\frac{\partial d}{\partial s'} = \begin{bmatrix} S_X^{-1} & 0 & b' \otimes S_X^{-1} \\ -2b' & 1 & b' \otimes b' \\ 0 & 0 & I_{g^2} \end{bmatrix},$$

and the probability limit of this is clearly

$$H \equiv \operatorname*{plim}_{N\to\infty} \frac{\partial d}{\partial s'} = \begin{bmatrix} \Sigma_X^{-1} & 0 & \kappa' \otimes \Sigma_X^{-1} \\ -2\kappa' & 1 & \kappa' \otimes \kappa' \\ 0 & 0 & I_{g^2} \end{bmatrix}.$$

Hence, the asymptotic covariance matrix of $\sqrt{N}(d - \delta_N)$ conditional on Ξ is $H\Psi H'$. After some tedious calculations, this turns out to be equivalent to

$$\begin{bmatrix} \gamma\Sigma_X^{-1} + \alpha\Sigma_X^{-1}\Sigma_\Xi\Sigma_X^{-1} - \zeta\zeta' & 2\alpha\zeta & 2(\omega'\Sigma_\Xi \otimes \Sigma_X^{-1}\Sigma_\Xi)Q_g \\ 2\alpha\zeta' & 2\gamma^2 - 2\alpha^2 & -2(\omega'\Sigma_\Xi \otimes \omega'\Sigma_\Xi) \\ 2Q_g(\Sigma_\Xi\omega \otimes \Sigma_\Xi\Sigma_X^{-1}) & -2(\Sigma_\Xi\omega \otimes \Sigma_\Xi\omega) & \Psi_{33} \end{bmatrix},$$

where $\alpha \equiv -\omega'\Sigma_\Xi\omega$, $\zeta \equiv \Sigma_X^{-1}\Sigma_\Xi\omega$, and $\omega = \kappa - \beta$, as defined before. On letting

$$C \equiv \begin{bmatrix} -\omega' \otimes \Sigma_X^{-1} \\ \omega' \otimes \omega' \\ I_{g^2} \end{bmatrix}, \tag{4.6}$$

we find that

$$\text{AVar}\bigl(\sqrt{N}(d - \delta_N) \mid \Xi\bigr) = \mathcal{I}_0^+ - 2CQ_g(\Sigma_\Xi \otimes \Sigma_\Xi)C'. \tag{4.7}$$

This result will prove useful later on when we discuss consistent estimators of the structural parameters when additional information is available.

4.3 Maximum likelihood estimation in the functional model

In the functional model, a characteristic property of the likelihood L_{func} is that it has no proper maximum. It is unbounded from above. So if the first-order conditions for a maximum have a solution, it must correspond to a local maximum, a saddlepoint, or a minimum of the likelihood function, but not to a global maximum.

The unboundedness of the likelihood function can be seen as follows. L_{func} as given by (4.1) and (4.2) is a function of β, σ_ε^2, Ω, and Ξ given the observations y and X. Note that σ_ε^2 occurs in only two terms of L_{func}, in $-\frac{N}{2}\log\sigma_\varepsilon^2$ and in the term containing $y - \Xi\beta$. In the parameter subspace where $y = \Xi\beta$ the latter term vanishes and σ_ε^2 appears only in $-\frac{N}{2}\log\sigma_\varepsilon^2$. It is clear that this term approaches infinity when σ_ε^2 approaches zero. In other words, we can choose Ξ and β such that $y = \Xi\beta$, and next let σ_ε^2 tend to zero. Then L_{func} diverges to infinity. Analogously, in the subspace where $X = \Xi$, we can let $|\Omega|$ approach zero, which indicates another singularity of L_{func}. Therefore, it may seem irrelevant to inspect L_{func} any further. It turns out, however, that L_{func} does have stationary points and, although these can not correspond to a global maximum of the likelihood, they still may lead to a consistent estimator. We will investigate this now.

The first-order conditions corresponding to stationary points of L_{func} can be found by differentiation:

$$\frac{\partial L_{\text{func}}}{\partial \beta} = -\sigma_\varepsilon^{-2}\Xi'(y - \Xi\beta) = 0 \tag{4.8a}$$

$$\frac{\partial L_{\text{func}}}{\partial \sigma_\varepsilon^2} = -\frac{N}{2}\sigma_\varepsilon^{-2} + \tfrac{1}{2}\sigma_\varepsilon^{-4}(y - \Xi\beta)'(y - \Xi\beta) = 0 \tag{4.8b}$$

$$\frac{\partial L_{\text{func}}}{\partial \Omega} = -\frac{N}{2}\Omega^{-1} + \tfrac{1}{2}\Omega^{-1}(X - \Xi)'(X - \Xi)\Omega^{-1} = 0 \tag{4.8c}$$

$$\frac{\partial L_{\text{func}}}{\partial \Xi} = \sigma_\varepsilon^{-2}(y - \Xi\beta)\beta' + (X - \Xi)\Omega^{-1} = 0. \tag{4.8d}$$

In order to try to solve this system, premultiply (4.8d) by $\Omega^{-1}(X - \Xi)'$ and combine the outcome with (4.8c). This yields

$$\sigma_\varepsilon^{-2}\Omega^{-1}(X - \Xi)'(y - \Xi\beta)\beta' = -N\Omega^{-1}.$$

The left-hand side of this equation is a matrix of rank one and the right-hand side of this equation is a matrix of rank g. Hence, the equation system is inconsistent if $g > 1$. Therefore, we restrict our attention to the case $g = 1$.

The case of a single regressor

For the case $g = 1$ we adapt the notation slightly and write x, ξ, and σ_v^2 instead of X, Ξ, and Ω and note that β is a scalar. The loglikelihood, (4.1) combined with (4.2), then becomes

$$\begin{aligned} L_{\text{func}} = {} & -N\log(2\pi) - \frac{N}{2}\log\sigma_\varepsilon^2 - \tfrac{1}{2}\sigma_\varepsilon^{-2}(y - \xi\beta)'(y - \xi\beta) \\ & - \frac{N}{2}\log\sigma_v^2 - \tfrac{1}{2}\sigma_v^{-2}(x - \xi)'(x - \xi), \end{aligned} \tag{4.9}$$

and the first-order conditions from (4.8) yield

$$\xi'y = \xi'\xi\beta \tag{4.10a}$$

$$N\sigma_\varepsilon^2 = (y - \xi\beta)'(y - \xi\beta) \tag{4.10b}$$

$$N\sigma_v^2 = (x - \xi)'(x - \xi) \tag{4.10c}$$

$$x - \xi = -(y - \xi\beta)\sigma_v^2\beta/\sigma_\varepsilon^2. \tag{4.10d}$$

Substitution of (4.10b) and (4.10d) into (4.10c) yields $\sigma_\varepsilon^2 = \sigma_v^2\beta^2$. Substitution into (4.10d) then implies $x - \xi = -y/\beta + \xi$ or

$$2\xi = x + y/\beta. \tag{4.11}$$

Substitution of this in (4.10a) yields the estimator

$$\hat{\beta}^2 = \frac{y'y}{x'x}. \tag{4.12}$$

This determines $\hat{\beta}$ up to the choice of sign. We will discuss the choice of sign below. To obtain estimators for σ_ε^2 and σ_v^2 we use

$$\begin{aligned} y - \xi\beta &= \tfrac{1}{2}(y - x\beta) \\ x - \xi &= x - \tfrac{1}{2}(x + y/\beta) \\ &= \tfrac{1}{2}(x - y/\beta). \end{aligned}$$

Thus, (4.10b) implies

$$\begin{aligned}2N\sigma_\varepsilon^2 &= 2(y-\xi\beta)'(y-\xi\beta)\\ &= \tfrac{1}{2}(y-x\beta)'(y-x\beta)\\ &= \tfrac{1}{2}(y'y-2\beta x'y+\beta^2x'x)\\ &= y'y-\beta x'y,\end{aligned}$$

and (4.10c) implies

$$\begin{aligned}2N\sigma_v^2 &= 2(x-\xi)'(x-\xi)\\ &= \tfrac{1}{2}(x-y/\beta)'(x-y/\beta)\\ &= \tfrac{1}{2}(x'x-2x'y/\beta+y'y/\beta^2)\\ &= x'x-x'y/\beta\\ &= 2N\sigma_\varepsilon^2/\beta^2\end{aligned}$$

At this solution, L_{func} follows by substitution of (4.10b) and (4.10c) into (4.9): $L_{\text{func}} = -N\log(2\pi) - \frac{N}{2}\log\sigma_\varepsilon^2 - \frac{N}{2}\log\sigma_v^2 - N$. We can now settle the choice of $\hat{\beta}$. Recall that $\hat{\beta}$ is determined by (4.12), which has two roots. Given the way σ_ε^2 and σ_v^2 depend on β and $x'y$, the root of (4.12) that has the same sign as $x'y$ yields the highest value of L_{func}. We denote this root by $\hat{\beta}$.

Clearly, the solution for $\hat{\beta}$ is an inconsistent estimator of β. The right-hand side of (4.12) converges to the ratio of $\beta^2\sigma_\xi^2 + \sigma_\varepsilon^2$ and $\sigma_\xi^2 + \sigma_v^2$, where σ_ξ^2 is the limit of $\xi'\xi/N$. The solution for $\hat{\beta}$ is not even consistent in the absence of measurement error. Note that it was assumed from the outset that Ω is positive definite, which translates to $\sigma_v^2 > 0$ in this case. This assumption has been used implicitly in the derivations, which may explain why $\hat{\beta}$ is not consistent when $\sigma_v^2 = 0$.

Why is the solution a saddlepoint?

We have noted above that this likelihood-based solution can not be a global maximum of L_{func}, because L_{func} is unbounded from above. It is not even a local maximum of L_{func}, but a saddlepoint. This can be seen as follows. We consider the subspace of the parameter space where $\beta = \hat{\beta}$ and where σ_ε^2 and σ_v^2 are such that (4.10b) and (4.10c) are satisfied. Then we investigate the behavior of L_{func} as a function of ξ:

$$L_{\text{func}}(\xi) = -N\log(2\pi) - \frac{N}{2}\log\sigma_\varepsilon^2 - \frac{N}{2}\log\sigma_v^2 - N$$

$$
\begin{aligned}
&= -N\log(2\pi) - \frac{N}{2}\log\frac{(y-\xi\hat{\beta})'(y-\xi\hat{\beta})}{N} \\
&\qquad - \frac{N}{2}\log\frac{(x-\xi)'(x-\xi)}{N} - N \\
&= \text{constant} - N\log\|x-\xi\|\;\|\xi - y/\hat{\beta}\|.
\end{aligned}
$$

Denote the likelihood-based solution (4.11) for ξ by ξ_0. This is the midpoint of the line segment joining x and $y/\hat{\beta}$. Let us first consider whether along this line segment ξ_0 represents a maximum. Insert $\xi = \nu x + (1-\nu)(y/\hat{\beta})$ into the loglikelihood to obtain

$$L_{\text{func}}(\nu) = \text{constant} - N\log\|x - y/\hat{\beta}\|^2 - N\log\nu(1-\nu).$$

Clearly, $L_{\text{func}}(\nu)$ is at a local *minimum* for $\nu = \frac{1}{2}$, i.e., for $\xi = \xi_0$. Hence, $L_{\text{func}}(\xi_0)$ is either a local minimum of the likelihood or a saddlepoint. It is the latter, because if ξ_1 is some point on the line passing through ξ_0 and perpendicular to the line passing through x and $y/\hat{\beta}$, $\|x-\xi_1\| > \|x-\xi_0\|$ and $\|\xi_1 - y/\hat{\beta}\| > \|\xi_0 - y/\hat{\beta}\|$, so $L_{\text{func}}(\xi_0) > L_{\text{func}}(\xi_1)$. Thus, when moving from the stationary point ξ_0, L_{func} increases in the direction of x or $y/\hat{\beta}$ and decreases in the direction of ξ_1. See figure 4.1 for an illustration.

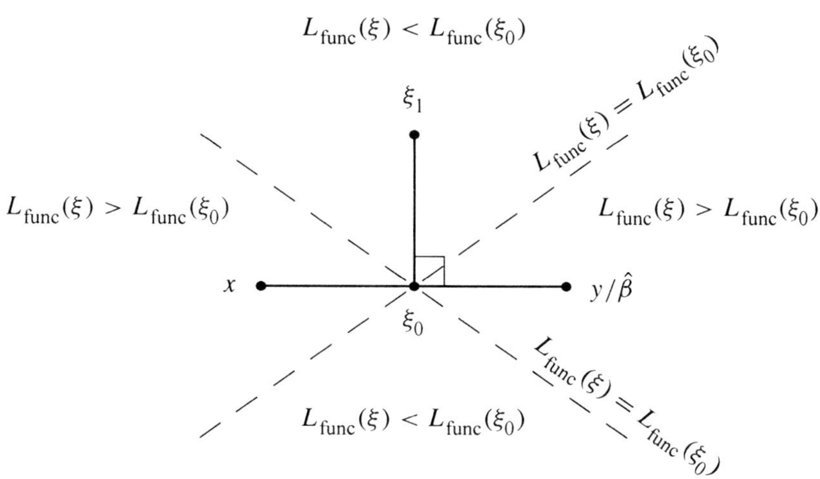

Figure 4.1 *The saddlepoint solution.*

4.4 General identification theory

Identification of parametric models is an important topic in econometric research. This is especially true in models with measurement error. In order to put the discussion into perspective we discuss in this section some basics of identification. In particular we formulate and prove a useful result that links identification to the rank of the information matrix.

Assume that we may observe a random vector y, and a model for y implies a distribution function $F(y;\theta)$ for y, which depends on a parameter vector θ that has to be estimated. Let the set $\mathcal{S}$ denote the domain of y. It is assumed that $\mathcal{S}$ does not depend on the specific model one is interested in. Then, two models with implied distribution functions $F_1(y;\theta_1)$ and $F_2(y;\theta_2)$ are called *observationally equivalent* if $F_1(y;\theta_1) = F_2(y;\theta_2)$ for all $y \in \mathcal{S}$. Clearly, if two models lead to the same distribution of the observable variables, we will not be able to distinguish between them statistically.

For example, if $F_1(y;\sigma^2)$ is the distribution function of a $\mathcal{N}(0,\sigma^2)$ variable with $\sigma^2 > 0$, and $F_2(y;\tau^2)$ is the distribution function of a $\mathcal{N}(0, 1/\tau^2)$ variable, then these two models for y are obviously observationally equivalent.

We will encounter situations in which F_1 and F_2 are functions of such different parameterizations in section 8.7, but here we will discuss the regular case in which only one parameterization is considered, but different values of θ lead to the same distribution. For example, if $F(y;\mu_1,\mu_2)$ is the distribution function of a $\mathcal{N}(\mu_1 - \mu_2, 1)$ variable, this function depends only on the difference $\mu_1 - \mu_2$ and hence, different choices of μ_1 and μ_2 lead to the same distribution, as long as $\mu_1 - \mu_2$ is the same.

We assume that $F(y;\theta)$ is continuously differentiable in y and θ. This implies that we assume that y is continuously distributed with a density function f, but this is not essential. The function f may also be considered the probability mass function of a discrete random variable y.

Let $f(y;\theta)$ be the density function parameterized by the parameter vector θ, where the domain of θ is the open set Θ. In this setup, two points θ_1 and θ_2 are observationally equivalent if $f(y;\theta_1) = f(y;\theta_2)$ for all $y \in \mathcal{S}$. A point θ_0 in Θ is said to be *globally identified* if there is no other θ in Θ that is observationally equivalent. A parameter point θ_0 is *locally identified* if there exists an open neighborhood of θ_0 in which no element is observationally equivalent to θ_0. Under certain conditions, there is a close connection between the local identification of θ_0 and the rank of the information matrix in θ_0.

Theorem 4.1 (Rothenberg). Let θ_0 be a regular point of the information matrix $\mathcal{I}(\theta)$, i.e., $\mathcal{I}(\theta)$ has constant rank in an open neighborhood $\mathcal{T}$ of θ_0. Assume that the support $\mathcal{S}$ of $f(y;\theta)$ is the same for all $\theta \in \mathcal{T}$, and $f(y;\theta)$ and $\log f(y;\theta)$

are continuously differentiable in θ for all $\theta \in \mathcal{T}$ and for all y. Then θ_0 is locally identified if and only if $\mathcal{I}(\theta_0)$ is nonsingular.

Proof. First, let us define

$$g(y;\theta) \equiv \log f(y;\theta)$$
$$h(y;\theta) \equiv \partial \log f(y;\theta)/\partial\theta.$$

Then, the mean value theorem implies

$$g(y;\theta) - g(y;\theta_0) = h(y;\theta^*)'(\theta - \theta_0), \tag{4.13}$$

for all θ in a neighborhood of θ_0, for all y, and with θ^* between θ and θ_0 (although θ^* may depend on y). Now, suppose that θ_0 is *not* locally identified. Then any open neighborhood of θ_0 will contain parameter points that are observationally equivalent to θ_0. Hence, we can construct an infinite sequence $\theta^1, \theta^2, \ldots, \theta^k, \ldots$, such that $\lim_{k\to\infty} \theta^k = \theta_0$, with the property that $g(y;\theta^k) = g(y;\theta_0)$, for all k and all y. It then follows from (4.13) that for all k and all y there exist points θ^{*k} (which again may depend on y), such that

$$h(y;\theta^{*k})'\delta^k \equiv h(y;\theta^{*k})'(\theta^k - \theta_0)/\|\theta^k - \theta_0\| = 0, \tag{4.14}$$

with θ^{*k} between θ^k and θ_0. From $\theta^k \to \theta_0$, it follows that $\theta^{*k} \to \theta_0$ for all y. Furthermore, the sequence $\delta^1, \delta^2, \ldots, \delta^k, \ldots$, is an infinite sequence on the unit sphere, which is a bounded closed set, so that there must be at least one limit point on the unit sphere. Let δ_0 be such a limit point. Then (4.14) implies that $h(y;\theta_0)'\delta_0 = 0$ for all y. Hence,

$$\mathrm{E}\big(h(y;\theta_0)'\delta_0\big)^2 = \delta_0' \,\mathrm{E}\big(h(y;\theta_0)h(y;\theta_0)'\big)\delta_0 = \delta_0'\mathcal{I}(\theta_0)\delta_0 = 0,$$

so that nonidentification of θ_0 implies singularity of the information matrix.

Conversely, if θ_0 is a regular point but $\mathcal{I}(\theta_0)$ is singular, then there exists a vector function $\delta(\theta)$ of θ such that in an open neighborhood of θ_0

$$\delta(\theta)'\mathcal{I}(\theta)\delta(\theta) = \mathrm{E}\big(h(y;\theta)'\delta(\theta)\big)^2 = 0.$$

This implies, for all θ in this neighborhood, that $h(y;\theta)'\delta(\theta) = 0$ for all y. Because $\mathcal{I}(\theta)$ is continuous and of constant rank, $\delta(\theta)$ can be chosen to be continuous in a neighborhood of θ_0. We use this property to define a curve $\theta(t)$ which solves for $0 \le t \le t_*$ the differential equation $\mathrm{d}\theta(t)/\,\mathrm{d}t = \delta(\theta)$, with $\theta(0) = \theta_0$. This gives

$$\frac{\mathrm{d}g(y;\theta)}{\mathrm{d}t} = h(y;\theta)'\frac{\mathrm{d}\theta}{\mathrm{d}t} = h(y;\theta)'\delta(\theta) = 0$$

for all y. So $g(y;\theta)$ is constant along the curve $\theta(t)$ for $0 \le t \le t_*$, and hence θ_0 is not locally identified. □

The Jacobian matrix criterion

The advantage of theorem 4.1 is that we do not have to operate on the joint probability distribution of the underlying random variables directly when analyzing the identification of a particular model. It suffices to consider the information matrix. There is a further simplification possible when the underlying distribution is from the exponential family. A probability density (or mass) function is a member of the exponential family if it can be written as

$$f(y;\theta) = \exp\bigl(a(\theta)'s(y) + \beta(\theta) + c(y)\bigr),$$

where y is a vector of random variables with a domain that does not depend on the parameters, θ is a vector of parameters, $a(\cdot)$ and $s(\cdot)$ are vector-valued functions, and $\beta(\cdot)$ and $c(\cdot)$ are scalar functions of their respective arguments. It is assumed that $a(\cdot)$ is a differentiable function. Many well-known distributions belong to the exponential family, e.g., the (multivariate) normal, lognormal, gamma, beta, and Poisson distributions. The vector $a(\theta)$ is often called the vector of canonical parameters, or just the canonical parameter for short. Without loss of generality we assume that the covariance matrix Ψ of $s(y)$ is nonsingular.

For observations $y_1, \ldots, y_N$ and $s_N \equiv \sum_{n=1}^{N} s(y)/N$, the first-order derivative of the loglikelihood is

$$\frac{\partial \log \mathcal{L}(\theta)}{\partial\theta} = N\left(A(\theta)'s_N + \frac{\partial\beta(\theta)}{\partial\theta}\right),$$

where $A(\theta)$ is the Jacobian matrix with the derivatives of the canonical parameters with respect to the structural parameters,

$$A(\theta) \equiv \frac{\partial a(\theta)}{\partial\theta'}. \tag{4.15}$$

Under general regularity assumptions, $\mathrm{E}\,\partial \log \mathcal{L}(\theta)/\partial\theta = 0$, and the information matrix is given by the variance of the derivative of the loglikelihood and is proportional to $\mathcal{I}_0 = A(\theta)'\Psi A(\theta)$. Because Ψ is of full rank, the information matrix is of full rank if and only if $A(\theta)$ is of full column rank. Thus, we have established the result that, if $f(y;\theta)$ belongs to the exponential family and θ_0 is a regular point of $A(\theta)$, then θ_0 is locally identified if and only if $A(\theta_0)$ has full column rank.

This constitutes the Jacobian matrix criterion (or condition) for identification, or just the rank condition for identification. Obviously, a necessary order condition is that $A(\theta)$ has at least as many rows as columns. Note that the canonical parameter $a(\theta)$ is always identified, because the corresponding information matrix is simply the covariance matrix of $s(y)$, which was assumed to be of full rank.

This result is not restricted to the exponential family, but applies to any density function $f(y;\theta)$ that depends on θ only through $a(\theta)$, provided $a(\theta)$ is identified. The identification of the parameters from the underlying distribution can be thought to be transmitted through $a(\theta)$.

Sometimes, prior information may be available on the parameter vector θ. Let this be of the form $r(\theta_0) = r_0$. Such information will generally improve the identification status of the parameters. Redefine $A(\theta)$ from (4.15) as

$$A(\theta) \equiv \begin{bmatrix} \dfrac{\partial a(\theta)}{\partial \theta'} \\ \dfrac{\partial r(\theta)}{\partial \theta'} \end{bmatrix}.$$

After thus redefining the Jacobian matrix, the rank and order conditions for identification remain the same.

The normal distribution

An important application of this result concerns the M-dimensional normal distribution with parameters μ and Σ, which are are functions of a parameter vector θ. The density is

$$\begin{aligned} f(y;\theta) &= (2\pi)^{-M/2}|\Sigma|^{-1/2}\exp\left(-\tfrac{1}{2}(y-\mu)'\Sigma^{-1}(y-\mu)\right) \\ &= (2\pi)^{-M/2}\exp\Big(\big(y', -\tfrac{1}{2}y'\otimes y'\big)\big(\mu'\Sigma^{-1}, (\operatorname{vec}\Sigma^{-1})'\big)' \\ &\quad - \tfrac{1}{2}\log|\Sigma| - \tfrac{1}{2}\mu'\Sigma^{-1}\mu\Big). \end{aligned}$$

This gives the normal distribution in the form of the exponential family, but the term $y \otimes y$ contains redundant elements and hence its covariance matrix is singular. To eliminate this singularity, note that $y\otimes y = Q_M(y\otimes y) = D_M D_M^+(y\otimes y)$, where Q_M is the symmetrization matrix, and D_M is the duplication matrix (see section A.4). Hence, we can write

$$(y\otimes y)'\operatorname{vec}\Sigma^{-1} = \big(D_M^+(y\otimes y)\big)' D_M' \operatorname{vec}\Sigma^{-1}.$$

The transformed vector $D_M^+(y \otimes y)$ does not have redundant elements and has a nonsingular covariance matrix. Thus, the normal density fits in the p-dimensional exponential family with $p = M + M(M+1)/2$,

$$s(y) = \begin{bmatrix} y \\ -\frac{1}{2} D_M^+(y \otimes y) \end{bmatrix}, \qquad \text{and} \qquad a(\theta) = \begin{bmatrix} \Sigma^{-1}\mu \\ D_M' \operatorname{vec} \Sigma^{-1} \end{bmatrix}.$$

The identification of a normality-based model with parameterized mean and variance hence depends on the column rank of the matrix of derivatives of $a(\theta)$ with respect to θ', or, equivalently, on the column rank of the matrix of derivatives of

$$\sigma(\theta) \equiv \begin{bmatrix} \mu \\ D_M^+ \operatorname{vec} \Sigma \end{bmatrix}. \tag{4.16}$$

The equivalence is due to the fact that the Jacobian matrix of the transformation from $a(\theta)$ to $\sigma(\theta)$ is equal to

$$\frac{\partial a}{\partial \sigma'} = \begin{bmatrix} \Sigma^{-1} & -(\mu'\Sigma^{-1} \otimes \Sigma^{-1}) D_M \\ 0 & -D_M'(\Sigma^{-1} \otimes \Sigma^{-1}) D_M \end{bmatrix}$$

and is hence nonsingular. Furthermore, the matrix of derivatives of $\sigma(\theta)$ is of full column rank if and only if the matrix of derivatives of $\tilde{\sigma}(\theta) \equiv (\mu', (\operatorname{vec} \Sigma)')'$ is of full column rank, because adding or removing redundant rows obviously does not change the column rank.

If, as is often the case in practice, the mean of the distribution is zero, (4.16) reduces to $\sigma(\theta) = D_M^+ \operatorname{vec} \Sigma$. Therefore, the identification of a model when the underlying distribution is multivariate normal with zero means depends on the structure of the covariance matrix only and is determined by the rank of $\partial \operatorname{vec} \Sigma / \partial \theta'$.

While frequently normality is an assumption of convenience, not justified by theory or data, it should be stressed that, when dealing with problems of identification, it is also a conservative assumption. When the underlying distribution is nonnormal, models that are not identified under normality may still be identified, because higher order moments can then be added to $\sigma(\theta)$, which either leaves the rank of the Jacobian matrix unaffected or increases it.

4.5 Identification of the measurement error model under normality

After this general discussion of aspects of identification, we consider again the measurement error model under normality. We investigate first the identification of the structural model and next the identification of the functional model.

There are two ways to see that the structural model is not identified. First, the distribution of $(y, X) = \Xi(\beta, I_g) + (\varepsilon, V)$, where the rows of Ξ have covariance matrix Σ_Ξ and the rows of V have covariance matrix Ω, is indistinguishable from the distribution of $(y, X) = X(\kappa, I_g) + (\varepsilon, 0)$. Hence, different parameter values imply the same distribution of the data and thus the model is by definition not identified. Alternatively, the Jacobian matrix $A(\theta)$ in (4.15) is, in the case of the measurement error model, of order $(g+1)(g+2)/2 \times (g+1)^2$. Hence, the order condition for identification is not satisfied.

We investigate the identification of the functional model by inspection of the rank of the information matrix. This matrix can be derived as follows. We reconsider (4.8) and write ε for $y - \Xi\beta$ and V for $X - \Xi$. Furthermore, we write the equation for Ω as a vector and remove redundancy due to symmetry by premultiplication with D_g^+. This yields

$$\begin{aligned}
\frac{\partial L_{\text{func}}}{\partial \beta} &= -\sigma_\varepsilon^{-2}\Xi'\varepsilon \\
\frac{\partial L_{\text{func}}}{\partial \sigma_\varepsilon^2} &= \frac{N}{2}\sigma_\varepsilon^{-4}(\varepsilon'\varepsilon/N - \sigma_\varepsilon^2) \\
D_g^+\frac{\partial L_{\text{func}}}{\partial \operatorname{vec}\Omega} &= \frac{N}{2}D_g^+(\Omega^{-1}\otimes\Omega^{-1})(\operatorname{vec}V'V/N - \operatorname{vec}\Omega) \\
\frac{\partial L_{\text{func}}}{\partial \operatorname{vec}\Xi} &= \sigma_\varepsilon^{-2}\beta\otimes\varepsilon + (\Omega^{-1}\otimes I_N)\operatorname{vec}V.
\end{aligned}$$

Taking the expectation of the outer product of this vector with its transpose yields the information matrix

$$\mathcal{I}_0 = \begin{bmatrix} \sigma_\varepsilon^{-2}\Xi'\Xi & 0 & 0 & \sigma_\varepsilon^{-2}(\beta\otimes\Xi)' \\ 0 & \frac{1}{2}N\sigma_\varepsilon^{-4} & 0 & 0 \\ 0 & 0 & \frac{1}{2}N\Phi & 0 \\ \sigma_\varepsilon^{-2}(\beta\otimes\Xi) & 0 & 0 & (\sigma_\varepsilon^{-2}\beta\beta' + \Omega^{-1})\otimes I_N \end{bmatrix},$$

with $\Phi \equiv D_g^+(\Omega^{-1}\otimes\Omega^{-1})D_g^{+\prime}$, which is nonsingular. Let

$$\tilde{\mathcal{I}} \equiv \begin{bmatrix} \sigma_\varepsilon^{-2}\Xi'\Xi & \sigma_\varepsilon^{-2}(\beta\otimes\Xi)' \\ \sigma_\varepsilon^{-2}(\beta\otimes\Xi) & (\sigma_\varepsilon^{-2}\beta\beta' + \Omega^{-1})\otimes I_N \end{bmatrix},$$

then it follows immediately that

$$\begin{aligned}
|\mathcal{I}_0| &= \tfrac{1}{2}N\sigma_\varepsilon^{-4}\cdot|\tfrac{1}{2}N\Phi|\cdot|\tilde{\mathcal{I}}| \\
&= (N/2)^{g(g+1)/2+1}\sigma_\varepsilon^{-4}|\Xi'\Xi|\,|\Omega|^{-N}(1+\beta'\Omega\beta)^{N-g},
\end{aligned}$$

where the determinantal formulas from section A.1 have been used. Hence, $\mathcal{I}_0$ is positive definite if Ξ is of full column rank, which is almost everywhere in the parameter space. Therefore, the functional model is identified.

This can also be seen in an alternative way. First, $\mathrm{E}(X \mid \Xi) = \Xi$, so Ξ is identified. We can not change Ξ without changing the distribution of X. Next, $\mathrm{E}(y \mid \Xi\beta) = \Xi\beta$, so that β is identified as well, in view of the fact that Ξ is identified. By similar arguments, Ω and σ_ε^2 can also be seen to be identified.

Does this mean that the functional model can be consistently estimated? The result on identification may suggest this. Identification and the existence of a consistent estimator are by and large the same. This is intuitively obvious by the following reasoning. Let $F(y; \theta)$ be a distribution function parameterized by θ. A distribution function can be consistently estimated under mild regularity conditions. Let $\hat{F}(y)$ be such a consistent estimator and let θ_0 again denote the true value of θ. Suppose that θ_0 is identified. This implies that for any other value of θ, θ_1, say, there exists a value y_1, say, of y such that $F(y_1; \theta_1) \neq F(y_1; \theta_0)$. Because $\operatorname{plim}_{N\to\infty} \hat{F}(y_1) = F(y_1; \theta_0) \neq F(y_1; \theta_1)$, we can rule out θ_1 in the limit. Clearly, the identification rules all values of θ out in the limit, except θ_0 and hence, we find a consistent estimator.

Conversely, if we estimate a model that is not identified, there exists a parameter value θ_1, say, such that $F(y; \theta_1) = F(y; \theta_0)$ for all y. Obviously, we can not infer θ from anything else than the distribution function of y, because, if two distribution functions are the same, they are equally likely to have generated the data. If the implied distribution functions are equivalent for θ_1 and θ_2, we can never know which of the two underlies the data, so there can be no consistency.

This argument becomes dubious in the presence of incidental parameters. In the limit we obtain more information on the distribution function but the number of parameters increases at the same speed. Indeed, the functional model can not be consistently estimated. This follows from the result that, if the functional model can be consistently estimated, the structural model can also be consistently estimated for any distribution of the ξ. But we know that the structural model under normality can not be consistently estimated, and hence that the functional model can not be consistently estimated. We now turn to a general formulation of this result.

Consistent estimation in functional and structural models

Assume that for every observation n, we have an observable (vector valued) random variable y_n. The distribution of y_n is assumed to depend on a (univariate) structural parameter of interest θ and on a set of (possibly vector valued) parameters ξ_m, $m = 1, \ldots, n$. The parameters ξ_m may be incidental parameters, but may also contain structural parameters. Hence, if we are interested in the consistent estimation of a parameter vector, we can let θ denote any of its elements and let ξ_1 contain the other structural parameters, and cycle over the structural parameters to check the consistency of each one in turn. Note that y_n may depend on "previous" parameters ξ_m, $m < n$, but not on "future" parameters ($m > n$).

The question is whether there exists a consistent estimator of θ. It is assumed that $a \leq \theta \leq b$ for known constants a and b. (We will come back to this assumption later.) Let $\hat{\theta}$ be an estimator of θ; $\hat{\theta}$ is a function of $y_1, \ldots, y_N$, but for notational convenience we leave this dependence implicit. Clearly, we may restrict ourselves to $\hat{\theta}$ that only assume values between a and b. Then, in the functional model, $\hat{\theta}$ is a consistent estimator of θ if and only if

$$\lim_{N\to\infty} r_N(\theta, \xi_1, \ldots, \xi_N) = 0$$

for all θ and for all $\xi_1, \xi_2, \ldots$, where

$$r_N(\theta, \xi_1, \ldots, \xi_N) \equiv \mathrm{E}\big((\hat{\theta} - \theta)^2 \mid \theta, \xi_1, \ldots, \xi_N\big).$$

Obviously, this means that $\hat{\theta}$ is a consistent estimator of θ if and only if $\lim_{N\to\infty} R_N = 0$, where

$$R_N \equiv \max_{\theta, \xi_1, \ldots, \xi_N} r_N(\theta, \xi_1, \ldots, \xi_N).$$

Now, let $F_N(\xi_1, \ldots, \xi_N)$ be any distribution function defined on $\xi_1, \ldots, \xi_N$ and let $\mathcal{D}$ be the domain of F_N. Note that F_N does not necessarily restrict $\xi_1, \ldots, \xi_N$ to be independently or identically distributed. Define

$$\rho_N(\theta; F_N) \equiv \mathrm{E}\big((\hat{\theta} - \theta)^2 \mid \theta, F_N\big).$$

Evidently, $\hat{\theta}$ is a consistent estimator of θ in the structural model if and only if $\lim_{N\to\infty} \rho_N(\theta; F_N^0) = 0$ for all θ, where F_N^0 is the true distribution of $\xi_1, \ldots, \xi_N$. But we have

$$\begin{aligned}
\rho_N(\theta; F_N) &= \int_{\mathcal{D}} r_N(\theta, \xi_1, \ldots, \xi_N)\, \mathrm{d}F_N(\xi_1, \ldots, \xi_N) \\
&= \mathrm{E}_{\xi_1, \ldots, \xi_N}\big(r_N(\theta, \xi_1, \ldots, \xi_N); F_N\big) \\
&\leq \max_{\xi_1, \ldots, \xi_N} r_N(\theta, \xi_1, \ldots, \xi_N) \\
&\leq \max_{\theta, \xi_1, \ldots, \xi_N} r_N(\theta, \xi_1, \ldots, \xi_N) \\
&= R_N.
\end{aligned}$$

Hence, $\lim_{N\to\infty} R_N = 0$ implies $\lim_{N\to\infty} \rho_N(\theta; F_N) = 0$ for all θ and all F_N. Thus, if $\hat{\theta}$ is a consistent estimator in the functional model, it is also a consistent estimator in the structural model, for any distribution F_N of $\xi_1, \ldots, \xi_N$. Conversely, if there exists a distribution $\tilde{F}_N$, say, of $\xi_1, \ldots, \xi_N$ for which $\hat{\theta}$ is not consistent in the structural model, then $\hat{\theta}$ is also not consistent in the functional model. The parameter θ can be consistently estimated if there exists a consistent estimator $\hat{\theta}^*$, say.

The discussion above shows that, if a parameter can be consistently estimated in the functional model, then it can also be consistently estimated in the structural model, regardless of the distribution of $\xi_1, \ldots, \xi_N$. If a parameter can not be consistently estimated in the structural model for some distribution $\tilde{F}_N$, then the parameter can also not be consistently estimated in the functional model.

In the derivation of this result, we used the assumptions that $a \leq \theta \leq b$ and $a \leq \hat{\theta} \leq b$ implicitly. These assumptions assure that the mean squared error $\mathrm{E}(\hat{\theta} - \theta)^2$ exists and is finite and that the maximum R_N exists and is attained for some value of θ. If the assumption $a \leq \theta \leq b$ can not be made, then in many cases the mean squared error will still exist and R_N will also still exist. We will not attempt to find the weakest set of sufficient assumptions, however, but note that in practice, a possibly unbounded parameter value will typically not be relevant, so that the assumption is not very strong.

4.6 A general identification condition in the structural model

Up till now, the discussion of the structural measurement error model was limited by the assumption of normality of the ξ_n. It was shown that the structural model is not identified under normality. In section 4.4, however, we have seen that normality is a conservative assumption from an identification point of view. Hence, under alternative distributional assumptions, the model may be identified. In this section we look into this and consider the question what lack of identification implies about the distribution of the ξ_n. We essentially obtain the result that the model is not identified only under normality. There is a subtle difference here between the case of a single regressor and the multiple regression case. Hence we consider first the single regressor case and next the multiple regression case.

The single regressor case

The model is $y_n = \xi_n\beta + \varepsilon_n$ and $x_n = \xi_n + v_n$ and we conservatively assume that $\varepsilon_n \sim \mathcal{N}(0, \sigma_\varepsilon^2)$ and $v_n \sim \mathcal{N}(0, \sigma_v^2)$, both i.i.d. The ξ_n are also i.i.d., with zero expectation, but have an otherwise unspecified nondegenerate distribution. Note that we use again the notation σ_v^2 instead of Ω in this case with a single regressor. In the sequel we will omit the indices to x, y, ξ, ε, and v.

Theorem 4.2 (Reiersøl). If the parameters are not identified, ξ is normally distributed.

Proof. The proof is based on the notion of the characteristic function. In general, the characteristic function of a (possibly vector-valued) random variable x in a point t is defined as $\varphi_x(t) = \mathrm{E}\big(\exp(it'x)\big)$. We exploit the following properties of characteristic functions. First, $\varphi(0) = 1$. Second, characteristic functions determine distribution functions uniquely, and vice versa. Third, let $x = (x_1', x_2')'$ and $t = (t_1', t_2')'$ accordingly. Stochastic independence of x_1 and x_2 is equivalent to the factorization $\varphi_x(t) = \varphi_{x_1}(t_1)\varphi_{x_2}(t_2)$. Fourth, the characteristic function of the marginal distribution of x_1 is obtained by putting $t_2 = 0$. Fifth, if $x \sim \mathcal{N}(\mu, \Sigma)$, then

$$\varphi_x(t) = \exp\big(-\tfrac{1}{2}(t'\mu + t'\Sigma t)\big).$$

For the single regressor errors-in-variables case the characteristic function of the joint distribution of y and x satisfies

$$\begin{aligned}
\varphi_{y.x}(s,t) &= \mathrm{E}\exp(i(sy + tx)) \\
&= \mathrm{E}\exp\big(i\big(s(\xi\beta + \varepsilon) + t(\xi + v)\big)\big) \\
&= \mathrm{E}\exp\big(i(s\beta + t)\xi\big)\exp(is\varepsilon)\exp(itv) \\
&= \varphi_\xi(s\beta + t)\exp\Big(-\tfrac{1}{2}\big(s^2\sigma_\varepsilon^2 + t^2\sigma_v^2\big)\Big),
\end{aligned} \tag{4.17}$$

where the last equality rests on the normality of ε and v. If β is not identified, there exist parameter sets $\{\beta, \sigma_\varepsilon^2, \sigma_v^2\}$ and $\{\beta^*, \sigma_\varepsilon^{2*}, \sigma_v^{2*}\}$ with $\beta \neq \beta^*$ generating the same distribution and hence the same characteristic function. Then, (4.17) implies

$$\begin{aligned}
&\varphi_\xi(s\beta + t)\exp\Big(-\tfrac{1}{2}\big(s^2\sigma_\varepsilon^2 + t^2\sigma_v^2\big)\Big) \\
&\qquad = \varphi_\xi^*(s\beta^* + t)\exp\Big(-\tfrac{1}{2}\big(s^2\sigma_\varepsilon^{2*} + t^2\sigma_v^{2*}\big)\Big).
\end{aligned} \tag{4.18}$$

Note that we have introduced a separate characteristic function φ_ξ^*, because in general a different set of structural parameters will only give the same distribution of the observables if the distribution of ξ is also different in both cases. Now, let m be arbitrary and let t and s vary such that

$$s\beta^* + t = 0 \tag{4.19a}$$

$$s\beta + t = m \tag{4.19b}$$

so that $s = -m/(\beta^* - \beta)$ and $t = m\beta^*/(\beta^* - \beta)$, and (4.18) reduces to

$$\varphi_\xi(m)\exp\Bigl(-\tfrac{1}{2}\bigl(s^2\sigma_\varepsilon^2 + t^2\sigma_v^2\bigr)\Bigr) = \exp\Bigl(-\tfrac{1}{2}\bigl(s^2\sigma_\varepsilon^{2*} + t^2\sigma_v^{2*}\bigr)\Bigr).$$

This implies that the characteristic function of ξ is $\varphi_\xi(m) = \exp(-\frac{1}{2}cm^2)$, where

$$c \equiv \frac{\bigl(\sigma_\varepsilon^{2*} - \sigma_\varepsilon^2\bigr) + \bigl(\sigma_v^{2*} - \sigma_v^2\bigr)\beta^{*2}}{\bigl(\beta^* - \beta\bigr)^2}.$$

Clearly, $\varphi_\xi(m)$ is the characteristic function of a normal distribution. This means that nonidentification implies a normal distribution of ξ. □

The converse, that normality of ξ implies nonidentification has already been noted in section 4.5, so the two are equivalent in this simple model.

The multiple regression case

We next turn to the multiple regression case, with $y_n = \xi_n'\beta + \varepsilon_n$ and $x_n = \xi_n + v_n$. Now, ξ_n and β are g-vectors. The generalization to the multiple regression case is nontrivial.

Theorem 4.3 (Bekker). The parameter vector β is identified if and only if there does not exist a nonsingular matrix $A = (a_1, A_2)$ such that $\xi' a_1$ is distributed normally and independently of $\xi' A_2$.

Proof. We start the proof again from nonidentification. The beginning of the proof is a straightforward generalization of the proof in the single regressor case. Letting t now be a g-vector, we arrive analogous to (4.17) at

$$\varphi_{y,x}(s,t) = \varphi_\xi(s\beta + t)\exp\Bigl(-\tfrac{1}{2}\bigl(s^2\sigma_\varepsilon^2 + t'\Omega t\bigr)\Bigr). \tag{4.20}$$

We consider again the implications of nonidentification. Analogous to (4.18) there now must exist parameter sets $\{\beta, \sigma_\varepsilon^2, \Omega\}$ and $\{\beta^*, \sigma_\varepsilon^{2*}, \Omega^*\}$ with $\beta \neq \beta^*$ such that

$$\begin{aligned}\varphi_\xi(s\beta + t)&\exp\Bigl(-\tfrac{1}{2}\bigl(s^2\sigma_\varepsilon^2 + t'\Omega t\bigr)\Bigr)\\ &= \varphi_\xi^*(s\beta^* + t)\exp\Bigl(-\tfrac{1}{2}\bigl(s^2\sigma_\varepsilon^{2*} + t'\Omega^* t\bigr)\Bigr).\end{aligned} \tag{4.21}$$

We can not, however, generalize (4.19) to the multiple regression case and now proceed differently.

Let $l \equiv s\beta^* + t$, then

$$\varphi_\xi(s\beta + t) = \varphi_\xi\big(s(\beta - \beta^*) + l\big) = \varphi_{\xi'(\beta-\beta^*),\xi}(s, l).$$

This enables us to rewrite (4.21) as

$$\varphi_{\xi'(\beta-\beta^*),\xi}(s, l) = \exp\Big(-\tfrac{1}{2}\big(s^2(\sigma_\varepsilon^{2*} - \sigma_\varepsilon^2) + (l - \beta^* s)'(\Omega^* - \Omega)(l - \beta^* s)\big)\Big)\varphi_\xi^*(l). \quad (4.22)$$

From this we can derive the characteristic function of the marginal distribution of $\xi'(\beta - \beta^*)$ and that of ξ, by putting $l = 0$ and $s = 0$, respectively:

$$\varphi_{\xi'(\beta-\beta^*)}(s) = \exp\Big(-\tfrac{1}{2}s^2\big((\sigma_\varepsilon^{2*} - \sigma_\varepsilon^2) + \beta^{*\prime}(\Omega^* - \Omega)\beta^*\big)\Big) \quad (4.23a)$$

$$\varphi_\xi(l) = \exp\big(-\tfrac{1}{2}l'(\Omega^* - \Omega)l\big)\varphi_\xi^*(l). \quad (4.23b)$$

Substituting these expressions into (4.22) yields

$$\varphi_{\xi'(\beta-\beta^*),\xi}(s, l) = \varphi_{\xi'(\beta-\beta^*)}(s)\,\varphi_\xi(l)\exp\big(s\beta^{*\prime}(\Omega^* - \Omega)l\big).$$

Now, let l vary such that $l = Bm$, where m is a $(g-1)$-vector and B is a $g\times(g-1)$ matrix of full column rank such that $\beta^{*\prime}(\Omega^* - \Omega)B = 0$. Then

$$\varphi_{\xi'(\beta-\beta^*),\xi}(s, Bm) = \varphi_{\xi'(\beta-\beta^*)}(s)\,\varphi_\xi(Bm),$$

or, equivalently,

$$\varphi_{\xi'(\beta-\beta^*,B)}(s, m) = \varphi_{\xi'(\beta-\beta^*)}(s)\,\varphi_{\xi'B}(m). \quad (4.24)$$

So nonidentification of β implies the existence of a matrix $(\beta - \beta^*, B)$ such that $\xi'(\beta - \beta^*)$ is distributed independently of $\xi'B$. Furthermore, it follows from (4.23a) that $\xi'(\beta - \beta^*)$ is normally distributed with mean zero and variance equal to the term in braces in the exponent in (4.23a). If $(\beta - \beta^*, B)$ is of full rank, it can serve as a choice of A as mentioned in the theorem. If its rank is deficient (i.e., $g - 1$), then $\beta - \beta^*$ is in the column space of B and (4.24) implies that a linear combination of $\xi'B$ is distributed independently of $\xi'B$. This can only be true if $\xi'(\beta - \beta^*)$ is zero with probability one, which can also be considered a normal distribution. Then we may choose for A any nonsingular matrix with first column $\beta - \beta^*$.

This completes one direction of the proof, and we now consider the converse: the existence of a nonsingular matrix $A = (a_1, A_2)$ such that $\xi'a_1$ is distributed normally and independently of $\xi'A_2$ implies nonidentification of β. Let

$$\tilde{t} \equiv \begin{bmatrix} \tilde{t}_1 \\ \tilde{t}_2 \end{bmatrix} \equiv A^{-1}t \qquad \text{and} \qquad \tilde{\beta} \equiv \begin{bmatrix} \tilde{\beta}_1 \\ \tilde{\beta}_2 \end{bmatrix} \equiv A^{-1}\beta,$$

where $\tilde{t}_1$ and $\tilde{\beta}_1$ are scalars, and $\tilde{t}_2$ and $\tilde{\beta}_2$ are $(g-1)$-vectors. Then

$$\begin{aligned} t &= A\tilde{t} = a_1\tilde{t}_1 + A_2\tilde{t}_2 \\ \beta &= A\tilde{\beta} = a_1\tilde{\beta}_1 + A_2\tilde{\beta}_2. \end{aligned}$$

We can now rewrite (4.20) as

$$\begin{aligned} \varphi_{y,x}(s,t) &= \varphi_{y,x}(s, A\tilde{t}) \\ &= \varphi_\xi\big(A(s\tilde{\beta}+\tilde{t})\big)\exp\Big(-\tfrac{1}{2}\big(s^2\sigma_\varepsilon^2 + t'\Omega t\big)\Big) \\ &= \varphi_{\xi' A}(s\tilde{\beta}+\tilde{t})\exp\Big(-\tfrac{1}{2}\big(s^2\sigma_\varepsilon^2 + t'\Omega t\big)\Big) \\ &= \varphi_{\xi' a_1}(s\tilde{\beta}_1+\tilde{t}_1)\varphi_{\xi' A_2}(s\tilde{\beta}_2+\tilde{t}_2)\exp\Big(-\tfrac{1}{2}\big(s^2\sigma_\varepsilon^2 + t'\Omega t\big)\Big) \\ &= \exp\Big(-\tfrac{1}{2}(s\tilde{\beta}_1+\tilde{t}_1)^2\sigma^2_{\xi' a_1}\Big)\varphi_{\xi' A_2}(s\tilde{\beta}_2+\tilde{t}_2) \\ &\qquad \times \exp\Big(-\tfrac{1}{2}\big(s^2\sigma_\varepsilon^2 + \tilde{t}'A'\Omega A\tilde{t}\big)\Big) \\ &= \exp\big(-\tfrac{1}{2}(s,\tilde{t}')C(s,\tilde{t}')'\big)\varphi_{\xi' A_2}(s\tilde{\beta}_2+\tilde{t}_2), \end{aligned}$$

where

$$C \equiv \begin{bmatrix} \sigma_\varepsilon^2 & 0 \\ 0 & A'\Omega A \end{bmatrix} + \sigma^2_{\xi' a_1}\begin{bmatrix} \tilde{\beta}_1 \\ e_1 \end{bmatrix}(\tilde{\beta}_1, e_1')$$

and e_1 denotes the first unit vector. The $\frac{1}{2}g(g+1)+2$ different nonzero elements of C are functions of the $\frac{1}{2}g(g+1)+3$ parameters in σ_ε^2, Ω, $\tilde{\beta}_1$, and $\sigma^2_{\xi' a_1}$. These parameters do not occur in $\varphi_{\xi' A_2}(s\tilde{\beta}_2+\tilde{t}_2)$. So we can vary the parameters in σ_ε^2, Ω, $\tilde{\beta}_1$, and $\sigma^2_{\xi' a_1}$ without altering the characteristic function, and hence the distribution function, of the observables x and y, which proves that these parameters are not identified. □

Note that this theorem implies that if ξ is normally distributed, β is not identified. This follows of course already from inspection of the Jacobian matrix, we would not need theorem 4.3 for that. Moreover, note that the independence between $\xi' a_1$ and $\xi' A_2$ is essential; the mere fact that there exists a normally distributed linear function of ξ, $\xi' a_1$, is insufficient to spoil identification of β. For example if $g = 2$ and $\xi_1 \sim \mathcal{N}(0, \sigma^2)$ and $\xi_2 = \xi_1^2 - \sigma^2$, then ξ_1 is a normally distributed linear function of ξ, but there is of course no $A = (a_1, a_2)$ such that $\xi' a_1$ and $\xi' a_2$ are stochastically independent. In fact, in section 11.2, it will be shown that this model is identified.

The theorem clearly rests on the assumed normality of ε and v. If these random variables follow different distributions, a normally distributed ξ need not spoil identification. It seems, however, wise to be conservative with respect to the distributions of the errors. These may frequently be approximately normally distributed due to some central limit theorem argument.

The proposition also has implications for the functional model where ξ are considered to be fixed unknown constants. As discussed in section 4.5, there will exist, in the functional model, a consistent estimator of β if and only if β can be estimated consistently in the structural model under *any* distributional assumption regarding ξ. Under the normality assumption regarding ε and v, the theorem implies that normality is the worst possible assumption for ξ. Thus the extraneous information that will be required to estimate β consistently in the structural model with normally distributed ξ is identical to that which is needed to guarantee the existence of a consistent estimator of β in the functional model.

4.7 Bibliographical notes

4.1 Apart from the functional and structural models, there is also the ultrastructural model, due to Dolby and Freeman (1975) and Dolby (1976c), which may be a useful umbrella in case when both the structural and the functional model need to be discussed at once or in cases with mixed functional and structural components, such as quasi-experimentation, see the main text. In the ultrastructural model, it is assumed that the ξ_n are independently nonidentically distributed with means μ_n and common variance Ω. Thus, the structural model is obtained if $\mu_n = \mu (= 0)$ for all n, whereas the functional model is obtained if $\Omega = 0$ and the μ_n are free parameters. Note that the ultrastructural model also allows different special cases, like $\mu_n = \alpha_0 + \alpha_1 n$ (a linear trend), or $\mu_n = \alpha' w_n$, where w_n is a vector of observed explanatory variables. This leads us to models discussed in chapter 8. Further papers investigating various aspects and extensions of the ultrastructural model are Patefield (1978), L. K. Chan and Mak (1979a), and Gleser (1985).

4.2 The conditional and marginal interpretations of the likelihoods have been discussed by Kendall and Stuart (1973) and Leamer (1978).

4.3 This section is based on Solari (1969). See also Sprent (1970) and Copas (1972). For the factor analysis model with fixed factors, i.e., factor analysis under functional assumptions, Anderson and Rubin (1956) have already noted the unboundedness of the likelihood.

4.4 For identification in parametric models, see e.g. Fisher (1966), Rothenberg (1971), Bowden (1973), Richmond (1974), Hsiao (1983, 1987), and Bekker,

Merckens, and Wansbeek (1994). The pioneering work in the field is due to Haavelmo (1944), which contained the first identification theory for stochastic models to be developed in econometrics. See Aldrich (1994) for an extensive discussion. The theory was further formalized by Koopmans and Reiersøl (1950).

Identification is hardly an issue from a Bayesian perspective. See Poirier (1998) for a discussion of the simple errors-in-variables model from a Bayesian point of view. Further references are Lindley and El-Sayyad (1968), Florens, Mouchart, and Richard (1974), Reilly and Patino-Leal (1985), and Erickson (1989).

Theorem 4.1 is due to Rothenberg (1971). The relationship between local identification and the rank of the information matrix has been derived in an information theoretic context by Bowden (1973).

4.5 The result linking consistent estimation in the functional and structural models is based on Wald (1948).

4.6 The result on identification in the case of a single regressor is due to Reiersøl (1950). The multiple regression extension given in theorem 4.3 is due to Bekker (1986). It corrects Kapteyn and Wansbeek (1984).

Chapter 5

Consistent adjusted least squares

An important conclusion from the previous chapter is that the regression model with normally distributed errors in the variables and in the equation is not identified, for both the functional model and the structural model with normally distributed regressors. In this chapter we consider statistical inference in the linear regression model when the model is identified. In particular, we consider the case that there are a sufficient number of restrictions on the parameters to render the model identified. These restrictions can be combined with the statistics from OLS to yield a consistent estimator for the model parameters. This estimation method is called consistent adjusted least squares (CALS), and forms the topic of this chapter.

A special case of CALS has been discussed in the beginning of section 3.1 in a simple regression setting, where the ratio of the measurement error to equation error was assumed known. Here we consider a more general situation, multiple regression, and a more general form of prior information. This includes the important case that Ω is known from outside the model.

The general description of CALS is given in section 5.1, including a derivation of the asymptotic distribution of the CALS estimator. The special case of known Ω is discussed in section 5.2. As an even more special case we focus on the situation where there is just one regressor measured with error. This case is of empirical relevance, because often in cross-sectional regression analysis one regressor is of special interest and is at the same time imprecisely measured as it is an imperfect reflection of a theoretical ideal. The theory of CALS estimation is employed to deduce, quickly and easily, the adaptation that has to be made to the OLS estimates and the t-value for any admissible value of the single measurement error variance.

The chapter concludes with a brief discussion of two closely related methods, weighted regression and orthogonal regression. With weighted regression, discussed in section 5.3, σ_ε^2 and Ω are assumed known up to a scale factor. This fits into the CALS framework and can be seen as least squares where the distances from the observations to the regression plane are measured under a given angle. A special case of this is orthogonal regression, discussed in section 5.4. There, the distances are measured perpendicular to the regression plane.

5.1 The CALS estimator

Equations (2.9) and (2.12b) show that the inconsistency of b and s_ε^2 could be removed if Ω were known. For example, rather than b we would take $(I_g - S_X^{-1}\Omega)^{-1}b$ as an estimator of β, and from (2.9) it is clear this estimator is consistent. The resulting statistic is a least squares estimator that is adjusted to attain consistency.

A generalization of this procedure is to assume that a system of g^2 identifying restrictions on the unknown parameters β, σ_ε^2, and Ω is available:

$$r(\beta, \sigma_\varepsilon^2, \Omega) = r_0, \tag{5.1}$$

with r a totally differentiable vector function of order g^2. Of course, in view of the symmetry of Ω, $\frac{1}{2}g(g-1)$ of the restrictions in (5.1) may be of the form $\Omega_{ij} - \Omega_{ji} = 0$.

If we combine the sample information with the prior information and add hats to indicate estimators, we obtain the following system of equations:

$$(I_g - S_X^{-1}\hat{\Omega})\hat{\beta} - b = 0 \tag{5.2a}$$

$$\hat{\sigma}_\varepsilon^2 + \hat{\beta}'\hat{\Omega}b - s_\varepsilon^2 = 0 \tag{5.2b}$$

$$r(\hat{\beta}, \hat{\sigma}_\varepsilon^2, \hat{\Omega}) - r_0 = 0. \tag{5.2c}$$

When r is such that this system has a unique solution

$$\hat{\theta} \equiv \left(\hat{\beta}', \hat{\sigma}_\varepsilon^2, (\operatorname{vec}\hat{\Omega})'\right)',$$

this solution is a consistent estimator of

$$\theta \equiv \left(\beta', \sigma_\varepsilon^2, (\operatorname{vec}\Omega)'\right)',$$

because, asymptotically, S_X tends to Σ_X and the system then represents the relationship between the true parameters on the one hand and the probability limits of b and of s_ε^2 on the other hand. The estimator $\hat{\theta}$ is called the *consistent adjusted least squares* (CALS) estimator. Below, we will elaborate its properties.

Before we do so we note that the CALS estimator is easy to implement. One can use a standard regression program to obtain b and s_ε^2 and then employ a computer program for the solution of a system of nonlinear equations. In many cases it will be possible to find an explicit solution for (5.2), which then obviates the necessity of using a computer program for the solution of nonlinear equations. Some examples will be given in section 5.2.

Asymptotic distribution of the CALS estimator

In order to derive the asymptotic distribution of the CALS estimator, we need some notation and some intermediate results. We first rewrite (5.2) in a condensed way in one vector of order $\ell \equiv g + 1 + g^2$ as

$$h(d, \hat{\theta}) = 0,$$

where d contains the OLS statistics and the covariance matrix of the observed regressors,

$$d \equiv \left(b', s_\varepsilon^2, (\operatorname{vec} S_X)'\right)'.$$

It will turn out that the asymptotic distribution of the CALS estimator is the same under functional and structural assumptions. Because $\hat{\theta}$ is a function of d, whose asymptotic distribution was derived in section 4.2 under both structural and functional assumptions, we can use the delta method (see section A.5) to derive the asymptotic distribution of the CALS estimator from that of d. In order to do so, we need an expression for

$$\operatorname*{plim}_{N\to\infty} \frac{\partial \hat{\theta}}{\partial d'} = -H_\theta^{-1} H_\delta,$$

where

$$H_\delta \equiv \operatorname*{plim}_{N\to\infty} \frac{\partial h}{\partial d'} \qquad \text{and} \qquad H_\theta \equiv \operatorname*{plim}_{N\to\infty} \frac{\partial h}{\partial \hat{\theta}'},$$

both of order $\ell \times \ell$. We assume that H_θ is nonsingular in an open set around the true value of θ, which will be the case if the restrictions $r(\cdot)$ are sufficient to identify the parameters.

Let R_β $(\ell \times g)$, $R_{\sigma_\varepsilon^2}$ $(\ell \times 1)$, and R_Ω $(\ell \times g^2)$ denote the probability limits of the derivatives of r with respect to $\hat{\beta}'$, $\hat{\sigma}_\varepsilon^2$, and $(\operatorname{vec} \hat{\Omega})'$, respectively. Then H_θ

and H_δ can be written as

$$H_\theta = \begin{bmatrix} \Sigma_X^{-1}\Sigma_\Xi & 0 & -\beta' \otimes \Sigma_X^{-1} \\ \kappa'\Omega & 1 & \kappa' \otimes \beta' \\ R_\beta & R_{\sigma_\varepsilon^2} & R_\Omega \end{bmatrix} \tag{5.3a}$$

$$\equiv \begin{bmatrix} H_1 & H_2 \\ H_3 & R_\Omega \end{bmatrix} \tag{5.3b}$$

$$H_\delta = \begin{bmatrix} -I_g & 0 & -(\omega' \otimes \Sigma_X^{-1})Q_g \\ \beta'\Omega & -1 & 0 \\ 0 & 0 & 0 \end{bmatrix}, \tag{5.3c}$$

where Σ_X, Σ_Ξ, Ω, κ, and ω are as defined in section 2.1, and Q_g is the symmetrization matrix defined in section A.4. (The partitioning of H_θ into H_1, H_2, H_3, and R_Ω will be used later on.) The expressions (5.3a) and (5.3c) follow from (5.2). Only one of the derivatives appearing in H_δ and H_θ is nontrivial to derive:

$$\begin{aligned} \frac{\partial\big((I_g - S_X^{-1}\hat{\Omega})\hat{\beta} - b\big)}{\partial(\operatorname{vec} S_X)'} &= -\frac{\partial S_X^{-1}\hat{\Omega}\hat{\beta}}{\partial(\operatorname{vec} S_X)'} \\ &= -\frac{\partial(\hat{\beta}'\hat{\Omega} \otimes I_g)\operatorname{vec} S_X^{-1}}{\partial(\operatorname{vec} S_X)'} \\ &= (\hat{\beta}'\hat{\Omega} \otimes I_g)(S_X^{-1} \otimes S_X^{-1})Q_g \\ &= (\hat{\beta}'\hat{\Omega}S_X^{-1} \otimes S_X^{-1})Q_g, \end{aligned}$$

which converges in probability to $-(\omega' \otimes \Sigma_X^{-1})Q_g$.

Combining (5.3a) and (5.3c) yields an expression for $H_\theta^{-1}H_\delta$. In the structural model, d is according to (4.4) asymptotically normally distributed with asymptotic covariance matrix $\mathcal{I}_0^+$, which was given in (4.5). The asymptotic distribution of $\hat{\theta}$ is

$$\sqrt{N}(\hat{\theta} - \theta) \xrightarrow{d} \mathcal{N}_\ell\big(0, H_\theta^{-1}H_\delta\mathcal{I}_0^+H_\delta'(H_\theta^{-1})'\big). \tag{5.4}$$

In the functional model, $\hat{\theta}$ has virtually the same asymptotic distribution. This follows from (4.7), where we had

$$\operatorname{AVar}\big(\sqrt{N}(d - \delta_N) \mid \Xi\big) = \mathcal{I}_0^+ - 2CQ_g(\Sigma_\Xi \otimes \Sigma_\Xi)C', \tag{5.5}$$

with C defined in (4.6). From inspection of H_δ in (5.3c) and C as above it immediately follows that $H_\delta CQ_g = 0$, and hence that the asymptotic covariance matrix of $\hat{\theta}$, conditional on Ξ, is the same as in the structural model

(5.4). The only difference is that the asymptotic mean of $\hat{\theta}$ is different. Of course, $\text{plim}_{N\to\infty} \hat{\theta} = \theta$ in the functional model, as it is in the structural model. However, in (5.5), δ_N is used instead of δ. Hence, the mean of the asymptotic distribution of $\sqrt{N}(\hat{\theta} - \theta)$ conditional on Ξ is not zero unless

$$\operatorname*{plim}_{N\to\infty} \sqrt{N} H_\theta^{-1} H_\delta (\delta_N - \delta) = 0.$$

By straightforward computation, we find that

$$H_\delta(\delta_N - \delta) = \begin{bmatrix} -(S_\Xi + \Omega)^{-1}(S_\Xi - \Sigma_\Xi)\Sigma_X^{-1}(S_\Xi - \Sigma_\Xi)\omega \\ 0 \\ 0 \end{bmatrix},$$

which is apparently not zero. However, it contains two factors $(S_\Xi - \Sigma_\Xi)$, so that the conditional asymptotic distribution of the CALS estimator under the functional model is equivalent to (5.4) if $\text{plim}_{N\to\infty} N^{1/4}(S_\Xi - \Sigma_\Xi) = 0$, which is a considerably weaker assumption than $\text{plim}_{N\to\infty} N^{1/2}(S_\Xi - \Sigma_\Xi) = 0$. Therefore, in most cases, we may assume that the asymptotic distribution of the CALS estimator under the functional model is (5.4).

A further elaboration

The asymptotic variance of the CALS estimator depends on $H_\theta^{-1} H_\delta$. The matrix H_θ has R_Ω as its lower-right block. In most instances of CALS, R_Ω is nonsingular. This makes it possible to elaborate $H_\theta^{-1} H_\delta$. From (5.3), we have

$$H_\theta^{-1} H_\delta = \begin{bmatrix} I_{g+1} \\ -L_2 \end{bmatrix} L_3 L_1,$$

with

$$\begin{aligned} L_1 &\equiv \begin{bmatrix} \Sigma_\Xi^{-1}\Sigma_X & 0 & (\omega' \otimes \Sigma_\Xi^{-1})Q_g \\ -2\beta'\Omega & 1 & \omega' \otimes \omega' \end{bmatrix} \\ L_2 &\equiv R_\Omega^{-1}(R_\beta, R_{\sigma_\varepsilon^2}) \\ L_3 &\equiv \left(\begin{bmatrix} -\beta' \otimes \Sigma_\Xi^{-1} \\ \kappa' \otimes \beta' - \beta' \otimes \omega' \end{bmatrix} L_2 - I_{g+1} \right)^{-1}. \end{aligned}$$

This can be shown as follows. Using the partitioning of H_θ as given in (5.3b), and noting that $\Omega\Sigma_X^{-1}\Sigma_\Xi = \Sigma_\Xi\Sigma_X^{-1}\Omega$, which can be easily verified, it follows that

$$\begin{aligned} H_1^{-1}H_2 &= \begin{bmatrix} \Sigma_\Xi^{-1}\Sigma_X & 0 \\ -\beta'\Omega & 1 \end{bmatrix} \begin{bmatrix} -\beta' \otimes \Sigma_X^{-1} \\ \kappa' \otimes \beta' \end{bmatrix} \\ &= \begin{bmatrix} -\beta' \otimes \Sigma_\Xi^{-1} \\ \kappa' \otimes \beta' - \beta' \otimes \omega' \end{bmatrix}, \end{aligned}$$

and L_1, L_2, and L_3 satisfy the following relations:

$$\begin{aligned} H_\delta &= -\begin{bmatrix} H_1 \\ 0 \end{bmatrix} L_1 \\ R_\Omega^{-1}H_3 &= L_2 \\ H_1L_3^{-1} &= -H_1(I_{g+1} - H_1^{-1}H_2L_2) \\ &= -(H_1 - H_2R_\Omega^{-1}H_3). \end{aligned}$$

Then

$$\begin{aligned} H_\theta^{-1}H_\delta &= -H_\theta^{-1}\begin{bmatrix} H_1 \\ 0 \end{bmatrix} L_1 \\ &= -H_\theta^{-1}\begin{bmatrix} H_1L_3^{-1} \\ 0 \end{bmatrix} L_3L_1 \\ &= H_\theta^{-1}\begin{bmatrix} H_1 - H_2R_\Omega^{-1}H_3 \\ H_3 - H_3 \end{bmatrix} L_3L_1 \\ &= H_\theta^{-1}\begin{bmatrix} H_1 & H_2 \\ H_3 & R_\Omega \end{bmatrix} \begin{bmatrix} I_{g+1} \\ -R_\Omega^{-1}H_3 \end{bmatrix} L_3L_1 \\ &= \begin{bmatrix} I_{g+1} \\ -L_2 \end{bmatrix} L_3L_1. \end{aligned}$$

These expressions are useful when elaborating the asymptotic variance of the CALS estimator for those cases where R_Ω is nonsingular. The expressions further simplify when Ω is known. Then $R_\Omega = I_{g^2}$, $R_{\sigma_\varepsilon^2} = 0$, and $R_\beta = 0$, implying $L_2 = 0$, $L_3 = -I_{g+1}$, and $H_\theta^{-1}H_\delta = -(L_1', 0)'$.

5.2 Measurement error variance known

A number of important models are special cases of the general CALS estimator. We start with the case where Ω is known.

In the case that Ω is known the CALS procedure is very simple. Equations (5.2a) and (5.2b) immediately give $\hat{\beta}$ and $\hat{\sigma}_\varepsilon^2$:

$$\hat{\beta} \equiv (S_X - \Omega)^{-1} S_X b \tag{5.6}$$

$$\hat{\sigma}_\varepsilon^2 \equiv s_\varepsilon^2 - \hat{\beta}'\Omega b. \tag{5.7}$$

Given the structure that knowledge of Ω puts on the various matrices as described above, the asymptotic covariance matrix is

$$L_1 \mathcal{I}_0^+ L_1' = \begin{bmatrix} \tilde{\gamma}\Sigma_\Xi^{-1}\Sigma_X\Sigma_\Xi^{-1} + \tilde{\omega}\tilde{\omega}' & 2\tilde{\gamma}\tilde{\omega} \\ 2\tilde{\gamma}\tilde{\omega}' & 2\tilde{\gamma}^2 \end{bmatrix}, \tag{5.8}$$

with $\tilde{\gamma} \equiv \sigma_\varepsilon^2 + \beta'\Omega\beta$ and $\tilde{\omega} \equiv -\Sigma_\Xi^{-1}\Omega\beta$. A leading example of known Ω is the case where it has a single nonzero element only. We inspect this case in some detail.

Measurement error in a single regressor

In regression analysis one often encounters the case where the regressors include control variables to account for population heterogeneity in addition to one regressor focal to the topic under study. This variable is often theory-based and is not directly observable. Examples include consumption models relating consumption to permanent income, labor supply models relating hours to wage per hour, and investment models relating investment to Tobin's q. The case of multiple regression with measurement error in a single but interesting regressor (the first one, say) is hence important.

When only the first regressor is mismeasured, the covariance matrix of measurement errors Ω is of the form

$$\Omega = \varphi e_1 e_1', \tag{5.9}$$

with e_1 the first unit vector, and φ the variance of the measurement error in the first regressor. We derive a number of results from applying CALS by assuming that φ is known. The results, which depend of course on φ, which in practice will usually be unknown, can be used to see what to expect when different values of φ are considered.

We will use the following notation for this special case:

$$a \equiv S_X^{-1} e_1$$

$$z \equiv e_1' S_X^{-1} e_1$$

$$m \equiv \frac{1}{1 - \varphi z}$$

with properties $S_X a = e_1$ and

$$m = 1 + m\varphi z \tag{5.10a}$$

$$m^2 = 1 + m(m+1)\varphi z \tag{5.10b}$$

$$I_g + m\varphi a e_1' = (S_X - \varphi e_1 e_1')^{-1} S_X \tag{5.10c}$$

$$ma = (S_X - \varphi e_1 e_1')^{-1} e_1; \tag{5.10d}$$

(5.10c) and (5.10d) follow by multiplying both sides by $S_X - \varphi e_1 e_1'$. We assume $m > 1$, which holds in the limit, because $\operatorname{plim}_{N\to\infty} z = \sigma_X^{11}$ and $0 < \varphi\sigma_X^{11} < 1$, as we have seen in section 2.4.

Substitution of (5.9) in (5.6) using (5.10c) gives the CALS estimator

$$\hat{\beta} = (S_X - \varphi e_1 e_1')^{-1} S_X b = (I_g + m\varphi a e_1')b = b + \lambda a, \tag{5.11}$$

where b_1 the first element of b and λ is defined as

$$\lambda \equiv m\varphi b_1. \tag{5.12}$$

In particular, for the first element $\hat{\beta}_1$ of $\hat{\beta}$, we have

$$\hat{\beta}_1 = (1 + m\varphi z)b_1 = mb_1. \tag{5.13}$$

Because $m > 1$, $\hat{\beta}_1$ has the same sign as b_1, but is larger in magnitude. Thus, (5.13) illustrates the correction for the bias towards zero when estimating β_1 by OLS if there is measurement error, and (5.11) shows, for all elements of β jointly, that this correction is along a line in β-space, from b in the direction given by the first column of the inverse of $X'X$.

We now consider the estimation of σ_ε^2. Substitution of (5.9) in (5.7) using (5.12) and (5.13) gives

$$\hat{\sigma}_\varepsilon^2 = s_\varepsilon^2 - \varphi\hat{\beta}' e_1 e_1' b = s_\varepsilon^2 - \varphi\hat{\beta}_1 b_1 = s_\varepsilon^2 - \lambda b_1 \tag{5.14}$$

as a consistent estimator for a given value of φ. Restricting this estimator to nonnegative values imposes an upper limit on the values of φ that one may wish to consider. Putting (5.14) to zero and solving gives

$$\varphi_{\max} = \frac{1}{z + b_1^2/s_\varepsilon^2}, \tag{5.15}$$

because then $m_{\max} = 1/(1 - \varphi_{\max} z) = 1 + z/(b_1^2/s_\varepsilon^2)$. Hence,

$$\lambda_{\max} = m_{\max}\varphi_{\max} b_1 = \frac{s_\varepsilon^2}{b_1},$$

which solves (5.14) for $\hat{\sigma}_\varepsilon^2 = 0$. This gives

$$\hat{\beta}_{1,\,\max} = m_{\max} b_1 = b_1 + \frac{z}{b_1} s_\varepsilon^2$$

as the upper bound on the estimator of β_1.

To illustrate this graphically, we notice that in general, for Ω not restricted to be of the form $\varphi e_1 e_1'$, $\hat{\beta}$ satisfies

$$0 \le (\hat{\beta} - b)' S_X b \le s_\varepsilon^2.$$

These inequalities are the finite-sample analogues of (2.17) and (2.20), which are in asymptotic terms, with β, κ, γ, and Σ_X instead of $\hat{\beta}$, b, s_ε^2, and S_X, respectively. The inequalities show that, whatever Ω may be, the CALS estimator based on a particular value for Ω lies in β-space between the two parallel hyperplanes $(\hat{\beta} - b)' S_X b = 0$ and $(\hat{\beta} - b)' S_X b = s_\varepsilon^2$. These hyperplanes are perpendicular to the vector $S_X b$.

The situation is illustrated in figure 5.1. The set of $\hat{\beta}$'s compatible with $\Omega = \varphi e_1 e_1'$ is given by the line segment between the two planes, ranging from b to $b + \lambda_{\max} a$.

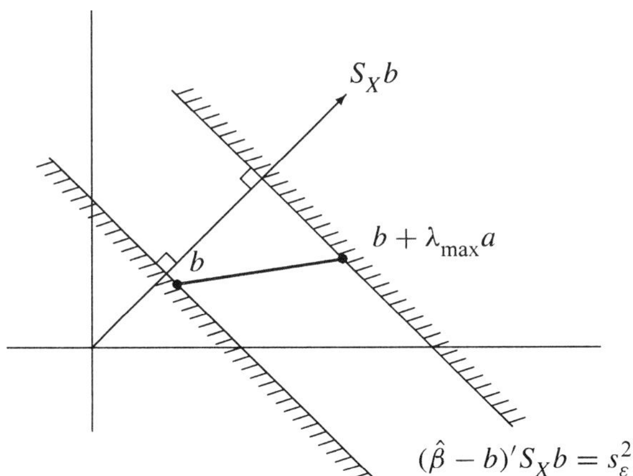

Figure 5.1 *Admissible values of $\hat{\beta}$.*

Estimating the asymptotic variance

For Ω as in (5.9) with given φ, we can derive the asymptotic variance of $\hat{\beta}$ by elaborating (5.8). We give a consistent estimator of this asymptotic variance based on the consistent estimators for β and σ_ε^2. We consider the various terms in (5.8) in turn.

First, using (5.10a) and (5.12), a consistent estimator of $\tilde{\gamma} \equiv \sigma_\varepsilon^2 + \beta'\Omega\beta = \sigma_\varepsilon^2 + \varphi\beta_1^2$ is given by

$$\begin{aligned}
\hat{\sigma}_\varepsilon^2 + \varphi\hat{\beta}_1^2 &= s_\varepsilon^2 - \lambda b_1 + m^2\varphi b_1^2 \\
&= s_\varepsilon^2 - \lambda b_1 + m\lambda b_1 \\
&= s_\varepsilon^2 + (m-1)\lambda b_1 \\
&= s_\varepsilon^2 + m\varphi z\lambda b_1 \\
&= s_\varepsilon^2 + \lambda^2 z.
\end{aligned}$$

Next, using (5.10d) and (5.13), $-\tilde{\omega} = \Sigma_\Xi^{-1}\Omega\beta = \varphi(\Sigma_X - \varphi e_1 e_1')^{-1} e_1 e_1'\beta$ is consistently estimated by

$$\begin{aligned}
\varphi(S_X - \varphi e_1 e_1')^{-1} e_1 e_1'\hat{\beta} &= m\varphi\hat{\beta}_1 a \\
&= m^2\varphi b_1 a \\
&= m\lambda a,
\end{aligned}$$

and, using (5.10a)–(5.10c), $\Sigma_\Xi^{-1}\Sigma_X\Sigma_\Xi^{-1} = (\Sigma_X - \varphi e_1 e_1')^{-1}\Sigma_X(\Sigma_X - \varphi e_1 e_1')^{-1}$ is estimated by

$$\begin{aligned}
(S_X - \varphi e_1 e_1')^{-1} S_X (S_X - \varphi e_1 e_1')^{-1} &= (I_g + m\varphi a e_1') S_X^{-1} (I_g + m\varphi e_1 a') \\
&= S_X^{-1} + (2m + m\varphi z) a a' \\
&= S_X^{-1} + m\varphi(2 + (m-1)) a a' \\
&= S_X^{-1} + m(m+1)\varphi a a'.
\end{aligned}$$

Combining these results gives as a consistent estimator of the asymptotic variance of $\hat{\beta}$:

$$\widehat{\text{AVar}}(\hat{\beta}) = (s_\varepsilon^2 + \lambda^2 z)\left(S_X^{-1} + m(m+1)\varphi a a'\right) + m^2\lambda^2 a a', \tag{5.16}$$

which of course reduces to $s_\varepsilon^2 S_X^{-1}$ when there is no measurement error.

The t-value for the first regression coefficient

When making statistical inference with respect to the first regression coefficient, the t-statistic is of interest. We express this statistic in the terms of our analysis.

From (5.16) we have

$$\begin{aligned}\widehat{\text{AVar}}(\hat{\beta}_1) &= (s_\varepsilon^2 + \lambda^2 z)\big(z + m(m+1)\varphi z^2\big) + m^2\lambda^2 z^2 \\ &= (s_\varepsilon^2 + \lambda^2 z)m^2 z + m^2\lambda^2 z^2 \\ &= m^2 z(s_\varepsilon^2 + 2\lambda^2 z).\end{aligned}$$

The t-statistic of the OLS estimator of the first element of β if there is no measurement error is $t_0 = b_1\sqrt{N}/\sqrt{s_\varepsilon^2 z}$. Hence,

$$s_\varepsilon^2 = \frac{b_1^2 N}{t_0^2 z}. \tag{5.17}$$

The t-statistic corresponding with a measurement error variance of size φ is, using (5.13) and (5.17), given by

$$\begin{aligned}t_\varphi &= \frac{\hat{\beta}_1\sqrt{N}}{\sqrt{\widehat{\text{AVar}}(\hat{\beta}_1)}} \\ &= \frac{mb_1\sqrt{N}}{m\sqrt{z}\sqrt{s_\varepsilon^2 + 2\lambda^2 z}} \\ &= \frac{t_0}{\sqrt{1 + 2\lambda^2 z/s_\varepsilon^2}} \\ &= \frac{t_0}{\sqrt{1 + \frac{2}{N}(\lambda z t_0/b_1)^2}} \\ &= \frac{t_0}{\sqrt{1 + \frac{2}{N}h_\varphi^2}},\end{aligned} \tag{5.18}$$

with $h_\varphi \equiv \lambda z t_0/b_1 = (m-1)t_0$. By straightforward differentiation, it follows immediately that t_φ decreases (in absolute sense) monotonically in φ. Figure 5.2 illustrates the behavior of t_φ, for $z = 1$ and $N = 100$, for various values of t_0. Substitution of (5.17) in (5.15) gives

$$\varphi_{\max} = \frac{1}{z\left(1 + t_0^2/N\right)},$$

so the relevant parts of the curves in figure 5.2 end to the left of $\varphi = 1/z \equiv 1$, and the minimal t-values are above zero.

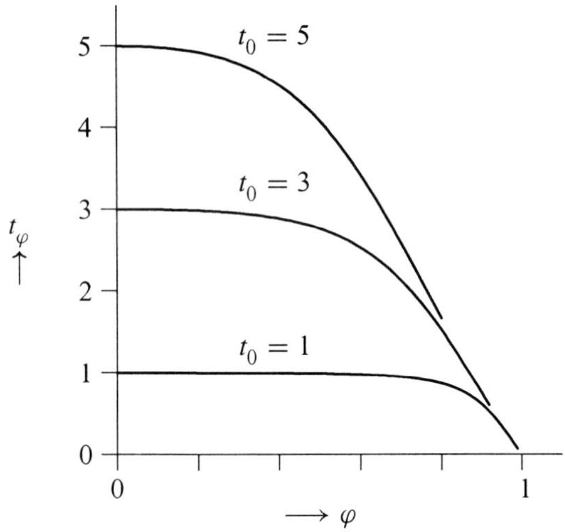

Figure 5.2 *The value of t_φ as a function of φ and t_0.*

One may be interested to see which level of φ corresponds with a given t-value. Let this value be t_*. This corresponds with $\varphi = \varphi_*$ satisfying

$$t_* = \frac{t_0}{\sqrt{1 + \frac{2}{N} h_{\varphi_*}^2}}, \tag{5.19}$$

cf. (5.18). Let

$$w \equiv \left(\frac{N}{2} \left[\left(\frac{t_0}{t_*} \right)^2 - 1 \right] \right)^{1/2},$$

then (5.19) implies that $h_{\varphi_*} = w$, or

$$\varphi_* = \frac{1}{z} \frac{w}{w + t_0}.$$

By way of an informal specification diagnostic, we may put t_* at the conventional value of 2, to see at what level of noise in a variable its estimated coefficient becomes insignificant.

5.3 Weighted regression

Among the models that can be interpreted as instances of CALS, the case that has received most attention in the literature is *weighted regression* (WR), where σ_ε^2 and Ω are known up to a multiplicative constant. WR is closely connected with orthogonal regression, where the sum of squared distances from the observations to the regression plane is minimized. We first consider WR.

Knowing σ_ε^2 and Ω up to a multiplicative constant amounts to knowing the matrix $\Omega_0 \equiv \sigma_\varepsilon^{-2}\Omega$. Here, we assume that Ω_0 is of full rank. If that is not the case, the formulas become somewhat more complicated, but the discussion remains largely the same. See the sections 7.5 and 7.6 for an elaboration of this.

The identifying restrictions (5.2c) now become

$$\hat{\sigma}_\varepsilon^{-2} \operatorname{vec} \hat{\Omega} - \operatorname{vec} \Omega_0 = 0.$$

We start by solving (5.2), by substituting $\hat{\sigma}_\varepsilon^2 \Omega_0$ for $\hat{\Omega}$ in (5.2a) and (5.2b). Then

$$\begin{aligned}
&\hat{\sigma}_\varepsilon^2 + \hat{\beta}'\hat{\Omega} b - s_\varepsilon^2 \\
&= \hat{\sigma}_\varepsilon^2 + b' S_X (S_X - \hat{\Omega})^{-1} \hat{\Omega} b - s_\varepsilon^2 \\
&= \hat{\sigma}_\varepsilon^2 + b' S_X (S_X - \hat{\Omega})^{-1} S_X b - b' S_X b - s_\varepsilon^2 \\
&= \hat{\sigma}_\varepsilon^2 + b' S_X (S_X - \hat{\sigma}_\varepsilon^2 \Omega_0)^{-1} S_X b - b' S_X b - s_\varepsilon^2 \\
&= -\left(\frac{1}{N} y'y - \hat{\sigma}_\varepsilon^2 - \frac{1}{N^2} y'X \left(\frac{1}{N} X'X - \hat{\sigma}_\varepsilon^2 \Omega_0 \right)^{-1} X'y \right) \qquad (5.20) \\
&= 0,
\end{aligned}$$

where the equalities $S_X b = X'y/N$ and $s_\varepsilon^2 + b' S_X b = y'y/N$ have been used. On defining

$$S \equiv \frac{1}{N} \begin{bmatrix} y'y & y'X \\ X'y & X'X \end{bmatrix} \quad \text{and} \quad \Sigma_0 \equiv \begin{bmatrix} 1 & 0' \\ 0 & \Omega_0 \end{bmatrix}, \qquad (5.21)$$

and using the formula for the determinant of a partitioned matrix (see section A.1), (5.20) can be seen to be equivalent to the following determinantal equation:

$$|S - \lambda \Sigma_0| = 0, \qquad (5.22)$$

with $\lambda = \hat{\sigma}_\varepsilon^2$, provided that $|S_X - \hat{\sigma}_\varepsilon^2 \Omega_0| \neq 0$, but this should evidently be the case, because $S_X - \hat{\sigma}_\varepsilon^2 \Omega_0 = \hat{\Sigma}_\Xi$, and it was assumed that $\Sigma_\Xi > 0$. As we will sketch below, the *smallest* positive eigenvalue λ of equation (5.22) is a consistent estimator of σ_ε^2. Multiplying Ω_0 by this estimator gives an estimator of Ω. The properly scaled corresponding eigenvector converges in probability to $(1, -\beta')'$.

Consistency

We now sketch the core of the argument that proves the consistency of the WR estimator. The matrix S converges to

$$\operatorname*{plim}_{N\to\infty} S = \begin{bmatrix} \beta' \\ I_g \end{bmatrix} \Sigma_\Xi (\beta, I_g) + \sigma_\varepsilon^2 \Sigma_0.$$

Therefore, asymptotically, the determinantal equation can be written as

$$\left| \begin{bmatrix} \beta' \\ I_g \end{bmatrix} \Sigma_\Xi (\beta, I_g) - (\lambda - \sigma_\varepsilon^2)\Sigma_0 \right| = 0. \tag{5.23}$$

On letting

$$M \equiv \Sigma_0^{-1/2} \begin{bmatrix} \beta' \\ I_g \end{bmatrix} \Sigma_\Xi (\beta, I_g) \Sigma_0^{-1/2},$$

equation (5.23) can be written as

$$\left| M - (\lambda - \sigma_\varepsilon^2) I_{g+1} \right| = 0. \tag{5.24}$$

The vector $\Sigma_0^{1/2}(1, -\beta')'$ is an eigenvector of M corresponding with an eigenvalue 0. Because $M \geq 0$ and M has rank g, all other g eigenvalues of M are positive. Therefore, the estimator for β can be derived from the eigenvector corresponding with the smallest eigenvalue in (5.22), and from (5.24) it is clear that this eigenvalue gives a consistent estimator of σ_ε^2. The properly scaled eigenvector is a consistent estimator of $(1, -\beta')'$. In figure 5.3, the WR estimated line (with $\Sigma_0 = I_2$) is compared to the OLS estimated line for the data of figure 2.1. The WR estimate of β is 1.088, which is close to the true value 1.

Variance

The variance of the WR estimator is $L_3 L_1 \mathcal{I}_0^+ L_1' L_3'$, with $L_1 \mathcal{I}_0^+ L_1'$ given in (5.8), and it remains to evaluate $L_3 L_1 \mathcal{I}_0^+ L_1' L_3'$. Now, $R_\Omega = \sigma_\varepsilon^{-2} I_{g^2}$, $R_\beta = 0$, and $R_{\sigma_\varepsilon^2} = -\sigma_\varepsilon^{-4} \operatorname{vec} \Omega$. Thus,

$$L_2 = (0, -\sigma_\varepsilon^{-2} \operatorname{vec} \Omega)$$

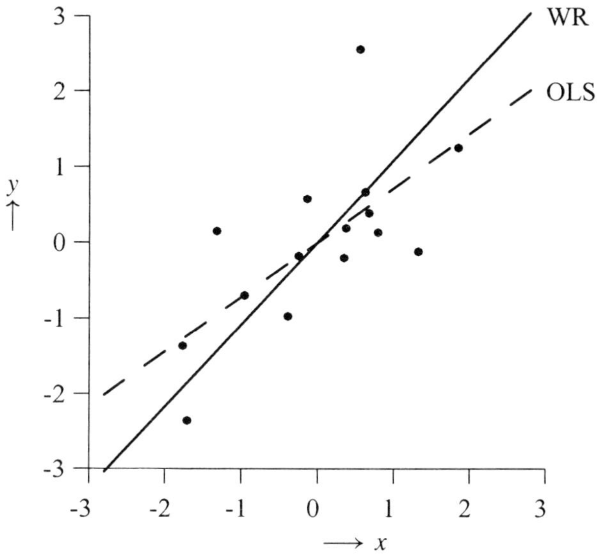

Figure 5.3 *Weighted regression.*

$$L_3 = \left(\begin{bmatrix} -\beta' \otimes \Sigma_\Xi^{-1} \\ \kappa' \otimes \beta' - \beta' \otimes \omega' \end{bmatrix} (0, -\sigma_\varepsilon^{-2} \operatorname{vec} \Omega) - I_{g+1} \right)^{-1}$$
$$= - \begin{bmatrix} I_g & -\sigma_\varepsilon^{-2} \Sigma_\Xi^{-1} \Omega \beta \\ 0 & \sigma_\varepsilon^{-2} \beta' \Omega \beta + 1 \end{bmatrix}^{-1}$$
$$= - \frac{1}{\sigma_\varepsilon^2 + \beta' \Omega \beta} \begin{bmatrix} (\sigma_\varepsilon^2 + \beta' \Omega \beta) I_g & \Sigma_\Xi^{-1} \Omega \beta \\ 0 & \sigma_\varepsilon^2 \end{bmatrix}$$
$$= - \frac{1}{\tilde{\gamma}} \begin{bmatrix} \tilde{\gamma} I_g & -\tilde{\omega} \\ 0 & \sigma_\varepsilon^2 \end{bmatrix}.$$

Given these results the asymptotic variance now readily follows as

$$L_3 L_1 \mathcal{I}_0^+ L_1' L_3' = \begin{bmatrix} \tilde{\gamma} \Sigma_\Xi^{-1} \Sigma_X \Sigma_\Xi^{-1} - \tilde{\omega}\tilde{\omega}' & 0 \\ 0 & 2\sigma_\varepsilon^4 \end{bmatrix}$$
$$= \begin{bmatrix} \Sigma_\Xi^{-1} \left((\sigma_\varepsilon^2 + \beta' \Omega \beta) \Sigma_X - \Omega \beta \beta' \Omega \right) \Sigma_\Xi^{-1} & 0 \\ 0 & 2\sigma_\varepsilon^4 \end{bmatrix}.$$

So in this case, unlike equation (5.8) for the case where Ω is known completely, the estimators of β and σ_ε^2 are asymptotically uncorrelated.

5.4 Orthogonal regression

One way to estimate regression coefficients is to fit a hyperplane such that the sum of the squared distances from the observations to that hyperplane are minimal. That implies that the distances are measured perpendicular to that plane, which is illustrated in figure 5.4 for the data of figure 2.1. This contrasts with the usual way regression is performed, where the distances are measured vertically. For obvious reasons such a method is called *orthogonal regression* (OR), but sometimes also *total least squares*. It will appear below that OR leads to an eigenequation problem that is a special case of (5.22), so there is some logic in discussing the method in the context of WR. Yet using OR has a different character from classical econometric practice. There, the quest is for estimators of parameters in fully specified models where the numerical size of these parameters is the only unknown quantity. Now OR will be seen equivalent to a particular choice for Σ_0, cf. (5.21). But this choice is just an implication of a particular estimation (or rather, fitting) method, and does not reflect prior knowledge about the value of a particular set of parameters. So OR should primarily be seen as a data analysis method and not as an estimation method for a parametric model.

To derive OR, we rewrite the errors-in-variables model (2.1)–(2.2) for a typical observation n as

$$(1, -\beta')\begin{bmatrix}\eta_n\\ \xi_n\end{bmatrix} = \alpha'\zeta_n = 0 \tag{5.25}$$

$$\begin{aligned} y_n &= \eta_n + \varepsilon_n \\ x_n &= \xi_n + v_n. \end{aligned}$$

We still have all variables in deviations from their mean. Equation (5.25) characterizes a g-dimensional hyperplane in $(g+1)$-dimensional space. In that space, the observations are the points $z_n \equiv (y_n, x_n')'$, $n = 1, \ldots, N$, and the sum of squared differences from these N points to the plane is to be minimized. That is, we want to minimize

$$\sum_{n=1}^{N}(z_n - \zeta_n)'(z_n - \zeta_n) \tag{5.26}$$

subject to $\alpha'\zeta_n = 0, n = 1, \ldots, N$. We do this by first choosing ζ_n optimally for a given α and next determining the optimal α. Clearly, (5.26) is minimized if for each n separately we minimize $(z_n - \zeta_n)'(z_n - \zeta_n)$.

So we first minimize the distance from z_n to ζ_n subject to (5.25). The Lagrange function is

$$\tfrac{1}{2}(z_n - \zeta_n)'(z_n - \zeta_n) + \lambda_n\alpha'\zeta_n, \tag{5.27}$$

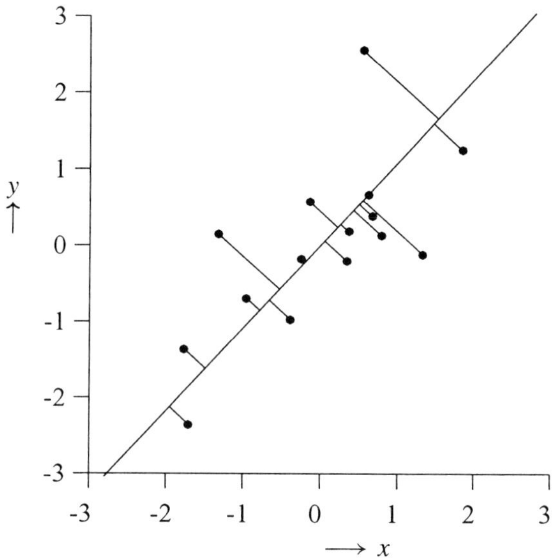

Figure 5.4 *Orthogonal regression.*

with λ_n a Lagrange multiplier. Hence, the first-order condition, upon differentiating with respect to ζ_n, is

$$z_n - \zeta_n = \lambda_n \alpha. \tag{5.28}$$

Although the first element of α has been normalized to 1, cf. (5.25), it is simpler to normalize α alternatively, but without loss of generality, as $\alpha'\alpha = 1$. Then, premultiplication of (5.28) by α' gives

$$\lambda_n = \alpha'(z_n - \zeta_n) = \alpha' z_n, \tag{5.29}$$

because $\alpha'\zeta_n = 0$, cf. (5.25). Combining (5.28) and (5.29) gives

$$\zeta_n = (I_{g+1} - \alpha\alpha')z_n. \tag{5.30}$$

The squared distance from z_n to the hyperplane $\alpha' z_n$ follows directly from (5.28):

$$(z_n - \zeta_n)'(z_n - \zeta_n) = \lambda_n^2 = \alpha' z_n z_n' \alpha,$$

and the sum of squared distances is then $N \cdot \alpha' S \alpha$, with $S \equiv \sum_{n=1}^{N} z_n z_n' / N$. Next, α is found by minimizing this subject to $\alpha'\alpha = 1$. The Lagrange function corresponding with this problem leads to the eigenvalue equation

$$(S - \mu I_{g+1})\alpha = 0, \tag{5.31}$$

so $\hat{\alpha}$ is an eigenvector of S. In the optimum, $\alpha' S \alpha = \mu \alpha' \alpha = \mu$. Therefore, the eigenvector corresponding with the smallest eigenvalue should be taken. The same choice was made with WR, as was argued above, but the arguments leading to the choice of the smallest eigenvalue differ. Because OR is based on a minimization criterion, which was not available with WR, the proof is simpler.

WR and OR compared

The above might be taken to suggest that WR can not be based on a minimization criterion. This is not true, though, and it is instructive to consider how WR can be seen as the solution of a minimization problem. If we generalize (5.27) to

$$\tfrac{1}{2}(z_n - \zeta_n)' \Sigma_0^{-1} (z_n - \zeta_n) + \lambda_n \alpha' \zeta_n,$$

and impose the normalization $\alpha' \Sigma_0 \alpha = 1$ instead of $\alpha' \alpha = 1$, it is a matter of straightforward generalization of the OR derivation to show that $(S - \mu \Sigma_0)\alpha = 0$ becomes the eigenvalue equation generalizing (5.31). This equation leads to the WR solution, cf. (5.22).

Thus, WR can be seen as a generalization of OR where the angle of projection onto the hyperplane is not 90°. The angle implied by a particular Σ_0 can be seen as follows. The *weighted regression* projection of a point z_n on the hyperplane, analogous to (5.30), is given by

$$\zeta_n = (I_{g+1} - \Sigma_0 \alpha \alpha') z_n.$$

Its *orthogonal* projection is

$$\hat{z}_n \equiv \left(I_{g+1} - \frac{1}{\alpha' \alpha} \alpha \alpha' \right) z_n.$$

Hence, the angle ϕ, say, under which the observations are projected onto the hyperplane by the regression is obtained from

$$(\sin \phi)^2 = \frac{\|z_n - \hat{z}_n\|^2}{\|z_n - \zeta_n\|^2} = \frac{1}{(\alpha' \alpha)(\alpha' \Sigma_0^2 \alpha)}.$$

This is illustrated in figure 5.5.

Note that, because $\Sigma_0 = I_2$ in figure 5.3, $\alpha = 90°$ and the fitted WR line in that figure is actually equivalent to the fitted OR line in figure 5.4. Had y been measured in different units, however, the results would have been different. For example, if $\tilde{y}_n \equiv 10 y_n$ had been the dependent variable, $\tilde{\beta} \equiv 10$ is the corresponding true regression coefficient instead of $\beta \equiv 1$, and WR with

$$\tilde{\Sigma}_0 \equiv \begin{bmatrix} 1 & 0 \\ 0 & 0.01 \end{bmatrix}$$

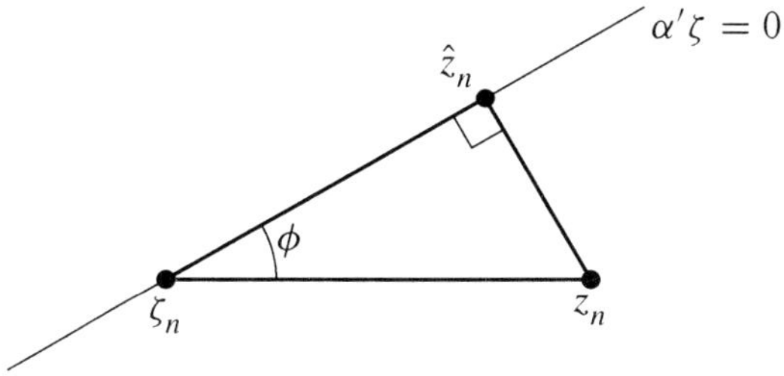

Figure 5.5 *The angle of projection of z_n onto the hyperplane $\alpha'\zeta = 0$ with weighted regression.*

gives consistent estimators, whereas OR, which implicitly takes $\tilde{\Sigma}_0 = I_2$, gives inconsistent estimators.

5.5 Bibliographical notes

5.1 The CALS estimator was introduced by Kapteyn and Wansbeek (1984). The application of special cases of CALS estimators to standard linear models and to models that may in some respects be more general, e.g., heteroskedastic or nonlinear, has been discussed by numerous authors, e.g., L. K. Chan and Mak (1979b, 1984), N. N. Chan and Mak (1983, 1984), Bickel and Ritov (1987), Fuller (1987), and Cheng and Van Ness (1999).

5.2 The results of this section are due to Meijer and Wansbeek (2000). Complementary results have been obtained by Kroch (1988), who studied the case with two variables in which one is measured without error and one is mismeasured, and the coefficient of the variable measured without error is of primary interest.

5.3 The case where $\sigma_\varepsilon^{-2}\Omega$ is known generalizes the case with a single regressor where the error variances are known. See the bibliographical notes to section 3.1 for remarks on this special case. The general case has been discussed in a large number of papers, see, e.g., Van Uven (1930), Sprent (1966), Malinvaud (1970, chapter 10), DeGracie and Fuller (1972), Dolby (1972), Copas (1972), Casson (1974), Robertson (1974), Schneeweiss (1976), Madansky (1976), Nussbaum (1977), Moberg and Sundberg (1978), Höschel (1978), and Fuller (1980). Fuller and Hidiroglou (1978) look at the same case but with Ω diagonal and extract consistent estimators by adjusting for inconsistencies. They consider a structural model with normally distributed latent variables but also make slightly more general distributional assumptions than with CALS. A similar approach is taken by DeGracie and Fuller (1972), who consider a simple analysis-of-variance model where the concomitant variable is measured with error. The model is functional and an extraneous estimate of the covariance matrix of the errors is assumed to be available. Their estimator is similar to CALS but in addition they correct for its small-sample bias up to order r^{-2}, where r is the number of replications for each treatment.

5.4 Orthogonal regression was introduced by Pearson (1901b). It was discussed, among others, by Malinvaud (1970), Golub and Van Loan (1980), and Van Huffel and Vandewalle (1991). See also section 7.6. Computational aspects have been discussed by Boggs, Donaldson, Schnabel, and Spiegelman (1988). Orthogonal regression by minimizing the sum of absolute distances, as opposed to the sum of squared distances, has been discussed by Nyquist (1988).

Chapter 6

Instrumental variables

As we saw in chapter 2, a regression model with errors in the regressors suffers from a correlation between the regressors and the disturbance term, rendering ordinary least squares inconsistent. This problem occurs in a wide variety of regression contexts, measurement error being one of these. The major approach chosen in econometrics is application of the method of instrumental variables (IV). By assumption, instrumental variables are correlated with the regressors (in particular, with the true values when we are in the measurement error setting), but are not correlated with the disturbance term.

Given the importance of the method of IV in general and in the measurement error setting in particular we consider a number of issues around IV in this chapter. In section 6.1, we present the basic theory of IV estimation. In section 6.2, this theory is applied to the linear regression model with measurement error, highlighting some aspects specific for this model. In particular, we investigate how the difference between the OLS and IV estimates can be used for testing for the presence of measurement error.

Because we concentrate on analyzing cross-sectional data, heteroskedasticity can be a source of complications. The IV method can be adapted to handle it, in two ways. First, the standard errors of the estimator of the regression coefficient can be made robust to the possible presence of heteroskedasticity. Second, the estimator itself can be adapted to improve its asymptotic efficiency. Section 6.3 is devoted to this topic.

An intriguing application of IV concerns the situation where the data come from two sources, one data set providing the cross products of the instruments and the dependent variable, and the other data set providing the cross-products of the instruments and the regressors. As is shown in section 6.4, combining these two allows for consistent estimation of the regression coefficient.

So far the analytical framework has been asymptotic. As is increasingly appreciated, the small-sample properties of IV estimators can be unsatisfactory. The limited information maximum likelihood (LIML) estimator, which is introduced in section 6.5, tends to have better small-sample properties than the IV estimator under quite general conditions. In section 6.6, the LIML estimator is derived from a different perspective, suggesting the rationale of its possibly superior performance.

An important issue in the application of the IV method is the origin of the instrumental variables. The remainder of the chapter considers three situations in which the context suggests instruments. First, in some cases, the observations can be considered to be grouped. Under certain conditions, the group indicator can be used as an instrumental variable. This is discussed in section 6.7, where it is also shown that under normality this does not alleviate the measurement error problem if the grouping is based on the data. Second, the data may be nonnormally distributed. As we saw in chapter 4.5, normality is unfavorable from an identification point of view. In section 6.8 we first show, through a simple example, how nonnormality helps and we indicate how instrumental variables can be constructed that allow for consistent estimation under nonnormality. Third, we consider the context of panel data, that is, repeated observations over time for the same observational units. In section 6.9 we show the bias that measurement error induces in panel data estimators. However, the structure over time inherent in panel data allow for consistent estimation. The resulting estimator can be given an IV interpretation.

6.1 Assumptions and estimation

To introduce the notion of instrumental variables, it is useful to start from the model (2.5): $y = X\beta + u$, for which consistent estimation was hampered by the correlation between X and u. Assume that we have observed a matrix Z, say, of the same order as X, whose columns correspond with variables that are correlated with the variables in X but not with u. Consider the equation $Z'y/N = Z'X\beta/N + Z'u/N$. Because $Z'u/N$ will vanish in the limit, solving the normal equations $Z'y = Z'X\hat{\beta}$ should give a sensible estimator of β.

This is the idea behind instrumental variables (IV) estimation. Of all the methods used to obtain consistent estimators in models with measurement error, or with regressors that are correlated with the disturbance term in general, this is undisputably the most popular one. We first discuss the basic theory, then derive an optimal approach for the case that there are more instruments available than needed, and finally consider estimating the error variances.

Basic theory

A matrix Z ($N \times h$, where $h \geq g$) is called a matrix of instrumental variables if the following conditions are satisfied:

(i) $\Sigma_{ZX} \equiv \operatorname*{plim}_{N\to\infty} \frac{1}{N} Z'X$ and $\Sigma_{ZZ} \equiv \operatorname*{plim}_{N\to\infty} \frac{1}{N} Z'Z$ both exist and are of full rank;

(ii) $\operatorname*{plim}_{N\to\infty} \frac{1}{N} Z'u = 0$;

(iii) $\frac{1}{\sqrt{N}} Z'u \xrightarrow{d} \mathcal{N}_h(0, \sigma_u^2 \Sigma_{ZZ})$.

In the simplest situation, where $h = g$, the instrumental variable estimator b_{IV} of β is defined as

$$b_{\mathrm{IV}} \equiv (Z'X)^{-1} Z'y. \tag{6.1}$$

The essential property of b_{IV} is that it is a consistent estimator of β,

$$\operatorname*{plim}_{N\to\infty} b_{\mathrm{IV}} = \beta + \operatorname*{plim}_{N\to\infty} \left(\frac{Z'X}{N}\right)^{-1} \frac{Z'u}{N} = \beta + \Sigma_{ZX}^{-1} \cdot 0 = \beta.$$

Moreover, given our assumptions, b_{IV} is asymptotically normally distributed,

$$\sqrt{N}(b_{\mathrm{IV}} - \beta) \xrightarrow{d} \mathcal{N}_g\left(0, \sigma_u^2 \Sigma_{ZX}^{-1} \Sigma_{ZZ} \Sigma_{XZ}^{-1}\right), \tag{6.2}$$

where we have used the notation $\Sigma_{XZ} = \Sigma'_{ZX}$.

When X is not correlated with u, the choice $Z = X$ suggests itself. When some of the variables collected in X are correlated with u and the other variables collected in X are not, the latter may be incorporated in Z. This does, of course, only give a partial answer to the question how to obtain IV's. The answer to this question very much depends on the context. For the case of measurement error, we give a number of possibilities for obtaining IV's at the end of this chapter.

More instruments than regressors

The IV estimator b_{IV} in (6.1) was defined for the case that there are as many instruments as regressors, $h = g$. When $h > g$, the above approach is inapplicable, because $Z'X$ is not a square matrix and hence not invertible. In order to make this approach applicable we consider the following procedure: choose g linear combinations of the h columns of Z and use these as instruments, so use ZC

with C a matrix of order $h \times g$. As long as the rank of ZC is g, any choice for C will do.

Naturally, the question arises what choice for C is optimal. From (6.2) we see that, apart from a scalar constant, the asymptotic variance of b_{IV} with ZC as instruments is proportional to $(C'Z'X)^{-1}C'Z'ZC(X'ZC)^{-1}$. The optimal choice for C is such that this expression is as small as possible (in the Löwner sense, see section A.3) or that its inverse is as large as possible. The Cauchy-Schwarz inequality (A.14) implies

$$X'ZC(C'Z'ZC)^{-1}C'Z'X \leq X'Z(Z'Z)^{-1}Z'X. \tag{6.3}$$

If C is chosen to be

$$C_* \equiv (Z'Z)^{-1}Z'X, \tag{6.4}$$

inequality (6.3) becomes an equality. Therefore, C_* is an optimal choice for C in the sense that the asymptotic variance of b_{IV} based on C_* is not greater (in the Löwner sense) than that based on any other linear combination of instruments. Notice that C_* is not the only solution. Let T be an orthonormal $g \times g$ matrix, so that $TT' = T'T = I_g$. For any such T, the choice $C = C_*T$ turns (6.3) into an equality .

Given the choice of C, we can give an explicit expression for b_{IV}. Let $P_Z \equiv Z(Z'Z)^{-1}Z'$ denote the projector on the space spanned by the columns of Z. From (6.4), we can write $ZC = P_Z X$ and

$$\begin{aligned} b_{\mathrm{IV}} &= (C'Z'X)^{-1}C'Z'y \\ &= (X'Z(Z'Z)^{-1}Z'X)^{-1}X'Z(Z'Z)^{-1}Z'y \\ &= (X'P_Z X)^{-1}X'P_Z y. \end{aligned} \tag{6.5}$$

Note that for each orthonormal matrix T defined above, the choice $C = C_*T$ leads to the same estimator (6.5). Moreover, for $h = g$, this evidently reduces to (6.1). If we let $\hat{X} \equiv P_Z X$, an alternative expression for b_{IV} is

$$b_{\mathrm{IV}} = (\hat{X}'\hat{X})^{-1}\hat{X}'y.$$

Thus, we can compute b_{IV} by transforming X and next performing OLS. The transformation is easy to do because $\hat{X}$ is the predicted value of X after regressing each of its columns on Z. Computing the IV estimator in this way leads to a two-stage procedure. Hence, IV is also often called two-stage least squares (2SLS), especially in the context of estimating a single equation from a system of simultaneous equations. Then, Z consists of all exogenous variables in the system.

Another way to look at IV is to transform the model $y = X\beta + u$ by premultiplication with Z' to obtain

$$Z'y = Z'X\beta + Z'u, \tag{6.6}$$

which can be considered as a regression model with h observations and a GLS structure, because the error covariance matrix (conditional on Z) is $\sigma_u^2 Z'Z$. Note that the errors in the transformed model are (asymptotically) uncorrelated with the regressors,

$$\operatorname*{plim}_{N\to\infty} \left(\frac{1}{N}Z'X\right)'\left(\frac{1}{N}Z'u\right) = 0.$$

It follows that the optimal estimator of β is the GLS estimator for the model (6.6), which is (6.5).

The asymptotic distribution of b_{IV} is given by

$$\sqrt{N}(b_{\text{IV}} - \beta) \xrightarrow{d} \mathcal{N}_g(0, \sigma_u^2\Gamma^{-1}), \tag{6.7}$$

with

$$\Gamma \equiv \operatorname*{plim}_{N\to\infty} \frac{1}{N}X'P_Z X = \Sigma_{XZ}\Sigma_{ZZ}^{-1}\Sigma_{ZX}.$$

For practical purposes, this means that b_{IV} is taken to be normally distributed around the true value with estimated covariance matrix $\hat{\sigma}_u^2\left(X'Z(Z'Z)^{-1}Z'X\right)^{-1}$, where $\hat{\sigma}_u^2$ is a consistent estimator of σ_u^2. It remains to find such an estimator.

Estimating the residual variance

Consistent estimation of σ_u^2 requires some care, at least when β has been estimated by 2SLS, so by regressing y on $\hat{X}$. By analogy with the procedure for the standard regression model, a natural approach is to estimate σ_u^2 by the average of the squared residuals. However, the residuals $\tilde{u} \equiv y - \hat{X}b_{\text{IV}}$ are not orthogonal to X,

$$\tilde{u} = (I_N - P_Z)X\beta + \left(I_N - P_Z X(X'P_Z X)^{-1}X'P_Z\right)u,$$

and the first term on the right-hand side does not vanish. As a result, $\tilde{u}'\tilde{u}/N$ does not converge to σ_u^2. However, if we use $\hat{u} \equiv y - Xb_{\text{IV}}$, then a consistent estimator of σ_u^2 is readily obtained as $\hat{\sigma}_u^2 \equiv \hat{u}'\hat{u}/N$, because

$$\hat{u} = \left(I_N - X(X'P_Z X)^{-1}X'P_Z\right)u,$$

and hence $\operatorname{plim}_{N\to\infty} \hat{\sigma}_u^2 = \sigma_u^2$, using $\operatorname{plim}_{N\to\infty} Z'u/N = 0$.

6.2 Application to the measurement error model

Having discussed the general theory of IV estimation, let us now return to the linear regression model with measurement error, i.e., $y = X\beta + u$, $X = \Xi + V$, and $u = \varepsilon - V\beta$. The conditions for the instrumental variables matrix Z can be translated into

(i*) $\Sigma_{Z\Xi} \equiv \operatorname*{plim}_{N\to\infty} \frac{1}{N} Z'\Xi$ and $\Sigma_{ZZ} \equiv \operatorname*{plim}_{N\to\infty} \frac{1}{N} Z'Z$ both exist and are of full rank;

(ii*) $\operatorname*{plim}_{N\to\infty} \frac{1}{N} Z'\varepsilon = 0$ and $\operatorname*{plim}_{N\to\infty} \frac{1}{N} Z'V = 0$;

(iii*) $\frac{1}{\sqrt{N}} Z'u \xrightarrow{d} \mathcal{N}_h(0, \sigma_u^2 \Sigma_{ZZ})$, where $\sigma_u^2 = \sigma_\varepsilon^2 + \beta'\Omega\beta$.

The condition on $\Sigma_{Z\Xi}$ follows from the condition on Σ_{ZX} and the condition on $\operatorname{plim}_{N\to\infty} Z'V/N$. The conditions (ii*) follow from the condition (ii) and the assumed independence of ε and V. Condition (iii*) is a straightforward application of condition (iii) to the measurement error model. Conversely, (i), (ii), and (iii) follow immediately from (i*), (ii*), and (iii*).

As we have seen in the previous section, β and σ_u^2 can be estimated consistently by the IV estimator and the mean squared residual based on it, respectively. We may now wonder whether σ_ε^2, Ω, and Σ_Ξ can be estimated consistently as well. Consider σ_ε^2 first. This can be estimated consistently by $\hat{\sigma}_\varepsilon^2 \equiv y'(y - Xb_{\text{IV}})/N$. This can be seen as follows,

$$
\begin{aligned}
\operatorname*{plim}_{N\to\infty} \hat{\sigma}_\varepsilon^2 &= \operatorname*{plim}_{N\to\infty} \frac{1}{N} y'(y - Xb_{\text{IV}}) \\
&= \operatorname*{plim}_{N\to\infty} \frac{1}{N} y'y - \operatorname*{plim}_{N\to\infty} \frac{1}{N} y'X \operatorname*{plim}_{N\to\infty} b_{\text{IV}} \\
&= \operatorname*{plim}_{N\to\infty} \frac{1}{N} \left(\beta'\Xi'\Xi\beta + \varepsilon'\Xi\beta + \beta'\Xi'\varepsilon + \varepsilon'\varepsilon\right) \\
&\quad - \operatorname*{plim}_{N\to\infty} \frac{1}{N} \left(\beta'\Xi'\Xi + \varepsilon'\Xi + \beta'\Xi'V + \varepsilon'V\right) \operatorname*{plim}_{N\to\infty} b_{\text{IV}} \\
&= \beta'\Sigma_\Xi\beta + \sigma_\varepsilon^2 - (\beta'\Sigma_\Xi)\beta \\
&= \sigma_\varepsilon^2,
\end{aligned}
$$

where the consistency of b_{IV} and the mutual independence of ε, Ξ, and V have been used in the fourth equality. Note that $y'(y - Xb_{\text{IV}})/N$ converges to a different value than $(y - Xb_{\mathrm{IV}})'(y - Xb_{\mathrm{IV}})/N$, because the IV residuals $y - Xb_{\mathrm{IV}}$ are not orthogonal to the regressors X, unlike the OLS residuals.

The measurement error covariance matrix Ω can not be estimated consistently without further assumptions. The reason for this is that, if we do not want to rule out the assumption that the data are jointly normally distributed, then a parameter can only be consistently estimated if it can be written as a unique function of $\Sigma_{ZX}, \Sigma_{ZZ}, \Sigma_{Zy} \equiv \mathrm{plim}_{N\to\infty} Z'y/N$, $\Sigma_X, \Sigma_{Xy} \equiv \mathrm{plim}_{N\to\infty} X'y/N$, and $\sigma_y^2 \equiv \mathrm{plim}_{N\to\infty} y'y/N$. Given the assumptions, expressions of these covariances in terms of underlying parameters are

$$\begin{aligned}
\Sigma_{ZX} &= \Sigma_{Z\Xi} \\
\Sigma_{ZZ} &= \Sigma_{ZZ} \\
\Sigma_{Zy} &= \Sigma_{Z\Xi}\beta \\
\Sigma_X &= \Sigma_\Xi + \Omega \\
\Sigma_{Xy} &= \Sigma_\Xi\beta \\
\sigma_y^2 &= \beta'\Sigma_\Xi\beta + \sigma_\varepsilon^2 = \Sigma_{Xy}'\beta + \sigma_\varepsilon^2.
\end{aligned}$$

Note that the assumptions about Z do not tell us anything about Σ_{ZZ} and $\Sigma_{Z\Xi}$, except that they are of full rank. Hence, they must be treated as nuisance parameters. Obviously, $\Sigma_{Z\Xi}$ and Σ_{ZZ} can be consistently estimated from the sample equivalents of the first two equations. As we have seen above, β and σ_ε^2 can be consistently estimated by b_{IV} and $\hat{\sigma}_\varepsilon^2$, which use sample equivalents of the first three equations and the last. The remaining parameters are Ω and Σ_Ξ, which have to be estimated from sample versions of the fourth and fifth equation, where b_{IV} may be inserted for β in the fifth equation. The number of independent parameters in Ω and Σ_Ξ is $g(g+1)$, whereas the number of independent equations (i.e., elements of Σ_X and Σ_{Xy}) is $g(g+1)/2 + g$. Thus, the number of parameters is larger than the number of equations and therefore, the parameters can not be estimated consistently. Any positive definite matrix M that satisfies the restrictions $M\beta = \Sigma_{Xy}$ and $M \leq \Sigma_X$ gives a solution for Σ_Ξ, with $\Omega = \Sigma_X - M$. The solution is in general not unique, precluding consistent estimation.

Obtaining a unique solution requires additional assumptions. One might for example be willing to assume that the measurement errors of different regressors are independent. Then, Ω is a diagonal matrix. From (2.9) we know that the inconsistency of the OLS estimator is given by

$$\kappa = \Sigma_X^{-1}(\Sigma_X - \Omega)\beta, \tag{6.8}$$

where κ is the probability limit of the OLS estimator. Let δ be the g-vector with the measurement error variances (the diagonal elements of Ω), and let B be the diagonal matrix with the elements of β on its diagonal. Then $\Omega\beta = B\delta$. Using this equality after substitution in (6.8) gives $\Sigma_X^{-1} B\delta = \beta - \kappa$, or

$$\delta = B^{-1}\Sigma_X(\beta - \kappa).$$

A consistent estimator of δ is obtained by replacing the various quantities at the right-hand side by consistent estimators, that is, b_{OLS} is substituted for κ, b_{IV} for β, b_{IV} in diagonal form for B, and $X'X/N$ for Σ_X.

Testing for measurement error

The availability of instrumental variables is not only useful for consistent estimation in the presence of measurement error, it can also offer the scope for testing whether measurement error is present. An obvious testing strategy is to compare b_{OLS} with b_{IV} and to see whether they differ significantly. Under the null hypothesis of no measurement error, the difference between the two will be purely random, but because they have different probability limits under the alternative hypothesis, a significant difference may be indicative of the presence of measurement error.

We assume the following context. There exists a partitioning of X and Z according to

$$\begin{aligned} X &= (X_1, X_2) \\ Z &= (X_2, X_3), \end{aligned}$$

with X_i of rank g_i, $i = 1, 2, 3$. A necessary order condition for IV to exist is $g_3 \geq g_1$. As the notation suggests, X_1 possibly contains measurement error, X_2 is assumed error-free, and X_3 contains instruments that are not regressors in the model. The quantity of interest is

$$\begin{aligned} b_{\text{OLS}} - b_{\text{IV}} &= \left((X'X)^{-1}X' - (X'P_Z X)^{-1}X'P_Z\right)y \\ &= \left((X'X)^{-1}X' - (X'P_Z X)^{-1}X'P_Z\right)u \\ &\equiv L'u, \end{aligned} \tag{6.9}$$

with L implicitly defined. Let A be the covariance matrix of $b_{\text{OLS}} - b_{\text{IV}}$ under the null hypothesis of no measurement error. Then

$$A = \sigma_u^2 L'L = \sigma_u^2\left((X'P_Z X)^{-1} - (X'X)^{-1}\right).$$

When $g_2 > 0$, this covariance matrix is singular and requires some care. Because X_2 is part of Z, $P_Z X_2 = X_2$, and

$$X'P_Z X = \begin{bmatrix} X_1'P_Z X_1 & X_1'X_2 \\ X_2'X_1 & X_2'X_2 \end{bmatrix}.$$

Consequently,

$$X'X - X'P_Z X = \begin{bmatrix} I_{g_1} \\ 0 \end{bmatrix} X_1' M_Z X_1 (I_{g_1}, 0),$$

with $M_Z \equiv I_N - P_Z = I_N - Z(Z'Z)^{-1}Z'$. On partitioning

$$I_g = \begin{bmatrix} I_{g_1} & 0 \\ 0 & I_{g_2} \end{bmatrix} \equiv (U_1, U_2),$$

the covariance matrix of the difference of the two estimators under the null hypothesis can be written as

$$\begin{aligned} A &= \sigma_u^2 L'L \\ &= \sigma_u^2 (X'P_Z X)^{-1}(X'X - X'P_Z X)(X'X)^{-1} \\ &= \sigma_u^2 (X'P_Z X)^{-1} U_1 X_1' M_Z X_1 U_1' (X'X)^{-1}, \end{aligned} \tag{6.10}$$

which implies that $AX'XU_2 = 0$ and $U_2'X'P_Z XA = 0$. Because $X'X$ and $X'P_Z X$ are assumed nonsingular and U_2 is of full rank, this shows that A is singular.

Under the null hypothesis and the assumption that the disturbance term u is normally distributed, it follows from (6.9) and from section B.3 that, for any choice of generalized inverse A^- of A,

$$\begin{aligned} \frac{1}{\sigma_u^2} q &\equiv (b_{\mathrm{OLS}} - b_{\mathrm{IV}})' A^- (b_{\mathrm{OLS}} - b_{\mathrm{IV}}) \\ &= \frac{1}{\sigma_u^2} (b_{\mathrm{OLS}} - b_{\mathrm{IV}})' (L'L)^- (b_{\mathrm{OLS}} - b_{\mathrm{IV}}) \\ &= \frac{1}{\sigma_u^2} u'L(L'L)^- L'u \\ &= \frac{1}{\sigma_u^2} u'P_L u \\ &\sim \chi^2_{g_1}, \end{aligned} \tag{6.11}$$

where the number of degrees of freedom equals the rank of P_L or of L, which is g_1. Under H_0, we also have

$$\begin{aligned} \frac{1}{\sigma_u^2} q^* &\equiv \frac{1}{\sigma_u^2} (y - Xb_{\mathrm{OLS}})'(y - Xb_{\mathrm{OLS}}) \\ &= \frac{1}{\sigma_u^2} u'M_X u \\ &\sim \chi^2_{N-g}, \end{aligned}$$

where $M_X \equiv I_N - X(X'X)^{-1}X'$, which has rank $N - g$. Because $X'L = 0$, $M_X L = L$, so $M_X P_L = P_L$ or $(M_X - P_L)P_L = 0$. Hence, P_L and $M_X - P_L$ are mutually orthogonal and idempotent, of ranks g and $N - 2g$, respectively. This means that under H_0

$$\frac{q/g}{(q - q^*)/(N - 2g)} \sim F_{g,N-2g}, \tag{6.12}$$

providing us with a test statistic. When the assumption of normality does not hold, an approximate chi-square test can be obtained from (6.11) after substitution of a consistent estimator for σ_u^2.

An alternative form of the test can be obtained by using an explicit expression for the generalized inverse of $L'L$. One choice is

$$(L'L)^- = X'XU_1\left(X_1'M_Z X_1\right)^{-1}U_1'X'P_Z X,$$

as can be readily verified using (6.10). From

$$\begin{aligned} X(b_{\text{OLS}} - b_{\text{IV}}) &= (y - Xb_{\text{IV}}) - (y - Xb_{\text{OLS}}) \\ &\equiv \hat{u}_{\text{IV}} - \hat{u}_{\text{OLS}}, \end{aligned}$$

i.e., the difference between the residuals from IV and OLS estimation, and from $XU_1 = X_1$, we obtain

$$\frac{1}{\sigma_u^2}(\hat{u}_{\text{IV}} - \hat{u}_{\text{OLS}})'X_1\left(X_1'M_Z X_1\right)^{-1}X_1'P_Z(\hat{u}_{\text{IV}} - \hat{u}_{\text{OLS}}) \sim \chi^2_{g_1} \tag{6.13}$$

as an equivalent expression to (6.11). Note that $X_1'\hat{u}_{\text{OLS}} = 0$ and $X_1'P_Z\hat{u}_{\text{IV}} = 0$. Hence we also have

$$\frac{1}{\sigma_u^2}\hat{u}_{\text{IV}}'X_1(X_1'M_Z X_1)^{-1}X_1'P_Z\hat{u}_{\text{OLS}} \sim \chi^2_{g_1}. \tag{6.14}$$

Notice that (6.11), (6.13), and (6.14) lead to numerically identical results.

6.3 Heteroskedasticity

Up till now we have been concerned with homoskedastic models, where the variance of the error term in the regression equation is assumed identical for all observations. In cross-sectional research this is often an assumption that is hard to justify. A lot of attention has been paid in the econometric literature to relaxing this assumption. Originally, this literature focused on modeling heteroskedasticity by introducing parameterized functions relating the error variance to the regressors. Estimation then usually takes place in two steps. In the first step, OLS is performed and the squared residuals (or a function of these) are related to the regressors. The results are employed to approximate the error standard deviation of each individual observation. In the second step, feasible GLS (i.e., OLS after dividing the observations by their estimated error standard deviations) is performed to obtain an asymptotically efficient estimator of the regression coefficients.

This approach suffers from two potential drawbacks. First, the assumed parametric specification of the error variance may be incorrect. Second, the quality of the two-step estimator is overestimated because the random nature of the predicted error variance is neglected. Hence, applied work is nowadays often based on an approach whereby the nature of the heteroskedasticity is left unspecified. The idea is to use the OLS estimator as it is but to correct the estimated variance for the presence of heteroskedasticity of unknown form. This approach at least meets the first mentioned drawback.

This idea can be incorporated into IV in a straightforward way. To accommodate it, assumption (iii) is replaced by

(iii′) $\frac{1}{\sqrt{N}} Z'u \xrightarrow{d} \mathcal{N}_h(0, \Psi)$,

where the asymptotic covariance matrix Ψ is defined as

$$\Psi \equiv \lim_{N\to\infty} \mathrm{E}\left(\frac{1}{N} Z'uu'Z\right) = \operatorname*{plim}_{N\to\infty} \frac{1}{N} Z'\Upsilon Z,$$

and Υ is a diagonal matrix with n-th diagonal element equal to $\Upsilon_{nn} \equiv u_n^2 = (y_n - x_n'\beta)^2$. Under these assumptions,

$$\sqrt{N}(b_{\mathrm{IV}} - \beta) \xrightarrow{d} \mathcal{N}_g\left(0, \Gamma^{-1}\Sigma_{XZ}\Sigma_{ZZ}^{-1}\Psi\Sigma_{ZZ}^{-1}\Sigma_{ZX}\Gamma^{-1}\right). \tag{6.15}$$

This reduces to (6.7) in the homoskedastic case where $\Psi = \sigma_u^2\Sigma_{ZZ}$. When using this estimator in practice, Ψ is replaced by $\hat{\Psi} \equiv Z'\hat{\Upsilon}Z/N$, where $\hat{\Upsilon}$ is diagonal with n-th diagonal element equal to $(y_n - x_n'b_{\mathrm{IV}})^2$. Evidently, $\hat{\Upsilon}$ is not a consistent estimator of Υ. However, under fairly general assumptions, $\hat{\Psi}$ will be a consistent estimator of the nonrandom matrix Ψ. The reason for this is that $\hat{\Psi}$ is a matrix of fixed dimensions $(h \times h)$ of averages, with (i, j)-th element

$$\hat{\Psi}_{ij} \equiv \frac{1}{N}\sum_{n=1}^{N}(y_n - x_n'b_{\mathrm{IV}})^2 z_{ni}z_{nj}.$$

Because b_{IV} converges to β, $(y_n - x_n'b_{\mathrm{IV}})^2$ converges to u_n^2, and $\hat{\Psi}_{ij}$ converges to the mean of $u_n^2 z_{ni}z_{nj}$, which exists under general assumptions and is equal to Ψ_{ij} in that case.

A more efficient estimator

We just presented, for the standard IV estimator, the asymptotic distribution under heteroskedasticity of unspecified form. In other words, we adapted the second-order properties of the IV estimator for heteroskedasticity. This suggests an even better approach, which is to adapt the first-order properties and to derive an estimator that takes heteroskedasticity into account directly.

The approach is suggested by the discussion above where we considered, for the homoskedastic case, the transformed model $Z'y = Z'X\beta + Z'u$ and noted that this is a GLS model with disturbance covariance matrix proportional to $Z'Z$ (conditional on Z). In the heteroskedastic case, it is proportional to Ψ. This suggests the feasible GLS estimator

$$\tilde{\beta}_{\mathrm{IV}} = \left(X'Z\hat{\Psi}^{-1}Z'X\right)^{-1} X'Z\hat{\Psi}^{-1}Z'y,$$

where $\hat{\Psi}$ is constructed as above. The asymptotic distribution of this estimator is given by

$$\sqrt{N}(\tilde{\beta}_{\mathrm{IV}} - \beta) \xrightarrow{d} \mathcal{N}_g\left(0, (\Sigma_{XZ}\Psi^{-1}\Sigma_{ZX})^{-1}\right). \tag{6.16}$$

Comparing the asymptotic variances in (6.15) and (6.16), we notice that the Cauchy-Schwarz inequality (A.13) implies

$$\left(\Sigma_{XZ}\Psi^{-1}\Sigma_{ZX}\right)^{-1} \leq \Gamma^{-1}\Sigma_{XZ}\Sigma_{ZZ}^{-1}\Psi\Sigma_{ZZ}^{-1}\Sigma_{ZX}\Gamma^{-1},$$

with $\Gamma \equiv \Sigma_{XZ}\Sigma_{ZZ}^{-1}\Sigma_{ZX}$ as before. Hence $\tilde{\beta}_{\mathrm{IV}}$ is asymptotically more efficient than b_{IV}, as was to be expected.

6.4 Combining data from various sources

An interesting use of the idea of IV that has found a number of empirical applications concerns the case where y and X come from different sources. In addition to y and X, there are some variables (denoted by Z, say) on which both sources contain information. As the notation already suggests, these shared variables can be used as instruments.

We let subscripts to variables denote the sample (I or II) from which the observations come. In this notation, sample I contains y_{I} and Z_{I} and sample II contains X_{II} and Z_{II}. The numbers of observations are N_{I} and N_{II}, respectively. The model is

$$\begin{aligned} y_{\mathrm{I}} &= X_{\mathrm{I}}\beta + u_{\mathrm{I}} \\ y_{\mathrm{II}} &= X_{\mathrm{II}}\beta + u_{\mathrm{II}}, \end{aligned}$$

where u denotes a vector of residuals. Note that the model can not be estimated directly because X is not observed for the first equation and y is not observed for the second. However, for the model to make sense these variables should exist in principle. Assume that

(i) $\operatorname*{plim}_{N_\mathrm{I}\to\infty} \frac{1}{N_\mathrm{I}} Z_\mathrm{I}' X_\mathrm{I} = \operatorname*{plim}_{N_\mathrm{II}\to\infty} \frac{1}{N_\mathrm{II}} Z_\mathrm{II}' X_\mathrm{II} = \Sigma_{ZX}$, which exists and is of full rank;

(ii) $\operatorname*{plim}_{N_\mathrm{I}\to\infty} \frac{1}{N_\mathrm{I}} Z_\mathrm{I}' u_\mathrm{I} = 0.$

Obviously, the idea is to use an IV estimator with $Z_\mathrm{II}' X_\mathrm{II}/N_\mathrm{II}$ as a substitute for the unobserved $Z_\mathrm{I}' X_\mathrm{I}/N_\mathrm{I}$, because it is assumed that they converge to the same limit. When the number of variables in X and Z is the same, an obvious estimator of β is given by

$$\hat\beta_{2\mathrm{SIV}} = \left(\frac{Z_\mathrm{II}' X_\mathrm{II}}{N_\mathrm{II}}\right)^{-1} \frac{Z_\mathrm{I}' y_\mathrm{I}}{N_\mathrm{I}}. \tag{6.17}$$

It is called the *two-sample IV* (2SIV) estimator. Given the assumptions (i) and (ii), $\hat\beta_{2\mathrm{SIV}}$ is consistent when both N_I and N_II go to infinity. This conveys the general idea how the instruments can be elegantly used to combine the data from the two sources.

We consider the properties of this estimator in a more general setting. As before, we consider the case of more instruments than regressors and take heteroskedasticity into account. Let $\hat\Psi$ be a data-dependent $h \times h$ weight matrix, to be discussed below, then the natural extension of (6.17) is

$$\hat\beta_{2\mathrm{SIV}} = \left(\frac{X_\mathrm{II}' Z_\mathrm{II}}{N_\mathrm{II}} \hat\Psi^{-1} \frac{Z_\mathrm{II}' X_\mathrm{II}}{N_\mathrm{II}}\right)^{-1} \frac{X_\mathrm{II}' Z_\mathrm{II}}{N_\mathrm{II}} \hat\Psi^{-1} \frac{Z_\mathrm{I}' y_\mathrm{I}}{N_\mathrm{I}}. \tag{6.18}$$

To derive the asymptotic properties of this estimator, we let N_I and N_II go to infinity with $\hat k \equiv N_\mathrm{I}/N_\mathrm{II} \to k$, say, where k is finite and nonzero. Define

$$\begin{aligned}
d &\equiv \frac{1}{N_\mathrm{I}} Z_\mathrm{I}' y_\mathrm{I} - \frac{1}{N_\mathrm{II}} Z_\mathrm{II}' X_\mathrm{II}\beta \\
d_\mathrm{I} &\equiv \frac{1}{N_\mathrm{I}} Z_\mathrm{I}' y_\mathrm{I} - \Sigma_{ZX}\beta \\
d_\mathrm{II} &\equiv \frac{1}{N_\mathrm{II}} Z_\mathrm{II}' X_\mathrm{II}\beta - \Sigma_{ZX}\beta.
\end{aligned}$$

It follows that

$$\sqrt{N_{\mathrm{I}}}\, d = \sqrt{N_{\mathrm{I}}}\, d_{\mathrm{I}} - \sqrt{\hat{k}}\, \sqrt{N_{\mathrm{II}}}\, d_{\mathrm{II}}.$$

Because d_{I} and d_{II} are based on data from different sources, we may assume that they are independent. Furthermore, assume that

$$\begin{aligned} \sqrt{N_{\mathrm{I}}}\, d_{\mathrm{I}} &\xrightarrow{d} \mathcal{N}_h(0, \Psi_{\mathrm{I}}) \\ \sqrt{N_{\mathrm{II}}}\, d_{\mathrm{II}} &\xrightarrow{d} \mathcal{N}_h(0, \Psi_{\mathrm{II}}). \end{aligned}$$

This usually holds under fairly weak assumptions due to some form of the central limit theorem. Now, using Slutsky's theorem, we obtain

$$\sqrt{N_{\mathrm{I}}}\, d \xrightarrow{d} \mathcal{N}_h(0, \Psi_{\mathrm{I}} + k\Psi_{\mathrm{II}}).$$

Substitution of $Z'_{\mathrm{II}}X_{\mathrm{II}}\beta/N_{\mathrm{II}} + d$ for $Z'_{\mathrm{I}}y_{\mathrm{I}}/N_{\mathrm{I}}$ in (6.18) gives

$$\hat{\beta}_{\mathrm{2SIV}} = \beta + \left(\frac{X'_{\mathrm{II}}Z_{\mathrm{II}}}{N_{\mathrm{II}}} \hat{\Psi}^{-1} \frac{Z'_{\mathrm{II}}X_{\mathrm{II}}}{N_{\mathrm{II}}} \right)^{-1} \frac{X'_{\mathrm{II}}Z_{\mathrm{II}}}{N_{\mathrm{II}}} \hat{\Psi}^{-1} d.$$

Thus, the estimator is consistent if $\hat{\Psi}$ converges to a positive definite matrix. The efficient choice is to choose it such that it converges to $\Psi \equiv \Psi_{\mathrm{I}} + k\Psi_{\mathrm{II}}$. Then

$$\sqrt{N_{\mathrm{I}}}\, (\hat{\beta}_{\mathrm{2SIV}} - \beta) \xrightarrow{d} \mathcal{N}_g\Big(0, (\Sigma_{XZ}\Psi^{-1}\Sigma_{ZX})^{-1}\Big).$$

To achieve this, estimate Ψ_{I} by the sample variance of the columns of $Z'_{\mathrm{I}}y_{\mathrm{I}}$, and estimate Ψ_{II} by the sample variance of the columns of $Z'_{\mathrm{II}}X_{\mathrm{II}}\tilde{\beta}$, where $\tilde{\beta}$ is a consistent estimator of β, for example the estimator (6.18) with the suboptimal choice $\hat{\Psi} = I_h$. Specifically, let $\mu \equiv \Sigma_{ZX}\beta$, which can be estimated in both samples as $\hat{\mu}_{\mathrm{I}} \equiv Z'_{\mathrm{I}}y_{\mathrm{I}}/N_{\mathrm{I}}$ and $\hat{\mu}_{\mathrm{II}} \equiv Z'_{\mathrm{II}}X_{\mathrm{II}}\tilde{\beta}/N_{\mathrm{I}}$. Then

$$\begin{aligned} \hat{\Psi}_{\mathrm{I}} &\equiv \frac{1}{N_{\mathrm{I}}} \sum_{n=1}^{N_{\mathrm{I}}} (Z_{\mathrm{I}n}y_{\mathrm{I}n} - \hat{\mu}_{\mathrm{I}})(Z_{\mathrm{I}n}y_{\mathrm{I}n} - \hat{\mu}_{\mathrm{I}})' \\ &= \frac{1}{N_{\mathrm{I}}} \sum_{n=1}^{N_{\mathrm{I}}} Z_{\mathrm{I}n}y_{\mathrm{I}n}^2 Z'_{\mathrm{I}n} - \hat{\mu}_{\mathrm{I}}\hat{\mu}'_{\mathrm{I}} \\ &= \frac{1}{N_{\mathrm{I}}} Z'_{\mathrm{I}}\Upsilon_{\mathrm{I}}Z_{\mathrm{I}}, \end{aligned}$$

where $\Upsilon_{\rm I}$ is a matrix with (n, n)-th element $(N_{\rm I} - 1)y_{{\rm I}n}^2/N_{\rm I}$ and with (m, n)-th element $-y_{{\rm I}m}y_{{\rm I}n}/N_{\rm I}$ $(m \neq n)$, so $\Upsilon_{\rm I} = Y_{\rm I} - y_{\rm I}y_{\rm I}'/N_{\rm I}$, where $Y_{\rm I}$ is the diagonal matrix with the squared elements of $y_{\rm I}$ on its diagonal. Analogously,

$$\begin{aligned}\hat{\Psi}_{\rm II} &\equiv \frac{1}{N_{\rm II}}\sum_{n=1}^{N_{\rm II}}(Z_{{\rm II}n}X_{{\rm II}n}'\tilde{\beta} - \hat{\mu}_{\rm II})(Z_{{\rm II}n}X_{{\rm II}n}'\tilde{\beta} - \hat{\mu}_{\rm II})' \\ &= \frac{1}{N_{\rm II}}\sum_{n=1}^{N_{\rm II}} Z_{{\rm II}n}(X_{{\rm II}n}'\tilde{\beta})^2 Z_{{\rm II}n}' - \hat{\mu}_{\rm II}\hat{\mu}_{\rm II}' \\ &= \frac{1}{N_{\rm II}} Z_{\rm II}'\Upsilon_{\rm II}Z_{\rm II},\end{aligned}$$

where $\Upsilon_{\rm II}$ is a matrix with (n, n)-th element $(N_{\rm II} - 1)(X_{{\rm II}n}'\tilde{\beta})^2/N_{\rm II}$ and (m, n)-th element $-(X_{{\rm II}m}'\tilde{\beta})(X_{{\rm II}n}'\tilde{\beta})/N_{\rm II}$ $(m \neq n)$, so $\Upsilon_{\rm II} = Y_{\rm II} - X_{\rm II}\tilde{\beta}\tilde{\beta}'X_{\rm II}'/N_{\rm II}$, where $Y_{\rm II}$ is the diagonal matrix with the squared elements of $X_{\rm II}\tilde{\beta}$ on its diagonal. So, (6.18) with $\hat{\Psi} = \hat{\Psi}_{\rm I} + (N_{\rm I}/N_{\rm II})\hat{\Psi}_{\rm II}$ gives an asymptotically efficient estimator.

6.5 Limited information maximum likelihood

Limited information maximum likelihood (LIML) is an important alternative to IV or 2SLS. In this section we give a derivation of the LIML estimator. In the next section we discuss its qualities.

The aim of LIML estimation is to estimate β in the equation

$$y = X_1\beta_1 + X_2\beta_2 + u = X\beta + u, \tag{6.19}$$

where X_1 $(N \times g_1)$ is a matrix of regressors that are correlated with u and X_2 $(N \times g_2)$ is a matrix of regressors that are not. We assume that (6.19) is one equation from a system of simultaneous equations, and that the system is completed with

$$X_1 = X_2\Pi_2 + X_3\Pi_3 + E = Z\Pi + E, \tag{6.20}$$

where E $(N \times g_1)$ is a disturbance matrix orthogonal to $Z \equiv (X_2, X_3)$, and Π_2 $(g_2 \times g_1)$ and Π_3 $(g_3 \times g_1)$ are coefficient matrices with $\text{rank}(\Pi_3) = g_1$. Equation (6.20) can be considered the reduced-form equation for the endogenous variables X_1 as derived from the system. As a result, Π will be structured through the underlying structural parameters of the simultaneous system. Evidently, (6.19) and (6.20) together form a complete system of simultaneous equations.

Let (u_n, e_n') be the n-th row of (u, E), distributed $\mathcal{N}_{g_1+1}(0, \Phi)$. The LIML estimator of β is the ML estimator, in the complete simultaneous system (6.19) and (6.20), that is obtained by neglecting any structure inherent in Π through the simultaneous system.

According to (A.19), minus the logarithm of the density of u and E is, apart from constants, equal to $L = \log|\Phi| + \mathrm{tr}(\Phi^{-1}F)$, with $F \equiv (u, E)'(u, E)/N$. On substitution of $y - X\beta$ for u and $X_1 - Z\Pi$ for E, this is also minus the log-likelihood, again apart from constants, since the Jacobian of the transformation of (u, E) to (y, X_1) is 1.

We minimize L with respect to the parameters by first concentrating out Φ. Because $\partial L/\partial\Phi = \Phi^{-1} - \Phi^{-1}F\Phi^{-1}$, the optimal value for Φ is F. On substitution in the likelihood, we obtain the LIML estimator from the minimization of the expression

$$q_1 \equiv |(u, X_1 - Z\Pi)'(u, X_1 - Z\Pi)|, \tag{6.21}$$

where u is used here and in the remainder of this section as short-hand notation for $y - X\beta$.

Define $R \equiv (Z, u)$, $h \equiv g_2 + g_3$, and $P \equiv (I_h, 0)(R'R)^{-1}R'X_1$. Furthermore, let M_A again denote the projection matrix orthogonal to A for any matrix A, $M_A \equiv I - A(A'A)^{-1}A'$, where I is the identity matrix of appropriate order. Then, we can write

$$\begin{aligned} X_1 - Z\Pi &= M_R X_1 + R(R'R)^{-1}R'X_1 - Z\Pi \\ &= M_R X_1 + (Z, u)\left(\begin{bmatrix} I_h & 0 \\ 0' & 1 \end{bmatrix}(R'R)^{-1}R'X_1 - \begin{bmatrix} \Pi \\ 0' \end{bmatrix}\right) \\ &= M_R X_1 + R\begin{bmatrix} P - \Pi \\ (0', 1)(R'R)^{-1}R'X_1 \end{bmatrix} \\ &\equiv M_R X_1 + RD, \end{aligned} \tag{6.22}$$

with D implicitly defined. Note that $M_R R = 0$, which implies $M_R u = 0$, because u is a column of R. Substitution of (6.22) in (6.21) gives

$$\begin{aligned} q_1 &= |(u, M_R X_1 + RD)'(u, M_R X_1 + RD)| \\ &= \left|\begin{bmatrix} u'u & u'RD \\ D'R'u & X_1'M_R X_1 + D'R'RD \end{bmatrix}\right| \\ &= u'u|X_1'M_R X_1 + D'R'M_u RD|, \end{aligned}$$

where the expression for the determinant of a partitioned matrix has been used, see section A.1. Because $X_1'M_R X_1$ is a symmetric positive definite matrix and $D'R'M_u RD$ is a symmetric positive semidefinite matrix, it follows from theorem A.16 that q_1 is minimized over Π if $D'R'M_u RD = 0$. Now, $M_u RD =$

$(M_u Z, 0)D = M_u Z(P - \Pi)$, which implies that q_1 is minimized by the choice $\Pi = P$.

On doing so, the problem becomes one of minimizing $u'u|X_1' M_R X_1|$ over β. Using $M_R = M_Z - M_Z uu' M_Z / u' M_Z u$, the expression for the determinant of the sum of two matrices gives

$$\begin{aligned}|X_1' M_R X_1| &= |X_1' M_Z X_1| \left(1 - \frac{u' M_Z X_1 (X_1' M_Z X_1)^{-1} X_1' M_Z u}{u' M_Z u}\right) \\ &= |X_1' M_Z X_1| \frac{u' M_{(X_1, Z)} u}{u' M_Z u}.\end{aligned}$$

Because $(X_1, Z) = (X, X_3)$, we can write $M_{(X_1,Z)} u = M_{(X,X_3)}(y - X\beta) = M_{(X_1,Z)} y$, so $u' M_{(X_1,Z)} u = y' M_{(X_1,Z)} y$ and hence does not depend on β. Moreover, $X_1' M_Z X_1$ clearly does not depend on β as well. Consequently, minimization of q_1 is equivalent to minimization of

$$q_2 \equiv \frac{u'u}{u' M_Z u} = \frac{u'(P_Z + M_Z)u}{u' M_Z u}, \tag{6.23}$$

with $P_Z = Z(Z'Z)^{-1} Z'$ as before. Thus, the LIML estimator of β is found by minimizing the *ratio* of $u'u$ and $u' M_Z u$, whereas the IV estimator is found by minimizing the *difference* $u'u - u' M_Z u = u' P_Z u$. From (6.23), we see immediately that minimization of q_2 is equivalent to minimization of

$$q_3 \equiv q_2 - 1 = \frac{u' P_Z u}{u' M_Z u}.$$

Define

$$\delta \equiv \begin{bmatrix} 1 \\ -\beta \end{bmatrix}, \tag{6.24}$$

so that $u = y - X\beta = (y, X)\delta$. On letting

$$S \equiv (y, X)' P_Z (y, X) \tag{6.25}$$

$$\begin{aligned} S_\perp &\equiv (y, X)' M_Z (y, X) \\ &= (y, X_1, X_2)' M_{(X_2, X_3)} (y, X_1, X_2) \\ &= (y, X_1, 0)' M_{(X_2, X_3)} (y, X_1, 0), \end{aligned} \tag{6.26}$$

we can reformulate q_3 as

$$q_3 = \frac{\delta' S \delta}{\delta' S_\perp \delta}.$$

Thus, the LIML estimator follows from the vector δ that minimizes q_3, normalized according to (6.24). Clearly, the minimum of q_3 does not depend on the normalization of δ. It proves convenient to use a different normalization ($\delta' S_\perp \delta = 1$) in the minimization process and to renormalize afterwards. Using this normalization, $q_3 = \delta' S \delta$ and the Lagrange function is $\delta' S\delta + \lambda(\delta' S_\perp \delta - 1)$. This leads to the first-order condition

$$(S - \hat{\lambda} S_\perp)\hat{\delta}_{\text{LIML}} = 0. \tag{6.27}$$

The optimal δ is a solution of this generalized eigenequation. Premultiplication of (6.27) by $\hat{\delta}'_{\text{LIML}}$ and substitution of the normalization gives $\hat{\delta}'_{\text{LIML}} S \hat{\delta}_{\text{LIML}} = \hat{\lambda}$. Therefore, in the optimum, $q_3 = \hat{\lambda}$. Because q_3 has to be minimized, $\hat{\lambda}$ should be chosen as the smallest value for which $|S - \hat{\lambda} S_\perp| = 0$.

Determining $\hat{\lambda}$ is not entirely straightforward, because $S_\perp$ is singular. As is apparent from (6.26), only its upper left submatrix of order $(1 + g_1) \times (1 + g_1)$ corresponding with (y, X_1) is nonzero (and nonsingular). Partitioning S and $S_\perp$ accordingly, we have

$$\begin{aligned} \left| S - \hat{\lambda} S_\perp \right| &= \left| \begin{bmatrix} S_{11} - \hat{\lambda} S_{\perp,11} & S_{12} \\ S_{21} & S_{22} \end{bmatrix} \right| \\ &= \left| S_{11} - S_{12} S_{22}^{-1} S_{21} - \hat{\lambda} S_{\perp,11} \right| \, |S_{22}|, \end{aligned}$$

so $\hat{\lambda}$ should be chosen as the smallest generalized eigenvalue of the determinantal equation $|S_{11.2} - \hat{\lambda} S_{\perp,11}| = 0$, with $S_{11.2} \equiv S_{11} - S_{12} S_{22}^{-1} S_{21}$. Because $P_Z X_2 = X_2$ and

$$\begin{aligned} S_{11} &= (y, X_1)' P_Z (y, X_1) \\ S_{12} &= (y, X_1)' P_Z X_2 = (y, X_1)' X_2 = S_{21}' \\ S_{22} &= X_2' P_Z X_2 = X_2' X_2, \end{aligned}$$

we can rewrite $S_{11.2}$ as $(y, X_1)'(P_Z - P_{X_2})(y, X_1)$. In order to find an explicit form of the LIML estimator of β, substitute the definitions for S, $S_\perp$, and δ in (6.27) and renormalize δ according to (6.24) to obtain

$$\left((y, X)' P_Z (y, X) - \hat{\lambda} (y, X)' M_Z (y, X) \right) \begin{bmatrix} 1 \\ -\hat{\beta}_{\text{LIML}} \end{bmatrix} = 0. \tag{6.28}$$

Solving this system for $\hat{\beta}_{\text{LIML}}$ yields

$$\hat{\beta}_{\text{LIML}} = \left(X'(P_Z - \hat{\lambda} M_Z) X \right)^{-1} X'(P_Z - \hat{\lambda} M_Z) y$$

as the expression for the LIML estimator. This expression reduces to the IV estimator for $\hat{\lambda} = 0$.

The consistency of the LIML estimator follows from the consistency of ML estimators in general. It can also be verified directly by noting that $\hat{\lambda}$ converges to zero for $N \to \infty$. This is sufficient for consistency, because

$$\begin{aligned}
\operatorname*{plim}_{N\to\infty} \hat{\beta}_{\text{LIML}} &= \operatorname*{plim}_{N\to\infty} \left(\frac{X'(P_Z - \hat{\lambda} M_Z)X}{N} \right)^{-1} \operatorname*{plim}_{N\to\infty} \left(\frac{X'(P_Z - \hat{\lambda} M_Z)y}{N} \right) \\
&= \left(\operatorname*{plim}_{N\to\infty} \frac{X'P_Z X}{N} - \operatorname*{plim}_{N\to\infty} \hat{\lambda} \operatorname*{plim}_{N\to\infty} \frac{X'M_Z X}{N} \right)^{-1} \\
&\quad \times \left(\operatorname*{plim}_{N\to\infty} \frac{X'P_Z y}{N} - \operatorname*{plim}_{N\to\infty} \hat{\lambda} \operatorname*{plim}_{N\to\infty} \frac{X'M_Z y}{N} \right) \\
&= \left(\Sigma_{XZ} \Sigma_{ZZ}^{-1} \Sigma_{ZX} + 0 \cdot (\Sigma_X - \Sigma_{XZ} \Sigma_{ZZ}^{-1} \Sigma_{ZX}) \right)^{-1} \\
&\quad \times \left(\Sigma_{XZ} \Sigma_{ZZ}^{-1} \Sigma_{ZX} \beta + 0 \cdot (\Sigma_X - \Sigma_{XZ} \Sigma_{ZZ}^{-1} \Sigma_{ZX}) \beta \right) \\
&= \beta.
\end{aligned}$$

The argument for the convergence of $\hat{\lambda}$ to zero is as follows. Write $q_3 \equiv q_3(\beta)$ explicitly as a function of β and let β_0 be the true value of β and u_0 be defined accordingly. By the IV assumptions, we have that $N^{-1/2} Z' u_0$ converges in distribution to a normally distributed variate with mean zero and finite covariance matrix $\sigma_u^2 \Sigma_{ZZ}$. Hence, $N^{-(1+\varepsilon)/2} Z' u_0$ converges in probability to zero for any $\varepsilon > 0$. Furthermore, $u_0' u_0 / N$ converges in probability to σ_u^2 and $Z'Z/N$ converges in probability to Σ_{ZZ}. Thus,

$$N^{1-\varepsilon} q_3(\beta_0) = \frac{(N^{-(1+\varepsilon)/2} Z' u_0)' (Z'Z/N)^{-1} (N^{-(1+\varepsilon)/2} Z' u_0)}{u_0' u_0 / N - (u_0' Z/N)(Z'Z/N)^{-1}(Z' u_0 / N)},$$

from which it follows immediately that $N^{1-\varepsilon} q_3(\beta_0)$ converges to zero for any positive ε. Now, $\hat{\lambda}$ is just the minimum of q_3 over β and should hence converge at least equally fast.

By extending this argument we can also show that the LIML estimator has the same asymptotic distribution as the IV estimator. Obviously,

$$\sqrt{N}(\hat{\beta}_{\text{LIML}} - \beta_0) = \sqrt{N}(b_{\text{IV}} - \beta_0) + \sqrt{N}(\hat{\beta}_{\text{LIML}} - b_{\text{IV}}).$$

Straightforward computation shows that the last term in the right-hand side of this equation can be rewritten as

$$\sqrt{N}(\hat{\beta}_{\text{LIML}} - b_{\text{IV}}) = -(\sqrt{N}\hat{\lambda}) \left(\frac{X'(P_Z - \hat{\lambda} M_Z)X}{N} \right)^{-1} \times \left(\frac{X' M_Z y}{N} - \frac{X' M_Z X}{N} b_{\text{IV}} \right).$$

It was derived above that $\operatorname{plim}_{N\to\infty} \sqrt{N}\hat{\lambda} = 0$. Furthermore,

$$\operatorname*{plim}_{N\to\infty} \frac{X'(P_Z - \hat{\lambda} M_Z)X}{N} = \Sigma_{XZ}\Sigma_{ZZ}^{-1}\Sigma_{ZX} \tag{6.29}$$

$$\operatorname*{plim}_{N\to\infty} \frac{X' M_Z y}{N} = \Sigma_{Xy} - \Sigma_{XZ}\Sigma_{ZZ}^{-1}\Sigma_{ZX}\beta$$

$$\operatorname*{plim}_{N\to\infty} \frac{X' M_Z X}{N} = \Sigma_{X} - \Sigma_{XZ}\Sigma_{ZZ}^{-1}\Sigma_{ZX}$$

$$\operatorname*{plim}_{N\to\infty} b_{\text{IV}} = \beta_0,$$

which are all assumed finite and (6.29) is assumed nonsingular. Consequently, $\operatorname{plim}_{N\to\infty} \sqrt{N}(\hat{\beta}_{\text{LIML}} - b_{\text{IV}}) = 0$ and thus, by Slutsky's theorem, the asymptotic distribution of $\sqrt{N}(\hat{\beta}_{\text{LIML}} - \beta_0)$ is the same as the asymptotic distribution of $\sqrt{N}(b_{\text{IV}} - \beta_0)$.

6.6 LIML and weak instruments

As we have seen above, the LIML estimator has the same asymptotic distribution as the IV estimator. Hence, one may wonder why the LIML estimator deserves attention at all. It is more complicated to derive than the IV estimator and its use in practice involves more computations, whereas the asymptotic distribution is the same. To the extent that the asymptotic distribution provides a good approximation to the exact, finite sample, distribution of both estimators, there is no statistical reason to prefer one over the other, and simplicity would then favor the IV estimator.

The previous observation suggests the core of the matter. Asymptotic distributions are considered because they offer approximations to often untractable exact distributions, and they should be judged by the quality of the approximation. The IV literature provides ample evidence that the quality of the approximation can be low when the instruments are weak, that is, when the correlation between the instruments and the regressors is low. In particular, the asymptotic distribution does not bring out the considerable median bias that is likely to occur in such cases, and will often suggest a too optimistic picture of the precision of the estimate. Moreover, the shape of the exact distribution can deviate strongly from the bell-shaped curve of the approximating normal distribution and can even be bimodal.

We will now argue heuristically that the LIML estimator offers a better inferential context than the IV estimator. To that end, we consider again the original model (6.19) and (6.20) and derive an important implication of this model. From (6.20) we have

$$\begin{aligned} X &= (X_1, X_2) \\ &= (X_2\Pi_2 + X_3\Pi_3, X_2) + (E, 0) \\ &= (X_2, X_3)\begin{bmatrix} \Pi_2 & I_{g_2} \\ \Pi_3 & 0 \end{bmatrix} + (E, 0) \\ &\equiv Z\tilde{\Pi} + (E, 0), \end{aligned}$$

with $\tilde{\Pi}$ implicitly defined. Let $V \equiv \big(u + (E, 0)\beta, E, 0\big)$. Then $\mathrm{E}(Z'V) = 0$ and

$$(y, X) = Z\tilde{\Pi}(\beta, I_g) + V.$$

Let $h = g_2 + g_3$, and let the rows of V be i.i.d. with variance Ψ. Then

$$\Sigma \equiv \mathrm{E}(S) = (\beta, I_g)'\tilde{\Pi}'Z'Z\tilde{\Pi}(\beta, I_g) + h\Psi \tag{6.30a}$$

$$\Sigma_\perp \equiv \mathrm{E}(S_\perp) = (N - h)\Psi. \tag{6.30b}$$

Let $\lambda \equiv h/(N - h)$. Notice that

$$(\beta, I_g)\begin{bmatrix} 1 \\ -\beta \end{bmatrix} = 0. \tag{6.31}$$

Substituting (6.30b) in (6.30a) gives

$$\Sigma = (\beta, I_g)'\tilde{\Pi}'Z'Z\tilde{\Pi}(\beta, I_g) + \lambda\Sigma_\perp, \tag{6.32}$$

and rearranging and using (6.31) gives

$$(\Sigma - \lambda\Sigma_\perp)\begin{bmatrix} 1 \\ -\beta \end{bmatrix} = 0. \tag{6.33}$$

Note that λ is the smallest value for which $\Sigma - \lambda\Sigma_\perp$ is singular, cf. theorem A.14.

Another implication of the model is obtained by omitting the first row of (6.33) and rearranging the remainder into

$$\sigma_{21} - \lambda\sigma_{\perp,21} = (\Sigma_{22} - \lambda\Sigma_{\perp,22})\beta,$$

using obvious notation. Premultiplication by Σ_{22}^{-1} gives, after another rearrangement of terms and using (6.30b),

$$\Sigma_{22}^{-1}\sigma_{21} = \beta + \frac{\lambda}{\lambda+1}\Sigma_{22}^{-1}(\psi_{21} - \Psi_{22}\beta), \tag{6.34}$$

again in obvious notation.

The first conclusion from the above is that the LIML estimator is the sample analogue of (6.33) because it is obtained by substituting S, $S_\perp$, and $\hat{\lambda}$ for Σ, $\Sigma_\perp$, and λ, respectively, cf. (6.24) and (6.27). In this sense, the LIML estimator stays, informally speaking, closer to the data than the IV estimator. For reasons of comparison, the latter can be written in the format of (6.33) by substituting $\mu e_1 e_1'$ for $\lambda\Sigma_\perp$, with e_1 a vector with the first element equal to unity and the other elements are zero. This is at variance with the model, at least in a finite sample context. This suggests a better performance of LIML over IV.

Evidently, the difference between IV and LIML is small when λ is small. This is the case when N is large or when the instruments are not weak; in that case, the instruments do a good job in explaining the regressors, so the elements of Ψ (apart from the upper-left element corresponding with the error in the equation) can be neglected at no great cost.

This observation has an implication for the investigation of the asymptotic behavior of the estimators. An asymptotic distribution is based on parameter sequences. The choice of such sequences should be motivated by the quality of the approximation that the asymptotic distribution provides to the exact distribution of the estimators. It is desirable to design the parameter sequence such that it generates acceptable approximations of known distributional properties of related statistics. This suggests studying the asymptotic behavior of LIML and IV under alternative asymptotics that stays close to (6.33), where in particular $\hat{\lambda}$ does not vanish in the limit, at least when there are weak instruments.

It is interesting to consider the IV estimator under such asymptotics. To that end we use the second implication of the model, i.e., (6.34). The left-hand side is the population counterpart of the IV estimator. The right-hand side equals β plus a term that vanishes under the traditional asymptotics but not under the alternative asymptotics. Under the latter, which arguably gives a better approximation of the exact distribution, IV is inconsistent unless λ is neglected.

Under traditional asymptotics, the asymptotic covariance matrix of the LIML estimator is equal to the asymptotic covariance matrix of the IV estimator, as shown at the end of section 6.5. A consistent estimator of this covariance matrix follows from (6.7), which is, using the definition of S as given in (6.25),

$$\widehat{\text{AVar}}(\hat{\beta}_{\text{LIML}}) = \hat{\sigma}_u^2 \left(S_{22}\right)^{-1},$$

where S_{22} denotes the lower right submatrix of S of order $g \times g$, and where

$$\hat{\sigma}_u^2 = \frac{\hat{u}'\hat{u}}{N} = \frac{(y - X\hat{\beta}_{\text{LIML}})'(y - X\hat{\beta}_{\text{LIML}})}{N}.$$

Alternative asymptotics lead to a different expression for the asymptotic covariance matrix. An estimator that is consistent under alternative asymptotics, still assuming normality, is given by

$$\widehat{\text{AVar}}(\hat{\beta}_{\text{LIML}}) = \hat{\sigma}_u^2 \left(B_{22}\right)^{-1} \left(C_{22} + \hat{\lambda}\left(C_{22} - B_{22}\right)\right) \left(B_{22}\right)^{-1},$$

with

$$B \equiv S - \hat{\lambda} S_{\perp}$$
$$C \equiv S - \hat{\lambda} \frac{S_{\perp}(1, -\hat{\beta}'_{\text{LIML}})'(1, -\hat{\beta}'_{\text{LIML}})S_{\perp}}{(1, -\hat{\beta}'_{\text{LIML}})S_{\perp}(1, -\hat{\beta}'_{\text{LIML}})'}.$$

Under traditional asymptotics, $\hat{\lambda}$ is zero and this expression reduces to the previous one. The expression under alternative asymptotics is larger but will give a more realistic idea about the estimation uncertainty in $\hat{\beta}$ when the instrumens are weak. For a derivation and further details, see Bekker (1994).

6.7 Grouping

Sometimes, it is known to a researcher that the observations in a regression analysis come from various subsets or groups. If so, a quick-and-dirty way to estimate the regression coefficient is to use the group indicator as an instrument. In the case of a single regressor, this amounts to estimating β by the slope of the line passing through the means of the two groups in the (x, y)-plane.

To illustrate this approach, assume that, in the single regressor model $y = x\beta + u$, the regressor vector x has the following structure:

$$x = (\mu_{\text{I}} + w_{\text{I},1}, \ldots, \mu_{\text{I}} + w_{\text{I},N}, \mu_{\text{II}} + w_{\text{II},1}, \ldots, \mu_{\text{II}} + w_{\text{II},N})',$$

so there are $2N$ observations, N from group I and N from group II, where we take the groups equally large for simplicity. The w_{I}'s are assumed independent random variables with mean zero and variance σ_{I}^2 and the w_{II}'s are assumed independent random variables with mean zero and variance σ_{II}^2. At this point, we assume that there is no measurement error, i.e., u and x are uncorrelated.

Estimating β by the slope of the line passing through the means of the two groups in the (x, y)-plane is equivalent to IV estimation with the instrumental variable $z = (-\iota_N', \iota_N')'$, with ι_N a vector of N ones. This instrument satisfies the requirements of an IV and hence it leads to a consistent estimator. In order to derive the asymptotic variance of this IV estimator, consider

$$\begin{aligned}
\operatorname*{plim}_{N\to\infty} \frac{1}{2N} x'x &= \tfrac{1}{2}(\mu_{\mathrm{I}}^2 + \mu_{\mathrm{II}}^2 + \sigma_{\mathrm{I}}^2 + \sigma_{\mathrm{II}}^2) \\
\operatorname*{plim}_{N\to\infty} \frac{1}{2N} x'z &= \tfrac{1}{2}(\mu_{\mathrm{II}} - \mu_{\mathrm{I}}) \\
\operatorname*{plim}_{N\to\infty} \frac{1}{2N} z'z &= 1.
\end{aligned}$$

Hence, using (6.2), it follows that

$$\sqrt{2N}(b_{\mathrm{IV}} - \beta) \xrightarrow{d} \mathcal{N}\left(0, \sigma_u^2 \frac{4}{(\mu_{\mathrm{II}} - \mu_{\mathrm{I}})^2}\right).$$

For the sake of comparison, notice that

$$\sqrt{2N}(b_{\mathrm{OLS}} - \beta) \xrightarrow{d} \mathcal{N}\left(0, \sigma_u^2 \frac{2}{\mu_{\mathrm{I}}^2 + \mu_{\mathrm{II}}^2 + \sigma_{\mathrm{I}}^2 + \sigma_{\mathrm{II}}^2}\right).$$

The inequalities

$$\frac{2}{\mu_{\mathrm{I}}^2 + \mu_{\mathrm{II}}^2 + \sigma_{\mathrm{I}}^2 + \sigma_{\mathrm{II}}^2} \leq \frac{2}{\mu_{\mathrm{I}}^2 + \mu_{\mathrm{II}}^2} \leq \frac{4}{(\mu_{\mathrm{II}} - \mu_{\mathrm{I}})^2},$$

which are easy to check, show the loss of efficiency of this simple method as compared to OLS.

Grouping and measurement error

The above shows the link between grouping and IV in a situation where a group indicator is available and there is no measurement error. We now consider the presence of measurement error and combine it with a different basis for grouping, that is, grouping by numerical size of the observations.

We still look at the case of a single regressor. We use the standard notation $y = \xi\beta + \varepsilon$ and $x = \xi + v$ and make the usual stochastic assumptions. Groups are created by ordering the observed x's. This is illustrated for the data of figure 2.1 in figure 6.1. Let A and B ($A \leq B$) be two real numbers and consider the sets of observations $\mathcal{A}$ and $\mathcal{B}$ with x-values smaller than A and larger than B, respectively. Let $(\bar{x}_A, \bar{y}_A)$ and $(\bar{x}_B, \bar{y}_B)$ be the arithmetic means of the points in $\mathcal{A}$ and $\mathcal{B}$, respectively. Then the grouping estimator b_G of β is defined as

$$b_G \equiv \frac{\bar{y}_B - \bar{y}_A}{\bar{x}_B - \bar{x}_A}.$$

This is an IV estimator where the IV takes on the value 1, -1, or 0 for x in $\mathcal{B}$, $\mathcal{A}$, or neither $\mathcal{A}$ nor $\mathcal{B}$, respectively.

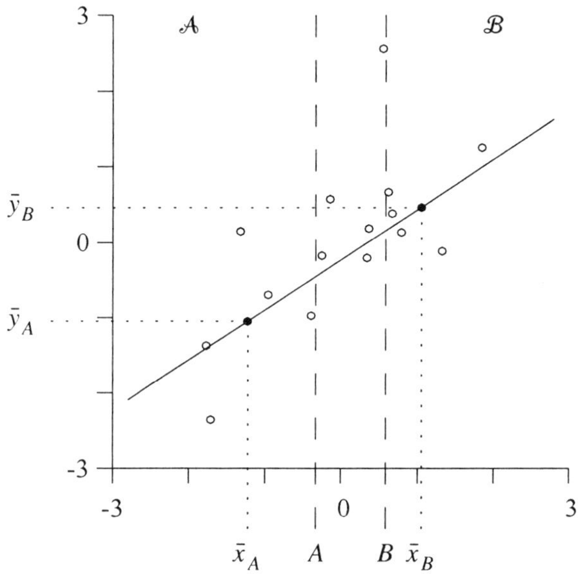

Figure 6.1 *The grouping-based estimator.*

The asymptotic behavior of b_G is of interest. Consistency of b_G requires that the instrument should be uncorrelated with ε and v. This means in particular that the allocation of observations to groups is independent of the measurement error, which is a strong requirement. In order to see what happens if this requirement is not met we reason as follows. Using self-evident notation, we write

$$\begin{aligned}\bar{y}_A &= \beta\bar{\xi}_A + \bar{\varepsilon}_A \\ &= \beta\bar{x}_A + \bar{\varepsilon}_A - \beta\bar{v}_A,\end{aligned}$$

and likewise for B, so that

$$\bar{y}_B - \bar{y}_A = \beta(\bar{x}_B - \bar{x}_A) + (\bar{\varepsilon}_B - \bar{\varepsilon}_A) - \beta(\bar{v}_B - \bar{v}_A),$$

and thus

$$b_G = \beta + \frac{\bar{\varepsilon}_B - \bar{\varepsilon}_A}{\bar{x}_B - \bar{x}_A} - \beta\frac{\bar{v}_B - \bar{v}_A}{\bar{x}_B - \bar{x}_A}. \tag{6.35}$$

In the right-hand side of (6.35), the middle term vanishes asymptotically, because both $\bar{\varepsilon}_A$ and $\bar{\varepsilon}_B$ vanish in the limit. The last term is the interesting one. If there is no measurement error, it equals zero, showing that we can estimate β consistently by this simple procedure without the need for outside information on a group structure. When there is measurement error, $\bar{v}_B > 0$ is likely to hold for any sample size, reflecting an overrepresentation of observations with positive measurement error among the set of largest observations. Analogously, we will have $\bar{v}_A < 0$ with high probability. So we may expect a bias in b_G. When the absolute size of the measurement error is known to be bounded and smaller than the gap separating $\mathcal{A}$ and $\mathcal{B}$, the bias might be moderate.

However, in general the grouping estimator is of doubtful quality. It is illuminating to consider the case where x_n and v_n are normally distributed,

$$\begin{bmatrix} x_n \\ v_n \end{bmatrix} \sim \mathcal{N}_2\left(0, \begin{bmatrix} \sigma_x^2 & \sigma_v^2 \\ \sigma_v^2 & \sigma_v^2 \end{bmatrix}\right).$$

Using a result on the conditional normal distribution (cf. section A.5), this implies that

$$\mathrm{E}(v_n \mid x_n) = \frac{\sigma_v^2}{\sigma_x^2} x_n.$$

Hence,

$$\begin{aligned} \operatorname*{plim}_{N\to\infty} \bar{v}_A &= \mathrm{E}(v_n \mid x_n < A) \\ &= \mathrm{E}_x\left(\mathrm{E}_v(v_n \mid x_n) \mid x_n < A\right) \\ &= \frac{\sigma_v^2}{\sigma_x^2} \operatorname*{plim}_{N\to\infty} \bar{x}_A. \end{aligned} \tag{6.36}$$

Obviously, the analogous expression for $\bar{v}_B$ is

$$\operatorname*{plim}_{N\to\infty} \bar{v}_B = \frac{\sigma_v^2}{\sigma_x^2} \operatorname*{plim}_{N\to\infty} \bar{x}_B. \tag{6.37}$$

Taking probability limits in (6.35), using (6.36) and (6.37), yields

$$\operatorname*{plim}_{N\to\infty} b_G = \left(1 - \frac{\sigma_v^2}{\sigma_x^2}\right)\beta = \frac{\sigma_\xi^2 \beta}{\sigma_x^2},$$

so the grouping estimator has the same bias as the OLS estimator, cf. (2.10). This result may seem surprising at first sight because, by using the group means, one might intuitively expect the impact of measurement error to be "averaged out" to some extent.

6.8 Instrumental variables and nonnormality

As we have seen in section 4.5, normality of the random variables in the measurement error model is an unfavorable situation from an identification point of view. When the variables are nonnormal, the scope for identification is improved. In this section, we illustrate this idea by a simple example. We next show how we can construct instrumental variables in a nonnormal setting.

To illustrate how nonnormality is beneficial for identification and consistent estimation, we reconsider the simplest measurement error model, written for a typical observation,

$$y_n = \xi_n \beta + \varepsilon_n \tag{6.38a}$$

$$x_n = \xi_n + v_n, \tag{6.38b}$$

where y_n, x_n, ξ_n, ε_n, and v_n have mean zero, ξ_n, ε_n, and v_n are mutually independent, and ε_n and v_n are normally distributed.

We now assume that the distribution of the latent variable ξ_n has zero skewness, as in the normal case, but that it has nonzero kurtosis, unlike in the normal case, and define

$$\psi \equiv \mathrm{E}(\xi_n^4) - 3(\sigma_\xi^2)^2 \tag{6.39}$$

as the kurtosis multiplied by $(\sigma_\xi^2)^2$. Under normality, $\psi = 0$. From (6.38), it follows that the second-order population moments are

$$\sigma_y^2 = \beta^2 \sigma_\xi^2 + \sigma_\varepsilon^2 \tag{6.40a}$$

$$\sigma_x^2 = \sigma_\xi^2 + \sigma_v^2 \tag{6.40b}$$

$$\sigma_{xy} = \beta \sigma_\xi^2. \tag{6.40c}$$

Furthermore, from (6.38), (6.39), and (6.40), it follows that the fourth-order moments are

$$\mathrm{E}(x_n^4) = 3(\sigma_x^2)^2 + \psi \tag{6.41a}$$

$$\mathrm{E}(x_n^3 y_n) = 3\sigma_x^2 \sigma_{xy} + \beta\psi \tag{6.41b}$$

$$\mathrm{E}(x_n^2 y_n^2) = \sigma_x^2 \sigma_y^2 + 2(\sigma_{xy})^2 + \beta^2\psi \tag{6.41c}$$

$$\mathrm{E}(x_n y_n^3) = 3\sigma_y^2 \sigma_{xy} + \beta^3\psi \tag{6.41d}$$

$$\mathrm{E}(y_n^4) = 3(\sigma_y^2)^2 + \beta^4\psi. \tag{6.41e}$$

There is a variety of ways to use these equations to obtain consistent estimators. Each of the equations relates the unknown parameters β and ψ to moments of observables, which can be consistently estimated by their sample counterparts. This suggests a simple approach to estimation, which is to pick two of the equations of (6.41) and solve these for β using also (6.40). Replacing the population moments by corresponding sample moments then yields a consistent estimator. For example, solving (6.41a) and (6.41b) for β yields

$$\beta = \frac{\mathrm{E}(x_n^3 y_n) - 3\sigma_x^2 \sigma_{xy}}{\mathrm{E}(x_n^4) - 3(\sigma_x^2)^2},$$

so a consistent estimator that exploits the nonnormality is obtained by replacing the population moments by their sample analogues,

$$\hat{\beta} = \frac{\sum_{n=1}^{N} x_n^3 y_n - \frac{3}{N}\left(\sum_{n=1}^{N} x_n^2\right)\left(\sum_{n=1}^{N} x_n y_n\right)}{\sum_{n=1}^{N} x_n^4 - \frac{3}{N}\left(\sum_{n=1}^{N} x_n^2\right)^2}.$$

Notice that this approach breaks down under normality. In an analogous way we can obtain a different estimator if we take a different set of two of the equations (6.41). For example, a combination of (6.41a) and (6.41c) yields

$$\beta = \sqrt{\frac{\mathrm{E}(x_n^2 y_n^2) - \sigma_x^2 \sigma_y^2 - 2(\sigma_{xy})^2}{\mathrm{E}(x_n^4) - 3(\sigma_x^2)^2}}.$$

From the sample analogue of this expression, a different consistent estimator is obtained. By combining any two of the five equations (6.41), a total of ten of such consistent estimators can be constructed. Because each of these estimators uses only part of the information, they are not efficient. An increase in efficiency can be obtained by combining the moment conditions in some optimal way. The general principle is discussed in chapter 9. The topic is not pursued here, because the example is only meant to illustrate identification under nonnormality. The assumed symmetry of ξ_n is likely to make the details of the current approach of very limited practical relevance, but the ideas can be used in more general contexts, as we will see below.

Consistent estimation under nonnormality by IV

A simple and practically feasible approach to consistent estimation when the regressor is nonnormal is through instrumental variables. Under nonnormality it is possible to derive valid instruments from the data already at hand without using external variables. Consider again the simplest model, (6.38). The reduced form is $y = x\beta + u$ with $u = \varepsilon - v\beta$. Now, consider the Hadamard (element-by-element) product of x and y, $x * y$. We can write

$$\mathrm{E}\big((x_n y_n)x_n\big) = \mathrm{E}\big((\xi_n\beta + \varepsilon_n)(\xi_n + v_n)^2\big) = \beta\,\mathrm{E}(\xi_n^3),$$

which, for all practical purposes, is nonzero if the distribution of ξ_n is asymmetric. Furthermore, under the assumption $\mathrm{E}(\xi_n) = 0$,

$$\mathrm{E}\big((x_n y_n)u_n\big) = \mathrm{E}\big((\xi_n + v_n)(\xi_n\beta + \varepsilon_n)(\varepsilon_n - v_n\beta)\big) = 0.$$

Consequently, when the third-order moment of ξ does not vanish, $x * y$ is a valid instrument.

An extension of this idea is provided by the following results now also involving the third-order moments of the measurement error and the error in the equation:

$$\begin{aligned}
\mathrm{E}\big((x_n^2)x_n\big) &= \mathrm{E}(\xi_n^3) + \mathrm{E}(v_n^3)\\
\mathrm{E}\big((x_n^2)u_n\big) &= -\beta\,\mathrm{E}(v_n^3)\\
\mathrm{E}\big((y_n^2)x_n\big) &= \beta^2\,\mathrm{E}(\xi_n^3)\\
\mathrm{E}\big((y_n^2)u_n\big) &= -\beta\,\mathrm{E}(\varepsilon_n^3).
\end{aligned}$$

These results show that $x * x$ is a valid instrument if the third-order moment of v vanishes but the third-order moment of ξ does not. Also, $y * y$ is a valid instrument if the third-order moment of ε vanishes but the third-order moment of ξ does not.

In the same spirit, but now involving nonlinearity, we can obtain additional valid instruments when the model contains additional, correctly measured, regressors. Let z_n be one such regressor. Then, any nonlinear fuction f of z can of course be used as an instrument provided that it is correlated with x. Moreover, any function f that has mean zero can be used to create $f * x$ and $f * y$ as instruments, at least if they are correlated with x.

6.9 Measurement error in panel data

By panel data, also known as longitudinal data, we denote repeated observations over time pertaining to the same observational units, such as individuals, households, or firms. The analysis of panel data has become a major research topic in econometrics. As will become clear below, the scope for consistent estimation in the presence of measurement error is widened when the data are not a single cross-section but have a panel data structure.

Let the number of observations per variable in a panel data set be NT, where N denotes the number of individual observational units (individuals, for short) and T denotes the number of waves of the panel, i.e., the number of time points at which these individuals have been observed. Therefore, the data in a panel data set have two indices, $n = 1, \ldots, N$ and $t = 1, \ldots, T$. In many practical situations, $N \gg T$. Hence, when deriving asymptotic results below, we keep T fixed and let N go to infinity.

Due to the panel data character of the NT data points, it is extremely unlikely that the regressors are independently distributed in both dimensions of the data set. Independence may be a reasonable assumption for the distributions for different individuals, but observations per individual are likely to be highly correlated over time.

In order to concentrate on essentials, we consider a model with a single regressor only. Blending elements from measurement error and panel data modeling, the simplest linear model for an observation indexed by n and t is

$$y_{nt} = \alpha_n + \xi_{nt}\beta + \varepsilon_{nt} \tag{6.42a}$$

$$x_{nt} = \xi_{nt} + v_{nt}. \tag{6.42b}$$

We consider the structural model and assume that the ε_{nt}, ξ_{nt}, and v_{nt} have zero mean, are mutually independent and are independent for different individuals. The observable variables are the y_{nt} and x_{nt}. The random term α_n denotes the individual effect of individual n, capturing unobservable heterogeneity. It has mean zero and may be correlated with $\xi_{n1}, \ldots, \xi_{nT}$. The T-vectors $x_n \equiv (x_{n1}, \ldots, x_{nT})'$, $\xi_n \equiv (\xi_{n1}, \ldots, \xi_{nT})'$, and $v_n \equiv (v_{n1}, \ldots, v_{nT})'$ have covariance matrices Σ_x, Σ_ξ, and Σ_v, respectively, with $\Sigma_x = \Sigma_\xi + \Sigma_v$.

We now consider estimation of this model. Substituting for ξ, the model in matrix notation for all NT observations jointly is

$$y = \iota_T \otimes \alpha + x\beta + u$$
$$u = \varepsilon - v\beta,$$

where ι_T is a T-vector of ones and α denotes the N-vector containing the individual effects α_n. The vectors y, x, u, ε, and v are $NT \times 1$. Due to the correlation that exists in many instances between the individual effects and the regressor, we restrict our attention to estimators of β that are based on the elimination of the individual effects.

Let Q be a $T \times T$ matrix such that $Q\iota_T = 0$, for example, $Q = M_\iota \equiv I_T - \iota_T\iota_T'/T$, the centering matrix that transforms a vector with T elements into deviations from its mean, or $Q = DD'$ with D' the $(T-1) \times T$ matrix that takes first differences,

$$D' \equiv \begin{bmatrix} -1 & 1 & & & \\ & -1 & 1 & & \\ & & \ddots & \ddots & \\ & & & -1 & 1 \end{bmatrix}.$$

The individual effects can be eliminated by multiplying each individual time series of T observations by Q. We consider estimators of the form

$$\begin{aligned} \hat{\beta} &= \frac{x'(Q \otimes I_N)y}{x'(Q \otimes I_N)x} \\ &= \beta + \frac{x'(Q \otimes I_N)u}{x'(Q \otimes I_N)x}. \end{aligned} \tag{6.43}$$

We evaluate the probability limit of such estimators by taking expectations of numerator and denominator:

$$\begin{aligned} \frac{1}{N}\,\mathrm{E}\big(x'(Q \otimes I_N)u\big) &= \frac{1}{N}\,\mathrm{E}\big((\xi + v)'(Q \otimes I_N)(\varepsilon - v\beta)\big) \\ &= -\frac{1}{N}\beta\,\mathrm{tr}\big((Q \otimes I_N)\,\mathrm{E}(vv')\big) \\ &= -\beta\,\mathrm{tr}(Q\Sigma_v) \\ \frac{1}{N}\,\mathrm{E}\big(x'(Q \otimes I_N)x\big) &= \frac{1}{N}\,\mathrm{tr}\big((Q \otimes I_N)(\Sigma_x \otimes I_N)\big) \\ &= \mathrm{tr}(Q\Sigma_x). \end{aligned}$$

As discussed above, we use asymptotic results based on T fixed and $N \to \infty$. Doing so in (6.43) gives

$$\operatorname*{plim}_{N\to\infty} \hat{\beta} = \beta \left(1 - \frac{\operatorname{tr}(Q\Sigma_{\upsilon})}{\operatorname{tr}(Q\Sigma_x)}\right). \tag{6.44}$$

Not surprisingly, this is again an inconsistent estimator. The bias when using the panel data may even be larger than when we would have used a single cross section. This is the case, intuitively speaking, when the regressor is more correlated over time than the measurement error. In most practical instances this will be the case. The transformation by Q will eliminate a larger part of the variance of x than of the variance of υ, and

$$\frac{\operatorname{tr}(Q\Sigma_{\upsilon})}{\operatorname{tr}(Q\Sigma_x)} > \frac{\operatorname{tr}(\Sigma_{\upsilon})}{\operatorname{tr}(\Sigma_x)},$$

the latter being the bias factor without the transformation, assuming that the regressor is independent of the individual effect.

Biases compared

We can formalize this reasoning as follows. Let us assume, for each individual, that the measurement error and the true regressor values follow an AR(1) process. That is, let $\Sigma_{\upsilon} = \sigma_{\upsilon}^2\Psi_{\upsilon}$ and $\Sigma_{\xi} = \sigma_{\xi}^2\Psi_{\xi}$, where Ψ_{υ} is the matrix with (i, j)-th element equal to $\rho_{\upsilon}^{|i-j|}$ and where Ψ_{ξ} is the matrix with (i, j)-th element equal to $\rho_{\xi}^{|i-j|}$, where ρ_{υ} is the autocorrelation in the measurement error and ρ_{ξ} is the autocorrelation in the true value of the regressor. As stated above, in most practical instances, it is likely that $0 < \rho_{\upsilon} < \rho_{\xi} < 1$. After some tedious but straightforward algebraic calculations, we find that

$$\begin{aligned}
\psi_{\upsilon} &\equiv \operatorname{tr}(M_{\iota}\Psi_{\upsilon}) = T - 1 - 2\frac{\rho_{\upsilon}}{1-\rho_{\upsilon}}\phi_{\upsilon} \\
\phi_{\upsilon} &\equiv 1 - \frac{1}{T}\frac{1-\rho_{\upsilon}^T}{1-\rho_{\upsilon}} \\
\operatorname{tr}(DD'\Psi_{\upsilon}) &= 2(T-1)(1-\rho_{\upsilon}).
\end{aligned}$$

Analogous results hold for ξ. We can now derive the probability limits of the estimator (6.43) with $Q = M_{\iota}$ and with $Q = DD'$. As a benchmark we add the probability limit of the OLS estimator, under the assumption that the individual effects are not correlated with the regressor. We have

$$\begin{aligned}
\operatorname*{plim}_{N\to\infty} \hat{\beta}_{\text{OLS}} &= \beta - \beta \frac{\sigma_v^2}{\sigma_\xi^2 + \sigma_v^2} \\
\operatorname*{plim}_{N\to\infty} \hat{\beta}_{M_\iota} &= \beta - \beta \frac{\sigma_v^2 \psi_v}{\sigma_\xi^2 \psi_\xi + \sigma_v^2 \psi_v} \\
\operatorname*{plim}_{N\to\infty} \hat{\beta}_{DD'} &= \beta - \beta \frac{\sigma_v^2 (1 - \rho_v)}{\sigma_\xi^2 (1 - \rho_\xi) + \sigma_v^2 (1 - \rho_v)}.
\end{aligned}$$

Now ψ_v is a decreasing function in ρ_v and $\psi_v/(1 - \rho_v)$ is an increasing function in ρ_v. In the empirically likely case that $\rho_\xi > \rho_v$, in which the true value of the regressor is more correlated over time than the measurement error, this implies

$$0 < \left|\text{bias}(\hat{\beta}_{\text{OLS}})\right| < \left|\text{bias}(\hat{\beta}_{M_\iota})\right| < \left|\text{bias}(\hat{\beta}_{DD'})\right| < |\beta| . \tag{6.45}$$

The last two inequalities become equalities when $\rho_\xi \to 1$, i.e., ξ tends to a time-constant variable. We see that OLS gives a better result than the two frequently used panel data estimators $\hat{\beta}_{M_\iota}$ and $\hat{\beta}_{DD'}$. Somewhat informally expressed, the bias due to measurement error increases when the individual effects are eliminated, because the transformation to eliminate the individual effects removes more of the signal than of the noise in the data. Of course, this conclusion is still only valid when the individual effects are not correlated with the regressor.

In many situations in practice, the individual effects are correlated with the regressors. If this correlation is positive, OLS gives a result that is biased away from zero. This compensates to some extent a bias towards zero due to measurement error. This compensation is absent when one of the estimators that eliminate the individual effects are used. This means that methods that give consistent estimators when even when the data may be mismeasured deserve particular consideration in the context of panel data.

Consistent estimation

Although the problems created by measurement error may be exacerbated with panel data, the structure over time inherent in such data often allows for consistent estimation. When estimating a panel data model with measurement error in the regressors in practice, programs for structural equation models (cf. chapter 8) are usually convenient. In section 8.3 we show how our simple panel data model (6.42) can be translated in terms of structural equation models. In the remainder of this section, we illustrate the principle of consistent estimation with panel data and show how a consistent estimator can be obtained, which assumes the form of an IV estimator.

To see how the panel data structure can be exploited to construct a consistent estimator of β, it is instructive to consider the case where the structure of v is simple. In particular, we take the measurement error to be homoskedastic and uncorrelated over time. Then, $\Sigma_v = \sigma_v^2 I_T$ and (6.44) becomes

$$\operatorname*{plim}_{N\to\infty} \hat{\beta} = \beta(1 - \sigma_v^2 q), \tag{6.46}$$

with

$$q \equiv \frac{\operatorname{tr}(Q)}{\operatorname{tr}(Q\Sigma_x)}. \tag{6.47}$$

Recall that Q is symmetric but otherwise arbitrary except for the condition that $Q\iota_T = 0$. So by varying the choice of Q we can obtain different estimators with different probability limits. By combining these (inconsistent) estimators we can construct a consistent estimator of β, and also of σ_v^2. Let Q_1 and Q_2 be two different choices that are not a scalar multiple of each other, which is possible if $T > 2$, let $q_i \equiv \operatorname{tr}(Q_i)/\operatorname{tr}(Q_i\Sigma_x)$, $i = 1, 2$ be the corresponding values of q as defined in (6.47), and let the corresponding estimators of β be $\hat{\beta}_1$ and $\hat{\beta}_2$. Then, from (6.46), $\beta_i \equiv \operatorname{plim}_{N\to\infty} \hat{\beta}_i = \beta(1 - \sigma_v^2 q_i)$, for $i = 1, 2$. These two equations can be solved to yield

$$\beta = \frac{q_1\beta_2 - q_2\beta_1}{q_1 - q_2} \tag{6.48}$$

$$\sigma_v^2 = \frac{\beta_2 - \beta_1}{q_1\beta_2 - q_2\beta_1}, \tag{6.49}$$

and consistent estimators follow by replacing β_1 and β_2 at the right-hand sides of (6.48) and (6.49) by their consistent estimators $\hat{\beta}_1$ and $\hat{\beta}_2$ and by replacing the q's by consistent estimators, obtained by substitution of the sample analogue of Σ_x. There is, however, no guarantee that the estimator of σ_v^2 will be nonnegative in small samples.

Notice that (6.48) only exists if $q_1 \neq q_2$. In the (unlikely) case that the regressors would behave as white noise over time, i.e., $\Sigma_x = \sigma_x^2 I_T$, then $q_i = 1/\sigma_x^2$ for $i = 1, 2$, and our approach does not yield a consistent estimator. This is not surprising because then the panel data satisfy the standard measurement error model, albeit with NT rather than N observations. Thus, the structure of x over time plays an essential role in consistent estimation.

The above shows that the panel data context is rich enough to allow for consistent estimation. Furthermore, the context allows for the construction of instrumental variables. This can be illustrated as follows. From (6.46) and (6.47) it is clear that $\hat{\beta}$ is consistent if Q is chosen such that $\operatorname{tr}(Q) = 0$. Take $T = 2$ for simplicity. Then Q is uniquely determined (apart from sign and a scaling factor) as $Q = \iota_2(1, -1)$, and elaborating (6.43) gives

$$\hat{\beta} = \frac{(x_1 + x_2)'(y_1 - y_2)}{(x_1 + x_2)'(x_1 - x_2)},$$

with x_1 the N-vector of observations on the regressor for $T = 1$, and so forth. The consistency of this estimator follows from $\mathrm{E}(x_{n1} + x_{n2})(u_{n1} - u_{n2}) = \mathrm{E}(x_{n1}u_{n1}) - \mathrm{E}(x_{n2}u_{n2}) = 0$. This is the IV estimator in the regression of $y_1 - y_2$ on $x_1 - x_2$ with $x_1 + x_2$ as instrument.

6.10 Bibliographical notes

6.1 Bowden and Turkington (1984) is a monograph devoted to instrumental variables, including a brief overview of the history of the subject. The expression "instrumental variables" is due to Reiersøl (1941) and was elaborated in Reiersøl (1945). Goldberger (1972b) argued that methods that came later to be known as instrumental variables were already developed in the twenties.

How to optimally handle more instruments than regressors was shown by Sargan (1958, 1964). The IV estimator has an optimality property beyond the one derived in section 6.1 on the optimal use of instruments. Holly and Magnus (1988) showed, in the system (6.19)–(6.20) that the IV estimator has the same asymptotic variance as the maximum likelihood estimator based on the complete system, and is hence asymptotically efficient, if Π has no structure. Dijkstra and Wansbeek (1990) provided a short proof of this finding.

6.2 The test for measurement error is from Wu (1973). See also Liviatan (1961, 1963), Hausman (1978), and Reynolds (1982).

6.3 The approach to heteroskedasticity discussed here was popularized in the standard OLS case in the seminal contribution by White (1980), but the main results were already obtained by Eicker (1963, 1967). The generalization to the IV case was provided by White (1982). For an elaborate discussion on heteroskedasticity in an IV context, see Davidson and MacKinnon (1993).

6.4 The idea of applying instrumental variables to combine data from two sources is due to Angrist and Krueger (1992) and Arellano and Meghir (1992).

6.5 LIML was introduced by Anderson and Rubin (1949, 1950). It had not seen many applications until it was resurrected by Bekker (1994), who linked it to the case of many weak instruments. The recent upsurge of LIML is mainly a result of this insight. LIML is not the only alternative to IV that has been proposed for its better small-sample properties. Other alternatives are split-sample IV (SSIV; Angrist and Krueger, 1995), which is related to two-sample IV, jackknife IV (JIVE; Angrist, Imbens, and Krueger, 1999), which is in its turn based on SSIV, and symmetrically normalized IV(Alonso-Borrego and Arellano, 1999).

Blomquist and Dahlberg (1999) compared IV (2SLS), SSIV, JIVE, and LIML in a Monte Carlo simulation study with many weak instruments and found that neither dominates the others in terms of MSE. The 2SLS estimator tends to have a larger bias and the JIVE and LIML estimators have larger variances. They found, however, that LIML has the best coverage rates at small samples.

6.6 The derivation of LIML as given here is adapted from Bekker (1994). The problem of weak instruments was studied by Nelson and Startz (1990a, 1990b), Bound, Jaeger, and Baker (1995), and Staiger and Stock (1997).

6.7 The grouping approach is due to Wald (1940). It was extended to a multiple regression setting by Hooper and Theil (1958). It has spawned a large literature; see for example Theil (1971) for a discussion. The argument showing the behavior of the grouping method under normality is adapted from Pakes (1982). If the conditions for the use of the grouping estimator are satisfied, several variations are possible, like groups of unequal size and more than two groups. See for example Bartlett (1949), Theil and Van IJzeren (1956), Gibson and Jowett (1957a, 1957b), Dorff and Gurland (1961a), Ware (1972), Kendall and Stuart (1973), and Pal and Bhaumik (1981). Small-sample properties have been investigated by Dorff and Gurland (1961b). Ketellapper (1981) considered estimation of an Engel function where the income variable is measured with error but where a correct *income group* variable is available. He showed that the group based estimator will have a smaller MSE than the one based on "noisy" income even with a small number of groups. Note that if outside information about the income distribution is available, this case can be reduced to a Berkson model, see section 2.5.

Richardson and Wu (1970) analyzed properties of estimators in a single regressor model where grouping takes place through a criterion that is correlated with the true value but not with the measurement error.

6.8 There is an elaborate literature on exploiting nonnormality. Pal (1980) developed consistent estimators based on higher order cumulants and moments for the single regressor case. Van Montfort, Mooijaart, and De Leeuw (1987) and Van Montfort (1989) developed a general "BGLS" (i.e., GMM with optimal weighting, see chapter 9) estimation theory based on an arbitrary set of second- and higher order moments. The method of constructing additional instruments under nonnormality is due to Dagenais and Dagenais (1997) and Lewbel (1997).

Van Montfort, Mooijaart, and De Leeuw (1989) use the empirical characteristic function approach due to Feuerverger and Mureika (1977). Ronner and

Steerneman (1985) presented a method of moments estimator for the single regressor case with nonnormal measurement error. In particular they elaborated the case where measurement error *is* normal but occurs per observation with a fixed but unknown probability only. For an assessment by simulation see Ronner, Steerneman, and Kuper (1985).

One particular case of a regressor being nonnormal is a dichotomous regressor. The regressor is then a dummy variable and measurement error can then be viewed as a classification error. This model was studied by Aigner (1973), who derived a consistent estimator using exogenous information on the classification error process. Mouchart (1977) presented a Bayesian analysis. Klepper (1988a) derived bounds on the coefficients in the spirit of chapter 3. These results were generalized by Bollinger (1996). Bekker, Van Montfort, and Mooijaart (1991) investigated identification by inspecting the characteristic function. They showed that the model is locally identified but not globally identified unless the probability of misclassification is less than $1/2$.

On misclassification in a panel data setting see Freeman (1984), generalized by Krueger and Summers (1988). The misclassified variable in these studies is union membership.

6.9 The seminal paper on measurement error in a panel data setting is Griliches and Hausman (1986). Wansbeek and Koning (1991) elaborated some of the ideas. For a further elaboration, see Hsiao and Taylor (1991) and Biørn (1992a, 1992b).

There are various empirical studies where measurement error in panel data is taken into account. For example, Himmelberg and Petersen (1994) employ a model of the permanent income-type to explain R&D expenditures of firms by their "permanent" cash flow, which is a latent variable. The most frequent application of measurement error techniques in panel data has to do with estimating investment models using Tobin's q, the ratio of the market valuation of a firm and the replacement value of its assets. Because the operationalization of q is not clear-cut and unambiguous, estimation obviously poses a measurement error problem. See, e.g., Fazzari and Petersen (1993), Cummins, Hassett, and Hubbard (1994), and especially Blundell, Bond, Devereux, and Schiantarelli (1992).

Aasness, Biørn, and Skjerpen (1993) formulated a demand system for panel data where total expenditures is the exogenous variable measured with error.

Dagenais (1994) studied a time series regression model with measurement errors and first-order autocorrelations in all random terms, and showed that in many cases the bias, due to measurement error, of the OLS estimator is smaller than the bias of the ML estimator that takes the autocorrelation in the equation error into account. This result is in the same spirit as (6.45).

A model that is in spirit closely related to those for panel data is given by

Chamberlain and Griliches (1975), where observations on individuals are correlated due to kinship rather than repeated observation over time. This type of data is called multilevel data, and the models are called multilevel models (Goldstein, 1995; Muthén and Satorra, 1989).

The panel data context is a generalization of a type of models that have attracted attention in the statistics literature, viz. those pertaining to models with *replication*. See, e.g., Barnett (1970).

Chapter 7

Factor analysis and related methods

As we have seen in chapter 4, the standard errors-in-variables model is not identified when the regressors and the disturbance term are assumed to be normally distributed. There are a variety of ways to cope with this problem. One way is to relax the assumption of normality. Higher order moments then become available for estimation. This idea has been explored in section 6.8. Another possible way out is offered if we can embed the error-ridden equation in a system of equations. Then, often, natural restrictions arise that aid identification. The present chapter explores various aspects of this.

The simplest possible case of one latent variable is introduced in section 7.1. We extend the model by one equation and obtain what appears to be the simplest possible factor analysis model. Adding an arbitrary number of equations yields a more general one-factor FA model. Section 7.2 discusses estimation in this model. This results in an eigenvalue problem.

When there is more than one latent variable, the multiple factor analysis model suggests itself. This is the topic of section 7.3. We first address estimation in this model, which is a straightforward extension of the one-factor case. However, there are a number of issues that only arise in the multiple factor setting, in particular rotation. Section 7.4 presents an application of multiple factor analysis.

As just stated, the estimation of factor analysis entails an eigenvalue problem. In this sense, factor analysis belongs to a wide class of methods that result in eigenvalues, all of which can somehow be related to underlying latent variables. Section 7.5 presents an underlying dichotomy in the kind of modeling concerned, and section 7.6 describes various methods that fall into one of these two classes.

7.1 Towards factor analysis

In this section, we introduce the factor analysis model as a generalization of the linear regression model with measurement errors. Consider again the simplest possible measurement error model

$$y_n = \beta\xi_n + \varepsilon_n \tag{7.1a}$$
$$x_n = \xi_n + v_n, \tag{7.1b}$$

for a typical observational unit n, where the unobservable random variables ξ_n, ε_n, and v_n are assumed to be mutually independent with expectation zero. The variables y_n and x_n are observable. Now, let us assume that there is a third observable variable, z_n, say, that is linearly related to ξ_n in the same way as y_n is related to ξ_n:

$$z_n = \gamma\xi_n + u_n, \tag{7.1c}$$

where u_n is independent of all the other random variables (except z_n of course) and has also mean zero. The new variable z can be used as an instrumental variable because it is correlated with ξ but not with v and ε, but we will follow a different strategy here.

From this extended model, we can derive the implied variances and covariances. This leads to the following so-called covariance equations or moment equations

$$\begin{aligned}
&\sigma_y^2 = \sigma_\xi^2\beta^2 + \sigma_\varepsilon^2 && && \\
&\sigma_{yx} = \sigma_\xi^2\beta && \sigma_x^2 = \sigma_\xi^2 + \sigma_v^2 && \\
&\sigma_{yz} = \sigma_\xi^2\beta\gamma && \sigma_{xz} = \sigma_\xi^2\gamma && \sigma_z^2 = \sigma_\xi^2\gamma^2 + \sigma_u^2.
\end{aligned}$$

This system of six equations in six unknown parameters can be solved uniquely for the unknown parameters. The left-hand variables are obviously consistently estimated by their sample counterparts. Hence, on adding hats to the parameters at the right-hand side, consistent estimators for the regression coefficients follow immediately as

$$\hat{\beta} = \frac{y'z}{x'z} \quad \text{and} \quad \hat{\gamma} = \frac{y'z}{y'x}.$$

Note that $\hat{\beta}$ is the usual IV estimator, with z as instrumental variable. Some straightforward algebra shows that the corresponding estimators of the variances of the random terms in the model are

$$\hat{\sigma}_\xi^2 = \frac{1}{N}\frac{y'xx'z}{y'z}$$

$$\hat{\sigma}_\varepsilon^2 = \frac{1}{N}\left(y'y - \frac{x'yy'z}{x'z}\right)$$

$$\hat{\sigma}_v^2 = \frac{1}{N}\left(x'x - \frac{y'xx'z}{y'z}\right)$$

$$\hat{\sigma}_u^2 = \frac{1}{N}\left(z'z - \frac{y'zz'x}{y'x}\right).$$

Consequently, the introduction of the equation containing z renders the model identified. The variance estimators may appear to be negative in finite samples.

Because the number of equations is equal to the number of parameters, the solution of the moment equations gives the ML estimator of the parameters under the hypothesis of normality of all random variables in the model. This statement is subject to a minor qualification if at least one of the variance estimates turns out to be negative. This can obviously not be the ML estimator, because it is an inadmissible value. In that case, the ML estimator of the "negative" variances is zero.

A reparameterization

A generalization of model (7.1) is obvious. To obtain it, first rewrite the three equations in the condensed form

$$y_n = \beta\xi_n + \varepsilon_n, \tag{7.2}$$

with a somewhat different notation, where the 3-vectors y_n, β, and ε_n are defined as $y_n \equiv (y_n, x_n, z_n)'$, $\beta \equiv (\beta, 1, \gamma)'$, and $\varepsilon_n \equiv (\varepsilon_n, v_n, u_n)'$. Note that y_n, ε_n, and β have been redefined. The three equations are asymmetric in the sense that the second element of β (after redefinition) is fixed at 1 and is not a parameter like the other elements. This asymmetry is easily eliminated by reparameterizing the model. We can normalize the variance of ξ_n at 1 and let all elements of β be free parameters. Of course this reparameterization is inconsequential in the sense that it has no observational implications. The old and the new version of the model are equivalent, except that now the sign of β may be reversed. This has no interpretational consequences, because the sign of ξ_n will then be reversed at the same time.

Given this reparameterization a more general model suggests itself. Instead of considering y_n, β, and ε_n as vectors with three elements we let them be vectors with number of elements equal to M, say, keeping the variance of ξ_n equal to 1. Under the assumption of normality of both ξ_n and ε_n, the model is then

$$y_n = \beta\xi_n + \varepsilon_n \tag{7.3a}$$

$$\xi_n \sim \mathcal{N}(0, 1) \tag{7.3b}$$

$$\varepsilon_n \sim \mathcal{N}_M(0, \Omega), \tag{7.3c}$$

with ξ_n and ε_n independent and Ω a diagonal matrix of order $M \times M$. This implies that $y_n \sim \mathcal{N}_M(0, \Sigma)$, where

$$\Sigma \equiv \beta\beta' + \Omega. \tag{7.4}$$

This is the one-factor factor analysis (FA) model. The structure that it imposes on the covariance matrix of the observations is that of a diagonal matrix (Ω) plus a matrix of rank one ($\beta\beta'$). The diagonality of Ω implies that any correlation that may exist between different elements of y is solely due to the common factor. The M-vector β is called the vector of *factor loadings*, the variables that constitute the elements of y_n are called the *indicators* of ξ_n, and the values of ξ_n are called the *factor scores*.

When the FA model holds, the variance of an indicator, i.e., a diagonal element of Σ, is split up into two parts, the variance accounted for by the factor, which is called the *common variance* and is represented by the square of the corresponding element of β, and what is called the *unique variance*, i.e., the corresponding element of Ω:

$$\Sigma_{ii} = \beta_i^2 + \Omega_{ii}. \tag{7.5}$$

The *communality* of an indicator is the common variance expressed as a fraction of the total variance and indicates the extent to which the factor accounts for the variance of that indicator. Thus, it is the R^2 of the regression of the indicator on the factor.

A path diagram representation

Figure 7.1 gives a transparent graphical representation of the factor analysis model in the form of a so-called *path diagram*. In a path diagram, circled variables denote latent (unobserved) variables. Variables in square boxes denote observed variables, such as the indicators. Variables that are not circled and not in square boxes are errors or residuals. An arrow with one arrowhead denotes a (hypothesized) causal dependency, i.e., a factor loading or regression coefficient, and an arrow with arrowheads on both sides (not shown in this figure) denotes an undirected dependence, i.e., covariance.

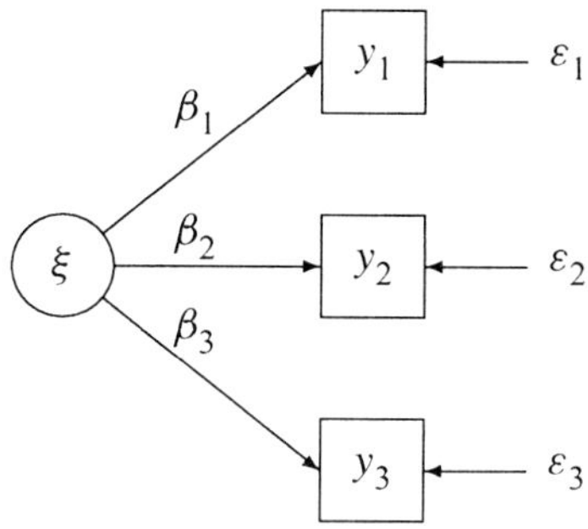

Figure 7.1 *Path diagram of the one-factor model with $M = 3$.*

7.2 Estimation in the one-factor FA model

In the course of this chapter and the next one we will introduce a number of models that generalize the one-factor FA model in many respects. When discussing these models, we concentrate on formulation, use, and interpretation, and defer a general treatment of statistical inference to later chapters. Yet it is useful to discuss estimation by maximum likelihood of the one-factor FA model already at this stage because it will appear to involve the solution of an eigenvalue equation. Eigenvalue analysis plays an important role by itself in models for latent variables.

Let Σ be as given in (7.4) and let S be the corresponding covariance matrix of the observations,

$$S \equiv \frac{1}{N} \sum_{n=1}^{N} y_n y_n' = \frac{1}{N} Y'Y, \tag{7.6}$$

where Y is the $N \times M$ matrix with typical row y_n'. From (A.19), the loglikelihood appears to be, apart from an additive constant and a (negative) multiplicative constant,

$$L = \log|\Sigma| + \operatorname{tr}(\Sigma^{-1} S). \tag{7.7}$$

The ML estimator for β and Ω is obtained by minimizing L over the parameter space. Let θ_h denote any of the parameters of Σ (here, the elements of β and the diagonal elements of Ω), and let Σ_h be the $M \times M$ matrix of first derivatives of the elements of Σ with respect to θ_h. Then the first-order condition is found by the chain rule as

$$\begin{aligned}
\frac{\partial L}{\partial \theta_h} &= \frac{\partial L}{\partial (\operatorname{vec} \Sigma)'} \frac{\partial \operatorname{vec} \Sigma}{\partial \theta_h} \\
&= \left(\frac{\partial \log |\Sigma|}{\partial (\operatorname{vec} \Sigma)'} + \frac{\partial \operatorname{tr}(\Sigma^{-1} S)}{\partial (\operatorname{vec} \Sigma)'} \right) \operatorname{vec} \frac{\partial \Sigma}{\partial \theta_h} \\
&= \left(\operatorname{vec} \Sigma^{-1} - \operatorname{vec} \Sigma^{-1} S \Sigma^{-1}\right)' \operatorname{vec} \Sigma_h \\
&= \left(\operatorname{vec} \Sigma^{-1} (\Sigma - S) \Sigma^{-1}\right)' \operatorname{vec} \Sigma_h \\
&= \operatorname{tr}\left(\Sigma^{-1} (\Sigma - S) \Sigma^{-1} \Sigma_h\right) && \text{(7.8a)} \\
&= 0. && \text{(7.8b)}
\end{aligned}$$

(See section A.1 for the relevant results on matrix differentiation.) Notice that this expression is quite general because it applies to any parameterized covariance function. We will elaborate the expression for β and Ω for the specific case of factor analysis with one factor. We omit hats indicating estimators in order not to clutter notation.

Estimating the factor loadings

The derivative of Σ with respect to β_h, the h-th element of β, is

$$\Sigma_h = \beta e_h' + e_h \beta', \tag{7.9}$$

where e_h denotes the h-th unit vector. Substitution of (7.9) in (7.8) and using the rule $\operatorname{tr}(ab') = a'b$ for vectors a and b of equal dimensions yields $e_h' \Sigma^{-1}(\Sigma - S)\Sigma^{-1}\beta = 0$ as first-order condition for a typical element of β. Hence, for all elements of β jointly, the first-order condition is

$$\Sigma^{-1}(\Sigma - S)\Sigma^{-1}\beta = 0. \tag{7.10}$$

To elaborate this, we define

$$\lambda \equiv 1 + \beta' \Omega^{-1} \beta \tag{7.11}$$

and note that $\Sigma \Omega^{-1} \beta = (\beta\beta' + \Omega)\Omega^{-1}\beta = \lambda\beta$, and consequently,

$$\Sigma^{-1}\beta = \frac{1}{\lambda}\Omega^{-1}\beta. \tag{7.12}$$

After substitution of this in (7.10) and premultiplication of the result by $\lambda\Sigma$, we obtain

$$(\Sigma - S)\Omega^{-1}\beta = 0, \tag{7.13}$$

or

$$(S\Omega^{-1} - \lambda I_M)\beta = 0. \tag{7.14}$$

Thus, given a value of Ω, β follows as the solution of an eigenequation. It is an eigenvector of $S\Omega^{-1}$, with corresponding eigenvalue λ. Because (7.14) is equivalent to

$$\Omega^{1/2}(\Omega^{-1/2}S\Omega^{-1/2} - \lambda I_M)\Omega^{-1/2}\beta = 0,$$

or

$$(\Omega^{-1/2}S\Omega^{-1/2} - \lambda I_M)\Omega^{-1/2}\beta = 0,$$

we may equivalently derive $\Omega^{-1/2}\beta$ as an eigenvector of $\bar{S} \equiv \Omega^{-1/2}S\Omega^{-1/2}$. The solution for β then follows immediately. The matrix $\bar{S}$ is symmetric and positive definite. The computation of eigenvalues and eigenvectors for symmetric positive definite matrices is numerically easier than for asymmetric matrices, so when M is large this alternative formulation can be useful.

The eigenvalue λ that results from the procedure serves to determine the length of β. Let $\tilde{\beta}$ be the eigenvector as given by a computer program and normalized in the way specific to that program, for example, such that its length or its first element equals one. Then we have to find a proportionality factor δ, say, such that $\beta = \delta\tilde{\beta}$ is the correct solution. From the definition,

$$\lambda \equiv 1 + \beta'\Omega^{-1}\beta = 1 + \delta^2\tilde{\beta}'\Omega^{-1}\tilde{\beta}, \tag{7.15}$$

and because λ and $\tilde{\beta}'\Omega^{-1}\tilde{\beta}$ are given, we obtain $\delta = (\lambda - 1)/\tilde{\beta}'\Omega^{-1}\tilde{\beta}$.

The choice of eigenvalue

The eigenequation has in general M solutions. Therefore, we still have to determine which eigenvalue and which eigenvector to choose. We now address this question.

Recall the loglikelihood (7.7). Using the formulas for the determinant and inverse of the sum of two matrices (cf. section A.1), this can be rewritten as

$$\begin{aligned} L &= \log|\Sigma| + \operatorname{tr}(\Sigma^{-1}S) \\ &= \log\big(|\Omega|\,(1 + \beta'\Omega^{-1}\beta)\big) + \operatorname{tr}\left[\left(\Omega^{-1} - \frac{\Omega^{-1}\beta\beta'\Omega^{-1}}{1 + \beta'\Omega^{-1}\beta}\right)S\right] \\ &= \log(1 + \beta'\Omega^{-1}\beta) - \frac{\beta'\Omega^{-1}S\Omega^{-1}\beta}{1 + \beta'\Omega^{-1}\beta} + c, \end{aligned} \tag{7.16}$$

with c not a function of β. Premultiplication of (7.14) by $\beta'\Omega^{-1}$ and using $\lambda = 1 + \beta'\Omega^{-1}\beta$, which holds in the optimum, yields

$$\beta'\Omega^{-1}S\Omega^{-1}\beta = \lambda\beta'\Omega^{-1}\beta = \lambda(\lambda - 1).$$

Thus, omitting an additive constant and still conditional on Ω, the loglikelihood (7.16), considered as a function of the eigenvalue, can be rewritten in a stationary point as $L(\lambda) = \log\lambda - \lambda$. This function is depicted in figure 7.2. Because $\lambda = 1 + \beta'\Omega^{-1}\beta \geq 1$, only the decreasing part of the curve is relevant, and because maximization of the likelihood is equivalent to minimization of $L(\lambda)$, we have to take the largest eigenvalue and estimate β by the corresponding eigenvector.

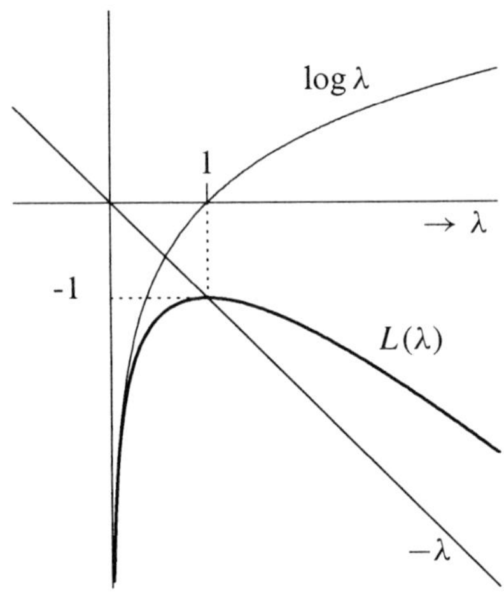

Figure 7.2 *Choice of eigenvalue for the one-factor model.*

Estimating the unique variances

Let θ_h now denote the h-th diagonal element of Ω. Then $\Sigma_h = e_h e_h'$, and (7.8) becomes

$$0 = \text{tr}\big(\Sigma^{-1}(\Sigma - S)\Sigma^{-1}e_h e_h'\big) = \big(\Sigma^{-1}(\Sigma - S)\Sigma^{-1}\big)_{hh}. \tag{7.17}$$

This can be simplified, because at a point where the first-order condition for β is satisfied, (7.13) implies

$$(\Sigma - S)\Omega^{-1}\Sigma = (\Sigma - S)\Omega^{-1}(\beta\beta' + \Omega) = \Sigma - S. \tag{7.18}$$

Hence,

$$(\Sigma - S)\Sigma^{-1} = (\Sigma - S)\Omega^{-1}, \tag{7.19}$$

and (7.17) becomes $\left(\Omega^{-1}(\Sigma - S)\Omega^{-1}\right)_{hh} = 0$, or, because Ω is diagonal,

$$(\Sigma - S)_{hh} = 0. \tag{7.20}$$

Therefore, given the current value of β, Ω is estimated by the diagonal elements of $S - \beta\beta'$, which results in the equality

$$S_{ii} = \hat{\beta}_i^2 + \hat{\Omega}_{ii}, \tag{7.21}$$

cf. (7.5). To estimate both β and Ω, an iterative procedure suggests itself, that is based on switching between solving an eigenvalue equation for the vector β and updating the matrix Ω.

Predicting the factor scores

After estimation of the FA model, one is often interested in making statements about the values for the latent variable for each of the individual observations, i.e., for the the factor scores. Because these values are considered random, we should speak of predicting rather than estimating these. An intuitively appealing approach is to exploit the joint normality of the random variables in the model to derive the conditional expectation of the factor scores and to use this as the predictor for the factor scores. We assume here that all parameters are known and hence abstract from estimation uncertainty. This obviously oversimplifies matters. However, if instead of the true parameter values consistent estimators are used, the formulas to be presented below are still asymptotically correct. Therefore, the formulas should be considered as asymptotic properties.

From (7.3), it follows that

$$\begin{bmatrix} y_n \\ \xi_n \end{bmatrix} \sim \mathcal{N}_{M+1}\left(0, \begin{bmatrix} \Sigma & \beta \\ \beta' & 1 \end{bmatrix}\right).$$

Using (7.11), (7.12), and the expression for the conditional normal distribution (see section A.5), we obtain

$$\begin{aligned} \xi_n \mid y_n &\sim \mathcal{N}\left(\beta'\Sigma^{-1}y_n, 1 - \beta'\Sigma^{-1}\beta\right) \\ &= \mathcal{N}\left(\beta'\Omega^{-1}y_n/\lambda, 1/\lambda\right), \end{aligned}$$

and the predictor $\hat{\xi}_n$ of ξ_n is given as

$$\hat{\xi}_n \equiv \mathrm{E}(\xi_n \mid y_n) = \beta'\Omega^{-1}y_n/\lambda,$$

or, for all observations together,

$$\hat{\xi} \equiv \mathrm{E}(\xi \mid Y) \equiv Y\Omega^{-1}\beta/\lambda. \tag{7.22}$$

As will appear in a more general setting in the next section, the predictor (7.22) is optimal in the sense of having minimal mean squared error. Moreover, the expression is intuitively appealing. In scalar form, the result is that the predictor is a weighted average of the columns of Y, where the i-th column of Y is weighted by β_i/Ω_{ii} (apart from the proportionality factor given by the eigenvalue). This weight is large when β_i is relatively large compared to Ω_{ii}, i.e., when the indicator measures the factor with a relatively small error.

Principal components analysis

As we have seen above, the factor analysis model implies a particular simple structure of the covariance matrix. To a certain extent, this also carries over to the data matrix Y itself. Under the factor analysis model, this can be written as

$$Y = \xi\beta' + E, \tag{7.23}$$

with obvious notation, where ξ and E are independently distributed, the elements of ξ are i.i.d. standard normally distributed, and the rows of E are i.i.d. multivariate normally distributed with mean zero and diagonal covariance matrix Ω. Clearly, this model contains a lot of assumptions that may not be satisfied. Therefore, we may drop the assumptions altogether and take (7.23) as our starting point and wonder whether we can find vectors ξ and β so that the resulting errors are small in some sense. Given a definition of "average smallness" of the errors, this leads to a criterion that can be optimized with respect to ξ and β. A convenient criterion is the sum of squared errors

$$\sum_{n=1}^{N}\sum_{i=1}^{M}\varepsilon_{ni}^2 = \mathrm{tr}(E'E) = \mathrm{tr}\big((Y - \xi\beta')'(Y - \xi\beta')\big).$$

Before we attempt to find the solution for ξ and β that minimizes this criterion, we note that ξ can be multiplied by a nonzero constant c and β can accordingly be divided by c without altering the result. Hence, to avoid an indeterminacy, we need to impose a restriction on ξ and β. When a solution has been found, it can always be rescaled again without altering the sum of squared errors. It turns out that it is convenient to use a different restriction to obtain the solution than the restriction that is interpretationally preferable. Therefore, we change notation at this point and search for the minimum of $\mathrm{tr}(Y - ba')'(Y - ba')$, where b is a vector of dimension N and a is a vector of dimension M, and a and b have to be determined.

To find a solution, a convenient restriction is $a'a = 1$. Hence, we minimize $\operatorname{tr}(Y - ba')'(Y - ba')$ subject to $a'a = 1$. The Lagrange function is

$$L = \operatorname{tr} Y'Y - 2b'Ya + b'b + \mu(a'a - 1),$$

where μ is a Lagrange multiplier. Differentiation with respect to b gives the condition $-2Ya + 2b = 0$ or $b = Ya$, and differentiation with respect to a gives

$$\begin{aligned} \frac{\partial L}{\partial a} &= -2Y'b + 2\mu a \\ &= -2Y'Ya + 2\mu a \qquad (\text{using } b = Ya) \\ &= -2\big(Y'Y - \mu I_M\big)a = 0 \end{aligned}$$

as the first-order condition for a with the optimum value of b inserted. Thus, a is an eigenvector of $Y'Y$ with eigenvalue μ. In the optimum, we have

$$\begin{aligned} \operatorname{tr}(Y - ba')'(Y - ba') &= \operatorname{tr} Y'Y - 2b'Ya + b'b \\ &= \operatorname{tr} Y'Y - 2a'Y'Ya + a'Y'Ya \\ &= \operatorname{tr} Y'Y - a'Y'Ya \\ &= \operatorname{tr} Y'Y - \mu, \end{aligned}$$

where we have used $Y'Ya = \mu a$ and $a'a = 1$. Clearly, this expression is minimized if μ is taken to be the largest eigenvalue of $Y'Y$ and a is the corresponding eigenvector. It was derived above that the solution for b given a is found as $b = Ya$, so that the complete solution for a and b has now been found.

This solution is closely related to the *singular value decomposition* (SVD) of the matrix Y. Any $N \times M$ matrix Y of rank r can be written as

$$Y = U \Lambda V', \tag{7.24}$$

where $U'U = V'V = I_r$ and Λ is a positive definite diagonal matrix with the diagonal elements in descending order, $\lambda_1 \geq \lambda_2 \geq \ldots \geq \lambda_r > 0$. The decomposition (7.24) is the SVD of Y. In the generic case that we assume here, $r = M$, which also implies that $VV' = I_M$. Finding U, Λ, and V can be seen as an eigenvalue problem, because (7.24) implies $Y'Y = V\Lambda^2 V'$, so that the columns of V are the eigenvectors of $Y'Y$ and the diagonal matrix Λ^2 contains the eigenvalues of $Y'Y$. If we maintain the convention of transforming all observations into deviations from their means, $Y'Y$ is proportional to the sample covariance matrix S. Analogously, the columns of U can be computed as the eigenvectors of YY' corresponding to the nonzero eigenvalues. Usually $N \gg M$, so that it is advantageous from a computational point of view to compute V first and then U subsequently as

$$U = YV\Lambda^{-1},$$

which follows directly from (7.24) by postmultiplication of both sides by $V\Lambda^{-1}$. This usually involves less computation than the computation of the eigenvectors of YY'. However, it may be noted that it is generally numerically preferable to compute the SVD directly and jointly from Y.

Let $U = (u_1, \ldots, u_M)$ and $V = (v_1, \ldots, v_M)$. Then, the SVD can also be written as

$$Y = \sum_{i=1}^{M} \lambda_i u_i v_i'. \tag{7.25}$$

Earlier, we saw that a is the eigenvector of $Y'Y$ corresponding to its largest eigenvalue. Given the eigenvalue decomposition $Y'Y = V\Lambda^2 V'$, it follows immediately that $a = v_1$ and $b = Ya = U\Lambda V'v_1 = \lambda_1 u_1$, and the best approximation of rank one is given by

$$\tilde{Y} = ba' = \lambda_1 u_1 v_1', \tag{7.26}$$

which is the first term of the sum in (7.25).

Recall that the discussion started with the equation (7.23), which was derived from the FA model. In the FA model, it is assumed that the variance of the elements of ξ is one (in the population), whereas β is completely free. This contradicts with the results obtained thus far, because a was restricted to have length one and b was unrestricted. Therefore, it is useful to enlarge the correspondence with the FA model by rescaling such that the sample variance of ξ is 1, i.e., $\xi'\xi/N = 1$, and β is not restricted. The solution is to take $\xi = \sqrt{N}u_1$ and $\beta = (\lambda_1/\sqrt{N})v_1$. Note that ξ is a linear combination of the columns of Y, because $u_1 = Yv_1/\lambda_1$. Hence, if Y is measured in deviation from the mean, which implies that $\iota_N' Y = 0$, where ι_N is an N-vector of ones, ξ is also in deviation of the mean, because $\iota_N'\xi = \iota_N' Y v_1 \sqrt{N}/\lambda_1 = 0$.

The vector ξ is called the first *principal component* of Y and the total method is accordingly called principal components analysis (PCA). Contrary to FA, no assumptions are made in the analysis and PCA is therefore a (descriptive) data analysis method rather than a model. Furthermore, the principal component ξ is uniquely obtained as a linear combination of the observed variables, whereas the factor scores can only be predicted with limited precision.

However, PCA has disadvantages as well, compared to FA, which follows from another link between FA and PCA. We can interpret the computation of the first principal component as following from a specific FA model. To be specific, PCA gives the ML estimator for β in the FA model for the case where Ω is scalar, i.e., $\Omega = \omega I_M$, for some scalar ω. Then, the first-order condition (7.14) implies $(S - \tilde{\lambda} I_M)\beta = 0$, with

$$\tilde{\lambda} \equiv \omega\lambda = \omega(1 + \beta'\Omega^{-1}\beta) = \omega + \beta'\beta,$$

so that β is the eigenvector corresponding with the largest eigenvalue of S, which leads to the PCA solution.

Thus, PCA is a special case of FA, obtained by taking $\Omega = \omega I_M$. This choice also implies a rigidity of PCA that may be considered a weakness compared to FA. This pertains to scaling. If we rescale in a FA model the variables under observation, Σ is replaced by $\Delta\Sigma\Delta$, where Δ is some diagonal matrix containing the (nonzero) scaling factors, and (7.2) becomes

$$\Sigma^* \equiv \Delta\Sigma\Delta = \Delta\beta\beta'\Delta + \Delta\Omega\Delta = \beta^*\beta^{*\prime} + \Omega^*,$$

with β^* an M-vector and Ω^* an $M \times M$ nonnegative diagonal matrix. Hence, the rescaled covariance matrix has the same structure as before, $\Delta\Sigma\Delta$ is the sum of a rank-one matrix and a nonnegative diagonal matrix. The estimators in the rescaled model are simply the rescaled estimators of the original model, $\hat{\beta}^* = \Delta\hat{\beta}$ and $\hat{\Omega}^* = \Delta\hat{\Omega}\Delta$. In this sense, FA is scale invariant. In particular, this means that factor analysis using the correlation matrix instead of the covariance matrix leads to essentially the same estimators. Scale invariance does not hold for PCA because $\Delta\Omega\Delta$ with $\Omega = \omega I_M$ is after rescaling not proportional to a unit matrix anymore if the diagonal elements of Δ are not all equal. To avoid arbitrariness in the results, PCA is therefore almost exclusively performed on the correlation matrix, which also assures that in most cases the scales of the errors will be relatively homogeneous.

Note that, paradoxically, although PCA does not use any assumptions, which should be one of its strengths compared to FA, it is mathematically equivalent to a form of FA with very restrictive assumptions. Despite the various differences between PCA and FA, however, their solutions tend to be quite similar if M is not very small. This can be derived more formally, because it can be proved that as $M \to \infty$, then the solutions will become equivalent.

7.3 Multiple factor analysis

Up till now we considered the case of a number of indicators of a single latent variable, i.e., in (7.3), ξ_n is a scalar. In this section we consider an obvious generalization of this model, where we allow for more than one latent variable (or factor) underlying the indicators. We denote this number by k. The model with multiple factors is

$$y_n = B\xi_n + \varepsilon_n, \tag{7.27}$$

where B is a matrix of order $M \times k$ assumed to be of full column rank. It is called the matrix of factor loadings, and generalizes the vector β of factor loadings in the model with a single factor. We maintain the assumptions made on ε. The factors ξ are assumed to be normal with mean zero and covariance matrix Φ, which is assumed positive definite. This extended model is the multiple factor analysis (MFA) model. Under this model, the indicators y_n are i.i.d. with

$$y_n \sim \mathcal{N}_M(0, \Sigma),$$

where

$$\Sigma = B\Phi B' + \Omega \tag{7.28}$$

is the covariance matrix implied by the assumptions of the MFA model.

Broadly speaking, there are two different situations where the MFA model is encountered, leading to what is commonly described by exploratory factor analysis (EFA) and by confirmatory factor analysis (CFA). The first one, EFA, follows from the observation that under the MFA model the covariance matrix of the indicators, Σ is structured as the sum of a diagonal matrix and a matrix of rank k. When k is a small number, the elements of Σ are highly structured and the correlation between the indicators can be represented in a parsimonious way. The essence of EFA is to investigate, given a data set Y, whether the observed covariance matrix of the indicators can be approximated by such a structure for a small value of k. If this is the case, it suggests that the observed variables can be considered imperfect reflections of only a few underlying latent variables, which leads to a more parsimonious representation of the data. This use of factor analysis is purely exploratory (hence its name) and does not use subject matter theory to restrict the parameters.

Confirmatory factor analysis, by contrast, takes subject matter theory as its point of departure. Theory implies structure, and there are many situations in the social sciences where the implied structure is the MFA model with restrictions (most notably, exclusion restrictions) on B and Φ. Statistical inference in the thus restricted MFA model involves the verification of the underlying subject matter theory. When the inference process does not lead to a rejection of the theory, the theory may be considered confirmed (although this is methodologically a dubious word), and hence restricted MFA is called CFA.

The next chapter deals with CFA. In the remainder of this chapter we concentrate on EFA and extend the results obtained for the one-factor case to MFA. Before we turn to details, we note a simplification of the MFA model that can be made in EFA but not in CFA due to the absence of restrictions on B and Φ. The simplification is that we are free to put $\Phi = I_k$. This can be seen as follows. Let L be a matrix of order $k \times k$ such that $\Phi = LL'$. Because the indicators are assumed to be normal with mean zero, their distribution is entirely determined by $\Sigma = B\Phi B' + \Omega = (BL)(BL)' + \Omega = \tilde{B}\tilde{B}' + \Omega$. For $\Phi = I_k$, we have $\Sigma = BB' + \Omega$. Clearly, if B and Φ are unrestricted, so is $\tilde{B}$. This implies that the model with $\Phi = I_k$ generates the same possible distributions for the indicators as the model with unrestricted Φ.

Estimation in MFA

The discussion of estimation in MFA in general is a straightforward extension of estimation in the one-factor model. We now discuss each of the aspects of the one-factor model and see how they have to be adapted for MFA. We maintain the assumption of normality and again first consider estimating B given Ω. As previously, we omit hats.

From $\Sigma = BB' + \Omega$, we obtain two alternative versions for the stacked version of Σ, namely

$$\begin{aligned}
\operatorname{vec}\Sigma &= (B \otimes I_M)\operatorname{vec}B + \operatorname{vec}\Omega; \\
\operatorname{vec}\Sigma &= (I_M \otimes B)\operatorname{vec}(B') + \operatorname{vec}\Omega \\
&= (I_M \otimes B)P_{k,M}\operatorname{vec}B + \operatorname{vec}\Omega \\
&= P_{M,M}(B \otimes I_M)\operatorname{vec}B + \operatorname{vec}\Omega,
\end{aligned}$$

where $P_{k,M}$ and $P_{M,M}$ denote commutation matrices (see section A.4). Hence,

$$\frac{\partial \operatorname{vec}\Sigma}{\partial(\operatorname{vec}B)'} = 2Q_M(B \otimes I_M), \tag{7.29}$$

where $Q_M \equiv \frac{1}{2}(I_{M^2} + P_{M,M})$ is the symmetrization matrix (see section A.4). Using (7.8), this gives the first-order condition

$$\begin{aligned}
\frac{\partial L}{\partial(\operatorname{vec}B)'} &= \frac{\partial L}{\partial(\operatorname{vec}\Sigma)'}\frac{\partial \operatorname{vec}\Sigma}{\partial(\operatorname{vec}B)'} \\
&= 2\big(\operatorname{vec}\Sigma^{-1}(\Sigma - S)\Sigma^{-1}\big)'Q_M(B \otimes I_M) \\
&= 2\big(\operatorname{vec}\Sigma^{-1}(\Sigma - S)\Sigma^{-1}B\big)' \\
&= 0.
\end{aligned}$$

In the third equality, the properties $Q_M \operatorname{vec} A = \operatorname{vec} A$ for any symmetric $M \times M$ matrix A and $\operatorname{vec}(ABC) = (C' \otimes A) \operatorname{vec} B$ for arbitrary matrices A, B, and C have been used (see sections A.1 and A.4). Thus, for MFA, (7.10) generalizes to

$$\Sigma^{-1}(\Sigma - S)\Sigma^{-1}B = 0. \tag{7.30}$$

Moreover,

$$\begin{aligned} \Sigma\Omega^{-1}B &= (BB' + \Omega)\Omega^{-1}B \\ &= B(I_k + B'\Omega^{-1}B) \\ &= B\Lambda, \end{aligned} \tag{7.31}$$

with $\Lambda \equiv I_k + B'\Omega^{-1}B$, so $\Sigma^{-1}B = \Omega^{-1}B\Lambda^{-1}$. Substitution in (7.30) and premultiplication of the result by Σ and postmultiplication by Λ gives

$$(\Sigma - S)\Omega^{-1}B = 0.$$

Using (7.31) then yields $B\Lambda - S\Omega^{-1}B = 0$, which implies

$$\Omega^{-1/2}S\Omega^{-1/2} \cdot \Omega^{-1/2}B - \Omega^{-1/2}B\Lambda = 0. \tag{7.32}$$

Let $\bar{S} \equiv \Omega^{-1/2}S\Omega^{-1/2}$ and $\bar{B} \equiv \Omega^{-1/2}B$. Then (7.32) can be written as

$$\bar{S}\bar{B} - \bar{B}\Lambda = 0. \tag{7.33}$$

The solution of this equation is given by taking for $\bar{B}$ a set of k (orthogonal) eigenvectors of $\bar{S}$ and by taking for $\Lambda \equiv I_k + B'\Omega^{-1}B = I_k + \bar{B}'\bar{B}$ the diagonal matrix of corresponding eigenvalues.

We now consider the scaling of the eigenvectors. Let $\tilde{B}$ be the value of B as produced by the computer as the solution of (7.33) premultiplied by $\Omega^{1/2}$. Let Δ be a diagonal matrix of order $k \times k$ to be determined such that $B = \tilde{B}\Delta$ is of appropriate length. Then

$$\begin{aligned} \Lambda &= I_k + B'\Omega^{-1}B \\ &= I_k + \Delta\tilde{B}'\Omega^{-1}\tilde{B}\Delta, \end{aligned}$$

where $\tilde{B}'\Omega^{-1}\tilde{B}$ is diagonal. This implies that

$$\Delta_{jj} = \left(\frac{\lambda_j - 1}{(\tilde{B}'\Omega^{-1}\tilde{B})_{jj}} \right)^{1/2}$$

provides the appropriate scaling, or $\Delta^2 = (\Lambda - I_k)(\tilde{B}'\Omega^{-1}\tilde{B})^{-1}$.

Directly extending the derivation for the one-factor case, the value of the loglikelihood in the optimum is $\sum_{j=1}^{k}(\log\lambda_j - \lambda_j)$, with λ_j the j-th diagonal element of Λ. Hence, choosing the k largest eigenvalues and the corresponding eigenvectors is optimal.

Estimation of the unique variances for MFA requires little adaptation from the one-factor case. In (7.18), BB' should be substituted for $\beta\beta'$ but this does not affect (7.20), and

$$S_{ii} = \sum_{j=1}^{k} \hat{B}_{ij}^2 + \hat{\Omega}_{ii}$$

provides the generalization of (7.21) to the MFA setting.

Factor score prediction in the MFA case

We now discuss the topic of prediction for MFA. As in the one-factor FA case we take the parameter values as given. We may hence equally well include the covariance matrix of the factors, Φ, here. This covers prediction for models that are more general than the EFA model discussed thus far. In these models, to be discussed in the sequel, the covariance matrix Φ does play a distinctive role.

Just as in the one-factor case we derive the predictor as a conditional expectation. We assume normality, but we will relax this later on. Then

$$\begin{bmatrix} y_n \\ \xi_n \end{bmatrix} \sim \mathcal{N}_{M+k}\left(0, \begin{bmatrix} \Sigma & B\Phi \\ \Phi B' & \Phi \end{bmatrix}\right).$$

Using the results on the conditional expectation for the normal distribution as given in section A.5, we obtain

$$\xi_n \mid y_n \sim \mathcal{N}_k\big(\Phi B'\Sigma^{-1} y_n, \Phi - \Phi B'\Sigma^{-1} B\Phi\big). \tag{7.34}$$

The matrices appearing in (7.34) can be simplified in the following way. Redefine $\Lambda \equiv \Phi^{-1} + B'\Omega^{-1}B$, then

$$\begin{aligned} \Sigma\Omega^{-1}B &= (B\Phi B' + \Omega)\Omega^{-1}B \\ &= B\Phi(\Phi^{-1} + B'\Omega^{-1}B) \\ &= B\Phi\Lambda. \end{aligned}$$

On premultiplying by Σ^{-1} and postmultiplying by Λ^{-1}, this gives

$$\Omega^{-1}B\Lambda^{-1} = \Sigma^{-1}B\Phi. \tag{7.35}$$

Hence,

$$\begin{aligned}\Phi B'\Sigma^{-1}B\Phi &= \Phi B'\Omega^{-1}B\Lambda^{-1}\\ &= \Phi(\Lambda - \Phi^{-1})\Lambda^{-1}\\ &= \Phi - \Lambda^{-1},\end{aligned}$$

which can be rearranged as

$$\Lambda^{-1} = \Phi - \Phi B'\Sigma^{-1}B\Phi. \tag{7.36}$$

Inserting (7.35) and (7.36) into (7.34) gives the simplified expression

$$\xi_n \mid y_n \sim \mathcal{N}_k(\Lambda^{-1}B'\Omega^{-1}y_n, \Lambda^{-1})$$

for the conditional distribution. It leads to the natural predictor

$$\hat{\xi}_n^R \equiv \mathrm{E}(\xi_n \mid y_n) = \Lambda^{-1}B'\Omega^{-1}y_n, \tag{7.37}$$

which is called the *regression* predictor, because it is the predictor based on the regression of ξ_n on y_n, in the classical sense that it is its conditional expectation. It has conditional mean square error of prediction

$$\mathrm{E}\big((\hat{\xi}_n^R - \xi_n)(\hat{\xi}_n^R - \xi_n)' \mid y_n\big) = \Lambda^{-1},$$

which is also the marginal mean squared error (MSE), because it does not depend on y_n. In a sense, this is again a predictor that weights observations inversely proportional to the unique variances, although the interpretation is less straightforward than in the one-factor case.

In order to further assess the properties of this predictor, we drop the assumption of normality and consider the prediction problem from a different angle. We consider predictors that are linear in y_n, i.e., are of the form $L'y_n$, where L is an $M \times k$ matrix to be determined. In order to assess the quality of such predictors we investigate their MSE. From

$$\begin{aligned}\hat{\xi}_n - \xi_n &= L'y_n - \xi_n\\ &= (L'B - I_k)\xi_n + L'\varepsilon_n,\end{aligned} \tag{7.38}$$

we obtain

$$\begin{aligned}\mathrm{MSE}(\hat{\xi}_n) &\equiv \mathrm{E}\big((\hat{\xi}_n - \xi_n)(\hat{\xi}_n - \xi_n)'\big)\\ &= (L'B - I_k)\Phi(B'L - I_k) + L'\Omega L\\ &= L'B\Phi B'L - \Phi B'L - L'B\Phi + \Phi + L'\Omega L\\ &= L'\Sigma L - \Phi B'L - L'B\Phi + \Phi\\ &= (L'\Sigma - \Phi B')\Sigma^{-1}(\Sigma L - B\Phi) + \Phi - \Phi B'\Sigma^{-1}B\Phi\\ &= (L'\Sigma - \Phi B')\Sigma^{-1}(\Sigma L - B\Phi) + \Lambda^{-1}.\end{aligned} \tag{7.39}$$

The positive definite matrix Λ^{-1} does not depend on L. Hence, because Σ^{-1} is positive definite, the MSE is minimized in the Löwner sense (see section A.1) when L is chosen such that $L'\Sigma - \Phi B' = 0$, or

$$(L^R)' = \Phi B'\Sigma^{-1} = \Lambda^{-1}B'\Omega^{-1}, \tag{7.40}$$

where the last step is based on (7.35). By this choice, the first term at the right-hand side of (7.39), which is positive semidefinite, vanishes and the MSE reaches its minimum. This choice of L yields precisely the normality-based predictor (7.37), which explains the usage of the superscript R. This proves the minimum MSE property of the conditional mean of the normal distribution.

The conditional expectation approach (or the minimum MSE approach) is intuitively appealing but has a property that may be deemed unattractive. This is the bias inherent in the predictor. From (7.38) and (7.40) we have

$$\mathrm{E}\left(\hat{\xi}_n^R - \xi_n \mid \xi_n\right) = (\Lambda^{-1}B'\Omega^{-1}B - I_k)\xi_n = -\Lambda^{-1}\Phi^{-1}\xi_n \neq 0, \tag{7.41}$$

i.e., the predictor is biased in this sense, although $\mathrm{E}\left(\hat{\xi}_n^R - \xi_n \mid y_n\right) = 0$, so that it is unbiased in another sense. However, (7.41) may suggest an alternative approach, where the MSE is minimized under the restriction that the predictor is unbiased in the sense that $\mathrm{E}\left(\hat{\xi}_n - \xi_n \mid \xi_n\right) = 0$. In view of (7.38) this implies $L'B = I_k$ as a restriction on L. Finding the minimum MSE predictor under this restriction is easy because we can consider (7.27) as a regression model with M observations, where B is the matrix of the regressors and ξ_n the vector of regression coefficients. Because the disturbances in this system have a nonscalar covariance matrix Ω, the Gauss-Markov theorem implies that the GLS estimator is optimal and hence that the choice

$$(L^B)' \equiv (B'\Omega^{-1}B)^{-1}B'\Omega^{-1} \tag{7.42}$$

leads to the best linear unbiased predictor. This predictor is called the Bartlett predictor, after Bartlett (1937). (Note that this predictor is, of course, also based on regression.) If the distribution of ε_n is normal, the Bartlett predictor is even best unbiased. Note that substitution of $\Lambda = \Phi^{-1} + B'\Omega^{-1}B$ in (7.40) gives

$$(L^R)' = (\Phi^{-1} + B'\Omega^{-1}B)^{-1}B'\Omega^{-1}, \tag{7.43}$$

which means that it invokes a kind of *shrinkage* compared to the Bartlett predictor. This becomes clear in the one-factor case. From the comparison of (7.43) and (7.42), it follows immediately that in the one-factor case, the weights are equal, except for a proportionality factor. The regression predictor is more shrunken towards zero, with shrinkage factor

$$\frac{\hat{\xi}_n^R}{\hat{\xi}_n^B} = \frac{\beta'\Omega^{-1}\beta}{\phi^{-1} + \beta'\Omega^{-1}\beta},$$

in which the symbols ϕ and β have been used instead of Φ and B to indicate the one-factor case.

The MSE of the Bartlett predictor equals the conditional variance, for which we can write

$$\begin{aligned}
\text{MSE}(\hat{\xi}_n^B) &= \text{E}_\xi\, \text{E}_\varepsilon\Big((\hat{\xi}_n^B - \xi_n)(\hat{\xi}_n^B - \xi_n)' \mid \xi_n\Big) \\
&= \text{E}_\varepsilon\Big((\hat{\xi}_n^B - \xi_n)(\hat{\xi}_n^B - \xi_n)' \mid \xi_n\Big) \\
&= (B'\Omega^{-1}B)^{-1} \\
&= (\Lambda - \Phi^{-1})^{-1} \\
&= \Phi(\Phi - \Lambda^{-1})^{-1}\Lambda^{-1} \\
&= (\Phi - \Lambda^{-1})(\Phi - \Lambda^{-1})^{-1}\Lambda^{-1} + \Lambda^{-1}(\Phi - \Lambda^{-1})^{-1}\Lambda^{-1} \\
&= \Lambda^{-1} + \Lambda^{-1}(\Phi - \Lambda^{-1})^{-1}\Lambda^{-1}.
\end{aligned} \tag{7.44}$$

The last member of (7.44) shows the loss in terms of MSE of imposing the restriction of conditional unbiasedness, because $\text{MSE}(\hat{\xi}_n^R) = \Lambda^{-1}$ and the last term in (7.44) is positive definite because of (7.36).

PCA with more principal components

The discussion of principal components analysis extends directly to more dimensions as well. We now look for the best rank-k approximation of Y, which can be seen to be

$$\tilde{Y} = \sum_{j=1}^{k} \lambda_j u_j v_j' = U_{(k)}\Lambda_{(k)}V_{(k)}',$$

where $U_{(k)}$ is the $N \times k$ matrix of the first k columns of U, $V_{(k)}$ is the $M \times k$ matrix of the first k columns of V, and $\Lambda_{(k)}$ is the $k \times k$ upper left submatrix of Λ. This means that the sum in (7.25) is truncated after the first k terms, rather than after the first term as in (7.26). The resulting matrix Ξ of the first k principal components is $\Xi = \sqrt{N}U_{(k)}$ and the component loading matrix B is $B = V_{(k)}\Lambda_{(k)}/\sqrt{N}$. Of course, $\tilde{Y} = \Xi B'$ again.

Rotation

Up till now, the discussion of MFA led to a direct extension of results for the one-factor model. An important issue that arises only if $k > 1$ involves an indeterminacy of the factor loadings matrix B. The distribution of the y_n depends on B only through BB'. Hence, this distribution is not affected when B is replaced by BT, where T is an orthonormal $k \times k$ matrix (i.e., a matrix satisfying $T' = T^{-1}$ or $TT' = T'T = I_k$), because $BB' = BTT'B' = BT(BT)'$. So the data can not be used to discriminate between B and BT for any orthonormal matrix T. In other words, B and BT imply the same distribution of the y_n and hence B is not identified. The number of free elements in an orthonormal matrix of order k is $k(k-1)/2$, which is thus the number of restrictions that may be imposed on B without consequence. The freedom to replace B by BT is commonly expressed by stating that the factor loadings matrix is open to rotation. When the MFA model is estimated the estimator $\hat{B}$ can be replaced by any linear combination $\hat{B}T$ without affecting the value of the likelihood.

This rotational freedom and the indeterminacy that it reflects may seem a nuisance, because in the estimation of B the researcher has to impose, implicitly or explicitly, essentially untestable restrictions on B. Yet this freedom may also be considered attractive, because it can be used to obtain a meaningful interpretation of the outcomes of the estimation procedure. In particular, it is appealing to try to rotate B (or rather, $\hat{B}$ but we disregard the distinction) in such a way that it shows a simple structure, that is, a clear pattern. Ideally, the variance of a particular variable is accounted for by the smallest possible number of factors or, in other words, each indicator is correlated with as few factors as possible. At least one factor should, if possible, *not* contribute to a particular variable.

As a concrete example, let $M = 6$ and $k = 3$. A simple structure could be

$$\begin{bmatrix} * & \cdot & \cdot \\ * & \cdot & \cdot \\ \cdot & * & \cdot \\ \cdot & * & \cdot \\ \cdot & * & \cdot \\ \cdot & \cdot & * \end{bmatrix},$$

where an asterisk indicates a substantially nonzero entry, and a dot indicates a small number. Each indicator correlates substantially with only one factor. Trying to obtain such a simple structure is done by inspecting BT over all possible orthonormal matrices T. Generally, this can not be done by manual inspection of all these solutions. We need some objective criterion to judge the simplicity of the solution. Different criteria lead to different rotation methods.

The rotation method most frequently employed in practice is the varimax method. The point of departure is the definition of simplicity of the measurement of the j-th, say, factor,

$$v_j \equiv \frac{1}{M}\sum_{i=1}^{M}(b_{ij}^2)^2 - \left(\frac{1}{M}\sum_{i=1}^{M} b_{ij}^2\right)^2,$$

for $j = 1, \ldots, k$, where b_{ij} denotes element (i, j) of BT for the *raw* varimax criterion and b_{ij} denotes element (i, j) of BT divided by the square root of its communality for the varimax criterion with Kaiser normalization, which is usually simply called varimax. In words, the simplicity is the variance of the squared (normalized) factor loadings in the j-th column of BT. The simplicity is high when there are both large factor loadings (in absolute value) and factor loadings near zero. The criterion employed for the varimax rotation is

$$v \equiv \frac{1}{k}\sum_{j=1}^{k} v_j,$$

i.e., the average of the simplicities taken over the variables. This criterion has to be maximized over all orthonormal matrices T. For $k > 2$ there is no explicit solution for the varimax problem and the optimal rotation has to be found by iteration.

Up till now in MFA we have assumed $\Phi = I_k$, i.e., the factors are considered uncorrelated. This orthogonality of factors is maintained under rotation. The desirability of this is doubtful, for two reasons. The first one reflects on the subject matter. An important objective when striving for a simple structure is to see which indicators correlate with a particular factor. This sheds light on the interpretation of the factor. Considering the meaning of the indicators that correlate most with a factor is often helpful in interpreting the factor. When the various factors have thus been given a meaning, subject matter considerations may make it doubtful that these latent variables are indeed uncorrelated. Another reason why orthogonal factors may be deemed undesirable comes from the objective to obtain a simple structure. When a wider class of rotations is considered than the class of orthogonal rotations, a more transparent structure on B can be achieved.

A rotation that introduces nonorthogonality is called an *oblique* rotation. It is based on the structure (7.28) for the covariance matrix. As the scales of the various columns of B do not contribute to the interpretation of the solution, the covariance matrix Φ of the factors is restricted to have ones on its diagonal, which means that it is a correlation matrix. Let the oblique transformation be characterized by the nonsingular $k \times k$ transformation matrix F. So we have

$\Sigma = BB' + \Omega = (BF)\Phi(BF)' + \Omega$, which implies that $F\Phi F' = I_k$, or $\Phi = (F'F)^{-1}$. The restriction on Φ translates in a restriction on the transformation matrix F,

$$\operatorname{diag}\bigl((F'F)^{-1}\bigr) = I_k. \tag{7.45}$$

Evidently, this includes orthonormal matrices T as a special case because (7.45) is then trivially satisfied, but the class of matrices satisfying (7.45) is larger. The optimal transformation matrix F has to be determined according to some criterion. The most frequently used oblique rotation method is *direct oblimin*, which minimizes

$$D \equiv \sum_{j=1}^{k} \sum_{h=1}^{j-1} \left[\frac{1}{M} \sum_{i=1}^{M} b_{ij}^2 b_{ih}^2 - \delta \left(\frac{1}{M} \sum_{i=1}^{M} b_{ij}^2 \right) \left(\frac{1}{M} \sum_{i=1}^{M} b_{ih}^2 \right) \right],$$

where b_{ij} is the (i, j)-th element of BF and δ is a constant to be chosen by the researcher. Apparently, the most popular choice is $\delta \equiv 0$. The idea behind oblimin is that it minimizes the correlation between columns of the factor loadings matrix and hence tends to have zeros in one column if there is a high value in another column in the same row.

The Ledermann bound

Apart from rotational freedom, there is another identification problem in the context of MFA. When discussing one-factor FA we saw that it was identified when $M \geq 3$. With multiple FA the situation is more complex. However, a simple necessary condition for identification is easily obtained by noting that the number of sample covariances should be at least as large as the number of parameters in the model. This counting should take into account the symmetry of the sample covariance matrix (we may only count its nonduplicated elements) and the rotational freedom in B.

The number of nonduplicated elements in a symmetric matrix of order $M \times M$ is $M(M+1)/2$. The number of elements of B is Mk, with the rotational freedom accounting for $k(k-1)/2$ of these, and the number of diagonal elements in Ω is M. Therefore, a necessary condition for identification (except for rotational freedom) is

$$\tfrac{1}{2}M(M+1) \geq Mk - \tfrac{1}{2}k(k-1) + M,$$

or, after rearrangement,

$$(M-k)^2 \geq M + k. \tag{7.46}$$

This is known as the *Ledermann bound* (Ledermann, 1937). It can be shown that, in addition to being a necessary condition for identification, it is also sufficient almost everywhere in the parameter space.

Choice of the number of factors

Evidently, in an EFA context, the number k of factors that are to be "extracted" must be chosen. This choice can be made on the basis of several arguments. First, we may view this as a problem of model selection. This is a subject we will discuss more extensively in section 10.5. Here, we only note that this usually involves computing some fit statistic for several competing models and choosing a model that has an optimal fit in some sense, or a model that has acceptable fit, but is easier to interpret. Note that some of the fit statistics that are discussed in that section use the degrees of freedom of the model and it should be kept in mind that the rotational freedom of the EFA reduces the number of degrees of freedom by $k(k-1)/2$, so that the number of degrees of freedom becomes $(M-k)^2-(M+k)$, cf. (7.46).

Second, there are two commonly applied rules for the choice of the number of factors, both of which are related to the eigenvalues of the correlation matrix, which is the covariance matrix of the standardized variables. Hence, every standardized variable has a variance of 1 and if we would define this variable to be a factor, it accounts for a common variance of at least 1. Therefore, the argument is that a common factor is only substantially relevant if it explains a common variance of more than 1. In PCA, each component explains a variance equal to the corresponding eigenvalue of the correlation matrix, and hence relevant components correspond to eigenvalues larger than 1. Given the similarity between PCA and FA, this criterion may also be used as a guideline for choosing the number of factors.

The other eigenvalue-based rule is based on the so-called *scree plot*. This is a plot of the points (i, μ_i), $i = 1, \ldots, M$, where μ_i is the i-th largest eigenvalue of the correlation matrix. These points are joined by straight lines. Frequently, such a plot shows a "kink" somewhere. Before the kink, the eigenvalues drop rapidly and after the kink, they decline only gradually. The eigenvalues after the kink are viewed as unimportant departures from pure noise, which can be ignored. The number of factors is thus the number of eigenvalues before the kink. The drawback inherent to this "eyeballing" criterion is that it is somewhat subjective. Sometimes, multiple kinks may be observed and different researchers will often not agree about where the important kink lies. Of course, statistical model building is highly subjective anyway, so whether this is really a problem is doubtful.

7.4 An example of factor analysis

To illustrate the various concepts we now turn to an empirical example of exploratory factor analysis. The example concerns data on television network viewership in the Netherlands. The data matrix contains data, for $N = 2154$ individuals and $M = 7$ networks. The seven networks include the three public networks (NL1, TV2, and NL3) and the four major commercial networks (RTL4, RTL5, Veronica, and SBS6). The elements in the matrix are integers ranging from 0 to 7 and denote the number of days in one particular week that an individual has watched a network. We neglect the fact that these data are evidently not normally distributed. This does not affect consistency of the estimators (see the sections 9.2 and 9.5 for elaborations of this point). The correlation matrix derived from the data matrix is given in table 7.1.

Table 7.1 *Correlation matrix of the TV network viewing data.*

	NL1	TV2	NL3	RTL4	RTL5	Veronica	SBS6
NL1	1.000						
TV2	.661	1.000					
NL3	.610	.648	1.000				
RTL4	.378	.433	.368	1.000			
RTL5	.381	.441	.363	.542	1.000		
Veronica	.332	.428	.343	.581	.602	1.000	
SBS6	.317	.383	.301	.469	.569	.598	1.000

In order to get an idea of the number of factors to be included in the analysis, we first consider the seven eigenvalues of the correlation matrix. They are 3.791, 1.187, 0.527, 0.417, 0.396, 0.364, and 0.319. The scree plot of the eigenvalues is given in figure 7.3. The eigenvalues add up to $M = 7$ as they should, because the sum of the eigenvalues of a symmetric matrix equals the trace of the matrix, which consists of ones here because we work on a correlation matrix. The average eigenvalue equals 1. Two eigenvalues exceed 1, one considerably and the other slightly, which we take as a justification to consider two factors.

The results before rotation for MFA with two factors are given in table 7.2. The unrotated factor loadings are given in the second and third column and the error variances in the last column. Note that for each indicator the sum of the squared factor loadings plus the error variance, i.e., the corresponding diagonal element of $\hat{\Omega}$, add up to 1 because the data are from a correlation matrix. For the same reason, each communality equals 1 minus the corresponding error variance. The two factors jointly account for 50 to 70 percent of the variances in the

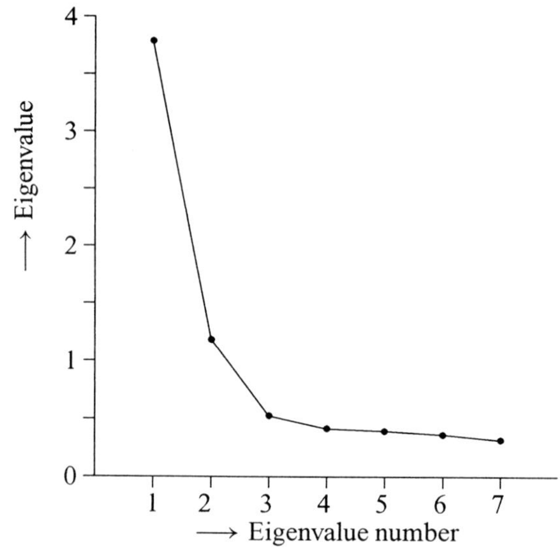

Figure 7.3 *Scree plot of the eigenvalues.*

network viewership variables.

The unrotated loadings are shown graphically in figure 7.4. The axes correspond with the two factors, and the two factor loadings of each indicator supply the coordinates. Two very pronounced clusters appear from the figure, one corresponding to the public networks, and one corresponding to the commercial networks. The distance from each point to the origin equals the square root of the communality, which lies between 0 and 1. Thus, a larger distance indicates

Table 7.2 *FA solutions of the TV network viewing example.*

variable	factor loadings						error variance
	unrotated		varimax		oblimin		
NL1	.697	−.373	.230	.757	−.024	.805	.375
TV2	.777	−.318	.326	.774	.083	.788	.295
NL3	.683	−.362	.228	.739	−.020	.785	.402
RTL4	.661	.236	.635	.300	.635	.104	.507
RTL5	.698	.302	.707	.279	.729	.050	.422
Veronica	.710	.405	.789	.215	.851	−.058	.332
SBS6	.636	.353	.699	.199	.751	−.041	.472

a larger correlation between the indicator concerned on the one hand and the factors on the other. Notice that for this example the coordinates of the indicators corresponding with viewership of NL1 and NL3 are nearly identical. This does not mean that the data are nearly identical. In fact, they differ a lot, because the correlation between these indicators is only 0.610.

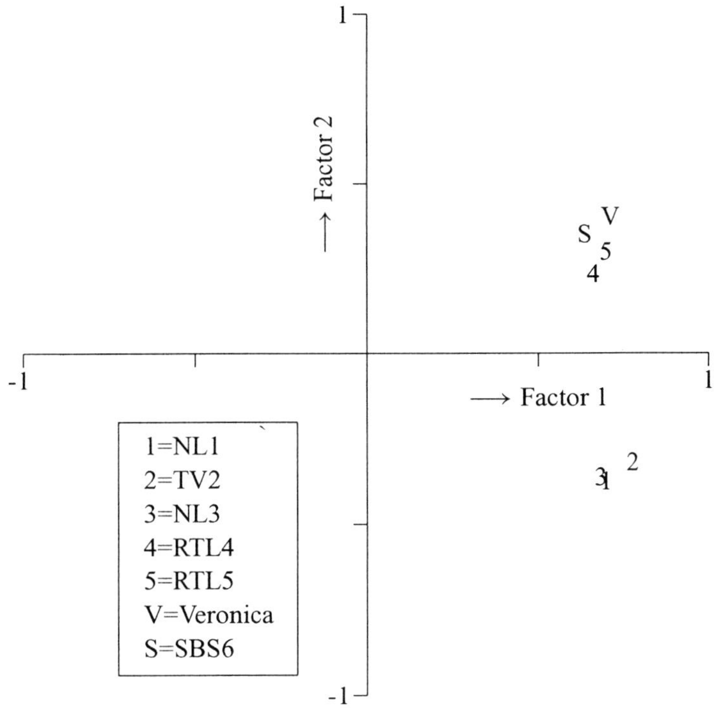

Figure 7.4 *Plot of the unrotated factor loadings of the TV network viewing data.*

In order to obtain a simpler structure the results were subjected to a varimax rotation. The factor loadings after performing this rotation are given in columns 4 and 5 of table 7.2 and are shown graphically in figure 7.5. Note that the rotation includes a reflection of the second factor. The rotation matrix is

$$T = \begin{bmatrix} .708 & .706 \\ .706 & -.708 \end{bmatrix},$$

so the angle of rotation is almost exactly 45°. This value was to be expected given the symmetry relative to the first axis in figure 7.4. The structure of the factor loadings matrix has indeed become simpler after the rotation. Each column contains elements that are either small (ranging from 0.2 to 0.3) or large (ranging from 0.7 to 0.8), and each row contains one large and one small figure.

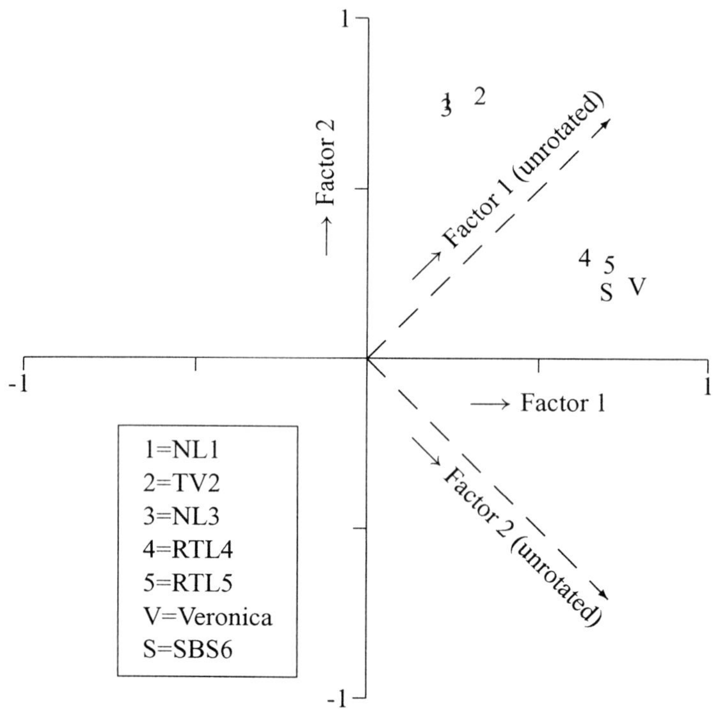

Figure 7.5 *Plot of the varimax rotated factor loadings for the TV network viewing data.*

The first three indicators, corresponding to the three public networks, are primarily correlated with the second factor and not with the first factor, and the converse holds for the four indicators of commercial network viewership. These results corroborate the existence of two factors. The first factor can be interpreted as the tendency to view the commercial networks, and the second factor as the tendency to view the public networks.

These results can be interpreted as follows. Each individual in the data set is characterized by two factor scores, one for each of the two factors. These are not directly observed and each vary over individuals from low to high and are uncorrelated. If the two-factor model is taken as a model of the data generation process, we have that for a particular individual the observation on, for example, the first indicator, viewership of NL1, has been generated as the sum of 0.230 times his or her score on the first factor, 0.757 times his or her score on the second factor, and a draw from a distribution with mean zero and variance 0.375. (Again, we abstract from complications introduced by the nonnormality of the data and the integer character of the observations.)

From the interpretation of the two factors it is clear that the imposition of a zero correlation between the two is not satisfactory. If such factors are at work in the viewers' minds, common sense suggests that they may be correlated. Inspection of the figures suggests that an even simpler structure can be obtained by an oblique rotation, with the axes transecting the clusters. The result of a direct oblimin rotation, given in columns 6 and 7 of table 7.2, brings this out clearly. The correlation between the two factors is 0.599. This means that people who watch the public channels frequently also tend to watch the commercial channels more frequently and vice versa. Apparently, the distinction between frequent viewers and infrequent viewers is more important than the distinction between commercial networks and public networks. We emphasize, though, that the latter distinction remains an important characteristic, which is clear from the figures.

7.5 Principal relations and principal factors

As we saw above, estimation in the MFA model entails the solution of an eigenvalue problem. Similarly, in the sections 5.3 and 5.4, we encountered estimators as the solution of an eigenvalue problem in the discussion of weighted and orthogonal regression, and in the sections 6.5 and 6.6, we showed that the LIML estimator is also the solution to an eigenvalue problem. In this section we take a general look at eigenvalue problems and discuss two versions of the linear measurement error model where estimation leads to an eigenvalue problem. One version is based on linear relations that restrict the space of latent variables, the other one is based on underlying factors that span the space of the latent variables. Maximum likelihood estimators for both versions are derived. In the next section a number of multivariate methods are interpreted in terms of the measurement error model, each time by imposing a certain formulation for the covariance matrix of the disturbances.

The basic linear measurement error model adopted in this section and the next one is as follows. Let there be N individuals under observation, for each of which a vector of $M < N$ variables is measured. As before, variables are assumed to be measured as deviations from the mean. The measurements are grouped into an $N \times M$ matrix Y of rank M (with probability 1), and are subject to measurement error. Let $\tilde{Y}$ be the conformable matrix of true values and E be the matrix of measurement errors, which implies the equality

$$Y = \tilde{Y} + E. \tag{7.47}$$

The elements of $\tilde{Y}$ can be either stochastic or nonstochastic, and the rows of E are assumed i.i.d. with zero expectation and covariance matrix Ω. In the sequel, we will assume that Ω is known up to a proportionality factor σ^2, except when explicitly stated otherwise.

The model is concerned with the rank of the matrix $\tilde{Y}$. Therefore, we are interested in the linear relations that exist between the columns of $\tilde{Y}$. These relations may take on either of two forms. Under the principal relations (PR) specification, there exists an $M \times l$ matrix A, with $l < M$, of full column rank such that

$$\tilde{Y}A = 0, \tag{7.48}$$

i.e., the columns of $\tilde{Y}$ are restricted to lie in an $(M - l)$-dimensional subspace. Under the principal factors (PF) specification, we view the structure in a complementary way and assume the existence of an $N \times k$ matrix Ξ and an $M \times k$ matrix B, with $k < M$ and $\operatorname{rank}(B) = \operatorname{rank}(\Xi) = k$, such that

$$\tilde{Y} = \Xi B',$$

i.e., the columns of $\tilde{Y}$ are a linear combination of the columns of Ξ, called the factors of $\tilde{Y}$. When Ω is diagonal and unknown, the PF model is the MFA model discussed earlier in this chapter. PR and PF are equivalent in the sense that they are able to impose the same restrictions on $\tilde{Y}$ when $M = k + l$.

Maximum likelihood estimation

When E is assumed to be normally distributed, the ML estimator of A (for PR) and B (for PF) can be derived. We do so first for Ω nonsingular. For PR, ML estimation of A amounts to minimizing

$$\operatorname{tr}(Y - \tilde{Y})\Omega^{-1}(Y - \tilde{Y})' \tag{7.49}$$

subject to $\tilde{Y}A = 0$. Let K $(N \times l)$ be a matrix of Lagrange multipliers, then the Lagrange function is

$$L = \operatorname{tr}(Y - \tilde{Y})\Omega^{-1}(Y - \tilde{Y})' + 2\operatorname{tr}(K'\tilde{Y}A).$$

The first-order condition with respect to $\tilde{Y}$ is $\tilde{Y}\Omega^{-1} = Y\Omega^{-1} - KA'$. Hence, $K = YA(A'\Omega A)^{-1}$ and $Y - \tilde{Y} = YA(A'\Omega A)^{-1}A'\Omega$. Substitution of this expression into (7.49) yields

$$\operatorname{tr} A'Y'YA(A'\Omega A)^{-1} \tag{7.50}$$

as the expression that has to be minimized. Let T be the $M \times M$ matrix of all generalized eigenvectors of $Y'Y$ in the metric of Ω^{-1}, normalized according to $T'\Omega T = I_M$. In other words, $Y'YT = \Omega T\Lambda$, with Λ the diagonal $M \times M$ matrix with corresponding roots $\lambda_1 > \ldots > \lambda_M$. So $T'Y'YT = T'\Omega T\Lambda = \Lambda$. (It is assumed that all roots are different in order to avoid further indeterminacies.) Without loss of generality, we can write $A = TC$, where C is some $M \times l$ matrix of rank l, and (7.50) can be rewritten as

$$\begin{aligned}
\operatorname{tr} A'Y'YA(A'\Omega A)^{-1} &= \operatorname{tr} C'T'Y'YTC(C'T'\Omega TC)^{-1} \\
&= \operatorname{tr} C'\Lambda C(C'C)^{-1} \\
&= \operatorname{tr} \Lambda C(C'C)^{-1}C' \\
&= \sum_{i=1}^{M} \lambda_i c_{ii},
\end{aligned} \tag{7.51}$$

with c_{ii} the i-th diagonal element of the idempotent matrix $C(C'C)^{-1}C'$, so $0 \leq c_{ii} \leq 1$ for any choice of C and $\sum_{i=1}^{M} c_{ii} = l$. Consequently, (7.51), and hence (7.49), is minimal when C is chosen such that $c_{M-l+1,M-l+1} = \cdots = c_{MM} = 1$, and all other c_{ii} equal to zero. This requires that the first $M - l$ rows of C be zero. Thus, A is some linear combination of the last l columns of T, and the minimum value of (7.49) is $\sum_{i=M-l+1}^{M} \lambda_i$. The solution A is not unique because it is open to rotation.

Under PF, we have to minimize (7.49) with $\tilde{Y} = \Xi B'$. Thus, the function that has to be minimized is

$$\operatorname{tr}(Y - \Xi B')\Omega^{-1}(Y - \Xi B')'. \tag{7.52}$$

The first-order condition with respect to Ξ is $Y\Omega^{-1}B = \Xi B'\Omega^{-1}B$. Hence,

$$\Xi = Y\Omega^{-1}B(B'\Omega^{-1}B)^{-1}.$$

Substitution in (7.52) yields

$$\operatorname{tr} B'\Omega^{-1}Y'Y\Omega^{-1}B(B'\Omega^{-1}B)^{-1} \tag{7.53}$$

as the expression that has to be *maximized* with respect to B. This contrasts with the expression in (7.50), which had to be *minimized*. On defining $A = \Omega^{-1}B$, (7.53) reduces to (7.50). The only difference is that now we have to maximize a trace, which means that the eigenvectors corresponding to the *largest* roots should be chosen.

Some of the models dealt with below are cases of PR with singular Ω. This requires an adaptation of the proof. Let Ω be of rank s ($l \leq s \leq M$), then its eigenvalue decomposition can be written as $\Omega = U\Delta U'$, with U an $M \times s$ matrix of eigenvectors of Ω corresponding to its nonzero eigenvalues, which are the elements of the diagonal matrix Δ, and, of course, $U'U = I_s$. Let V be an $M \times (M - s)$ matrix of eigenvectors of Ω corresponding to its zero roots. Thus, we have $V'V = I_{M-s}$, $U'V = 0$, and $UU' + VV' = I_M$. As $YV = \tilde{Y}V + EV$ and $EV = 0$ by definition, $YV = \tilde{Y}V$.

For PR, ML estimation of A amounts to minimizing $\operatorname{tr}(Y - \tilde{Y})\Omega^+(Y - \tilde{Y})'$ subject to $\tilde{Y}A = 0$ and $YV = \tilde{Y}V$, where Ω^+ is the Moore-Penrose inverse of Ω. Let K_1 ($N \times l$) and K_2 ($N \times M - s$) be matrices of Lagrange multipliers, then the Lagrange function is

$$L = \operatorname{tr}(Y - \tilde{Y})\Omega^+(Y - \tilde{Y})' + 2\operatorname{tr}(K_1'\tilde{Y}A) + 2\operatorname{tr}K_2'(Y - \tilde{Y})V.$$

The first-order condition with respect to $\tilde{Y}$ is $\tilde{Y}\Omega^+ = Y\Omega^+ - K_1A' + K_2V'$. Postmultiplication by $U\Delta$ and using $\Omega^+ = U\Delta^{-1}U'$ yields $\tilde{Y}U = YU - K_1A'U\Delta$. Combining this with $\tilde{Y}V = YV$ gives $\tilde{Y}(U, V) = Y(U, V) - (K_1A'U\Delta, 0)$. Postmultiplication by the inverse of (U, V), i.e., by $(U, V)'$ in view of the orthonormality of this matrix, yields

$$\tilde{Y} = Y - (K_1A'U\Delta, 0)\begin{bmatrix} U' \\ V' \end{bmatrix} = Y - K_1A'\Omega.$$

Thus, $\tilde{Y}A = YA - K_1A'\Omega A$. As $\tilde{Y}A = 0$, it follows that $K_1 = YA(A'\Omega A)^{-1}$. Substitution in the objective function yields (7.50), and the remainder of the derivation is the same as in the case of Ω being of full rank.

7.6 A taxonomy of eigenvalue-based methods

We now turn to a number of models and methods that fit into the PR or PF class. A variable will be called endogenous if the corresponding diagonal element of Ω is positive. If it is zero, the corresponding variable is called exogenous. In this case, the entire corresponding row and column of Ω are zero and hence, Ω is of deficient rank.

Table 7.3 captures the main characteristics of the models discussed in this section. It shows the method, the number of endogenous variables, the number of exogenous variables, whether there are one or two sets of variables, whether or not these sets play a symmetric role, and the type (PR or PF) to which the method belongs.

Table 7.3 *Summary of the various methods discussed.*

method	number of variables: endogenous	number of variables: exogenous	1 or 2 sets	Sym.? (if 2 sets)	PR or PF
Factor analysis	M	0	1	–	PF
OLS	1	$M-1$	2	asym.	PR
Measurement error	M	0	2	sym.	PR
Weighted regression	M	0	1	–	PR
Orthogonal regression	M	0	1	–	PR
PCA	M	0	1	–	PF
Canonical correlation	$M = M_1 + M_2$	0	2	sym.	PF
Canonical regression	M_1	M_2	2	asym.	PR
LIML*	$M = 1 + g$	0	2	sym.	PR
IV*	1	$M - 1 = g$	2	asym.	PR

* With LIML and IV, the variables are first projected onto the space of the instruments.

Factor analysis

Evidently, factor analysis is the standard case of PF with Ω diagonal, except that in FA Ω is not known. Hence, the PF problem is a subproblem of the FA problem, the other subproblem being the estimation of Ω. As stated earlier in this chapter, estimators can be obtained by iteratively switching between the two subproblems.

Linear regression

Ordinary linear regression of one endogenous variable (the i-th, say) on all the other (exogenous) variables is derived from the PR model by letting $l = 1$ and $\Omega = \sigma^2 e_i e_i'$, with e_i the i-th unit vector. Take $i = 1$ for simplicity, normalize $A = \alpha = (1, -\beta')'$ and write $Y = (y, X)$, $\tilde{Y} = (\tilde{y}, X)$ and $E = (\varepsilon, 0)$. Then, (7.48) becomes $\tilde{Y}\alpha = \tilde{y} - X\beta = 0$, so $\tilde{y} = X\beta$, and from (7.47),

$$y = \tilde{y} + \varepsilon = X\beta + \varepsilon.$$

Taking $i = 1, \ldots, M$ successively defines linear regression of each of the columns of Y on the other columns. Note that the choice of the nonzero elements in Ω determines which variables are exogenous and which variable is endogenous. It is easy to show that the OLS estimator coincides with the ML estimator in the PR case thus defined for $\Omega = \sigma^2 e_i e_i'$ and $l = 1$.

The single equation measurement error model arises when Ω has the structure

$$\Omega = \sigma^2 \begin{bmatrix} 1 & 0 \\ 0 & \Omega_0 \end{bmatrix},$$

with Ω_0 representing the presence of measurement errors in the regressors. The model with Ω_0 unknown was discussed in detail in chapter 2. The model with known Ω_0 was discussed in section 5.3 on weighted regression.

Note that all variables are assumed to be measured in deviations from the mean, instead of from zero origin. If the variables are measured from zero origin, the same results can be arrived at if we add a column of ones to Y, which is assumed to be "measured" without error. The same statement also holds for the other methods in this section.

Orthogonal regression and principal components

For $\Omega = \sigma^2 I_M$ and $l = 1$, all variables are dealt with in a symmetric way and we have to solve

$$\left(Y'Y - \lambda I_M\right)\alpha = 0, \tag{7.54}$$

for λ minimal, which is the orthogonal regression model discussed in section 5.4. Distances are measured perpendicular to the $(M - 1)$-dimensional hyperplane $\tilde{Y}\alpha = 0$. The complement of α, i.e., the set of eigenvectors corresponding to the $(M - 1)$ largest roots of $Y'Y$, corresponds with the set of $(M - 1)$ first principal components of Y. PCA was introduced earlier in this chapter. In other words, orthogonal regression corresponds with the last principal component of Y. The first principal component $\Xi = Y\alpha$ corresponds with the models $\tilde{Y}A = 0$, $\text{rank}(A) = M - 1$ (PR) and $\tilde{Y} = \Xi B'$, $\text{rank}(\Xi) = 1$ (PF); α follows from (7.54) with λ maximal.

As was already noted in section 7.2, a problem with PCA is its dependence on the scale of Y. Given the close connection between PCA and OR just discussed, this problem holds for OR as well. This dependence is obvious, because E is measured in the same units as Y is, and a change in scale of Y should affect Ω. A possible solution is to take Ω proportional to the diagonal matrix containing the diagonal elements of $Y'Y$. This solution makes OR and PCA invariant to scale values, as the error variances are now assumed to be proportional to the sample variances. This results in PCA on the correlation matrix.

Canonical correlation and canonical regression

Let Y be partitioned according to $Y = (Y_{(1)}, Y_{(2)})$, where $Y_{(1)}$ has M_1 columns and $Y_{(2)}$ has M_2 columns. We consider the case where the errors are correlated within the sets but the errors are uncorrelated between the sets. Furthermore, the error variances are assumed to be proportional to the sample variances. Thus, we obtain

$$\Omega = \sigma^2 \begin{bmatrix} Y'_{(1)}Y_{(1)} & 0 \\ 0 & Y'_{(2)}Y_{(2)} \end{bmatrix}. \tag{7.55}$$

Solving the PF problem with $l = 1$ and Ω as specified in (7.55) is equivalent to the method of maximizing the canonical correlation between the two sets. The canonical loadings $\alpha' = (\alpha'_{(1)}, \alpha'_{(2)})$ follow from $(Y'Y - \lambda\Omega)\alpha = 0$, with Ω as in (7.55) and λ maximal. Due to the two-way structure of Ω, the PR solution for α (corresponding to λ minimal) equals the PF (and canonical correlation) solution, except for the sign of $\alpha_{(2)}$.

If there are two sets of variables as in canonical correlation, but one of them is taken to be nonstochastic, as in OLS, one arrives at what is sometimes called *canonical regression*. This is defined as the PR model in which Ω is taken to be

$$\Omega = \sigma^2 \begin{bmatrix} Y'_{(1)}Y_{(1)} & 0 \\ 0 & 0 \end{bmatrix}.$$

Canonical regression is a regression model with $M_1 > 1$ endogenous variables, which are to be scaled such that their linear combination has maximum correlation with the M_2 exogenous variables. It can easily be shown that the canonical regression solution equals the canonical correlation solution except for a different normalization on the subvector of coefficients corresponding with $Y_{(2)}$.

LIML and IV

The LIML estimator was derived in section 6.5 as the solution to the generalized eigenproblem

$$(S - \lambda S_{\perp})\delta = 0,$$

with $S \equiv (y, X)'P_Z(y, X)$, $S_{\perp} \equiv (y, X)'M_Z(y, X)$, $\delta \equiv (1, -\beta')'$, and λ minimal. Although the similarity with the current framework is striking, this does not appear to fit straightforwardly into one of the classes. After a transformation of variables, however, it does. Choose $Y \equiv P_Z(y, X)$, $\alpha \equiv \delta$, and $\Omega \equiv (y, X)'M_Z(y, X)$, then we obtain

$$(Y'Y - \lambda\Omega)\alpha = 0,$$

and LIML is a special case of PR on the transformed variables, i.e., with y and X first projected onto the space spanned by the columns of Z. IV is obtained with the same choice of Y, but with $\Omega = \sigma^2 e_1 e_1'$, which confirms that IV is OLS after projection onto the space of Z.

7.7 Bibliographical notes

7.1 The problem of negative variances in the one-factor model with three indicators was studied extensively by Dijkstra (1992). He also derived explicit formulas for the ML estimator in this case. Solutions with negative variances (or variances that are estimated to be zero, if the nonnegativity is explicitly imposed) are called *Heywood cases* after Heywood (1931). These are discussed in most textbooks about factor analysis. Other references include Van Driel (1978), Rindskopf (1984a), and Boomsma (1985).

Factor analysis has its roots in psychometrics, more specifically in the measurement of (different forms of) intelligence (Spearman, 1904). For a basic description highlighting the relevance for econometrics, see Goldberger (1971).

A simple but extensive and useful introduction to the topic of multiple indicators is Sullivan and Feldman (1979). Path diagrams were developed by Wright (1918, 1920, 1921). An early review of the method is Wright (1934). Originally, the method was devised for regression and correlation methods for observed variables. Later, the basic principles were extended to incorporate latent variables.

7.2 Maximum likelihood estimation of FA as an iterative switching between solving the eigenvalue problem and updating Ω has a long history, but eigenvalue problems are computationally intensive, which has hampered the application of ML for a long time. The breakthrough in the application of ML to FA came with the theoretical work of Jöreskog (1967), who proposed to optimize the loglikelihood function by the fast Davidon-Fletcher-Powell method (see, e.g., Gill, Murray, and Wright, 1981). He also provided a series of computer programs since the late 1960s, which eventually culminated in the well-known LISREL program, see chapter 8.

PCA, like orthogonal regression, can be traced back to Pearson (1901b), but the method was reintroduced and popularized by Hotelling (1933). An important development was the discovery of the singular value decomposition by Eckart and Young (1936). There are several criteria that lead to the principal components solution. The one presented as based on approximating a matrix by one of lower rank is due to Eckart and Young (1936). Others are based on maximizing the variance of the components (with a restricted in length) or the correlation between the components and the variables. An extensive discussion of these issues can be found in Ten Berge and Kiers (1996); see also Cadima and Jolliffe (1997) and Ten Berge and Kiers (1997). Ten Berge (1993) derived the PCA solution as a global minimum without relying on first-order derivative conditions. The computation of the SVD is discussed in detail by Golub and Van Loan (1996).

Discussions of PCA can generally be found in the same books on multivariate analysis that also discuss factor analysis. The relationships and differences between PCA and FA have been explored in Velicer and Jackson (1990), Schneeweiss and Mathes (1995), and Ogasawara (2000).

One situation where PCA has been advocated in econometrics is in the context of simultaneous equations models with insufficient observations. See, e.g., Kloek and Mennes (1960) or Amemiya (1966).

7.3 The literature on factor analysis is enormous. Textbooks with applied introductions include Harman (1976), Loehlin (1987), and Lewis-Beck (1994). More statistical textbooks are Lawley and Maxwell (1971), Mulaik (1972), Gorsuch (1974), McDonald (1985), Basilevsky (1994), and Bartholomew and Knott (1999). FA is also generally treated in books on multivariate analysis, e.g., Anderson (1984b) or Morrison (1990).

Identification and the Ledermann bound are treated in Shapiro (1985c) and, in particular, by Bekker and Ten Berge (1997). They showed, in addition to the identification result mentioned in the text, that if M and k are such that (7.46) is a *strict* inequality, the identification is global almost everywhere. If M and k are exactly on the Ledermann bound, i.e., such that (7.46) is an equality, then there are multiple solutions in many cases.

Mooijaart (1985) showed that if the variables are nonnormally distributed and the factors are assumed independent rather than just uncorrelated, the EFA model is generally identified without rotational freedom. This result was further extended by Meijer (1998, p. 17).

As mentioned above, maximum likelihood estimation has been extensively discussed by Jöreskog (1967). For estimation by instrumental variables, see Hägglund (1982).

Overviews of factor score predictors have been given by McDonald and Burr (1967) and Krijnen, Wansbeek, and Ten Berge (1996). The regression predictor was proposed by Thurstone (1935). As mentioned in the text, the Bartlett predictor is due to Bartlett (1937). Meijer and Wansbeek (1999) showed that, if the variables are nonnormally distributed, an asymptotically more efficient predictor can be obtained as a quadratic function of the indicators. This uses higher order moments of the variables.

A somewhat annoying feature of most factor score predictors is that, although the assumed covariance matrix of the factors is Φ, the covariance matrix of the predictors is not Φ, but, $\Phi - \Lambda^{-1} < \Phi$ for the regression predictor and $\Phi + (B'\Omega^{-1}B)^{-1} > \Phi$ for the Bartlett predictor. It is sometimes deemed desirable that the covariance matrix of the predictors is exactly equal to the estimated covariance matrix of the factors, so $\mathrm{E}(\hat{\xi}_n \hat{\xi}_n') = \mathrm{E}(\xi_n \xi_n')$ or $L'\Sigma L = \Phi$. Minimizing the MSE (7.39) under this restriction on L leads to prediction methods that are called covariance (or correlation) preserving. A discussion of these methods can be found in Ten Berge, Krijnen, Wansbeek, and Shapiro (1999).

A brief review of aspects of indeterminacy and interpretation is given by Elffers, Bethlehem, and Gill (1978). As to a simple structure, Thurstone (1947) gave five desirable characteristics as to what a simple structure should look like. Rotations are discussed in most books that treat factor analysis, e.g., Lawley and Maxwell (1971, chapter 6) or Loehlin (1987, chapter 6). The varimax method is due to Kaiser (1958). Nevels (1986) gives an explicit expression for the varimax solution in the two-factor case. Direct oblimin was introduced by Jennrich and Sampson (1966).

7.4 The data used in the example are from the "Continu Kijkonderzoek" of Intomart BV.

7.5 This section and the following one are based on Keller and Wansbeek (1983). They also discussed the case where the variables are categorical, and scale values, to be estimated jointly with the structural parameters, are assigned to the various categories. A similar discussion was given by Anderson (1984a).

7.6 A more extensive description of some of the methods discussed here can be found in books on multivariate analysis, e.g., Anderson (1984b) or Morrison (1990). The incorporation of LIML into the current framework is similar to Keller (1975), who derived a class of LIML-related estimators by considering different choices of Ω.

Chapter 8

Structural equation models

In this chapter we follow on the discussion of the factor analysis model in the previous chapter. Two kinds of factor analysis were distinguished, exploratory factor analysis (EFA) and confirmatory factor analysis (CFA). EFA was dealt with in the previous chapter, CFA being deferred until the present chapter. In section 8.1 we start out by giving two examples of CFA models, followed by a discussion of identification in CFA. In section 8.2, the model is extended with explanatory variables, called multiple causes in this context, which leads to the MIMIC model and the related reduced rank regression model.

In section 8.3, a general model system called the LISREL model is introduced, which encompasses most of the models discussed previously in this book as special cases. Other equally general parameterizations, the EQS and RAM models, are discussed in section 8.4, where it is shown that the three specifications are all equivalent. The pros and cons of the various specifications are briefly indicated. The general model class, of which LISREL, EQS, and RAM are different but equivalent operationalizations, is called (linear) *structural equation models*, frequently abbreviated as SEM.

In section 7.2, we already encountered the concept of scale invariance of a model and the resulting possibility to estimate the model from the correlation matrix. In section 8.5, we will come back to this issue and discuss the various aspects of scaling of the variables for general structural equation models.

In most cases, means of variables and intercepts of regression equations are either uninteresting or straightforward to estimate from sample means. Therefore, structural equation models are usually specified for variables with zero means. In some cases, however, there is reason to consider means and intercepts explicitly, most notably in panel data models. This implies that the models are extended with mean structures, which are discussed in section 8.6. Finally, the substantively important but usually ignored problem of equivalent models is discussed briefly in section 8.7.

At this point, it may be noted that there is an unfortunate duplication of terminology, because "structural" has two different meanings. The first is the opposite of "functional" and means that the (exogenous) variables are considered random variables with a certain distribution, and the second denotes the "structural" form of a simultaneous equation regression model as opposed to the "reduced" form. In SEM, "structural" is considered in the latter sense, although in the vast majority of cases, structural assumptions in the former sense are also made concerning the variables. This is, however, not always the case. In particular, for exogenous variables that are measured without error, functional assumptions may be more relevant and are easily incorporated.

8.1 Confirmatory factor analysis

As discussed in the previous chapter, EFA, which basically is one of the many tools from the toolbox for exploratory data analysis, contrasts with CFA, where the parameter matrices are structured by subject matter theory or at least some prior thoughts about relations between the variables. The structure implied usually takes on the form of (linear) restrictions on the parameter matrices B, Φ, and Ω in the factor analytic structure $\Sigma = B\Phi B' + \Omega$. Hence, CFA is also referred to as restricted factor analysis. In order to illustrate how restricted matrices arise we will first mention a few examples of confirmatory FA. Next we deal with the issue of identification. Estimation can be done rather straightforwardly by maximum likelihood, as discussed in the sections 7.2 and 7.3 for exploratory FA. Alternative estimation methods are given in chapter 9, and statistical inference is discussed in chapter 10. Given the estimates of the parameter matrices, factor score prediction in the CFA model has already been discussed in section 7.3.

Examples of confirmatory FA

As a first example of CFA we reconsider the TV viewership data from section 7.4. We saw that it was possible to obtain, through oblique rotation introducing a correlation between the factors, a structure with in each row of the estimate of B one large element and one element close to zero. As another approach, one could imagine that some kind of theory would suggest the existence of two correlated latent variables driving the attention given to public and commercial networks, to be measured through separate sets of indicators. Then, the model that has to be estimated is a CFA model, that is, an MFA model where B and Φ are structured according to

$$B = \begin{bmatrix} * & 0 \\ * & 0 \\ * & 0 \\ 0 & * \\ 0 & * \\ 0 & * \\ 0 & * \end{bmatrix} \qquad \text{and} \qquad \Phi = \begin{bmatrix} 1 & * \\ * & 1 \end{bmatrix},$$

where an asterisk indicates a free element, with the understanding that the two free elements in Φ are of course identical. A path diagram of this model is given in figure 8.1. Path diagrams were introduced in section 7.1. In addition to the conventions in drawing path diagrams discussed there, we use a curved, two-headed arrow to indicate a correlation between two variables.

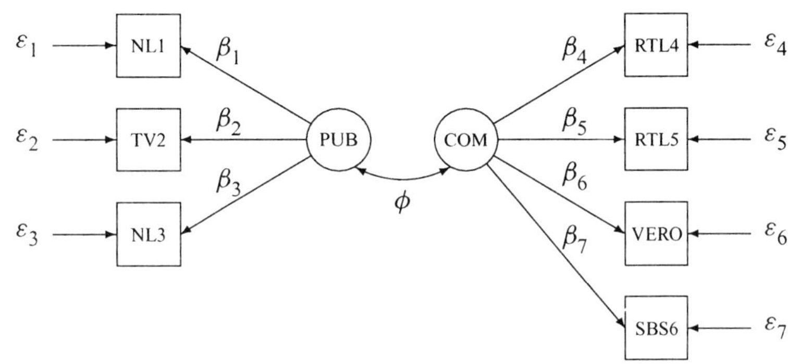

Figure 8.1 *Path diagram for the network viewership model.*

To compare CFA with oblimin rotated MFA, we present the CFA estimation results for B and Ω in table 8.1. As was to be expected, these results closely resemble the oblimin results presented in table 7.2. The estimator of the off-diagonal element of Φ equals 0.625, which is also close to the oblimin value, which equals 0.599.

We introduce a second example of CFA directly through its path diagram, which is given in figure 8.2. This model fits in a line of research on central bank independence (CBI), where differences between countries in CBI are related to macro-economic performance, in particular the degree of inflation. A crucial issue is to assess whether countries where the central banks are less independent from the political process are more open to political pressure to spend and as a result to have higher inflation.

Table 8.1 *CFA solution of the TV network viewing model.*

variable	factor loadings		error variance
NL1	.777		.396
TV2	.856		.267
NL3	.763		.418
RTL4		.710	.496
RTL5		.770	.407
Veronica		.800	.360
SBS6		.719	.483

In this literature, two variables may be considered, one (LEG in the path diagram) denoting the independence of central banks as institutionalized in its legal status, and the other (CON) the degree of conservatism of the central banks. Both variables are evidently latent variables, and indicators are required for empirical research.

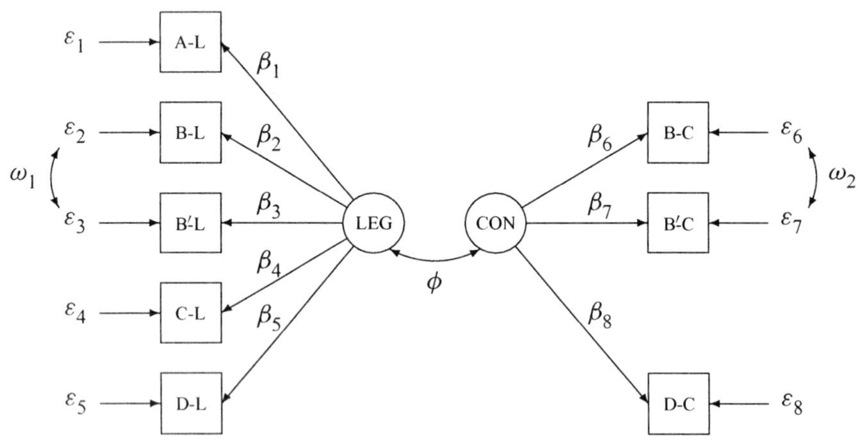

Figure 8.2 *Path diagram of the CBI model.*

The path diagram shows five indicators for LEG and three for CON. The indicators are the observable counterparts of the latent variables as proposed by a number of authors, with a letter after the hyphen denoting the latent variable involved. These authors (or groups of authors) are denoted by A, B, B', C, and D. The groups of authors behind B and B' overlap, and the two resulting indicators are actually differently weighted combinations of the same underlying variables. This suggests a correlation between the indicators not solely due to communality, i.e., correlation with the underlying latent variable, but also a correlation between the error terms. Therefore, the figure exhibits a correlation between ε_2 and ε_3, and between ε_6 and ε_7.

This CFA model seems to be at variance with the general MFA structure, where Ω was taken to be diagonal from the outset. By a redefinition of variables, however, it is possible to let this model fit the MFA specification. This is obtained by considering ε_2, ε_3, ε_6, and ε_7 as "factors" rather than error terms, so in terms of the general formulation $y_n = B\xi_n + \varepsilon_n$ as elements of ξ. The corresponding elements of the redefined ε are zero (with probability one) by restricting their variance to zero. On doing so, Φ becomes a 6×6 matrix with three 2×2 blocks on the diagonal, where the off-diagonal elements in the three blocks contain the correlation between LEG and CON, the covariance between ε_2 and ε_3, and the covariance between ε_6 and ε_7. The expansion of ξ requires a corresponding expansion of B. Four columns should be added to B. The first additional column contains the factor loadings for ε_2. This column has 1 as its second element, the other elements being zero. The other three additional columns are structured analogously. The general conclusion is that the CFA formulation has a wider applicability than may be apparent at first sight.

In practice, however, CFA models are redefined by freeing the off-diagonal elements of Ω directly, whenever applicable, rather than by this somewhat clumsy reparameterization into the restrictive framework. The general principles behind this reparameterization, however, are useful, because they can be applied to fit nonstandard models in a standard framework. These principles will also be used in section 8.4.

Identification in CFA

Identification of a particular instance of the CFA model depends on the number and position of the restrictions on the parameter matrices. In many cases it can be established quickly. For example, in the first example given above, the number of parameters to be estimated equals 15 and the number of covariance or moment equations is 21, so a necessary condition for identification is easily established. In fact the model can be seen to be identified. The factor analytic submodels that are implied for the public networks and the commercial networks separately are one-factor models with three and four indicators, respectively, which are identified, and thus serve to identify B and Ω. The remaining parameter is the off-diagonal element of Φ. This parameter can be consistently estimated (and hence is identified) from the correlation between one arbitrarily chosen indicator for public network viewership and one arbitrarily chosen indicator of commercial network viewership, rescaled by the estimates of the corresponding factor loadings. The nonuniqueness of this estimator does of course not affect the argument on identification.

In the second, somewhat more complicated, example given above, the situation is less transparent and a more general treatment is called for. Let us assume that the data are normally distributed. This is a conservative assumption from the point of view of identification, as we have seen in chapter 4, because in that case only the matrix of second-order moments supplies information on the parameters.

We first consider a general case where B, Φ, and Ω depend on a parameter vector θ. According to section 4.4, the identification in such a case can be assessed by determining the rank of the Jacobian matrix

$$\begin{aligned} A(\theta) &= \frac{\partial \operatorname{vec}\left(B\Phi B' + \Omega\right)}{\partial \theta'} \\ &= 2Q_M(B\Phi \otimes I_M)B_\theta + (B \otimes B)\Phi_\theta + \Omega_\theta, \end{aligned} \tag{8.1}$$

where $B_\theta \equiv \partial \operatorname{vec} B/\partial\theta'$, $\Phi_\theta \equiv \partial \operatorname{vec} \Phi/\partial\theta'$, and $\Omega_\theta \equiv \partial \operatorname{vec} \Omega/\partial\theta'$; see (7.29) for the derivation of the partial derivatives of $\operatorname{vec} \Sigma$ with respect to the elements of B. If the true value θ_0 of θ is a regular point of $A(\theta)$, then the model is identified if and only if $A(\theta)$ has full column rank in θ_0.

In CFA, the parameter matrices are usually linearly restricted and B_θ, Φ_θ, and Ω_θ are fixed matrices, C_B, C_Φ, and C_Ω, say. A simplification of the identification condition is possible if Ω on the one hand and B and Φ on the other involve different parameters, which will often be the case. We write the restrictions on Ω as $R'_\Omega \operatorname{vec} \Omega = r_\Omega$, with R_Ω (a complement of C_Ω, so $R'_\Omega C_\Omega = 0$) a fixed matrix and r_Ω a fixed vector. If we redefine θ to pertain only to the free parameters in B and Φ (and adapt C_B and C_Φ accordingly), then identification of the model parameters is equivalent to the condition that the matrix

$$\tilde{A}(\theta) = R'_\Omega\left(2Q_M(B\Phi \otimes I_M)C_B + (B \otimes B)C_\Phi\right)$$

is of full column rank. This can be seen when $A(\theta)$ in (8.1) is premultiplied by the nonsingular matrix $(R_\Omega, C_\Omega^{+'})'$, with $C_\Omega^+ = (C'_\Omega C_\Omega)^{-1} C'_\Omega$. Because Ω on the one hand and B and Φ on the other hand do not share parameters, we may write $A(\theta)$ as $(A_1(\theta), C_\Omega)$. After the premultiplication, $A(\theta)$ becomes

$$\begin{bmatrix} \tilde{A}(\theta) & 0 \\ C_\Omega^+ A_1(\theta) & I \end{bmatrix}.$$

This matrix is of the same rank as $A(\theta)$ and is of full rank if and only if $\tilde{A}(\theta)$ is of full rank.

Checking the rank of such a Jacobian matrix by hand can be a formidable and even impossible job. A practical approach is to fill in numerical values for the parameters and checking the rank at that particular point. Although this will work in many instances, it is not a really satisfactory approach, because the choice of numerical values can be unfortunate, but especially because computing singular values of large matrices can be troubled by numerical inaccuracies.

An alternative approach is to use computer algebra to do the required computations analytically. This is most conveniently done by using the program IDFAC (see Bekker et al., 1994), which is tailor-made for the purpose. It requires as input the values of M and k plus the restrictions. It delivers as output a matrix spanning the null-space of the Jacobian. If the Jacobian is of full column rank, the null-space is empty, which implies that all parameters are identified. If the null-space is not empty, there are identification problems and the nonzero rows in the matrix that spans the null-space indicate the parameters that are not identified.

8.2 Multiple causes and the MIMIC model

Up till now, we have been concerned with an elaboration of equation (7.1c), which offered additional information about the otherwise unidentified parameters in the form of an additional indicator. The latent variable appeared once more as the exogenous variable in yet another regression equation. Another way in which additional information may be available is in the form of a regression equation where the latent variable appears as the *endogenous* variable, on the left-hand side. Instead of (or in addition to) an additional indicator, we now have a relation that explains ξ_n:

$$\xi_n = w_n'\alpha + u_n,$$

where w_n is the l-vector of observable variables that "cause" ξ_n, α is an l-vector of regression coefficients, and u_n is an i.i.d. disturbance term with mean zero and variance σ_u^2.

To mention one situation where such a model may be relevant, think of an Engel curve model where the expenditure on some good is explained by income. Income is imperfectly measured. The cause relationship then specifies the process by which income is generated. The vector w_n may contain variables like age, experience, and schooling. We now investigate how such an additional relation helps identification. To that end we collect the full model and write it down for all observations. This yields

$$\begin{aligned} y &= \xi\beta + \varepsilon \\ x &= \xi + v \\ \xi &= W\alpha + u. \end{aligned} \tag{8.2}$$

By eliminating ξ, we obtain

$$(y, x) = W(\alpha\beta, \alpha) + U, \tag{8.3}$$

where $U \equiv (\varepsilon + \beta u, v + u)$. The covariance matrix Σ_U of every row of U is

$$\Sigma_U = \begin{bmatrix} \sigma_\varepsilon^2 + \beta^2\sigma_u^2 & \beta\sigma_u^2 \\ \beta\sigma_u^2 & \sigma_v^2 + \sigma_u^2 \end{bmatrix}.$$

Thus, the model is a multiple equation model (8.3) that is subject to restrictions. The $l \times 2$ matrix of regression coefficients in the reduced form is of rank 1 because its two columns are proportional, they differ by a scalar factor β. This is, of course, only restrictive if $l > 1$. Evidently, α and β are identified as well as the parameters in Σ_U. We conclude that an additional relation that explains the latent variable renders the model identified.

As a more general case, consider the situation where M indicators of the latent variable ξ are available, as in the MFA model, so that we have

$$Y = \xi\beta' + E, \tag{8.4}$$

where the rows of E are i.i.d. as before, with covariance matrix Ω. The model consisting of (8.2) and (8.4) is known as the *multiple indicators multiple causes* (MIMIC) model. It relates a single unobservable to a number of indicators and a number of exogenous variables. A path diagram of the MIMIC model with $M = l = 3$ is given in figure 8.3. This figure shows the distinctive wasp-waisted character of MIMIC path diagrams and illustrates that the dependence of the indicators on the causes is channeled through the single latent variable. Note that the correlations among the exogenous variables are not shown in the figure, although they should be taken into account in the model specification.

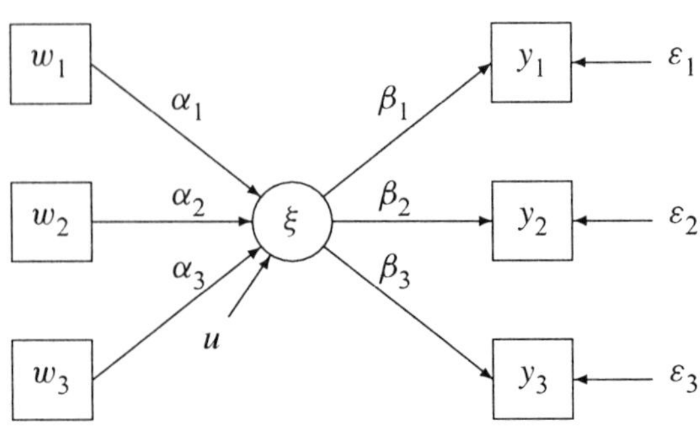

Figure 8.3 *Path diagram of the MIMIC model with $M = l = 3$.*

After substitution of (8.2) into (8.4), the MIMIC model reduces to

$$Y = W\alpha\beta' + (E + u\beta').$$

This multivariate regression system imposes two kinds of restrictions on its parameters. First, the matrix of regression coefficients has rank one. Second, the rows of the disturbance matrix have covariance matrix

$$\Sigma \equiv \Omega + \sigma_u^2 \beta\beta', \tag{8.5}$$

which is the sum of a diagonal matrix and a matrix of rank one.

There is an indeterminacy in the triplet α, β, and σ_u^2. The product $\alpha\beta'$ remains the same when α is multiplied by an arbitrary constant, β is divided by the same constant, and σ_u^2 is adapted likewise. This indeterminacy can be removed, for example, by the normalization $\sigma_u^2 = 1$.

The MIMIC model comprises several models as special cases. When no cause relation (8.2) is present, we have the one-factor FA model. If in (8.2) $u = 0$, i.e., the latent variable is an exact linear function of a set of explanatory variables, we obtain a model due to Zellner (1970). This model was inspired by the problem of dealing with permanent income as an explanatory variable. In this model, y denotes consumption, x observed income and ξ permanent income. By expressing permanent income as a function of variables like house value, educational attainment, and age, permanent income can be eliminated. Simultaneous estimation of the complete reduced form of the model, however, increases the precision of the estimates.

A restriction of the MIMIC model is the diagonality of Ω, the covariance matrix of the rows of E. This means that the indicators satisfy the usual factor analysis assumption that they are correlated only via the latent variable. This assumption may be unduly strong, and we may consider an unrestricted Ω as an alternative. This introduces a further indeterminacy, because

$$\Omega + \sigma_u^2 \beta\beta' = (\Omega + \varphi\beta\beta') + (\sigma_u^2 - \varphi)\beta\beta'$$

for any scalar φ. This indeterminacy may be solved by fixing σ_u^2 at some non-negative value, e.g., $\sigma_u^2 = 0$. This means that, in the case of Ω unrestricted, the model is observationally equivalent to a model without an error in the cause equation.

Reduced rank regression

A frequently used generalization of the MIMIC model is the *reduced rank regression* (RRR) model. It extends MIMIC in two ways. First, the rank of the coefficient matrix can be larger than one, and second, the error covariance matrix need not be structured. The resulting model equation is

$$Y = WAB' + E,$$

where A and B are $l \times r$ and $M \times r$ matrices, respectively, both of full column rank $r < \min(M, l)$, and E has i.i.d. rows with expectation zero and unrestricted covariance matrix Ω. In its general form, A and B are not identified, because $A^* B^{*\prime} \equiv (AF)(F^{-1}B') = AB'$ for every nonsingular $r \times r$ matrix F.

Part of the indeterminacy may be removed by requiring the columns of $\Xi \equiv WA$ to be orthonormal. This only leaves a rotation problem, which may be solved by optimizing a standard optimality criterion. In this case, the model can be viewed as a kind of principal components analysis with the additional restriction that the "components" should lie in the column space of the exogenous variables W. In some cases, substantive theory may impose restrictions on A, B, and Ω, which may resolve the identification problem. In other cases, an arbitrary normalization can be used.

The reduced rank regression model resembles some of the models discussed in section 7.6, but still does not seem to fit into the principal relations and principal factors framework described in section 7.5. It looks like a PF model with $\tilde{Y} = WAB'$ and $\Xi = WA$, where the latter is a PR restriction. As such, it may be viewed as a two-level PF/PR model. Note, however, that we can transform the model to $\tilde{Y}\tilde{B} - WA = 0$, where $\tilde{B} = B(B'B)^{-1}$. This is a matrix with as many elements as B and also unrestricted if B is unrestricted. Hence, this is a PR model. The full specification in terms of the PR model is now $Y^{\text{PR}} = (Y, W)^{\text{RRR}}$, $\tilde{Y}^{\text{PR}} = (WAB', W)^{\text{RRR}}$, and consequently

$$\Omega^{\text{PR}} = \begin{bmatrix} \Omega^{\text{RRR}} & 0 \\ 0 & 0 \end{bmatrix}$$

and $A^{\text{PR}} = (\tilde{B}', -A')^{\text{RRR}}$, where the superscripts PR and RRR refer to the principal relations and reduced rank regression notation, respectively. Note that, as in some other models, Ω is unknown and has to be estimated as well. After a solution has been obtained, the reduced rank regression matrix B can be recovered from $\tilde{B}$ as $B = \tilde{B}(\tilde{B}'\tilde{B})^{-1}$. Finally, the matrices A and B may have to be renormalized.

8.3 The LISREL model

We have been considering a variety of models for latent variables that all implied some sort of structure on the covariance matrix of the distribution from which the observations were assumed to be drawn. For a number of reasons, such as ease of application and the derivation of general statistical properties, it is useful to integrate these models into one model that encompasses all the models dealt with up till now as special cases. The LISREL model, after the widely used LISREL program in which it was first implemented, serves this purpose. The acronym LISREL stands for LInear Structural RELations.

The LISREL model consists of three parts. The core of the LISREL model is constituted by the *structural model*, which is a simultaneous equations regression model that has all the characteristics usually assumed to hold for such a model, except that the endogenous and exogenous variables are latent. These latent variables are linked to observable variables through factor analysis models. One factor analysis model concerns the endogenous variables, and the other factor analysis model concerns the exogenous variables. These two factor analysis models constitute the second and third parts of the model and these are jointly called the *measurement model*.

This implies that we have the following model equations, written again for a typical observation,

$$\eta_n = B\eta_n + \Gamma\xi_n + \zeta_n \tag{8.6a}$$

$$y_n = \Lambda_y \eta_n + \varepsilon_n \tag{8.6b}$$

$$x_n = \Lambda_x \xi_n + \delta_n, \tag{8.6c}$$

where we have used the standard LISREL notation. The vectors η_n and ξ_n contain the (latent) endogenous and exogenous variables, the vectors y_n and x_n contain the corresponding observed variables, the vector ζ_n contains the residuals or disturbances in the regression equations, and the vectors ε_n and δ_n contain the (measurement) errors. The matrices B and Γ contain regression coefficients and the matrices Λ_y and Λ_x contain factor loadings. The random vectors ξ_n, ζ_n, ε_n, and δ_n are assumed to be mutually uncorrelated with means zero and covariance matrices $\Phi \equiv \mathrm{E}(\xi_n \xi_n')$, $\Psi \equiv \mathrm{E}(\zeta_n \zeta_n')$, $\Theta_\varepsilon \equiv \mathrm{E}(\varepsilon_n \varepsilon_n')$, and $\Theta_\delta \equiv \mathrm{E}(\delta_n \delta_n')$, respectively.

In the standard LISREL notation, the dimensions of y_n and x_n are denoted by p and q, respectively, and the dimensions of η_n and ξ_n are denoted by m and n, respectively. The subscript n is evidently not used to denote an observation. Obviously, the dimensions of ζ_n, ε_n, and δ_n are equal to those of η_n, y_n, and x_n, respectively. Because the standard LISREL symbols for these dimensions conflict somewhat with our previous notation, we will use M for the dimension of y_n, l for the dimension of x_n, k for the dimension of ξ_n, and g for the dimension of η_n, which is more in agreement with the notation used in this book, although completely consistent notation is not possible.

Examples of models written as LISREL models

Most of the models discussed up till now can be written as special cases of the LISREL model, many even in different ways. The class of all models that can be written as a LISREL model is called *structural equation models*. Here we will discuss some examples. Evidently, the confirmatory factor analysis model is simply (8.6c), and the other two equations are not relevant.

Linear regression is obtained by specifying $\Lambda_x \equiv I_l$, $\Theta_\delta \equiv 0$, $\Phi \equiv \Sigma_X$, $M \equiv 1$ and $g \equiv 1$, $\Lambda_y \equiv 1$, $\Theta_\varepsilon \equiv \sigma_\varepsilon^2$, $B \equiv 0$, $\Gamma \equiv \beta'$, and $\Psi \equiv 0$. Linear regression with measurement error is a straightforward extension of this with $\Theta_\delta \equiv \Omega$. Simultaneous equations regression is obtained from the linear regression specification by taking $M > 1$, $\Lambda_y \equiv I_M$, $\Theta_\varepsilon \equiv \Sigma_\varepsilon$, and B and Γ as usual in such models. Simultaneous equations with measurement error is again a straightforward extension of this with $\Theta_\delta \equiv \Omega$.

A MIMIC specification is obtained from the linear regression specification by specifying $\Gamma \equiv \alpha'$, $\Psi \equiv \sigma_u^2$, $M > 1$, $\Lambda_y \equiv \beta$, and $\Theta_\varepsilon \equiv \Omega$. (Note that the same symbols have slightly different meanings in the different models.) Reduced rank regression follows by taking $g > 1$, with $\Gamma \equiv A'$, $\Lambda_y \equiv B$, Θ_ε (possibly) unrestricted, and $\Psi \equiv 0$.

Note that in some of the examples above, the x variables are exogenous, which is specified by $\Lambda_x \equiv I$ and $\Theta_\delta \equiv 0$. In the usual framework, however, they are still considered random, so structural assumptions are made, even if these variables can not be considered random. This does not affect consistency, but may slightly affect parameter estimates and standard errors. It is possible to use functional assumptions concerning x by restricting Φ to the sample covariance matrix of x. The LISREL program has a *fixed* x option for this.

Now, let us consider the case of instrumental variables. In its most general form, we have for each observation an endogenous variable y_n, a vector of g explanatory variables x_n, which is expected to be correlated with the residual u_n in the regression equation for y_n, and a vector of h instrumental variables z_n, which is correlated with the explanatory variables x_n but not with u_n. (Here, we use the IV notation from section 6.1, which uses partly the same symbols as LISREL, but sometimes in a different way.)

First, assume that all x variables are endogenous. One of the ways in which instrumental variables can be modeled as a LISREL model is by defining $\xi_n \equiv (u_n, x_n', z_n')$ and $\eta_n \equiv y_n$, where the right-hand side symbols are IV notation. The IV assumptions imply the restriction that

$$\Phi = \begin{bmatrix} \sigma_u^2 & \sigma_{xu}' & 0' \\ \sigma_{xu} & \Sigma_X & \Sigma_{XZ} \\ 0 & \Sigma_{ZX} & \Sigma_{ZZ} \end{bmatrix},$$

in obvious notation. Because x_n and z_n are observed and u_n is not, we have

$$\Lambda_x \equiv \begin{bmatrix} 0 & I_g & 0 \\ 0 & 0 & I_h \end{bmatrix}$$

and $\Theta_\delta \equiv 0$. By specifying $B \equiv 0$, $\Gamma \equiv (1, \beta', 0')$, $\Psi \equiv 0$, $\Lambda_y \equiv 1$, and $\Theta_\varepsilon \equiv 0$, we obtain the standard IV model. If the number of instruments is equal to the number of regressors (i.e., $h = g$), then it can be easily derived that the estimator of β is the standard IV estimator. This generally does not hold exactly if $h > g$.

If not all variables in x_n are endogenous, x_n can be partitioned as $x_n \equiv (x'_{1n}, x'_{2n})'$, where x_{1n} contains the endogenous regressors and x_{2n} contains the exogenous regressors. In this case, the latter are also part of z_n, so that we can write $z_n \equiv (x'_{2n}, x'_{3n})'$, where x_{3n} contains the additional instruments that are not part of x_n. Because singular covariance matrices are frequently problematic in the estimation process, the parameterization should recognize this situation. This is done by replacing z_n by x_{3n} in the above parameterization, and make the according changes in Φ. In Λ_x, I_h is replaced by I_{g_3}, where g_3 is the number of elements of x_3, and in Λ_x, Θ_δ, and Γ, the dimensions of some of the zero submatrices are reduced accordingly.

In case the endogeneity of the regressors is due to measurement error, which was our primary reason for discussing IV, the model can be alternatively parameterized in a more explicit form. Let, in line with the above partitioning, ξ_n and x_n be partitioned as $\xi_n \equiv (\xi'_{1n}, \xi'_{2n})'$ and $x_n \equiv (x'_{1n}, x'_{2n})'$, such that ξ_{1n} is measured with error by x_{1n} and $\xi_{2n} = x_{2n}$ is measured without error. The covariance matrix of the measurement errors in x_n is Ω_1 and the vector of instrumental variables is again $z_n \equiv (x'_{2n}, x'_{3n})'$. Now, we can choose, in obvious notation, $\xi_n^{\mathrm{LISREL}} \equiv (\xi'_{1n}, \xi'_{2n}, x'_{3n})'$, $\Lambda_x \equiv I_{g+g_3}$,

$$\Theta_\delta \equiv \begin{bmatrix} \Omega_1 & 0 & 0 \\ 0 & 0 & 0 \\ 0 & 0 & 0 \end{bmatrix}, \qquad \Phi \equiv \begin{bmatrix} \Sigma_{\Xi_1} & \Sigma_{X_1X_2} & \Sigma_{X_1X_3} \\ \Sigma_{X_2X_1} & \Sigma_{X_2} & \Sigma_{X_2X_3} \\ \Sigma_{X_3X_1} & \Sigma_{X_3X_2} & \Sigma_{X_3} \end{bmatrix},$$

$\eta_n \equiv \beta'\xi_n^{\mathrm{IV}}$, so that $\Gamma \equiv (\beta', 0'_{g_3})$, $B \equiv 0$, and $\Psi \equiv 0$, and $y_n = \beta'\xi_n^{\mathrm{IV}} + \varepsilon_n$, so that $\Lambda_y \equiv 1$, and $\Theta_\varepsilon \equiv \sigma_\varepsilon^2$. Without further restrictions, Σ_Ξ and Ω_1 are not identified, as discussed in section 6.2. The estimators of the other parameters are, however, consistent, although lack of identification of Σ_Ξ and Ω_1 may cause computational problems in the specific program, so that arbitrary identification restrictions may have to be imposed. If the number of instruments is equal to the number of regressors (i.e., $h = g$), then it can be easily derived that the estimator of β is the standard IV estimator. As with the parameterization above, this does generally not hold exactly if $h > g$. If Ω_1 is restricted to be diagonal, all parameters are identified. Again, with $h = g$, the estimators of all parameters are equivalent to those discussed in section 6.2.

LIML can be obtained straightforwardly from (6.19) and (6.20) by choosing $x_n^{\text{LISREL}} \equiv (x_{2n}', x_{3n}')'$, $\Lambda_x \equiv I_{g_2+g_3}$, $\Phi^{\text{LISREL}} \equiv \Sigma_{ZZ}$, $\Theta_\delta \equiv 0$, $y_n^{\text{LISREL}} \equiv (y_n^{\text{LIML}}, x_{1n}')'$, $\Lambda_y \equiv I_{1+g_1}$, $\Theta_\varepsilon \equiv 0$,

$$B \equiv \begin{bmatrix} 0 & \beta_1' \\ 0 & 0 \end{bmatrix}, \qquad \Gamma \equiv \begin{bmatrix} \beta_2' & 0 \\ \Pi_2' & \Pi_3' \end{bmatrix},$$

and $\Psi \equiv \Phi^{\text{LIML}}$. If $h = g$ or if the LISREL model is estimated with ML in the fixed x option, this gives exactly the LIML estimator.

Now, consider the panel data model (6.42), which we repeat here:

$$\begin{aligned} y_{nt} &= \alpha_n + \xi_{nt}\beta + \varepsilon_{nt} \\ x_{nt} &= \xi_{nt} + v_{nt}. \end{aligned}$$

Because the number T of time points is usually small compared to the number of observations N and the data are assumed dependent over time, but independent across observations, the variables y_{nt} and x_{nt}, $t = 1, \ldots, T$, are gathered in the two T-vectors y_n and x_n of the LISREL model. The random effect α_n is a random variable that is constant over time, but may be correlated with ξ_{nt}. Hence, the LISREL specification of ξ_n contains both α_n and ξ_{nt}, i.e., $\xi_n \equiv (\alpha_n, \xi_{n1}, \ldots, \xi_{nT})'$. The LISREL vector δ_n contains the measurement errors v_{nt} (note that Θ_δ need not be diagonal). The elements η_{tn} of the LISREL vector η_n are defined as $\eta_{tn} \equiv \alpha_n + \xi_{nt}\beta$, and the LISREL vector ε_n contains the disturbances ε_{nt}. The LISREL specification of this model is completed by taking $\Lambda_y \equiv I_T$, $\Theta_\varepsilon \equiv \sigma_\varepsilon^2 I_T$ (assuming that the ε_{nt} are i.i.d.), $B \equiv 0$, $\Gamma \equiv (\iota_T, \beta I_T)$, $\Psi \equiv 0$, $\Lambda_x \equiv (0, I_T)$, $\Theta_\delta \equiv \Sigma_v$, and

$$\Phi \equiv \begin{bmatrix} \sigma_\alpha^2 & \sigma_{\xi\alpha}' \\ \sigma_{\xi\alpha} & \Sigma_\xi \end{bmatrix}.$$

If it is desirable to stress that v is correlated over time, one may alternatively choose $\Theta_\delta \equiv 0$, $\Lambda_x \equiv (0, I_T, I_T)$, and

$$\Phi \equiv \begin{bmatrix} \sigma_\alpha^2 & \sigma_{\xi\alpha}' & 0 \\ \sigma_{\xi\alpha} & \Sigma_\xi & 0 \\ 0 & 0 & \Sigma_v \end{bmatrix}.$$

As discussed in section 6.9, an interesting restriction of this model is obtained if it is assumed that ξ_{nt} and v_{nt} follow independent AR(1) processes. The model can then be written as

$$\begin{aligned} y_{nt} &= \alpha_n + \xi_{nt}\beta + \varepsilon_{nt} \\ x_{nt} &= \xi_{nt} + v_{nt} \\ \xi_{nt} &= \rho_\xi \xi_{n,t-1} + w_{nt} \\ v_{nt} &= \rho_v v_{n,t-1} + u_{nt}, \end{aligned}$$

where u_{nt}, w_{nt}, and ε_{nt} are i.i.d. with variances σ_u^2, σ_w^2, and σ_ε^2, respectively, ρ_ξ, ρ_v, and β are regression coefficients, and α_n is the random effect, which may be correlated with w_{nt}. Let σ_α^2 be its variance and $\sigma_{w\alpha}$ be the vector containing its covariances with w_{nt}. The variances of ξ_{n0} and v_{n0} are $\sigma_{\xi_0}^2$ and $\sigma_{v_0}^2$, which are not restricted, so we do not have to make assumptions about the initial conditions.

This can be modeled using the above specification in LISREL terms, by explicit restrictions on the relevant elements of Φ and Θ_δ, but may also be modeled explicitly in the LISREL specification. We then have to subsume ξ_{nt} and v_{nt} in η_n, because they are now dependent variables, and similarly subsume x_{nt} in y_n. A possible specification is then $\xi_n \equiv (\xi_{n0}, v_{n0})'$,

$$\begin{aligned} \eta_n &\equiv (\alpha_n, \xi_{n1}, \ldots, \xi_{nT}, v_{n1}, \ldots, v_{nT})', \\ y_n &\equiv (y_{n1}, \ldots, y_{nT}, x_{n1}, \ldots, x_{nT})', \end{aligned}$$

and x_n is not defined in the LISREL specification. Hence, Λ_x and Θ_δ are also not defined. Furthermore, it is now obvious that

$$\Phi \equiv \begin{bmatrix} \sigma_{\xi_0}^2 & 0 \\ 0 & \sigma_{v_0}^2 \end{bmatrix}, \quad \Lambda_y \equiv \begin{bmatrix} \iota_T & \beta I_T & 0 \\ 0 & I_T & I_T \end{bmatrix}, \quad \text{and} \quad \Theta_\varepsilon \equiv \begin{bmatrix} \sigma_\varepsilon^2 I_T & 0 \\ 0 & 0 \end{bmatrix}.$$

The most interesting part of the specification of this model in LISREL form is the equation for η_n. The matrices B and Γ include the AR(1) regression coefficients ρ_ξ and ρ_v to reflect the dependencies among the elements of η_n and the dependences on the values for $t = 0$. The matrix Ψ contains the variances of the random effect α_n and the residuals w_{nt} and u_{nt}, and the covariances between α_n and w_{nt}. Hence, we have

$$B \equiv \begin{bmatrix} 0 & 0_{T-1}' & 0 & 0_{T-1}' & 0 \\ 0 & 0_{T-1}' & 0 & 0_{T-1}' & 0 \\ 0_{T-1} & \rho_\xi I_{T-1} & 0_{T-1} & 0_{(T-1)\times(T-1)} & 0_{T-1} \\ 0 & 0_{T-1}' & 0 & 0_{T-1}' & 0 \\ 0_{T-1} & 0_{(T-1)\times(T-1)} & 0_{T-1} & \rho_v I_{T-1} & 0_{T-1} \end{bmatrix},$$

$$\Gamma \equiv \begin{bmatrix} 0 & 0 \\ \rho_\xi & 0 \\ 0_{T-1} & 0_{T-1} \\ 0 & \rho_v \\ 0_{T-1} & 0_{T-1} \end{bmatrix}, \qquad \text{and} \qquad \Psi \equiv \begin{bmatrix} \sigma_\alpha^2 & \sigma_{w\alpha}' & 0_T' \\ \sigma_{w\alpha} & \sigma_w^2 I_T & 0_{T\times T} \\ 0_T & 0_{T\times T} & \sigma_u^2 I_T \end{bmatrix}.$$

This dynamic panel data model has now been written in LISREL form.

The examples illustrate the great advantage of the general specification. A great variety of models can be specified relatively easily and estimated using standard software.

The covariance structure

Just like the factor analysis models discussed earlier, the LISREL model is usually estimated by fitting the theoretical covariance structure to the sample covariance matrix. We will now derive the covariance structure of the LISREL model, i.e., the population covariance matrix of the $M+l$ vector $(y_n', x_n')'$ in terms of the parameters.

The reduced form of the structural part of the model is

$$\eta_n = (I_g - B)^{-1}\Gamma\xi_n + (I_g - B)^{-1}\zeta_n. \tag{8.7}$$

Hence, the covariance matrix of η_n is $(I_g - B)^{-1}(\Gamma\Phi\Gamma' + \Psi)(I_g - B')^{-1}$. As a specification issue, note that the endogeneity of η_n apparently implies that its variances are not parameters, but nonlinear functions of other parameters in the model. Hence, if we would keep the habit of restricting the variances of the latent variables to 1, we would have to impose nonlinear restrictions. This is usually complicated and hence undesirable. On the other hand, as discussed in section (7.1), it is necessary to restrict the scale of η_n. We could do this by restricting the diagonal elements of Ψ to 1, which is in line with the discussion of the MIMIC model, or by restricting one factor loading to 1 for each element of η_n. The latter is customary, for both η and ξ, and this brings us back to the somewhat asymmetric specification with which we started our discussion in section 7.1. This has the additional advantage that the indeterminacy of the sign of the factor is resolved. Of course, we have to be convinced that the restricted loading should be actually nonzero, because if it would be zero in the specification with unit variance of the factor, the model can not be reparameterized in this way.

If we substitute (8.7) for η_n in the measurement equation for y_n, we obtain

$$y_n = \Lambda_y\big((I_g - B)^{-1}\Gamma\xi_n + (I_g - B)^{-1}\zeta_n\big) + \varepsilon_n.$$

Hence, the covariance matrix of the observations is

$$\Sigma \equiv \begin{bmatrix} \Sigma_{yy} & \Sigma_{yx} \\ \Sigma_{xy} & \Sigma_{xx} \end{bmatrix}, \tag{8.8a}$$

with

$$\Sigma_{yy} \equiv \Lambda_y \big((I_g - B)^{-1} (\Gamma \Phi \Gamma' + \Psi)(I_g - B')^{-1} \big) \Lambda_y' + \Theta_\varepsilon \tag{8.8b}$$

$$\Sigma_{yx} \equiv \Sigma_{xy}' \equiv \Lambda_y (I_g - B)^{-1} \Gamma \Phi \Lambda_x' \tag{8.8c}$$

$$\Sigma_{xx} \equiv \Lambda_x \Phi \Lambda_x' + \Theta_\delta . \tag{8.8d}$$

When there are no restrictions on the parameters, the model is evidently highly underidentified. Therefore, restrictions on the parameters are needed to achieve identification. Of course, restrictions on the parameters are also needed to make the models theoretically interesting, and substantive theory usually implies many restrictions. Due to the nonlinear character of the reduced form, assessing identification is a complicated problem. There are two approaches. One is by trial and error, that is, choose a specification and select starting values. When the information matrix at that point appears to be singular (this becomes clear when trying to fit the model) there is a strong indication that the model is not identified. The other approach is to check identification analytically. Even for simple models this is sometimes impossible to do by hand. For models of moderate size, identification can be checked by the IDLIS computer program, which uses computer algebra (see Bekker et al., 1994).

Estimation of structural equation models is discussed, in a more general setting, in the next chapter. Here we only state the overall idea, which is based on a confrontation of S, the sample covariance matrix based on the N observations $(y_n', x_n')'$, $n = 1, \ldots, N$, with Σ. The parameters are chosen in such a way that Σ maximally resembles S. One possible estimation method is ML, which proceeds in the same way as ML for factor analysis models, as discussed earlier.

Because structural equation models generally use the model to put a structure on the covariance matrix of the observations and fit the covariance structure to the sample covariance matrix, this class of models is also frequently referred to as the *analysis of covariance structures*. This is, however, not entirely correct. In section 6.8, for example, we have seen that under nonnormality it may be advantageous to fit higher order moments in addition to covariances. Similarly, means may also be structured, as will be discussed in section 8.6. Conversely, it is quite well possible to specify models that do not fall into the class of structural equation models, but may still be estimated by fitting a covariance structure (although examples of these are infrequently met). Therefore, the term analysis of covariance structures is nowadays considered inappropriate if the class of structural equation models is meant and the term structural equation model or SEM should be used instead.

Similarly, it has been common usage to refer to the class of structural equation models as LISREL models, because the LISREL program was the first of its kind and maintained a dominant position for a long time. In the next section, we will see that there exist alternative equivalent parameterizations that are also widely used. The LISREL program has lost its dominant market position and has become simply one of the programs. Hence, referring to the class of structural equation models as LISREL models is now also considered inappropriate, unless one specifically means the specification (8.6).

Given the above considerations, we will use the term covariance structure for a function $\Sigma(\theta)$ of a parameter vector θ that results in a covariance matrix Σ. The term LISREL will be used if the specification (8.6) or the LISREL program is meant, and the term structural equation models will be used to refer to the general class of models.

8.4 Other important general parameterizations

As discussed above, the LISREL model is a very general model specification that includes many, if not all, linear models with or without latent variables as special cases. There are, however, other equally general specifications. The two most important ones are the Bentler-Weeks (or EQS) model and the reticular action model, which will be discussed in this section. It is instructive to see that they are actually equivalent specifications, although they are seemingly quite different, because the principles used in showing this are valuable tools in themselves to specify as special cases models that do not seem to fit well within the general framework.

The Bentler-Weeks (EQS) model

Another general latent variable model specification is the Bentler-Weeks model. The program EQS uses the model equations of this model and hence, this model may also be called the EQS model, although the user never sees the model equations explicitly in this form. The model equations are

$$\eta_n = \beta\eta_n + \gamma\xi_n \tag{8.9a}$$

$$y_n = G_y\eta_n \tag{8.9b}$$

$$x_n = G_x\xi_n, \tag{8.9c}$$

where η_n is a vector of observed and latent endogenous variables for subject n, ξ_n is a vector of observed and latent exogenous variables for subject n, including errors and residuals, and β and γ are matrices of regression coefficients. The observed variables are collected in y_n and x_n, and the matrices G_y and G_x are known matrices with zeros and ones that indicate which elements of η_n and ξ_n are observed. They may therefore be called *filter* matrices, because they filter the observed variables out. For example, if the second element of η_n is the first observed variable, then $(G_y)_{12} = 1$ and the remaining elements in the first row of G_y, as well as the remaining elements in the second column of G_y are zero. It is assumed that $\mathrm{E}(\xi_n) = 0$, and $\Phi \equiv \mathrm{E}(\xi_n \xi_n')$.

To show that any EQS model can be written as a LISREL model, let a superscript L denote a variable or matrix in the LISREL notation and let a superscript E denote a variable or matrix in the EQS notation. Clearly, if we choose

$$\begin{array}{llll} y_n^L \equiv y_n^E & \Lambda_y^L \equiv G_y^E & \Theta_\varepsilon^L \equiv 0 & (\text{so } \varepsilon_n^L = 0) \\ x_n^L \equiv x_n^E & \Lambda_x^L \equiv G_x^E & \Theta_\delta^L \equiv 0 & (\text{so } \delta_n^L = 0) \\ \eta_n^L \equiv \eta_n^E & B^L \equiv \beta^E & \Psi^L \equiv 0 & (\text{so } \zeta_n^L = 0) \\ \xi_n^L \equiv \xi_n^E & \Gamma^L \equiv \gamma^E & \Phi^L \equiv \Phi^E, & \end{array}$$

then the resulting LISREL model is equivalent to the EQS model. Consequently, any EQS model can be written as a LISREL model.

Showing the converse is somewhat more complicated. The LISREL model clearly contains more symbols than the EQS model. Hence, we have to find a way in which different LISREL symbols (vectors, matrices) are gathered in one EQS symbol. In order to do so, it is helpful to start with the description of the EQS model, and more specifically with its random variables. According to the description, there are only two "basic" random vectors in EQS, ξ_n and η_n, because x_n and y_n are simply subsets of these. By definition, ξ_n contains all exogenous variables (variables that are not modeled, i.e., appear only on the right-hand side of equations) and η_n contains all endogenous variables (variables that are modeled, i.e., appear somewhere on the left-hand side of an equation). Clearly, from the equations (8.6), in the LISREL model ξ_n, δ_n, ε_n, and ζ_n are exogenous and x_n, y_n, and η_n are endogenous. Thus, we have

$$\xi_n^E \equiv (\xi_n^L, \delta_n^L, \varepsilon_n^L, \zeta_n^L)' \qquad \text{and} \qquad \eta_n^E \equiv (x_n^L, y_n^L, \eta_n^L)'$$

Now, all we have to do is to specify the parameter matrices β, γ, and Φ, and the filter matrices G_y and G_x in the EQS model such that the LISREL relations are emulated. The matrix Φ in the EQS model is defined as $\Phi^E \equiv \mathrm{E}(\xi_n^E \xi_n^{E\prime})$, which, using the above definition, is straightforwardly computed as

$$\Phi^E \equiv \mathrm{E}\begin{bmatrix}\xi_n^L\\ \delta_n^L\\ \varepsilon_n^L\\ \zeta_n^L\end{bmatrix}\begin{bmatrix}\xi_n^L\\ \delta_n^L\\ \varepsilon_n^L\\ \zeta_n^L\end{bmatrix}' = \begin{bmatrix}\Phi^L & 0 & 0 & 0\\ 0 & \Theta_\delta^L & 0 & 0\\ 0 & 0 & \Theta_\varepsilon^L & 0\\ 0 & 0 & 0 & \Psi^L\end{bmatrix}.$$

The matrices γ^E and β^E contain the regression coefficients of η^E on ξ^E and the regression coefficients of η^E on itself, respectively,

$$\gamma^E \equiv \begin{bmatrix}\Lambda_x^L & I_l & 0 & 0\\ 0 & 0 & I_M & 0\\ \Gamma^L & 0 & 0 & I_g\end{bmatrix} \quad \text{and} \quad \beta^E \equiv \begin{bmatrix}0 & 0 & 0\\ 0 & 0 & \Lambda_y^L\\ 0 & 0 & B^L\end{bmatrix}.$$

At this point, only the filter matrices G_x and G_y remain to be defined. These select the observed variables x_n^E and y_n^E from the vectors ξ_n^E and η_n^E. The observed variables in the LISREL model are x_n^L and y_n^L. These are not contained in the vector ξ_n^E, so x_n^E and G_x^E are empty (do not exist). The vectors x_n^L and y_n^L are the first two subvectors of η_n^E, so we have

$$G_y^E \equiv \begin{bmatrix}I_l & 0 & 0\\ 0 & I_M & 0\end{bmatrix} \quad \text{and} \quad y_n^E \equiv \begin{bmatrix}x_n^L\\ y_n^L\end{bmatrix}.$$

This completes the definitions and the LISREL model has now been written as a special case of the EQS model. Consequently, the LISREL and EQS models are different specifications of the same model.

Given the model specification (8.9), the implied covariance structure of the EQS model is derived in completely the same way as the covariance structure of the LISREL model was derived. Estimation then also proceeds in the same way as for the LISREL model.

Obviously, as the specifications of the EQS and LISREL model are equivalent, they lead to the same implied covariance structure in any given specific case. Only the way to arrive at this structure differs considerably.

The reticular action model (RAM)

A third general model specification is the *reticular action model* (RAM), which stresses the relationship with path diagrams, because the word reticular refers to networks. The programs MX and SAS PROC CALIS use the model equations of this model. These are

$$v_n = Av_n + u_n \tag{8.10a}$$
$$g_n = Fv_n, \tag{8.10b}$$

where v_n is a vector of observed and latent endogenous variables for subject n, u_n is a vector of observed and latent exogenous variables for subject n, including errors and residuals, and A is a matrix of *asymmetric* (regression) coefficients. The observed variables are collected in g_n, and the matrix $F \equiv (I, 0)$ is a *fixed* (known) or *filter* matrix with zeros and ones that indicate which elements of v_n are observed. Hence, the vector v_n is partitioned as $v_n' \equiv (g_n', h_n')'$, with g_n observed, manifest, or *given* and h_n unobserved, latent, or *hidden*. It is assumed that $\mathrm{E}(u_n) = 0$, and $S \equiv \mathrm{E}(u_n u_n')$ is a matrix of *symmetric* coefficients (covariances). Evidently, the sample covariance matrix is not referred to as S in this model.

Showing that the RAM model is a special case of the LISREL model is again straightforward. We will denote by the superscript R the matrices from the RAM model. Now, choose

$$\begin{array}{llll}
y_n^L \equiv g_n^R & \Lambda_y^L \equiv F^R & \Theta_\varepsilon^L \equiv 0 & (\text{so } \varepsilon_n^L = 0) \\
\eta_n^L \equiv v_n^R & B^L \equiv A^R & & \\
\zeta_n^L \equiv u_n^R & \Psi^L \equiv S^R & & \\
 & \Lambda_x^L \equiv 0 & \Theta_\delta^L \equiv 0 & (\text{so } x_n^L = 0 \text{ and } \delta_n^L = 0) \\
 & \Gamma^L \equiv 0 & \Phi^L \equiv 0 & (\text{so } \xi_n^L = 0),
\end{array}$$

then the RAM model is a special case of the LISREL model.

As with the EQS model, showing the converse is a bit more tricky. The only covariance matrix that is estimated in RAM is S, the covariance matrix of u_n. Hence, all exogenous variables from LISREL must be part of u_n^R. This gives

$$u_n^R \equiv \begin{bmatrix} \delta_n^L \\ \varepsilon_n^L \\ \zeta_n^L \\ \xi_n^L \end{bmatrix} \quad \text{and} \quad S^R \equiv \begin{bmatrix} \Theta_\delta^L & 0 & 0 & 0 \\ 0 & \Theta_\varepsilon^L & 0 & 0 \\ 0 & 0 & \Psi^L & 0 \\ 0 & 0 & 0 & \Phi^L \end{bmatrix}.$$

By definition, all endogenous variables are gathered in v_n^R, with the observed variables first. This suggests that $v_n^R \equiv (x_n^{L\prime}, y_n^{L\prime}, \eta_n^{L\prime})'$. The problem is now that the regression coefficients of x_n^L and η_n^L on ξ_n^L are gathered in the matrices Λ_x^L and Γ^L, whereas the RAM specification does not allow regression coefficients of v_n on u_n other than the identity matrix. All "asymmetric" parameters (i.e., regression coefficients) are gathered in the matrix A^R. Hence, Λ_x^L and Γ^L must be submatrices of A^R, which implies that ξ_n^L must be a subvector of υ_n^R. Apparently, ξ_n^L is a subvector of both υ_n^R and u_n^R. These subvectors are defined equal by imposing the restriction that the corresponding submatrices of A^R are zero. The result is

$$\upsilon_n^R \equiv \begin{bmatrix} x_n^L \\ y_n^L \\ \eta_n^L \\ \xi_n^L \end{bmatrix} \quad \text{and} \quad A^R \equiv \begin{bmatrix} 0 & 0 & 0 & \Lambda_x^L \\ 0 & 0 & \Lambda_y^L & 0 \\ 0 & 0 & B^L & \Gamma^L \\ 0 & 0 & 0 & 0 \end{bmatrix}.$$

The filter matrix F^R filters the observed variables x_n^L and y_n^L from υ_n^R. Evidently,

$$F^R \equiv \begin{bmatrix} I_l & 0 & 0 & 0 \\ 0 & I_M & 0 & 0 \end{bmatrix}.$$

Note that the ordering of the elements of υ_n has to comply with the ordering of the elements of u_n, and that the observed variables must come first in υ_n by definition. This completes the definitions and the LISREL model has now been written as a special case of the RAM model. So all three specifications are equivalent.

Given the model specification (8.10), the implied covariance structure of the RAM model is derived in completely the same way as the covariance structure of the LISREL model was derived. Estimation then also proceeds in the same way as for the LISREL model. As noted in the context of the EQS model, the equivalence of the various model specifications means that they lead to the same implied covariance structure in any given specific case. Only the way in which this structure is found differs.

Comparison of the specifications

Given that the LISREL, EQS, and RAM specifications lead to the same model class, one may wonder why different specifications are used at all. The reason is that some specifications are more convenient or natural in some situations, whereas other specifications are preferable in other situations.

The LISREL model specification is often more natural to interpret and specify, with its explicit distinction between latent and observed variables and its explicit distinction between factors and errors. It is also more evident that it is a combination of an econometric simultaneous equations regression model and a psychometric factor analysis measurement model. The various parts are clearly recognizable and extensions of regression models to measurement error models and extensions of factor analysis models with directed relationships among the factors are immediately clear.

A disadvantage of the LISREL model, however, is its large number of different parameter matrices and random vectors. In many cases, this makes specification of a model less transparent. The EQS and RAM models have an advantage on this point. Furthermore, statistical derivations are usually easier for the EQS and RAM specifications, because the number of terms is much smaller, which results in much less "bookkeeping". Additionally, it is more straightforward with the EQS and RAM models to specify relationships that do not follow the LISREL principles closely. Examples of these are models with observed x variables that directly influence observed y variables, or correlations between random variables that are typically elements of different parameter vectors in LISREL.

With the increasing availability of user-friendly software with model specification based on building path diagrams in a graphical user interface, applied researchers are less required to learn the model equations themselves, and differences between the parameterizations are largely hidden from the user. Moreover, most statistical theory is nowadays based on very general concepts of parameter vectors and moment conditions, as will become apparent from the next two chapters. Therefore, the statistical development progresses without referring to specific model equations. Hence, the importance of the reasons for preferring one or another specification is declining.

8.5 Scaling of the variables

In section 7.2 we have seen that FA, unlike PCA, is insensitive to the scaling of the variables. This implies that the EFA solution is basically unaltered if the variables are scaled differently, whereas the PCA solution is not. Hence, PCA solutions may be completely different if the variables are scaled differently. Assume for example, that we have observed two variables, with sample covariance matrix

$$S = \begin{bmatrix} 2 & 0 \\ 0 & 1 \end{bmatrix},$$

which implies immediately that the first principal component is proportional to the first variable. If we multiply the second variable by 10, however, the first principal component is proportional to the second variable, which is orthogonal to the first variable. Thus, the solution is completely different. Because such arbitrariness is usually unwanted in a PCA analysis, it is typically performed on the correlation matrix. Similarly, EFA is also usually performed on the correlation matrix, because the scales of the variables are often arbitrary and the solution is much easier to interpret. For the one-factor model, for example, if the correlation matrix is analyzed, the factor loadings will be the correlations of the indicators with the factor, which are restricted to be between -1 and 1, and larger loadings (in an absolute sense) denote better indicators. If the analysis is performed on the covariance matrix, the quality of the indicators does not follow immediately from the estimation results.

Scale invariance

To analyze this in more detail, let us first try to define the concept of scale invariance of a model. The idea is that, if we have a model with arbitrary given parameter values and we multiply each of the observed variables by some nonzero number, then we can find other parameter values such that the transformed variables still satisfy the model. For a structural equation model that is fitted on the covariance matrix, the model implies that the population covariance matrix Σ is some function of a vector θ of parameters, $\Sigma \equiv \Sigma(\theta)$. Let $\mathcal{D} \subseteq \mathbb{R}^m$ denote the domain of θ, where m is the number of elements of θ. Compared to $\mathbb{R}^m$, $\mathcal{D}$ excludes values that are not allowed by the model, such as negative variances or explicit restrictions imposed on θ.

Is we scale the variables differently, this means that we premultiply the vector of observed variables for each observation by a diagonal matrix Δ, say. Then the population covariance matrix of the rescaled variables Σ^*, say, is $\Sigma^* \equiv \Delta\Sigma\Delta$. The model is scale invariant if, for each diagonal matrix Δ and each $\theta \in \mathcal{D}$, we can find an allowed parameter vector θ^*, say, such that $\Sigma^* = \Sigma(\theta^*)$.

For the EFA model, this is obviously true, because we can simply choose $B^* \equiv \Delta B$ and $\Omega^* \equiv \Delta\Omega\Delta$. Because the factor loading matrix B is unrestricted, B^* is an allowed value. Since Ω is restricted to be diagonal and positive semidefinite, the same holds for Ω^* for each diagonal matrix Δ. Hence, the EFA model is scale invariant. Consider now the simple one-factor CFA model with the restriction $\beta = \rho\iota_M$, where ρ is a scalar and ι_M is an M-vector of ones. The implied covariance matrix is

$$\Sigma = \rho^2\iota_M\iota_M' + \Omega, \tag{8.11}$$

where Ω is a diagonal matrix with nonnegative elements. The rescaled covariance matrix of this model is

$$\Sigma^* = \rho^2\delta\delta' + \Omega^*, \tag{8.12}$$

where $\delta \equiv \Delta\iota_M$ is the vector with the diagonal elements of Δ. Clearly, if $M > 2$ and the diagonal elements of Δ are different, (8.12) does not satisfy the model

(8.11). Hence, we have a very simple example of a CFA model that is not scale invariant. Therefore, we have to be careful.

Analyzing the correlation matrix

As discussed above, FA models are often estimated from the correlation matrix, because the resulting solution is easier to interpret. Evidently, a correlation matrix is a rescaled covariance matrix. Let S be the sample covariance matrix and R be the sample correlation matrix, then by definition

$$R = D_S^{-1/2} S D_S^{-1/2},$$

where D_S is the diagonal matrix with the same diagonal elements as S. A structural equation model implies a covariance structure and the model is fitted based on the principle that

$$\operatorname*{plim}_{N\to\infty} S = \Sigma = \Sigma(\theta).$$

We find a value of θ such that the difference between S and $\Sigma(\theta)$ is minimal in some sense, so that asymptotically, we find that the parameters are correctly recovered if the model is identified. Analogously, for the correlation matrix, we have

$$\operatorname*{plim}_{N\to\infty} R = \operatorname*{plim}_{N\to\infty} D_S^{-1/2} S D_S^{-1/2} = D_\Sigma^{-1/2} \Sigma D_\Sigma^{-1/2},$$

where D_Σ is the diagonal matrix with the same diagonal elements as Σ. Clearly, if the model is scale invariant, there exists a value θ^* of the parameters, such that

$$\operatorname*{plim}_{N\to\infty} R = \Sigma(\theta^*),$$

and $\Sigma(\theta^*)$ is the population correlation matrix. Hence, we may redefine θ^* as the true parameter value, which will be consistently estimated if the parameters are identified. Thus, scale invariance implies that we may sensibly analyze the correlation matrix.

However, it is now also clear that if the model is not scale invariant, the covariance structure $\Sigma(\theta)$ can not reproduce the population correlation matrix, and hence fitting the model to the correlation matrix does not make sense. The model is misspecified for the correlation matrix. In principle, it is possible to fit the model to the correlation matrix, but the correlation structure should then be respecified as

$$\Sigma^*(\theta) = D_{\Sigma(\theta)}^{-1/2} \Sigma(\theta) D_{\Sigma(\theta)}^{-1/2},$$

which generally involves imposing complicated nonlinear restrictions if the model is to be estimated with a program designed for fitting covariance structures. Clearly, it is much easier to estimate the model on the covariance matrix than to estimate it on the correlation matrix.

Inference using the correlation matrix

Because scale invariant models apply equally well to the correlation matrix as to the covariance matrix, they can be estimated consistently from the correlation matrix. However, if a correlation matrix is analyzed as if it were a covariance matrix, standard errors are typically overestimated.

An example may give some intuition for this phenomenon. Assume that we have observed a data set and the sample variance of the first variable is 1. We estimate a one-factor model and find $\beta_1 = 0.95$, with a standard error of 0.05. Thus, the 95% confidence interval is roughly [0.85, 1.05], which stretches beyond 1. This is perfectly sensible, because there is likely to be considerable variance in the estimator of the covariance matrix. If the data are normally distributed, for example, the variance of the sample variance is approximately $2/N$ if the population variance is 1. Hence, we are not so sure about our estimate 1 and as a consequence, β_1 may also be larger than 1. In fact, a formal statistical test whether $\beta_1 = 1.01$ will not be rejected.

If we measure the first variable in different units, by multiplying it by δ, the variance of the first sample variance must be multiplied by δ^4 and the standard error of the transformed estimate of β_1 will be multiplied by δ. (This depends somewhat on the estimation method, but we will not go into that.) Thus, if we multiply our variable by 10, the estimate of β_1 will be 9.5 with standard error 0.5, which clearly does not alter our interpretation of the solution.

However, if we standardize our variable, so that we fit a correlation matrix, the diagonal element is 1 by definition and thus has a variance of 0. The population value of β_1 is less than 1 by definition, so that $\beta_1 = 1.01$ should always be rejected. Apparently, it makes a large difference for the standard errors and the statistical inference whether a given matrix is a correlation matrix or a covariance matrix. The reason for this is that the rescaling is not a fixed rescaling that would be performed exactly the same for any data set (i.e., with the same factor), but a random rescaling depending on the actual outcome of the sample covariance matrix. A failure to recognize this will lead to errors in the conclusions based on the analysis. This can be corrected, but this requires complicated computations that are not generally performed by the available software, so that it is again easier to just analyze the covariance matrix. Moreover, as we will see in the next two chapters, correct standard errors and statistical inference require consistent estimates of the fourth-order moments of the data if the covariance matrix is fitted, so that even using the covariance matrix is not sufficient in most cases. Some programs compute the required fourth-order moments from the raw data, but in other programs these fourth-order moments must be computed before the analysis. When analyzing (correctly parameterized) correlation structures, we also need fourth-order moments of the data, but corrections are needed. The sample covariance matrix is sufficient for a correct analysis only if we know that the data are multivariate normally distributed.

Reasons why models may not be scale invariant

Many structural equation models are scale invariant, so if we are only interested in reasonable estimators and do not bother much about standard errors and statistical tests (as in EFA), we may analyze the correlation matrix. There are, however, important situations in which we would specify models that are not scale invariant. These situations occur if scales of the different variables are related. The leading case is an analysis of panel data, in which the same variable is measured on several occasions. Consider, for example, a simple dynamic panel data model with data from three occasions, specified by

$$y_{2n} = \beta_1 y_{1n} + \varepsilon_{2n} \tag{8.13a}$$

$$y_{3n} = \beta_2 y_{2n} + \varepsilon_{3n}. \tag{8.13b}$$

Obviously, a theoretically interesting restriction is $\beta_1 = \beta_2$. This implies that the model is not scale invariant and if the sample variances of y at the different occasions are different, it makes no sense to analyze the correlation matrix with this model. If the restriction is not imposed, the parameters can be consistently estimated from the correlation matrix, but the estimators of β_1 and β_2 will generally be different, even after retransforming to the original scales.

As another example, assume that we have observed the data at only two occasions, so that the model consists of only the equation (8.13a). This model is scale invariant, so we could estimate the model from the correlation matrix. The estimate of β_1 is then the sample correlation between y_1 and y_2. In this case, however, an important empirical question is whether $|\beta_1| < 1$, which means that the model is stationary, $|\beta_1| = 1$, which means that the system has a unit root, or $|\beta_1| > 1$, which means that the model is nonstationary. This pertains to the original scale, however. The correlation between y_1 and y_2 is always between -1 and 1, and we can not infer from this whether the model is stationary or not. Clearly, there is a strong theoretical substantive reason for analyzing the data on its original scale.

The standardized solution

The above examples showed that in some cases, models are easier to interpret and substantively meaningful on their original scales. In many other cases, however, the scales of variables are completely arbitrary. In the CBI model, for example, there is no natural scale for central bank independence. The scales of the different indicators differ considerably. In such cases, it is difficult to interpret the results. If the factor loading of one indicator is 2, say, and the factor loading of another indicator is 1, then this may imply that the former measures the latent variable better, but it may also imply that the scale of the former is larger than the scale of the latter. Therefore, we can not easily draw conclusions from the outcomes. Similarly, if expenses on durable goods are regressed on income and wealth, with regression coefficients 0.2 and 0.05, say, it is hard to say which regressor is more important in the sense of giving a better prediction or explaining more variance.

To interpret models easier, especially with variables that have no natural scale, it is common usage in the social sciences to compute the *standardized solution*. This is obtained from a certain model by (hypothetically) rescaling all variables in the model such that they have variance 1. The regression coefficients, factor loadings, and residual variances then have to be rescaled accordingly. This is most easily defined for the EQS model, but the modifications for the LISREL and RAM specifications are straightforward. The reduced form of the EQS model is given by

$$\eta_n = (I_g - \beta)^{-1} \gamma \xi_n,$$

where η_n is the vector of g endogenous variables, ξ_n is the vector of exogenous variables, including residuals, and β and γ are matrices of regression coefficients and factor loadings. The covariance matrix of ξ_n is Φ. For the standardized solution, ξ_n should be rescaled such that its elements all have variance 1. Hence, the standardized exogenous variables are

$$\tilde{\xi}_n \equiv D_\Phi^{-1/2} \xi_n,$$

where D_Φ is the diagonal matrix with the same diagonal elements as Φ. The covariance matrix of the standardized exogenous variables can accordingly be computed as

$$\tilde{\Phi} \equiv D_\Phi^{-1/2} \Phi D_\Phi^{-1/2},$$

which is a correlation matrix by definition. Let C be the covariance matrix of η_n. Then η_n is standardized analogously as

$$\tilde{\eta}_n \equiv D_C^{-1/2} \eta_n,$$

where D_C is the diagonal matrix with the same diagonal elements as C. The covariance matrix of $\tilde{\eta}_n$ is

$$\tilde{C} \equiv D_C^{-1/2} C D_C^{-1/2}.$$

However, C is not a parameter matrix, but a function of β, γ, and Φ. Hence, the transformation to $\tilde{C}$ should be translated into a transformation of β and γ, using the transformation of Φ to $\tilde{\Phi}$. From the reduced form equation, it follows that

$$\begin{aligned}
\tilde{\eta}_n &\equiv D_C^{-1/2} \eta_n \\
&= D_C^{-1/2} (I_g - \beta)^{-1} \gamma \xi_n \\
&= D_C^{-1/2} (I_g - \beta)^{-1} \gamma D_\Phi^{1/2} \tilde{\xi}_n \\
&= \left(I_g - D_C^{-1/2} \beta D_C^{1/2}\right)^{-1} D_C^{-1/2} \gamma D_\Phi^{1/2} \tilde{\xi}_n.
\end{aligned}$$

Consequently, the standardized solutions for β and γ are

$$\tilde{\beta} \equiv D_C^{-1/2} \beta D_C^{1/2} \qquad \text{and} \qquad \tilde{\gamma} \equiv D_C^{-1/2} \gamma D_\Phi^{1/2},$$

respectively. Note that the residuals are contained in ξ_n. In the usual specification, their variances are free parameters and their regression coefficients, which are elements of γ, are fixed to 1, although they would not normally be viewed as regression coefficients. In the standardized solution, however, their variances are fixed to 1 and they have associated nontrivial values of the regression coefficients as contained in $\tilde{\gamma}$.

For a model that is not scale invariant, the standardized solution does not satisfy the restrictions for the original model. Rather, it is just a reformulation of the original model. However, for scale invariant models, the standardized solution is usually equivalent to the model estimated on the correlation matrix, or a reparameterization thereof. The CFA model for the TV viewership data discussed in section 8.1, for example, is scale invariant and it was actually obtained as the standardized solution of the model in the original scales. In contrast, the oblimin-rotated solution discussed in section 7.4 was obtained from the correlation matrix. These solutions are almost equivalent, as was to be expected.

The standardized solution is usually much easier to interpret. For the one-factor model, for example, factor loadings of the standardized solution will be the correlations of the indicators with the factor, which makes interpretation particularly easy, as discussed above. Similarly, in a regression model, larger coefficients generally indicate more important regressors in the sense of explaining more variance, although with correlated regressors, this is a little more complicated. Note that in an unrestricted multiple regression model, the standardized solution is equivalent to the solution that is obtained by performing the regression on the correlation matrix.

In summary, our conclusion is that a correlation matrix should almost never be used to estimate a model. Only if a model is scale invariant and we are only interested in the estimates and not in standard errors or statistical tests, this can be done. We suggest that only EFA and PCA should be performed on the correlation matrix, EFA because it satisfies the conditions just mentioned and PCA because it is actually not based on a model and it is usually more interesting to find a simple approximation to the standardized data matrix than to the original data matrix. CFA models and all other structural equation models, with the exception of EFA, should be estimated on the covariance matrix. Correct standard errors and statistical tests can be obtained from the fourth-order moments of the data, as will become clear in the next two chapters. Virtually all theoretically interesting tests will be possible on the original scales, most importantly equality of regression coefficients and tests whether certain parameters are zero. For easier interpretation of models that are hard to interpret on their original scales, the standardized solution can be inspected.

8.6 Extensions of the model

As we have seen, structural equation models are very versatile and incorporate many important models. A given structural equation model implies a certain covariance structure and estimation can be done by fitting this covariance structure to the sample covariance matrix. Some important related model specifications do not fit into the general framework, however, but can be incorporated by relatively small and straightforward extensions of the model. In this section, we will discuss these extensions.

The first extension is the incorporation of nonzero means and intercepts in the model. In most situations, means and intercepts are uninteresting, but in some other situations, this is not the case. The leading example concerns a model for panel data.

The second extension is the analysis of a model for multiple subpopulations. In principle, a model could be estimated for each subpopulation separately, but in many cases, one would desire to impose some restrictions across subpopulations. This so-called multiple groups analysis is very powerful and can be applied to seemingly different problems, such as missing data. Multiple groups analysis usually also involves mean structures.

Similar to mean structures, higher order moment structures may also be specified as we have seen in section 6.8. These are, however, not nearly as important as mean structures. For this reason, and because higher order moment structures tend to lead to massive computational, mathematical, and statistical problems, without contributing much to the precision of the estimators, at least in moderate samples with moderately large models, higher order moment structures are not implemented in most software and will not be discussed here. In chapter 11, however, we will encounter some models where higher order moment structures have to be considered. It appears that these models can be reformulated such that they can yet be handled by standard software.

Mean structures

Thus far, we have assumed that all variables have zero means. The reason for this is that usually the means of the latent variables are not determined, so that they may be chosen freely. A choice of zero for the means of the latent variables is mathematically convenient. If the observed variables have nonzero means, we would generally specify an intercept term for each measurement equation. These intercepts are usually of little theoretical interest, but may be estimated straightforwardly through the sample means of the variables.

As we have seen above, the parameters are usually estimated by fitting the covariance structure to the sample covariance matrix. Shifting the sample mean does not change the sample covariance matrix or the fourth-order (central) moments, so that we might as well assume that the means of the observed variables are zero. Note that this contrasts with the scales of the variables. As discussed above, analysis of the correlation matrix produces results that differ from the results that are obtained when the covariance matrix is analyzed, even for scale invariant models.

There are, however, situations in which nonzero means and intercepts are theoretically interesting or statistically necessary tools. The leading case is when different indicators are measurements using the same measurement process. In a panel data study, for example, we may have observed M_1 indicators of productivity at T time points. It is reasonable to assume that the parameters of the measurement process, i.e., the factor loadings and the intercepts, are the same for the T different measurements of each indicator. If this is assumed, differences in observed means in the indicators are reflections of differences in average productivity. Due to the restrictions on the measurement model (the same intercepts and factor loadings at different time points), the means of the latent variables may be identified, and increases or decreases of productivity may be detected. Note, however, that always one mean or intercept parameter remains to be fixed, because otherwise the means and intercept parameters are not identified.

Based on these considerations, the three general structural equation model specifications have been extended to include mean and intercept parameters. In the LISREL model, the equations (8.6) are replaced by

$$
\begin{aligned}
\eta_n &= \alpha + B\eta_n + \Gamma\xi_n + \zeta_n \\
y_n &= \tau_y + \Lambda_y \eta_n + \varepsilon_n \\
x_n &= \tau_x + \Lambda_x \xi_n + \delta_n,
\end{aligned}
$$

where τ_x, τ_y, and α are vectors of intercepts. Furthermore, the assumption $\mathrm{E}(\xi_n) = 0$ is replaced by $\mathrm{E}(\xi_n) = \kappa$. The resulting mean structure is

$$
\mu \equiv \begin{bmatrix} \mu_y \\ \mu_x \end{bmatrix} \equiv \begin{bmatrix} \mathrm{E}(y) \\ \mathrm{E}(x) \end{bmatrix} = \begin{bmatrix} \tau_y + \Lambda_y (I_g - B)^{-1} \Gamma\kappa \\ \tau_x + \Lambda_x \kappa \end{bmatrix}.
$$

The estimation of the parameters now involves fitting the mean structure and the covariance structure jointly.

Similarly, for the EQS model, the assumption $\mathrm{E}(\xi_n) = 0$ is replaced by $\mathrm{E}(\xi_n) = \mu_\xi$, and an extra variable $x_{0n} \equiv \xi_{0n} \equiv 1$ is added, which has zero variance, i.e., this element is the constant 1. By specifying this as explanatory variable, the intercepts are obtained. In the program, this variable is called V999.

The RAM specification is extended completely analogous to the EQS specification. The assumption $\mathrm{E}(u_n) = 0$ is replaced by $\mathrm{E}(u_n) = \mu$. Intercept parameters are obtained by introducing one extra element u_{0n} with expectation 1 and variance 0. This constant is introduced in the vector v_n by restricting the corresponding row of A to zero. Intercepts are then obtained as regression coefficients with respect to this variable.

The mean structures of the EQS and RAM specifications can be derived straightforwardly. Again, estimation now involves fitting the mean structure and the covariance structure jointly.

Multiple groups and missing data

Frequently, we can identify several subpopulations in the sample, e.g., men versus women, age groups, subsamples from different geographical regions, and so forth. In such cases, we may be interested in specifying a structural equation model for each subgroup separately and investigating correspondences and differences among the subgroups.

We may do this by estimating a model for each subgroup separately, but usually, the interest lies in testing cross-group constraints and restricting parts of the models for the different groups to be equal or proportional, or imposing some other substantively meaningful restriction. Hence, we would like to estimate the models for the subgroups jointly and base statistical inference on this integrated analysis.

This turns out to be quite easy. If the subsamples are drawn independently, the joint likelihood is simply the product of the likelihoods of the subsamples and the joint loglikelihood is the sum of the loglikelihoods of the subsamples. Note, however, that in the combination of the (log)likelihoods, the sample sizes should not be eliminated, or the loglikelihoods should be weighted with weights proportional to their sample size. Similarly, if other estimation methods are used, the criterion function is simply the weighted sum of the criterion functions of the subgroups, i.e., if the criterion function for group j is $\bar{q}_j(\theta)$ (see the next chapter for a definition of an appropriate criterion function) and there are J subgroups, then the overall criterion function is

$$\bar{q}(\theta) \equiv \sum_{j=1}^{J} \frac{N_j}{N} \bar{q}_j(\theta),$$

where N_j is the sample size in the j-th subgroup and N is the overall sample size. Estimation and inference then proceeds straightforwardly.

The combination of models for different subpopulations is called *multiple groups analysis*. This is frequently combined with structured means, because multiple groups models are frequently used to estimate the average differences in some variables across subpopulations, and to test whether they differ significantly from zero.

For multiple groups analysis, it is not necessary that the observed and latent variables for the different subgroups are the same or that the models are related in any way. As long as the groups are independently sampled, different models may be specified for different subpopulations. Generally, however, it is of course most relevant if the models of the different subgroups are related.

An important application of multiple groups analysis with related but different models is the estimation of models with a considerable amount of missing data. If there are only a few missing data *patterns*, and if it is assumed that the occurrence of missing data is either completely coincidental or induced by known factors not related to the missing data but, e.g., due to different questionnaires for different data sources, then the model may be estimated as a multiple groups model, with one group for each missing data pattern. The missing data are then specified as latent variables or omitted if that does not influence the model for the variables that are not missing. Even if the separate models for the different subgroups are not identified, we may be able to identify the joint model by imposing the relevant cross-group constraints on the parameters.

In section 6.4, we have already encountered such as situation. There, a model $y = X\beta + u$ was hypothesized, but the sample consisted two subsamples, one in which X was not observed and one in which y was not observed. In both samples, however, variables Z were observed that could act as instrumental variables. This led to the development of the two-sample IV estimator. In section 8.3, we already saw that instrumental variables can be specified within the LISREL model. The extension to the two-sample IV case is straightforward. We start the development of the model for sample I by defining $\xi_n \equiv (u_n, x_n', z_n')$ and $\eta_n \equiv y_n$, where the right-hand side symbols are IV notation. As previously, the IV assumptions imply the restriction that

$$\Phi = \begin{bmatrix} \sigma_u^2 & \sigma_{xu}' & 0' \\ \sigma_{xu} & \Sigma_X & \Sigma_{ZX}' \\ 0 & \Sigma_{ZX} & \Sigma_{ZZ} \end{bmatrix}.$$

By specifying $B \equiv 0$, $\Gamma \equiv (1, \beta', 0')'$, and $\Psi \equiv 0$, the basic IV model is specified. In sample I, u_n and x_n are not observed and y_n and z_n are observed directly, which implies the specification $x_n^{\text{LISREL}} \equiv z_n$, $\Lambda_x \equiv (0, 0, I_h)$, $\Theta_\delta \equiv 0$, $\Lambda_y \equiv 1$, and $\Theta_\varepsilon \equiv 0$.

In sample II, x_n and z_n are observed and y_n and u_n are not. The only function of this sample is to provide estimators of Σ_{XX}, Σ_{ZX}, and Σ_{ZZ}. This leads to the simple specification $x_n^{\text{LISREL}} \equiv ((x_n^{\text{2SIV}})', z_n')'$,

$$\Phi \equiv \begin{bmatrix} \Sigma_X & \Sigma_{ZX}' \\ \Sigma_{ZX} & \Sigma_{ZZ} \end{bmatrix}.$$

$\Lambda_x \equiv I_{g+h}$, and $\Theta_\delta \equiv 0$. The endogenous variables y_n and η_n and corresponding variables and parameters are not defined. The cross-group restrictions that specify Σ_{XX}, Σ_{ZX}, and Σ_{ZZ} as equivalent in both subpopulations assure identification of the model.

8.7 Equivalent models

In section 3.1, it was shown that direct regression and reverse regression lead to the same value of R^2, namely the squared correlation coefficient. Judged by this criterion, there is no reason to prefer either one, because they have the same fit in any data set. One might say that these models are equivalent. To study this issue in more detail we consider the structural model without measurement error. Then the model corresponding to the direct regression is

$$y_n = \beta x_n + \varepsilon_n,$$

where x_n is i.i.d. with mean zero and variance σ_x^2 and ε_n is i.i.d. with mean zero and variance σ_ε^2, independent of x_n. Analogously, the model corresponding to the reverse regression is

$$x_n = \gamma y_n + \delta_n,$$

where y_n is i.i.d. with mean zero and variance σ_y^2 and δ_n is i.i.d. with mean zero and variance σ_δ^2, independent of y_n.

It can be easily seen that any positive definite 2×2 covariance matrix will be fitted perfectly by either regression. Hence, if we assume normality, these two models are observationally equivalent, cf. section 4.4. This is not due to an identification problem, because both models are clearly identified.

This problem of *equivalent models* is much wider ranging. For example, any multiple regression model with g, say, regressors and 1 dependent variable has g equivalent models with each of the other variables acting as dependent variable in turn. (As mentioned in section 3.3, these are called the $g + 1$ elementary regressions.) These regression models are all *saturated* in the sense that they have as many different covariances as there are parameters. The problem of equivalent models is not restricted to saturated models, however, as we will see below.

If there is a set of equivalent models, there is clearly no statistical argument to prefer one over another. The choice for one particular model must be theory based. If, for example, the value of a variable is set by the researcher in a controlled experiment, this variable can obviously not be the dependent variable in a regression equation. Similarly, variables like sex and age are generally not endogenous. In panel data, variables can only be influenced by variables from previous or contemporaneous time points and not by variables from later time points.

In many cases, however, plausible equivalent models remain, and this should be recognized by the researcher. Note also that the frequent occurrence of equivalent models illustrates that statistical analysis can never prove that one variable causes another. Based on the assumption that it does, the size of the effect can be estimated, and this may be small or large, but other explanations about the relation are statistically equally valid.

In structural equation models, the problem of equivalent models is even larger, because relationships among the latent variables can only be inferred indirectly, and examples exist of equivalent models with different numbers of latent variables. Moreover, it is sometimes hard to see whether two models are equivalent or not.

Formally, we consider two structural equation models equivalent if any covariance matrix that satisfies one model also satisfies the other. Let the covariance structures of two structural equation models be denoted by $\Sigma_1(\theta_1)$ and $\Sigma_2(\theta_2)$, respectively. These may be completely different functions of completely different parameter vectors. The only requirement is that any matrix resulting from these functions should be a covariance matrix. These models are equivalent if, for any value θ_1^* of θ_1, there exists a value θ_2^* of θ_2 such that $\Sigma_1(\theta_1^*) = \Sigma_2(\theta_2^*)$ and vice versa. It is important that this can be done for *any* value of the parameter vectors. For example, the regression models $y_n = \beta x_n + \varepsilon_n$ and $y_n = \beta x_n + \gamma z_n + \varepsilon_n$ produce the same set of covariance matrices for $\gamma = 0$, but it is clear that they are not equivalent. If $\gamma \neq 0$, the first model will generally not be able to reproduce the covariance matrix of the second model. Note that we have restricted ourselves to covariance structures. If mean structures are also specified, or multiple groups models, the definition should be adapted accordingly.

Two examples

We now consider two examples illustrating the intricacies involved with equivalent models. Each example consists of two alternative models, which are both identified and nonsaturated. In both examples, it is not immediately clear whether the models are equivalent indeed. The measurement models are the same in all cases and are identified. As a result, we may restrict our attention to the structural models. If the structural submodels are equivalent, the full models are equivalent as well. Moreover, we have the converse result that, if the structural models are nonequivalent, the full models are nonequivalent as well.

We will stay close to the symbols of the LISREL model, but drop the subscript n indicating observations. In all models, there are two endogenous variables, η_1 and η_2, and two exogenous variables ξ_1 and ξ_2. Let, for $i, j, k, l = 1, 2$, γ_{ij} and β_{ik} denote the regression coefficients of the regressions of ξ_j and η_k, respectively, on η_i, and let ϕ_{ij} and ψ_{kl} denote (co)variances among the elements of $\{\xi_1, \xi_2\}$ and $\{\zeta_1, \zeta_2\}$, respectively. We use the superscripts L and R to refer to a parameter in the left or right model, respectively, where left and right refer to their positions in the figures below.

In figure 8.4, the path diagrams of the first example are given. We will now show that these two models are equivalent. First, note that for both models, the covariance matrix of $(\xi_1, \xi_2, \eta_1)'$ is

$$\begin{bmatrix} \phi_{11} & & \\ \phi_{21} & \phi_{22} & \\ \gamma_{11}\phi_{11} & \gamma_{11}\phi_{11} & \gamma_{11}^2\phi_{11} + \psi_{11} \end{bmatrix},$$

from which it follows immediately that ϕ_{11}, ϕ_{21}, ϕ_{22}, γ_{11}, and ψ_{11} should be the same for both models if they should produce the same covariance matrix. Further, the requirements $\mathrm{E}(\eta_2^L\xi_1^L) = \mathrm{E}(\eta_2^R\xi_1^R)$ and $\mathrm{E}(\eta_2^L\xi_2^L) = \mathrm{E}(\eta_2^R\xi_2^R)$ lead to the restrictions

$$\pi_{21}^L\phi_{11} + \gamma_{22}^L\phi_{21} = \gamma_{21}^R\phi_{11} + \gamma_{22}^R\phi_{21}$$
$$\pi_{21}^L\phi_{21} + \gamma_{22}^L\phi_{22} = \gamma_{21}^R\phi_{21} + \gamma_{22}^R\phi_{22},$$

where $\pi_{21}^L \equiv \beta_{21}^L\gamma_{11} + \gamma_{21}^L$. This leads to the solutions $\gamma_{21}^R = \pi_{21}^L$ and, conversely, $\gamma_{21}^L = \gamma_{21}^R - \beta_{21}^L\gamma_{11}$ (where β_{21}^L remains to be solved) and γ_{22} is the same in both solutions. The requirement $\mathrm{E}(\eta_2^L\eta_1^L) = \mathrm{E}(\eta_2^R\eta_1^R)$ leads to the restriction

$$\pi_{21}^L\gamma_{11}\phi_{11} + \gamma_{22}\gamma_{11}\phi_{21} + \beta_{21}^L\psi_{11} = \gamma_{21}^R\gamma_{11}\phi_{11} + \gamma_{22}\gamma_{11}\phi_{21} + \psi_{21}^R,$$

which gives $\psi_{21}^R = \beta_{21}^L\psi_{11}$ and $\beta_{21}^L = \psi_{21}^R/\psi_{11}$. Finally, $\mathrm{E}(\eta_2^L)^2 = \mathrm{E}(\eta_2^R)^2$ leads to the restriction

$$(\pi_{21}^L)^2\phi_{11} + \gamma_{22}^2\phi_{22} + 2\pi_{21}^L\gamma_{22}\phi_{21} + (\beta_{21}^L)^2\psi_{11} + \psi_{22}^L$$
$$= (\gamma_{21}^R)^2\phi_{11} + \gamma_{22}^2\phi_{22} + 2\gamma_{21}^R\gamma_{22}\phi_{21} + \psi_{22}^R,$$

or $\psi_{22}^R = \psi_{22}^L + (\beta_{21}^L)^2\psi_{11}$ and $\psi_{22}^L = \psi_{22}^R - (\beta_{21}^L)^2\psi_{11}$. Thus, given a covariance matrix that satisfies one model, parameter values for the other model can be found that reproduce this covariance matrix. This implies that these models are equivalent, provided the parameter values thus obtained are always allowed. The only restriction that has not been taken into account explicitly or implicitly is that Ψ should be positive definite. It is easily seen that if Ψ^R is positive definite, then Ψ^L is also positive definite and vice versa, so we can conclude that these models are equivalent.

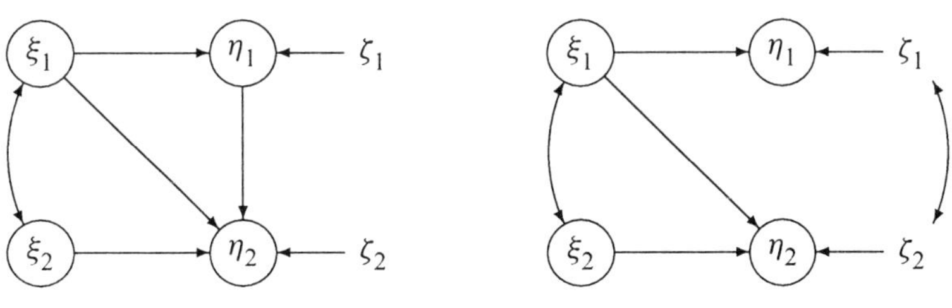

Figure 8.4 *Two equivalent models.*

In figure 8.5, the path diagrams of the second example are given. We will now show that these two models are not equivalent, despite their similarity with the first example. Again, note that for both models, the covariance matrix of $(\xi_1, \xi_2, \eta_1)'$ is the same, in this case

$$\begin{bmatrix} \phi_{11} & & \\ \phi_{21} & \phi_{22} & \\ \gamma_{11}\phi_{11} + \gamma_{12}\phi_{21} & \gamma_{11}\phi_{21} + \gamma_{12}\phi_{22} & \gamma_{11}^2\phi_{11} + \gamma_{12}^2\phi_{22} + 2\gamma_{11}\gamma_{12}\phi_{21} + \psi_{11} \end{bmatrix}$$

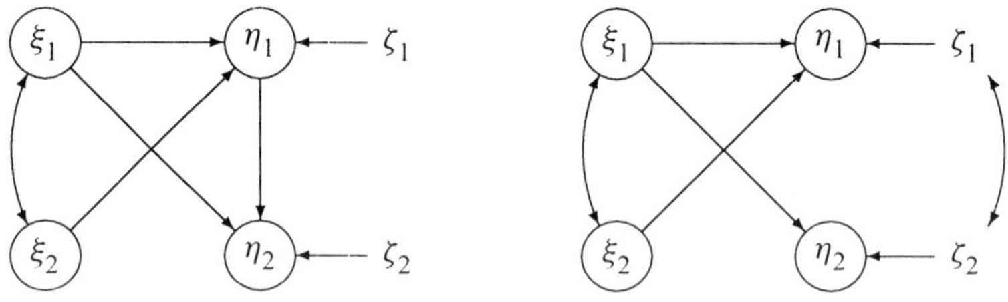

Figure 8.5 *Two nonequivalent models.*

and it follows immediately that $\phi_{11}, \phi_{21}, \phi_{22}, \gamma_{11}, \gamma_{12}$, and ψ_{11} should be same for both models if they should produce the same covariance matrix.

Now, the requirements $\mathrm{E}(\eta_2^L \xi_1^L) = \mathrm{E}(\eta_2^R \xi_1^R)$ and $\mathrm{E}(\eta_2^L \xi_2^L) = \mathrm{E}(\eta_2^R \xi_2^R)$ lead to the restrictions

$$\pi_{21}^L \phi_{11} + \pi_{22}^L \phi_{21} = \gamma_{21}^R \phi_{11}$$
$$\pi_{21}^L \phi_{21} + \pi_{22}^L \phi_{22} = \gamma_{21}^R \phi_{21},$$

where $\pi_{21}^L \equiv \beta_{21}^L \gamma_{11} + \gamma_{21}^L$ and $\pi_{22}^L \equiv \beta_{21}^L \gamma_{12}^L$. If we try to solve these two equations for γ_{21}^R in terms of the parameters of the left model, we obtain the two solutions

$$\gamma_{21}^R = \pi_{21}^L + \pi_{22}^L \phi_{21}/\phi_{11}$$
$$\gamma_{21}^R = \pi_{21}^L + \pi_{22}^L \phi_{22}/\phi_{21},$$

which can only be satisfied both if $\pi_{22}^L = 0$ or $\phi_{21}/\phi_{11} = \phi_{22}\phi_{21}$. The first of these conditions is equivalent to $\beta_{21}^L = 0$ or $\gamma_{12}^L = 0$, which is a restriction that will generally not be satisfied. Anyway, the left model allows these to be nonzero, so this condition will not be satisfied for *any* choice of possible parameter values of the left model. Hence, if the models are to be equivalent, the second condition should be satisfied. This condition can be rewritten as

$$\frac{\phi_{21}^2}{\phi_{11}\phi_{22}} = 1,$$

or the squared correlation between ξ_1 and ξ_2 should be 1. This is unlikely and certainly not satisfied for *any* choice of possible parameter values of the left model. We conclude that these models are not equivalent.

8.8 Bibliographical notes

8.1 On confirmatory FA, see Jöreskog (1969) and, in particular on identification issues, Anderson and Rubin (1956). The discussion on identification in the text is from Bekker (1989). See also Shapiro and Browne (1983). Rotation in a confirmatory context is dealt with by Jennrich (1978). Bollen and Jöreskog (1985) gave a nonpathological example to show that identification is not the same as lack of rotational freedom in CFA.

For a discussion about the legal independence and conservatism of central banks, see De Haan and Kooi (1997).

8.2 The MIMIC model builds on Zellner (1970) and Goldberger (1972a), where the central idea was introduced of expressing the latent variable as the dependent variable in a second model containing the observable causes as regressors. The MIMIC model was introduced by Goldberger (1974). On estimation see Jöreskog and Goldberger (1975). Chen (1981) discusses estimation using the EM approach where the value of the latent variable is explicitly predicted. Chamberlain (1977) presented an instrumental variable interpretation of identification in MIMIC. Attfield (1977) used the original framework by Zellner to estimate a permanent income model where only grouped data are available, inducing heteroskedasticity.

On reduced rank regression, see, e.g., Izenman (1975) and Tso (1981). Cragg and Donald (1997) discussed tests of the rank r of the matrix of regression coefficients. Bekker, Dobbelstein, and Wansbeek (1996) showed that the *arbitrage pricing theory* model can be written as an RRR model. Van der Leeden (1990) developed a version of the RRR model in which general covariance structures may be imposed on Ω (cf. section 8.3 below) and used this to model individual (biological) growth trajectories. Ten Berge (1993, section 4.6) and Reinsel and Velu (1998) gave an extensive discussion of the reduced rank regression model and its relations to other multivariate statistical methods.

8.3 The LISREL model was developed mainly in a series of papers by Karl G. Jöreskog, e.g., Jöreskog (1969, 1970, 1977). He also provided computer programs from the beginning on, culminating in the widely used LISREL program (e.g., Jöreskog and Sörbom, 1981, 1993). After the groundbreaking work of Jöreskog, researchers started to apply the model and the program, and alternative parameterizations and programs were developed.

The amount of literature on structural equation modeling has become enormous, and since 1994 there is even a journal (*Structural Equation Modeling: A Multidisciplinary Journal*) entirely devoted to this type of modeling. Applied introductions to structural equation models are, e.g., Dunn, Everitt, and Pickles (1993), Byrne (1994), and Mueller (1996). More technical overviews about SEM are Bollen (1989), Hoyle (1995), Marcoulides and Schumacker (1996), and Bentler and Dudgeon (1996).

A list of programs and their user's manuals is: LISREL (Jöreskog and Sörbom, 1993), EQS (Bentler, 1995), AMOS (Arbuckle, 1997), Mx (Neale,

Boker, Xie, and Maes, 1999), M*plus* (Muthén and Muthén, 1998), MECOSA (Arminger, Wittenberg, and Schepers, 1996), RAMONA (Browne, Mels, and Coward, 1994), LINCS (Schoenberg and Arminger, 1990), and PROC CALIS (SAS Institute, 1990).

The important subclass of simultaneous equations models with measurement errors has been studied extensively, see, e.g., Geraci (1976, 1977, 1983), Hausman (1977), Hsiao (1976), and Ketellapper (1982). On the identification of this model, see, in particular, Bekker et al. (1994). An extensive discussion of the use of structural equation models in panel data contexts is given in Bijleveld, Mooijaart, Van der Kamp, and Van der Kloot (1998).

Structural equation modeling has been strongly advocated in econometrics by Arthur S. Goldberger; see e.g. Goldberger (1971, 1972b, 1974), Hauser and Goldberger (1971), and Goldberger and Duncan (1973).

How to incorporate polynomial and inequality constraints in LISREL is shown by Rindskopf (1983, 1984b). He used *phantom* variables (latent variables without observable indicators) and *imaginary* variables (latent variables with negative variances) to impose all kinds of complicated restrictions. Although these methods are generally not necessary with current versions of the software, they are illuminating and illustrate the versatility of the specification.

The use of structural equation models has its pitfalls. Freedman (1987) illustrated some of these incisively and questioned the very use of this type of models. Breckler (1990) raised similar issues, but with a more positive view on the possibilities of meaningful empirical application of this type of models, and gave some guidelines on its application.

8.4 The Bentler-Weeks (or EQS) model is due to Bentler and Weeks (1980). The RAM model was developed by McArdle and McDonald (1984).

8.5 The subjects of scale invariance and analysis of correlation matrices have been discussed by, e.g., Swaminathan and Algina (1978), Krane and McDonald (1978), Jöreskog (1978), and Browne (1982). Shapiro and Browne (1990) gave a highly technical discussion of the subject, involving tangent planes.

The analysis of correlation matrices by structural equation models remains a tricky problem in which mistakes are easily made. Cudeck (1989) provided a clear and extensive analysis of the problem and cited a large number of distinguished authors who have drawn wrong conclusions based on the analysis of a correlation matrix. Hence our advice to avoid these problems by analyzing the covariance matrix, with the possible exception of EFA.

A simple derivation of the asymptotic covariance matrix of the elements of the sample correlation matrix is given by Neudecker and Wesselman (1990).

Standardization has a long history in the social sciences, where scales of variables are frequently arbitrary. Some discussion about the merits and drawbacks of standardization in different situations is given in Kim and Mueller (1976) and Kim and Ferree (1981).

8.6 Mean structures are discussed in most books about structural equation modeling and in the manuals of the various programs. An early discussion can be found in Sörbom (1982).

For references to the analysis of higher order moments in the errors in variables and exploratory factor analysis models, we refer to the bibliographic notes to chapters 6 and 7, respectively. Higher order moments are also useful to identify some nonlinear models, see chapter 11. Meijer and Mooijaart (1996) discussed estimation of factor analysis models with parametric forms of heteroskedasticity by analysing second- and third-order moments. Meijer (1998) studied the estimation of structural equation models with higher order moments extensively.

Multiple groups analysis is discussed in most books about structural equation modeling and in the manuals of the various programs. Some key publications developing the theory are Jöreskog (1971), Sörbom (1974), Bentler, Lee, and Weng (1997), Muthén (1989a), and Muthén (1989b).

The treatment of missing data in structural equation models has been discussed by Lee (1986, 1987), Allison (1987), Muthén, Kaplan, and Hollis (1987), and Arbuckle (1996).

8.7 The subject of equivalent models was studied in the context of changing one parameter of a given model by Luijben (1991) and Bekker et al. (1994). The latter authors also provided a computer program to check the equivalency of two models that are both obtained from the same base model by freeing one parameter. Their approach is based on a Jacobian matrix rank criterion extending the rank criterion for local identification.

Rules with which equivalent models can be found from a given model are provided by Stelzl (1986), Lee and Hershberger (1990), and Hershberger (1994).

A general analysis of the problem of equivalent models is given in Raykov and Penev (1999), from which our examples are derived. Williams, Bozdogan, and Aiman-Smith (1996) discussed some examples and proposed to use the ICOMP informational complexity criterion of Bozdogan (1988) as a guideline to choose among equivalent models. The importance of the subject was shown by MacCallum, Wegener, Uchino, and Fabrigar (1993), who surveyed the psychological literature in which structural equation models were used. Equivalent models were very rarely mentioned, although MacCallum et al. found that the median number of equivalent models varied between 12 and 21 in different subdisciplines, with large outliers up to 1.19×10^{18}. These large numbers usually occur when the model has large saturated blocks. In some of the examples that MacCallum et al. analyzed in more detail, they found equivalent models that provided theoretically plausible alternative explanations of the phenomena.

Chapter 9

Generalized method of moments

In the previous chapters, we have used a variety of estimation methods, in particular least squares, instrumental variables, and maximum likelihood. In this chapter, we consider a general class of estimation methods, the generalized method of moments (GMM), that encompasses most other methods and that is particularly relevant in the context of latent variables, warranting treatment at some level of generality.

As the name indicates, GMM extends the classical method of moments (MM). This is a simple and intuitively appealing estimation method where consistent estimators of the parameters of a probability distribution are found by equating corresponding population and sample moments. Section 9.1 starts with some simple examples, and indicates the problem that arises when more moments (or other statistics) are used than there are parameters in the model. Essentially, we then have a system of equations where the number of equations exceeds the number of unknown parameters. Some kind of compromise across the equations is then required where weights indicate the quality of the information conveyed by the respective equations. This approach constitutes the core of the GMM estimation method.

Section 9.2 defines GMM and introduces the notation. Then, in section 9.3 we consider the basic issues of identification, asymptotic distribution, and asymptotic efficiency of the GMM estimator. Asymptotic efficiency amounts to finding optimal weights. These weights are usually unknown, because they depend on the very parameters that are the topic of investigation. Without loss in asymptotic variance, however, consistent estimators can be substituted for the weights. Section 9.4 discusses how to find such estimators in general, and section 9.5 deals with the important special case of covariance structures.

In general, additional information can be employed to estimate a parameter more precisely, and GMM is no exception. When we employ more moments in the estimation procedure, the asymptotic variance of the GMM estimator is reduced, as is shown in section 9.6. An important caveat is that optimal weights should be used. Adding information with suboptimal weighting can actually lead to an estimator with an increased asymptotic variance.

In many situations in econometrics, we are concerned with conditional moments rather than unconditional moments. Conditional moment equations can be used in a flexible way to derive unconditional moment equations. This is discussed in section 9.7, where it is also shown that there is a lower bound to the asymptotic variance of the GMM estimator even if the number of moments increases without bound.

Some applications of GMM suffer from the problem that the population moments, being the expectation of the corresponding sample moments, can not be expressed in a convenient closed form as a function of the parameters. In section 9.8 it is shown how simulation can be employed in this case, and what the consequences are for the asymptotic variance of an estimator based on such a simulation.

Because GMM and maximum likelihood (ML) are the major estimation approaches used in econometrics, a discussion of their differences and agreements and of their relative merits is interesting. These issues are addressed in section 9.9. ML is well known to yield asymptotically efficient estimators, but we show that GMM need not underperform ML.

9.1 The method of moments

The method of moments (MM) is conceptually the simplest approach to parameter estimation. To get a feeling for the method, we consider the simple case of estimating the parameters of a lognormal distribution. The density function is

$$f(x) = \frac{1}{x\sqrt{2\pi}\sigma} \exp\left(-\frac{(\log x - \mu)^2}{2\sigma^2}\right)$$

for $x > 0$. There are two parameters, μ and σ^2. A property of this distribution is that the raw moments are given by

$$\mu_r \equiv \mathrm{E}\left(x^r\right) = \exp(r\mu + \tfrac{1}{2}r^2\sigma^2), \tag{9.1}$$

so, in particular, we have

$$\mu_1 \equiv \mathrm{E}(x) = \exp\left(\mu + \tfrac{1}{2}\sigma^2\right) \tag{9.2a}$$

$$\mu_2 \equiv \mathrm{E}\left(x^2\right) = \exp\left(2\mu + 2\sigma^2\right). \tag{9.2b}$$

The idea of MM is to replace expectations by their sample counterparts and defining estimators by solving the resulting system in terms of the parameters. These estimators are by definition MM estimators. The equations (9.2) are called the *moment equations* or *moment conditions*. Thus, given a sample $x_1, \ldots, x_N$, the MM estimators solve the *estimating equations*

$$m_1 \equiv \frac{1}{N}\sum_{n=1}^{N} x_n = \exp\left(\hat{\mu} + \tfrac{1}{2}\hat{\sigma}^2\right)$$

$$m_2 \equiv \frac{1}{N}\sum_{n=1}^{N} x_n^2 = \exp\left(2\hat{\mu} + 2\hat{\sigma}^2\right).$$

The solution of this system is readily obtained as

$$\hat{\mu} = 2\log m_1 - \tfrac{1}{2}\log m_2 \tag{9.3a}$$

$$\hat{\sigma}^2 = -2\log m_1 + \log m_2. \tag{9.3b}$$

This example can serve as a starting point to group various aspects of MM estimators.

First, MM estimators can often be obtained in a simple way and are by construction, invoking Slutsky's theorem, consistent under general conditions. Originally, this was their major virtue. The example of estimating the parameters of the lognormal distribution does not bring this out clearly, though, because for this particular distribution ML estimators, with their well-known optimality properties, are obtained easily. This can be seen by realizing that, if x is lognormal, $\log x$ is normal. However, when, for example, x is gamma distributed, $f(x) = x^{\theta-1}e^{-x}/\Gamma(\theta)$, and the ML estimator of θ follows from the nonlinear equation

$$\frac{1}{N}\sum_{n=1}^{N}\log x_n = \frac{\Gamma'(\hat{\theta})}{\Gamma(\hat{\theta})},$$

which has to be solved by numerical methods. The MM estimator, by contrast, is simply obtained by equating the first sample and population moment, which leads to $\hat{\theta} = \bar{x}$, the sample mean.

Second, MM estimators are not unique. We can alternatively estimate the two parameters in the lognormal case by considering, for example, the first- and third-order moments μ_1 and μ_3. This gives

$$\begin{aligned}\hat{\mu} &= \tfrac{3}{2}\log m_1 - \tfrac{1}{6}\log m_3\\ \hat{\sigma}^2 &= -\log m_1 + \tfrac{1}{3}\log m_3,\end{aligned}$$

with $m_3 \equiv \sum_{n=1}^{N} x_n^3/N$. These are different but also consistent estimators. This suggests an approach where, rather than choosing between estimators, the information conveyed by the three moments is combined to obtain a more efficient estimator. In that case, however, not all three estimating equations can be simultaneously solved for the two parameters. Therefore, some compromise has to be found, and this constitutes the essence of the generalized method of moments (GMM). Generally, by increasing the amount of information, more efficient estimators are found. In the limit, the estimators thus found may be equally efficient as ML estimators, which are well known to be asymptotically efficient under general conditions.

This raises a third issue, which is why ML estimators are not to be preferred anyhow. One reason was already hinted at, which is that MM (or in general GMM, from now on) estimators can be computationally easier to handle. This is nowadays usually not a convincing argument, however. The major argument in favor of GMM relative to ML is that, in order to be able to perform ML estimation, a full parametric specification of the model, including distributional assumptions on all random elements, is required. This contrasts with GMM estimation, which can be applied as soon as a sufficient number of estimating equations is available. In this sense, GMM is more robust to specification error than ML.

A simple illustration is offered by the linear regression model. To consider one form of this model, let $y_n = x_n'\beta + \varepsilon_n$, $n = 1, \ldots, N$, or, for all observations together, $y = X\beta + \varepsilon$, with the x_n i.i.d. with mean zero and covariance matrix Σ_X and with the ε_n i.i.d. with mean zero and variance σ_ε^2. Then the moment conditions are

$$\mathrm{E}\begin{bmatrix} y_n \\ x_n \end{bmatrix}(y_n, x_n') = \begin{bmatrix} \beta'\Sigma_X\beta + \sigma_\varepsilon^2 & \beta'\Sigma_X \\ \Sigma_X\beta & \Sigma_X \end{bmatrix},$$

which leads to estimators that solve the estimating equations

$$\frac{1}{N}\begin{bmatrix} y'y & y'X \\ X'y & X'X \end{bmatrix} = \begin{bmatrix} \hat{\beta}'\hat{\Sigma}_X\hat{\beta} + \hat{\sigma}_\varepsilon^2 & \hat{\beta}'\hat{\Sigma}_X \\ \hat{\Sigma}_X\hat{\beta} & \hat{\Sigma}_X \end{bmatrix}.$$

These estimators are, of course, the well-known estimators for β and σ_ε^2 (and $\hat{\Sigma}_X = X'X/N$ is the estimator of Σ_X), which would also be the ML estimators if we had imposed an assumption of normality on the x_n and the ε_n. However, to derive the estimators just implied, no assumption on the distributions of the random elements has been made.

As another illustration, consider the simple dynamic panel data model given by $y_{nt} = \gamma y_{n,t-1} + u_{nt}$ for observations y_{nt} with $t = 1, 2, 3$, and $n = 1, \ldots, N$. The disturbance term u_{nt} consists of two components, $u_{nt} = \alpha_n + \varepsilon_{nt}$, where α_n and ε_{nt} have mean zero and are mutually uncorrelated, and where the ε_{nt} are uncorrelated over time and uncorrelated with the y_{ns} for $s < t$. This model implies that α_n and the y_{nt} are correlated. Therefore, we have a model where the regressor and the disturbance term are correlated and hence estimation requires special care in order to avoid inconsistency. Consistent estimators for this model can be based on

$$\mathrm{E}\big((y_{n3} - y_{n2})y_{n1} - \gamma(y_{n2} - y_{n1})y_{n1}\big) = 0,$$

because $\mathrm{E}(u_{n3} - u_{n2})y_{n1} = 0$. This gives the estimating equation

$$\sum_{n=1}^{N}(y_{n3} - y_{n2})y_{n1} = \hat{\gamma}\sum_{n=1}^{N}(y_{n2} - y_{n1})y_{n1}, \tag{9.4}$$

from which a consistent estimator of γ follows readily. The interesting feature of this approach is that there is in particular no need to choose between the various ways proposed in the literature to specify the distribution of y_{n0}. Estimation of the model by ML, however, does require such a specification. A correct specification will result in an efficiency gain of ML over GMM when estimating γ, and when γ is close to 1 this gain is large. However, when an incorrect specification is chosen, the ML estimator is inconsistent. Thus, choosing between ML and GMM in estimating this model involves a trade-off between efficiency on the one hand and hedging against misspecification on the other hand.

Note that $\hat{\gamma}$ as derived from (9.4) is the IV estimator of the regression of $y_{n3} - y_{n2}$ on $y_{n2} - y_{n1}$, with y_{n1} as instrumental variable. This phenomenon occurs frequently, many GMM estimators can be interpreted as IV estimators. On the other hand, IV estimators form the leading case of GMM, based on the moment equation $\mathrm{E}(Z'y - Z'X\beta) = 0$ if the number of instruments is equal to the number of regressors, or $\mathrm{E}(X'P_Zy - X'P_ZX\beta) = 0$ if the number of instruments exceeds the number of regressors.

As a final example, note that from (6.30) and (6.33), it follows that the LIML estimator can also be interpreted as a GMM estimator.

9.2 Definition and notation

We now turn to a general formulation of GMM estimators. Let $\bar{g}$ be a p-vector of statistics, e.g., a number of sample moments, derived as the average of a sample of N observations g_n,

$$\bar{g} = \frac{1}{N} \sum_{n=1}^{N} g_n. \tag{9.5}$$

Let $\gamma \equiv \mathrm{E}(g_n) = \mathrm{E}(\bar{g})$. The expectation vector γ depends on a number of parameters collected in the m-vector θ, i.e., $\gamma = \gamma(\theta)$, with $m \leq p$.

In the previous section, we have already seen some examples of this. Another, important case that will get particular attention in this chapter is given by the covariance structure of a structural equation model. As we have seen from (8.8), a structural equation model implies a certain formula for the covariance matrix of the observed variables, $\mathrm{E}(z_n z_n') = \Sigma(\theta)$, where z_n is the vector of observed variables and $\Sigma(\theta)$ expresses the covariance matrix as a function of the parameter vector θ. For example, in a factor analysis model, $\Sigma(\theta) = B\Phi B' + \Omega$, where B is the matrix of factor loadings, Φ is the covariance matrix of the factors, and Ω is the covariance matrix of the errors. In this case, θ consists of the elements of B, Φ, and Ω that may be freely estimated, g_n consists of the nonduplicated elements of $z_n \otimes z_n$, $\bar{g}$ consists of the corresponding elements of the sample covariance matrix (assuming that the mean of z is zero), and $\gamma(\theta)$ consists of the corresponding elements of $\Sigma(\theta)$.

Let us now return to the general specification. We wish to estimate the true value θ_0 of θ. The moment equations are

$$\mathrm{E}\left(g_n - \gamma(\theta_0)\right) = 0, \tag{9.6}$$

and we search for an estimator $\hat{\theta}$ such that $\bar{g} - \gamma(\hat{\theta}) \approx 0$. The principle to be employed is to minimize the distance, measured in a certain metric, between $\bar{g}$ and $\gamma(\theta)$ over θ.

Let $\hat{W}$ be a matrix of order $p \times p$, chosen by the researcher. As suggested by the hat, this matrix may depend on the data. It is assumed that $\hat{W}$ is symmetric and positive definite with probability one. Then the GMM estimator $\hat{\theta}$ of θ_0 is defined as the minimizer of the distance between $\bar{g}$ and γ in the metric given by $\hat{W}$, so $\hat{\theta}$ is the minimizing argument of

$$\bar{q}(\theta) \equiv (\bar{g} - \gamma(\theta))' \hat{W} (\bar{g} - \gamma(\theta)). \tag{9.7}$$

For obvious reasons, $\hat{W}$ is called the weight matrix. As the form of (9.7) suggests, the GMM estimator can be interpreted as a minimum distance estimator. However, this term is unduly restrictive, because we can extend the form of moment equations within the scope of GMM theory beyond (9.6) to cases that do not directly suggest a distance. That is, we can generalize (9.6) to

$$\mathrm{E}\left(h_n(\theta_0)\right) = 0, \tag{9.8}$$

where h_n explicitly depends on parameters and implicitly on the data. For obvious reasons, we call (9.8) the *inclusive form* and (9.6) the *separated form*. In the inclusive form, we search for $\hat{\theta}$ such that

$$\bar{h}(\hat{\theta}) \equiv \frac{1}{N}\sum_{n=1}^{N} h_n(\hat{\theta}) \approx 0. \tag{9.9}$$

Therefore, more in general, the GMM estimator is the minimizing argument of

$$\bar{q}(\theta) \equiv \bar{h}(\theta)'\hat{W}\bar{h}(\theta). \tag{9.10}$$

We will often consider GMM theory for the more general formulation in terms of $\bar{h}$ but some results to be discussed in the sequel apply only to the more specific formulation in terms of $\bar{g}$ and γ.

To economize on notation, we will often write

$$\begin{aligned} \hat{\gamma} &\equiv \gamma(\hat{\theta}) \qquad & \hat{h} &\equiv \bar{h}(\hat{\theta}) \\ \gamma_0 &\equiv \gamma(\theta_0) \qquad & \bar{h}_0 &\equiv \bar{h}(\theta_0). \end{aligned}$$

We assume $\bar{h}$ in general and γ in particular to be at least twice continuously differentiable with respect to θ and write

$$\begin{aligned} \bar{G}(\theta) &\equiv \frac{\partial \bar{h}(\theta)}{\partial \theta'} \qquad & G(\theta) &\equiv \operatorname*{plim}_{N\to\infty} \bar{G}(\theta) \\ \hat{G} &\equiv \bar{G}(\hat{\theta}) \qquad & G_0 &\equiv G(\theta_0), \end{aligned} \tag{9.11}$$

all being of order $p \times m$. Note that in the separated case, the matrix of derivatives is given by $\bar{G}(\theta) = G(\theta) = -\partial\gamma/\partial\theta'$, which does not depend on the data.

Considering the more general formulation (9.10) rather than (9.7), the first-order condition for a minimum is

$$\hat{s} \equiv \hat{G}'\hat{W}\hat{h} = 0. \tag{9.12}$$

The vector $\hat{s}$ may be called the *pseudo score*, because it plays in GMM estimation the same role as the score vector (the derivative of the loglikelihood function) in ML estimation. The value $\hat{\theta}$ for which (9.12) holds and which is also the minimizing argument of (9.10) is by definition the GMM estimator $\hat{\theta}$ of θ.

To derive asymptotic properties of the GMM estimator, we make a few assumptions on the asymptotic behavior of $\hat{h}$ and $\hat{W}$. Under weak conditions, $\bar{h}_0$ converges to 0 in probability if (9.8) holds. Further, we assume that $\hat{W}$ converges in probability to a nonrandom symmetric positive definite matrix W_0, and we assume that

$$\sqrt{N}\,\bar{h}_0 \xrightarrow{d} \mathcal{N}_p(0, \Psi), \tag{9.13}$$

which is usually true for some Ψ under mild conditions. This follows by applying some form of central limit theorem to (9.9). Incidentally, many results in this chapter and chapter 10 only use (9.13), without reference to (9.9). It is assumed that Ψ is of full rank. Otherwise, some elements of $\bar{h}$ are linearly dependent and $\bar{h}$ can hence be reduced without losing information.

In the next section we discuss a number of basic properties of GMM. Before doing so, we show that GMM is much more general than may be apparent at first sight.

On the generality of GMM

As we saw above, GMM estimation in the separated case can be interpreted as a minimum distance estimator. The estimator was seen to be found by minimizing the distance between statistics and their parameterized expectations, where this distance was measured with a quadratic function. However, one could think of many other distance functions besides the quadratic one.

In order to discuss this point, we first need to be explicit about the notion of a distance function. We use the following definition. A function $d \equiv d(\bar{g}, \gamma)$ is said to be a distance function in the estimation of the parameter vector θ when it is nonnegative, twice continuously differentiable in both arguments, and when it is zero if and only if $\bar{g} = \gamma$.

Given this definition, we have the following result. Any distance function d can be expressed in the quadratic form

$$d\,(\bar{g}, \gamma) = (\bar{g} - \gamma)' V_{\bar{g},\gamma} (\bar{g} - \gamma),$$

where $V_{\bar{g}.\gamma}$ is the matrix with typical element

$$(V_{\bar{g}.\gamma})_{ij} \equiv \int_0^1 \int_0^1 t d''_{ij}\big(\gamma + ut(\bar{g} - \gamma), \gamma\big)\, \mathrm{d}u\, \mathrm{d}t,$$

where primes denote, here and below, derivatives taken with respect to the first argument of the function.

This result can be shown as follows. Fix the value of γ momentarily and let $\delta(t)$ be the scalar function of the scalar variable t defined by

$$\delta(t) \equiv d\big(\gamma + t(\bar{g} - \gamma), \gamma\big).$$

Hence, $\delta(0) = d(\gamma, \gamma) = 0$, and

$$d(\bar{g}, \gamma) = d(\bar{g}, \gamma) - d(\gamma, \gamma) = \delta(1) - \delta(0) = \int_0^1 \delta'(t)\, \mathrm{d}t. \tag{9.14}$$

Application of the chain rule yields

$$\delta'(t) = \sum_{i=1}^{p} (\bar{g}_i - \gamma_i) d_i'\big(\gamma + t(\bar{g} - \gamma), \gamma\big), \tag{9.15}$$

where $d_i'(\cdot, \gamma)$ denotes the partial derivative of d with respect to the i-th element of its first argument. Next, let $\zeta_i(u)$ be the scalar function of the scalar variable u defined by

$$\zeta_i(u) \equiv d_i'\big(\gamma + ut(\bar{g} - \gamma), \gamma\big).$$

Now, observe that the conditions on d imply that, given the value of γ, $d(\bar{g}, \gamma)$ has a unique global minimum in $\bar{g} = \gamma$, and is differentiable in that point. Hence, $\zeta_i(0) = d_i'(\gamma, \gamma) = 0$, and

$$d_i'\big(\gamma + t(\bar{g} - \gamma), \gamma\big) = \zeta_i(1) - \zeta_i(0) = \int_0^1 \zeta_i'(u)\, \mathrm{d}u. \tag{9.16}$$

Applying the chain rule once again gives

$$\zeta_i'(u) = \sum_{j=1}^{p} t(\bar{g}_j - \gamma_j) d_{ij}''\big(\gamma + ut(\bar{g} - \gamma), \gamma\big).$$

Combining this with (9.14)–(9.16) gives

$$d(\bar{g}, \gamma) = \sum_{i=1}^{p} \sum_{j=1}^{p} (\bar{g}_i - \gamma_i)(\bar{g}_j - \gamma_j) \times \int_0^1 \int_0^1 t d_{ij}''\big(\gamma + ut(\bar{g} - \gamma), \gamma\big)\, \mathrm{d}u\, \mathrm{d}t,$$

which proves the result that any distance function can be written as a quadratic function.

Notice that the weight matrix in the quadratic function, $V_{\bar{g},\gamma}$, depends on both $\bar{g}$ and γ. As we will see in the next section, the asymptotic distribution of the GMM estimator depends on the probability limit of the weight matrix rather than on the weight matrix proper and is hence not affected if γ is replaced by $\bar{g}$, provided the estimator is consistent, because then both $\operatorname{plim}_{N\to\infty} \bar{g} = \gamma$ and $\operatorname{plim}_{N\to\infty} \gamma(\hat{\theta}) = \gamma$. Then, the estimator has the same asymptotic distribution as the estimator with weight matrix $V_{\bar{g},\bar{g}}$, with elements

$$\left(V_{\bar{g},\bar{g}}\right)_{ij} = \int_0^1 \int_0^1 t d''_{ij}(\bar{g}, \bar{g})\, \mathrm{d}u\, \mathrm{d}t = \tfrac{1}{2} d''_{ij}(\bar{g}, \bar{g}), \tag{9.17}$$

instead of $V_{\bar{g},\gamma}$. Apparently, the asymptotic distribution of an estimator based on a particular distance function depends only on the second derivatives of this function. Note further that in the derivation, only the consistency of the estimator is used, to derive (9.17).

Up till now, we have considered the separated case. However, the result extends straightforwardly to the inclusive form. In the inclusive case, we only have one moment vector, $\bar{h}(\theta)$. The definition of a distance function to be used in this case is as follows. A function $\tilde{d} \equiv \tilde{d}(\bar{h})$ is said to be a distance function in the estimation of the parameter vector θ when it is nonnegative, twice continuously differentiable, and when it is zero if and only if $\bar{h} = 0$.

Let us now use the notation $d(\bar{h}, 0) \equiv \tilde{d}(\bar{h})$, then we see immediately that, given that the second argument is zero, d satisfies the conditions for a distance function in the separated case. If, in the derivation for the separated case above, we replace γ by 0 and $\bar{g}$ by $\bar{h}$, the entire derivation remains correct, as well as the result. Instead of (9.17), we now have

$$\left(\tilde{V}_0\right)_{ij} \equiv \tfrac{1}{2} \tilde{d}''_{ij}(0)$$

and it is now required that $\operatorname{plim}_{N\to\infty} \bar{h} = 0$. Because $\bar{h}$ is a function of θ, this means that the requirement is $\operatorname{plim}_{N\to\infty} \hat{h} = 0$. Again, this means that it must be proved first that the estimator is consistent.

9.3 Basic properties of GMM estimators

In this section, we discuss the basic properties of GMM estimators. We consider the consistency of the GMM estimator, raising of course the issue of identification. After that, the asymptotic distribution is derived. We consider linearized GMM, which can sometimes offer a simplification of the estimation of a model by GMM. We conclude with a discussion of the optimal choice for the weight matrix.

Identification and consistency

First, define the vector function $h(\theta) \equiv \text{plim}_{N\to\infty} \bar{h}(\theta)$, which implies that $h(\theta) = \text{E}(h_n(\theta))$ if the data are i.i.d., and observe that $h(\theta_0) = \text{plim}_{N\to\infty} \bar{h}_0 = 0$ by some law of large numbers. If there is another value of θ, θ_1, say, such that $h(\theta_1) = 0$, then (9.8) also holds for θ_1 and on the basis of the given moment conditions we can not decide whether θ_0 or θ_1 should be considered the true value. This situation is very similar to a lack of identification as discussed in chapter 4.

When introduced in section 4.2, the notion of identification was linked to the information matrix, which is a concept in the context of maximum likelihood estimation and which, hence, only has a meaning when the underlying parameterized probability distribution functions have been fully specified. In the context of GMM, however, we do not necessarily use this full specification, but rather work with a certain number of statistics, and the only role played by probability distributions in constructing an estimator is to derive the expectation of whatever statistics we happen to consider. If we consider identification as the notion that informs as to what can and can not be inferred about the parameters on the basis of the statistics collected in $\bar{g}$ or $\bar{h}$, we need a different definition. The above discussion makes it clear that a useful definition is that the parameters are (globally) identified if and only if the only value of θ that satisfies $h(\theta) = 0$ is $\theta = \theta_0$.

Now consider, for example, a factor analysis model. It is clear that we can reverse the signs of the elements in an arbitrary column of the factor loadings matrix without any distributional consequence, provided that column, and the corresponding off-diagonal elements of the factor covariance matrix, do not contain nonzero fixed values. If we do so, we get an observationally equivalent model that is also interpretationally equivalent. From a practitioner's point of view, there is no substantial issue at stake. According to the above definition, however, this means that the parameters are not identified. We may, however, impose some arbitrary restriction that excludes one of the solutions, for example, restrict one factor loading to be positive. This restriction may render the parameters identified.

It should be stressed, however, that the current definition of identification is conditional on the set of moment conditions. There may exist different choices of moment conditions, derived from the same underlying model, such that the model is identified using one choice and not identified using another.

Because $\hat{W}$ converges in probability to W_0, the GMM criterion function $\bar{q}(\theta)$ converges in probability to $q(\theta) = h(\theta)' W_0 h(\theta)$. Clearly, this expression attains a global minimum equal to zero for $h(\theta) = h(\theta_0) = 0$. Hence, if the model is identified, then under some fairly weak generality conditions, $\hat{\theta}$ converges to θ_0 and is therefore consistent.

In practice, it is difficult to check the (global) identification of the model. It would be desirable if we would have a criterion that is easier to check, such as the information matrix criterion discussed in chapter 4. From mathematical analysis, it is known that, if $F(x)$ is a twice continuously differentiable function of the vector variable x, x_0 is an interior point of its domain, and the rank of the Hessian matrix $\partial^2 F/\partial x\,\partial x'$ is constant in a neighborhood of x_0, then F has a local minimum in x_0 if and only if the gradient $\partial F/\partial x$ is zero in x_0 and the Hessian is positive definite in x_0. (See also the proof of theorem 4.1.)

The gradient of $q(\theta)$ in θ_0 is $G_0' W_0 h(\theta_0)$, which is obviously zero, because $h(\theta_0)$ is zero. Hence, if we assume that θ_0 is an interior point of its domain and the rank of the Hessian of $q(\theta)$ is constant in a neighborhood of θ_0, then $q(\theta)$ has a local minimum in θ_0 if and only if its Hessian is positive definite in θ_0. Given that $h(\theta_0) = 0$, the Hessian in θ_0 is $G_0' W_0 G_0$. Because W_0 is positive definite by assumption, this expression is positive definite if and only if G_0 is of full column rank in θ_0. Consequently, given the stated assumptions, local identification of θ is equivalent to the requirement that $G(\theta)$ is of full column rank in a neighborhood of θ_0. We will make this assumption in the rest of this chapter. (Note the similarity with the Jacobian matrix criterion in section 4.4.)

The asymptotic distribution of the GMM estimator

We now turn to the asymptotic distribution of the GMM estimator. We show that $\hat{\theta}$ is asymptotically normally distributed,

$$\sqrt{N}(\hat{\theta} - \theta_0) \xrightarrow{d} \mathcal{N}_m(0, V_W), \tag{9.18}$$

with asymptotic covariance matrix V_W,

$$V_W \equiv (G_0' W_0 G_0)^{-1} G_0' W_0 \Psi W_0 G_0 (G_0' W_0 G_0)^{-1} \tag{9.19}$$

and Ψ as in (9.13). Consider first the separated case. From (9.12) we obtain

$$\frac{\partial \hat{s}}{\partial \hat{\theta}'} = \hat{G}' \hat{W} \hat{G} + \big((\bar{g} - \hat{\gamma})' \hat{W} \otimes I_m\big) \frac{\partial \operatorname{vec} \hat{G}'}{\partial \hat{\theta}'},$$

where the result $\operatorname{vec}(ABC) = (C' \otimes A)\operatorname{vec}(B)$, see section A.1, has been used. As a result,

$$\operatorname*{plim}_{N\to\infty} \frac{\partial \hat{s}}{\partial \hat{\theta}'} = G_0' W_0 G_0.$$

Furthermore, $\partial\hat{s}/\partial\bar{g}' = \hat{G}'\hat{W}$, which converges in probability to $G_0'W_0$. The implicit function theorem implies that

$$\operatorname*{plim}_{N\to\infty} \frac{\partial\hat{\theta}}{\partial\bar{g}'} = -\operatorname*{plim}_{N\to\infty} \left(\frac{\partial\hat{s}}{\partial\hat{\theta}'}\right)^{-1} \frac{\partial\hat{s}}{\partial\bar{g}'} = -(G_0'W_0G_0)^{-1}G_0'W_0, \tag{9.20}$$

and straightforward application of the delta method leads to the desired result.

For the inclusive case, we have to adapt this derivation somewhat. By the mean value theorem, we have that

$$\bar{h}(\theta) = \bar{h}_0 + G^*(\theta - \theta_0),$$

where G^* is a matrix whose elements are

$$G^*_{ij} = \left(\bar{G}\left(\alpha_i\theta + (1-\alpha_i)\theta_0\right)\right)_{ij},$$

for some $\alpha_i \in [0, 1]$. Asymptotically, $\hat{\theta}$ will be an interior point of its domain if θ_0 is, because of its consistency. Hence, $\hat{\theta}$ is (asymptotically) a solution to $\hat{G}'\hat{W}\hat{h} = 0$. Analogously, both $\hat{G}$ and G^* will have full column rank asymptotically, given the local identification assumption, and thus, an explicit expression for $\hat{\theta}$ is

$$\hat{\theta} - \theta_0 = -(\hat{G}'\hat{W}G^*)^{-1}\hat{G}'\hat{W}\bar{h}_0. \tag{9.21}$$

Because of the consistency of $\hat{\theta}$, both $\hat{G}$ and G^* converge in probability to G_0. Therefore, and because $\hat{W}$ converges in probability to W_0, application of Slutsky's theorem to (9.21) and (9.13) gives the desired result.

Linearized GMM

Assume that an estimator $\hat{\theta}_1$ is easy to obtain and consistent but considered not yet attractive, for example, because its asymptotic distribution is hard to determine or because it is not asymptotically efficient. It may then be fruitful to use $\hat{\theta}_1$ as a starting point for obtaining more suitable GMM estimators. By the mean value theorem, we have that

$$\bar{h}(\theta) = \hat{h}_1 + G^{**}(\theta - \hat{\theta}_1),$$

where $\hat{h}_1 \equiv \bar{h}(\hat{\theta}_1)$ and G^{**} is a matrix whose elements are

$$G^{**}_{ij} = \left(\bar{G}\left(\alpha_i\theta + (1-\alpha_i)\hat{\theta}_1\right)\right)_{ij},$$

for some $\alpha_i \in [0, 1]$. Of course, these α_i's may be different from the α_i's used in the definition of G^*. Because we are interested in estimating θ_0, we are interested in the value of G^{**} in $\theta = \theta_0$. As $\hat{\theta}_{\mathrm{I}}$ is a consistent estimator of θ_0, this can be approximated (and consistently estimated) by $\hat{G}_{\mathrm{I}} \equiv \bar{G}(\hat{\theta}_{\mathrm{I}})$. Hence, given the initial estimator $\hat{\theta}_{\mathrm{I}}$, we can *linearize* the moment vector as

$$\bar{h}(\theta) \approx \hat{h}_{\mathrm{I}} + \hat{G}_{\mathrm{I}}(\theta - \hat{\theta}_{\mathrm{I}}),$$

and, consequently,

$$\bar{q}(\theta) \approx \bar{q}^*(\theta) \equiv \left(\hat{h}_{\mathrm{I}} + \hat{G}_{\mathrm{I}}(\theta - \hat{\theta}_{\mathrm{I}})\right)' \hat{W} \left(\hat{h}_{\mathrm{I}} + \hat{G}_{\mathrm{I}}(\theta - \hat{\theta}_{\mathrm{I}})\right). \tag{9.22}$$

Therefore, we may approximate the GMM estimator $\hat{\theta}$, which is found by minimizing $\bar{q}(\theta)$, by the linearized GMM (LGMM) estimator $\hat{\theta}_{\mathrm{LGMM}}$, which is found by minimizing $\bar{q}^*(\theta)$. It follows immediately from (9.22) that $\hat{\theta}_{\mathrm{LGMM}}$ can be written in explicit form as

$$\hat{\theta}_{\mathrm{LGMM}} = \hat{\theta}_{\mathrm{I}} - (\hat{G}_{\mathrm{I}}' \hat{W} \hat{G}_{\mathrm{I}})^{-1} \hat{G}_{\mathrm{I}}' \hat{W} \hat{h}_{\mathrm{I}}. \tag{9.23}$$

Thus, LGMM builds on a given consistent estimator and makes a one-step adaptation, based on the local approximation of the GMM criterion function by a quadratic function in θ. The LGMM estimator is the value of θ that minimizes this quadratic function.

To study the asymptotic distribution of $\hat{\theta}_{\mathrm{LGMM}}$, we first apply the mean value theorem to $\hat{h}_{\mathrm{I}}$:

$$\hat{h}_{\mathrm{I}} = \bar{h}_0 + G^{***}(\hat{\theta}_{\mathrm{I}} - \theta_0), \tag{9.24}$$

where G^{***} is a matrix whose elements are

$$G_{ij}^{***} = \left(\bar{G}(\alpha_i \hat{\theta}_{\mathrm{I}} + (1 - \alpha_i)\theta_0)\right)_{ij},$$

for some $\alpha_i \in [0, 1]$, of course again different from the previous α_i's. By inserting (9.24) into (9.23), we have

$$\begin{aligned} \hat{\theta}_{\mathrm{LGMM}} - \theta_0 &= (I_m - (\hat{G}_{\mathrm{I}}' \hat{W} \hat{G}_{\mathrm{I}})^{-1} \hat{G}_{\mathrm{I}}' \hat{W} G^{***})(\hat{\theta}_{\mathrm{I}} - \theta_0) \\ &\quad - (\hat{G}_{\mathrm{I}}' \hat{W} \hat{G}_{\mathrm{I}})^{-1} \hat{G}_{\mathrm{I}}' \hat{W} \bar{h}_0. \end{aligned} \tag{9.25}$$

Clearly, the matrix $I_m - (\hat{G}_{\mathrm{I}}' \hat{W} \hat{G}_{\mathrm{I}})^{-1} \hat{G}_{\mathrm{I}}' \hat{W} G^{***}$ converges to zero in probability, so if $\sqrt{N}(\hat{\theta}_{\mathrm{I}} - \theta_0)$ converges to a random variable that is bounded in probability (i.e., $\hat{\theta}_{\mathrm{I}}$ is root-N consistent), we have, by applying Slutsky's theorem to (9.25),

$$\sqrt{N}(\hat{\theta}_{\mathrm{LGMM}} - \theta_0) \xrightarrow{d} \mathcal{N}_m(0, V_W).$$

Thus, the LGMM estimator has the same asymptotic distribution as the GMM estimator based on the same weight matrix. Moreover, not only are their asymptotic distributions equivalent, but it is also immediately clear by comparing (9.25) to (9.21) that the LGMM and GMM estimators are asymptotically equivalent in the sense that

$$\sqrt{N}(\hat{\theta}_{\mathrm{LGMM}} - \hat{\theta}_{\mathrm{GMM}}) \xrightarrow{p} 0.$$

This means that all subsequent asymptotic results pertaining to GMM estimators also hold for the corresponding LGMM estimators. As long as it is root-N consistent, the choice of initial estimator $\hat{\theta}_{\mathrm{I}}$ is asymptotically irrelevant. The LGMM procedure is especially attractive when the computation of the GMM estimator can only be obtained as the solution of a nonlinear equation, calling for numerical methods, while at the same time it is possible to construct an estimator noniteratively that is root-N consistent and can hence act as initial estimator. Another application of LGMM is to use the unweighted GMM estimator with $\hat{W} = I_p$ as initial estimator and to improve it in one step towards efficiency.

The main advantage of the LGMM estimators is that they are computationally more efficient than their GMM counterparts. This computational efficiency is particularly useful in situations where the parameter vector θ has to be estimated repeatedly, such as for jackknife and bootstrap procedures (for bias correction, nonparametric confidence intervals and the like) or for multiple LM or LR tests (see section 10.1).

Asymptotic efficiency

The discussion of the consistency of the GMM estimator showed that the choice of $\hat{W}$ has no bearing on consistency. From the expression of the asymptotic distribution, however, it is evident that the choice does affect the asymptotic variance of the GMM estimator. The question remains what choice for $\hat{W}$ leads to a GMM estimator with minimal asymptotic variance, where minimal means that the asymptotic covariance matrix is dominated, in the Löwner sense (cf. section A.3), by that of any other consistent estimator based on $\bar{h}$. The weight matrix $\hat{W}$ is optimal if

$$W_0 \equiv \operatorname*{plim}_{N\to\infty} \hat{W} = \Psi^{-1}.$$

The asymptotic covariance matrix for the GMM estimator then attains its lower bound, which is

$$V_{\Psi^{-1}} = \left(G_0'\Psi^{-1}G_0\right)^{-1}. \tag{9.26}$$

This follows from the Cauchy-Schwarz inequality (A.13), which implies that

$$(G_0' W_0 G_0)^{-1} G_0' W_0 \Psi W_0 G_0 (G_0' W_0 G_0)^{-1} \geq (G_0' \Psi^{-1} G_0)^{-1}. \tag{9.27}$$

The left-hand side is the asymptotic covariance matrix of the GMM estimator based on a weight matrix $\hat{W}$ that converges to the matrix W_0, as given in (9.19), and the right-hand side is the covariance matrix of the GMM estimator based on a weight matrix $\hat{W}$ that converges to Ψ^{-1}, the inverse of the asymptotic covariance matrix of $\bar{h}_0$.

Although $W_0 = \Psi^{-1}$ is one choice for W_0 that leads to an optimal estimator, it is not the only one. From theorem B.1, it follows that a necessary and sufficient condition for (9.27) to become an equality is that

$$\Psi W_0 G_0 = G_0 D, \tag{9.28}$$

for some nonsingular matrix D, or equivalently, that

$$W_0^{-1} = \alpha \Psi + G_0 P G_0' + \Psi H_0 Q H_0' \Psi, \tag{9.29}$$

where α is an arbitrary nonnegative constant and P and Q are symmetric matrices which are arbitrary as long as W_0 is positive definite, and H_0 is such that (G_0, H_0) is a square matrix of full rank p and $G_0' H_0 = 0$.

Estimation of the asymptotic covariance matrix of the estimator

If $W_0 = \Psi^{-1}$, the asymptotic covariance matrix $V_{\Psi^{-1}}$ can obviously be estimated consistently by

$$\hat{V} \equiv (\hat{G}' \hat{W} \hat{G})^{-1}. \tag{9.30}$$

However, if $W_0 \neq \Psi^{-1}$, (9.30) is generally not a consistent estimator of the asymptotic covariance matrix, even under optimal weighting, i.e., even if (9.29) is satisfied, or, equivalently, (9.28) is satisfied. Evidently, (9.30) is a consistent estimator of the asymptotic covariance matrix of $\hat{\theta}$ if and only if

$$(G_0' W_0 G_0)^{-1} = (G_0' W_0 G_0)^{-1} G_0' W_0 \Psi W_0 G_0 (G_0' W_0 G_0)^{-1},$$

cf. (9.19). This condition is equivalent with

$$G_0' W_0 G_0 = G_0' W_0 \Psi W_0 G_0. \tag{9.31}$$

The precise condition under which this holds is given (in slightly different notation) in theorem B.2.

If this condition is not satisfied, the asymptotic covariance matrix must be estimated by inserting consistent estimators in (9.26) if (9.29) is satisfied, or in (9.19) in the general case. Using (9.19) does not rely on the efficiency requirement (9.29), which is sometimes hard to check, and may therefore be preferred to using (9.26), which does rely on the efficiency requirement. Note that both estimators of the asymptotic covariance matrix require a consistent estimator of Ψ. In section 9.4, the estimation of Ψ will be discussed. If estimation of Ψ is problematic, due to computational or statistical problems, a satisfactory consistent estimator of the asymptotic covariance matrix may be found by bootstrap or jackknife methods.

9.4 Estimation of the covariance matrix of the sample moments

As we have seen in the previous section, for the consistent estimation of the asymptotic covariance matrix and for an optimal weight matrix, we generally need a consistent estimator of Ψ. In the standard i.i.d. case, there are several straightforward options that give a consistent estimator. Some are specific to certain situations and others are more generally applicable. GMM is, however, frequently applied in the econometrics literature to problems with data that are not i.i.d., such as time series and heteroskedastic data. Although this is somewhat outside the scope of this book, the topic is very important in the general application of GMM and we will therefore devote some attention to it. Hence, in this section, we consider estimation of Ψ in various cases.

Explicit expression for the weight matrix

A simple case occurs when it is possible to express the elements of Ψ directly in terms of the parameters of the model. This holds for the example of the lognormal distribution from the beginning of this chapter. From (9.1) it follows directly that

$$\begin{aligned}
\Psi_{rs} &\equiv N \operatorname{Cov}\left(\frac{1}{N}\sum_{n=1}^{N} x_n^r, \frac{1}{N}\sum_{n=1}^{N} x_n^s\right) \\
&= \mathrm{E}(x_n^{r+s}) - \mathrm{E}(x_n^r)\,\mathrm{E}(x_n^s) \\
&= \exp\bigl((r+s)\mu + \tfrac{1}{2}(r^2+s^2)\sigma^2\bigr)\bigl(\exp(rs\sigma^2) - 1\bigr). \qquad (9.32)
\end{aligned}$$

A consistent estimator of the (r, s)-th element of Ψ can be found by inserting consistent estimators of μ and σ^2, e.g., those from (9.3), in (9.32). An optimal GMM estimator is found by setting $\hat{W} = \hat{\Psi}^{-1}$, where $\hat{\Psi}$ is the consistent estimator of Ψ just constructed.

The separated case

In the more general case where the moment equations are of the form (9.6) and the observations are assumed independent, two choices for the estimator of Ψ suggest themselves naturally. These are

$$\hat{\Psi}_1 \equiv \frac{1}{N}\sum_{n=1}^{N}(g_n - \gamma(\tilde{\theta}))(g_n - \gamma(\tilde{\theta}))' \tag{9.33a}$$

$$\hat{\Psi}_2 \equiv \frac{1}{N}\sum_{n=1}^{N}(g_n - \bar{g})(g_n - \bar{g})', \tag{9.33b}$$

where $\tilde{\theta}$ is an initial consistent estimator of θ, typically a GMM estimator based on a nonoptimal weight matrix such as the identity matrix. Both estimators use the second-order moment of the observations as a consistent estimator of their variance, but they differ in the way they deal with the problem that the mean γ of g_n is unknown. In $\hat{\Psi}_1$, a consistent estimator is substituted, whereas in $\hat{\Psi}_2$ the sample mean is substituted, and no initial consistent estimator of θ is required. Note that $\hat{\Psi}_2$ is a consistent estimator of the asymptotic covariance matrix of $\bar{g}$ whether or not the model is specified correctly, whereas $\hat{\Psi}_1$ is generally only consistent if the model is specified correctly.

There is an interesting relationship between the two approaches if $\hat{\theta}_2$, the GMM estimator based on the weight matrix $\hat{W}_2 \equiv \hat{\Psi}_2^{-1}$, is used as an initial consistent estimator in $\hat{\Psi}_1$, leading to the GMM estimator $\hat{\theta}_1$ based on the weight matrix $\hat{W}_1 \equiv \hat{\Psi}_1^{-1}$. Let, for the sake of brevity, $\hat{\gamma}_i \equiv \gamma(\hat{\theta}_i)$, $\hat{G}_i \equiv \bar{G}(\hat{\theta}_i)$, and $\hat{q}_i \equiv (\bar{g} - \hat{\gamma}_i)'\hat{W}_i(\bar{g} - \hat{\gamma}_i)$, for $i = 1, 2$. Then

$$\begin{aligned}
\hat{W}_1^{-1} &= \frac{1}{N}\sum_{n=1}^{N}(g_n - \hat{\gamma}_2)(g_n - \hat{\gamma}_2)' \\
&= \frac{1}{N}\sum_{n=1}^{N}(g_n - \bar{g} + \bar{g} - \hat{\gamma}_2)(g_n - \bar{g} + \bar{g} - \hat{\gamma}_2)' \\
&= \frac{1}{N}\sum_{n=1}^{N}(g_n - \bar{g})(g_n - \bar{g})' + (\bar{g} - \hat{\gamma}_2)(\bar{g} - \hat{\gamma}_2)' \\
&= \hat{W}_2^{-1} + (\bar{g} - \hat{\gamma}_2)(\bar{g} - \hat{\gamma}_2)'.
\end{aligned}$$

On premultiplication by $\hat{W}_1$ and postmultiplication by $\hat{W}_2(\bar{g} - \hat{\gamma}_2)$, this yields

$$\hat{W}_2(\bar{g} - \hat{\gamma}_2) = \hat{W}_1(\bar{g} - \hat{\gamma}_2) + \hat{W}_1(\bar{g} - \hat{\gamma}_2)(\bar{g} - \hat{\gamma}_2)'\hat{W}_2(\bar{g} - \hat{\gamma}_2)$$

$$= (1 + \hat{q}_2)\hat{W}_1(\bar{g} - \hat{\gamma}_2). \tag{9.34}$$

This implies that taking $\hat{\theta}_1$ equal to $\hat{\theta}_2$ solves the first-order condition for GMM because then $\hat{\gamma}_1 = \hat{\gamma}_2$ and $\hat{G}_1 = \hat{G}_2$, so that premultiplication of (9.34) with $\hat{G}_i$ yields

$$\hat{G}_2'\hat{W}_2(\bar{g} - \hat{\gamma}_2) = (1 + \hat{q}_2)\hat{G}_1'\hat{W}_1(\bar{g} - \hat{\gamma}_1) = 0.$$

Moreover, premultiplication of (9.34) by $(\bar{g} - \hat{\gamma}_1)'$, which equals $(\bar{g} - \hat{\gamma}_2)'$, yields $\hat{q}_2 = \hat{q}_1(1 + \hat{q}_2)$, or

$$\hat{q}_1 = \frac{\hat{q}_2}{1 + \hat{q}_2} < \hat{q}_2. \tag{9.35}$$

Consequently, the minimum of the GMM criterion function differs between these two estimators, although they lead to the same estimator. This result will play a role when we discuss testing procedures in section 10.3.

The inclusive case

The estimators $\hat{\Psi}_1$ and $\hat{\Psi}_2$ defined for the separated case can be adapted to the inclusive case. For the matrix $\hat{\Psi}_1$, this is evident by observing that $(g_n - \gamma(\tilde{\theta}))$ is a special case of the moment $h_n(\tilde{\theta})$. Hence, we obtain immediately

$$\hat{\Psi}_1 \equiv \frac{1}{N}\sum_{n=1}^{N} h_n(\tilde{\theta})h_n(\tilde{\theta})'. \tag{9.36}$$

The generalization of $\hat{\Psi}_2$ is somewhat less immediate, because the mean of h can generally not be estimated without an initial estimator of θ_0. After realizing this, it follows that

$$\hat{\Psi}_2 \equiv \frac{1}{N}\sum_{n=1}^{N}(h_n(\tilde{\theta}) - \bar{h}(\tilde{\theta}))(h_n(\tilde{\theta}) - \bar{h}(\tilde{\theta}))', \tag{9.37}$$

where $\tilde{\theta}$ is an initial consistent estimator of θ, typically a GMM estimator based on a nonoptimal weight matrix such as the identity matrix. From (9.37), we see immediately that if $h_n(\theta) = g_n - \gamma(\theta)$, then $\hat{\Psi}_2$ as defined in (9.37) reduces to $\hat{\Psi}_2$ as defined in (9.33b), which justifies the use of the same notation. Note that in this case the initial estimator drops out of the equation.

As in the separated case, $\hat{\Psi}_2$ is a consistent estimator of the asymptotic covariance matrix of $\bar{h}$ whether or not the model is specified correctly, whereas $\hat{\Psi}_1$

is generally only a consistent estimator of Ψ if the model is specified correctly. This may be important in some situations, but note that the asymptotic covariance matrix of $\bar{h}$ in the case of $\hat{\Psi}_2$ has to be evaluated for $\theta = \text{plim}_{N\to\infty}\hat{\theta}$, which is generally different from θ_0. It may actually be questioned whether θ_0 can be meaningfully defined if the model is misspecified, but in many situations, this is possible, at least for some elements of θ. We will further leave these philosophical issues aside.

As we have seen above, both estimators of Ψ lead to the same estimator in the separated case, if $\hat{\theta}_2$ is used as an initial consistent estimator in $\hat{\Psi}_1$. In the inclusive case, both estimators of Ψ need an initial consistent estimator. Let $\tilde{\theta}$ be a suitable initial consistent estimator. We can then consider $\hat{\Psi}_1$ based on $\tilde{\theta}$ and $\hat{\Psi}_2$ based on $\hat{\theta}_1$ or $\hat{\Psi}_2$ based on $\tilde{\theta}$ and $\hat{\Psi}_1$ based on $\hat{\theta}_2$. It is straightforward to check that generally neither of these two options gives $\hat{\theta}_1 = \hat{\theta}_2$ exactly, although the differences will generally be small.

Iterative reweighting and continuous updating

From the discussion above, it is clear that, in the inclusive case, an initial consistent estimator $\tilde{\theta}$ is needed for the consistent estimation of Ψ. The inverse of the resulting estimator (9.36) or (9.37) of Ψ can then be used as a weight matrix to obtain an asymptotically optimal estimator. Hence, this estimator is computed in a two-step procedure. In the first step, a consistent but (generally) not asymptotically efficient estimator is computed, which gives a consistent estimator of Ψ. In the second step, an asymptotically efficient estimator is computed using the inverse of the consistent estimator of Ψ as weight matrix. Therefore, the resulting GMM estimator may be termed the two-step GMM estimator.

Evidently, given the two-step GMM estimator, we can compute a new consistent estimator for Ψ based on (9.36) or (9.37), with the two-step GMM estimator as $\tilde{\theta}$. This may be more efficient, because the two-step GMM estimator is more efficient than the initial estimator. Based on this new estimator of Ψ, a new GMM estimator can be computed, which may be called the three-step estimator, and so forth. After convergence of this process, the resulting estimator is the *iteratively reweighted* GMM estimator, or IGMM estimator.

To formally introduce the IGMM estimator, we start from the criterion used for GMM estimation in (9.10), $\bar{q}(\theta) \equiv \bar{h}(\theta)'\hat{W}\bar{h}(\theta)$. We rewrite it slightly to bring out the dependence of the weight matrix on θ:

$$\bar{q}(\theta) \equiv \bar{h}(\theta)'\hat{W}(\theta)\bar{h}(\theta). \tag{9.38}$$

When using the two-step estimator, an initial consistent estimator $\tilde{\theta} \equiv \hat{\theta}_{(1)}$, say, is substituted for θ in $\hat{W}(\theta)$ in (9.38), leading to the estimator $\hat{\theta}_{(2)}$, say. This procedure can be repeated until convergence. Let $\hat{\theta}_{(k)}$ be the value of θ obtained in the k-th step. Then, the next value is obtained from minimizing

$$\bar{h}(\hat{\theta}_{(k+1)})'\hat{W}(\hat{\theta}_{(k)})\bar{h}(\hat{\theta}_{(k+1)}) \tag{9.39}$$

with respect to $\hat{\theta}_{(k+1)}$. After convergence, the resulting estimator $\hat{\theta}_{(\infty)}$, say, is the IGMM estimator.

Evidently, the iteratively reweighted GMM estimator may be based on (sequential updates of) $\hat{\Psi}_1$ or (sequential updates of) $\hat{\Psi}_2$, defining the estimators $\hat{\theta}_{1(\infty)}$ and $\hat{\theta}_{2(\infty)}$. It now follows straightforwardly that, by computation of

$$\hat{\Psi}_2 = \hat{W}(\hat{\theta}_{1(\infty)})^{-1},$$

we find that $\hat{\theta}_{2(2)} = \hat{\theta}_{2(1)} = \hat{\theta}_{1(\infty)}$ satisfies the first-order condition, as in the separated case, and thus $\hat{\theta}_{2(\infty)} = \hat{\theta}_{1(\infty)}$. Analogously, by starting with computing $\hat{\theta}_{2(\infty)}$, we find that $\hat{\theta}_{1(\infty)} = \hat{\theta}_{2(\infty)}$. In both cases, we obtain again (9.35).

By comparing (9.39) with (9.38) and noting that, after convergence, $\hat{\theta}_{(\infty)}$ should be inserted for both $\hat{\theta}_{(k)}$ and $\hat{\theta}_{(k+1)}$, one might surmise that the IGMM estimator is the minimizing argument over θ of (9.38). This is, however, not the case. Yet, we can certainly consider an estimator of θ thus defined, i.e., the estimator that is obtained when the weight matrix in each step is not taken as given but when (9.38) is minimized over θ both in $\bar{h}(\theta)$ and $\hat{W}(\theta)$. This estimator is called the *continuous-updating* GMM estimator. Under weak conditions, this estimator is asymptotically equivalent to the two-step and iteratively reweighted estimators, because the weight matrices of these estimators all converge to Ψ^{-1}.

Notwithstanding their asymptotic equivalence, the various estimators will behave differently in finite samples, although the differences vanish when the sample size increases. In particular, the differences between the IGMM estimator and the continuous-updating estimator are noteworthy. On convergence, the IGMM estimator satisfies

$$\bar{G}(\hat{\theta}_{(\infty)})'\hat{W}(\hat{\theta}_{(\infty)})\bar{h}(\hat{\theta}_{(\infty)}) = 0,$$

whereas the continuous-updating estimator satisfies

$$\bar{G}(\hat{\theta}_{\mathrm{CU}})'\hat{W}(\hat{\theta}_{\mathrm{CU}})\bar{h}(\hat{\theta}_{\mathrm{CU}}) + \tfrac{1}{2}\frac{\partial\left(\operatorname{vec}\hat{W}(\hat{\theta}_{\mathrm{CU}})\right)'}{\partial\theta}\left(\bar{h}(\hat{\theta}_{\mathrm{CU}}) \otimes \bar{h}(\hat{\theta}_{\mathrm{CU}})\right) = 0.$$

Therefore, equality of the two estimators requires the last term to vanish. For both forms (9.36) and (9.37) of the inverse of the weight matrix, this last term reduces to

$$-\frac{1}{N}\sum_{n=1}^{N}(\hat{h}'_{\mathrm{CU}}\hat{W}_{\mathrm{CU}}h_n(\hat{\theta}_{\mathrm{CU}}))(G_n(\hat{\theta}_{\mathrm{CU}})'\hat{W}_{\mathrm{CU}}\hat{h}_{\mathrm{CU}}),$$

where $\hat{h}_{\mathrm{CU}} \equiv \bar{h}(\hat{\theta}_{\mathrm{CU}})$, $\hat{W}_{\mathrm{CU}} \equiv \hat{W}(\hat{\theta}_{\mathrm{CU}})$, and $G_n(\theta) \equiv \partial h_n/\partial\theta'$. Hence, this term vanishes if h_n and G_n are uncorrelated when evaluated in $\hat{\theta}_{\mathrm{CU}}$. In general, however, this term will not vanish in finite samples, although it may be close to zero if the model fits well. There is some evidence that the continuous-updating estimator has good small-sample properties.

As with the previous types of GMM estimators, we can compare the estimators based on the forms (9.36) and (9.37) of the inverse of the weight matrix, and the corresponding minima of the GMM criterion functions. Evidently, for all values of θ,

$$\hat{W}_2(\theta)^{-1} = \hat{W}_1(\theta)^{-1} - \bar{h}(\theta)\bar{h}(\theta)',$$

or, by premultiplication with $\hat{W}_1(\theta)$ and postmultiplication with $\hat{W}_2(\theta)$,

$$\hat{W}_2(\theta) = \hat{W}_1(\theta) + \hat{W}_1(\theta)\bar{h}(\theta)\bar{h}(\theta)'\hat{W}_2(\theta),$$

which, by pre- and postmultiplication with $\bar{h}(\theta)$, leads to

$$\bar{q}_1(\theta) = \frac{\bar{q}_2(\theta)}{1+\bar{q}_2(\theta)}.$$

This is a monotonically increasing function and hence, both forms lead to the same estimator with the by now familiar relationship between the corresponding minima of the criterion functions.

Finally, note that iterative reweighting and continuous updating are only relevant for the inclusive case. In the separated case, the estimator based on $\hat{W}_2$ does not use an initial consistent estimator and hence, there is nothing to update, whether iteratively or continuously. Because the two-step estimator based on $\hat{W}_1$, with the estimator based on $\hat{W}_2$ as initial consistent estimator, is equivalent to the latter, i.e., the two-step estimator is equivalent to the one-step estimator, the iteratively reweighted estimator has already converged in the second step and the IGMM and two-step estimators are equivalent. Furthermore, in the separated case, $G_n(\theta) = \bar{G}(\theta) = G(\theta) = -\partial\gamma/\partial\theta'$, which clearly does not depend on the data. Hence, G_n and h_n are uncorrelated and the continuous-updating estimator is equivalent to the IGMM estimator.

Heteroskedasticity and autocorrelation

Up till now, we have assumed that g_n or h_n are independent and identically distributed. In many econometric applications of GMM, however, this is not the case. GMM owes much of its popularity to its relatively easy application in time series models or with heteroskedastic data. In such cases, estimation of Ψ is less straightforward. Although somewhat out of the scope of this book, we will mention the main results here because of their importance for GMM estimation in general.

In (9.13), Ψ was defined as the asymptotic covariance matrix of $\sqrt{N}\,\bar{h}_0 \equiv \sqrt{N}\big(\sum_{n=1}^{N} h_n(\theta_0)/N\big)$. Now, define $\Psi_{nm} \equiv \mathrm{E}\big(h_n(\theta_0)h_m(\theta_0)'\big)$. Clearly, in the i.i.d. case, $\Psi_{nn} = \Psi$ for all n and $\Psi_{nm} = 0$ for all (m, n) such that $m \neq n$. More in general, assuming that $\mathrm{E}(h_n(\theta_0)) = 0$ for all n,

$$\begin{aligned}
\Psi &\equiv \lim_{N\to\infty} N\,\mathrm{E}\left(\frac{1}{N}\sum_{n=1}^{N} h_n(\theta_0)\right)\left(\frac{1}{N}\sum_{m=1}^{N} h_m(\theta_0)'\right) \\
&= \lim_{N\to\infty} \frac{1}{N}\sum_{n=1}^{N}\sum_{m=1}^{N} \mathrm{E}\left(h_n(\theta_0)h_m(\theta_0)'\right) \\
&\equiv \lim_{N\to\infty} \frac{1}{N}\sum_{n=1}^{N}\sum_{m=1}^{N} \Psi_{nm} \\
&= \lim_{N\to\infty} \frac{1}{N}\sum_{n=1}^{N} \Psi_{nn} + \lim_{N\to\infty} \frac{1}{N}\sum_{n=1}^{N}\sum_{m=1}^{n-1}(\Psi_{nm} + \Psi_{mn}).
\end{aligned} \tag{9.40}$$

Obviously, the definition of Ψ is only meaningful if the limit exists. We will not discuss explicitly the conditions under which the limit exists, but confine ourselves to two straightforward observations. First, the limit only exists if Ψ_{mn} goes to zero sufficiently fast as $|n - m| \to \infty$. Otherwise, the second term in (9.40) would diverge to infinity because the number of terms grows quadratically with N, whereas the denominator is only N. Second, for any given value of j, the mean of $\Psi_{n,n-j}$ should converge to some finite value, Ψ_j, say, and given the first condition, Ψ_j should converge to zero fast enough as j goes to plus or minus infinity. Note that in this case, we have $\Psi_{-j} = \Psi_j'$. Then, Ψ can be rewritten as

$$\Psi = \Psi_0 + \sum_{j=1}^{\infty}(\Psi_j + \Psi_j'). \tag{9.41}$$

A consistent estimator of Ψ_0 is of course given by $\hat{\Psi}_1$ or $\hat{\Psi}_2$ as defined in (9.36) and (9.37), respectively. These may be denoted by $\hat{\Psi}_{01}$ and $\hat{\Psi}_{02}$ in the present context. We note that, with heteroskedastic but independent data, these estimators are still consistent. Similarly, obvious consistent estimators of Ψ_j are given by the expressions

$$\hat{\Psi}_{j1} \equiv \frac{1}{N} \sum_{n=j+1}^{N} h_n(\tilde{\theta}) h_{n-j}(\tilde{\theta})'$$

$$\hat{\Psi}_{j2} \equiv \frac{1}{N} \sum_{n=j+1}^{N} \big(h_n(\tilde{\theta}) - \bar{h}(\tilde{\theta})\big)\big(h_{n-j}(\tilde{\theta}) - \bar{h}(\tilde{\theta})\big)'.$$

Although $N - j$ may seem more logical to use in the denominator of these estimators, N is usually proposed. A straightforward estimator of Ψ may now be defined as

$$\hat{\Psi}_{\mathrm{TR}} \equiv \hat{\Psi}_0 + \sum_{j=1}^{M} (\hat{\Psi}_j + \hat{\Psi}_j'), \tag{9.42}$$

where $\hat{\Psi}_0$ may denote either $\hat{\Psi}_{01}$ or $\hat{\Psi}_{02}$ and similarly for $\hat{\Psi}_j$, and M is the so-called *lag truncation parameter*. The subscript TR points to this truncation. It may seem logical to use $M = N - 1$, but the resulting $\hat{\Psi}_{N-1}$ only depends on one combination of observations, which is not very reliable. It is generally found that a much smaller value of M gives a better estimator of Ψ. Note, however, that $\hat{\Psi}_{\mathrm{TR}}$ is only consistent under the weakest assumptions if M is allowed to increase (slowly) with N.

A disadvantage of the estimator (9.42) is that it is not necessarily positive semidefinite. This can be seen by writing it as $\hat{\Psi}_{\mathrm{TR}} = \tilde{H}' V \tilde{H} / N$, where V is an $N \times N$ matrix with elements equal to $V_{nm} = 1$ if $|n - m| \leq M$ for $n, m = 1, \ldots, N$, and $V_{nm} = 0$ otherwise, and $\tilde{H} \equiv (h_1(\tilde{\theta}), \ldots, h_N(\tilde{\theta}))'$ if $\hat{\Psi}_{j1}$ is used for $j = 0, \ldots, M$. If $\hat{\Psi}_{j2}$ is used, $\tilde{H}$ has to be centered. The matrix V is indefinite. For example, for $N = 3$ and $M = 1$,

$$V = \begin{bmatrix} 1 & 1 & 0 \\ 1 & 1 & 1 \\ 0 & 1 & 1 \end{bmatrix},$$

which has eigenvalues 1 and $1 \pm \sqrt{2}$ and is hence indefinite. This indefiniteness carries over to $\tilde{H}' V \tilde{H}$, which means that $\hat{\Psi}_{\mathrm{TR}}$ can not be used in the estimation process, because $\hat{W} \equiv \hat{\Psi}_{\mathrm{TR}}^{-1}$ is not positive definite, and it may create problems in the inferential process.

An alternative consistent estimator of Ψ that is guaranteed to be positive semidefinite (and generally positive definite) is

$$\hat{\Psi}_{\mathrm{BT}} \equiv \hat{\Psi}_0 + \sum_{j=1}^{M} \left(1 - \frac{j}{M+1}\right) (\hat{\Psi}_j + \hat{\Psi}_j'), \tag{9.43}$$

where the weights $1-j/(M+1)$ are the so-called Bartlett weights, which explains the subscript BT. The matrix $\hat{\Psi}_{\mathrm{BT}}$ can also be written in the form $\tilde{H}'V\tilde{H}/N$, but in this case V is a matrix with (n, m)-th element $(M + 1 - |n - m|)/(M + 1)$ if $|n - m| \leq M$ and 0 otherwise. For example, for $N = 5$ and $M = 2$,

$$V = \frac{1}{3}\begin{bmatrix} 3 & 2 & 1 & 0 & 0 \\ 2 & 3 & 2 & 1 & 0 \\ 1 & 2 & 3 & 2 & 1 \\ 0 & 1 & 2 & 3 & 2 \\ 0 & 0 & 1 & 2 & 3 \end{bmatrix},$$

which is the covariance matrix of the moving average process $y_n = \varepsilon_n + \varepsilon_{n-1} + \varepsilon_{n-2}$, with the ε_n i.i.d. with mean zero and variance $1/3$, and is hence positive definite. This argument extends immediately to arbitrary values of M and N.

Obviously, if $M \to \infty$ as $N \to \infty$, then $1 - j/(M + 1) \uparrow 1$ for all j, which is necessary for consistency given (9.41). Under the given assumptions, this estimator is consistent if $M \to \infty$ slowly enough.

From (9.42) and (9.43), we easily derive a general formula for a class of estimators of Ψ as

$$\hat{\Psi}_w \equiv \hat{\Psi}_0 + \sum_{j=1}^{M} w(j, M, N) \left(\hat{\Psi}_j + \hat{\Psi}_j'\right), \tag{9.44}$$

where $w(j, M, N)$ is some weight function that is a function of j, M, and possibly N. As we have already discussed above, consistency requires that, with $N \to \infty$, $M \to \infty$ and for all j, $w(j, M, N) \uparrow 1$. Note that the choice of weight function w and lag truncation parameter M is a joint one, because we can define $w(j, M, N) = 0$ for $j > M$ and subsequently replace M by $N - 1$ in (9.44) without altering the result.

We will not go into discussions about which weight function w is best in some sense or how the lag truncation parameter M should be chosen, but refer to the literature for this. Note, however, that the asymptotic results in this chapter and chapter 10 only require the estimator of Ψ to be consistent. Any discussion about rates of convergence, optimal estimators of Ψ in some sense, and so forth, is thus irrelevant for our asymptotic results. Of course, this does not mean that it is not important. In any practical situation, we only have a finite sample with a given sample size, and the quality of GMM estimators and their corresponding statistical inference may differ considerably among the various possible GMM estimators based on different estimators of Ψ.

9.5 Covariance structures

As stated in section 9.2, structural equation models are usually estimated by GMM in separated form, where $\bar{g}$ consists of the sample covariances and $\gamma(\theta)$ consists of the corresponding elements of the covariance structure. This situation has some special implications for the estimation of Ψ and the resulting GMM estimators.

Let z_n be the vector of observed variables for the n-th individual, and assume that these vectors are i.i.d. for $n = 1, \ldots, N$. As usual, assume that $\mathrm{E}(z_n) = 0$ and $\mathrm{E}(z_n z_n') = \Sigma(\theta_0)$ for a given covariance structure $\Sigma(\theta)$, depending on the parameter vector θ with true value θ_0. Let $\bar{g}_{ij}$ denote the element of $\bar{g}$ defined by

$$\bar{g}_{ij} \equiv \frac{1}{N} \sum_{n=1}^{N} z_{ni} z_{nj},$$

i.e., $\bar{g}_{ij}$ is the (i, j)-th element of the sample covariance matrix. Obviously, $\mathrm{E}(\bar{g}_{ij}) = \sigma_{ij}$, the (i, j)-th element of the population covariance matrix $\Sigma(\theta_0)$. From (9.13), we have that the elements of Ψ are the asymptotic covariances of $\sqrt{N}\bar{g}_{ij}$ and $\sqrt{N}\bar{g}_{kl}$, or

$$\begin{aligned}\Psi_{ij,kl} &\equiv \lim_{N\to\infty} N \operatorname{Cov}(\bar{g}_{ij}, \bar{g}_{kl}) \\ &= \lim_{N\to\infty} N \mathrm{E}\big((\bar{g}_{ij} - \sigma_{ij})(\bar{g}_{kl} - \sigma_{kl})\big) \\ &= \sigma_{ijkl} - \sigma_{ij}\sigma_{kl},\end{aligned}$$

where $\sigma_{ijkl} \equiv \mathrm{E}(z_{ni} z_{nj} z_{nk} z_{nl})$. Obviously, σ_{ijkl} can be consistently estimated by

$$\bar{g}_{ijkl} \equiv \frac{1}{N} \sum_{n=1}^{N} z_{ni} z_{nj} z_{nk} z_{nl}$$

and σ_{ij} and σ_{kl} can be consistently estimated by $\bar{g}_{ij}$ and $\bar{g}_{kl}$, respectively. The estimator of Ψ thus obtained is $\hat{\Psi}_2$ as defined in (9.33b).

Up till now, we took the observed variables to have zero means. Of course, this is generally not the case, but we can center the variables by subtracting their sample means. Assume that we observe the variables $\tilde{z}_n$, with $\mathrm{E}(\tilde{z}_n) = \mu$ and $\mathrm{Cov}(\tilde{z}_n) = \Sigma(\theta_0)$. Then we can compute the sample mean $\bar{z}$, define $z_n \equiv \tilde{z}_n - \bar{z}$, and define g_n as the vector with elements $g_{nij} \equiv z_{ni}z_{nj}$. Hence, $\bar{g}$ consists of the elements of

$$\tilde{S} \equiv \frac{1}{N}\sum_{n=1}^{N} z_n z_n' = \frac{1}{N}\sum_{n=1}^{N}(\tilde{z}_n - \bar{z})(\tilde{z}_n - \bar{z})'.$$

It is well known that $\tilde{S}$ is a biased estimator of Σ, with $\mathrm{E}(\tilde{S}) = ((N-1)/N)\Sigma$. Therefore, $\gamma(\theta)$ consists of the elements of $((N-1)/N)\Sigma$. Alternatively, we may multiply the moment conditions by $N/(N-1)$, so that $\gamma(\theta)$ consists of the elements of Σ and $\bar{g}$ consists of the elements of the unbiased sample covariance matrix $S \equiv (N/(N-1))\tilde{S}$. The factor $N/(N-1)$ is negligible in large samples and, hence, it is asymptotically irrelevant whether we use $\tilde{S}$ or S.

Let s_{ij} denote a typical element of S. Then, tedious but straightforward computation shows that

$$\Psi_{ij,kl} \equiv \lim_{N\to\infty} N\,\mathrm{Cov}(s_{ij}, s_{kl}) = \sigma_{ijkl} - \sigma_{ij}\sigma_{kl}, \tag{9.45}$$

where σ_{ijkl} is now redefined as

$$\sigma_{ijkl} \equiv \mathrm{E}((\tilde{z}_{ni} - \mu_i)(\tilde{z}_{nj} - \mu_j)(\tilde{z}_{nk} - \mu_k)(\tilde{z}_{nl} - \mu_l)).$$

Evidently, we can estimate this consistently by

$$(\hat{\Psi}_3)_{ij,kl} \equiv s_{ijkl} - s_{ij}s_{kl},$$

where

$$\begin{aligned} s_{ijkl} &\equiv \frac{1}{N}\sum_{n=1}^{N}(\tilde{z}_{ni} - \bar{z}_i)(\tilde{z}_{nj} - \bar{z}_j)(\tilde{z}_{nk} - \bar{z}_k)(\tilde{z}_{nl} - \bar{z}_l) \\ &= \frac{1}{N}\sum_{n=1}^{N} z_{ni}z_{nj}z_{nk}z_{nl}, \end{aligned}$$

which is a consistent estimator of σ_{ijkl}. Given the consistency of $\hat{\Psi}_3$, the matrix $\hat{W}_3 \equiv \hat{\Psi}_3^{-1}$ is an asymptotically optimal weight matrix. This is called the *asymptotically distribution free* (ADF) weight matrix and the corresponding estimator is analogously called the ADF estimator, because the estimator does not use any assumption about the distribution of $\tilde{z}_n$ and all inference about θ is asymptotically correct regardless of the distribution of $\tilde{z}_n$. The only requirement on the distribution of $\tilde{z}_n$ is that its fourth-order moments must be finite.

This approach is equivalent (except for a factor of $N-1$ instead of N in the denominator, which is irrelevant asymptotically) to subtracting the sample mean from $\tilde{z}_n$ and then continuing as if the resulting vectors z_n are i.i.d. with mean zero and covariance matrix $\Sigma(\theta)$. This shows that the assumption that the observed variables have mean zero, which is generally made in this book, is harmless.

Normality

If it is assumed that $z_n \sim \mathcal{N}_J(0, \Sigma)$, where J is the number of observed variables (the dimension of z_n), then the resulting formulas become much simpler. It is convenient to use matrix notation now. Let $s \equiv \text{vec}(S)$ and $\sigma(\theta) \equiv \text{vec}(\Sigma(\theta))$. Because S and Σ are symmetric, their off-diagonal elements are contained twice in s and σ and one of these copies is redundant. Moreover, if we would use $\bar{g} = s$, then Ψ would be singular because of these redundant elements. Therefore, $\bar{g}$ should consist of the *nonduplicated* elements of s, i.e., with one copy of each. One way to achieve this is to define $\bar{g} \equiv D_J^+ s$ and, accordingly, $\gamma(\theta) \equiv D_J^+ \sigma(\theta)$, where D_J^+ is the Moore-Penrose inverse of the duplication matrix as defined in section A.4. Alternatively, we could maintain the duplicated elements in $\bar{g}$ and use a generalized inverse of the singular matrix $\hat{\Psi}$ as weight matrix. It turns out that this gives the same estimators, but the theory, although elegant, is somewhat more complicated. Therefore, we do not pursue this further.

We will now derive a concise formula for the GMM criterion function under normality. From (A.20), it follows that

$$\lim_{N\to\infty} N\,\text{Cov}(s) = 2Q_J(\Sigma \otimes \Sigma),$$

where Q_J is the symmetrization matrix (see section A.4). Hence,

$$\begin{aligned}\Psi &\equiv \lim_{N\to\infty} N\,\text{Cov}(\bar{g}) \\ &= D_J^+\big(\lim_{N\to\infty} N\,\text{Cov}(s)\big)(D_J^+)' \\ &= 2D_J^+ Q_J(\Sigma \otimes \Sigma)(D_J^+)' \\ &= 2D_J^+(\Sigma \otimes \Sigma)(D_J^+)',\end{aligned}$$

where the last equality follows from $D_J^+ Q_J = D_J^+$. Therefore, Ψ can be estimated consistently by

$$\hat{\Psi}_4 = 2D_J^+(S \otimes S)(D_J^+)'.$$

Thus, the corresponding weight matrix is

$$\hat{W}_4 = \tfrac{1}{2}\left(D_J^+(S \otimes S)(D_J^+)'\right)^{-1} = \tfrac{1}{2}D_J'(S^{-1} \otimes S^{-1})D_J.$$

The GMM criterion function can now be written as

$$\begin{aligned}
\bar{q}_4(\theta) &= \big(\bar{g} - \gamma(\theta)\big)'\hat{W}_4\big(\bar{g} - \gamma(\theta)\big) \\
&= \tfrac{1}{2}\Big(\mathrm{vec}\big(S - \Sigma(\theta)\big)\Big)'(D_J^+)'D_J'\big(S^{-1} \otimes S^{-1}\big)D_J D_J^+\Big(\mathrm{vec}\big(S - \Sigma(\theta)\big)\Big) \\
&= \tfrac{1}{2}\Big(\mathrm{vec}\big(S - \Sigma(\theta)\big)\Big)' Q_J\big(S^{-1} \otimes S^{-1}\big)Q_J\Big(\mathrm{vec}\big(S - \Sigma(\theta)\big)\Big) \\
&= \tfrac{1}{2}\Big(\mathrm{vec}\big(S - \Sigma(\theta)\big)\Big)'\big(S^{-1} \otimes S^{-1}\big)\Big(\mathrm{vec}\big(S - \Sigma(\theta)\big)\Big) \\
&= \tfrac{1}{2}\,\mathrm{tr}\Big(\big(S - \Sigma(\theta)\big)S^{-1}\Big)^2 . \qquad (9.46)
\end{aligned}$$

The expression (9.46) is computationally highly efficient. The estimator that minimizes (9.46) is called the (normal-theory) *generalized least squares* (GLS) estimator.

As discussed in section 9.4, the matrix Ψ can sometimes be explicitly written as a function of the parameters, $\Psi = \Psi(\theta_0)$. Then, if we have an initial consistent estimator $\tilde{\theta}$, an asymptotically optimal weight matrix is

$$\hat{W}_5 \equiv \Psi(\tilde{\theta})^{-1}.$$

An estimator based on $\hat{W}_5$ may be more efficient in small or moderate samples than the previously discussed estimators. Evidently, in the case of covariance structures under normality, this means replacing (9.46) by

$$\bar{q}_5(\theta) = \tfrac{1}{2}\,\mathrm{tr}\Big(\big(S - \Sigma(\theta)\big)\Sigma(\tilde{\theta})^{-1}\Big)^2 .$$

Analogous to the iteratively reweighted GMM estimator, this process can be iterated, where the function that is minimized in the k-th step is

$$\bar{q}_{5(k)}(\theta) \equiv \tfrac{1}{2}\,\mathrm{tr}\Big(\big(S - \Sigma(\theta)\big)\Sigma(\hat{\theta}_{(k-1)})^{-1}\Big)^2 . \qquad (9.47)$$

This estimation method is called iteratively reweighted generalized least squares (IGLS). The resulting estimator is equivalent to the maximum likelihood estimator under normality, which can be seen as follows. In section 7.2, the first-order condition with respect to the h-th parameter

$$\mathrm{tr}\big(\hat{\Sigma}^{-1}(\hat{\Sigma} - S)\hat{\Sigma}^{-1}\hat{\Sigma}_h\big) = 0 \qquad (9.48)$$

was derived for the maximum likelihood estimator of a factor analysis model, cf. (7.8). Hats have now been added to indicate matrices with estimators substituted for parameters as the distinction will become relevant later on. Expression

(9.48) is valid in a much more general setting. When Σ stands for *any* structured covariance matrix, not just the one for the FA model, and Σ_h stands for the derivative of Σ with respect to the h-th parameter, we evidently still have the same expression (9.48) for the first-order condition.

By differentiation of (9.47), we obtain the first-order condition

$$\operatorname{tr}\left(\hat{\Sigma}_{(k-1)}^{-1}\left(\hat{\Sigma}_{(k)} - S\right)\hat{\Sigma}_{(k-1)}^{-1}\hat{\Sigma}_{h(k)}\right) = 0, \tag{9.49}$$

where the subscripts $(k-1)$ and (k) indicate whether the matrix is evaluated in $\hat{\theta}_{(k-1)}$ or $\hat{\theta}_{(k)}$. After convergence, we obviously have $\hat{\theta}_{(k-1)} = \hat{\theta}_{(k)}$, so that (9.49) is equivalent to (9.48) and the IGLS estimator is identical to the ML estimator. There does not seem to be a simple relationship between the minimum values of the corresponding criterion functions, however. See section 9.9 for a more elaborate discussion of GMM versus ML.

Given the analogy between IGMM and IGLS, it is now also obvious that we could define a type of continuous-updating estimator for covariance structures under normality. This estimator is the minimizing argument of the function

$$\bar{q}_6(\theta) \equiv \tfrac{1}{2}\operatorname{tr}\left(\left(S - \Sigma(\theta)\right)\Sigma(\theta)^{-1}\right)^2.$$

There is an interesting relationship between this criterion function and the GLS criterion function $\bar{q}_4(\theta)$ from (9.46). The latter can be rewritten as

$$\bar{q}_4(\theta) = \tfrac{1}{2}\operatorname{tr}\left(I_J - \Sigma(\theta)S^{-1}\right)^2,$$

whereas the continuous-updating GLS function can be written as

$$\bar{q}_6(\theta) = \tfrac{1}{2}\operatorname{tr}\left(I_J - \Sigma(\theta)^{-1}S\right)^2.$$

Therefore, the continuous-updating GLS estimator may also be called the inverse GLS estimator.

As with the IGMM and continuous-updating GMM estimators, the iteratively reweighted GLS and continuous-updating GLS estimators are generally not equivalent. The first-order condition for the latter is

$$\operatorname{tr}\left(\hat{\Sigma}^{-1}(\hat{\Sigma} - S)\hat{\Sigma}^{-1}S\hat{\Sigma}^{-1}\hat{\Sigma}_h\right) = 0,$$

which differs from the first-order condition (9.48) for the iteratively reweighted GLS and ML estimators. In general, the estimators differ, but they are asymptotically equivalent, so that in large samples, they will be very similar.

9.6 Asymptotic efficiency and additional information

In this section, we consider the effect on the asymptotic distribution of the GMM estimator when additional moment conditions are used. The focus will be on GMM estimators that use an optimal weight matrix, and as before denote the vector of parameters to be estimated by θ. Let $\bar{h}_1$ be a vector function (of order p_1) of θ and the data, and let let $\bar{h}_2$ be a vector function (of order p_2) of θ and the data. Let a subscript zero denote evaluation at the true parameter value. Assume that $\bar{h}_{10}$ and $\bar{h}_{20}$ have mean zero, and for their joint asymptotic distribution, assume that

$$\sqrt{N}\begin{bmatrix}\bar{h}_{10}\\ \bar{h}_{20}\end{bmatrix} \xrightarrow{d} \mathcal{N}_{p_1+p_2}\left(0, \begin{bmatrix}\Psi_{11} & \Psi_{12}\\ \Psi_{21} & \Psi_{22}\end{bmatrix}\right).$$

Let us now compare the asymptotic covariance matrices of two estimators of θ, one (labeled I) based on $\bar{h}_1$, and the other (labeled II) based on both $\bar{h}_1$ and $\bar{h}_2$. Let $h_1 \equiv \text{plim}_{N\to\infty} \bar{h}_1$ and $h_2 \equiv \text{plim}_{N\to\infty} \bar{h}_2$ and

$$G = \begin{bmatrix}G_1\\ G_2\end{bmatrix} = \begin{bmatrix}\dfrac{\partial h_1}{\partial \theta'}\\ \dfrac{\partial h_2}{\partial \theta'}\end{bmatrix}. \tag{9.50}$$

Then the asymptotic covariance matrices of the two estimators are given by

$$\text{AVar}(\hat{\theta}_{\text{I}}) = \left(G'_{10}\Psi_{11}^{-1}G_{10}\right)^{-1} \tag{9.51a}$$

$$\text{AVar}(\hat{\theta}_{\text{II}}) = \left(G'_0\Psi^{-1}G_0\right)^{-1}. \tag{9.51b}$$

To compare these two expressions, we apply the expression for the inverse of a partitioned matrix (cf. section A.1) to obtain

$$\begin{aligned}
G'_0\Psi^{-1}G_0 &= (G'_{10}, G'_{20})\begin{bmatrix}\Psi_{11}^{-1} & 0\\ 0 & 0\end{bmatrix}\begin{bmatrix}G_{10}\\ G_{20}\end{bmatrix}\\
&\quad + \left(G_{20} - \Psi_{21}\Psi_{11}^{-1}G_{10}\right)'\left(\Psi_{22} - \Psi_{21}\Psi_{11}^{-1}\Psi_{12}\right)^{-1}\\
&\quad \times \left(G_{20} - \Psi_{21}\Psi_{11}^{-1}G_{10}\right)\\
&\equiv G'_{10}\Psi_{11}^{-1}G_{10} + B_0U^{-1}B'_0\\
&\geq G'_{10}\Psi_{11}^{-1}G_{10},
\end{aligned}$$

with B_0 and U implicitly defined, and noting that U and hence $B_0UB'_0$ are positive semidefinite. The conclusion is that adding moments in an optimal GMM procedure lowers the asymptotic variances.

Nuisance parameters

In many situations, additional moments involve additional parameters. The derivation just given does not capture this case and hence the conclusion may require qualification. Let us assume that $\bar{h}_2$ involves not only the m parameters contained in the vector θ but also the l parameters contained in a vector ζ. Our interest is still in θ, we consider the parameters in ζ as nuisance parameters. We assume $l \leq p_2$, i.e., the number of nuisance parameters does not exceed the number of additional moment conditions. Otherwise, ζ is not identified.

In order to describe the asymptotic variances for this more complicated case, we expand the definition of G as given in (9.50):

$$G^{\dagger} = \begin{bmatrix} \dfrac{\partial h_1}{\partial \theta'} & \dfrac{\partial h_1}{\partial \zeta'} \\ \dfrac{\partial h_2}{\partial \theta'} & \dfrac{\partial h_2}{\partial \zeta'} \end{bmatrix} = \begin{bmatrix} G_1 & 0 \\ G_2 & G_3 \end{bmatrix}.$$

The asymptotic covariance matrix of $\hat{\theta}_{\mathrm{I}}$ is still given by (9.51a), but (9.51b) has to be adapted to

$$\mathrm{AVar}(\hat{\theta}_{\mathrm{II}}) = (I_m, 0)\left(G_0^{\dagger\prime}\Psi^{-1}G_0^{\dagger}\right)^{-1}(I_m, 0)'. \tag{9.52}$$

In order to compare the asymptotic covariance matrices for this case, let $V \equiv G_{10}'\Psi_{11}^{-1}G_{10}$ for short. Then,

$$G_0^{\dagger\prime}\Psi^{-1}G_0^{\dagger} = \begin{bmatrix} V & 0 \\ 0 & 0 \end{bmatrix} + \begin{bmatrix} B_0 \\ G_0' \end{bmatrix} U^{-1}(B_0', G_0).$$

This is the sum of two positive semidefinite matrices of order $(m+l) \times (m+l)$. The first matrix has rank m, and the second matrix has rank $r = \min(p_2, m+l)$. In the case that $r = p_2$, the number of nuisance parameters equals the number of additional moment conditions. Application of theorem A.6 (with $X = (I_m, 0)'$) directly shows that (9.52) equals $V^{-1} = (G_0'\Psi_{11}^{-1}G_0)^{-1}$. So the conclusion is, not surprisingly, that the additional moments are essentially used to estimate the nuisance parameters, which are the same in number, and do not contribute to improved estimation of θ. They can be considered redundant for the purpose of estimating θ.

For the case of a surplus of additional moment conditions, so $p_2 > l$, it follows immediately from applying theorem A.15 with $X = (I_m, 0)'$ that

$$(I_m, 0)(G_0^{\dagger\prime}\Psi^{-1}G_0^{\dagger})^{-1}(I_m, 0)' \leq V^{-1}.$$

The left-hand side of this inequality is the asymptotic covariance matrix of $\hat{\theta}_{\text{II}}$ and the right-hand side is the asymptotic covariance matrix of $\hat{\theta}_{\text{I}}$. It follows that $\hat{\theta}_{\text{II}}$ is asymptotically more efficient than $\hat{\theta}_{\text{I}}$ if there are more additional moment conditions than additional parameters.

Worse estimation with more moments?

The conclusion that adding moment conditions increases efficiency requires a qualification. That is, when the weighting is not optimal, adding moment conditions may in fact increase the asymptotic variances of the estimators. A simple example illustrates this point. Consider the case of a scalar parameter θ, say. Let $\bar{h}_1$ be a scalar function of this parameter and of the data, with expectation zero at the true value θ_0 and with variance v_1, and let h_1 be its probability limit. Let c_1 be a measure of the information provided by $\bar{h}_1$,

$$c_1 \equiv \frac{1}{v_1}\left(\frac{\partial h_1}{\partial \theta}\right)^2\bigg|_{\theta=\theta_0}.$$

Let $\bar{h}_2$, v_2, h_2, and c_2 be defined analogously, and let $\text{E}(\bar{h}_1\bar{h}_2) = 0$. Then the MM estimator of θ based on $\bar{h}_1$ has asymptotic variance $1/c_1$, and the MM estimator of θ based on $\bar{h}_2$ has asymptotic variance $1/c_2$. Assume that $c_1 > c_2$, meaning that the first moment condition is more informative for θ than the second one.

The optimal GMM estimator based on both $\bar{h}_1$ and $\bar{h}_2$ has asymptotic variance $1/(c_1 + c_2)$, which is evidently smaller than the asymptotic variance of either one of the two MM estimators. In terms of our previously used notation, the GMM estimator is based on the weight matrix

$$\Psi^{-1} = \begin{bmatrix} 1/v_1 & 0 \\ 0 & 1/v_2 \end{bmatrix}.$$

Now, consider the case of a suboptimal GMM estimator that is based on a weight matrix $\hat{W}$ that converges to

$$W_0 \equiv \begin{bmatrix} 1/v_1 & 0 \\ 0 & \pi/v_2 \end{bmatrix},$$

with π some positive scalar; $\pi = 1$ corresponds with the optimal GMM estimator. Applying (9.19) yields that this estimator has asymptotic variance

$$\frac{c_1 + \pi^2 c_2}{(c_1 + \pi c_2)^2}.$$

When comparing this asymptotic variance of the estimator based on the first and the second moment condition jointly to the asymptotic variance of the estimator based on only the first moment condition, some simple algebra shows that the asymptotic variance of the latter is smaller if

$$\pi > \frac{2c_1}{c_1 - c_2}.$$

If, for example, h_1 is twice as informative as h_2, the suboptimal GMM estimator performs worse than the MM estimator based on h_1 if $\pi > 4$, i.e., the less informative moment condition is weighted four times stronger than would be optimal.

Reducing the set of moment conditions

As a corollary to the result that adding moment conditions is in general helpful in reducing the asymptotic variance, it is clear that reducing the set of moment conditions has the opposite effect. Yet, it is useful to consider this result separately. Let p_1 be an integer such that $m \leq p_1 \leq p$ and let L be a $p \times p_1$ matrix of constants and of full column rank. We can estimate θ on the reduced set of moment conditions $L'\bar{h}(\theta)$. When we do so optimally, with a weight matrix that converges to $(L'\Psi L)^{-1}$, the asymptotic covariance matrix of the resulting estimator is

$$\mathrm{AVar}(\hat{\theta}) = \left(G_0' L (L'\Psi L)^{-1} L' G_0\right)^{-1}.$$

From theorem A.7, it follows that

$$L(L'\Psi L)^{-1}L' = \Psi^{-1} - \Psi^{-1}K\left(K'\Psi^{-1}K\right)^{-1}K'\Psi^{-1} \leq \Psi^{-1},$$

where K is a matrix such that $K'L = 0$ and (L, K) is a square nonsingular matrix. Consequently,

$$G_0'\Psi^{-1}G_0 \geq G_0' L (L'\Psi L)^{-1} L' G_0. \tag{9.53}$$

Inversion of this inequality shows the harmful effect of reducing the set of moment conditions. In particular, this holds when p_1 is chosen to be equal to m, the number of parameters. One such choice is $L = (I_m, 0)'$, possibly after a reordering of the rows of $\bar{h}$ if θ is not identified from the first m moments. By such a choice, GMM reduces to MM, because then the number of moment conditions is reduced to the number of parameters. This may make the estimation procedure simpler, but at a cost in efficiency.

There is no efficiency loss when L is chosen such that (9.53) holds with equality. This is trivially the case when $L = \Psi^{-1}G_0 Q$ for Q a nonsingular $m \times m$ matrix, but there are more solutions. To see this, write (9.53) with equality as

$$G_0'\Psi^{-1/2}\big(I_p - \Psi^{1/2}L(L'\Psi L)^{-1}L'\Psi^{1/2}\big)\Psi^{-1/2}G_0 = 0.$$

So $\Psi^{-1/2}G_0$ lies in the space spanned by $\Psi^{1/2}L$. Hence, there exists a matrix R, say, of order $p_1 \times m$, such that $\Psi^{-1/2}G_0 = \Psi^{1/2}LR(R'R)^{-1}$. In other words, L has to satisfy $\Psi LR(R'R)^{-1} = G_0$ for (9.53) to be an equality. The general solution of this equation in L is

$$L = \Psi^{-1}G_0 R' + FM_R, \tag{9.54}$$

with F an arbitrary matrix of order $p \times p_1$ and $M_R \equiv I_{p_1} - R(R'R)^{-1}R'$. When L is taken to have as many columns as G_0, R is square and M_R vanishes.

9.7 Conditional moments

Many applications of GMM are in the context of instrumental variables. To concentrate on the case of a single equation for simplicity, the orthogonality condition is then often in the form

$$\mathrm{E}(u \mid \mathcal{S}) = 0, \tag{9.55}$$

where u is an N-vector depending on the data and the parameter vector θ, typically a vector of regression disturbance terms of the form $u = y - X\beta$, and $\mathcal{S}$ is a set of variables. Let Z be a matrix of variables contained in $\mathcal{S}$, or functions thereof. Then the conditional moment restriction (9.55) implies the set of unconditional moment conditions

$$\mathrm{E}(Z'u) = 0.$$

Let $\Upsilon \equiv \mathrm{E}(uu' \mid \mathcal{S})$, then $\mathrm{Var}(Z'u \mid \mathcal{S}) = Z'\Upsilon Z$. As we have seen in section 6.3, Υ can generally not be consistently estimated, but by inserting a certain inconsistent estimator $\hat{\Upsilon}$ for Υ, $Z'\hat{\Upsilon}Z$ is a consistent estimator of $Z'\Upsilon Z$. Hence, the GMM estimator of θ is found by minimizing $u'Z(Z'\hat{\Upsilon}Z)^{-1}Z'u$. This estimator has conditional asymptotic covariance matrix

$$\mathrm{AVar}(\hat{\theta} \mid Z) = \operatorname*{plim}_{N\to\infty} N\big(D'Z(Z'\Upsilon Z)^{-1}Z'D\big)^{-1},$$

where $D \equiv \mathrm{E}(\partial u/\partial\theta' \mid Z)$. This procedure has an arbitrary aspect. It is based on an instrument matrix Z containing variables in $\mathcal{S}$ and functions thereof. We can increase at will the number of instruments, because the number of functions is unbounded. Hence, we can increase the number of moment conditions as we please. As we have seen in section 9.6, increasing the number of moments decreases in general the asymptotic variance of the GMM estimator. However, the asymptotic variance can not be reduced to an arbitrarily low level. It has a lower bound, the so-called GMM bound, over all possible Z's, because

$$\left(D'\Upsilon^{-1}D\right)^{-1} \leq \left(D'Z(Z'\Upsilon Z)^{-1}Z'D\right)^{-1},$$

which is analogous to (9.53). This inequality becomes an equality if $Z = \Upsilon^{-1}DQ$ when Q is a square, nonsingular matrix. However, as we have seen above, there are more solutions, with general characterization

$$Z = \Upsilon^{-1}DR' + FM_{R'} \tag{9.56}$$

where R is now an arbitrary $h \times m$ matrix, $M_R \equiv I_h - R(R'R)^{-1}R'$, and F is arbitrary of appropriate order. This indicates the way to optimal instruments.

If D is known up to some parameters, optimal instruments Z can frequently be constructed from (9.56) after estimating the parameters in D by regression, because it has the form of a conditional expectation. To illustrate this by a very simple example, consider estimation of the model $y = X\beta + u$ under homoskedasticity, so that Υ is proportional to the unit matrix, with instruments $\tilde{Z}$ satisfying $X = \tilde{Z}\Pi + E$ and $\mathrm{E}(E \mid \tilde{Z}) = 0$. Then $\partial u/\partial\beta' = -X$ and $D = -\mathrm{E}(X \mid \tilde{Z}) = \tilde{Z}\Pi$. After substitution of the estimator $(\tilde{Z}'\tilde{Z})^{-1}\tilde{Z}'X$ for Π, we obtain $\hat{D} = \tilde{Z}(\tilde{Z}'\tilde{Z})^{-1}\tilde{Z}'X$, and one choice for the estimated optimal instruments is $\hat{Z} \equiv \hat{D}$. This choice obviously leads to the usual IV estimator. For cases where the functional form of D in terms of $\tilde{Z}$ is not fully specified, nonparametric methods are called for.

9.8 Simulated GMM

Consider GMM estimation in the separated case: for each observation, we have a vector g_n of random variables. Its sample mean is a vector $\bar{g}$ of sample moments that do not depend on the parameters, and its expectation $\gamma(\theta)$ does not depend on the data. As before, we assume that the g_n are i.i.d. with covariance matrix Ψ. Sometimes, $\gamma(\theta)$ can not be easily computed, typically because it contains multidimensional integrals that have no closed form solution. In many cases, however, it is possible to simulate random variables that, given θ, have mean $\gamma(\theta)$. Under fairly general conditions, these random variables can take the role of $\gamma(\theta)$ to produce consistent estimators, thereby avoiding the difficulties with the computation of $\gamma(\theta)$.

To be specific, let $\{t_{nr}(\theta), r = 1, \ldots, R\}$ be a set of R i.i.d. random vectors generated by the researcher, such that $\mathrm{E}(t_{nr}(\theta)) = \gamma(\theta)$ and $t_{nr}(\theta)$ is independent of the actual data. In the standard case, the vectors $t_{nr}(\theta)$ are generated in the same way that g_n is generated according to the model, given the value of θ. In that case,

$$\mathrm{E}\left(\left(t_{nr}(\theta) - \gamma(\theta)\right)\left(t_{nr}(\theta) - \gamma(\theta)\right)'\right) = \Psi.$$

Furthermore, define

$$t_n(\theta) \equiv \frac{1}{R}\sum_{r=1}^{R} t_{nr}(\theta).$$

Because the expectation of g_n is $\gamma(\theta_0)$, where θ_0 is the true value of θ,

$$\mathrm{E}\left(g_n - t_n(\theta_0)\right) = 0.$$

Apparently, this is a valid moment condition with covariance matrix

$$\begin{aligned}
\Psi_{\mathrm{sim}} &= \mathrm{E}\left(g_n - t_n(\theta_0)\right)\left(g_n - t_n(\theta_0)\right)' \\
&= \mathrm{E}\left(\left(g_n - \gamma(\theta_0)\right) - \left(t_n(\theta_0) - \gamma(\theta_0)\right)\right) \\
&\qquad \times \left(\left(g_n - \gamma(\theta_0)\right) - \left(t_n(\theta_0) - \gamma(\theta_0)\right)\right)' \\
&= \mathrm{E}\big(g_n - \gamma(\theta_0)\big)\big(g_n - \gamma(\theta_0)\big)' \\
&\qquad + \mathrm{E}\big(t_n(\theta_0) - \gamma(\theta_0)\big)\big(t_n(\theta_0) - \gamma(\theta_0)\big)' \\
&= \Psi + \frac{1}{R}\Psi \\
&= \left(1 + \frac{1}{R}\right)\Psi,
\end{aligned}$$

where the mutual independence of the $t_{nr}(\theta)$ and their independence of g_n have been used. Because $\mathrm{E}\big(t_n(\theta)\big) = \gamma(\theta)$, some law of large numbers ensures that

$$\operatorname*{plim}_{N\to\infty} \frac{1}{N}\sum_{n=1}^{N} t_n(\theta) = \gamma(\theta).$$

Hence, if $t_{nr}(\theta)$ is a differentiable function of θ,

$$\operatorname*{plim}_{N\to\infty} \frac{1}{N}\sum_{n=1}^{N} \frac{\partial t_n(\theta)}{\partial \theta'} = -G(\theta),$$

where $G(\theta) \equiv -\partial\gamma(\theta)/\partial\theta'$. Define

$$\bar{h}(\theta) \equiv \frac{1}{N}\sum_{n=1}^{N}(g_n - t_n(\theta))$$

and let the simulated GMM estimator $\hat{\theta}_{\text{SGMM}}$ be defined as the minimizing argument of $\bar{h}(\theta)'\hat{W}\bar{h}(\theta)$. Combining the results derived above with standard GMM theory, we find that, with asymptotically optimal weighting,

$$\sqrt{N}\left(\hat{\theta}_{\text{SGMM}} - \theta_0\right) \xrightarrow{d} \mathcal{N}_m\left(0, V_{\text{sim}}\right),$$

where

$$V_{\text{sim}} = \left(G_0'\Psi_{\text{sim}}^{-1}G_0\right)^{-1} = \left(1 + \frac{1}{R}\right)\left(G_0'\Psi^{-1}G_0\right)^{-1},$$

and $G_0 \equiv G(\theta_0)$. From standard GMM theory, we have that, if we had been able to use $\gamma(\theta)$ directly instead of the simulated values, the asymptotic covariance matrix would have been $(G_0'\Psi^{-1}G_0)^{-1}$, which implies that the efficiency loss of the simulation amounts to an increase in the covariance matrix by a factor of $(1 + 1/R)$, which is a small efficiency loss even with R as small as 10. Note, however, that the SGMM estimator is already consistent for $R = 1$.

Simulation in practice

To give some idea about how the simulation is used in practice, let us consider a nonlinear latent variable model, with a one-dimensional standard normally distributed latent variable ξ_n and $\text{E}(g_n \mid \xi_n) = \mu(\xi_n; \beta)$, where $\mu(\xi_n; \beta)$ is a nonlinear function of ξ_n and a parameter vector β. We will encounter models of this kind in chapter 11. For this model, we have

$$\gamma(\beta) \equiv \text{E}(g_n) = \text{E}\left(\text{E}(g_n \mid \xi_n)\right) = \int_{-\infty}^{+\infty} \mu(\xi_n; \beta)\phi(\xi_n)\,\text{d}\xi_n, \tag{9.57}$$

where $\phi(\cdot)$ is the standard normal density function. For nonlinear functions $\mu(\xi_n; \beta)$, this integral can generally not be expressed in closed form. It is, however, easy to generate standard normally distributed random variables ξ_{nr}. Clearly, if we define $t_{nr}(\beta) \equiv \mu(\xi_{nr}; \beta)$, then $\text{E}\left(t_{nr}(\beta)\right) = \gamma(\beta)$. Hence, we can simply generate R standard normally distributed variables ξ_{nr}, $r = 1, \ldots, R$ for each observation, define $t_{nr}(\beta)$ as a function of β and the correspondingly generated value of ξ_{nr}, and proceed as discussed above.

Now, assume that $\xi_n \sim \mathcal{N}(\alpha, \sigma^2)$, where α and σ^2 are parameters that have to be estimated as well (assuming that they are identified). Then, we can not straightforwardly generate ξ_{nr}, because its distribution depends on the parameter we wish to estimate. In this case, however, we can obviously write $\xi_{nr} = \alpha + \sigma z_{nr}$, where z_{nr} is standard normally distributed. Consequently, we can generate values of z_{nr} and define $t_{nr}(\beta, \alpha, \sigma^2) \equiv \mu(\alpha + \sigma z_{nr}; \beta)$ and proceed as before. Note that γ is now a function of $(\beta, \alpha, \sigma^2)$.

In principle, all random variables can be written as transformations of random variables with known distributions, where the transformations may depend on the parameters. In fact, random variables are usually generated in this way on a computer, starting with a uniformly distributed variable on the interval (0, 1). This procedure may, however, be difficult or inconvenient. For example, let, analogous to (9.57), the expectation γ be defined as

$$\gamma(\beta, \alpha) = \int_{\mathcal{D}} \mu(\xi_n; \beta) f(\xi_n; \alpha) \, \mathrm{d}\xi_n,$$

where $f(\xi_n; \alpha)$ is the density function of ξ_n, depending on the parameter vector α, and $\mathcal{D}$ is the support of f, i.e., the set of values of ξ for which $f(\xi; \alpha) > 0$. If it is difficult to generate random variables with the corresponding distribution, we can write

$$\gamma(\beta, \alpha) = \int_{\mathcal{D}} \frac{\mu(\xi_n; \beta) f(\xi_n; \alpha)}{f^*(\xi_n)} f^*(\xi_n) \, \mathrm{d}\xi_n = \int_{\mathcal{D}} \mu^*(\xi_n; \beta, \alpha) f^*(\xi_n) \, \mathrm{d}\xi_n,$$

where $f^*(\cdot)$ is the density function of a distribution from which it is convenient to generate random variables and μ^* is defined implicitly. Clearly, this is the expectation of the function μ^* of a random variable ξ_n^* that has density function $f^*(\cdot)$. It is now obvious that we can generate values of ξ_{nr}^* from the distribution with density $f^*(\cdot)$ and define $t_{nr}(\beta, \alpha) \equiv \mu^*(\xi_{nr}^*; \beta, \alpha)$ and proceed as before. There are, however, some restrictions on the density function $f^*(\cdot)$. In particular, $f^*(\cdot)$ should have the same support as $f(\cdot\,; \alpha)$ and should be bounded in some sense. We will not further discuss these details.

Further issues

The transformation of the problem in μ and f to the problem in μ^* and f^* is called importance sampling. In some leading cases, such as the multinomial probit model, the most obvious candidate for $t_{nr}(\theta)$ is not differentiable. However, in these cases, importance sampling techniques can be used as well, by which $t_{nr}(\theta)$ becomes a differentiable function of θ. Moreover, with these techniques, as well as other efficient simulation methods like antithetic sampling and the use of control variates, the variance of $t_{nr}(\theta)$ may be reduced considerably, which also reduces the variance of the estimator. Of course, the lower bound of the asymptotic covariance matrix of the estimator remains $(G_0'\Psi^{-1}G_0)^{-1}$.

Thus far, simulated GMM was discussed in the context of an unconditional moment vector in the separated form. The ideas extend, however, straightforwardly to conditional moments. This is particularly simple if the conditional moments can be written as $\mathrm{E}(y_n \mid z_n) = \gamma(\theta; z_n)$. Then, we can simulate $\tilde{t}_{nr}(\theta; z_n)$ such that

$$\mathrm{E}\big(\tilde{t}_{nr}(\theta; z_n) \mid z_n\big) = \gamma(\theta; z_n).$$

Given this definition, an unconditional simulated moment vector is given by

$$h_n(\theta) \equiv z_n\big(y_n - \tilde{t}_{nr}(\theta; z_n)\big),$$

and the estimation proceeds as before. Similarly, it is possible to extend simulation techniques to the inclusive case.

Simulated GMM is applied in a wide variety of econometric models, most notably models with qualitative or limited-dependent endogenous variables and random coefficient models, especially with panel data. In these models, high-dimensional integrals that can not be computed satisfactorily in a reasonable amount of computer time are approximated by simulation of the random variables that underlie these, which is usually quite easy. As indicated above, we will encounter another class of models that may benefit from SGMM, namely nonlinear latent variable models, in chapter 11.

9.9 The efficiency of GMM and ML

In section 9.3, it was shown that GMM is optimal, in the sense of yielding an estimator with maximal asymptotic efficiency, if the weight matrix $\hat{W}$ in the GMM criterion function is chosen such that it converges to the inverse of the covariance matrix Ψ of the statistics that are used in the GMM estimation procedure. This leaves open a wider question, which concerns the overall asymptotic efficiency of the GMM estimator relative to the sampling framework. In this section we address this question of efficiency. We will find that, if the underlying distribution of the data is a member of the *exponential family*, the GMM estimator has the same asymptotic covariance matrix as the ML estimator (and is hence asymptotically efficient overall) if GMM is applied using the sufficient statistics with an optimal weight matrix.

The exponential family

As mentioned in section 4.4, a probability density is a member of the exponential family if it can be written as

$$f(y;\theta) = \exp\left(a(\theta)'s(y) + \beta(\theta) + c(y)\right), \tag{9.58}$$

where y is a vector of random variables with domain $\mathcal{S}$, which does not depend on parameters, θ is a vector of parameters, $a(\cdot)$ and $s(\cdot)$ are vector-valued functions, and $\beta(\cdot)$ and $c(\cdot)$ are scalar functions of their respective arguments. It is assumed that $a(\cdot)$ is a differentiable function. Many well-known distributions belong to the exponential family, e.g., the (multivariate) normal, lognormal, gamma, and beta distributions. Many discrete distributions are also members of the exponential family, but we confine ourselves here to continuous distributions.

Because f is a density, it integrates to 1. Hence, from

$$\int_{\mathcal{S}} f(y;\theta)\,\mathrm{d}y = 1 \tag{9.59}$$

it follows that $\beta(\theta)$ is given by

$$\beta(\theta) = -\log \int_{\mathcal{S}} \exp\left(a(\theta)'s(y) + c(y)\right)\,\mathrm{d}y.$$

Assume we have observed a sample $\{y_n, n = 1, \ldots, N\}$, from f, where N is the sample size. Let

$$\bar{s} \equiv \frac{1}{N}\sum_{n=1}^{N} s(y_n) \qquad \text{and} \qquad \bar{c} \equiv \frac{1}{N}\sum_{n=1}^{N} c(y_n). \tag{9.60}$$

The vector $\bar{s}$ is a *sufficient statistic*. By definition, this means that the conditional distribution of a sample given $\bar{s}$ does not depend on the parameters. In that sense, the sufficient statistic contains all information on the parameters. Hence, we may conjecture that GMM based on the sufficient statistic and optimal weighting is efficient. We substantiate this below.

By and large, the exponential family contains most well-known densities that allow a sufficient statistic with a fixed number of elements, i.e., a number of elements that does not depend on sample size. (The data themselves always trivially provide a sufficient statistic with a number of elements that increases with the number of observations.) Therefore, the exponential family is of particular interest when discussing GMM. However, note that there exist densities that do not belong to the exponential family that still allow for a sufficient statistic with a fixed number of elements. For example, the uniform distribution with support

$[\theta_1, \theta_2]$ is evidently not a member of the exponential family because $\mathcal{S}$ depends on θ_1 and θ_2, but it can be shown straightforwardly that the sample minimum and the sample maximum together are a two-dimensional sufficient statistic.

Proof of the sufficiency

We first show that $\bar{s}$ is a sufficient statistic. Assume that there exists a differentiable one-to-one mapping between $y \equiv (y_1', \ldots, y_N')'$ and $(\bar{s}', z')'$, where z is a vector with auxiliary random variables, such that the numbers of elements of y and $(\bar{s}', z')'$ are the same. If $\bar{s}$ does not contain redundant elements, such a mapping usually exists. Let $J(\bar{s}, z)$ denote the absolute value of the determinant of the matrix $\partial y / \partial(\bar{s}', z')$, which is positive for almost all values of $\bar{s}$ and z under the assumptions stated. The joint density of $\bar{s}$ and z is

$$f_{\bar{S},Z}(\bar{s}, z) = J(\bar{s}, z) \exp\big(a(\theta)'\bar{s} + \beta(\theta) + \bar{c}\big),$$

where $\bar{c}$ is now implicitly a function of $\bar{s}$ and z (through y). Hence, the marginal density of $\bar{s}$ is

$$\begin{aligned} f_{\bar{S}}(\bar{s}) &= \int_{\mathcal{D}} J(\bar{s}, z) \exp\big(a(\theta)'\bar{s} + \beta(\theta) + \bar{c}\big)\, \mathrm{d}z \\ &= \exp\big(a(\theta)'\bar{s} + \beta(\theta)\big) \int_{\mathcal{D}} J(\bar{s}, z) \exp(\bar{c})\, \mathrm{d}z, \end{aligned}$$

where $\mathcal{D}$ is the domain of z. Consequently, the conditional density of the random variable Z given $\bar{S}$ is

$$\begin{aligned} f_{Z|\bar{S}}(z \mid \bar{s}) &\equiv \frac{f_{\bar{S},Z}(\bar{s}, z)}{f_{\bar{S}}(\bar{s})} \\ &= \frac{\exp\big(a(\theta)'\bar{s} + \beta(\theta)\big) J(\bar{s}, z) \exp(\bar{c})}{\exp\big(a(\theta)'\bar{s} + \beta(\theta)\big) \int_{\mathcal{D}} J(\bar{s}, z) \exp(\bar{c})\, \mathrm{d}z} \\ &= \frac{J(\bar{s}, z) \exp(\bar{c})}{\int_{\mathcal{D}} J(\bar{s}, z) \exp(\bar{c})\, \mathrm{d}z}, \end{aligned}$$

which apparently does not depend on θ. The conditional distribution function of Y given $\bar{S}$ is

$$F_{Y|\bar{S}}(y \mid \bar{s}) = \Pr(Y \leq y \mid \bar{S} = \bar{s}) = \int_{\mathcal{D}} I(Y \leq y) f_{Z|\bar{S}}(z \mid \bar{s})\, \mathrm{d}z,$$

where $I(\cdot)$ is the indicator function and Y is implicitly regarded as a function of $\bar{s}$ and z. Because $F_{Y|\bar{S}}(y \mid \bar{s})$ does not depend on θ, $\bar{s}$ is a sufficient statistic.

The maximum likelihood estimator

In order to have a yardstick to judge the quality of the GMM estimator based on a sufficient statistic by, we first consider the asymptotic distribution of the ML estimator, which is well known to be asymptotically efficient.

The contribution to the loglikelihood of observation y_n is given by

$$\begin{aligned} L(\theta; y_n) &\equiv \log f(y_n; \theta) \\ &= a(\theta)' s(y_n) + \beta(\theta) + c(y_n). \end{aligned}$$

The loglikelihood corresponding with the sample is

$$\begin{aligned} L(\theta; \bar{s}, \bar{c}) &\equiv \sum_{n=1}^{N} L(\theta; y_n) \\ &= N\big(a(\theta)'\bar{s} + \beta(\theta) + \bar{c}\big). \end{aligned}$$

To derive the score vector, i.e., the derivative of the loglikelihood function with respect to the parameter vector θ, we define

$$A(\theta) \equiv \frac{\partial a(\theta)}{\partial \theta'} \qquad \text{and} \qquad b(\theta) \equiv \frac{\partial \beta(\theta)}{\partial \theta}.$$

From (9.59) we obtain

$$\int_{\mathcal{S}} \frac{\partial \log f(y; \theta)}{\partial \theta} f(y; \theta)\, \mathrm{d}y = \frac{\partial}{\partial \theta} \int_{\mathcal{S}} f(y; \theta)\, \mathrm{d}y = 0,$$

and substituting the density from (9.58) gives

$$\int_{\mathcal{S}} \big(A(\theta)' s(y) + b(\theta)\big) f(y; \theta)\, \mathrm{d}y = 0,$$

which on defining

$$\sigma(\theta) \equiv \mathrm{E}\big(s(y); \theta\big) = \int_{\mathcal{S}} s(y) f(y; \theta)\, \mathrm{d}y$$

can be succinctly expressed as

$$A(\theta)'\sigma(\theta) = -b(\theta).$$

The score vector is

$$\begin{aligned} \bar{h}(\theta; \bar{s}) &\equiv \frac{\partial L(\theta; \bar{s}, \bar{c})}{\partial \theta} \\ &= N\big(A(\theta)'\bar{s} + b(\theta)\big) \\ &= N A(\theta)'\big(\bar{s} - \sigma(\theta)\big). \end{aligned}$$

The maximum likelihood estimator is found by setting the score vector equal to zero and solving for θ. From (9.60), it follows immediately that $\mathrm{E}(\bar{s};\theta) = \mathrm{E}\big(s(y);\theta\big) = \sigma(\theta)$, which proves that $\mathrm{E}\big(\bar{h}(\theta;\bar{s});\theta\big) = 0$, which essentially holds for all score vectors when the domain of $f(\cdot)$ does not depend on parameters.

Note that the ML estimator depends on the parameters only through $\bar{s}$. Hence, the analysis of section 9.2 already implies that the ML estimator is asymptotically equivalent to a GMM estimator based on $\bar{s}$. We will derive this explicitly below.

Let the covariance matrix of $s(y)$ be written as a function of θ,

$$\Psi(\theta) \equiv \mathrm{E}\left(\big(s(y) - \sigma(\theta)\big)\big(s(y) - \sigma(\theta)\big)'\,;\theta\right).$$

Let θ_0 be the true value of θ and let $\Psi \equiv \Psi(\theta_0)$. Without loss of generality, we assume that Ψ is of full rank, and hence positive definite, in an open neighborhood of θ_0. Otherwise, $s(y)$ would contain redundant elements which could be removed at no cost, cf. section 4.4. Obviously,

$$\mathrm{E}\left(\big(\bar{s} - \sigma(\theta_0)\big)\big(\bar{s} - \sigma(\theta_0)\big)'\right) = \frac{1}{N}\Psi.$$

We assume that $A(\theta)$ is of full column rank in an open neighborhood of θ_0. Hence, in particular, $A_0 \equiv A(\theta_0)$ is of full column rank. The information matrix becomes

$$\begin{aligned}\mathcal{I}_0 &\equiv \mathrm{E}\left(g(\theta_0;\bar{s})g(\theta_0;\bar{s})'\,;\theta_0\right)\\ &= NA_0'\Psi A_0.\end{aligned}$$

Note that, given the assumptions on the rank of A_0 and Ψ, this information matrix is of full rank and hence θ is identified, cf. theorem 4.1.

Letting $\hat{\theta}$ denote the ML estimator, it holds that

$$\sqrt{N}(\hat{\theta} - \theta_0) \xrightarrow{d} \mathcal{N}_m(0, N\mathcal{I}_0^{-1}) = \mathcal{N}_m\big(0, (A_0'\Psi A_0)^{-1}\big). \tag{9.61}$$

The ML estimator is asymptotically efficient in the sense that it has the smallest asymptotic variance within the class of all consistent asymptotically normal estimators.

The GMM estimator

After having discussed ML, we now turn to GMM. In particular, we will consider GMM based on the sufficient statistic $\bar{s}$ and an as yet unspecified weight matrix $\hat{W}$. The moment condition then is $\mathrm{E}\big(\bar{s} - \sigma(\theta)\big) = 0$, and the GMM estimator $\tilde{\theta}$ of θ is the minimizing argument of

$$\bar{q}(\theta) = \big(\bar{s} - \sigma(\theta)\big)'\hat{W}\big(\bar{s} - \sigma(\theta)\big).$$

As derived above,

$$\frac{\partial \log f(y;\theta)}{\partial \theta} = A(\theta)' s(y) + b(\theta) = A(\theta)'\big(s(y) - \sigma(\theta)\big),$$

from which it follows that

$$\begin{aligned}
-G(\theta)' &\equiv \frac{\partial \sigma(\theta)'}{\partial \theta} \\
&= \frac{\partial}{\partial \theta} \mathrm{E}\big(s(y)' ; \theta\big) \\
&= \frac{\partial}{\partial \theta} \int_{\mathcal{S}} s(y)' f(y;\theta)\, \mathrm{d}y \\
&= \int_{\mathcal{S}} \frac{\partial \log f(y;\theta)}{\partial \theta} s(y)' f(y;\theta)\, \mathrm{d}y \\
&= A(\theta)' \int_{\mathcal{S}} \big(s(y) - \sigma(\theta)\big) s(y)' f(y;\theta)\, \mathrm{d}y \\
&= A(\theta)' \,\mathrm{E}\left(\big(s(y) - \sigma(\theta)\big) s(y)'; \theta\right) \\
&= A(\theta)' \,\mathrm{E}\left(\big(s(y) - \sigma(\theta)\big)\big(s(y) - \sigma(\theta)\big)'; \theta\right) \\
&= A(\theta)' \Psi(\theta).
\end{aligned}$$

Given the assumptions above, $G(\theta)$ is of full column rank in an open neighborhood of θ_0. Letting $G_0 = G(\theta_0)$, we obtain a basic result linking the elements from GMM and ML, which is

$$G_0 = -\Psi A_0. \tag{9.62}$$

This result allows us to compare the efficiency of ML and GMM directly.

The first-order condition of the GMM estimator $\tilde{\theta}$ is

$$G(\tilde{\theta})' \hat{W} \big(\bar{s} - \sigma(\tilde{\theta})\big) = 0.$$

Let $W_0 \equiv \mathrm{plim}_{N\to\infty} \hat{W}$. Then, as discussed in section 9.3, an optimal GMM estimator is obtained if we set $W_0 = \Psi^{-1}$. Then, from (9.18) and (9.26), it follows that

$$\sqrt{N}(\tilde{\theta} - \theta_0) \xrightarrow{d} \mathcal{N}_m\left(0, \big(G_0' \Psi^{-1} G_0\big)^{-1}\right). \tag{9.63}$$

In view of (9.62), $G_0' \Psi^{-1} G_0 = A_0' \Psi A_0$. Hence, we see, on comparing (9.61) and (9.63), that ML and GMM based on a weight matrix that converges to Ψ^{-1} lead to estimators with the same asymptotic distribution and hence, GMM is also asymptotically efficient among the class of all consistent asymptotically normal estimators.

A further comparison

We have proved above that the GMM and ML estimators have the same asymptotic distribution. We will presently show that these estimators are even more intimately linked. Note only do $\sqrt{N}(\hat{\theta} - \theta_0)$ and $\sqrt{N}(\tilde{\theta} - \theta_0)$ have the same asymptotic distribution, but they are also asymptotically equivalent, i.e., the probability limit of their difference converges to zero, which is obviously a much stronger result. This result can be shown as follows.

The ML estimator is defined by the first-order condition

$$A(\hat{\theta})'\big(\bar{s} - \sigma(\hat{\theta})\big) = 0,$$

whereas the GMM estimator is defined by the first-order condition

$$G(\tilde{\theta})'\hat{W}\big(\bar{s} - \sigma(\tilde{\theta})\big) = 0.$$

By the mean value theorem, we can write

$$\begin{aligned} \sigma(\hat{\theta}) &= \sigma(\theta_0) - G^*(\hat{\theta} - \theta_0) \\ \sigma(\tilde{\theta}) &= \sigma(\theta_0) - G^\bullet(\tilde{\theta} - \theta_0), \end{aligned}$$

where the matrices G^* and $G^\bullet$ have elements

$$\begin{aligned} G^*_{ij} &= \Big(\bar{G}\big(\alpha_i\hat{\theta} + (1 - \alpha_i)\theta_0\big)\Big)_{ij} \\ G^\bullet_{kl} &= \Big(\bar{G}\big(\alpha_k\tilde{\theta} + (1 - \alpha_k)\theta_0\big)\Big)_{kl}, \end{aligned}$$

for some $\alpha_i, \alpha_k \in [0, 1]$. (Note that $G(\theta) = -\partial\sigma/\partial\theta'$.) Write $\sigma_0 \equiv \sigma(\theta_0)$, $\hat{A} \equiv A(\hat{\theta})$, and $\tilde{G} \equiv G(\tilde{\theta})$. Then,

$$\begin{aligned} \sqrt{N}(\hat{\theta} - \theta_0) &= -\big(\hat{A}'G^*\big)^{-1}\hat{A}'\big(\sqrt{N}(\bar{s} - \sigma_0)\big) \\ \sqrt{N}(\tilde{\theta} - \theta_0) &= -\big(\tilde{G}'\hat{W}G^\bullet\big)^{-1}\tilde{G}'\hat{W}\big(\sqrt{N}(\bar{s} - \sigma_0)\big). \end{aligned}$$

Clearly, $\sqrt{N}(\bar{s} - \sigma_0)$ converges to a nondegenerate normal distribution. Therefore, by Slutsky's theorem, the probability limit of the difference of $\sqrt{N}(\hat{\theta} - \theta_0)$ and $\sqrt{N}(\tilde{\theta} - \theta_0)$ is zero if

$$\operatorname*{plim}_{N\to\infty}\Big(\big(\hat{A}'G^*\big)^{-1}\hat{A}' - \big(\tilde{G}'\hat{W}G^\bullet\big)^{-1}\tilde{G}'\hat{W}\Big) = 0.$$

That this is indeed the case follows straightforwardly from (9.62) and the observation that G^*, $G^\bullet$, and $\tilde{G}$ converge to G_0, $\hat{A}$ converges to A_0, and $\hat{W}$ converges to Ψ^{-1}.

In practice, this result means that the ML and GMM estimators will be very close, whereas they may not be close to the true value. Note, however, that we have confined ourselves in this section to the exponential family. ML estimators are asymptotically efficient under much more general conditions (they usually attain the Cramér-Rao lower bound asymptotically), but there may not exist a sufficient statistic of fixed dimension in those cases. Hence, it may not be straightforward to define globally asymptotically efficient GMM estimators, apart from the trivial MM estimator defined as the solution to the first-order condition of the ML estimator.

9.10 Bibliographical notes

9.1 The method of moments dates back to the work of Pearson (1894). For a discussion of the theory of estimating equations, also called estimating functions, see, e.g., Godambe (1991). The interpretation of the LIML estimator as an MM estimator is due to Bekker (1994). Note that the method of moments does not necessarily lead to a unique solution, as was already shown by Pearson.

9.2 Much of the theory discussed in this chapter has also been discussed by Ferguson (1958), Hansen (1982), Bentler and Dijkstra (1985), Shapiro (1983, 1986), Manski (1988), Davidson and MacKinnon (1993, chapter 17), Hamilton (1994, chapter 14), Newey and McFadden (1994), Gouriéroux and Monfort (1995, chapter 9), and Meijer (1998, chapter 2). Note that the GMM estimator can generally not be found in closed form and has to be computed by a numerical optimization method.

The estimation of covariance structures with the separated form of GMM (confusingly called GLS in this context) was introduced for the particular case of factor analysis by Jöreskog and Goldberger (1972) and for general covariance structures by Browne (1974). For a general introduction to the estimation of structural equation models by fitting moment structures, see Browne (1982, 1984), Bentler (1983b, 1983a), Bollen (1989), Bentler (1989, chapter 10), or Meijer (1998, chapter2). A complete derivation of the asymptotic theory was given by Shapiro (1983).

Note that some authors (e.g., Browne, 1982; Shapiro, 1983; Bates and White, 1985; Newey, 1988) prefer the term *discrepancy function* to the term distance function, because the requirements on this function do not necessarily imply that it satisfies certain requirements usually imposed on distance functions, such as the triangle inequality. We are less strict (and, hence, mathematically less correct) in this respect.

The method presented that shows how to transform any distance function into a quadratic form is due to Shapiro (1985b). The proof closely follows his.

The basic results were, however, already given in Chiang (1956). Basically the same point has been made by Newey (1988), who gave a different proof for the inclusive case. Newey and McFadden (1994), however, stressed that this asymptotic equivalence only holds locally, which implies that the result only holds asymptotically *conditional on* the consistency of the estimator.

An important nonquadratic distance function is, of course, the minus loglikelihood function for covariance structures. Other possibly nonquadratic distance functions have been proposed by Swain (1975), Manski (1983), and Bates and White (1985).

9.3 The minimum distance estimator was introduced by Chiang (1956) and Ferguson (1958). Subsequently, the theory has been expanded, generalized, and sometimes independently rediscovered by a wide variety of authors, such as Chamberlain (1982) and Gouriéroux, Monfort, and Trognon (1985), who call it asymptotic least squares. The term generalized method of moments is due to Hansen (1982), which is the seminal contribution that extended the theory to dependent data, leading to the present popularity of the method. A clear and succinct treatment of the conditions for consistency of GMM in the separated case was given by Shapiro (1984).

Linearized estimation methods have been discussed for minimum distance methods by Ferguson (1958) and Bentler and Dijkstra (1985), who also note its usefulness for bootstrap and jackknife procedures. Linearized GMM is the standard estimation method in EQS for ADF estimators. Estimation subject to functional restrictions was discussed by Lee (1980), Lee and Bentler (1980), and Bentler and Dijkstra (1985).

Given the discussion on optimal weighting in the text, a natural question to ask is whether we would ever consider using GMM with nonoptimal weighting. The answer is in the affirmative. The optimality of optimal weighting is asymptotic. To the extent that the asymptotic distribution is a reasonable approximation of the exact distribution, optimal weighting is of course to be preferred. However, there is ample evidence that, especially when the sample used is not too large, the approximation can be poor. GMM estimators may then be severely biased and inference based on them can be highly unreliable. One cause of this phenomenon is due to the fact that the data are used twice, to construct $\hat{h}$ but also to construct $\hat{W}$, which induces a correlation between these elements. This correlation leads to a negative bias in the case of covariance structures, which was was shown by Altonji and Segal (1996). Angrist et al. (1999) obtained similar results for IV estimators, which are a subclass of GMM estimators. Carroll, Wu, and Ruppert (1988) showed the analogous problems associated with estimating the weight matrix in a weighted least squares regression context. General results on the finite-sample distribution of GMM estimators are, however, hard to give.

A large number of estimators have been proposed that should be asymptotically similar to some "standard" GMM estimators, but should have better small-sample properties. Some of these have been discussed already in chapter 6. A promising recent development is given in Imbens (1997), who transformed a GMM problem with more moment conditions than parameters, to an MM problem using empirical likelihood principles. The resulting moment estimators are asymptotically efficient, even though no weight matrix has to be estimated (although for standard errors, hypothesis tests, and confidence intervals this is still necessary) and appear to perform better in small samples.

Yuan and Bentler (1997a) proposed corrections to the estimated asymptotic covariance matrix in order to obtain better small-sample properties.

9.4 The equivalence of the estimators based on $\hat{\Psi}_1$ and $\hat{\Psi}_2$ is due to Yuan and Bentler (1997b), who also showed the relationship between the corresponding values of the criterion function.

The continous-updating estimator was introduced by Hansen, Heaton, and Yaron (1996). They also investigated the small-sample behavior of this estimator vis-à-vis the iteratively reweighted and two-step estimators through simulation, in the context of asset pricing models.

Estimation of heteroskedasticity and autocorrelation consistent (HAC) covariance matrices is discussed by many authors, such as Eicker (1967), White (1980), Hansen (1982), Cumby, Huizinga, and Obstfeld (1983), White and Domowitz (1984), and White (1984, section VI.4). Newey and West (1987) proposed the estimator (9.43). Andrews (1991) discussed estimation in a general framework and studied the properties of the different weight functions. Andrews and Monahan (1992) proposed an estimator based on prewhitening of the $h_n(\tilde{\theta})$ values. Selection of the lag truncation parameter has been discussed by Newey and West (1994). A very general consistency result has been given by De Jong and Davidson (2000).

9.5 The estimation of the asymptotic covariance matrix of the covariances and the corresponding optimal weight matrix has been discussed by numerous authors, Browne (1974) for covariance structures under the normality assumption and Browne (1984) for covariance structures under arbitrary distribution of the observed variables (the ADF estimator).

An estimator of the covariance matrix (9.45) of the covariances that is not only consistent but also unbiased was provided by Browne (1984). See Koning, Neudecker, and Wansbeek (1992) for a formulation in matrix format and a direct proof. Chan, Yung, and Bentler (1995) performed a simulation study and found that the results based the unbiased weight matrix were highly similar to the results based on the usual weight matrix.

Note that ADF is called AGLS in EQS (Bentler, 1989) and WLS in LISREL

(Jöreskog and Sörbom, 1993). Mooijaart (1985) extended the ADF method to both second- and third-order moments in the sample moment vector. Mooijaart and Bentler (1985) discussed using a parameterized weight matrix in the analysis of covariance structures, which leads to IGLS or continuous-updating estimators.

The equivalence of the ML and IGLS estimators of covariance structures was shown by Lee and Jennrich (1979). ML estimators are computed in this way by the software package EQS (Bentler, 1989). An extensive discussion of the importance of IGLS can be found in Del Pino (1989) and McCullagh and Nelder (1989). The continuous-updating estimator for covariance structures was briefly mentioned by Amemiya and Anderson (1990), but not further studied.

There have been several proposals for alternative estimators for covariance structures that should have better small-sample properties. For example, Bentler and Dijkstra (1985, p. 20) proposed an analytic bias-correction term. Meijer (1998) studied bias-correction through the bootstrap in a number of settings with not only covariance structures, but also higher order moment structures, and found some improvements, but still considerable remaining bias.

Koning, Neudecker, and Wansbeek (1993) proposed an estimator for covariance structure models with a weight matrix that has the same structure as the weight matrix $\hat{W}_4$ under normality, i.e.,

$$\hat{W}_{\text{KNW}} \equiv \tfrac{1}{2} D'_J (\hat{A}^{-1} \otimes \hat{A}^{-1}) D_J,$$

but where $\hat{A}$ is not necessarily equal to S. They proposed to choose $\hat{A}$ such that $\hat{A} \otimes \hat{A}$ is as close as possible to a consistent estimator $\hat{\Psi}$ of Ψ, in the sense that $\operatorname{tr}(A \otimes A - \hat{\Psi})^2$ is minimized, which leads to an eigenvalue problem. Given this setup, the GMM criterion function $\bar{q}(\theta)$ reduces to the convenient form

$$\bar{q}_{\text{KNW}}(\theta) = \tfrac{1}{2} \operatorname{tr}\left(\big(S - \Sigma(\theta)\big) \hat{A}^{-1} \right)^2.$$

The resulting GMM estimator of θ is a compromise between the normality-based estimator and the asymptotically efficient estimator. It shares the computational convenience with the former, but should be more efficient asymptotically. It is generally not asymptotically optimal, but should have better small-sample properties than asymptotically optimal estimators typically have. See section 10.4 and its corresponding bibliographical notes for more on small-sample properties, in particular for covariance structures.

9.6 The efficiency gains from adding moment conditions despite the introduction of additional nuisance parameters have been analyzed by Kemp (1992) and Kano, Bentler, and Mooijaart (1993). Meijer (1998) contains many examples in which one choice of moment conditions does not identify the model, whereas another choice does identify the model. Breusch, Qian, Schmidt, and Wyhowski (1999) derived conditions under which moment conditions are redundant.

9.7 For a general discussion of efficiency bounds with conditional moment restrictions, see Chamberlain (1987). Newey (1990, 1993) discussed the problem of constructing $\hat{D}$ when the functional form of D is not fully specified. He showed how this can be done by two nonparametric methods, nearest neighbor estimation and nonparametric estimation by series approximation.

9.8 The method of simulated moments was introduced by McFadden (1989) and Pakes and Pollard (1989), although the general idea dates back to Lerman and Manski (1981). The idea of using simulation to approximate an integral is much older, see, e.g., the overviews in Hammersley and Handscomb (1964) and Halton (1970). The principal observation of McFadden and Pakes and Pollard was that the approximation errors of the separate integrals of different observations tend to cancel each other out, so that a small number of draws per observation is sufficient.

The theory of simulation-based estimators has been extensively discussed by Gouriéroux and Monfort (1991). Overviews of simulation-based estimators and some of their main fields of application can be found in Gouriéroux and Monfort (1993, 1996), Hajivassiliou (1993), Hajivassiliou and Ruud (1994), McFadden and Ruud (1994), and Stern (1997). Mariano and Brown (1993) discussed the application of simulation-based estimators to nonlinear errors-in-variables models (see also chapter 11).

Simulation-based estimation methods are closely related to some Bayesian estimators, such as the Gibbs sampler (Geman and Geman, 1984; Casella and George, 1992), and to bootstrap methods (Efron, 1979; Stine, 1990; Hall, 1992; Efron and Tibshirani, 1993; Davison and Hinkley, 1997), especially the parametric bootstrap.

9.9 The asymptotic efficiency of the minimum distance estimator based on a sufficient statistic was already shown by Barankin and Gurland (1951) for a general class of problems. Links between ML and MM have been discussed by Serrecchia (1980). Arguments in favor of MM relative to ML have been brought forward forcefully by Berkson (1980). The lack of efficiency of MM relative to ML was discussed by Fisher (1921), quoted by, for instance, Cramér (1946). Soong (1969) and Kendall and Stuart (1973, pp. 69–72), among others, contain detailed examples comparing the relative inefficiency of MM for particular cases. Hansen and Singleton (1982) gave an example of a model containing a random variable whose distribution needs to be specified for ML to be applicable but not for MM.

Chapter 10

Model evaluation

If a model has been estimated, statistical inference usually proceeds in a number of steps. An important step is the performance of statistical tests whether certain restrictions on the parameters that have been imposed in the estimation were actually imposed correctly, or, conversely, whether theoretically interesting restrictions that have not been imposed may hold in the population. In section 10.1, the three major types of statistical tests will be derived, and they are compared in section 10.2.

If the number of moments is larger than the number of estimated parameters, GMM is equipped with an omnibus model test, the test of overidentifying restrictions, also simply called chi-square test. This test is the subject of section 10.3, where it is derived under optimal and nonoptimal weighting, and some asymptotically equivalent alternatives are given. Furthermore, it is investigated under what conditions the test designed for optimal weighting is still valid under nonoptimal weighting. This is called (asymptotic) robustness, which is discussed in section 10.4. An important application is a test for a structural equation model based on the normality assumption when the variables are not normally distributed.

A closely related question is how well the model fits the data. This may be judged by the chi-square test, but a disadvantage of this procedure is that with larger sample sizes, the power of this test increases and that with large samples, this test may detect theoretically irrelevant minor deviations from the model. Moreover, frequently, theory only specifies a broad outline of the model and several models may be consistent with theory. In that case, the problem is which model should be chosen from the set of plausible models.

To assess the fit of a model and compare the fit of different competing models, we can look at fit indexes, which are similar to the R^2 statistic. The (mean) values of these are supposed to be less dependent on sample size and hence may tell us more about the quality of the different models. These fit indexes will be treated in section 10.5.

Throughout this chapter, the focus will be on models that are estimated by GMM. Therefore, the notation of chapter 9 will be used largely without introduction. However, as we have seen in section 9.2, most estimators encountered in practice are asymptotically equivalent to GMM estimators. Similarly, the theory discussed in the current chapter may be applied in a much wider context.

10.1 Specification tests

In many cases, the applied researcher is interested whether specific functions of the parameters satisfy certain conditions. The simplest example is whether a certain parameter (e.g., a regression coefficient) is zero. Other, more complicated, examples are whether a substitution elasticity is one, whether a firm (or an industry) faces constant returns to scale, or whether regression coefficients are equal across subpopulations. These conditions can be put in the general form of a vector-valued equality restriction on a possibly nonlinear function of the parameter vector θ,

$$r(\theta) = r_1. \tag{10.1}$$

Let $R(\theta) \equiv \partial r(\theta)/\partial\theta'$ and let the number of restrictions in (10.1) be ν. Without loss of generality, we assume that the rank of $R(\theta)$ is ν for almost all θ. Otherwise, at least one restriction is implied by the other restrictions and hence can be removed, or the system of restrictions does not have a solution.

The parameter vector θ can be estimated without imposing the restriction or it can be estimated under the explicit restriction that (10.1) is satisfied. If the restrictions are imposed correctly, the difference between the restricted and unrestricted solutions will be small. Both the unrestricted estimator $\hat{\theta}$ and the restricted estimator $\tilde{\theta}$ will converge to θ_0, the true value of θ. If the restrictions are not imposed correctly, the difference between the restricted and unrestricted estimators will be larger. Therefore, a test whether the restriction is satisfied is based on some difference between a function of the two resulting solutions.

The first important test is based on the difference $r(\hat{\theta}) - r_1$, which is equivalent to $r(\hat{\theta}) - r(\tilde{\theta})$. This leads to a Wald test, which is a straightforward test whether the restrictions are correct.

The second important test is based on the derivative of the objective function at the minimum. For the unrestricted estimator, this derivative is obviously zero.

For the restricted estimator, the derivative will generally be nonzero and the restrictions will be binding. If the restrictions are imposed correctly, however, the restrictions will asymptotically not be binding and the derivative will converge to zero, because the restricted and unrestricted estimators both converge to the same value. Hence, we may construct a test statistic based on the derivative of the criterion function at the restricted estimator, $\partial\tilde{q}/\partial\theta$, where $\tilde{q} \equiv \bar{q}(\tilde{\theta})$. The resulting test is called the (pseudo) score test, because it was originally defined for maximum likelihood estimators and the score is the derivative of the loglikelihood function. Alternatively, note that if the restrictions are binding, the Lagrange multipliers associated with them are nonzero, whereas if they are not binding, the Lagrange multipliers are zero. Hence, we may base a test on the Lagrange multipliers and thus obtain the LM test, which turns out to be numerically equivalent to the score test. The term LM test is generally used in econometrics. Observe that the unrestricted estimator generally satisfies $\partial\hat{q}/\partial\theta = 0$, where $\hat{q} \equiv \bar{q}(\hat{\theta})$. Therefore, the LM test statistic can be viewed as being based on the difference between the derivatives at the restricted and unrestricted minima, respectively.

The third type of test is a straightforward generalization of the likelihood ratio test, which is well known in maximum likelihood. It is based on the idea that, if the weight matrices that are used for the restricted and unrestricted estimators are (asymptotically) the same, then the unrestricted estimator leads to a smaller minimum value of the criterion function than the restricted estimator. If the restrictions are correct, however, they will not be binding asymptotically and both the restricted and the unrestricted minimum will be close to zero in large samples. Hence, a test statistic may be constructed based on the difference between the restricted and the unrestricted minima, $\tilde{q}-\hat{q}$. This leads to a chi-square difference test, frequently called LR test, because it is a generalization of the likelihood ratio test for maximum likelihood estimators.

The three types of test just mentioned are sometimes, for obvious reasons, called the *trinity* and they will be discussed extensively below. The trinity is not exhaustive, though. There are variations on these tests and there exist alternative tests. Many of the alternatives are numerically equivalent under some commonly occurring situations or asymptotically equivalent in more general situations. They will not be discussed here.

Throughout this section, we use the subscripts 0 and 1 to refer to true or limit values in the unconstrained and constrained cases, respectively. Similarly, we use hats (ˆ) to denote estimated values in the unconstrained case and tildes (˜) to denote estimated values in the constrained case. If it is assumed that the restrictions are imposed correctly, the constrained and unconstrained limit values will often be the same, and we use the subscript 0 in restricted situations as well.

Wald test

Arguably the simplest test is the *Wald test*. The Wald test can be computed without the need to compute the restricted estimator. This is a great advantage if the restricted estimator is difficult to compute or if several different sets of restrictions of a common unrestricted model need to be tested.

If θ is estimated as a completely free parameter vector, we have from (9.18), with V_0 substituted for V_W, following the notational convention we have just introduced, that

$$\sqrt{N}(\hat{\theta} - \theta_0) \xrightarrow{d} \mathcal{N}_m(0, V_0), \tag{10.2}$$

with

$$V_0 \equiv (G_0' W_0 G_0)^{-1} G_0' W_0 \Psi W_0 G_0 (G_0' W_0 G_0)^{-1}.$$

The asymptotic covariance matrix V_0 is consistently estimated by $\hat{V}$, which is an estimator of V_0 that is obtained by replacing the matrices G_0, Ψ, and W_0 by $\hat{G}$, $\hat{\Psi}$, and $\hat{W}$, respectively, where $\hat{G} = G(\hat{\theta})$, and $\hat{\Psi}$ and $\hat{W}$ are consistent estimators of Ψ and W_0, respectively. By application of the delta method to (10.2), we conclude that

$$\sqrt{N}\big(r(\hat{\theta}) - r(\theta_0)\big) \xrightarrow{d} \mathcal{N}_\nu\big(0, R_0 V_0 R_0'\big),$$

where $R_0 \equiv R(\theta_0)$, which is estimated consistently by $\hat{R} \equiv R(\hat{\theta})$. Hence, by applying Slutsky's theorem, we have

$$(\hat{R}\hat{V}\hat{R}')^{-1/2}\sqrt{N}\big(r(\hat{\theta}) - r(\theta_0)\big) \xrightarrow{d} \mathcal{N}_\nu(0, I_\nu),$$

and

$$N\big(r(\hat{\theta}) - r(\theta_0)\big)'\big(\hat{R}\hat{V}\hat{R}'\big)^{-1}\big(r(\hat{\theta}) - r(\theta_0)\big) \xrightarrow{d} \chi^2_\nu.$$

Clearly, this can be used to test the hypothesis (10.1), by replacing $r(\theta_0)$ by its hypothesized value, r_1. This gives the Wald test statistic

$$T_W(r_1) \equiv N\big(r(\hat{\theta}) - r_1\big)'\big(\hat{R}\hat{V}\hat{R}'\big)^{-1}\big(r(\hat{\theta}) - r_1\big). \tag{10.3}$$

The null hypothesis is rejected at level α if $T_W(r_1)$ exceeds the $(1-\alpha)$-th quantile of the χ^2_ν distribution.

LM test

The *Lagrange multiplier test* or LM test can be used if the model is estimated subject to the constraints. This is very useful if the restricted estimator is easier to compute than the unrestricted estimator, or if several sets of extensions of a common restricted model have to be tested for significance. A typical example is the estimation of a linear regression model with only a few regressors and homoskedastic errors. Then, LM tests can be used to test whether additional regressors have to be added, or nonlinear terms, or whether there is heteroskedasticity present.

Assume that the restricted model is estimated. This means that θ is estimated such that it satisfies the restrictions (10.1). This requires the minimization of

$$\tilde{q}(\theta) \equiv \bar{h}(\theta)' \tilde{W} \bar{h}(\theta)$$

under equality constraints, where $\tilde{W}$ is a symmetric weight matrix that converges in probability to some nonrandom positive definite matrix W_1. Note that we allow $\tilde{W}$ and W_1 to be different from $\hat{W}$ and W_0, respectively. The reason for this is that $\tilde{W}$ may be based on an initial restricted estimator, whereas $\hat{W}$ may be based on an initial unrestricted estimator. In the separated case, the weight matrix can be estimated without an initial estimator, so $\hat{W}$ and $\tilde{W}$ will coincide in that case.

The Lagrange function for computing the restricted estimator is

$$\begin{aligned} L(\theta) &\equiv \tfrac{1}{2}\tilde{q}(\theta) + \lambda' \left(r(\theta) - r_1\right) \\ &= \tfrac{1}{2}\bar{h}(\theta)' \tilde{W} \bar{h}(\theta) + \lambda' \left(r(\theta) - r_1\right). \end{aligned}$$

In the constrained minimum, the derivatives of $L(\theta)$ with respect to the parameter vector θ and the vector of Lagrange multipliers λ should be zero. Thus, the restricted estimator satisfies the following first-order conditions:

$$\bar{G}(\theta)' \tilde{W} \bar{h}(\theta) + R(\theta)'\lambda = 0 \qquad (10.4a)$$

$$r(\theta) - r_1 = 0. \qquad (10.4b)$$

Let $\tilde{\theta}$ and $\tilde{\lambda}$ be the solutions to (10.4), where $\tilde{\theta}$ is the constrained estimator of θ. Clearly, $\tilde{\theta}$ and $\tilde{\lambda}$ converge to θ_1 and λ_1, respectively, which are the solutions to the equations

$$G(\theta)' W_1 h(\theta) + R(\theta)'\lambda = 0 \qquad (10.5a)$$

$$r(\theta) - r_1 = 0. \qquad (10.5b)$$

If the restrictions are correct, it follows immediately that $\theta_1 = \theta_0$ and $\lambda_1 = 0$. If the restrictions are incorrect, $\theta_1 \neq \theta_0$, and hence $h(\theta_1) \neq h(\theta_0) = 0$ because θ is assumed identified. Manipulation of (10.5a) gives an explicit expression for λ_1:

$$\lambda_1 = -\left(R_1 U_1^{-1} R_1'\right)^{-1} R_1 U_1^{-1} G_1' W_1 h_1, \tag{10.6}$$

where $U_1 \equiv G_1' W_1 G_1$, $G_1 \equiv G(\theta_1)$, $h_1 \equiv h(\theta_1)$, and $R_1 \equiv R(\theta_1)$. It follows that generally $\lambda_1 \neq 0$ in this case. Therefore, a test of the restrictions can be based on a test whether the vector λ of Lagrange multipliers is zero. We will now derive the associated test statistic. By the mean value theorem, we can write

$$\begin{aligned} \bar{h}(\tilde{\theta}) - \bar{h}(\theta_1) &= G^{\bullet}(\tilde{\theta} - \theta_1) \\ r(\tilde{\theta}) - r(\theta_1) &= R^{\bullet}(\tilde{\theta} - \theta_1), \end{aligned} \tag{10.7}$$

where

$$\begin{aligned} G_{ij}^{\bullet} &= \left(\bar{G}\left(\alpha_i \tilde{\theta} + (1 - \alpha_i)\theta_1\right)\right)_{ij} \\ R_{kl}^{\bullet} &= \left(R\left(\alpha_k \tilde{\theta} + (1 - \alpha_k)\theta_1\right)\right)_{kl}, \end{aligned}$$

for some $\alpha_i, \alpha_k \in [0, 1]$. Furthermore, let $\tilde{G} \equiv \bar{G}(\tilde{\theta})$ and $\tilde{R} \equiv R(\tilde{\theta})$, and let $\bar{h}_1 \equiv \bar{h}(\theta_1)$. The first-order conditions (10.4) can now be written as

$$\begin{bmatrix} \tilde{G}' \tilde{W} G^{\bullet} & \tilde{R}' \\ R^{\bullet} & 0 \end{bmatrix} \begin{bmatrix} \tilde{\theta} - \theta_1 \\ \tilde{\lambda} \end{bmatrix} = \begin{bmatrix} -\tilde{G}' \tilde{W} \bar{h}_1 \\ 0 \end{bmatrix}, \tag{10.8}$$

where $r(\theta_1) - r_1 = 0$ has been used. Now, let $U^{\bullet} \equiv \tilde{G}' \tilde{W} G^{\bullet}$ and

$$\Upsilon^{\bullet} \equiv U^{\bullet -1} - U^{\bullet -1} \tilde{R}' \left(R^{\bullet} U^{\bullet -1} \tilde{R}'\right)^{-1} R^{\bullet} U^{\bullet -1}.$$

Then, (10.8) leads to the solution

$$\begin{bmatrix} \tilde{\theta} - \theta_1 \\ \tilde{\lambda} \end{bmatrix} = -\begin{bmatrix} \Upsilon^{\bullet} \\ \left(R^{\bullet} U^{\bullet -1} \tilde{R}'\right)^{-1} R^{\bullet} U^{\bullet -1} \end{bmatrix} \tilde{G}' \tilde{W} \bar{h}_1. \tag{10.9}$$

Obviously, $\tilde{R}$ and $R^{\bullet}$ converge in probability to R_1. Furthermore, $\tilde{G}$ and $G^{\bullet}$ converge in probability to G_1. Let $\tilde{U} \equiv \tilde{G}' \tilde{W} \tilde{G}$ and

$$\tilde{\Upsilon} \equiv \tilde{U}^{-1} - \tilde{U}^{-1} \tilde{R}' \left(\tilde{R} \tilde{U}^{-1} \tilde{R}'\right)^{-1} \tilde{R} \tilde{U}^{-1}.$$

Then, $\tilde{U}$ and $U^{\bullet}$ converge in probability to U_1, and $\tilde{\Upsilon}$ and $\Upsilon^{\bullet}$ converge in probability to

$$\Upsilon_1 \equiv U_1^{-1} - U_1^{-1} R_1' (R_1 U_1^{-1} R_1')^{-1} R_1 U_1^{-1}.$$

Under the null hypothesis, $\theta_1 = \theta_0$ and hence, $\bar{h}_1 = \bar{h}_0$, and so forth. Therefore, by applying Slutsky's theorem to (10.9), and using (10.6) and (9.13), we find that under the null hypothesis,

$$\sqrt{N}(\tilde{\theta} - \theta_0) \xrightarrow{d} \mathcal{N}_m(0, V_1)$$
$$\sqrt{N}\,\tilde{\lambda} \xrightarrow{d} \mathcal{N}_\nu(0, C_1),$$

with

$$V_1 \equiv \Upsilon_0 \Delta_0 \Upsilon_0$$
$$C_1 \equiv (R_0 U_0^{-1} R_0')^{-1} R_0 U_0^{-1} \Delta_0 U_0^{-1} R_0' (R_0 U_0^{-1} R_0')^{-1},$$

where $\Delta_0 \equiv G_0' W_0 \Psi W_0 G_0$. If the condition

$$R_0 U_0^{-1} R_0' = R_0 U_0^{-1} \Delta_0 U_0^{-1} R_0' \tag{10.10}$$

is satisfied, C_1 reduces to $(R_0 U_0^{-1} R_0')^{-1}$, from which it follows that $V_1 = \Upsilon_0 \leq U_0^{-1} = V_0$. The restricted estimator $\tilde{\theta}$ is more efficient than the unrestricted estimator $\hat{\theta}$. The condition (10.10) is satisfied if, but not only if, $W_0 = \Psi^{-1}$, i.e., with optimal weighting. More general conditions on W_0 that satisfy (10.10) can be derived from theorem B.2. Under nonoptimal weighting, the restricted estimator is not necessarily more efficient than the unrestricted estimator, which may be counterintuitive. This is similar to the situation discussed in section 9.6.

Let $\tilde{\Psi}$ be a consistent estimator of Ψ. Then, the asymptotic covariance matrices V_1 and C_1 are consistently estimated by $\tilde{V}$ and $\tilde{C}$, respectively, which are obtained by replacing the matrices R_0, G_0, U_0, Ψ, Υ_0, and W_0 by $\tilde{R}$, $\tilde{G}$, $\tilde{U}$, $\tilde{\Psi}$, $\tilde{\Upsilon}$, and $\tilde{W}$, respectively. Hence, by applying Slutsky's theorem once more, we find that under the null hypothesis

$$\tilde{C}^{-1/2}\sqrt{N}\,\tilde{\lambda} \xrightarrow{d} \mathcal{N}_\nu(0, I_\nu),$$

and

$$T_{\text{LM}}(r_1) \equiv N\tilde{\lambda}'\tilde{C}^{-1}\tilde{\lambda} \xrightarrow{d} \chi^2_\nu. \tag{10.11}$$

If the null hypothesis is not satisfied, the asymptotic distribution is more complicated, but it is clear that $T_{\text{LM}}(r_1)$ tends to be larger when the null hypothesis is not satisfied than when it is. Therefore, $T_{\text{LM}}(r_1)$ leads to a useful test. The null hypothesis is rejected at level α if $T_{\text{LM}}(r_1)$ exceeds the $(1-\alpha)$-th quantile of the χ^2_ν distribution. This test is called the Lagrange multiplier test, or LM test.

An expression for $T_{\mathrm{LM}}(r_1)$ that does not compute the Lagrange multipliers explicitly can be obtained as follows. From (10.4), we have

$$\tilde{G}'\tilde{W}\tilde{h} + \tilde{R}'\tilde{\lambda} = 0,$$

which gives

$$\tilde{\lambda} = -\big(\tilde{R}\tilde{U}^{-1}\tilde{R}'\big)^{-1}\tilde{R}\tilde{U}^{-1}\tilde{G}'\tilde{W}\tilde{h}.$$

Inserting this in (10.11) gives

$$T_{\mathrm{LM}}(r_1) \equiv N\tilde{h}'\tilde{W}\tilde{G}\tilde{U}^{-1}\tilde{R}'\big(\tilde{R}\tilde{U}^{-1}\tilde{\Delta}\tilde{U}^{-1}\tilde{R}'\big)^{-1}\tilde{R}\tilde{U}^{-1}\tilde{G}'\tilde{W}\tilde{h}, \tag{10.12}$$

where $\tilde{\Delta} \equiv \tilde{G}'\tilde{W}\tilde{\Psi}\tilde{W}\tilde{G}$. From this expression, it may be observed that the LM test can also be regarded as a test whether the probability limit of the pseudo score vector

$$\tilde{s} \equiv \frac{1}{2}\frac{\partial \tilde{q}(\theta)}{\partial \theta'}\bigg|_{\theta=\tilde{\theta}} = \tilde{G}'\tilde{W}\tilde{h}$$

is zero under the restrictions imposed by (10.1). Therefore, this test is also called the (pseudo) *score test*. Straightforward matrix algebra shows that a simpler equivalent expression of the test statistic is

$$T_{\mathrm{LM}}(r_1) \equiv N\tilde{s}'\tilde{U}^{-1}\tilde{s}, \tag{10.13}$$

provided that (10.10) is satisfied. If (10.10) does not hold, an expression analogous to (10.13) can be derived, but this is not simpler than the general formula for the test statistic.

Chi-square difference or LR test

As is well known, with maximum likelihood estimation, restrictions on the parameters can be tested by the likelihood ratio test. Let $\mathcal{L}_0$ be the unrestricted maximum of the likelihood function and let $\mathcal{L}_1$ be the maximum of the likelihood function over the subset of the domain of θ for which the restrictions are satisfied (the restricted maximum). The likelihood ratio is defined as the ratio of these two maxima: $\mathrm{LR} \equiv \mathcal{L}_1/\mathcal{L}_0$. Evidently, $\mathrm{LR} < 1$. The test statistic is $T_{\mathrm{LR}} \equiv -2\log\mathrm{LR}$, which is asymptotically chi-squared distributed under the null hypothesis. Alternatively, T_{LR} can be rewritten as $T_{\mathrm{LR}} = (-2\log\mathcal{L}_1) - (-2\log\mathcal{L}_0)$. The function $-2\log\mathcal{L}(\theta)$ is minimized by the ML estimators and in this representation, T_{LR} is the difference between the restricted and unrestricted minima of this criterion function.

This principle can also be applied to GMM estimators. The difference between the restricted and unrestricted minima of the GMM criterion function can be used as a basis for a test statistic, which is called the *chi-square difference* (CD) test statistic in structural equation modeling, and is usually called LR test statistic in GMM terminology. Evidently, this difference is only relevant when both estimators are based on the same weight matrix. Therefore, we will now assume that $\tilde{W} = \hat{W}$, although the results remain correct as long as the weight matrices of the restricted and unrestricted estimator converge in probability to the same matrix.

Under the null hypothesis, both the restricted and the unrestricted minimum of the GMM criterion function converge to zero and, consequently, their difference converges in probability to zero as well. In order to arrive at a test statistic with a nondegenerate distribution under the null hypothesis, we have to multiply the difference by the sample size, as will become clear below. Hence, the test statistic is

$$T_{\mathrm{CD}}(r_1) \equiv N(\tilde{q} - \hat{q}) = N(\tilde{h}'\tilde{W}\tilde{h} - \hat{h}'\hat{W}\hat{h}).$$

We will now study the properties of this test statistic. In order to do so, we need some intermediate results. First, from (10.7) and (10.9), we have that $\tilde{h} = \bar{h}_1 + G^\bullet(\tilde{\theta} - \theta_1)$, and $\tilde{\theta} - \theta_1 = -\Upsilon^\bullet\tilde{G}'\tilde{W}\bar{h}_1$. Hence,

$$\tilde{h} = (I_p - Q^\bullet)\bar{h}_1, \tag{10.14}$$

with $Q^\bullet \equiv G^\bullet\Upsilon^\bullet\tilde{G}'\tilde{W}$. Similarly, it was seen in section 9.2 that $\hat{h} = \bar{h}_0 + G^*(\hat{\theta} - \theta_0)$, and $\hat{\theta} - \theta_0 = -U^{*-1}\hat{G}'\hat{W}\bar{h}_0$, with $U^* = \hat{G}'\hat{W}G^*$. Hence,

$$\hat{h} = (I_p - P^*)\bar{h}_0,$$

with $P^* \equiv G^*U^{*-1}\hat{G}'\hat{W}$. Consequently,

$$\begin{aligned}
\hat{q} &\equiv \hat{h}'\hat{W}\hat{h} = \bar{h}_0'(I_p - P^*)'\hat{W}(I_p - P^*)\bar{h}_0 \\
\tilde{q} &\equiv \tilde{h}'\tilde{W}\tilde{h} = \bar{h}_1'(I_p - Q^\bullet)'\tilde{W}(I_p - Q^\bullet)\bar{h}_1.
\end{aligned}$$

Under the null hypothesis, $\theta_1 = \theta_0$ and hence $\bar{h}_1 = \bar{h}_0$. The test statistic then reduces to $T_{\mathrm{CD}}(r_1) = N\bar{h}_0'\hat{\Theta}\bar{h}_0$, with

$$\hat{\Theta} \equiv (I_p - Q^\bullet)'\tilde{W}(I_p - Q^\bullet) - (I_p - P^*)'\hat{W}(I_p - P^*).$$

Using the assumption that $\operatorname{plim}_{N\to\infty}\tilde{W} = \operatorname{plim}_{N\to\infty}\hat{W} = W_0$, we obtain $\operatorname{plim}_{N\to\infty} Q^\bullet = G_0\Upsilon_0G_0'W_0 \equiv Q_0$ and $\operatorname{plim}_{N\to\infty} P^* = G_0U_0^{-1}G_0'W_0 \equiv$

P_0. Straightforward calculations now show that, under the null hypothesis, $\text{plim}_{N\to\infty} \hat{\Theta} = \Theta_0$, with

$$\begin{aligned}
\Theta_0 &\equiv (I_p - Q_0)' W_0 (I_p - Q_0) - (I_p - P_0)' W_0 (I_p - P_0) \\
&= (W_0 - W_0 G_0 \Upsilon_0 G_0' W_0) - (W_0 - W_0 G_0 U_0^{-1} G_0' W_0) \\
&= W_0 G_0 (U_0^{-1} - \Upsilon_0) G_0' W_0 \\
&= W_0 G_0 U_0^{-1} R_0' (R_0 U_0^{-1} R_0')^{-1} R_0 U_0^{-1} G_0' W_0,
\end{aligned}$$

where all matrices are evaluated in θ_0. Therefore, by using Slutsky's theorem, we find that $T_{\text{CD}}(r_1)$ has the same asymptotic distribution as $N\bar{h}_0' \Theta_0 \bar{h}_0$. From the discussion in section B.3, it now follows that $T_{\text{CD}}(r_1)$ is asymptotically chi-squared distributed under the null hypothesis if and only if

$$\Psi \Theta_0 \Psi \Theta_0 \Psi = \Psi \Theta_0 \Psi.$$

This equation reduces to the condition (10.10). If this condition is satisfied, then $\text{tr}(\Theta_0 \Psi) = \nu$ and, consequently,

$$T_{\text{CD}}(r_1) \xrightarrow{d} \chi^2_\nu .$$

If the null hypothesis is not satisfied, the test statistic does not converge to a chi-square variate. The value of $T_{\text{CD}}(r_1)$ is generally larger in that case than if the null hypothesis is correct. Hence, using $T_{\text{CD}}(r_1)$ leads to a sensible test, which is known in the literature on structural equation models as the *chi-square difference* (CD) test. In the GMM literature, alternative names are used as well, such as distance metric (DM) test, or LR test to denote its relationship with the likelihood ratio test.

Note that the asymptotic chi-square distribution requires that the condition (10.10) is satisfied. If this condition is not satisfied, the test statistic converges in distribution to a weighted sum of χ^2_1 variates, as derived in section B.2. There seems to be no easy-to-use alternative form under nonoptimal weighting, so that an LM test or Wald test must be used in that case.

Further topics in testing

Before we compare the properties of the three test statistics derived above, we will discuss a few other issues briefly. Up till now, the test situation we have considered was that of testing H_0: $r(\theta) = r_1$ against an unrestricted alternative, partly because this problem is the most common, but also partly because it is statistically the easiest. In practice, however, other types of testing problems are also important. We may be interested in testing the *inequality constraints* H_0: $r(\theta) \leq r_1$ against an unrestricted alternative, or we may be interested in *nonnested* testing of H_0: $r^{(1)}(\theta) = r_1$ against the restricted alternative H_1: $r^{(2)}(\theta) = r_2$. Examples of the former are testing whether a certain price elasticity is smaller than 1 or testing whether a company faces decreasing marginal returns. An example of the latter is testing whether a certain regression follows a linear regression model or a loglinear regression model.

These problems are quite complicated and their solutions are outside the scope of this book. Hence, we will not discuss the details of these testing problems here, but only recognize their existence and importance.

Another problem we have not discussed so far is the testing of restrictions in situations where the model is only identified under the null hypothesis or only identified under the alternative. Consider, for example, a factor analysis model $y_n = B\xi_n + \varepsilon_n$, where $\mathrm{E}(\xi_n \xi_n') = \Phi$ is unrestricted and B is identified. If we want to test the null hypothesis $\Phi = 0$, then B is not identified under the null hypothesis, because it does not appear in the model. Conversely, if we want to test the null hypothesis $\Phi = \iota_2 \iota_2'$ in a factor analysis model with

$$B = \begin{bmatrix} \beta_1 & 0 \\ \beta_2 & 0 \\ 0 & \beta_3 \end{bmatrix},$$

then B and Φ are not identified under the alternative hypothesis. In such cases, the test can still be performed by adjusting the degrees of freedom of the test by the number of parameters that have to be fixed to render the model identified. In the first example above, this means that we additionally fix all free parameters in B to some arbitrary value. The estimates of the identified parameters (the error variances) and the values of the test statistics are not altered by this additional restriction, but now the restricted model is identified and the correct number of degrees of freedom is obtained.

The second example above is more complicated, because the natural alternative hypothesis is that

$$\Phi = \begin{bmatrix} 1 & \rho \\ \rho & 1 \end{bmatrix},$$

so that under the alternative, only one parameter is relaxed. If the number of degrees of freedom has to be reduced to cope with the nonidentification of the model, the resulting number of degrees of freedom is nonpositive. The cause of this is the value of ρ under the null hypothesis, which is 1. Clearly, ρ can not be greater than 1, because then Φ is not a covariance matrix. Hence, the hypothesized true value of ρ is a *boundary* value.

The presence of boundary values induces its own problems in statistical inference. Assume, for example, that $r(\theta) \geq r_1$ for all $\theta \in \mathcal{D}$, where $\mathcal{D}$ is the domain of θ. Then the asymptotic distribution of $\sqrt{N}(r(\hat{\theta}) - r_1)$ can not have a zero mean, because $\sqrt{N}(r(\hat{\theta}) - r_1)$ can not be negative for any sample size. Consequently, the Wald test statistic does not have an asymptotic chi-square distribution in this case.

Boundary values are quite common in econometrics. For example, in a model with latent variables or random coefficients, we may want to test that the variances of some of these are zero. Of course, variances are restricted to be nonnegative, so that zero is a boundary value. Another example is a correlation coefficient, such as discussed above, or a unit root test in time series analysis. Again, these problems are quite complicated and their solutions are outside the scope of this book.

10.2 Comparison of the three tests

Apparently, all three test statistics defined in section 10.1 have an asymptotic chi-square distribution with ν degrees of freedom under the null hypothesis. Therefore, the choice which one to use must be based on the asymptotic distribution under the alternative hypothesis, on small-sample properties, or on practical considerations. To start with the latter, it may be observed that the Wald test only requires the computation of the unrestricted estimate and the LM test only requires the computation of the restricted estimate, whereas the CD test requires the computation of both. Therefore, if the unrestricted estimate is easy to compute, the Wald test may be preferred on practical grounds and if the restricted estimate is easy to compute, the LM test may be preferred on practical grounds. Moreover, the CD test is not easily applicable under nonoptimal weighting. Clearly, the CD test is the least preferred on practical grounds.

Next, we will show that the three test statistics are asymptotically equivalent, which means that the difference between any two of them converges in probability to zero. As a result, they will lead to the same conclusions in large samples. Hence, the most relevant differences from a theoretical standpoint are the small-sample properties of the tests. Small-sample properties will be discussed subsequently.

Asymptotic equivalence

From (10.12) and (10.14), it follows that

$$\operatorname*{plim}_{N\to\infty} T_{\mathrm{LM}}(r_1) = N\bar{h}_1'(I_p - Q_1)'\Theta_1(I_p - Q_1)\bar{h}_1,$$

where $Q_1 \equiv \text{plim}_{N\to\infty}(Q^\bullet) = G_1\Upsilon_1 G_1' W_1$, and

$$\Theta_1 \equiv W_1 G_1 U_1^{-1} R_1' \left(R_1 U_1^{-1} \Delta_1 U_1^{-1} R_1'\right)^{-1} R_1 U_1^{-1} G_1' W_1, \tag{10.15}$$

where $\Delta_1 \equiv G_1' W_1 \Psi W_1 G_1$. (Note that the probability limit of $T_{\text{LM}}(r_1)$ is still a random variable and not a constant.) Straightforward multiplication shows that $(I_p - Q_1)'\Theta_1(I_p - Q_1) = \Theta_1$. Obviously, under the null hypothesis and (10.10), it follows that $\Theta_1 = \Theta_0$, so that the LM and CD test statistics are asymptotically equivalent. To show the asymptotic equivalence of the Wald test statistic to these test statistics, we first write, using the mean value theorem,

$$r(\hat{\theta}) - r(\theta_0) = R^*(\hat{\theta} - \theta_0),$$

where

$$R_{kl}^* = \left(R\left(\alpha_k \hat{\theta} + (1 - \alpha_k)\theta_0\right)\right)_{kl},$$

for some $\alpha_k \in [0, 1]$. Furthermore, as seen above, $\hat{\theta} - \theta_0 = -U^{*-1}\hat{G}'\hat{W}\bar{h}_0$, so that under the null hypothesis that $r(\theta_0) = r_1$ holds, the Wald test statistic can be written as

$$T_{\text{W}}(r_1) = N\bar{h}_0'\hat{W}\hat{G}(U^{*-1})'R^{*\prime}\left(\hat{R}\hat{V}\hat{R}'\right)^{-1} R^* U^{*-1}\hat{G}'\hat{W}\bar{h}_0,$$

which converges to

$$N\bar{h}_0' W_0 G_0 U_0^{-1} R_0' \left(R_0 U_0^{-1} \Delta_0 U_0^{-1} R_0'\right)^{-1} R_0 U_0^{-1} G_0' W_0 \bar{h}_0.$$

By comparison with (10.15), it follows that under the null hypothesis, the Wald test statistic and the LM test statistic are asymptotically equivalent under arbitrary weighting, and both are equivalent to the CD test statistic if (10.10) holds.

As stated several times in section 10.1, if the restrictions are not satisfied, the asymptotic distributions of the test statistics are more complicated. However, it is clear that all three test statistics diverge to infinity rapidly if the restrictions are not approximately satisfied. It is therefore customary to study the asymptotic distribution of the test statistics under the alternative hypothesis, and hence the asymptotic power of the tests, by assuming that the restrictions are approximately satisfied. This is operationalized by using the artificial construction that

$$r_0 \equiv r(\theta_0) = r_1 + \delta_0/\sqrt{N}.$$

This construction is called a *local alternative*. Obviously, it is not a realistic assumption that as the sample size increases, the restrictions will be satisfied in the end, but in many cases the asymptotic distribution of the test statistic derived from this assumption may be a reasonable approximation to the finite sample distribution of the test statistic, which is the sole justification of considering asymptotic methods at all.

Under such local alternatives and if (10.10) holds, all three test statistics are asymptotically distributed as a noncentral chi-square variate with ν degrees of freedom and noncentrality parameter $\delta_0'(R_0 U_0^{-1} R_0')^{-1}\delta_0$. Under arbitrary weighting, the LM and Wald test statistics are asymptotically noncentrally chi-squared distributed with ν degrees of freedom and noncentrality parameter $\delta_0'(R_0 U_0^{-1}\Delta_0 U_0^{-1} R_0')^{-1}\delta_0$. Moreover, the test statistics do not only have the same asymptotic distribution, but they are also asymptotically equivalent. This was already shown above under the null hypothesis, but the derivation extends straightforwardly to the alternative hypothesis under a local alternative. It is important that they are asymptotically equivalent, because it means that the three test statistics tend to lead to the same conclusions in large samples. If the test statistics would have the same asymptotic distribution, but were not asymptotically equivalent, the probability that they would give conflicting information would not vanish with increasing sample size. For example, if T_{W} and T_{LM} would be asymptotically *independent*, the probability that their corresponding tests with $\alpha = 0.05$ would give conflicting information is approximately $2(1-0.05)(0.05) = 0.095$ in large samples under the null hypothesis. Given the asymptotic equivalence, this probability tends to zero.

Small-sample properties

A major disadvantage of the Wald test statistic is that it is not invariant under reparameterizations of the restrictions. Consider, for example, the following situation. We have estimated a parameter θ from a given sample of size N. The estimate is $\hat{\theta}$ and the estimate of its asymptotic variance is $\hat{v}$. We want to test whether $\theta = \theta_1$. The Wald test statistic is

$$T_{\mathrm{W}} = \frac{N}{\hat{v}}(\hat{\theta} - \theta_1)^2.$$

We could also test whether $r(\theta) \equiv \exp(\gamma(\theta - \theta_1)) = 1$, where γ is a nonzero number. Clearly, $r(\theta) = 1$ if and only if $\theta = \theta_1$, so the two restrictions are algebraically equivalent. However, in the second parameterization, the Wald test statistic is

$$T_{\mathrm{W}}(\gamma) = \frac{N}{\hat{v}}\left(\frac{\exp(\gamma(\hat{\theta} - \theta_1)) - 1}{\gamma\exp(\gamma(\hat{\theta} - \theta_1))}\right)^2 = \frac{N}{\hat{v}}\left(\frac{1 - \exp(-\gamma(\hat{\theta} - \theta_1))}{\gamma}\right)^2,$$

the value of which depends on γ. If, for our given sample, $\hat{\theta}$ happens to be (slightly) larger than θ_1, then it is easily seen that, if $\gamma \to +\infty$, then $T_W(\gamma) \to 0$. Analogously, if $\gamma \to -\infty$, then $T_W(\gamma) \to +\infty$. If, on the other hand, for our given sample, $\hat{\theta}$ happens to be (slightly) smaller than θ_1, then, if $\gamma \to +\infty$, then $T_W(\gamma) \to +\infty$ and if $\gamma \to -\infty$, then $T_W(\gamma) \to 0$. Hence, given the sample, we can always find a γ such that the Wald statistic is significant at a given level and for the same sample, we can always find another γ such that the Wald statistic is not significant at the given level.

It is obvious that this basic principle can be generalized to an arbitrary set of nonlinear restrictions. The problem is that the application of asymptotic theory requires that the form of the restrictions, and in particular γ in our example, is given and $N \to \infty$. In practice, however, the sample is given, and in particular the sample size N, and γ can be manipulated.

Now, let us consider the effect of reparameterizations of the restrictions on the other test statistics. First, note that reparameterization does not alter the restricted estimator $\tilde{\theta}$, because for $\tilde{\theta}$, the restrictions are exactly satisfied, regardless of how they are parameterized. The minimum function value that can be attained of course does not depend on how the restrictions are parameterized as well. The CD test statistic is unaltered by the reparameterization, because the unrestricted minimum does not depend on the restrictions at all.

The formula (10.13) for the LM test statistic depends on the restrictions only through $\tilde{\theta}$. Neither $r(\tilde{\theta})$ nor $\tilde{R}$ enters this expression. Hence, in this case, the value of the LM test statistic does not depend on how the restrictions are parameterized. For the general case, this is somewhat more complicated, because $\tilde{R}$ does enter the general formula (10.12). By application of the implicit function theorem to two different parameterizations of the restrictions, it is straightforward to show that they yield the same value of the test statistic. We will not prove this here. However, note that, if the second parameterization is obtained from the first by a one-to-one function $r^*(\theta) \equiv r^*(r(\theta))$ or $r^*(\theta) = r^*(r(\theta) - r_1)$, then in (10.12), the matrix $\tilde{R}$ should be replaced by $R^* \equiv \tilde{J}\tilde{R}$, where $\tilde{J}$ is the matrix of first partial derivatives of r^*, evaluated in $r(\tilde{\theta}) = r_1$. This matrix is square and nonsingular, because r^* is a one-to-one function. Thus, $\tilde{J}$ drops out of the expression and the value of the test statistic is unaltered.

The discussion here may seem a little far-fetched, given the unnatural transformation that is applied, but it should be noted that any nonlinear transformation of the restriction will in general give a different Wald test statistic, although linear transformations leave the test statistic unaltered. In practice, especially with nonlinear restrictions, there may not be an obvious natural specification and even if such a natural specification exists, it may not be the one that is best in the sense that its distribution converges the fastest to the asymptotic chi-square distribution. The problems with the Wald test are generally corroborated in empirical studies. In typical empirical (simulation) studies, the Wald test tends to perform worse in small to moderate samples than the other tests. The chi-square difference test tends to perform best.

Apart from a reparameterization of the restrictions, we could also redefine the parameters, by considering $\phi \equiv f(\theta)$ as the vector of parameters, where f is a one-to-one vector function. This means that the estimates are obtained by minimizing the function $\bar{q}_\phi(\phi) \equiv \bar{q}(f^{-1}(\phi))$. Obviously, this leads to the same minimum and to the estimator $\hat{\phi} = f(\hat{\theta})$. Clearly, the CD test is again invariant under such reparameterizations. For the Wald test, observe that, in (10.3), $\hat{R}$ should be replaced by

$$\frac{\partial r(f^{-1}(\phi))}{\partial \phi'}\bigg|_{\phi=\hat{\phi}} = \left(\frac{\partial r(\theta)}{\partial \theta'}\bigg|_{\theta=f^{-1}(\hat{\phi})}\right)\left(\frac{\partial \theta}{\partial \phi'}\bigg|_{\phi=\hat{\phi}}\right) \equiv \hat{R}\hat{K},$$

where the square nonsingular matrix $\hat{K}$ is implicitly defined. Furthermore, $\hat{G}$ occurring in $\hat{V}$ in (10.3) should be replaced by

$$\frac{\partial \bar{h}(f^{-1}(\phi))}{\partial \phi'}\bigg|_{\phi=\hat{\phi}} = \left(\frac{\partial \bar{h}(\theta)}{\partial \theta'}\bigg|_{\theta=f^{-1}(\hat{\phi})}\right)\left(\frac{\partial \theta}{\partial \phi'}\bigg|_{\phi=\hat{\phi}}\right) = \hat{G}\hat{K}.$$

Hence, $\hat{K}^{-1}\hat{V}(\hat{K}^{-1})'$ should be substituted for $\hat{V}$. It follows that the Wald test is invariant under such reparameterizations. Using the same framework for the restricted estimator yields immediately that the LM test is invariant under such reparameterizations as well and we conclude that such reparameterizations do not affect any of the three test statistics. This holds, of course, under the condition that the restrictions are not simultaneously reparameterized, which may be the natural thing to do in practice.

Confidence sets

In typical estimation problems, the (point) estimate of a parameter θ is accompanied by an indication of the precision with which the parameter is estimated, usually its standard error. The point estimate and its standard error can then be combined into a confidence interval, which, given a level of significance α (= 0.05, say), provides an interval within which the true value of the parameter is likely to be situated, with probability $1 - \alpha$. Note that the probability refers to the randomness of the interval, because the true value of the parameter is a given but unknown constant in a frequentist view. This way of obtaining a confidence interval is closely related to the Wald test, as we will show below.

Confidence intervals need not be constructed in this way, however. For example, some types of confidence intervals based on the bootstrap method do not require a point estimate of the parameter. Furthermore, the concept of a confidence interval can be generalized to a confidence set for a multivariate function of the parameters. We will focus on confidence sets that are derived from test statistics. Given a significance level α, we define a $100(1-\alpha)\%$ confidence set for $r(\theta)$ formally as the set

$$\mathcal{S} \equiv \left\{ r_1 \in \mathbb{R}^\nu \;\middle|\; T(r_1) \leq \chi^2_\nu(1-\alpha) \right\}, \tag{10.16}$$

where $\chi^2_\nu(1-\alpha)$ is the $(1-\alpha)$-th quantile of the χ^2_ν distribution and $T(r_1)$ is a test statistic for the null hypothesis $r(\theta) = r_1$ that converges to a χ^2_ν distribution if the null hypothesis is true. In words, this means that a confidence set is the set of values of r_1 for which the null hypothesis $r(\theta) = r_1$ is not rejected. As mentioned above, the typical application of this is the estimation of a confidence interval for a single parameter θ_j based on the Wald test. In this case, the confidence set (10.16) reduces to

$$\begin{aligned}
\mathcal{S} &\equiv \left\{ r_1 \in \mathbb{R} \;\middle|\; T_W(r_1) \leq \chi^2_1(1-\alpha) \right\} \\
&= \left\{ r_1 \in \mathbb{R} \;\middle|\; \frac{N(\hat{\theta}_j - r_1)^2}{\hat{V}_{jj}} \leq \chi^2_1(1-\alpha) \right\} \\
&= \left\{ r_1 \in \mathbb{R} \;\middle|\; \frac{|\hat{\theta}_j - r_1|}{\sqrt{\hat{V}_{jj}/N}} \leq z(1-\tfrac{1}{2}\alpha) \right\} \\
&= \left[\hat{\theta}_j - z(1-\tfrac{1}{2}\alpha)\sqrt{\hat{V}_{jj}/N}\, ;\; \hat{\theta}_j + z(1-\tfrac{1}{2}\alpha)\sqrt{\hat{V}_{jj}/N} \right],
\end{aligned} \tag{10.17}$$

where $z(1-\frac{1}{2}\alpha)$ is the $(1-\frac{1}{2}\alpha)$-th quantile of the standard normal distribution. Evidently, (10.17) is the standard confidence interval for a parameter θ_j with an asymptotically normal estimator $\hat{\theta}_j$ with standard error $\surd(\hat{V}_{jj}/N)$. Because this confidence interval is based on the Wald test statistic, it has the same drawbacks as the Wald test. It is not invariant under reparameterization and its small-sample properties are not very good. Consequently, confidence intervals based on the LM test or the CD test may be preferred, although their computation is more complicated because restricted models have to be estimated repeatedly. In the MX computer program for structural equation modeling, confidence intervals are based on the CD test.

10.3 Test of overidentifying restrictions

One test that is of particular interest in the context of GMM estimation is an overall test of model adequacy based on the distance of the estimated moment vector $\hat{h}$ from zero. If the model is correctly specified this should, generally speaking, not be too large. In the case of model misspecification, a larger value of $\hat{h}$ may result. Apparently, the null hypothesis is $\mathrm{E}\big(\bar{h}(\theta_0)\big) = 0$ and the alternative hypothesis is $\mathrm{E}\big(\bar{h}(\theta_0)\big) \neq 0$. This does not seem to fit into the framework developed in section 10.1, because there it was assumed that the moment conditions are correct, but the additional nonstochastic restrictions on θ are possibly incorrect. We can, however, put the current problem into that framework by defining an additional p-vector ϕ of parameters and augment the definition of the moment conditions to

$$\mathrm{E}\big(\bar{h}_{\mathrm{aug}}(\theta_0, \phi_0)\big) \equiv \mathrm{E}\big(\bar{h}(\theta_0) - \phi_0\big) = 0.$$

Obviously, this moment condition is always true for some ϕ_0.

Because the number of parameters $(p + m)$ is now greater than the number of moment conditions (p), the model is not identified. Frequently, however, it is possible to define an explicit function $\phi(\eta)$ of a $(p - m)$-dimensional parameter vector η such that there always exists a solution to

$$\bar{h}(\theta) - \phi(\eta) = 0.$$

If such an explicit expression is not available, it still follows from the implicit function theorem that the number of free parameters in ϕ can be reduced by m, because these m are implicit functions of the remaining $p - m$ elements of ϕ and the m elements of θ (at least locally). The model thus defined, with p parameters, is called the *saturated model*.

Now, we can take the saturated model as the unrestricted model, for which the moment conditions are clearly correct, and the model we are interested in (the *target model*) as the restricted model. If the target model is correct, $\mathrm{plim}_{N\to\infty}\, \bar{h}(\theta_0) = 0$ and hence, we should have $\phi(\eta_0) = 0$ for some η_0. Given the discussion above, it follows that the restrictions are given by the equation $r(\theta, \eta) = r_1$, with $r(\theta, \eta) = \eta$ and $r_1 = \eta_0$. The number of restrictions is $\nu = p - m$.

Direct application of the ideas discussed so far is generally far from straightforward, because an explicit expression of $\phi(\eta)$ may not be available and the value η_0 is generally unknown. It will, however, turn out that these problems disappear if the chi-square difference test is chosen to test the null hypothesis. Note, however, that this test is only useful under optimal weighting in the sense that (10.10) is satisfied. The chi-square difference test statistic is then defined as

$$T_{\mathrm{CD}} \equiv N\tilde{h}'\hat{W}\tilde{h} - N\hat{h}'\hat{W}\hat{h},$$

where $\tilde{h}$ is the vector of moment conditions evaluated in the restricted estimator and $\hat{h}$ is the vector of moment conditions evaluated in the unrestricted estimator. In the current situation, the vector of moment conditions is $\bar{h}_{\mathrm{aug}}(\theta, \phi)$. In the restricted solution, $\phi = 0$, $\theta = \hat{\theta}$, and $\bar{h}_{\mathrm{aug}}(\theta, \phi) = \bar{h}(\hat{\theta})$. In the unrestricted solution, $\bar{h}_{\mathrm{aug}}(\theta, \phi) = 0$, as discussed above. Hence, the second term in the definition is zero and the first is $N\hat{q} = N\bar{q}(\hat{\theta})$, i.e., N times the minimum of the GMM criterion function. If the model is correct, $N\hat{q}$ is asymptotically chi-squared distributed with $p - m$ degrees of freedom.

A direct derivation of the asymptotic distribution

Because the above derivation was somewhat complicated and we want to study some generalizations of this test statistic, we will now give a direct derivation of its asymptotic distribution. Consider first the separated case. It turns out to be useful to have the joint asymptotic distribution of $\bar{g}$ and $\hat{\gamma}$. To that end, we consider

$$\begin{aligned} \operatorname*{plim}_{N\to\infty} \frac{\partial \hat{\gamma}}{\partial \bar{g}'} &= \operatorname*{plim}_{N\to\infty} \frac{\partial \hat{\gamma}}{\partial \hat{\theta}'} \operatorname*{plim}_{N\to\infty} \frac{\partial \hat{\theta}}{\partial \bar{g}'} \\ &= G_0(G_0' W_0 G_0)^{-1} G_0' W_0 = P_0, \end{aligned} \tag{10.18}$$

using (9.11) and (9.20). It follows that the joint asymptotic distribution of $\bar{g}$ and $\hat{\gamma}$ is

$$\sqrt{N}\left(\begin{bmatrix} \bar{g} - \gamma(\theta_0) \\ \hat{\gamma} - \gamma(\theta_0) \end{bmatrix}\right) \xrightarrow{d} \mathcal{N}_{2p}\left(0, \begin{bmatrix} I_p \\ P_0 \end{bmatrix} \Psi (I_p, P_0')\right).$$

Hence,

$$\sqrt{N}(\bar{g} - \hat{\gamma}) \xrightarrow{d} \mathcal{N}_p(0, \Pi), \tag{10.19}$$

where $\Pi \equiv (I_p - P_0)\Psi(I_p - P_0)'$. If an asymptotically efficient estimator for $\hat{\theta}$ is used, then (10.18) becomes $P_0 = G_0(G_0'\Psi^{-1}G_0)^{-1}G_0'\Psi^{-1}$, and, consequently,

$$\begin{aligned} \Pi &= (I_p - P_0)\Psi(I_p - P_0)' \\ &= \Psi - G_0(G_0'\Psi^{-1}G_0)^{-1}G_0' \\ &= \Psi^{1/2}\left(I_p - \Psi^{-1/2}G_0\left(G_0'\Psi^{-1}G_0\right)^{-1}G_0'\Psi^{-1/2}\right)\Psi^{1/2} \\ &\equiv \Psi^{1/2} M \Psi^{1/2}, \end{aligned}$$

with M a symmetric idempotent matrix of rank $p - m$ that is implicitly defined. Therefore,

$$\Psi^{-1/2}\sqrt{N}(\bar{g} - \hat{\gamma}) \xrightarrow{d} \mathcal{N}_p(0, M).$$

It follows from section B.3 that

$$N(\bar{g} - \hat{\gamma})'\Psi^{-1}(\bar{g} - \hat{\gamma}) \xrightarrow{d} \chi^2_{p-m}. \tag{10.20}$$

In order to turn this into a test statistic a consistent estimator of Ψ has to be substituted in (10.20). By Slutsky's theorem, this does not affect the asymptotic distribution of the test statistic. The resulting test statistic is N times the minimum of the GMM criterion function.

To study the inclusive case, note that, as discussed in section 10.1,

$$\hat{h} \equiv \bar{h}(\hat{\theta}) = (I_p - P^*)\bar{h}_0,$$

with $P^* \equiv G^* U^{*-1} \hat{G}' \hat{W}$, which converges to P_0. Using the asymptotic distribution of $\sqrt{N}\,\bar{h}_0$ as given in (9.13) and Slutsky's theorem, we obtain the asymptotic distribution of $\sqrt{N}\,\hat{h}$,

$$\sqrt{N}\,\hat{h} \xrightarrow{d} \mathcal{N}_p(0, \Pi), \tag{10.21}$$

which is completely analogous to (10.19). Again, it follows that

$$N\hat{h}'\hat{W}\hat{h} \xrightarrow{d} \chi^2_{p-m},$$

and the left-hand side of this can be used as a test statistic.

Summary of the properties under optimal weighting

Summarizing the above discussion, we find that, if we denote by $\hat{q}$ the value of $q(\theta)$ evaluated in $\hat{\theta}$ using a weight matrix $\hat{W}$ that converges to Ψ^{-1}, then

$$\chi^2 \equiv N\hat{q} \xrightarrow{d} \chi^2_{p-m}.$$

The statistic χ^2 is called the *chi-square test statistic*, frequently abbreviated as chi-square statistic or simply chi-square. This explains the use of the term chi-square difference test in section 10.1. The chi-square difference test statistic is evidently the difference of the chi-square test statistics of the restricted and unrestricted models.

Frequently, $N - 1$, instead of N, is used to define χ^2, but this has no consequences for the asymptotic distribution. Because the asymptotic distribution of this statistic was derived under the hypothesis of correct model specification, a high value of the test statistic may indicate a specification error. Thus, χ^2 can be used to test whether the model is true. If χ^2 exceeds the $(1 - \alpha)$-th quantile of the χ^2_{p-m} distribution, then the null hypothesis that the model is true is rejected at significance level α. This test is simply called the *chi-square test* in structural equation modeling language. It is usually called the *test of overidentifying restrictions* in GMM language. The reason for this is, that with a *just-identified* model, i.e., with the number of moment conditions equal to the number of parameters, the GMM estimator reduces to MM and the estimated moment conditions are exactly satisfied: $\hat{h} = 0$. Additional moment conditions increase the number of moment conditions beyond the number of parameters. In that case, generally, $\hat{h} = 0$ can not be obtained exactly. The model is now called *overidentified*, and a nonzero value of $\hat{h}$ is due to the addition of these so-called overidentifying moment restrictions.

In section 9.4, it was shown that, in many cases, the two choices $\hat{W}_1 \equiv \hat{\Psi}_1^{-1}$ and $\hat{W}_2 \equiv \hat{\Psi}_2^{-1}$ yield the same GMM estimator. It was shown that the minima of the corresponding GMM criterion functions are not equivalent in these cases, but $\hat{q}_1 = \hat{q}_2/(1 + \hat{q}_2)$. Consequently, the corresponding chi-square statistics satisfy the relationship

$$\chi_1^2 \equiv N\hat{q}_1 = \frac{N\hat{q}_2}{1 + \hat{q}_2} \equiv \frac{\chi_2^2}{1 + \chi_2^2/N} < \chi_2^2.$$

Hence, the chi-square test based on χ_1^2 is more conservative in finite samples. Asymptotically, both tests are equivalent, but in moderately sized samples, χ_1^2 tends to perform better than χ_2^2. Note that computation of χ_1^2 is typically based on $\hat{\theta}_2$.

Nonoptimal weighting

If a nonoptimal weight matrix is used, the chi-square statistic is distributed as a weighted sum of χ_1^2 variates under the null hypothesis, see section B.2. Although it is possible to estimate the weights and compute p-values on the basis of the resulting estimated null distribution, this is quite complicated. However, we can still devise a test statistic based on $\hat{h}$ that is asymptotically chi-squared distributed under the null hypothesis. This test statistic follows from the asymptotic distribution of $\hat{h}$ in (10.21). Clearly, a test statistic of the form $N\hat{h}'\hat{A}\hat{h}$ is asymptotically chi-squared distributed under the null hypothesis if $\Pi A_0 \Pi A_0 \Pi = \Pi A_0 \Pi$, where

$A_0 = \text{plim}_{N\to\infty} \hat{A}$. It can be straightforwardly verified that

$$A_0 \equiv \Psi^{-1} - \Psi^{-1}G_0(G_0'\Psi^{-1}G_0)^{-1}G_0'\Psi^{-1}$$

is a generalized inverse of Π, and $\text{tr}(A_0\Pi) = \text{tr}(I_p - P_0) = p - m$, and thus

$$N\hat{h}'\hat{A}\hat{h} \xrightarrow{d} \chi^2_{p-m}, \tag{10.22}$$

where $\hat{A}$ is a consistent estimator of A_0. Hence, the left-hand side of this can be used as a basis for a test of overidentifying restrictions under nonoptimal weighting. From theorem A.7, it follows that $A_0 = H_0(H_0'\Psi H_0)^{-1}H_0'$, which may be computationally more convenient in some situations. Using this formula, it follows from a derivation completely analogous to the derivation in section 9.4 leading to (9.35) that there are two versions of the test statistic (10.22). The first one is based on $\hat{\Psi}_2$ and is called the *residual-based ADF test statistic* in the context of structural equation modeling. It is denoted by T_{B}, where the subscript B refers to Browne (1984). The second one is based on $\hat{\Psi}_1$ and is denoted by T_{YB}, after Yuan and Bentler (1998a). The two statistics satisfy the relationship

$$T_{\text{YB}} = \frac{T_{\text{B}}}{1 + T_{\text{B}}/N}.$$

The test statistic T_{YB} has better small-sample properties and should hence be preferred.

An alternative test statistic is the *Satorra-Bentler scaled test statistic*, after Satorra and Bentler (1988, 1994). This is based on the observation that the mean of the null distribution of the chi-square statistic is $\text{tr}(W_0\Pi) = \text{tr}(B_0\Psi)$, see section B.1, where $B_0 = W_0 - W_0G_0(G_0'W_0G_0)^{-1}G_0'W_0$. The mean of the asymptotic chi-square distribution that can be used with optimal weighting is $p - m$. The Satorra-Bentler scaled test statistic corrects the chi-square such that its asymptotic mean is also $p - m$,

$$T_{\text{SB}} \equiv \frac{p-m}{\text{tr}(\hat{B}\hat{\Psi}_2)}\chi_2^2,$$

where $\hat{B}$ is the consistent estimator of B_0 obtained by replacing W_0 and G_0 in the definition of B_0 by their consistent estimators $\hat{W}$ and $\hat{G}$. Although the Satorra-Bentler scaled test statistic is not generally asymptotically chi-squared distributed, it tends to give satisfactory results (typically better than T_{B}) in finite samples when compared to a chi-square distribution. The test statistic T_{YB} is, however, superior to T_{SB} in most cases. Note that both the residual-based test statistics and the Satorra-Bentler scaled test statistic require a consistent estimate of Ψ. If such an estimate is unavailable, the bootstrap may be used to obtain an estimate of the null distribution of the test statistic.

10.4 Robustness

The properties of estimators and test statistics are usually derived under various conditions, e.g., under the condition of homoskedasticity of the errors, or under the condition that the distributions of some key variables are correctly specified. If these conditions do not hold, the derived properties of the estimators and test statistics may not hold as well. If the derived properties still hold under some violations of the assumptions, the properties are *robust* to these violations. For example, the OLS estimator is typically derived under the homoskedasticity assumption regarding the errors. Under this condition, the OLS estimator is best linear unbiased. Under heteroskedasticity, OLS is still unbiased, but not efficient. Thus, the unbiasedness of the OLS estimator is robust to heteroskedasticity, but the efficiency is not robust to heteroskedasticity.

Robustness is a rather vague term that applies to many different situations. There are different kinds of robustness and different degrees of robustness. We have already discussed one form of robustness in section 9.3. In that section, it was shown that the weight matrix $\hat{W}$ does not have to converge to Ψ^{-1} to ensure asymptotic efficiency of the GMM estimator $\hat{\theta}$. Analogously, $W_0 = \Psi^{-1}$ is not a necessary condition for the asymptotic chi-square distribution of the chi-square statistic. From (10.21) and section B.3, it follows that $N\hat{h}'\hat{W}\hat{h}$ is asymptotically chi-squared distributed if and only if $\Pi W_0 \Pi W_0 \Pi = \Pi W_0 \Pi$, which, according to theorem B.4, is equivalent to

$$W_0^{-1} = \Psi + G_0 C' + C G_0', \tag{10.23}$$

where C is an arbitrary $p \times m$ matrix, provided that the expression in the right-hand side yields a positive definite matrix.

Note that both forms of robustness (asymptotic efficiency of the estimator and asymptotic chi-square distribution of the chi-square statistic) apply if and only if both (9.29) and (10.23) hold. From theorem B.5, we have that this is the case if and only if

$$W_0^{-1} = \Psi + G_0 D G_0', \tag{10.24}$$

where D is an arbitrary symmetric $m \times m$ matrix. We will now discuss a situation in which this condition is satisfied.

Robustness to nonnormality

Often, the assumption of normality is an assumption of convenience. Models are frequently estimated under a patently unwarranted assumption of normality. In such cases, the condition (10.24) can be employed to assess whether the estimator is still asymptotically efficient (given the moment conditions) and whether the chi-square test statistic is still asymptotically chi-squared distributed. As we have seen in section 9.5, assuming normality amounts to taking $W_0^{-1} = \Psi_{\mathrm{N}}$, the asymptotic covariance matrix of the covariances under the normality assumption, which was shown to be

$$\Psi_{\mathrm{N}} \equiv 2D_J^{+}(\Sigma \otimes \Sigma)(D_J^{+})',$$

where J is the number of observed variables. So the results are robust to nonnormality if we can find a matrix D such that $\Psi - \Psi_{\mathrm{N}} = G_0 D G_0'$.

To illustrate this important principle, we consider a confirmatory factor analysis (CFA) model with nonnormal data. Let y_n be a vector of M observed variables for subject n and assume that y_n satisfies a CFA model

$$y_n = B\xi_n + \varepsilon_n,$$

with the usual notation and assumptions, cf. section 8.1. Let $\Sigma = B\Phi B' + \Omega$ be the covariance matrix of y_n, written as a function of the parameter vector θ, which consists of the free elements of B and the free elements of Φ and Ω, which are the covariance matrices of ξ_n and ε_n, respectively.

If ε_n and ξ_n are *independently* distributed, which is stronger than the usual requirement $\mathrm{E}(\varepsilon_n \mid \xi_n) = 0$, then straightforward computations show that Ψ can be written explicitly as

$$\Psi = D_M^{+}\big((B \otimes B)\Psi_\xi (B \otimes B)' + 4(B\Phi B' \otimes \Omega) + \Psi_\varepsilon\big)(D_M^{+})',$$

where Ψ_ξ and Ψ_ε are the covariance matrices of $\xi_n \otimes \xi_n$ and $\varepsilon_n \otimes \varepsilon_n$, respectively,

$$\Psi_\xi \equiv \mathrm{E}(\xi_n \otimes \xi_n)(\xi_n \otimes \xi_n)' - (\operatorname{vec}\Phi)(\operatorname{vec}\Phi)',$$
$$\Psi_\varepsilon \equiv \mathrm{E}(\varepsilon_n \otimes \varepsilon_n)(\varepsilon_n \otimes \varepsilon_n)' - (\operatorname{vec}\Omega)(\operatorname{vec}\Omega)'.$$

Assume now that Φ is completely free (except for its symmetry), ε_{ni} and ε_{nj} are independent for $i \neq j$, so that Ω is diagonal but otherwise free, and B, Φ, and Ω have no parameters in common. These are standard assumptions for a confirmatory factor analysis model, but also hold for some more general structural equation models. Then,

$$G_0 \equiv -\left(\frac{\partial\gamma}{\partial\beta'}, \frac{\partial\gamma}{\partial\phi'}, \frac{\partial\gamma}{\partial\omega'}\right) = -D_M^{+}\big(2(B\Phi \otimes I_M)C_B, (B \otimes B)D_k, H_M\big),$$

where γ is the vector of nonduplicated elements of Σ, β is the vector of free parameters in B, $C_B \equiv \partial \operatorname{vec} B / \partial\beta'$, $\phi \equiv D_k^+ \operatorname{vec} \Phi$ is the vector of nonduplicated elements of Φ, D_k is the duplication matrix of order k, which is the number of factors, ω consists of the diagonal elements of Ω, and H_M is the *diagonalization* matrix (see section A.4). Under the given assumptions,

$$\begin{aligned}
\Psi_\xi &= Q_k \Psi_\xi Q_k = D_k D_k^+ \Psi_\xi (D_k^+)' D_k' \\
\Psi_\varepsilon &= H_M(\Omega_4 - 2\Omega^2) H_M' + 2Q_M(\Omega \otimes \Omega) \\
\Phi \otimes \Phi &= D_k D_k^+ (\Phi \otimes \Phi)(D_k^+)' D_k',
\end{aligned}$$

where Ω_4 is the diagonal matrix with diagonal elements $\mathrm{E}(\varepsilon_{ni}^4)$. Combining the various elements, we find that

$$\begin{aligned}
\Psi - \Psi_{\mathrm{N}} &= D_M^+(B \otimes B) D_k \left(D_k^+ (\Psi_\xi - 2(\Phi \otimes \Phi))(D_k^+)' \right) D_k' (B \otimes B)'(D_M^+)' \\
&\quad + D_M^+ H_M (\Omega_4 - 2\Omega^2) H_M' (D_M^+)' \\
&= G_0 \begin{bmatrix} 0 & 0 & 0 \\ 0 & D_k^+ (\Psi_\xi - 2(\Phi \otimes \Phi))(D_k^+)' & 0 \\ 0 & 0 & \Omega_4 - 2\Omega^2 \end{bmatrix} G_0' \\
&\equiv G_0 D G_0',
\end{aligned}$$

which shows that the normality-based estimators are asymptotically efficient (given the set of moment conditions), and the corresponding chi-square statistics can be used to test the model.

This result is not restricted to the CFA model, but applies to a wide range of structural equation models. Unfortunately, there is no simple operational characterization of the class of the models for which this holds. To show the subtlety of this, reconsider the relatively simple CFA model as discussed above. Here, the robustness condition will generally not hold if restrictions are imposed on Φ or if ε_n is not independent of ξ_n even if they are uncorrelated, inducing heteroskedasticity.

It must be stressed, however, that, even if the robustness condition (10.24) holds, the normality-based standard errors are incorrect under nonnormality. Asymptotically correct standard errors must be based on a consistent estimator of (9.19).

10.5 Model fit and model selection

In practice, one generally does not have one prespecified model, which is then formally tested for its correctness. Usually, one considers, either explicitly or implicitly, a set of plausible models and wants to select the best in some sense. Furthermore, the results from the previous sections have been derived under the hypothesis that the model is true. However, models are never true. They are at best a good approximation. Consequently, the chi-square test tends to reject every nonsaturated model with large sample sizes, and whether or not the model will be rejected is more a question about sample size than about model fit.

In regression analysis, applied researchers rarely use a formal test whether the model is correct in the population. The correctness of the inclusion or exclusion of certain variables is tested by means of an F-test. Furthermore, residual plots are studied to detect deviations from linearity and homoskedasticity. The overall fit of the model is judged by the R^2.

The GMM equivalents of the F-test have been discussed in section 10.1. Residual analysis in GMM means an analysis of the sizes of the elements of the estimated moment vector $\hat{h}$. Large elements can help the researcher in the process of identifying important model misspecifications. In structural equation modeling, modification indexes may also be used to detect model misspecifications. These modification indexes are LM tests (with one degree of freedom) for each element of the parameter matrices discussed in chapter 8 that is fixed to a certain value, and for each cross-parameter restriction that is imposed. These tests are not used in a formal way, but their values are judged informally to find model modifications that are theoretically sound and are likely to improve the model fit considerably.

Fit indexes

To find a GMM equivalent of the R^2 statistic, consider a linear regression model that is not in deviation of its mean, i.e., the variables have nonzero means and an intercept term is included in the model. The model can then be written in matrix notation as $y = X\beta + \varepsilon$, where the first column of X is ι_N, an N-vector of ones, where N is the sample size, as usual. The R^2 can then be written as

$$R^2 \equiv \frac{(y - \iota_N \bar{y})'(y - \iota_N \bar{y}) - (y - X\hat{\beta})'(y - X\hat{\beta})}{(y - \iota_N \bar{y})'(y - \iota_N \bar{y})}$$

$$= \frac{(y - X\hat{\beta}_{\text{null}})'(y - X\hat{\beta}_{\text{null}}) - (y - X\hat{\beta}_{\text{t}})'(y - X\hat{\beta}_{\text{t}})}{(y - X\hat{\beta}_{\text{null}})'(y - X\hat{\beta}_{\text{null}})},$$

where $\hat{\beta}_{\text{null}} \equiv (\bar{y}, 0')'$ is the estimator of β for a highly restrictive *null model*, namely the model with only a constant, and $\hat{\beta}_{\text{t}} \equiv \hat{\beta}$ is the estimator of β for the *target model*, i.e., the model one is considering. From this formula, it can be observed that R^2 is the difference between the minima of the criterion functions of the null model and target model, respectively, as a proportion of the minimum of the criterion function of the null model.

The GMM equivalent is now obvious. First, we define a highly restrictive baseline or null model, which should be more restricted than the models one wishes to consider. For structural equation models, this is usually the model in which all variables are assumed independently distributed, the *independence model*. As discussed in the previous chapter, for structural equation models, the moment vector is in separated form, where $\bar{g}$ contains the nonduplicated elements of the sample covariance matrix and $\gamma(\theta)$ contains the corresponding elements of the population covariance matrix of the observable variables as functions of the parameters. In the independence model, the covariances in $\gamma(\theta)$ are fixed to zero and the variances in $\gamma(\theta)$ are free parameters.

Second, the minimum of the criterion function of the null model is computed. Let this be $\hat{q}_{\text{null}} \equiv \bar{q}(\hat{\theta}_{\text{null}})$. Third, the minimum of the criterion function of the model under consideration, the target model, is computed, which is similarly denoted by $\hat{q}_{\text{t}} \equiv \bar{q}(\hat{\theta}_{\text{t}})$. Finally, the fit index is

$$\text{NFI} \equiv \frac{\hat{q}_{\text{null}} - \hat{q}_{\text{t}}}{\hat{q}_{\text{null}}} = \frac{\chi^2_{\text{null}} - \chi^2_{\text{t}}}{\chi^2_{\text{null}}},$$

where $\chi^2_{\text{null}} \equiv N\hat{q}_{\text{null}}$ and $\chi^2_{\text{t}} \equiv N\hat{q}_{\text{t}}$ are the chi-square statistics of the null model and target model, respectively. This fit index is called the *normed fit index* (NFI), because its value is necessarily between 0 and 1, as with the R^2.

That the NFI is normed follows from the observation that $\hat{q}_{\text{null}}$ is always at least as large as $\hat{q}_{\text{t}}$, because the null model is designed to be a restricted version of the target model, and $\bar{q}(\theta)$ is minimized with respect to the free parameters. Therefore, any value of $\hat{q}_{\text{null}}$ can be attained by the target model by simply setting the appropriate free parameters to their restricted values. Obviously, NFI values close to 1 indicate good fit of the target model and NFI values close to 0 indicate bad fit of the target model.

A similar fit index is the *goodness of fit index* (GFI), which is only defined for the separated case. Its formula is

$$\text{GFI} \equiv 1 - \frac{(\bar{g} - \gamma(\hat{\theta}_{\text{t}}))'\hat{W}(\bar{g} - \gamma(\hat{\theta}_{\text{t}}))}{\bar{g}'\hat{W}\bar{g}} = 1 - \frac{\hat{q}_{\text{t}}}{\bar{g}'\hat{W}\bar{g}} = \frac{\bar{g}'\hat{W}\bar{g} - \hat{q}_{\text{t}}}{\bar{g}'\hat{W}\bar{g}}.$$

From the last of these expressions, it can be seen that this is a special type of normed fit index, with the null model being $\gamma = 0$. Because $\hat{q}_{\text{null}} \leq \bar{g}'\hat{W}\bar{g}$, we have that $1 \geq \text{GFI} \geq \text{NFI}$.

An unfortunate property of the NFI (and GFI, but we will concentrate on the NFI from now on) is that its mean depends strongly on sample size, despite its aim to be an indication of model fit that is relatively independent of sample size. The NFI value tends to be higher for larger samples, so that models appear to fit better in large samples. We will now discuss the cause of this problem, and a possible solution.

In order to do so, we consider the NFI as an estimator of a parameter. To that end, note that $\hat{q}$ converges to the minimum of the function

$$q(\theta) \equiv h(\theta)' W_0 h(\theta),$$

where $h(\theta)$ is defined as

$$h(\theta) \equiv \operatorname*{plim}_{N\to\infty} \bar{h}(\theta),$$

cf. section 9.2. Hence, we may consider $\hat{q}$ as an estimator of the minimum of $q(\theta)$. If the model is true, by definition there exists a θ_0 such that $h_0 \equiv h(\theta_0) = 0$ and the minimum of $q(\theta)$ is zero.

However, as stated at the beginning of this section, models are not true, but at best useful approximations. In that case, there does not exist a θ such that $h(\theta) = 0$, and we define $\theta_0 \equiv \text{plim}_{N\to\infty} \hat{\theta}$, which is the minimizing argument of $q(\theta)$. Analogously, $q_0 \equiv q(\theta_0)$. Obviously, for the null and target models, q_0 will be different, with $q_{0,\text{null}} > q_{0,\text{t}}$. It is now evident that the NFI is a consistent estimator of

$$\rho^2 \equiv \frac{q_{0,\text{null}} - q_{0,\text{t}}}{q_{0,\text{null}}}.$$

It is, however, a biased estimator. The cause of the bias can be seen by considering approximate chi-square distributions for its constituent elements. In section 10.3, we have seen that, if the model is true and $W_0 = \Psi^{-1}$, then $N\hat{q}$ follows an asymptotic (central) chi-square distribution with $p - m$ degrees of freedom.

Similar to the discussion in section 10.1 of the Wald, LM, and chi-square difference test statistics when the restrictions are not true, we may now consider a so-called local alternative. Under such a local alternative, it is assumed that $h_0 = \phi/\sqrt{N}$, which is hardly a tenable assumption. It implies that the population value of h depends on the sample size and that the model is asymptotically true. Of course, this assumption is rather unrealistic, but the noncentral chi-square distribution may be a good approximation to the distribution of $N\hat{q}$ if there is a $h^* \equiv h(\theta^*)$ close to h_0. Under the local alternative, if $W_0 = \Psi^{-1}$, then $N\hat{q}$ follows an asymptotic noncentral chi-square distribution with df $\equiv p-m$ degrees of freedom and noncentrality parameter δ, say, where $\delta \equiv \lim_{N\to\infty} Nq_0$.

From section B.3, it then follows that asymptotically, the mean of $N\hat{q}$ is $Nq_0 + \text{df}$. Hence, the denominator of the NFI is overestimated by df_{null}. The numerator is also overestimated, by $\text{df}_{\text{null}} - \text{df}_{\text{t}}$. In the typical case,

$$\frac{Nq_{\text{t}}}{\text{df}_{\text{t}}} \ll \frac{Nq_{\text{null}}}{\text{df}_{\text{null}}},$$

and some simple algebra now immediately leads to the downward bias of NFI in small and moderate samples. The bias diminishes in large samples, because df will then become negligible compared to Nq_0. Therefore, the mean of the NFI is an increasing function of N. However, this analysis also immediately leads to an improved formula. Apparently, an unbiased estimator of the noncentrality parameter δ is $\hat{\delta} \equiv N\hat{q} - \text{df}$. The quantity ρ^2 can then be estimated with less bias by the *relative noncentrality index* (RNI)

$$\text{RNI} \equiv \frac{\hat{\delta}_{\text{null}} - \hat{\delta}_{\text{t}}}{\hat{\delta}_{\text{null}}}.$$

The RNI is normed in the population, that is, ρ^2 is always between 0 and 1. In finite samples, however, its value may not be between 0 and 1. Moreover, $\hat{\delta}$ may not be positive. Therefore, we may prefer the *comparative fit index* (CFI)

$$\text{CFI} \equiv \frac{\delta^*_{\text{null}} - \delta^*_{\text{t}}}{\delta^*_{\text{null}}},$$

where $\delta^*_{\text{null}} \equiv \max(\hat{\delta}_{\text{null}}, \hat{\delta}_{\text{t}}, 0)$ and $\delta^*_{\text{t}} \equiv \max(\hat{\delta}_{\text{t}}, 0)$. The idea is that generally $0 \leq \text{RNI} = \text{CFI} \leq 1$, and the most likely other cases are those where $\text{RNI} > 1 = \text{CFI}$ or $\text{RNI} < 0 = \text{CFI}$. The CFI and RNI have proven to be valuable tools for assessing model fit and for comparing the fit of competing target models.

Parsimony and information criteria

Given the choice of the null model, and given the minimum of its asymptotic criterion function, $q_{0,\text{null}}$, the parameter ρ^2 is maximized by the probability limit of the estimator of the target model. A consequence of this is that, if we add a parameter to the target model, the value of ρ^2 for this new model will be higher than for the previous target model. This is analogous to the linear regression situation, where R^2 always increases by adding regressors. As with linear regression, this may hamper interpretation of the fit index. These indexes, like the chi-square statistic itself, may lead a researcher to propose a more complex model. It is generally believed that a model should be relatively simple, which usually means *parsimonious*, that is, with as few parameters as possible.

For that reason, in linear regression, the adjusted R^2 is sometimes used, which adjusts the R^2 with a penalty for overfitting. Its formula is

$$\bar{R}^2 \equiv 1 - \frac{N}{N-g}\left(1 - R^2\right).$$

If the number of regressors g is increased, but the R^2 does not increase much, $\bar{R}^2$ may not increase, but decrease. Obviously, the definition of ρ^2 can be adjusted in a completely analogous way. The formula is

$$\bar{\rho}^2 \equiv 1 - \frac{p}{\mathrm{df}}\left(1 - \rho^2\right) = 1 - \frac{p}{p-m}\left(1 - \rho^2\right).$$

The adjustments to be made to the various fit indexes are now obvious.

Other penalties for the introduction of additional parameters can be imposed as well. The *Tucker-Lewis index* (TLI), after Tucker and Lewis (1973), also contains a penalty for additional parameters, but in a different way than statistics based on $\bar{\rho}^2$. Its formula is

$$\mathrm{TLI} \equiv \frac{\dfrac{\chi^2_{\mathrm{null}}}{\mathrm{df}_{\mathrm{null}}} - \dfrac{\chi^2_{\mathrm{t}}}{\mathrm{df}_{\mathrm{t}}}}{\dfrac{\chi^2_{\mathrm{null}}}{\mathrm{df}_{\mathrm{null}}} - 1}.$$

This index compares the ratio of the chi-square statistic and its degrees of freedom of the target model to that of the null model. The idea behind using this ratio is that its mean should not depend on the number of degrees of freedom, so this fit measure should be equally applicable to large and small models.

If the target model is true (and the null model is not), the denominator is the expectation of the numerator. Because the target model is not necessarily hypothesized to be true, and the null model is generally far from true, so that $\chi^2_{\mathrm{null}} \gg \mathrm{df}_{\mathrm{null}}$, the TLI is generally between 0 and 1, 0 indicating bad fit and 1 indicating excellent fit. If the target model fits very well, with $\chi^2_t < \mathrm{df}_{\mathrm{t}}$, its value can be greater than 1, and if the target model fits very badly, with $\chi^2_{\mathrm{t}}/\mathrm{df}_{\mathrm{t}} > \chi^2_{\mathrm{null}}/\mathrm{df}_{\mathrm{null}}$, its value can be less than 0. Hence, this fit index is not normed and is therefore also called the *nonnormed fit index*. To overcome this apparent problem, we may use the *normed Tucker-Lewis index* (NTLI), defined as

1. If TLI < 0 or $\chi^2_{\mathrm{null}} \leq \mathrm{df}_{\mathrm{null}}$ then NTLI $\equiv 0$, but

2. If TLI > 1 or $\chi^2_{\mathrm{t}} \leq \mathrm{df}_{\mathrm{t}}$ (including $\mathrm{df}_{\mathrm{t}} = 0$, and both $\chi^2_{\mathrm{null}} \leq \mathrm{df}_{\mathrm{null}}$ and $\chi^2_{\mathrm{t}} \leq \mathrm{df}_{\mathrm{t}}$) then NTLI $\equiv 1$;

3. otherwise NTLI $\equiv$ TLI.

The idea of looking at the chi-square divided by its degrees of freedom also underlies the *root mean square error of approximation* (RMSEA). This is defined in the population as

$$\varepsilon_a \equiv \sqrt{\frac{q_0}{\mathrm{df}}}$$

and can be used as a standalone population measure of fit. It measures the lack of fit per degree of freedom and thus incorporates a penalty for overparameterizing. From the above discussion, it follows that an unbiased estimator of q_0 is $\hat{q}_0 \equiv \hat{q} - \mathrm{df}/N$. Because q_0 is always nonnegative and the argument of a square root must be nonnegative, an obvious estimator of the RMSEA is

$$\hat{\varepsilon}_a \equiv \sqrt{\max\left\{\left(\frac{\hat{q}_0}{\mathrm{df}} - \frac{1}{N}\right), 0\right\}},$$

which always exists and is always nonnegative.

A well-known class of criteria that incorporate a penalty for additional parameters is the class of information criteria. Information criteria were especially devised for model selection. The best-known information criterion is *Akaike's information criterion* (AIC), which has its origins in time series modeling. If the models under consideration are autoregressive models of different orders and if time series data up to time point N are available, then the model with the smallest AIC value is the model that has the smallest mean square prediction error of the (as yet unknown) data point at time point $N + 1$. A generalization to the field of structural equation modeling can be obtained by considering the prediction of the expectation of the so-called Kullback-Leibler information of an additional data point. We will not derive these complicated statistical results, but only give the formula of the AIC, which is

$$\mathrm{AIC} \equiv \chi^2 - 2\mathrm{df} = \chi^2 + 2m - 2p. \tag{10.25}$$

Although the AIC was originally only defined for maximum likelihood estimators, the formula (10.25) is currently also applied to other estimators, such as GMM estimators. The AIC is also sometimes defined without the constant term $-2p$ or divided by the sample size. These operations do not affect the comparison of different models using the same data and the same moment conditions, which is the primary aim of the AIC.

If it is assumed that there is a true model among the models that are considered, a desirable property of a model selection rule is that asymptotically, it selects the true model and in finite samples, it has a high probability of selecting the true model. It turns out that this is not generally the case with the AIC. AIC is more appropriate if it is not assumed that there exists a true model, but one is only trying to find a suitable model in some sense. If it is assumed that there is a true model, an alternative to the AIC, the *Consistent AIC* (CAIC) can be used. Its formula is

$$\mathrm{CAIC} \equiv \chi^2 + (1 + \log N)m.$$

Model selection on the basis of this criterion will asymptotically lead to the true model, if it is in the set of models under consideration.

Guidelines

Having defined a large number of statistics that measure model fit to a certain extent, the question remains how these statistics should be used in practice to select the best model. This question can not be answered unambiguously, but a few guidelines can be given.

First, a model should always be theoretically plausible. If parameters have the wrong sign or if theoretically essential parameters are omitted, this is an indication of misspecification. Such a model is useless in practice.

Second, once a model has been estimated, it can be tested whether certain free parameters are significantly different from zero or any other theoretically relevant value by means of t-values (or, more generally, Wald test statistics). It can also be tested whether certain fixed parameters should be relaxed by means of LM tests. However, the previous point should always be kept in mind, and one should relate the significance of the test to the sample size to avoid overfitting in large samples and underfitting in small samples.

Third, the fit of models should be assessed by checking several fit measures. No single fit measure is the best. It is generally recommended to use at least the chi-square statistic and the RNI (or CFI). Rules of thumb for interpreting the values of these statistics are that χ^2 values less than 2df indicate good fit with moderately large sample sizes (a few hundred) and values of the RNI of .90 or larger are indicative of good fit. There are, however, situations in which these rules of thumb are not satisfactory (notably when factors and errors are dependent but uncorrelated, as in the case of heteroskedasticity). A parsimony fit index or information criterion can be used in addition to the mentioned statistics, but simply selecting the model with the best value of this statistic is too rigid and not recommended.

Finally, in all situations, the expert eye of the researcher is important. Fit indexes are helpful in determining the best model, but theoretical plausibility and degrees of freedom (parsimony) are also important. Usually, a number of plausible target models remain and the researcher finally has to decide, based on fit indexes, significance tests, numbers of free parameters, and estimated values of these parameters, which model will be chosen.

10.6 Bibliographical notes

10.1 The three basic tests were reviewed in a maximum likelihood context by Engle (1984), in a covariance structures context by Satorra (1989), and in a general GMM context by Newey and McFadden (1994, section 9). The latter defined several alternative, but asymptotically equivalent, forms of the Wald and LM tests as well. Newey (1985) gave a very general framework for developing tests from GMM estimators, which includes the tests given here, Hausman tests (cf. Hausman, 1978), and the test of overidentifying restrictions of section 10.3. Another general framework was provided by Gouriéroux and Monfort (1989). Bollen and Long (1993) is a book-length discussion about tests and model fit in the context of structural equation models.

The three classical tests have all been introduced first in a maximum likelihood context. The likelihood ratio test was introduced by Neyman and Pearson (1928, 1933) and its asymptotic distribution was derived by Wilks (1938). The score test was introduced by Rao (1948) and the numerically equivalent Lagrange multiplier test was introduced by Aitchison and Silvey (1958) and Silvey (1959). The Wald test was introduced by Wald (1943) in the context of maximum likelihood estimation and generalized to arbitrary asymptotically normal estimators by Stroud (1971).

Shapiro (1987, proposition 4.1) showed that the condition (10.10) is equivalent to the expression

$$\Psi = W_0^{-1} + G_0 Z_0' C_1' + C_1 Z_0 G_0' + W_0^{-1} H_0 C_2' + C_2 H_0' W_0^{-1},$$

where C_1 and C_2 are arbitrary matrices of appropriate orders, and Z_0 is an $(m - \nu) \times m$ matrix such that (R_0', Z_0') is a square nonsingular matrix and $Z_0 R_0' = 0$.

Tests of inequality restrictions have been discussed by Shapiro (1985a), Gouriéroux, Holly, and Monfort (1982), and Wolak (1989a, 1989b). Dijkstra (1992) considered the related problem of statistical inference on the boundary of the parameter space. Inference in nonidentified cases was discussed by Shapiro (1986). Tests of nonnested hypotheses have been discussed by Gouriéroux and Monfort (1994) and, specifically in the context of GMM, by Smith (1992). Testing a linear regression specification versus a logarithmic specification was discussed by Aneuryn-Evans and Deaton (1980).

10.2 The inferior small-sample properties of the Wald test and its lack of invariance to reparameterization have been discussed by, among others, Gregory and Veall (1985), Breusch and Schmidt (1988), and Phillips and Park (1988). Dagenais and Dufour (1991) discussed the invariance properties of the various test statistics at length.

The link between hypothesis tests and confidence intervals was examined by Ferguson (1967, section 5.8). Hypothesis tests and confidence sets can also be based on the bootstrap, see, e.g., Hall (1992), Efron and Tibshirani (1993), and Davison and Hinkley (1997).

10.3 The test of overidentifying restrictions was given in a GMM framework by Hansen (1982). The chi-square statistic is, however, much older. The term chi-square or chi-square statistic (or, χ^2 or χ^2 statistic, rather) was already used in a minimum distance context by Ferguson (1958), who noted that it is a generalization of the well-known Pearson χ^2 that is commonly used in the analysis of contingency tables.

As mentioned above, the relationship between χ_1^2 and χ_2^2 is due to Yuan and Bentler (1997b). Because χ_2^2 tends to overreject in moderate samples, they advocated the use of χ_1^2, which is more conservative. Yuan and Bentler (1999) developed a scaled version of the chi-square statistic χ_2^2 that is a generalization of the F-test in linear regression. Its formula is

$$\frac{N-(p-m)}{(p-m)}\hat{q}_2,$$

and it should be compared to the quantiles of an F-distribution with $p-m$ and $N-(p-m)$ degrees of freedom. This test is also better in small and moderate samples than the chi-square test based on χ_2^2.

The residual-based ADF test statistic is due to Browne (1984). The correction based on $\hat{\Psi}_1$ was proposed by Yuan and Bentler (1998a) and may hence be called the Yuan-Bentler residual-based test statistic. They also proposed an F-variant, which may be called the residual-based F-statistic,

$$T_{\mathrm{F}} \equiv \frac{N-(p-m)}{(p-m)} T_{\mathrm{B}}/N,$$

which is analogous to the F-statistic discussed above and should also be compared to the quantiles of an F-distribution with $p-m$ and $N-(p-m)$ degrees of freedom.

The Satorra-Bentler scaled test statistic is due to Satorra and Bentler (1988, 1994). It is routinely computed in EQS (Bentler, 1995). Yuan and Bentler (1997a) developed a nontrivial class of distributions for which the Satorra-Bentler scaled chi-square is asymptotically chi-squared distributed. Satorra and Bentler also developed another scaled chi-square, called the *Satorra-Bentler adjusted test statistic*, which has the same mean *and* variance as a chi-square variate in the general case, possibly with noninteger degrees of freedom, but this has apparently not been used in practice. See also the bibliographical notes to section B.1.

Yuan and Bentler (1998a) and Bentler and Yuan (1999) studied the properties of the various test statistics in moderate and small samples by means of simulation. They advocated using ML to obtain the estimators and using the residual-based F-statistic for samples up to $N = 200$ and the Yuan-Bentler residual-based test statistic for samples above 200, although the residual-based F-statistic performed relatively well for these sample sizes as well.

Bollen and Stine (1992) proposed using the bootstrap to estimate the null distribution of the chi-square statistic in small samples, using a technique also proposed by Beran and Srivastava (1985). This bootstrap method is implemented in the software package AMOS (Arbuckle, 1997).

10.4 The study of robustness of estimators and test statistics for structural equation models was started by the extensive simulations of Boomsma (1983). Following that, a large number of other simulation studies have been published, in which the effects were studied of distributional misspecifications, small sample size, and occasionally model misspecifications, on convergence, improper solutions, properties of various estimators, standard errors, test statistics, and fit indexes, and on model selection (e.g., Cudeck and Browne, 1983; Anderson and Gerbing, 1984; Gerbing and Anderson, 1985; Muthén and Kaplan, 1985, 1992; Marsh, Balla, and McDonald, 1988; Hu, Bentler, and Kano, 1992; Hu and Bentler, 1995; Meijer, 1998). An overview of much of the (empirical) robustness literature is given by Hoogland and Boomsma (1998). Hu and Bentler (1995) demonstrated that ML with robust standard errors is generally preferable to ADF in small or moderate samples. Meijer and Mooijaart (1996) demonstrated that ML is not robust to heteroskedasticity.

Asymptotically correct standard errors can be obtained in EQS by using the ROBUST option, whereas in AMOS, asymptotically correct standard errors can be obtained by using a nonparametric bootstrap option. LISREL apparently does not provide any robustness options.

The theoretical robustness results presented here have been described by, among others, Shapiro (1986, 1987), Browne (1987), Anderson and Amemiya (1988), Amemiya and Anderson (1990), Mooijaart and Bentler (1991), and Satorra and Bentler (1990).

The CFA example discussed in the text, in which estimators are asymptotically efficient and the chi-square test is asymptotically chi-squared distributed, has been described by many of the authors mentioned above. It is a special case of a large class of structural equation models for which this robustness result holds, and which was described by Browne and Shapiro (1988) and Satorra and Bentler (1990). This class can be characterized as follows. First, let x be a generic l-variate random variable with mean μ_x and covariance matrix Σ_x. Let

$$\Psi_x \equiv \mathrm{E}\big(\mathrm{vec}(x-\mu_x)(x-\mu_x)'\big)\big(\mathrm{vec}(x-\mu_x)(x-\mu_x)'\big)' - (\mathrm{vec}\,\Sigma_x)(\mathrm{vec}\,\Sigma_x)'$$

be the asymptotic covariance matrix of the sample covariance matrix of x, and let

$$K_x \equiv \Psi_x - 2Q_l(\Sigma_x \otimes \Sigma_x)$$

be the matrix of fourth-order cumulants of x, where Q_l is the symmetrization matrix defined in section A.4. The matrix K_x is zero if, but not only if, x is normally distributed. Second, given these definitions, let y be the generic vector of observed variables, and assume that y can be written as

$$y = \mu_y + \sum_{i=1}^{I} \Lambda_i \xi_i,$$

where ξ_i, $i = 1, \ldots, I$ is a set of mutually independent random vectors, which may or may not be latent, with mean zero and covariance matrices Σ_{ξ_i}. The means μ_y are unrestricted and estimated by $\hat{\mu}_y \equiv \bar{y}$. The (other) parameters in the model are collected in the vector θ, and Λ_i and Σ_{ξ_i}, $i = 1, \ldots, I$, are functions of θ. If, for all $i = 1, \ldots, I$, either (i) $K_{\xi_i} = 0$, or (ii) the elements of Σ_{ξ_i} are completely free (except for the requirements of symmetry and positive definiteness) and none of the elements of the other matrices Λ_j and Σ_{ξ_j}, $j = 1, \ldots, I$, and Λ_i, is a function of one or more elements of Σ_{ξ_i}, then the GMM estimator based on the normality assumption is asymptotically efficient and the chi-square statistic is asymptotically chi-squared distributed. Note that for the GMM estimator based on the normality assumption (usually called normal-theory GLS estimator), the ML estimator may be substituted.

Given this result, an immediate extension of the CFA example is the full LISREL model, with $\xi_1 \equiv \xi$, $\xi_2 \equiv \zeta$, and the other ξ_j's all consist of a single measurement error δ_i or ε_i. If Φ is free and none of the other parameter matrices depends functionally on Φ, Ψ is free and none of the other parameter matrices depends functionally on Ψ, the variances of the elements of δ and ε are all free and none of the other parameter matrices depends functionally on these variances, and all random variates ξ_j thus defined are independent, then the normality based estimators are asymptotically efficient and their corresponding chi-square statistics are asymptotically chi-squared distributed.

Note that a large subfield of statistics is devoted to so-called *robust statistics*, which means something different than robustness as discussed in this chapter.

Robust statistics studies estimators that are more robust to outliers, in the sense that the influence of single observations on the estimator is limited, see, e.g., Hampel, Ronchetti, Rousseeuw, and Stahel (1986). Lehmann (1983, chapter 5) gave an overview of some robust location estimators, namely median, trimmed mean, L-, M-, and R-estimators. He showed that these may have good asymptotic and finite-sample properties. Under some conditions, these estimators are asymptotically normally distributed and they may be more efficient than the mean. Because the moment vector is also a sample average, these robust estimators may also be used in GMM estimation. Yuan and Bentler (1998b), for example, developed robust estimation procedures for structural equation models based on M-estimators and S-estimators of the sample moments.

10.5 This section relies heavily on the conception that models are not true. This view was put forward forcefully by Bentler and Bonett (1980), De Leeuw (1988), and Browne and Cudeck (1992).

Modification indexes are due to Sörbom (1989). A general discussion about specification search was given by Leamer (1978), and for structural equation models by MacCallum (1986).

The NFI was introduced by Bentler and Bonett (1980), and the GFI was proposed by Jöreskog and Sörbom (1981) for normality based estimators, and extended to general estimators by Bentler (1983b) and Tanaka and Huba (1985).

The NFI has the same form as the pseudo-R^2 for logit models proposed by McFadden (1974) and the R^2_{KL} based on the Kullback-Leibler divergence proposed by Cameron and Windmeijer (1997). In fact, for structural equation models estimated with ML, the NFI is identical to R^2_{KL}. However, for other types of models estimated with ML, for which no fixed-dimensional sufficient statistics exist, such as the logit model, the properties of R^2_{KL} and McFadden's pseudo-R^2 may not be comparable to those of the NFI, because the loglikelihood or the Kullback-Leibler divergence in the denominator of these statistics, even under the null hypothesis, do not generally converge to a (noncentral) chi-squared distributed variate with a finite number of degrees of freedom.

The theory based on local alternatives was introduced into the field of structural equation modeling by Shapiro (1983). The RNI was proposed by McDonald and Marsh (1990) and Bentler (1990). Bentler (1990) also defined the CFI, although Meijer (1998, p. 42) showed that its definition is not unambiguous, because it may result in the expression $0/0$.

The relation between parsimony and precision of estimators was studied by Bentler and Mooijaart (1989). The adjusted versions of the fit indexes were proposed by Jöreskog and Sörbom (1981) for the GFI, which leads to the adjusted goodness of fit index (AGFI), and for general fit indexes by Bentler (1983b). The TLI was introduced as a guideline for choosing the number of factors in exploratory factor analysis models by Tucker and Lewis (1973) and extended to general structural equation models by Bentler and Bonett (1980), who called it the nonnormed fit index (NNFI). Bentler (1990) showed that the RNI is linearly related to the TLI in the following way:

$$\mathrm{RNI} = \left(1 - \frac{\mathrm{df_t}}{\mathrm{df_{null}}}\right) + \frac{\mathrm{df_t}}{\mathrm{df_{null}}}\mathrm{TLI}.$$

The normed TLI is due to Marsh, Balla, and Hau (1996).

The RMSEA was defined by Steiger (1990) and extensively studied by Browne and Cudeck (1992), who advocated constructing a confidence interval for ε_a based on the quantiles of the approximating noncentral chi-square distribution of $N\hat{q}$. Based on this, they introduced a corresponding test of close fit, or $\varepsilon_a \leq \varepsilon$, with a typical value of 0.05 for ε, denoting the "upper limit of a close fitting model".

The AIC was introduced into the field of structural equation modeling by Akaike (1987). Bozdogan (1987) proposed the CAIC and derived several properties of the AIC and CAIC. Van Casteren (1994) studied a general class of information measures in a broader context.

As mentioned in the text, the means of the NFI and GFI are increasing functions of sample size. From the simulation study of Marsh et al. (1988), it is known that the mean of the TLI is largely unaffected by sample size. Because the RNI is a linear transformation of the TLI, this must also hold for the RNI. Moreover, because $0 < \mathrm{df_t}/\mathrm{df_{null}} < 1$, the variance of the RNI is smaller than that of the TLI, and it is therefore a more accurate measure of fit (Bentler, 1990). A small simulation study by Hu and Bentler (1995) confirmed the expected good behavior of the RNI and CFI, although if factors and errors are dependent (e.g., with heteroskedastic errors), these fit indexes did not behave well for sample sizes of 500 or less. It appears difficult to find a satisfactory fit measure for such smaller samples.

A large number of other descriptive fit measures have been proposed in the literature. They will not be discussed here, as they are now generally regarded inappropriate and they are not frequently used in practice. Furthermore, a number of other information criteria have been proposed, but will not be discussed here. An overview of the information criteria discussed here and other information criteria is given by Bozdogan (1987) and Van Casteren (1994, pp. 45–49).

Chapter 11

Nonlinear latent variable models

The models discussed so far have all been linear. The problem of measurement error is, however, obviously not restricted to linear models. Furthermore, there is no compelling reason why latent variable models should be exclusively linear. Therefore, in this chapter, we will study the implications of measurement error in nonlinear models, and discuss several types of structural equation models that incorporate nonlinear relations.

In principle, it is possible to study all aspects of the measurement error problem as discussed in the previous chapters for every proposed nonlinear model. Thus, bias and inconsistency of OLS estimators may be studied, bounds may be derived for the true coefficients given inconsistent estimators and other observable information, CALS estimators and instrumental variables estimators may be developed (although the latter is nontrivial in nonlinear models), and nonlinear structural equation models may be developed. Indeed, the literature contains many such studies.

In this chapter, the discussion will be rather eclectic. We study some basic nonlinear measurement error models, and for the rest concentrate on latent variables models where indicators are available. To set the stage, we consider in section 11.1 a nonlinear version of the simplest linear measurement error model, and in section 11.2 we move to polynomial models. We concentrate on quadratic models, because they are suitable to convey the essence. Section 11.3 deals with a major class of nonlinear econometric models, that is, the class of limited-dependent variables models including binary choice models. These models are essentially linear but the dependent variable is only observable through a nonlinear filter.

This scope is widened in section 11.4, where we discuss the LISCOMP model. This model generalizes the linear structural equation model, discussed in chapter 8, to the situation where the dependent variables are filtered. The underlying structural relations are still linear. The situation is reversed in section 11.5, where we consider the case where the dependent variable is observed but the structural relationship itself is nonlinear.

11.1 A simple nonlinear model

The simple linear regression model under normality is not identified, as was discussed in section 4.5. Here, we consider a simple nonlinear version of the linear normal model. The aim is to show that standard estimation still gives an inconsistent result but the nonlinearity allows the construction of a consistent estimator. The model is

$$\begin{aligned} y_n &= \alpha + \beta e^{\xi_n} + \varepsilon_n \\ x_n &= \xi_n + v_n, \end{aligned}$$

for $n = 1, \ldots, N$, with the y_n and x_n observed. We make simple assumptions on distribution and independence:

$$\begin{bmatrix} \varepsilon_n \\ x_n \\ \xi_n \\ v_n \end{bmatrix} \sim \mathcal{N}_4 \left(0, \begin{bmatrix} \sigma_\varepsilon^2 & 0 & 0 & 0 \\ 0 & \sigma_x^2 & \sigma_\xi^2 & \sigma_v^2 \\ 0 & \sigma_\xi^2 & \sigma_\xi^2 & 0 \\ 0 & \sigma_v^2 & 0 & \sigma_v^2 \end{bmatrix} \right).$$

The model can be considered linear with a lognormally distributed regressor but with a multiplicative measurement error. Let $f \equiv \mathrm{E}(e^{x_n})$ and $\phi \equiv \mathrm{E}(e^{\xi_n})$, then the moment generating function of the normal distribution has $\mathrm{E}(e^{t x_n}) = f^{t^2}$ and $\mathrm{E}(e^{t \xi_n}) = \phi^{t^2}$. Furthermore, $\mathrm{E}(e^{v_n}) = f/\phi$ and $\mathrm{E}(e^{x_n + \xi_n}) = f\phi^3$.

We now consider OLS of y on e^x. This gives in the limit

$$\begin{aligned} \operatorname*{plim}_{N \to \infty} \begin{bmatrix} \hat{\alpha} \\ \hat{\beta} \end{bmatrix} &= \left(\mathrm{E} \begin{bmatrix} 1 \\ e^{x_n} \end{bmatrix} (1, e^{x_n}) \right)^{-1} \mathrm{E} \begin{bmatrix} 1 \\ e^{x_n} \end{bmatrix} y_n \\ &= \begin{bmatrix} 1 & f \\ f & f^4 \end{bmatrix}^{-1} \begin{bmatrix} \alpha + \beta\phi \\ \alpha f + \beta f \phi^3 \end{bmatrix} \\ &= \begin{bmatrix} \alpha + \beta\phi \dfrac{f^2 - \phi^2}{f^2 - 1} \\ \beta \dfrac{\phi}{f} \dfrac{\phi^2 - 1}{f^2 - 1} \end{bmatrix}. \end{aligned}$$

Thus, assuming $\beta > 0$, we see that the intercept is estimated with an upward bias and the regression coefficient with a downward bias when there is measurement error, i.e., $f > \phi > 1$.

In this context the nonlinearity allows us to derive consistent estimators for the model parameters. We can base such estimators on

$$m_t \equiv \frac{\mathrm{E}(e^{tx_n} y_n)}{\mathrm{E}(e^{tx_n})} = \alpha + \beta \exp\left(\frac{2t+1}{2}\sigma_\xi^2\right).$$

Hence, m_0, m_1, and m_2 can be expressed in the three parameters α, β, and ϕ. These equations can be solved to yield

$$\alpha = \frac{m_0 m_2 - m_1^2}{m_0 - 2m_1 + m_2}$$
$$\beta = \frac{(m_1 - m_0)^{5/2}}{(m_0 - 2m_1 + m_2)(m_2 - m_1)}$$
$$\sigma_\xi^2 = \log\left(\frac{m_2 - m_1}{m_1 - m_0}\right).$$

Replacing the expectations of functions of observables by their sample counterparts gives estimators that are, by construction, consistent.

Broadly speaking, this example illustrates the scope offered for identification and consistent estimation when the model is nonlinear rather than linear. Identification problems are more likely to arise in a linear model. As we have seen in section 4.5, the structural model is not identified under normality. Normal distributions have linear conditional expectations. In this sense normality, linearity, and nonidentification are interrelated, suggesting an analogous interrelation between nonnormality, nonlinearity, and identification.

11.2 Polynomial models

Arguably the most natural step from linear models to nonlinear models is through *polynomial models*. In polynomial regression models, the expectation of the dependent variable conditional on the explanatory variables is a polynomial function of the explanatory variables. Polynomial regression models are easy to understand, easy to estimate, and they approximate many moderately nonlinear regression models well, especially if the explanatory variables are bounded. The latter follows from a local Taylor series expansion. We consider a simple, quadratic regression model first, then a factor analysis model where the factor enters in a quadratic rather than a linear fashion, and conclude the section with a two-factor model that includes interaction between the two factors. The extensions to higher degree polynomials are straightforward.

Quadratic regression

We first investigate the behavior of OLS in a model that is quadratic in the mismeasured variable. To concentrate on the essence, we assume a structural model under the assumption of normality and do not consider the possible presence of other regressors. Then, the model is

$$\begin{aligned} y_n &= \alpha + \beta\xi_n + \gamma\xi_n^2 + \varepsilon_n \\ x_n &= \xi_n + v_n, \end{aligned}$$

for $n = 1, \ldots, N$. The y_n and x_n are observed; ε_n, ξ_n, and v_n are assumed mutually independent and normally distributed. Without loss of generality, all variables are assumed to have mean zero. This implies $\alpha = -\gamma\sigma_\xi^2$, which allows the model to be rewritten as

$$y_n = \beta\xi_n + \gamma(\xi_n^2 - \sigma_\xi^2) + \varepsilon_n.$$

Then

$$\begin{aligned} \left(\mathrm{E} \begin{bmatrix} 1 \\ x_n \\ x_n^2 \end{bmatrix} (1, x_n, x_n^2) \right)^{-1} &= \begin{bmatrix} 1 & 0 & \sigma_x^2 \\ 0 & \sigma_x^2 & 0 \\ \sigma_x^2 & 0 & 3\sigma_x^4 \end{bmatrix}^{-1} \\ &= \frac{1}{2} \begin{bmatrix} 3 & 0 & -\sigma_x^{-2} \\ 0 & 2\sigma_x^{-2} & 0 \\ -\sigma_x^{-2} & 0 & \sigma_x^{-4} \end{bmatrix}; \\ \mathrm{E} \begin{bmatrix} 1 \\ x_n \\ x_n^2 \end{bmatrix} y_n &= \begin{bmatrix} 0 \\ \beta\sigma_\xi^2 \\ 2\gamma\sigma_\xi^4 \end{bmatrix}. \end{aligned}$$

Let the reliability of x be given by $\lambda \equiv \sigma_\xi^2/\sigma_x^2$. Then, OLS of regressing y on a constant, x, and x^2 yields an estimator with property

$$\operatorname*{plim}_{N\to\infty} \begin{bmatrix} \hat{\alpha} \\ \hat{\beta} \\ \hat{\gamma} \end{bmatrix} = \left(\mathrm{E} \begin{bmatrix} 1 \\ x_n \\ x_n^2 \end{bmatrix} (1, x_n, x_n^2) \right)^{-1} \mathrm{E} \begin{bmatrix} 1 \\ x_n \\ x_n^2 \end{bmatrix} y_n = \begin{bmatrix} \alpha\lambda \\ \beta\lambda \\ \gamma\lambda^2 \end{bmatrix}. \tag{11.1}$$

Not surprisingly, OLS is inconsistent. The bias in the estimator of the coefficient of the linear term, β, is the same as the bias in the linear case. The bias in the estimator of the coefficient of the quadratic term, γ, is relatively more severe, because $0 < \lambda \leq 1$ implies that $\lambda^2 \leq \lambda$. Thus, if for example $\lambda = 0.8$, β is underestimated by 20% and γ by 36%.

Unlike the linear case, the model is identified because there exists a consistent estimator of the parameters when $\gamma \neq 0$. This estimator can be based on the following moments:

$$\mathrm{E}(x_n y_n^2) = 4\beta\gamma\sigma_\xi^4$$
$$\mathrm{E}(x_n^2 y_n) = 2\gamma\sigma_\xi^4.$$

Consequently, a consistent estimator of β is

$$\tilde{\beta} \equiv \tfrac{1}{2} \sum_{n=1}^{N} x_n y_n^2 \Big/ \sum_{n=1}^{N} x_n^2 y_n,$$

and, combining this with (11.1), consistent estimators for the other parameters follow directly. Just as in section 11.1, we have an extension of the linear, unidentified normal model to a nonlinear model that is identified. This finding again underpins the idea that nonlinearity is generally beneficial from an identification point of view.

It is interesting to note that, even though ξ_n is normally distributed, y_n is not normally distributed because of its nonlinear relation with ξ_n. This is utilized to obtain consistent estimators. Thus, contrary to the linear case, where normality of ξ_n inhibits consistent estimation of the parameters, in the quadratic model normality of ξ_n facilitates identification, although it can be shown that the model is also identified if ξ_n is not normally distributed.

Generalization of these findings to higher degree polynomials and vector-valued ξ_n, x_n, and y_n is straightforward. If appropriate independence assumptions can be made, the model can be estimated by fitting appropriately chosen (higher order) moments or cumulants.

Quadratic factor analysis

Both the simple quadratic regression model with measurement errors and the one-factor factor analysis model generalize to the quadratic factor analysis (QFA) model with a single factor that enters quadratically. The extension to more factors is straightforward but for expository reasons we restrict ourselves to the one-factor case here. The model is

$$y_{in} = \beta_{i0} + \beta_{i1}\xi_n + \beta_{i2}\xi_n^2 + \varepsilon_{in},$$

where $i = 1, \ldots, M$ indexes indicators and $n = 1, \ldots, N$ indexes observations. It is assumed that $\xi_n \sim \mathcal{N}(0, 1)$; analogous to the linear factor analysis model we may freely set the variance of ξ_n at one. If the means of the y_n are zero, $\beta_{i0} = -\beta_{i2}\,\mathrm{E}(\xi_n^2) = -\beta_{i2}$. Let $\zeta_n \equiv (\xi_n, \xi_n^2 - 1)'$, so $\mathrm{E}(\zeta_n) = 0$.

In self-evident notation the model can now be written as $y_n = B\zeta_n + \varepsilon_n$, which is the structure of the standard linear exploratory factor analysis (EFA) model. So we can estimate the QFA along the lines of section 7.3. It should be kept in mind, though, that

$$\Phi_2 \equiv \mathrm{E}(\zeta_n \zeta_n') = \begin{bmatrix} 1 & 0 \\ 0 & 2 \end{bmatrix},$$

whereas EFA takes this matrix to be the unit matrix of order two. So the second column of the estimate of B as delivered by EFA should be divided by $\sqrt{2}$.

However, this is just part of the story. It suggests that the estimate of B is open to the usual rotational freedom inherent in EFA. This is not the case. The QFA model is in fact identified, as we will presently show.

The identification follows from the nonnormality of the ξ_n^2. As a result, the third-order moments are also informative, unlike the normal case, where only the second-order moments are relevant. Consider

$$\Sigma_3 \equiv \mathrm{E}\big((y_n \otimes y_n)y_n'\big) = (B \otimes B)\Phi_3 B' + \Omega_3, \tag{11.2}$$

where $\Omega_3 \equiv \mathrm{E}\left(\varepsilon_n \otimes \varepsilon_n)\varepsilon_n'\right)$ and

$$\Phi_3 \equiv \mathrm{E}\left((\zeta_n \otimes \zeta_n)\zeta_n'\right) = \begin{bmatrix} 0 & 2 \\ 2 & 0 \\ 2 & 0 \\ 0 & 8 \end{bmatrix}.$$

Now, consider the model $\Sigma_2 \equiv \mathrm{E}(y_n y_n') = \Lambda\Lambda' + \Omega_2$, where $\Omega_2 \equiv \mathrm{E}(\varepsilon_n \varepsilon_n')$ is a diagonal matrix. Furthermore, let $\tilde{\Lambda}$ be a solution to this model. Then, every Λ that satisfies this model must satisfy $\Lambda = \tilde{\Lambda}T$, for some orthonormal matrix T. On letting $H \equiv \Phi_2^{-1/2}$, the resulting restriction on B is $B = \Lambda H = \tilde{\Lambda}TH$. Note that $\tilde{\Lambda}$ is given and only T is yet unknown. Equation (11.2) can now be rewritten as follows:

$$\Sigma_3 - \Omega_3 = (\tilde{\Lambda}TH \otimes \tilde{\Lambda}TH)\Phi_3 HT'\tilde{\Lambda}'.$$

Let $\tilde{T}$ be a choice of T that satisfies this equation. If $\tilde{T}$ is the *only* choice of T that satisfies this equation, T is identified and hence the model is identified. Thus, the model is identified if the only choice of T that satisfies the equation

$$(\tilde{\Lambda}\tilde{T}H \otimes \tilde{\Lambda}\tilde{T}H)\Phi_3 H\tilde{T}'\tilde{\Lambda}' = (\tilde{\Lambda}TH \otimes \tilde{\Lambda}TH)\Phi_3 HT'\tilde{\Lambda}'$$

is $T = \tilde{T}$. Assume that $\tilde{\Lambda}$ is of full column rank, which will nearly always be the case. Then we can premultiply the left- and right-hand sides of this equation with $(\tilde{T}' \otimes \tilde{T}')(\tilde{\Lambda}^+ \otimes \tilde{\Lambda}^+)$ and postmultiply the left- and right-hand sides of this equation with $(\tilde{\Lambda}')^+\tilde{T}$, where $\tilde{\Lambda}^+ = (\tilde{\Lambda}'\tilde{\Lambda})^{-1}\tilde{\Lambda}'$. This gives

$$(H \otimes H)\Phi_3 H = (U \otimes U)(H \otimes H)\Phi_3 H U',$$

where $U \equiv \tilde{T}'T$ is an orthonormal matrix. The model is identified if the only choice of U that satisfies the equation is the identity matrix. On substitution of the formulas for Φ_2 and Φ_3, postmultiplication by U, and dividing by $\sqrt{2}$, this equation for U becomes

$$\begin{bmatrix} 0 & 1 \\ 1 & 0 \\ 1 & 0 \\ 0 & 2 \end{bmatrix} U = (U \otimes U) \begin{bmatrix} 0 & 1 \\ 1 & 0 \\ 1 & 0 \\ 0 & 2 \end{bmatrix}. \tag{11.3}$$

Any 2×2 orthonormal matrix U can be written as

$$U_1 = \begin{bmatrix} c & -s \\ s & c \end{bmatrix} \quad \text{or} \quad U_2 = \begin{bmatrix} c & s \\ s & -c \end{bmatrix},$$

where $-1 \leq c \leq 1$, $-1 \leq s \leq 1$, and $s^2 + c^2 = 1$. The form U_1 represents a rotation, where c and s are the cosine and sine, respectively, of the rotation angle, and the form U_2 represents a rotation followed by a reflection. Combining this with (11.3) gives only two possible solutions for U, with $U_1 = I_2$, and

$$U_2 = \begin{bmatrix} -1 & 0 \\ 0 & 1 \end{bmatrix}.$$

These two choices of U lead to the following solutions of the model:

$$y_{in} = \beta_{i1}\xi_n + \beta_{i2}(\xi_n^2 - 1) + \varepsilon_{in},$$

or

$$y_{in} = \beta_{i1}(-\xi_n) + \beta_{i2}((-\xi_n)^2 - 1) + \varepsilon_{in}.$$

The second solution is equivalent to the first, except that the sign of the factor is reversed, which does not alter the substantive interpretation of the results and therefore we consider the model identified. Along the same lines, it can be shown that higher degree polynomial factor analysis models with a normally distributed are identified.

Interaction between factors

Another kind of polynomial model arises when we have a regression model with two latent explanatory variables that interact. That is, the product of the two latent variables enters into the relationship, too:

$$y_n = \alpha + \gamma_1 \xi_{1n} + \gamma_2 \xi_{2n} + \gamma_3 \xi_{1n} \xi_{2n} + \varepsilon_n, \tag{11.4}$$

where $n = 1, \ldots, N$ indexes observations. We assume the presence of indicators for the latent variables, of the usual factor analytic structure with normalizations imposed for the sake of identification:

$$\begin{bmatrix} x_{1n} \\ x_{2n} \\ x_{3n} \\ x_{4n} \end{bmatrix} = \begin{bmatrix} 1 & 0 \\ \lambda_2 & 0 \\ 0 & 1 \\ 0 & \lambda_4 \end{bmatrix} \begin{bmatrix} \xi_{1n} \\ \xi_{2n} \end{bmatrix} + \begin{bmatrix} \delta_{1n} \\ \delta_{2n} \\ \delta_{3n} \\ \delta_{4n} \end{bmatrix}$$

or $x_n = \Lambda \xi_n + \delta_n$ for short. This defines the so-called Kenny-Judd model, after Kenny and Judd (1984). The presence of the nonlinear interaction term distinguishes this model from a standard linear structural equation model. However, by a redefinition of variables, the Kenny-Judd model can be rewritten into a form that comes close to this model. This can be done as follows. Construct a new factor $\xi_{3n} \equiv \xi_{1n} \xi_{2n}$ and compute, for all n, $x_{5n} \equiv x_{1n} x_{4n}$ and $x_{6n} \equiv x_{2n} x_{3n}$. Hence,

$$\begin{aligned} x_{5n} &= x_{1n} x_{4n} \\ &= (\xi_{1n} + \delta_{1n})(\lambda_4 \xi_{2n} + \delta_{4n}) \\ &= \lambda_4 \xi_{1n} \xi_{2n} + \xi_{1n} \delta_{4n} + \lambda_4 \xi_{2n} \delta_{1n} + \delta_{1n} \delta_{4n}, \end{aligned}$$

or $x_{5n} = \lambda_4 \xi_{3n} + \delta_{5n}$, where $\delta_{5n} \equiv \xi_{1n} \delta_{4n} + \lambda_4 \xi_{2n} \delta_{1n} + \delta_{1n} \delta_{4n}$. Similarly, $x_{6n} = \lambda_2 \xi_{3n} + \delta_{6n}$, where $\delta_{6n} \equiv \lambda_2 \xi_{1n} \delta_{3n} + \xi_{2n} \delta_{2n} + \delta_{2n} \delta_{3n}$. Thus, the Kenny-Judd model can be written as

$$y_n = \alpha + \gamma_1 \xi_{1n} + \gamma_2 \xi_{2n} + \gamma_3 \xi_{3n} + \varepsilon_n$$

and

$$\begin{bmatrix} x_{1n} \\ x_{2n} \\ x_{3n} \\ x_{4n} \\ x_{5n} \\ x_{6n} \end{bmatrix} = \begin{bmatrix} 1 & 0 & 0 \\ \lambda_2 & 0 & 0 \\ 0 & 1 & 0 \\ 0 & \lambda_4 & 0 \\ 0 & 0 & \lambda_4 \\ 0 & 0 & \lambda_2 \end{bmatrix} \begin{bmatrix} \xi_{1n} \\ \xi_{2n} \\ \xi_{3n} \end{bmatrix} + \begin{bmatrix} \delta_{1n} \\ \delta_{2n} \\ \delta_{3n} \\ \delta_{4n} \\ \delta_{5n} \\ \delta_{6n} \end{bmatrix}$$

or $\tilde{x}_n = \tilde{\Lambda}\tilde{\xi}_n + \tilde{\delta}_n$, say, for short. This is clearly the specification of a linear structural equation model and can be estimated as such, which gives consistent estimators. However, for the results to be interpreted as pertaining to the interaction model, some nonlinear restrictions must be satisfied. Asymptotically, these will be satisfied, but for the sake of interpretation, they must be satisfied in finite samples as well.

To study the restrictions, note first that $\mathrm{E}(\xi_{3n}) = \mathrm{E}(\xi_{1n}\xi_{2n}) \equiv \phi_{21}$, say, which is generally nonzero. Similarly, $\mathrm{E}(x_{5n}) = \lambda_4\phi_{21}$ and $\mathrm{E}(x_{6n}) = \lambda_2\phi_{21}$. This suggests that a mean structure should be added to the model, because the means are functions of the same parameters as the covariances. However, from $x_{5n} = x_{1n}x_{4n}$ and $x_{6n} = x_{2n}x_{3n}$, it follows that these means are actually equivalent to covariances in other parts of the model. The exact equivalence holds both for the sample statistics and for their population counterparts. Hence, adding a mean structure would imply adding redundant moments and is therefore not necessary and computationally undesirable.

Now, assume as usual that δ_{1n}, δ_{2n}, δ_{3n}, and δ_{4n} are mutually independent with variances θ_1, θ_2, θ_3, and θ_4, respectively. Then it follows that δ_{5n} and δ_{6n} are uncorrelated with δ_{1n}–δ_{4n} and with each other, although evidently not independent, which has consequences for the statistical inference. The variances of δ_{5n} and δ_{6n} are $\phi_{11}\theta_4+\lambda_4^2\phi_{22}\theta_1+\theta_1\theta_4$, and $\lambda_2^2\phi_{11}\theta_3+\phi_{22}\theta_2+\theta_2\theta_3$, respectively, where $\phi_{11} \equiv \mathrm{E}(\xi_{1n}^2)$ and $\phi_{22} \equiv \mathrm{E}(\xi_{2n}^2)$. Furthermore, the covariance matrix of $(\xi_{1n}, \xi_{2n}, \xi_{3n})'$ is

$$\begin{bmatrix} \phi_{11} & \phi_{21} & \phi_{211} \\ \phi_{21} & \phi_{22} & \phi_{221} \\ \phi_{211} & \phi_{221} & \phi_{2211} - \phi_{21}^2 \end{bmatrix},$$

where $\phi_{211} \equiv \mathrm{E}(\xi_{1n}^2\xi_{2n})$, $\phi_{221} \equiv \mathrm{E}(\xi_{1n}\xi_{2n}^2)$, and $\phi_{2211} \equiv \mathrm{E}(\xi_{1n}^2\xi_{2n}^2)$. Depending on the distributional assumptions concerning ξ_n, this may impose additional restrictions. If ξ_n is assumed normally distributed, for example, $\phi_{211} = \phi_{221} = 0$ and $\phi_{2211} = \phi_{11}\phi_{22} + 2\phi_{21}^2$. Hence, the construction of the additional factor and indicators imposes nonlinear restrictions on the moments of the elements of $\tilde{\xi}_n$ and $\tilde{\delta}_n$. Even if the ξ_n, δ_n, and ε_n are assumed to be normally distributed, the $\tilde{\xi}_n$ and $\tilde{\delta}_n$ are certainly not normally distributed. The same holds for the y_n because of the interaction term. Therefore, GMM with optimal weighting seems to be the most appropriate estimation method.

11.3 Models for qualitative and limited-dependent variables

In applied microeconometric modeling, the dependent variables are often qualitative rather than quantitative in nature. Examples are the choice between several products or the state of an individual's employment. For such situations, qualitative response models have been developed and are widely used. In this section we focus on the logit model, which is often used to model the choice between two alternatives, and see how we can handle measurement error there. We conclude by making some comments on the more general class of limited-dependent variables.

Binary choice models

We first recapitulate the idea behind binary choice models. To that end, consider the choice between two products. Let $y_n = 1$ if product 1 is chosen and $y_n = 0$ if product 2 is chosen. We wish to model the expectation of y_n, or equivalently, the probability that $y_n = 1$, as a function of characteristics p_{1n} and p_{0n} of the products and w_n of the subject. For example, p_{jn} may contain the price of product j as faced by consumer n and w_n may contain the age of the subject, and may also contain a constant. Assume that the conditional indirect utilities of the products are

$$\begin{aligned} u_{1n} &= \alpha_1' w_n + \beta' p_{1n} + \varepsilon_{1n} \\ u_{0n} &= \alpha_0' w_n + \beta' p_{0n} + \varepsilon_{0n}, \end{aligned}$$

where α_1, α_0, and β are regression coefficients and ε_{1n} and ε_{0n} are random errors. Assume further that the consumer buys the product with the highest utility. Hence, we observe $y_n = 1$ if $u_{1n} > u_{0n}$ and $y_n = 0$ if $u_{1n} < u_{0n}$. So

$$\begin{aligned} \Pr(y_n = 1 \mid w_n, p_{1n}, p_{0n}) &= \Pr(u_{1n} > u_{0n} \mid w_n, p_{1n}, p_{0n}) \\ &= \Pr(\alpha' w_n + \beta' p_n + \varepsilon_n > 0 \mid w_n, p_n) \\ &= \Pr(\varepsilon_n > -\alpha' w_n - \beta' p_n \mid w_n, p_n) \\ &= 1 - \Pr(\varepsilon_n \leq -\alpha' w_n - \beta' p_n \mid w_n, p_n) \\ &= 1 - F_\varepsilon(-\alpha' w_n - \beta' p_n), \end{aligned}$$

where $\alpha \equiv \alpha_1 - \alpha_0$, $p_n \equiv p_{1n} - p_{0n}$, $\varepsilon_n \equiv \varepsilon_{1n} - \varepsilon_{0n}$, and $F_\varepsilon(\cdot)$ is the distribution function of ε_n. Note that if the distribution of ε is symmetric around zero, then this probability reduces to $F_\varepsilon(\alpha' w_n + \beta' p_n)$.

Clearly, α_0 and α_1 can not be identified separately; only α may be identified. Moreover, the variance of ε_n is also not identified, because a change in the variance of ε_n can always be counteracted by multiplying α and β by an appropriate constant without changing the probability that $y_n = 1$. Hence, we may fix the variance of ε_n at some convenient value. If ε_n is assumed to be standard logistically distributed, with mean zero and variance $\pi^2/3$, $F_\varepsilon(x) \equiv e^x/(1+e^x)$, and we obtain the (binary) *logit* model

$$\mathrm{E}(y_n \mid w_n, p_n) = \Pr(y_n = 1 \mid w_n, p_n) = \frac{\exp(\alpha' w_n + \beta' p_n)}{1 + \exp(\alpha' w_n + \beta' p_n)}.$$

This model is usually estimated by MLmaximum likelihood, but may also be estimated by GMM.

Measurement error

Now, assume that the exogenous variables in the logit model are not observed directly. For simplicity, we assume that we have only one explanatory variable ξ_n. Instead of ξ_n, we observe a vector of l indicators x_n and we assume a standard factor analytic structure. This leads to the model

$$\mathrm{E}(y_n \mid \xi_n) = \Pr(y_n = 1 \mid \xi_n) = \frac{\exp(\beta \xi_n)}{1 + \exp(\beta \xi_n)} \tag{11.5a}$$

$$x_n = \lambda \xi_n + v_n, \tag{11.5b}$$

where λ is a vector of factor loadings, v_n is a vector of random errors independent of ξ_n, and it is assumed that $\mathrm{E}(\xi_n) = 0$, $\mathrm{E}(\xi_n^2) = 1$, and $\mathrm{E}(v_n) = 0$. We let $\Omega \equiv \mathrm{E}(v_n v_n')$.

We can rewrite (11.5a) as

$$y_n = \frac{\exp(\beta \xi_n)}{1 + \exp(\beta \xi_n)} + \zeta_n = \mu(\beta \xi_n) + \zeta_n,$$

say, where $\mu(\beta \xi_n) \equiv \mathrm{E}(y_n \mid \xi_n)$ and ζ_n is a random error with mean zero and conditional variance

$$\mathrm{E}(\zeta_n^2 \mid \xi_n) = \mu(\beta \xi_n)[1 - \mu(\beta \xi_n)] = \frac{\exp(\beta \xi_n)}{[1 + \exp(\beta \xi_n)]^2}. \tag{11.6}$$

This provides us with the following (second order) moment conditions:

$$\begin{aligned}
\mathrm{E}(y_n^2) &= \mathrm{E}(y_n) \\
&= \mathrm{E}_\xi\left(\mathrm{E}_\zeta(y_n \mid \xi_n)\right) \\
&= \mathrm{E}_\xi\left(\frac{\exp(\beta \xi_n)}{1 + \exp(\beta \xi_n)}\right) & (11.7\mathrm{a}) \\
\mathrm{E}(y_n x_n) &= \mathrm{E}_\xi\left(\mathrm{E}_{\zeta,v}(y_n x_n \mid \xi_n)\right) \\
&= \lambda\ \mathrm{E}_\xi\left(\frac{\exp(\beta \xi_n)}{1 + \exp(\beta \xi_n)}\, \xi_n\right) & (11.7\mathrm{b}) \\
\mathrm{E}(x_n x_n') &= \lambda \lambda' + \Omega. & (11.7\mathrm{c})
\end{aligned}$$

Previously, when discussing linear models, we usually assumed, without loss of generality, that the means of the variables were zero. In the present case, transforming y_n to have zero mean would be inconvenient. Hence, we do not center y_n. The moment conditions (11.7) can be used to define a GMM estimator of the parameters β, λ, and Ω.

The expectations in (11.7a) and (11.7b) can be expressed as integrals with respect to the density of ξ_n. Due to the nonlinearity of the function $\mu(\cdot)$, the resulting expectations will be different for different distributions of ξ_n. Hence, we need to assume a specific distribution of ξ_n. Let us assume that ξ_n is standard normally distributed, then (11.7a) and (11.7b) can be further written as

$$\mathrm{E}(y_n^2) = \int_{-\infty}^{+\infty} \frac{\exp(\beta\xi_n)}{1+\exp(\beta\xi_n)} \phi(\xi_n)\,\mathrm{d}\xi_n$$

$$\mathrm{E}(y_n x_n) = \lambda \int_{-\infty}^{+\infty} \frac{\exp(\beta\xi_n)}{1+\exp(\beta\xi_n)} \xi_n\,\phi(\xi_n)\,\mathrm{d}\xi_n,$$

where $\phi(\cdot)$ is the standard normal density function. These integrals have no closed-form solution, but they can be evaluated numerically by Gaussian quadrature. Alternatively, simulated GMM can be used, which will typically be computationally more convenient.

Another possible estimation method is maximum likelihood. If ξ_n had been observed, the likelihood contribution of the n-th observation would be

$$\begin{aligned}
\mathcal{L}_n^* &= f_v(x_n \mid \xi_n) \Pr(y_n \mid \xi_n) \phi(\xi_n) \\
&= \frac{1}{(2\pi)^{l/2}|\Omega|^{1/2}} \exp(-\tfrac{1}{2}(x_n - \lambda\xi_n)'\Omega^{-1}(x_n - \lambda\xi_n)) \\
&\quad \times \left(\frac{\exp(\beta\xi_n)}{1+\exp(\beta\xi_n)}\right)^{y_n} \left(\frac{1}{1+\exp(\beta\xi_n)}\right)^{1-y_n} \left(\frac{1}{\sqrt{2\pi}} \exp\left(-\tfrac{1}{2}\xi_n^2\right)\right).
\end{aligned}$$

Because ξ_n is not observed, the likelihood contribution of the n-th observation is obtained from this expression by integrating ξ_n out:

$$\begin{aligned}
\mathcal{L}_n &= \int_{-\infty}^{+\infty} f_v(x_n \mid \xi_n) \Pr(y_n \mid \xi_n) \phi(\xi_n)\,\mathrm{d}\xi_n \\
&= \mathrm{E}_\xi\left(f_v(x_n \mid \xi_n) \Pr(y_n \mid \xi_n)\right) \\
&= \int_{-\infty}^{+\infty} \left(\frac{1}{(2\pi)^{M/2}|\Omega|^{1/2}} \exp(-\tfrac{1}{2}(x_n - \lambda\xi_n)'\Omega^{-1}(x_n - \lambda\xi_n))\right. \\
&\quad \times \left(\frac{\exp(\beta\xi_n)}{1+\exp(\beta\xi_n)}\right)^{y_n} \left(\frac{1}{1+\exp(\beta\xi_n)}\right)^{1-y_n}
\end{aligned}$$

$$\times \left(\frac{1}{\sqrt{2\pi}} \exp(-\tfrac{1}{2}\xi_n^2) \right) \, d\xi_n \, .$$

This integral does not have a closed-form solution and hence must also be evaluated numerically or through simulation. In the latter case the resulting estimator is the *simulated maximum likelihood* estimator, which is the ML analogue of simulated GMM estimator discussed in section 9.8.

Other forms of limited-dependent variables

From the derivations above, it follows immediately that the general form of the binary logit model can be defined by the following equations:

$$y_n^* = \beta' x_n + \varepsilon_n \tag{11.8a}$$

$$y_n = I(y_n^* > 0), \tag{11.8b}$$

where y_n^* is a *latent response variable*, x_n is an observed vector of exogenous variables, ε_n is a logistically distributed random error term, y_n is an observed endogenous variable, and $I(\cdot)$ is the indicator function, $I(E) \equiv 1$ if the expression E is true and $I(E) \equiv 0$ otherwise.

The system (11.8) can be straightforwardly adapted and extended to cover many econometric models for limited-dependent and qualitative variables. If, for example, ε_n is assumed standard normally distributed instead of logistically, the (binary) *probit* model is obtained. Additionally, y_n may be an *ordered categorical variable*, that is, it has $J > 2$ possible answer categories. For example, "customer satisfaction" may be "low" ($y_n = 0$), "medium" ($y_n = 1$), or "high" ($y_n = 2$). This may be modeled by changing (11.8b) to $y_n = H(y_n^*)$, where $H(y_n^*) \equiv 0$ if $y_n^* < 0$, $H(y_n^*) \equiv 1$ if $0 < y_n^* < \tau$, and $H(y_n^*) \equiv 2$ if $y_n^* > \tau$, where τ is a *threshold* parameter. The resulting model is the *ordered probit* model. Alternatively, ε_n may be normally distributed with variance σ_ε^2 and y_n may be defined as $y_n = G(y_n^*)$, where $G(y_n^*) \equiv 0$ if $y_n^* < 0$, and $G(y_n^*) \equiv y_n^*$ if $y_n^* > 0$. This model is called the *censored regression* model. Unlike the categorical cases, the variance of ε_n is identified in this case.

Clearly, these ideas can be adapted in a large number of ways to accommodate a broad class of models. The extension of these models to allow for measurement error or latent variables is straightforward and completely analogous to the inclusion of latent variables in the logit model as discussed above. The exogenous variables x_n are replaced by the latent exogenous variables ξ_n and a measurement equation $x_n = \Lambda\xi_n + v_n$ is added to the model. Then, the parameters can be estimated by (simulated) maximum likelihood or (simulated) GMM. These estimation procedures are obtained by a straightforward adaptation of the estimation procedure discussed above for the logit model with measurement error.

The Berkson model with limited-dependent variables

Finally, we consider the Berkson model with a limited-dependent endogenous variable. In section 2.5, we saw that the OLS estimators of the regression coefficients in the Berkson model are unbiased and consistent in the linear model. We will now show that this not necessarily carries over to models with limited-dependent endogenous variables. The important aspects are most easily understood for the probit model, and therefore, we discuss the details for this model.

In the probit model, the latent response variable y_n^* follows the linear regression model

$$y_n^* = \beta'\xi_n + \varepsilon_n.$$

We have not observed y_n^* directly, but only a binary indicator $y_n \equiv I(y_n^* \geq 0)$. It is assumed that ε_n is normally distributed and, for identification purposes, its variance is fixed at 1. Hence,

$$\Pr(y_n = 1 \mid \xi_n) = \Phi(\beta'\xi_n),$$

where $\Phi(\cdot)$ is the standard normal distribution function. Note that this model is similar to the logit model (11.5a). In the Berkson model, ξ_n is not observed, but x_n is, and the two are related by

$$\xi_n = x_n + v_n,$$

with $\mathrm{E}(v_n \mid x_n) = 0$. In the current context, we assume that v_n is normally distributed, with mean zero and covariance matrix Ω, and independent of x_n. It follows that

$$y_n^* = \beta'x_n + \varepsilon_n^*,$$

where $\varepsilon_n^* = \varepsilon_n + \beta'v_n$, which is normally distributed with variance $1 + \beta'\Omega\beta > 1$. Hence,

$$\Pr(y_n = 1 \mid x_n) = \Phi(\tilde{\beta}'x_n),$$

where $\tilde{\beta} = \beta/\sqrt{1 + \beta'\Omega\beta}$, which is proportional to β, with the same signs, but smaller in magnitude. Clearly, this defines a standard probit model with attenuated regression coefficients and hence, the standard probit ML estimator is inconsistent. It turns out that, if Ω is not identified from other sources, the model is not identified.

The properties of this model and the resulting attenuation can be viewed as a special case of omitted regressors that are uncorrelated with the regressors that are present. It is well known that this does not pose problems in linear regression, but gives attenuation in probit models.

11.4 The LISCOMP model

Thus far, we have assumed that we have only one limited-dependent or categorical endogenous variable and a linear factor analytic measurement model for the latent exogenous variables. However, we may have more categorical or limited-dependent endogenous variables and we may not have continuous indicators of the latent variables. This more general case is covered by what is commonly called the LISCOMP model, after the LISCOMP software program in which it was first implemented. Here, LIS refers to linear structural relations, as in LISREL, and COMP refers to comprehensive measurement. Throughout, the notation will resemble the LISREL notation closely.

We first describe the basic model. Due its generality, estimation is somewhat complicated and is usually done in two steps, that is, sequentially for two subsets of the entire set of parameters.

The basic model specification

Assume that all observed variables for the n-th subject are collected in the vector y_n of dimension M. The elements of y_n can be ordered categorical, censored, or continuous variables, but other data types can also be incorporated in principle. We assume that there is a continuously distributed vector of latent response variables y_n^* underlying the y_n. The relation between the observed variables y and the latent response variables y^* is

$$y_{in} = H_i(y_{in}^*;\, \tau_i), \tag{11.9}$$

where y_{in} is the i-th observed variable for the n-th subject, y_{in}^* is the corresponding latent response variable, and $H_i(y_{in}^*;\, \tau_i)$ is a known deterministic function of the latent response variable and a parameter vector τ_i. Typically, H_i is one of the functions that are commonly used for limited-dependent variables, i.e., a function that maps the real line onto a set of consecutive integers, or a function that censors the latent response variable, or it may be the identity function to accommodate dependent variables that are not censored or categorical. The parameter vector τ_i typically consists of (known or unknown) thresholds.

The latent response variables are assumed to follow a factor analysis model

$$y_n^* = \Lambda\eta_n + \varepsilon_n, \tag{11.10}$$

where Λ is a matrix of factor loadings, η_n is a g-vector of factors, and ε_n is a vector of random errors with $\mathrm{E}(\varepsilon_n) = 0$ and $\Theta \equiv \mathrm{E}(\varepsilon_n\varepsilon_n')$. The factors η_n are assumed to satisfy the following structural model:

$$\eta_n = B\eta_n + \zeta_n, \tag{11.11}$$

where B is a matrix of regression coefficients, and ζ_n is a vector of random errors with $\mathrm{E}(\zeta_n) = 0$ and $\Psi \equiv \mathrm{E}(\zeta_n \zeta_n')$. This equation does not contain latent exogenous variables (ξ_n), but they can be incorporated easily within the current parameterization. To that end, replace (11.11) by

$$\tilde{\eta}_n = \tilde{B}\tilde{\eta}_n + \tilde{\Gamma}\tilde{\xi}_n + \tilde{\zeta}_n,$$

where $\tilde{B}$ and $\tilde{\Gamma}$ are matrices of regression coefficients, $\tilde{\eta}_n$ and $\tilde{\xi}_n$ are vectors of latent endogenous and exogenous variables, respectively, with $\mathrm{E}(\tilde{\xi}_n) = 0$ and $\tilde{\Phi} \equiv \mathrm{E}(\tilde{\xi}_n \tilde{\xi}_n')$, and $\tilde{\zeta}_n$ is a vector of random errors with $\mathrm{E}(\zeta_n) = 0$ and $\tilde{\Psi} \equiv \mathrm{E}(\tilde{\zeta}_n \tilde{\zeta}_n')$. Now, define $\eta_n \equiv (\tilde{\eta}_n', \tilde{\xi}_n')'$, $\zeta_n \equiv (\tilde{\zeta}_n', \tilde{\xi}_n')'$,

$$B \equiv \begin{bmatrix} \tilde{B} & \tilde{\Gamma} \\ 0 & 0 \end{bmatrix} \quad \text{and} \quad \Psi \equiv \begin{bmatrix} \tilde{\Psi} & 0 \\ 0 & \tilde{\Phi} \end{bmatrix},$$

then we have evidently obtained a submodel of (11.11). Hence, there is no need to include latent exogenous variables ξ_n explicitly.

The reduced-form equation for η_n is

$$\eta_n = (I_g - B)^{-1}\zeta_n,$$

and thus the covariance structure of the latent response variables y_n^* is

$$\Sigma^* \equiv \mathrm{E}(y_n^* y_n^{*\prime}) = \Lambda(I_g - B)^{-1}\Psi(I_g - B')^{-1}\Lambda' + \Theta.$$

It is assumed that y^* is normally distributed, and that location and scale restrictions are imposed when needed. For example, the variance of y_i^* is not identified if y_i is categorical, so its scale must be fixed, for example by imposing the restriction that Σ_{ii}^* should be one. Also, either the mean or one of the thresholds should be set to a fixed value. Here, we assume that the mean of y_i^* is set to zero.

An attractive feature of the LISCOMP model is that the only nonlinearity in the model is induced by the observation equation (11.9). The model for the latent response variables is completely linear. This makes interpretation of the model easy, because interest usually focuses on the model for y^* or the model for η. The imperfect observation that induces the nonlinearity is regarded as a nuisance that is relatively uninteresting from a substantive viewpoint.

Estimation of the LISCOMP model

We now turn to estimation of the LISCOMP model. For clarity, we consider the case where the variables are ordered categorical. In principle, estimation can be done by maximum likelihood. The parameters enter the likelihood through expressions for the probabilities that the observations fall into the various categories. For example, for the i-th variable, the (marginal) probability of falling in category a, say, is given by

$$\Pr(y_{in} = a) \equiv \Pr(\tau_{i,a-1} < y_{in}^* \leq \tau_{i,a}) = \Phi(\tau_{i,a}) - \Phi(\tau_{i,a-1}), \tag{11.12}$$

where $\Phi(\cdot)$ is the standard normal distribution function and $\tau_{i,a-1}$ and $\tau_{i,a}$ are the thresholds surrounding the a-th category. Analogously, the bivariate marginal probability that the i-th variable falls in category a and the j-th variable falls in category b is

$$\begin{aligned}\Pr(y_{in} = a, y_{jn} = b) &\equiv \Pr(\tau_{i,a-1} < y_{in}^* \leq \tau_{i,a}, \tau_{j,b-1} < y_{jn}^* \leq \tau_{j,b}) \\ &= \int_{\tau_{i,a-1}}^{\tau_{i,a}} \int_{\tau_{j,b-1}}^{\tau_{j,b}} \phi_2(t, u; \rho_{ij})\,\mathrm{d}u\,\mathrm{d}t, \end{aligned} \tag{11.13}$$

where $\phi_2(\cdot\,,\cdot\,;\rho)$ is the bivariate standard normal density function with correlation ρ, and ρ_{ij} is the correlation between y_{in}^* and y_{jn}^*, which is the (i, j)-th element of Σ^*. This probability involves a two-dimensional integral of the bivariate normal distribution. If y_n consists of M categorical variables, the likelihood involves the joint probabilities for all M variables. Hence, the evaluation of the likelihood requires the evaluation of M-dimensional integrals of the M-variate standard normal density with correlation matrix Σ^*, which is a function of the parameters Λ, B, Ψ, and Θ. Even for moderate values of M, standard numerical integration is impossible. However, simulation of the probabilities is possible for relatively large values of M and then simulated maximum likelihood and simulated GMM estimation is feasible.

An alternative is to estimate the model in two steps. This induces a certain cost in efficiency but is much more convenient. In the first step, the correlations ρ and the thresholds τ are estimated. We call these parameters the *intermediate parameters*. In the second step, the estimates for the ρ's and the estimate for their asymptotic covariance matrix are used to estimate parameters Λ, B, Ψ, and Θ, which we call the *structural parameters*. We now turn to this approach.

Estimation of the intermediate parameters

We first consider the thresholds. From (11.12), we have that

$$\Pr(y_{in} \leq a) \equiv \Pr(y_{in}^* \leq \tau_{i,a}) = \Phi(\tau_{i,a}),$$

and hence the thresholds are given by $\tau_{i,a} = \Phi^{-1}\left(\Pr(y_{in} \leq a)\right)$. It follows that $\tau_{i,a}$ can be estimated consistently by

$$\tilde{\tau}_{i,a} \equiv \Phi^{-1}(P_{i,a}), \tag{11.14}$$

where $P_{i,a}$ is the sample proportion of $y_i \leq a$. Now, using only information from variable i and variable j, a partial likelihood function based on (11.13) is

$$\mathcal{L}_{ij}(\tau_i, \tau_j, \rho_{ij}) = \prod_a \prod_b \left(\int_{\tau_{i,a-1}}^{\tau_{i,a}} \int_{\tau_{j,b-1}}^{\tau_{j,b}} \phi_2(t, u; \rho_{ij}) \, \mathrm{d}u \, \mathrm{d}t \right)^{N_{ij,ab}}, \qquad (11.15)$$

where $N_{ij,ab}$ is the number of observations for which $y_{in} = a$ and $y_{jn} = b$. If the consistent estimators $\tilde{\tau}$ from (11.14) are inserted in (11.15), computation of the pseudo maximum likelihood estimator of ρ_{ij} involves only the minimization of a univariate function with two-dimensional integrals, which does not pose big numerical problems. Alternatively, the thresholds and correlations may be estimated jointly from (11.15). The differences in estimates are usually small, but simulation studies provide some indication that the latter method works better for inferential purposes.

By repeating this process for all combinations of i and j, a consistent estimator of Σ^* is obtained. If some of the variables are censored, truncated, unordered categorical, or continuous, similar procedures can be followed. Note that the consistent estimator of Σ^* thus obtained does not use the restrictions on the covariance structure.

The covariance matrix of the estimated correlations

Optimal estimation of the structural parameters to be obtained in the second step requires consistent estimators for the asymptotic covariances of the elements of Σ^*. Let $\hat{\sigma}^*$ be the vector of estimated elements of Σ^*, that is, its diagonal and subdiagonal elements except those variances that are fixed to 1 for identification purposes. This vector consists of the estimators of the correlations ρ_{ij} between the latent response variables y_{in}^* and y_{jn}^*, $i, j = 1, \ldots, M, i \neq j$.

In order to derive the covariance matrix of $\hat{\sigma}^*$, we need some notation and results. From (11.15), we obtain the partial loglikelihood function

$$\begin{aligned} L_{ij}(\tau_i, \tau_j, \rho_{ij}) &\equiv \log \mathcal{L}_{ij}(\tau_i, \tau_j, \rho_{ij}) \\ &= \sum_a \sum_b N_{ij,ab} \log \left(\int_{\tau_{i,a-1}}^{\tau_{i,a}} \int_{\tau_{j,b-1}}^{\tau_{j,b}} \phi_2(t, u; \rho_{ij}) \, \mathrm{d}u \, \mathrm{d}t \right) \\ &\equiv N \sum_a \sum_b p_{ij,ab} \log \Phi_{ij,ab}(\tau_i, \tau_j, \rho_{ij}), \end{aligned}$$

where $p_{ij,ab} \equiv N_{ij,ab}/N$ is the sample proportion of observations for which $y_{in} = a$ and $y_{jn} = b$, and $\Phi_{ij,ab}(\tau_i, \tau_j, \rho_{ij})$ is implicitly defined and is the corresponding population probability as a function of the parameters. Define $z^n_{ij,ab} \equiv I(y_{in} = a, y_{jn} = b)$. Then, the sample proportions can be written as

$$p_{ij,ab} \equiv \frac{1}{N} \sum_{n=1}^{N} z^n_{ij,ab}.$$

Let z_n be the indicator vector in which all the variables $z^n_{ij,ab}$ are stacked, let $\pi(\tau, \sigma^*)$ be its expectation, depending on the thresholds gathered in the vector τ and the correlations in σ^*, and let the true value of $\pi(\tau, \sigma^*)$ be π_0. Furthermore, let p be the vector that stacks all the sample proportions $p_{ij,ab}$. Clearly, p is the sample mean of a vector of i.i.d. bounded variables. Hence, by some form of central limit theorem,

$$\sqrt{N}(p - \pi_0) \xrightarrow{d} \mathcal{N}(0, R)$$

for some positive semidefinite matrix R. The matrix R can obviously be estimated consistently by

$$\hat{R} \equiv \frac{1}{N} \sum_{n=1}^{N} (z_n - p)(z_n - p)'.$$

the sample variance of the z_n. Note, however, that R and $\hat{R}$ are of deficient rank, because the proportions obviously sum to 1. This does not lead to problems later on, however.

Now, following on the discussion above, there are two cases to consider. In the first case, the threshold parameters are estimated from (11.14) and the correlations from (11.15), with the estimated thresholds from the previous step inserted. In the second case, the thresholds and correlations are estimated jointly from (11.15). In this case, however, every $\mathcal{L}_{ij}$ from (11.15), $j = 1, \ldots, M$, $j \neq i$, gives a different estimator of the thresholds τ_i. Therefore, the final estimator of the thresholds is obtained by (possibly weighted) averaging of the $M - 1$ different estimators.

In the first case, the estimators $\tilde{\tau}$ are obtained from

$$\tilde{\tau}_{i,a} \equiv \Phi^{-1}(P_{i,a}) = \Phi^{-1}\left(\sum_{a' \leq a} p_{i,a'}\right) = \Phi^{-1}\left(\sum_{a' \leq a} \sum_{b} p_{ij,a'b}\right)$$

for any j. The elements of the estimator $\hat{\sigma}^*$ are then obtained from the condition

$$\frac{\partial L_{ij}(\tilde{\tau}_i, \tilde{\tau}_j, \rho_{ij})}{\partial \rho_{ij}} = 0.$$

Hence, the estimators are defined jointly as the solution to the estimating equations $\tilde{F}(\tau, \sigma^*; p) = 0$, in which $\tilde{F} = (F_1', F_2')'$, where F_1 gathers the functions

$$\tilde{\tau}_{i,a} - \Phi^{-1}\left(\sum_{a' \leq a}\sum_b p_{ij,a'b}\right)$$

and F_2 gathers the functions $\partial L_{ij}/\partial \rho_{ij}$. Let $\tilde{\theta} \equiv (\tilde{\tau}', \hat{\sigma}^{*\prime})'$ and let θ_0 be its true value. Clearly, the estimator $\tilde{\theta}$ is an implicit function of p. From the implicit function theorem (section A.7), it follows that

$$\tilde{G}(\tilde{\theta}, p) \equiv \frac{\partial \tilde{\theta}}{\partial p'} = -\left(\frac{\partial \tilde{F}}{\partial \tilde{\theta}'}\right)^{-1} \frac{\partial \tilde{F}}{\partial p'}.$$

By applying the delta method it follows that the asymptotic distribution of $\tilde{\theta}$ is

$$\sqrt{N}(\tilde{\theta} - \theta_0) \xrightarrow{d} \mathcal{N}\left(0, \tilde{G}(\theta_0, \pi_0) R \tilde{G}(\theta_0, \pi_0)'\right).$$

Obviously, the asymptotic covariance matrix of $\tilde{\theta}$ can be consistently estimated by $\tilde{G}(\tilde{\theta}, p)\hat{R}\tilde{G}(\tilde{\theta}, p)'$, and the estimated asymptotic covariance matrix $\hat{C}$ of $\hat{\sigma}^*$ is the relevant submatrix of this.

We now turn to the second case. As mentioned above, for this case, we first obtain estimators $\tau_i^{(ij)}$, $\tau_j^{(ij)}$, and $\hat{\rho}_{ij}$ from the conditions

$$\frac{\partial L_{ij}(\tau_i, \tau_j, \rho_{ij})}{\partial \rho_{ij}} = 0$$

$$\frac{\partial L_{ij}(\tau_i, \tau_j, \rho_{ij})}{\partial \tau_i} = 0$$

$$\frac{\partial L_{ij}(\tau_i, \tau_j, \rho_{ij})}{\partial \tau_j} = 0.$$

Hence, these estimators are defined jointly as the solution to the estimating equations $F^*(\tau^*, \sigma^*; p) = 0$, where $F^* = (F_2', F_3')'$, with F_2 as defined above; F_3 gathers the functions $\partial L_{ij}/\partial \tau_i$ and $\partial L_{ij}/\partial \tau_j$, and τ^* gathers the estimators $\tau_i^{(ij)}$ and $\tau_j^{(ij)}$. Note that τ^* contains multiple estimators of the same thresholds.

Let $\theta^* \equiv (\tau^{*\prime}, \hat{\sigma}^{*\prime})'$. The estimator θ^* is also an implicit function of p. Hence, it follows that

$$G^*(\theta^*, p) \equiv \frac{\partial \theta^*}{\partial p'} = -\left(\frac{\partial F^*}{\partial \theta^{*\prime}}\right)^{-1} \frac{\partial F^*}{\partial p'}.$$

By applying the delta method, it follows that the asymptotic distribution of θ^* is

$$\sqrt{N}(\theta^* - \theta_0^*) \xrightarrow{d} \mathcal{N}\left(0, G^*(\theta_0^*, \pi_0) R G^*(\theta_0^*, \pi_0)'\right),$$

where θ_0^* is the true value of θ^*. The "final" threshold estimators are (possibly weighted) averages of the different threshold estimators in τ^*. Hence, the (unique) estimators $\hat{\theta}$, say, are obtained from θ^* as $\hat{\theta} = \hat{A}'\theta^*$, where $\hat{A}$ is a known (possibly random) averaging matrix that converges in probability to some nonrandom matrix A_0. By applying the delta method once again, it follows that the asymptotic distribution of $\hat{\theta}$ is

$$\sqrt{N}(\hat{\theta} - \theta_0) \xrightarrow{d} \mathcal{N}\left(0, A_0' G^*(\theta_0^*, \pi_0) R G^*(\theta_0^*, \pi_0)' A_0\right).$$

The asymptotic covariance matrix of $\hat{\theta}$ can be consistently estimated by the expression $\hat{A}'G^*(\theta^*, p)\hat{R}G^*(\theta^*, p)'\hat{A}$. As in the first case, the estimated asymptotic covariance matrix $\hat{C}$ of $\hat{\sigma}^*$ is the relevant submatrix of this.

In both cases discussed, the expressions for the derivatives can be elaborated and then simplified considerably when the structure that is present in the estimating equations is exploited. The computational burden can thus be alleviated. The same holds for the expression for the estimator of R. Because these elaborations do not provide more insight, they will not be given here.

Estimation of the structural parameters

We now turn to the second step in the estimation procedure for the LISCOMP model. Let $\hat{\sigma}^*$ again be the vector of estimated elements of Σ^*, and let $\sigma^*(\theta)$ be the corresponding vector of elements of Σ^* as a function of θ, which now denotes the vector of structural parameters. Let $\hat{C}$ be the consistent estimator of the asymptotic covariance matrix of $\hat{\sigma}^*$. Then, obviously,

$$\hat{C}^{-1/2}\sqrt{N}\left(\hat{\sigma}^* - \sigma^*(\theta_0)\right) \xrightarrow{d} \mathcal{N}(0, I). \tag{11.16}$$

Hence, the parameter vector θ can be estimated consistently by minimizing the distance function

$$q^*(\theta) \equiv \left(\hat{\sigma}^* - \sigma^*(\theta)\right)' \hat{C}^{-1} \left(\hat{\sigma}^* - \sigma^*(\theta)\right).$$

This function is a GMM criterion function in separated form, with $\bar{g}$ replaced by $\hat{\sigma}^*$, $\gamma(\theta)$ replaced by $\sigma^*(\theta)$, and $\hat{W}$ replaced by $\hat{C}^{-1}$, which is an optimal weight matrix. The only difference with the standard case is that $\hat{\sigma}^*$ is not a sample average like $\bar{g}$ in (9.5) and that (11.16) takes the role of (9.13). Consequently, statistical inference about the model and its parameters can be obtained completely analogous to inference in usual linear structural equation models, with $\hat{\sigma}^*$ taking the role of $\bar{g}$. Note, however, that for categorical variables, the scale of the latent response variable has to be fixed, for example by setting its variance to one. This implies that the same restriction must be imposed on the covariance structure $\sigma^*(\theta)$, which generally leads to nonlinear constraints.

Observed exogenous variables

Assume that we have also observed a vector x_n of exogenous variables for the n-th individual. The exogenous variables enter the model in an extension of the structural equation (11.11):

$$\eta_n = B\eta_n + \Gamma x_n + \zeta_n, \tag{11.17}$$

where Γ is a matrix of regression coefficients and x_n is an l-vector of "truly" exogenous variables, i.e., variables we wish to condition upon and the distributions of which are not modeled. Typical examples of these are demographic variables and experimental variables. Now, it is apparent why we did not explicitly include latent exogenous variables ξ_n in (11.11). This would have made (11.17) unnecessarily complicated or not a straightforward extension of (11.11).

In *linear* structural equation models, exogenous variables are simply defined by the restrictions (in LISREL notation) $\Lambda_x \equiv I_l$ and $\Theta_\delta \equiv 0$. In the current situation, this poses more problems, because of the normality assumption on the latent variables. This assumption is necessary for the estimators, but leads to inconsistency if it is not satisfied, which is very likely with typical exogenous variables. The normality assumption is unnecessary but relatively harmless in linear structural equation models.

Given the structural equation (11.17), the reduced-form equation for η_n is

$$\eta_n = (I_g - B)^{-1}\Gamma x_n + (I_g - B)^{-1}\zeta_n$$

and thus the latent response variables y_n^* satisfy the model

$$\begin{aligned} y_n^* &= \Lambda\eta_n + \varepsilon_n \\ &= \Lambda(I_g - B)^{-1}\Gamma x_n + \Lambda(I_g - B)^{-1}\zeta_n + \varepsilon_n \\ &= \Pi x_n + \delta_n, \end{aligned}$$

say, where $\Pi \equiv \Lambda(I_g - B)^{-1}\Gamma$ and δ_n is a random error with $\mathrm{E}(\delta_n) = 0$ and

$$\begin{aligned} \Sigma^* &\equiv \mathrm{E}(\delta_n\delta_n') \\ &= \Lambda(I_g - B)^{-1}\Psi(I_g - B)^{-1'}\Lambda' + \Theta. \end{aligned}$$

This model is equivalent to the model without exogenous variables, except that the mean of y_n^* is now Πx_n instead of zero. In this case, a sequential estimation procedure similar to the case without exogenous variables can be used. The differences are that, instead of (11.14), univariate probit models should be estimated and (11.15) should be replaced by a bivariate probit likelihood. The unrestricted estimator of Π is added to $\hat{\sigma}^*$ and the estimated covariance matrix $\hat{C}$ has to be adapted accordingly. Similar adjustments have to be made with censored, truncated, unordered categorical, or continuous variables. These are straightforward and will not be discussed here.

11.5 General parametric nonlinear regression

In section 11.3, we saw that the logit model with latent variables could be written in the form

$$y_n = \mu(\xi_n; \phi) + \varepsilon_n, \tag{11.18}$$

where $\mu(\xi_n; \phi) = \exp(\phi\xi_n)/(1 + \exp(\phi\xi_n))$, which is a known function of the latent variable ξ_n and a parameter ϕ, $\mathrm{E}(\varepsilon_n \mid \xi_n) = 0$, and ξ_n is only observed indirectly through a factor analytic measurement model. Obviously, the specification (11.18) can be redefined to include any known nonlinear function. The formulation then includes polynomial regression and other nonlinear regression models with errors in variables, and nonlinear factor analysis models. Depending on the assumptions that are made concerning ε_n, the distribution of ξ_n, and the measurement of ξ_n, several ways to estimate the model are possible. As in section 11.3, however, it will generally be necessary to make some restrictive distributional assumptions to be able to estimate the model. In this section, we will discuss some possible assumptions and feasible estimators under these assumptions. These cover some important cases and serve at the same time as examples from which estimators under different assumptions may be derived by analogy. In the following, all variables, functions, and parameters may be vector valued, unless otherwise stated.

In order to estimate this model, let us assume that ξ_n is continuously distributed with density function $f_\xi(\xi; \alpha)$, where α is a vector of parameters. Then, the expectation of y_n is

$$\mathrm{E}(y_n) = \int \mu(\xi; \phi)\, f_\xi(\xi; \alpha)\, \mathrm{d}\xi \equiv \gamma_1(\phi, \alpha), \tag{11.19}$$

with the function $\gamma_1(\cdot)$ implicitly defined. Clearly, this defines a moment equation in the separated form with $g_n = y_n$ and $\gamma(\theta) = \gamma_1(\phi, \alpha)$. The evaluation of γ_1

will frequently be a computational burden, because it contains a (multidimensional) integral that rarely has a closed-form solution. Simulation techniques like simulated GMM (cf. section 9.8) then have to be employed.

The moment condition (11.19) was based on the assumption $\mathrm{E}(\varepsilon_n \mid \xi_n) = 0$. Sometimes we are able to make the stronger assumption that the ε_n and ξ_n are independent, implying $\mathrm{E}(\varepsilon_n \mid \mu(\xi_n; \phi)) = 0$ for all $\mu(\cdot)$ and ϕ. This stronger assumption is, however, not innocuous. It does, for example, not hold for the logit model of section 11.3, because (11.6) shows that the variance of the residual depends on ξ_n.

Furthermore, let us assume that $\Theta_\varepsilon \equiv \mathrm{E}(\varepsilon_n \varepsilon_n')$ is a diagonal matrix. Then,

$$\mathrm{E}(y_n y_n') = \int \mu(\xi; \phi)\mu(\xi; \phi)' \, f_\xi(\xi; \alpha) \, \mathrm{d}\xi + \Theta_\varepsilon.$$

This defines a second moment equation, also in the separated form. If ϕ and α are identified from (11.19), adding this second moment condition in the estimation process improves the precision of the estimators. If they are not identified from (11.19), it may help closing the gap with identification. Evidently, under the stated assumptions, higher order moments of y_n provide possible additional moment conditions.

As a generalization, let us now assume that we do not know the unconditional distribution of ξ_n (apart from parameters), but that there exists an observable vector z_n of exogenous variables and that we know that the conditional distribution of ξ_n given z_n is $f_{\xi|z}(\xi \mid z_n; \beta)$, where β is a vector of parameters. For example, we may assume that $\xi_n = Bz_n + w_n$, where B is a matrix of regression coefficients and w_n is a vector of disturbances that is assumed to be normally distributed with mean zero and covariance matrix Θ_w. Hence, β consists of the free parameters in B and Θ_w, and

$$f_{\xi|z}(\xi \mid z_n; \beta) = (2\pi)^{-k/2} |\Theta_w|^{-1/2} \exp\bigl(-\tfrac{1}{2}(\xi - Bz_n)'\Theta_w^{-1}(\xi - Bz_n)\bigr),$$

where k is the dimension of ξ_n. If we assume that $\mathrm{E}(\varepsilon_n \mid \xi_n, z_n) = 0$, we obtain the conditional moment equation

$$\mathrm{E}(y_n \mid z_n) = \int \mu(\xi; \phi) \, f_{\xi|z}(\xi \mid z_n; \beta) \, \mathrm{d}\xi \equiv \gamma_2(z_n; \phi, \beta).$$

Analogous to the example above, second and higher conditional moment equations can be derived from additional assumptions regarding ε_n.

Conditioning on the indicators

Up till now, estimation of the general nonlinear model (11.18) has been based on treating the vector y_n of dependent variables as a whole. Frequently, however, a distinction can be made between a subvector of y_n that consists of the dependent variables of interest (typically only one), and another subvector that contains indicators of the latent variables ξ_n and are supposed to follows a standard factor analysis model. To avoid cluttering of notation, we redefine y_n to be the first subvector as mentioned above and define x_n as the vector of indicators of ξ_n. This leads to the augmented model

$$\begin{aligned} y_n &= \mu(\xi_n; \phi) + \varepsilon_n \\ x_n &= B\xi_n + v_n, \end{aligned}$$

where B is a matrix of factor loadings, and v_n is a vector of random errors. Of course, this model can be estimated along the lines discussed above, with y_n replaced by $(y_n', x_n')'$, but due to the linear structure of the indicators, we can alternatively approach this model through the implied conditional expectation of y_n given x_n and hence link it to the econometric tradition.

If it is assumed that ξ_n and v_n are independently normally distributed with means zero and covariance matrices Φ and Ω, respectively, the joint distribution of x_n, ξ_n, and v_n is given by

$$\begin{bmatrix} x_n \\ \xi_n \\ v_n \end{bmatrix} \sim \mathcal{N}_{2l+k}\left(0, \begin{bmatrix} B\Phi B' + \Omega & B\Phi & \Omega \\ \Phi B' & \Phi & 0 \\ \Omega & 0 & \Omega \end{bmatrix}\right),$$

where l is the dimension of x_n. From this, we obtain the conditional distribution of ξ_n given x_n as (cf. section A.5)

$$\xi_n \mid x_n \sim \mathcal{N}_k(L'x_n, \Phi_{\xi|x}), \tag{11.20}$$

where

$$\begin{aligned} L' &\equiv \Phi B'(B\Phi B' + \Omega)^{-1} \\ \Phi_{\xi|x} &\equiv \Phi - \Phi B'(B\Phi B' + \Omega)^{-1} B\Phi. \end{aligned}$$

If ε_n is independent of v_n, we may use this conditional distribution to derive a conditional moment equation

$$\mathrm{E}(y_n \mid x_n) = \int \mu(\xi; \phi)\, f_{\xi|x}(\xi \mid x_n; \zeta)\, \mathrm{d}\xi = \gamma_3(x_n; \phi, \zeta),$$

where ζ contains the free parameters in L and $\Phi_{\xi|x}$ and $f_{\xi|x}(\xi \mid x_n; \zeta)$ is the density function of the conditional normal distribution (11.20). Furthermore, assuming that the factor analysis model is identified, we can derive a consistent two-step estimator. In the first step, the factor analysis model is estimated. In the second step, the estimators $\hat{L}$ and $\hat{\Phi}_{\xi|x}$ constituting $\hat{\zeta}$ are fixed, and ϕ is estimated using the conditional moment equation

$$\hat{\mathrm{E}}(y_n \mid x_n) = \gamma_3(x_n; \phi, \hat{\zeta}).$$

The asymptotic properties of this estimator can be derived in a way similar to the derivation of the asymptotic properties of the estimators of the LISCOMP model in section 11.4.

Of course, the different assumptions discussed in this section constitute only a small subset of possible relevant assumptions. For example, if the distribution of ξ_n is not assumed to be normal, but some other specific distribution, the moment equations have to be adapted accordingly. Furthermore, one may have observed both exogenous variables z_n and indicators x_n. It may also be possible to use only weak assumptions about the distribution of ξ_n, along with the normality assumption regarding δ_n, to identify the model, or to use even weaker assumptions about all distributions and estimate them by some semiparametric or nonparametric method. The set of possibilities is virtually infinite and, as stated at the beginning of this section, general results are hard to give. Some of the basic principles from which many specific results can be derived have been discussed in this section.

11.6 Bibliographical notes

11.2 The observation that even slight nonlinearities in a model are sufficient to identify it was made by McManus (1992). The polynomial functional model was studied by L. K. Chan and Mak (1985).

The asymptotic behavior of the OLS estimators in a quadratic model under normality is due to Griliches and Ringstad (1970). The quadratic model was also considered by Wolter and Fuller (1982b). The consistent estimator (11.2) is given by Van Montfort (1989, chapter 2) and Cheng and Van Ness (1999, chapter 6). These authors also discuss identification and estimation of more general polynomial measurement error models by fitting higher order moments and/or cumulants.

Hausman, Newey, Ichimura, and Powell (1991) and Hausman, Newey, and Powell (1995) proposed to use polynomial regression models to estimate nonlinear Engel curves. They showed how, if the degree of the polynomial increases with sample size, consistent estimators are obtained of analytical functions $\mu(\cdot)$ of unknown form. The applicability of this idea is, however, limited, because the order of the moments that have to be fitted increases with the degree of the polynomial, and huge samples are needed to obtain relatively stable estimators of the parameters based on fitting higher order moments (Meijer, 1998). In most situations occurring in practice, it will not be possible tc obtain useful estimators of polynomials higher than second or third degree.

A theoretical rationale for quadratic regression models comes from Banks, Blundell, and Lewbel (1997), who studied models for systems of equations of expenditures on different goods. They showed that the only possible models that satisfy some regularity conditions derived from economic theory are quadratic in the logarithm of expenditure.

A recent discussion of polynomial factor analysis models is given by Meijer (1998, chapter 5). He discusses at length a model consisting of a polynomial part and a linear part, without assuming normality of the factor. Under some standard conditions, the model is identified and consistent estimators of the parameters can be obtained by a GMM procedure with the fitting of higher order moments. This is completely analogous to the discussion of the quadratic regression model in the main text, in which up to fourth-order moments were used.

The polynomial model without a linear part has been studied extensively by McDonald (1962, 1965, 1967). The estimation methods he proposed are, however, complicated and do not lead to consistent estimators. Mooijaart and Bentler (1986) assumed that ξ_n is standard normally distributed and proposed to estimate the parameters by the ADF method (see section 9.4) using second- and third-order moments. Meijer (1998, appendix 5.A) resolved the identification issue of this model. Under some regularity conditions, the model is identified from only second- and third-order moments, regardless of the degrees of the polynomials. These regularity conditions are usually met and can be easily checked.

The model (11.4) is due to Kenny and Judd (1984). They also proposed to estimate the model using standard software by introducing the product indicators, such as x_{5n}. A lot of authors have studied this model. Schumacker and Marcoulides (1998) is a recent book-length discussion of this model. In older versions of standard software, nonlinear restrictions could not be imposed explicitly. Based on the ideas of Rindskopf (1983, 1984b), Hayduk (1987, chapter 7) showed how the nonlinear restrictions of the interaction model could be imposed by introducing many phantom variables, see the bibliographic notes to chapter 8. In later versions of some structural equations programs, nonlinear constraints can be imposed explicitly, although this is sometimes quite complicated. Other structural equations programs still do not allow nonlinear constraints to be imposed explicitly, so for these programs phantom variables still have to be used.

Correct asymptotic inference with interaction models can be obtained by methods provided by Jöreskog and Yang (1996). They circumvented the near-singularity problem of the covariance matrix (due to high multicollinearity introduced by the product indicators) by fitting the so-called *augmented moment matrix* in LISREL. This matrix is defined as $A \equiv N^{-1} \sum_{n=1}^{N} (1, y_n', x_n')'(1, y_n', x_n')$, which contains all raw first- and second-order moments. With product indicators, this matrix is exactly singular, but it can be fitted by using a generalized inverse as weight matrix. This gives asymptotically optimal results, although it is computationally complicated.

Meijer (1998, chapter 6) discussed these and other approaches to the estimation of the interaction model. He also showed the (near) singularity of the optimal weight matrix with product indicators if, as usual, $x_{7n} \equiv x_{1n}x_{3n}$ and $x_{8n} \equiv x_{2n}x_{4n}$ are added to the model as well, and the covariance matrix is fitted instead of the augmented moment matrix. Furthermore, he developed a model with both quadratic and interaction terms and gave sufficient identification conditions using up to fourth-order moment conditions. Using these conditions, GMM estimators can be used with an optimal nonsingular weight matrix. Arminger and Muthén (1998) extended the Kenny-Judd model with general (parametric) nonlinear functions of ξ_n and proposed to estimate the model by Bayesian methods, using the Gibbs sampler.

11.3 The logit model with factor analytic measurement structure is due to Train, McFadden, and Goett (1987). Under the assumption of joint normality of the latent variables and their indicators, they estimated this model by numerically integrating the logit probability over the conditional distribution of the latent variables given the indicators, which was estimated from the factor model.

Logit models and other discrete choice models with errors in variables are discussed by Carroll, Spiegelman, Lan, Bailey, and Abbott (1984), and by Stefanski and Carroll (1985). The latter authors derived three estimators of β that are consistent under *small σ asymptotics*, which means that the measurement errors vanish asymptotically. This may not be a realistic assumption in typical economic applications, but, as discussed in section 6.6, the aim of asymptotics is to provide useful approximations and small σ asymptotics with few distributional assumptions may in some cases give better approximations than usual asymptotics with stronger assumptions. The approach of Stefanski and Carroll (1985) was extended to the broader class of generalized linear models by Stefanski and Carroll (1987) and Schafer (1987a). A general analysis, through small σ asymptotics, of the effects of measurement errors on the distributions of the observed variables was given by Chesher (1991).

The censored regression model with measurement error in the explanatory variables was studied by Weiss (1993). He developed consistent IV estimators by minimizing a censored least absolute deviations (CLAD) function. These estimators do not require a normality assumption. A CALS-type estimator for the censored regression model under normality with measurement error in the explanatory variables, where the reliability of the mismeasured regressors is known, was proposed by Wang (1998).

As discussed in section 2.5, in the usual linear regression model, measurement error on the *dependent* variable can be subsumed in the equation disturbance term without affecting the consistency of the estimators if the explanatory variables are measured without error. In the censored regression model, however, this is not the case anymore. This situation was studied by Stapleton and Young (1984). They developed several one- and two-stage nonlinear and probit least squares estimators that are consistent.

Elrod and Keane (1995) developed a multinomial probit model for panel data with a factor analysis structure on the residuals along the lines discussed in this section, and applied it to a marketing problem.

The discussion of the Berkson-probit model is based on Burr (1988). The omitted variables problem in probit models has been studied by Yatchew and Griliches (1985).

11.4 The LISCOMP model was developed in a number of papers, mainly by Bengt Muthén. Some of the key papers are Christoffersson (1975), Muthén (1978, 1979), Muthén and Christoffersson (1981), Muthén (1982, 1983, 1984), which culminated in the LISCOMP program (Muthén, 1987). Later additions are Muthén (1989c) and Muthén (1990). A discussion of the model on which the current section was based is given in Muthén and Satorra (1995). The LISCOMP program is now superseded by the M*plus* program (Muthén and Muthén, 1998).

Full maximum likelihood estimation of subsets of the LISCOMP model has been considered by Bock and Lieberman (1970), Bock and Aitkin (1981), Bock, Gibbons, and Muraki (1988), and Lee, Poon, and Bentler (1990a). The approach of these authors is, however, only feasible for very simple models with few observed variables.

Further extensions to the model and discussions of its estimation have been given by Lee, Poon, and Bentler (1989, 1990b, 1992, 1995), Poon and Lee (1992, 1999), Poon, Lee, and Tang (1997), Poon and Leung (1993), Reboussin and Liang (1998), and Tang and Bentler (1997).

LISCOMP-like models have also been implemented in other software for structural equation models, such as EQS (Bentler, 1995), LISREL (Jöreskog, 1990; Jöreskog and Sörbom, 1993), Mx (Neale et al., 1999), and MECOSA (Arminger and Küsters, 1988; Schepers, Arminger, and Küsters, 1992; Arminger et al., 1996),

General discussions about factor analysis with categorical data can be found in Bartholomew (1980) and Mislevy (1986). The consequences of estimating linear structural equation models when the indicators are categorical are discussed by Olsson (1979b), Boomsma (1983), Mooijaart (1983), and Muthén and Kaplan (1985). The conclusion is that categorical data should generally not be treated as continuous indicators, unless the number of categories is relatively large and the data are fairly symmetrically and unimodally distributed.

The correlation coefficients ρ_{ij} in Σ^* are called tetrachoric correlations if y_{in} and y_{jn} are both binary, polychoric correlations if they are both ordered categorical (so tetrachoric is a special case of polychoric), biserial correlations if one is binary and one is not limited-dependent (so $y_{jn} = y^*_{jn}$, say), and polyserial correlations if one is ordered categorical and one is not limited-dependent (again, biserial is a special case of polyserial). The tetrachoric correlation coefficient was introduced by by Pearson (1901a). Articles that discuss the estimation of these correlation coefficients and their asymptotic covariances include Divgi (1979), Olsson (1979a), Olsson, Drasgow, and Dorans (1982), Lee and Poon (1986, 1987), Poon and Lee (1987), Poon, Lee, and Bentler (1990), Jöreskog (1994), and Christoffersson and Gunsjö (1996). Evidently, the use of these correlation coefficients presumes the existence of underlying normally distributed latent response variables. A lively debate about the usefulness of this assumption can be found in Yule (1912) and Pearson and Heron (1913). Muthén and Hofacker (1988) discuss a test for this assumption, based on the restriction it imposes on three-way probabilities of the form $\Pr(y_{in} = a, y_{jn} = b, y_{kn} = c)$.

Apparently, the LISCOMP model is based on a linear model for y^*_n, and univariate deterministic transformations by which y_n is obtained from y^*_n: $y_{in} = H_i(y^*_{in}, \tau_i)$. The functions H_i are not invertible if the corresponding variables are limited-dependent, because H_i is then a step function, a censoring function, etc. If y_{in} would be continuous and H_i would be invertible, then we could write $y^*_{in} = G_i(y_{in}, \tau_i)$ with $G_i = H_i^{-1}$, and could specify a (possibly conditional) multivariate normal loglikelihood function for y^*_{in}. The loglikelihood for the observed variables is then simply this loglikelihood plus an additional term derived from the Jacobian of the transformation. The computational complexities of the model then diminish considerably. This idea was applied by Meijerink (1996). He developed a model in which the functions G_i are Box-Cox transformations or monotonic spline transformations. For the latent response variables y^*_{in}, he used essentially the same specification as in the LISCOMP model. The parameters of the structural equation model and the transformation parameters are estimated jointly by ML under the assumption that y^*_n is multivariate normally distributed conditionally on x_n. This approach stays close to the common practice in regression analysis to transform the variables before entering them in the regression model, so that, e.g., a linear regression model is specified with log(income) as the dependent variable.

11.5 The general ideas discussed in this section are primarily due to Hsiao (1989, 1992), although he mainly discussed estimation of the model using $\gamma_3(\cdot)$. Li (2000) and Hsiao and Wang (2000) discuss estimation of this model using simulation. An early study of nonlinear errors-in-variables models is Wolter and

Fuller (1982a).

Nonlinear models with errors in variables have also been studied by Dolby (1972, 1976a), and by Dolby and Lipton (1972) for replicated observations. Linssen (1977) used an orthogonal regression approach to the nonlinear functional model. Egerton and Laycock (1979) estimated the multivariate nonlinear functional model with maximum likelihood.

Amemiya (1985, 1990, 1993) developed instrumental variables estimators for general analytical functions $\mu(\cdot)$ of known form, which are consistent under small σ asymptotics. Generally, however, instrumental variables are of limited use in nonlinear models, because they do not lead to consistent estimators unless stronger assumptions are made. Related work on the nonlinear functional model is Amemiya and Fuller (1988).

Carroll, Ruppert, and Stefanski (1995) described two general algorithms for estimation of nonlinear regression functions with errors in variables and apply them mainly to generalized linear models. Their algorithms are based on extrapolations and approximations and are not generally consistent but give satisfactory results in many cases.

Levine (1985) presents a local sensitivity analysis of estimators in a nonlinear context, which inter alia generalizes the result due to Levi (1973) on the sign of the estimators of the other coefficients if one regressor is measured with error, which was discussed in section 2.4

Lewbel (1998) considered a very general nonlinear regression model that also may include latent variables, but explanatory variables and instruments must be available. The regression functions need not be kown, however, so semiparametric assumptions are sufficient for this model. He showed that many standard econometric models can be written as submodels of his model like, for example, censored regression models, models with endogenous regressors, and measurement error models. Further, he defined a general consistent asymptotically normal estimation procedure for this model. See Lewbel (1998) for the details of the estimator and the assumptions needed.

Fan and Truong (1993) gave some results for *nonparametric* regression with errors in variables. They assumed the distribution of the measurement errors known, so that the density function of ξ_n can be estimated by the deconvolution method. This estimated density can then be used to define a kernel regression function estimator. We refer to their paper for the details of the implementation and the asymptotic properties of this estimator.

Appendix A

Matrices, statistics, and calculus

We group in this appendix a number of very diverse technical results that are used scattered throughout the main text. These results pertain to matrix algebra, statistics, and calculus.

In section A.1, we give some results from matrix algebra and matrix calculus. These results involve in particular the vec operator for stacking the elements of a matrix into a vector, Kronecker products of matrices, matrix differentiation, and partitioned matrices. Section A.2 mainly contains a number of highly specific technical results and their proofs.

Because covariance matrices, which by nature are positive definite or semidefinite, play a large role in the main text, we have grouped some important properties of definite matrices in section A.3. We often need a vector that is the stacked version of a covariance matrix. Section A.4 contains results on 0-1 matrices that are convenient to handle such vectors. Some results on the normal distribution are contained in section A.5, such as the likelihood based on normality, the conditional normal distribution, and the covariance matrix of the sample covariance matrix.

Slutsky's theorem and the delta method are discussed in section A.6, and section A.7 contains the implicit function theorem and the mean value theorem.

A.1 Some results from matrix algebra

In the following rules, A, B, C, D, E, F, G denote matrices of fixed elements of appropriate order. We denote by $\operatorname{vec}(A)$ the vector obtained from the matrix A

by stacking its columns. Furthermore, if A is an $m \times n$ matrix and B is a $p \times q$ matrix, $A \otimes B$ denotes their Kronecker product, the $mp \times nq$ matrix

$$A \otimes B = \begin{bmatrix} a_{11}B & \cdots & a_{1n}B \\ \vdots & \ddots & \vdots \\ a_{m1}B & \cdots & a_{mn}B \end{bmatrix}.$$

We have the following elementary rules involving Kronecker products and vec operators:

$$\begin{aligned} (A \otimes B)(C \otimes D) &= AC \otimes BD \\ \text{tr}(A \otimes B) &= (\text{tr}\, A)(\text{tr}\, B) \\ \text{vec}(ABC) &= (C' \otimes A)\, \text{vec}\, B \\ \text{tr}(ABCD) &= (\text{vec}\, A')'(D' \otimes B)\, \text{vec}\, C, \end{aligned}$$

so for $B = I$, $D = I$,

$$\text{tr}\, AC = (\text{vec}\, A')'\, \text{vec}\, C.$$

If A is of order $m \times m$ and B is of order $n \times n$, then

$$|A \otimes B| = |A|^n \ |B|^m.$$

The expectation of random matrices

If Y is a random matrix with N rows with $\text{E}(Y) = M$ and $\text{Var}(\text{vec}\, Y) = \Sigma \otimes I_N$ (so the rows of Y are uncorrelated), then

$$\begin{aligned} \text{E}(Y'AY) &= (\text{tr}\, A)\Sigma + M'AM \\ \text{E}(YBY') &= (\text{tr}\, B\Sigma)I_N + MBM' \\ \text{E}(YC'Y) &= C\Sigma + MC'M \\ \text{E}(\text{tr}\, F'Y)(\text{tr}\, G'Y) &= \text{tr}\, F'G\Sigma + (\text{tr}\, F'M)(\text{tr}\, G'M). \end{aligned}$$

Matrix differentiation

If X is nonsingular,

$$\frac{\partial\, \text{vec}\left(X^{-1}\right)}{\partial (\text{vec}\, X)'} = \left(X^{-1}\right)' \otimes X^{-1}.$$

If X and C (constant) are symmetric, then

$$\frac{\partial\, \text{tr}\left(CX^{-1}\right)}{\partial X} = -X^{-1}CX^{-1}.$$

If X is positive definite, then

$$\frac{\partial \log |X|}{\partial X} = X^{-1}.$$

If f is a vector-valued function of the vector x and g is a vector-valued function of f, then the chain rule states that

$$\frac{\partial g}{\partial x'} = \frac{\partial g}{\partial f'} \frac{\partial f}{\partial x'}.$$

Inverses and determinants

There are two important results on the inverse and determinant of structured matrices. The first concerns the inverse of a partitioned matrix:

$$\begin{bmatrix} A & B \\ B' & C \end{bmatrix}^{-1} = \begin{bmatrix} A^{-1} & 0 \\ 0 & 0 \end{bmatrix} + \begin{bmatrix} A^{-1}B \\ -I \end{bmatrix} W^{-1} \left(B'A^{-1}, -I\right),$$

with

$$W \equiv C - B'A^{-1}B,$$

provided the various inverses exist. The matrix W is called the Schur complement of A. Under the same condition, the determinant can be written as

$$\left| \begin{bmatrix} A & B \\ B' & C \end{bmatrix} \right| = |A| \; |W|.$$

For the inverse and determinant of a sum of matrices, we have the formulas

$$(A + BCD')^{-1} = A^{-1} - A^{-1}B(C^{-1} + D'A^{-1}B)^{-1}D'A^{-1}$$
$$|A + BCD'| = |A| \; |I + CD'A^{-1}B|,$$

provided the inverses exist.

Generalized inverses

If $A \neq 0$, a generalized inverse (or g-inverse) of A is any matrix A^- such that $AA^-A = A$. If A is square nonsingular, A^- is unique, with $A^- = A^{-1}$, otherwise it is not. The Moore-Penrose inverse A^+ is a special kind of generalized inverse, satisfying $AA^+A = A$, $A^+AA^+ = A^+$, and AA^+ and A^+A symmetric, and is unique. If A is symmetric, A^+ is also symmetric, but in general A^- need not be symmetric. In the latter case, however, $A^{-\prime}$ is also a generalized inverse of A.

Theorem A.1. If $X = AYB$, where X, A, Y, and B are square matrices and A and B are nonsingular, then any generalized inverse X^- of X can be written as $X^- = B^{-1}Y^-A^{-1}$, for some generalized inverse Y^- of Y.

Proof. The proof is straightforward. Let G be a generalized inverse of X. Then, by definition,

$$
\begin{aligned}
& & XGX &= X & \\
&\text{or} & (AYB)G(AYB) &= AYB & \\
&\text{or} & Y(BGA)Y &= Y & &\text{(because } A \text{ and } B \text{ are nonsingular)}\\
&\text{or} & BGA &= Y^- & &\text{(by definition of a generalized inverse)}\\
&\text{or} & G &= B^{-1}Y^-A^{-1} & &\text{(because } A \text{ and } B \text{ are nonsingular).}
\end{aligned}
$$

□

Theorem A.2. If $A = XVY'$, where V is nonsingular and X and Y are of full column rank, then

$$
\begin{aligned}
A^+ &= Y(Y'Y)^{-1}V^{-1}(X'X)^{-1}X' \\
&= (Y')^+V^{-1}X^+ \\
&= Y(X'AY)^{-1}X'.
\end{aligned}
$$

Proof. This follows straightforwardly by checking the conditions in the definition of the Moore-Penrose inverse. □

The Frisch-Waugh theorem

The Frisch-Waugh theorem makes it possible to break down the OLS computation of a regression coefficients vector β into two steps, each giving the estimate of a subvector, β_1 and β_2, say, with $\beta = (\beta_1', \beta_2')$, corresponding with a partitioning of the regressors X, say, in $X = (X_1, X_2)$. Then,

$$y = X\beta + u = (X_1, X_2)\begin{bmatrix} \beta_1 \\ \beta_2 \end{bmatrix} + u = X_1\beta_1 + X_2\beta_2 + u.$$

Theorem A.3 (Frisch-Waugh). The OLS estimator $\hat{\beta} = (X'X)^{-1}X'y$ of β is equal to $(\hat{\beta}_1', \hat{\beta}_2')'$, with

$$\hat{\beta}_2 = (X_2'M_1X_2)^{-1}X_2'M_1y \tag{A.1a}$$

$$\hat{\beta}_1 = (X_1'X_1)^{-1}X_1'(y - X_2\hat{\beta}_2) \tag{A.1b}$$

where $M_1 \equiv I - X_1(X_1'X_1)^{-1}X_1'$ projects onto the null-space of X_1.

Proof. The result follows directly from the normal equations $X'X\hat{\beta} = X'y$. On partitioning X this can be rewritten as

$$X_1'X_1\hat{\beta}_1 + X_1'X_2\hat{\beta}_2 = X_1'y \tag{A.2a}$$

$$X_2'X_1\hat{\beta}_1 + X_2'X_2\hat{\beta}_2 = X_2'y. \tag{A.2b}$$

From (A.2a) we directly obtain (A.1b). Next, premultiply (A.1b) by X_1 to obtain $X_1\hat{\beta}_1 = (I - M_1)(y - X_2\hat{\beta}_2)$. Substituting this in (A.2b) gives

$$X_2'(I - M_1)(y - X_2\hat{\beta}_2) + X_2'X_2\hat{\beta}_2 = X_2'y.$$

After rearrangement of terms this gives (A.1a). □

A.2 Some specific results

Unless otherwise stated, the matrices in the following theorems are arbitrary provided that the products and inverses exist.

Theorem A.4. $\left(B'(A + BCB')^{-1}B\right)^{-1} = C + (B'A^{-1}B)^{-1}$.

Proof.

$$\begin{aligned} B'(A + BCB')^{-1}B &= B'A^{-1}B - B'A^{-1}B(C^{-1} + B'A^{-1}B)^{-1}B'A^{-1}B \\ &= B'A^{-1}B(C^{-1} + B'A^{-1}B)^{-1} \\ &\quad \times \left((C^{-1} + B'A^{-1}B) - B'A^{-1}B\right) \\ &= B'A^{-1}B(C^{-1} + B'A^{-1}B)^{-1}C^{-1} \\ &= \left(C(C^{-1} + B'A^{-1}B)(B'A^{-1}B)^{-1}\right)^{-1} \\ &= \left(C + (B'A^{-1}B)^{-1}\right)^{-1}. \end{aligned}$$

Inversion gives the desired result. □

Theorem A.5. If μ is a scalar with $0 \le \mu \le 1$, then

$$(A + \mu\beta\beta')^{-1} = \lambda A^{-1} + (1 - \lambda)(A + \beta\beta')^{-1}, \tag{A.3}$$

where

$$0 \le \lambda \equiv \frac{1 - \mu}{1 + \mu\beta'A\beta} \le 1. \tag{A.4}$$

Proof. The result follows from premultiplication of (A.3) by $A + \mu\beta\beta'$ and postmultiplication of (A.4) by $A + \beta\beta'$. □

Theorem A.6. Let X and Y be matrices such that (X, Y) is a square, nonsingular matrix and let V and W be nonsingular matrices. Furthermore, let $A = XVX' + YWY'$. Then A is nonsingular and $X'A^{-1}X = V^{-1}$.

Proof. To prove this, write A as

$$A = (X, Y)\begin{bmatrix} V & 0 \\ 0 & W \end{bmatrix}\begin{bmatrix} X' \\ Y' \end{bmatrix}.$$

Let the matrix G be of the same order as X, and let the matrix H be of the same order as Y, such that

$$(X, Y)^{-1} = \begin{bmatrix} G' \\ H' \end{bmatrix}.$$

Thus, $G'X = I$ and $H'X = 0$, and

$$\begin{aligned} A^{-1} &= \begin{bmatrix} X' \\ Y' \end{bmatrix}^{-1}\begin{bmatrix} V^{-1} & 0 \\ 0 & W^{-1} \end{bmatrix}(X, Y)^{-1} \\ &= (G, H)\begin{bmatrix} V^{-1} & 0 \\ 0 & W^{-1} \end{bmatrix}\begin{bmatrix} G' \\ H' \end{bmatrix}. \end{aligned}$$

Hence,

$$X'A^{-1}X = (I, 0)\begin{bmatrix} V^{-1} & 0 \\ 0 & W^{-1} \end{bmatrix}\begin{bmatrix} I \\ 0 \end{bmatrix} = V^{-1}.$$

Note that it is not necessary that $X'Y = 0$. □

Theorem A.7. Let W be a $p \times p$ symmetric nonsingular matrix, let G be a $p \times m$ matrix of full column rank $m \leq p$, and let H be a $p \times (p - m)$ natrix of full column rank such that $H'G = 0$. Then

$$W - WG(G'WG)^{-1}G'W = H(H'W^{-1}H)^{-1}H'. \tag{A.5}$$

Proof. Postmultiply both sides of (A.5) with the matrix $F \equiv (G, W^{-1}H)$. This gives for both the result $(0, H)$. Now, note that F is nonsingular with inverse

$$F^{-1} = \begin{bmatrix} (G'WG)^{-1}G'W \\ (H'W^{-1}H)^{-1}H' \end{bmatrix}.$$

The inverses in this equation exist because W is nonsingular and H and G are of full column rank by assumption. Given that both matrices, when postmultiplied by the same nonsingular matrix F, give the same result, postmultiplying again by F^{-1} shows that the original matrices are equivalent. □

Theorem A.8. Let m be a nonnegative integer, let μ_j, $j = 1, \ldots, 2^m$, be scalars satisfying $\mu_j \geq 0$ and $\sum_{j=1}^{2^m} \mu_j = 1$, let β_l, $l = 1, \ldots, m$ be arbitrary vectors, and let φ_l, $l = 1, \ldots, m$ be arbitrary scalars. Now, let A_j, $j = 1, \ldots, 2^m$, be symmetric nonsingular matrices such that $A_{i+2^k} = A_i + \varphi_{k+1}\beta_{k+1}\beta_{k+1}'$, for all integers i and k such that $0 \leq k \leq m-1$ and $1 \leq i \leq 2^k$. Then there exist scalars λ_j, $j = 1, \ldots, 2^m$, satisfying $\lambda_j \geq 0$ and $\sum_{j=1}^{2^m} \lambda_j = 1$, such that

$$\left[\sum_{j=1}^{2^m} \mu_j A_j\right]^{-1} = \sum_{j=1}^{2^m} \lambda_j A_j^{-1}. \tag{A.6}$$

Proof. The proof is by induction. Assume that (A.6) holds for a certain m. Then we show that it also holds for $m+1$. First, let $\tau_{jm} \equiv \mu_j + \mu_{j+2^m}$, and observe that

$$\begin{aligned}\sum_{j=1}^{2^{m+1}} \mu_j A_j &= \sum_{j=1}^{2^m} \mu_j A_j + \sum_{j=1}^{2^m} \mu_{j+2^m} A_{j+2^m} \\ &= \sum_{j=1}^{2^m} \tau_{jm} A_j + \left[\sum_{j=1}^{2^m} \mu_{j+2^m}\right] \varphi_{m+1}\beta_{m+1}\beta_{m+1}'.\end{aligned}$$

Hence, using (A.3) and (A.4), we find that

$$\begin{aligned}\left[\sum_{j=1}^{2^{m+1}} \mu_j A_j\right]^{-1} &= \lambda \left[\sum_{j=1}^{2^m} \tau_{jm} A_j\right]^{-1} \\ &\quad + (1-\lambda)\left[\sum_{j=1}^{2^m} \tau_{jm}(A_j + \varphi_{m+1}\beta_{m+1}\beta_{m+1}')\right]^{-1} \\ &= \lambda \left[\sum_{j=1}^{2^m} \tau_{jm} A_j\right]^{-1} + (1-\lambda)\left[\sum_{j=1}^{2^m} \tau_{jm} A_{j+2^m}\right]^{-1},\end{aligned} \tag{A.7}$$

with $0 \leq \lambda \leq 1$. Assuming that (A.6) holds for m, (A.7) implies that it also holds for $m+1$. Furthermore, (A.6) trivially holds for $m = 0$. □

A.3 Definite matrices

The notation $A \geq 0$ indicates that the matrix A is positive semidefinite, i.e., A is symmetric and $x'Ax \geq 0$ for all vectors x of appropriate order. If $A \geq 0$, then $B'AB \geq 0$, and $B'AB = 0$ is equivalent to $AB = 0$, for any B of an appropriate number of rows. The notation $A > 0$ indicates that A is positive definite, i.e., A is symmetric and $x'Ax > 0$ for all vectors $x \neq 0$ of appropriate order. We occasionally use the notation $A \geq B$ to indicate that $A - B \geq 0$. The ordering '$\geq$' is a partial ordering on the set of all symmetric matrices, and is also known as the Löwner ordering, after Löwner (1934).

Theorem A.9. Let the matrix W be partitioned as

$$W = \begin{bmatrix} A & B' \\ B & C \end{bmatrix}. \tag{A.8}$$

Then $W \geq 0$ is equivalent to (i) $C \geq 0$, (ii) $B = CC^{-}B$, and (iii) $A \geq B'C^{-}B$, for any choice of g-inverse.

Proof. (i) is trivial. For (ii), let $P' = (0, I - CC^{-})$, then $P'WP = 0$. Hence, $P'W = 0$, or $(I - CC^{-})B = 0$. As to (iii), let $R' \equiv (I, -(C^{-}B)')$, then by virtue of (ii)

$$0 \leq R'WR = (I, -(C^{-}B)') \begin{bmatrix} A - B'C^{-}B \\ 0 \end{bmatrix} = A - B'C^{-}B.$$

The converse follows from

$$W = \begin{bmatrix} I & B'C^{-} \\ 0 & I \end{bmatrix} \begin{bmatrix} A - B'C^{-}B & 0 \\ 0 & C \end{bmatrix} \begin{bmatrix} I & 0 \\ C^{-\prime}B & I \end{bmatrix} \geq 0, \tag{A.9}$$

using the fact that C is symmetric and hence $C^{-\prime}$ is a generalized inverse of C if C^{-} is a generalized inverse of C. □

Theorem A.10. If A and C are symmetric, then $0 \leq A \leq C$ is equivalent to $C \geq 0$, $A = CC^{-}A$ and $A \geq AC^{-}A \geq 0$.

Proof. Apply theorem A.9 to both

$$W_1 \equiv \begin{bmatrix} A & A \\ A & C \end{bmatrix} \tag{A.10}$$

and

$$W_2 \equiv \begin{bmatrix} C & A \\ A & A \end{bmatrix} = \begin{bmatrix} 0 & I \\ I & 0 \end{bmatrix} \begin{bmatrix} A & A \\ A & C \end{bmatrix} \begin{bmatrix} 0 & I \\ I & 0 \end{bmatrix}. \tag{A.11}$$

Hence, $W_1 \geq 0$ is equivalent to $W_2 \geq 0$. Now, $W_1 \geq 0$ is equivalent to $C \geq 0$, $A = CC^- A$, and $A \geq AC^- A$; and $W_2 \geq 0$ is equivalent to $A \geq 0$, $A = AA^- A$, and $C \geq AA^- A = A$. □

Theorems A.9 and A.10 simplify straightforwardly if C is positive definite.

Theorem A.11. Let W again be a matrix partitioned as

$$W = \begin{bmatrix} A & B' \\ B & C \end{bmatrix}.$$

If $C > 0$, then $W \geq 0$ is equivalent to $A \geq B'C^{-1}B$.

Theorem A.12. If A and C are symmetric, then $0 < A \leq C$ is equivalent to $A^{-1} \geq C^{-1} > 0$.

Theorem A.13. If C is a symmetric matrix and x is a vector, then $xx' \leq C$ is equivalent to $CC^- x = x$, $x'C^- x \leq 1$ and $C \geq 0$.

Proof. Apply theorem A.10 with $A = xx'$, and note that $xx' = CC^- xx'$ is equivalent to $x = CC^- x$ and $xx' \geq xx'C^- xx'$ is equivalent to $1 \geq x'C^- x$. □

Theorem A.14. Let A and B be matrices and λ a scalar such that $0 \leq \lambda A \leq B$ and let the vector δ be such that $(B - \lambda A)\delta = 0$. Then λ is the smallest eigenvalue of B in the metric of A.

Proof. Assume that μ is an eigenvalue of B in the metric of A such that $0 \leq \mu \leq \lambda$. Let ζ be the corresponding eigenvector. Then

$$0 = \zeta'(B - \mu A)\zeta = \zeta'(B - \lambda A)\zeta + (\lambda - \mu)\zeta' A \zeta.$$

The last two terms are both nonnegative and hence must be zero. So ζ is an eigenvector corresponding not only with μ but also with λ. Hence $\mu = \lambda$, and this is therefore the smallest eigenvalue. Furthermore, if the null-space of $B - \lambda A$ has dimension 1, then ζ and δ are evidently equal, except for a possible proportionality constant. □

Theorem A.15. Let V be a symmetric positive definite matrix, let W be a symmetric positive semidefinite matrix, and let X be a matrix of full column rank, and let $A = XVX' + W$ be nonsingular. Then $X'A^{-1}X \leq V^{-1}$.

Proof. Let $G \equiv (X'A^{-1}X)V(X'A^{-1}X)$ and note that G is symmetric and positive definite. Then

$$\begin{aligned} G &= X'A^{-1}(A - W)A^{-1}X \\ &= X'A^{-1}X - X'A^{-1}WA^{-1}X \\ &\leq X'A^{-1}X \\ &= (X'A^{-1}X)(X'A^{-1}X)^{-1}(X'A^{-1}X). \end{aligned}$$

Apparently, $0 < (X'A^{-1}X)V(X'A^{-1}X) \leq (X'A^{-1}X)(X'A^{-1}X)^{-1}(X'A^{-1}X)$, which is equivalent to $0 < V \leq (X'A^{-1}X)^{-1}$, which in its turn is equivalent to $0 < X'A^{-1}X \leq V^{-1}$. □

Theorem A.16. Let A and C be two symmetric positive definite $m \times m$ matrices with $C \geq A$. Then $|C| \geq |A|$ with equality if and only if $C = A$.

Proof. Define $B \equiv C - A \geq 0$. Then $C = A + B = A^{1/2}(I_m + E)A^{1/2}$, where $A^{1/2}$ is a symmetric positive definite matrix such that $A^{1/2}A^{1/2} = A$, and $E = A^{-1/2}BA^{-1/2}$. Consequently, $|C| = |A|\,|I_m + E|$. Let λ_j, $j = 1, \ldots, m$, denote the eigenvalues of E. Clearly, $E \geq 0$ and, therefore, $\lambda_j \geq 0$ for all j. Furthermore,

$$|C| = |A|\,|I_m + E| = |A| \prod_{j=1}^{m}(1 + \lambda_j) \geq |A|,$$

with equality if and only if all the λ_j are zero, i.e., if and only if $B = 0$. □

In the following, diag(a) is the diagonal matrix with the elements of the vector a on its diagonal.

Theorem A.17. Let W be a symmetric $m \times m$ matrix with typical element w_{ij}, let ι_m be an m-vector of ones, and let Λ be a diagonal $m \times m$ matrix with i-th diagonal element λ_i. (i) If $w_{ij} > 0$ for all $i \neq j$, then $\text{diag}(\Lambda W \Lambda \iota_m) \geq \Lambda W \Lambda$ is equivalent to $\lambda_i \lambda_j \geq 0$ for all i and j. (ii) Conversely, if $w_{ij} < 0$ for all $i \neq j$, then $\text{diag}(\Lambda W \Lambda \iota_m) \geq \Lambda W \Lambda$ implies that either all λ_i are zero or $\lambda_i \lambda_j < 0$ for some i and j.

Proof. Let x be an m-vector. Then

$$\begin{aligned} x'\big(\text{diag}(\Lambda W \Lambda \iota_m) - \Lambda W \Lambda\big)x &= \sum_{i=1}^{m}\sum_{j=1}^{m} w_{ij}\lambda_i\lambda_j(x_i^2 - x_i x_j) \\ &= \tfrac{1}{2}\sum_{i=1}^{m}\sum_{j=1}^{m} w_{ij}\lambda_i\lambda_j(x_i - x_j)^2. \qquad \text{(A.12)} \end{aligned}$$

(i) If $\lambda_i\lambda_j \geq 0$ for all $i \neq j$, then $w_{ij}\lambda_i\lambda_j(x_i - x_j)^2 \geq 0$ for all i and j. Hence, (A.12) is nonnegative for all vectors x and, therefore, $\text{diag}(\Lambda W \Lambda \iota_m) \geq \Lambda W \Lambda$. Conversely, assume that $\lambda_i\lambda_j < 0$ for some (i, j). Choose $x_i = \text{sign}(\lambda_i)$. Then, (A.12) is negative and it therefore does not hold that $\text{diag}(\Lambda W \Lambda \iota_m) \geq \Lambda W \Lambda$.

(ii) Because all w_{ij} $(i \neq j)$ are now negative, it follows from (A.12) that, if $\lambda_i\lambda_j \geq 0$ for all $i \neq j$, then $\text{diag}(\Lambda W \Lambda \iota_m) \leq \Lambda W \Lambda$. Thus, $\text{diag}(\Lambda W \Lambda \iota_m) \geq \Lambda W \Lambda$ only holds if either all λ_i are zero or $\lambda_i\lambda_j < 0$ for some i and j. □

Theorem A.18. Let $A > 0$ with off-diagonal elements negative. Then all elements of A^{-1} are positive.

Proof. Without loss of generality, we may assume that the diagonal elements of A are 1. Then the off-diagonal elements of $B \equiv I - A$ are positive and the diagonal elements of B are zero. Consequently, all elements of B^i are positive for $i \geq 2$. Because $B < I$, its largest eigenvalue $\lambda_{\max}$ has $\lambda_{\max} < 1$. Furthermore, B is indefinite, because all its diagonal elements are zero, which implies that $\text{tr}(B) = 0$, and thus the sum of the eigenvalues of B is zero. But B is nonzero, so it has at least one nonzero eigenvalue and, consequently, at least one positive and at least one negative eigenvalue.

Hence, $\lambda_{\max} > 0$. Let λ_* be such that $\lambda_{\max} < \lambda_* < 1$. Then $B < \lambda_* I$, and the matrices

$$\bar{B}_n \equiv \sum_{i=0}^{n} B^i < \sum_{i=0}^{n} \lambda_*^i I = \frac{1 - \lambda_*^{n+1}}{1 - \lambda_*} I$$

are bounded from above. They are also bounded from below, because all their elements are positive. Hence, $A^{-1} = \sum_{i=0}^{\infty} B^i$ converges and has positive elements. □

The Cauchy-Schwarz inequality

When comparing the covariance matrices of estimators, the matrix version of the Cauchy-Schwarz inequality is often used. We give a derivation.

Let Z be a matrix of full column rank. Then $I - Z(Z'Z)^{-1}Z' \geq 0$, because this is an idempotent matrix with eigenvalues 0 or 1. Let B be a positive definite matrix and let X be a matrix of full rank. Substitution of $B^{-1/2}X$ for Z yields

$$I \geq B^{-1/2}X(X'B^{-1}X)^{-1}X'B^{-1/2}.$$

Next, let A be a symmetric matrix such that $X'AX$ is nonsingular, and premultiply both sides of this inequality by $(X'AX)^{-1}X'AB^{1/2}$ and postmultiply both sides by its transpose, to obtain the matrix version of the Cauchy-Schwarz inequality:

$$(X'AX)^{-1}X'ABAX(X'AX)^{-1} \geq (X'B^{-1}X)^{-1}. \tag{A.13}$$

Given the derivation, B must be a symmetric positive definite matrix. If we let $A = B^{-1}$, then (A.13) becomes an equality. An alternative form is obtained by taking inverses in (A.13):

$$X'AX(X'ABAX)^{-1}X'AX \leq X'B^{-1}X. \tag{A.14}$$

An alternative proof of (A.13) is obtained as follows. Write the left-hand side of (A.13) as $V(A)$ to bring out the dependence on A. The right-hand side is then $V(B^{-1})$. Let $L \equiv (X'AX)^{-1}X'A - (X'B^{-1}X)^{-1}X'B^{-1}$. Then

$$V(A) - V(B^{-1}) = LBL',$$

as can be easily verified. This establishes $V(A) \geq V(B^{-1})$, because $B > 0$ and hence $LBL' \geq 0$.

Let us now show the equivalence of this form of the Cauchy-Schwarz inequality to the well-known form for vectors,

$$(p'q)^2 \leq (p'p)(q'q), \tag{A.15}$$

where p and q are vectors of equal dimensions.

First, start from (A.13) for all X, A, and B as above, and let p and q be arbitrary but given. If $p'q = 0$, (A.15) holds trivially. Therefore, assume that $p'q \neq 0$. Then, we can choose $X = p$ and choose A symmetric such that $q = Ap$. Such an A always exists. Furthermore, if we choose $B = I$, then (A.13) reduces to

$$(p'q)^{-1}(q'q)(p'q)^{-1} \geq (p'p)^{-1}.$$

Multiplying both sides with the positive quantity $(p'p)(p'q)^2$ gives (A.15).

Second, start from (A.15) for all p and q and let X, A, and B be as above, and let y be an arbitrary nonzero vector. Choose

$$p = B^{1/2}AX(X'AX)^{-1}y$$
$$q = B^{-1/2}X(X'B^{-1}X)^{-1}y,$$

then (A.15) implies that

$$\left(y'(X'B^{-1}X)^{-1}y\right)^2 \leq y'(X'B^{-1}X)^{-1}y \cdot y'(X'AX)^{-1}X'ABAX(X'AX)^{-1}y$$

and by dividing both sides by the positive quantity $y'(X'B^{-1}X)^{-1}y$ and noting that y is arbitrary, (A.13) follows.

A.4 0–1 matrices

A permutation matrix is a square matrix with a single unit element in each row and each column, the other elements being zero. If x is a k-vector and P $(k \times k)$ is some permutation matrix, then Px is the k-vector with elements of x permuted in the same way as the rows of I_k were permuted to obtain P. Some properties of P are $P'P = PP' = I_k$, $P' = P^{-1}$, and P^r is also a permutation matrix.

The commutation matrix

A particular type of permutation matrix with many applications in statistics is the commutation matrix. An implicit or operational definition of the commutation matrix $P_{n,m}$ of order $mn \times mn$ is $P_{n,m} \operatorname{vec} A = \operatorname{vec}(A')$ for any $m \times n$ matrix A. So $P_{n,m}$ changes the running order of a vector of double-indexed variables.

An explicit definition of $P_{n,m}$ is as follows. It consists of an array of $m \times n$ blocks each of order $n \times m$. The (i, j)-th block has a unit element in the (j, i)-th position and zeros elsewhere. Then

$$P_{n,m} \equiv \sum_{i=1}^{m} \sum_{j=1}^{n} e_i^m (e_j^n)' \otimes e_j^n (e_i^m)',$$

where e_i^m is the i-th unit vector of order m. Some useful properties are

$$\begin{aligned} P'_{n,m} &= P_{m,n}, \\ P_{n,m} P_{m,n} &= I_{mn}, \\ P_{n,1} &= P_{1,n} = I_n, \\ P_{m,p}(A \otimes B) P_{q,n} &= B \otimes A, \\ P_{m,p}(A \otimes B) &= (B \otimes A) P_{n,q}, \end{aligned}$$

with A of order $m \times n$ and B of order $p \times q$.

The symmetrization matrix

The symmetrization matrix of order $m^2 \times m^2$ is defined as

$$Q_m \equiv \tfrac{1}{2}(I_{m^2} + P_{m,m}). \tag{A.16}$$

We have the following properties of Q_m:

$$\begin{aligned} Q'_m &= Q_m \\ Q_m^2 &= Q_m \end{aligned}$$

$$\mathrm{rank}(Q_m) = \mathrm{tr}(Q_m) = \tfrac{1}{2}m(m+1)$$
$$Q_m \,\mathrm{vec}\, F = \tfrac{1}{2}\,\mathrm{vec}(F + F')$$

for any $m \times m$ matrix F. When M is a symmetric $m \times m$ matrix, then

$$Q_m \,\mathrm{vec}\, M = \mathrm{vec}\, M$$
$$(M \otimes M)Q_m = Q_m(M \otimes M) = Q_m(M \otimes M)Q_m.$$

When M is symmetric and nonsingular, then

$$\frac{\partial \,\mathrm{vec}\, M^{-1}}{\partial (\mathrm{vec}\, M)'} = -(M^{-1} \otimes M^{-1})Q_m.$$

If $A = Q_m B = B Q_m$ and B is nonsingular, then $A^+ = Q_m B^{-1}$.

The duplication matrix

Let μ be the vector of dimension $m(m+1)/2$ obtained from the symmetric matrix M by ordering its distinct elements in the order $(1, 1), (2, 1), \ldots, (m, 1), (2, 2), (3, 2), \ldots, (m, 2), \ldots, (m, m-1), (m, m)$. Clearly, the vector $\mathrm{vec}(M)$ of dimension m^2 contains the same elements as μ, but the off-diagonal elements are duplicated, i.e., they are collected twice in $\mathrm{vec}(M)$ and only once in μ. Hence, there is a unique $m^2 \times m(m+1)/2$ matrix D_m such that

$$\mathrm{vec}(M) = D_m \mu.$$

This matrix is called the duplication matrix. Let $i \geq j$, $p = (j-1)m + i$, $q = (i-1)m + j$, and $r = (j-1)(2m-j)/2 + i$. Then, the elements of the duplication matrix are $(D_m)_{pr} = (D_m)_{qr} = 1$, and all elements with indices that are not related in the way that p, q, and r are, are zero. Straightforward matrix multiplication shows that $D_m' D_m$ is a diagonal $m(m+1)/2 \times m(m+1)/2$ matrix with diagonal elements $(D_m' D_m)_{rr} = 1$ if $i = j$ and $(D_m' D_m)_{rr} = 2$ if $i > j$. Hence, $D_m' D_m$ is a nonsingular matrix, which implies that D_m is of full column rank and the Moore-Penrose inverse of D_m is

$$D_m^+ = (D_m' D_m)^{-1} D_m'.$$

Consequently,

$$D_m^+ \,\mathrm{vec}(M) = (D_m' D_m)^{-1} D_m' D_m \mu = \mu.$$

The vector of distinct or nonduplicated elements of a symmetric matrix can be obtained by premultiplying its vec by D_m^+.

Let v be an arbitrary vector of dimension $m(m+1)/2$. Then, $D_m v$ is obviously the vec of a symmetric matrix, and hence,

$$Q_m D_m v = D_m v.$$

If we let $v_1, \ldots, v_{m(m+1)/2}$ be the columns of $I_{m(m+1)/2}$, it follows that

$$Q_m D_m = D_m \qquad \text{and, consequently,} \qquad Q_m N_m = N_m,$$

where $N_m \equiv D_m D_m^+$. If A is an arbitrary $m \times m$ matrix, straightforward matrix multiplication shows that

$$N_m \operatorname{vec}(A) = (\operatorname{vec}(A) + \operatorname{vec}(A'))/2 = Q_m \operatorname{vec}(A).$$

Now, let $A_1, \ldots, A_{m^2}$ be the matrices $e_i e_j'$, where e_i and e_j are columns of I_m. Then, $\operatorname{vec}(A_1), \ldots, \operatorname{vec}(A_{m^2})$ are the columns of I_{m^2} and thus

$$N_m = N_m \left(\operatorname{vec}(A_1), \ldots, \operatorname{vec}(A_{m^2})\right) = Q_m \left(\operatorname{vec}(A_1), \ldots, \operatorname{vec}(A_{m^2})\right) = Q_m,$$

or

$$Q_m = D_m D_m^+.$$

This also implies immediately that $D_m^+ Q_m = D_m^+$, which will be used a few times in the main text.

The diagonalization matrix

If Δ is an $m \times m$ diagonal matrix, we may collect its diagonal elements in the m-vector δ. Similar to the duplication matrix, we now have a unique matrix H_m such that

$$\operatorname{vec}(\Delta) = H_m \delta.$$

The matrix H_m may be called the diagonalization matrix. A constructive definition is

$$H_m \equiv \sum_{i=1}^{m} e_i \otimes e_i e_i',$$

where e_i is the i-th unit vector of order m. It follows that the elements of the diagonalization matrix are given by $(H_m)_{(i-1)m+i,\, i} = 1$, and all other elements are zero. Let a be an arbitrary m-vector, let $\operatorname{diag}(a)$ be the diagonal matrix with the elements of a on its diagonal, and let A be an arbitrary $m \times m$ matrix with the elements of a on its diagonal. Then, some useful properties of the diagonalization matrix, which are straightforward to check, are as follows:

$$\begin{aligned} H_m' H_m &= I_m \\ P_{m,m} H_m &= H_m \\ Q_m H_m &= H_m \\ H_m' \operatorname{vec}(A) &= a \\ H_m'(a \otimes I_m) &= \operatorname{diag}(a) \\ H_m'(X \otimes Y) H_n &= X * Y, \end{aligned}$$

where X and Y are $m \times n$ matrices and $X * Y = (X_{ij} Y_{ij})$ is their Hadamard or elementwise product.

A.5 On the normal distribution

The loglikelihood

Let the random vector y of order k be normally distributed according to

$$y \sim \mathcal{N}_k(\mu, \Sigma). \tag{A.17}$$

Then $\mathrm{E}(y) = \mu$ and $\mathrm{Var}(y) = \Sigma$. If A is an $m \times k$ nonrandom matrix, then

$$Ay \sim \mathcal{N}_m(A\mu, A\Sigma A').$$

If Σ is of full rank, the density of y is given by

$$f(y) = (2\pi)^{-k/2} |\Sigma|^{-1/2} \exp\bigl(-\tfrac{1}{2}(y - \mu)'\Sigma^{-1}(y - \mu)\bigr).$$

Let $y_1, \ldots, y_N$ be a random sample from the distribution of y, collected in the matrix Y of order $N \times k$. Thus, y_n' is the n-th row of Y. Let M_ι denote the centering matrix of order $N \times N$ that transforms a vector with N elements into deviations from its mean. Then, $M_\iota = I_N - \iota_N \iota_N'/N$ with ι_N a vector of ones of order N. The matrix M_ι is idempotent of rank $N - 1$. Let K be any matrix of order $N \times (N - 1)$ such that $M_\iota = KK'$ and $K'K = I_{N-1}$. Then, the sample covariance matrix is

$$\begin{aligned} S &\equiv \frac{1}{N-1} \sum_{n=1}^{N} (y_n - \bar{y})(y_n - \bar{y})' \qquad \text{(A.18)} \\ &= \frac{1}{N-1} (M_\iota Y)'(M_\iota Y) \end{aligned}$$

$$= \frac{1}{N-1} Y' M_\iota Y$$
$$= \frac{1}{N-1} (K'Y)'(K'Y),$$

of order $k \times k$. Because

$$\text{vec}\, Y \sim \mathcal{N}_{Nk}(\mu \otimes \iota_N, \Sigma \otimes I_N),$$

the distribution of $K'Y$ is given by

$$\begin{aligned} \text{vec}(K'Y) &= (I_k \otimes K')\, \text{vec}\, Y \\ &\sim \mathcal{N}_{(N-1)k}(0, \Sigma \otimes I_{N-1}). \end{aligned}$$

From

$$\begin{aligned} (N-1)\, \text{tr}\big(\Sigma^{-1} S\big) &= \text{tr}\big(Y' K K' Y \Sigma^{-1}\big) \\ &= (\text{vec}\, K'Y)'\big(\Sigma^{-1} \otimes I_{N-1}\big)(\text{vec}\, K'Y), \end{aligned}$$

we obtain the density of vec $K'Y$ as

$$f(\text{vec}\, K'Y) = (2\pi)^{-(N-1)k/2} |\Sigma|^{-(N-1)/2} \exp\left(-\frac{N-1}{2}\, \text{tr}\big(\Sigma^{-1} S\big)\right).$$

When Σ is a function of a parameter vector θ, say, this density is the likelihood when considered as a function of θ. Hence, the loglikelihood is, omitting a (negative) multiplicative and additive constant, given by

$$L = \log|\Sigma| + \text{tr}\big(\Sigma^{-1} S\big). \tag{A.19}$$

When it is known that $\mu = 0$, S is defined slightly differently,

$$S \equiv \frac{1}{N} \sum_{n=1}^{N} y_n y_n' = \frac{1}{N} Y'Y.$$

The loglikelihood then takes on the same form (A.19), as is easily seen by an obvious adaptation of the derivation. When μ and Σ both depend on the same parameter vector θ, a slight adaptation of the proof shows that

$$L = \log|\Sigma| + \frac{N-1}{N}\, \text{tr}\big(\Sigma^{-1} S\big) + (\bar{y} - \mu)'\Sigma^{-1}(\bar{y} - \mu),$$

with S as in (A.18). Of course, the effect of the factor $(N-1)/N$ is negligible in large samples and therefore, this factor may be omitted. Alternatively, S could be redefined as

$$S \equiv \frac{1}{N} Y' M_\iota Y,$$

which is the unrestricted maximum likelihood estimator, which is biased. With S redefined in this way, the factor $(N-1)/N$ is removed.

Finally, let the mean of the y_n be a function of a vector x_n of exogenous variables and a vector β of parameters, $\mu_n = \mu(x_n, \beta)$. Let M be the $N \times k$ matrix with these means as elements. Assumed that the covariance matrix is the same for all observations. Then, the loglikelihood is

$$L = \log|\Sigma| + \operatorname{tr}\Big(\Sigma^{-1}\frac{1}{N}(Y-M)'(Y-M)\Big),$$

which reduces to previous cases if $M = \iota_N\mu'$ or $M = 0$. Of course, the leading example of this is (multivariate) linear regression, with $\mu_n = B'x_n$ and $\beta = \operatorname{vec} B$, where B is the $k \times g$ matrix of regression coefficients. The loglikelihood is then

$$L = \log|\Sigma| + \operatorname{tr}\Big(\Sigma^{-1}\frac{1}{N}(Y-XB)'(Y-XB)\Big),$$

where X is the $N \times g$ matrix with the values of the exogenous variables.

Repeated conditioning

The next topic concerns the evaluation of the expectation of fourth-order polynomial functions of normally distributed matrices. The method of repeated conditioning is useful here. Let Y be a random normal matrix. Let F be a fourth-degree polynomial in Y. We want to find $\mathrm{E}(F)$. The following method is then useful. Label the four Y's in F in some order as Y_1, Y_2, Y_3, and Y_4. Then, we can write

$$\mathrm{E}(F) = (\mathrm{E}_{12}\,\mathrm{E}_{34} + \mathrm{E}_{13}\,\mathrm{E}_{24} + \mathrm{E}_{14}\,\mathrm{E}_{23})(F),$$

where, e.g., $\mathrm{E}_{12}\,\mathrm{E}_{34}$ indicates the operator that first takes the expectation with respect to Y_3 and Y_4, taking Y_1 and Y_2 fixed, and next takes the expectation of the result with respect to Y_1 and Y_2. The method extends to expectations involving matrix functions in Y of any even power. For odd powers of Y, we note that their expectations are zero if $\mathrm{E}(Y) = 0$, otherwise the adaptation is straightforward.

Variance of the sample variance

One application of the method of repeated conditioning is when dealing with the variance of the sample covariance matrix in the context of the normal distribution. Let the observations Y, the centering matrix M_ι, and the sample covariance matrix $S = Y'M_\iota Y/(N-1)$ be as above. Because S depends on Y only through

$M_\iota Y$, we may freely take $\mathrm{E}(Y) = 0$. We use the following auxiliary results. Let F and G be fixed matrices, then

$$\begin{aligned}
\mathrm{E}(\operatorname{vec} F'Y)(\operatorname{vec} G'Y)' &= \mathrm{E}(I_k \otimes F')(\operatorname{vec} Y)(\operatorname{vec} Y)'(I_k \otimes G) \\
&= (I_k \otimes F')(\Sigma \otimes I_N)(I_k \otimes G) \\
&= \Sigma \otimes F'G \\
\mathrm{E}(\operatorname{vec} Y'F)(\operatorname{vec} G'Y)' &= P_{k,k}\, \mathrm{E}(\operatorname{vec} F'Y)(\operatorname{vec} G'Y)' \\
&= P_{k,k}(\Sigma \otimes F'G).
\end{aligned}$$

On letting $V \equiv (N-1)^2 \operatorname{Var}(\operatorname{vec} S)$, we find

$$\begin{aligned}
V &= \mathrm{E}(\operatorname{vec} YM_\iota Y)(\operatorname{vec} YM_\iota Y)' - (\mathrm{E} \operatorname{vec} YM_\iota Y)(\mathrm{E} \operatorname{vec} YM_\iota Y)' \\
&= \left(\mathrm{E}_{12}\,\mathrm{E}_{34} + \mathrm{E}_{13}\,\mathrm{E}_{24} + \mathrm{E}_{14}\,\mathrm{E}_{23}\right)\left(\operatorname{vec} Y_1'M_\iota Y_2\right)\left(\operatorname{vec} Y_3'M_\iota Y_4\right)' \\
&\qquad - \left(\mathrm{E}_{12} \operatorname{vec} Y_1'M_\iota Y_2\right)\left(\mathrm{E}_{34} \operatorname{vec} Y_3'M_\iota Y_4\right)' \\
&= \left(\mathrm{E}_{13}\,\mathrm{E}_{24} + \mathrm{E}_{14}\,\mathrm{E}_{23}\right)\left(\operatorname{vec} Y_1'M_\iota Y_2\right)\left(\operatorname{vec} Y_3'M_\iota Y_4\right)' \\
&= \mathrm{E}_{13}(\Sigma \otimes Y_1'M_\iota Y_3) + \mathrm{E}_{14}(\Sigma \otimes Y_1'M_\iota Y_4)P_{k,k}.
\end{aligned}$$

Hence, it follows that

$$\operatorname{Var}(\operatorname{vec} S) = \frac{1}{(N-1)^2} V = \frac{2}{N-1} Q_k(\Sigma \otimes \Sigma). \tag{A.20}$$

The conditional normal distribution

Let y be as in (A.17), and let it be partitioned as $(y_1', y_2')'$ of order k_1 and k_2, respectively, with

$$\begin{bmatrix} y_1 \\ y_2 \end{bmatrix} \sim \mathcal{N}_k\left(\begin{bmatrix} \mu_1 \\ \mu_2 \end{bmatrix}, \begin{bmatrix} \Sigma_{11} & \Sigma_{12} \\ \Sigma_{21} & \Sigma_{22} \end{bmatrix}\right).$$

Assume that Σ_{11} is of full rank. Let

$$R \equiv \begin{bmatrix} I_{k_1} & 0 \\ -\Sigma_{21}\Sigma_{11}^{-1} & I_{k_2} \end{bmatrix},$$

then

$$Ry = \begin{bmatrix} y_1 \\ y_2 - \Sigma_{21}\Sigma_{11}^{-1} y_1 \end{bmatrix}$$

$$R\mu = \begin{bmatrix} \mu_1 \\ \mu_2 - \Sigma_{21}\Sigma_{11}^{-1}\mu_1 \end{bmatrix}$$

$$R\Sigma R' = \begin{bmatrix} \Sigma_{11} & 0 \\ 0 & \Sigma_{22.1} \end{bmatrix},$$

with $\Sigma_{22.1} \equiv \Sigma_{22} - \Sigma_{21}\Sigma_{11}^{-1}\Sigma_{12}$. So y_1 and $y_2 - \Sigma_{21}\Sigma_{11}^{-1}y_1$ are uncorrelated and because both are normal, this means that they are also independent. If $\mathcal{L}(\cdot)$ denotes the distribution of a random variable, then

$$\begin{aligned} \mathcal{L}\big(y_2 - \Sigma_{21}\Sigma_{11}^{-1}y_1 \mid y_1\big) &= \mathcal{L}\big(y_2 - \Sigma_{21}\Sigma_{11}^{-1}y_1\big) \\ &= \mathcal{N}_{k_2}\big(\mu_2 - \Sigma_{21}\Sigma_{11}^{-1}\mu_1, \Sigma_{22.1}\big). \end{aligned}$$

Hence, on shifting the mean by $\Sigma_{21}\Sigma_{11}^{-1}y_1$,

$$\mathcal{L}\big(y_2 \mid y_1\big) = \mathcal{N}_{k_2}\big(\mu_2 + \Sigma_{21}\Sigma_{11}^{-1}(y_1 - \mu_1), \Sigma_{22.1}\big).$$

This gives in particular the mean and the variance of the conditional normal distribution.

The expectation of an inverse Wishart matrix

For the case that the rows $x_1', \ldots, x_N'$ of X are i.i.d. $\mathcal{N}_k(0, \Sigma)$, we can establish the following result on the expectation of $(X'X)^{-1}$. First, let the rows $y_1', \ldots, y_N'$ of Y be i.i.d. $\mathcal{N}_k(0, I_k)$. Let $\mathcal{L}(\cdot)$ denote the distribution of a random variable and let C be an arbitrary orthonormal matrix, so $C'C = I_k$. One well-known property of the standard normal distribution is $\mathcal{L}(C'y_n) = \mathcal{L}(y_n)$. Then,

$$\mathcal{L}(Y'Y) = \mathcal{L}(C'Y'YC).$$

Hence, because $C' = C^{-1}$,

$$\mathcal{L}\big((Y'Y)^{-1}\big) = \mathcal{L}\big(C'(Y'Y)^{-1}C\big),$$

and in particular

$$\mathrm{E}\big((Y'Y)^{-1}\big) = \mathrm{E}\big(C'(Y'Y)^{-1}C\big),$$

which implies that $\mathrm{E}(Y'Y)^{-1}$ must be of the form $\zeta \cdot I_k$, for some constant ζ. The value of ζ can be found as follows. Partition Y as $Y = (Z, y)$, where y is the last column of Y. Then, from the formulas for the inverse of a partitioned matrix, it follows that the lower-right element of $(Y'Y)^{-1}$ can be written as

$$(Y'Y)^{kk} = \big(y'y - y'Z(Z'Z)^{-1}Z'y\big)^{-1} = \big(y'M_Z y\big)^{-1},$$

with $M_Z \equiv I_N - Z(Z'Z)^{-1}Z'$, the symmetric idempotent matrix that projects onto the null-space of Z. By definition, $y \sim \mathcal{N}_N(0, I_N)$. Hence, if M_Z were a nonrandom matrix, $y'M_Z y$ would be chi-squared distributed with degrees of freedom equal to the rank of M_Z, which is $N - (k - 1)$ with probability one. Thus, conditional on Z, $y'M_Z y$ is chi-squared distributed with $N - k + 1$ degrees of freedom. But, as y and Z are independent, this distribution must also hold unconditionally. Furthermore, it is well-known from statistical theory (and easy to prove) that, if T is chi-squared distributed with $\nu > 2$ degrees of freedom, then $\mathrm{E}(1/T) = 1/(\nu - 2)$. Hence, $\mathrm{E}(y'M_Z y)^{-1} = 1/(N - k - 1)$, which is evidently also the value of ζ.

The expectation of $(X'X)^{-1}$ can be derived from the expectation of $(Y'Y)^{-1}$:

$$\begin{aligned}
\mathrm{E}(X'X)^{-1} &= \Sigma^{-1/2}\,\mathrm{E}\big(\Sigma^{-1/2}X'X\Sigma^{-1/2}\big)^{-1}\Sigma^{-1/2} \\
&= \Sigma^{-1/2}\,\mathrm{E}(Y'Y)^{-1}\Sigma^{-1/2} \\
&= \frac{1}{N - k - 1}\Sigma^{-1}.
\end{aligned}$$

A.6 Slutsky's theorem

In the main text, Slutsky's theorem is extensively used. Actually, there are several Slutsky theorems. Most econometricians probably consider the formula

$$\operatorname*{plim}_{N\to\infty} f(Y_N) = f(\operatorname*{plim}_{N\to\infty} Y_N), \tag{A.21}$$

where Y_N is a sequence of vector-valued random variables and $f(\cdot)$ is a continuous vector-valued function of its argument, as "the" Slutsky theorem. We frequently need more general results. The ones we need are summarized in the following theorem.

Theorem A.19 (Slutsky). Let X_N be a sequence of random vector variables which, as $N \to \infty$, converges in distribution to the random vector variable X and let Y_N be a sequence of random vector variables which, as $N \to \infty$, converges in probability to the constant vector c. Furthermore, let $f(x, y)$ be a vector-valued function of its two vector-valued arguments and let $\mathcal{C}$ be the set of points (x, y) at which $f(x, y)$ is continuous. Then,

$$f(X_N, Y_N) \xrightarrow{d} f(X, c),$$

provided that the probability that $(X, c) \in \mathcal{C}$ is 1.

We will not prove the theorem here, but refer to the literature instead. Note that X_N and Y_N are not required to be independent.

A frequently used application of this theorem is when the asymptotic distribution of an expression of the form $\sqrt{N}(\hat{\phi} - \phi_0)$ is needed, where $\hat{\phi}$ is some vector of estimators and ϕ_0 is its true value. In such cases, the expression can usually be written as

$$\sqrt{N}(\hat{\phi} - \phi_0) = A_N \sqrt{N}(\hat{\pi} - \pi_0),$$

where A_N is a random matrix that converges in probability to the constant matrix A and $\sqrt{N}(\hat{\pi} - \pi_0)$ is a random vector expression that converges in distribution to a multivariate normal distribution with mean zero and covariance matrix V. Then, the above theorem can be applied with $X_N = \sqrt{N}(\hat{\pi} - \pi_0)$, $X \sim \mathcal{N}(0, V)$, $Y_N = \text{vec}(A_N)$, $c = \text{vec}(A)$, and $f(X_N, Y_N) = A_N \sqrt{N}(\hat{\pi} - \pi_0)$. It follows that

$$\sqrt{N}(\hat{\phi} - \phi_0) \xrightarrow{d} \mathcal{N}(0, AVA').$$

This result underlies the delta method, see below.

A second important application of this theorem is when it is known that the random vector $X_N \equiv \sqrt{N}(\hat{\pi} - \pi_0)$ converges in distribution to a multivariate normal distribution with mean zero and covariance matrix V, which is unknown, but can be consistently estimated by the random matrix $\hat{V}$. Then, according to the above theorem, the asymptotic distribution of the expression $T \equiv N(\hat{\pi} - \pi_0)'\hat{V}^-(\hat{\pi} - \pi_0)$ is the distribution of $X'V^-X$, which is chi-squared with degrees of freedom equal to the rank of V, see section B.3. This result is important in the derivation of test statistics.

Finally, note that the theorem obviously implies (A.21).

The delta method

A major reason behind the combined popularity of the normal distribution and of asymptotics is the delta method, which offers a very simple tool for deriving the asymptotic distribution of possibly nonlinear functions of random variables.

Let $\hat{\theta}$ be a vector of random variables and θ_0 a corresponding vector of parameters. Assume

$$\sqrt{N}(\hat{\theta} - \theta_0) \xrightarrow{d} \mathcal{N}(0, \Sigma). \tag{A.22}$$

Let $g(\cdot)$ be a totally differentiable vector function of a vector-valued argument and define $G_0 \equiv \partial g / \partial \theta'$, evaluated in θ_0. Then

$$\sqrt{N}\big(g(\hat{\theta}) - g(\theta_0)\big) \xrightarrow{d} \mathcal{N}\big(0, G_0 \Sigma G_0'\big). \tag{A.23}$$

This will be proved below, using the mean value theorem.

A.7 The implicit function theorem

In the main text, we need the implicit function theorem a few times. We will state this theorem without proof.

Theorem A.20 (Implicit function theorem). Let $\mathcal{E}$ be an open set in $\mathbb{R}^{n+m}$. Consider a continuously differentiable vector function $f : \mathcal{E} \to \mathbb{R}^n$. Let for some point $(a, b) \in \mathcal{E}$ (a is an n-vector and b is an m-vector) $f(a, b) = 0$. Let $F_x \equiv \partial f / \partial x'$ $(n \times n)$, $F_y \equiv \partial f / \partial y'$ $(n \times m)$ be the derivatives of f with respect to its first n and last m arguments, respectively. Assume that F_x is of rank n in the point (a, b). Then there exist open sets $\mathcal{U} \subset \mathbb{R}^{n+m}$ and $\mathcal{W} \subset \mathbb{R}^m$, with $(a, b) \in \mathcal{U}$ and $b \in \mathcal{W}$, such that:

(i) To every $y \in \mathcal{W}$ corresponds a unique x such that

$$(x, y) \in \mathcal{U} \quad \text{and} \quad f(x, y) = 0$$

(ii) If this x is defined to be $g(y)$, then g is a continuously differentiable mapping of $\mathcal{W}$ into $\mathbb{R}^n$, $g(b) = a$,

$$f\big(g(y), y\big) = 0 \quad (y \in \mathcal{W})$$
$$\left.\frac{\partial g}{\partial y'}\right|_{y=b} = -(F_x)^{-1} F_y.$$

For a good understanding one should note that the implicit function theorem has only local validity. Consider, for instance, the equation

$$f(x, y) = x^2 + y^2 - 1 = 0, \tag{A.24}$$

with x and y scalars. Take $x = \frac{1}{2}\sqrt{2}$ and $y = \frac{1}{2}\sqrt{2}$. Then, in an open neighborhood of $x = \frac{1}{2}\sqrt{2}$, we can write $x = g(y) = \sqrt{1 - y^2}$, and we can calculate $dx/dy = -y/\sqrt{1 - y^2}$, either directly or via the implicit function theorem. However, the function $x = -\sqrt{1 - y^2}$ also satisfies $f(x, y) = 0$, but when inserting $y = \frac{1}{2}\sqrt{2}$, we obtain $x = -\frac{1}{2}\sqrt{2}$. In other words, there is only one function g that satisfies (A.24) *and* $\frac{1}{2}\sqrt{2} = g\left(\frac{1}{2}\sqrt{2}\right)$, but there is more than one function that satisfies (A.24) alone.

We use the implicit function theorem sometimes to argue that a system of equations $f(x, y) = 0$ has a locally unique solution for x, say x_0, given $y = y_0$. The condition for this is that F_x is nonsingular in an open neighborhood of x_0.

The mean value theorem

We frequently need the mean value theorem to derive the asymptotic distribution of an estimator or a test statistic. We will give the theorem for the scalar case first, and subsequently derive the theorem for the vector case as a result.

Theorem A.21 (Mean value theorem for scalar functions). Let $f(x)$ be a scalar function of a scalar variable x and assume that $f(x)$ is continuously differentiable on the interval $[a, b]$. Then, there exists a point $x^* \in [a, b]$ such that $f(b) - f(a) = g(x^*) \cdot (b - a)$, where $g(x)$ is the derivative of $f(x)$.

Proof. We will not give a formal proof here. It can be found in most text books on calculus. A particularly simple proof can be found in Apostol (1967, pp. 184–185). An intuitive argument can be found by observing that

$$\frac{f(b) - f(a)}{b - a}$$

is the slope of the line segment connecting the points $(a, f(a))$ and $(b, f(b))$. If the function f is continuously differentiable, a simple graph shows that there must be a point x^* in the connecting interval in which the slope of the tangent line is equal to this "average" slope, i.e., $g(x^*) = (f(b) - f(a))/(b - a)$. The result then follows immediately. Note, however, that the point x^* need not be unique, i.e., there may be more points with the same value of the derivative. □

Theorem A.22 (Mean value theorem for vector functions). Now, let $v(y)$ be a vector-valued function of a vector-valued variable y and assume that $v(y)$ is continuously differentiable in a convex set containing the points y_0 and y_1. Then, there exists a vector λ with elements $\lambda_i \in [0, 1]$ and a matrix J^* with elements

$$(J^*)_{ij} \equiv \frac{\partial v_i}{\partial y_j} \Big|_{y=(1-\lambda_i)y_0+\lambda_i y_1}$$

such that $v(y_1) - v(y_0) = J^*(y_1 - y_0)$.

Proof. Define a vector-valued function $\eta(x) \equiv (1 - x)y_0 + xy_1$ of a scalar variable x. Furthermore, define scalar-valued functions $f_i(x) \equiv v_i(\eta(x))$ of x. Obviously, $f_i(1) = v_i(y_1)$ and $f_i(0) = v_i(y_0)$. Moreover, under the conditions stated, $f_i(x)$ is continuously differentiable on the interval $[0, 1]$. Hence, we have that $f_i(1) - f_i(0) = g_i(x^*) \cdot (1 - 0) = g_i(x^*)$ for some point $x^* \in [0, 1]$, where $g_i(x)$ is the derivative of $f_i(x)$. Using the chain rule, we find that

$$g_i(z) \equiv \frac{\mathrm{d}f_i}{\mathrm{d}x} \Big|_{x=z}$$

$$= \frac{\partial v_i}{\partial y'} \Big|_{y=\eta(z)} \frac{\partial \eta}{\partial x} \Big|_{x=z}$$
$$= \frac{\partial v_i}{\partial y'} \Big|_{y=(1-z)y_0+zy_1} (y_1 - y_0).$$

Defining $\lambda_i \equiv x^*$, it follows immediately that $g_i(\lambda_i) = J_i^* \cdot (y_1 - y_0)$, where J_i^* is the i-th row of J^*. Repeating the process for all v_i, the result follows. Note that the different rows of J^* may be based on different values of λ, but that the different elements in the same row are based on the same λ. □

This theorem is especially useful in situations where y_1 is a random vector that converges in probability to the nonrandom vector y_0. Then, under the stated assumptions, $v(y_1)$ converges in probability to $v(y_0)$ and J^* converges in probability to $J(y_0)$, where $J(y) \equiv \partial v/\partial y'$. Hence, if

$$\sqrt{N}(y_1 - y_0) \xrightarrow{d} \mathcal{N}(0, A), \tag{A.25}$$

then by application of Slutsky's theorem,

$$\sqrt{N}(v(y_1) - v(y_0)) \xrightarrow{d} \mathcal{N}\big(0, J(y_0)AJ(y_0)'\big),$$

which shows the validity of the delta method. Furthermore, if $\hat{v}$ is some estimator of a parameter vector v with true value v_0, then $\hat{v}$ is usually defined as a solution to an equation $h(v, y) = 0$, where y is some observed data vector, e.g., a vector of sample moments. In many cases, $h(v, y)$ can in its turn be written as $h(v, y) = \partial q(v, y)/\partial v$, where q is some function that has to be optimized with respect to v (e.g., a loglikelihood function or a GMM criterion function). Assume that the model is correct in the sense that $h(v_0, y_0) = 0$, where y_0 is the probability limit of y. Using the implicit function theorem, we have that $\hat{v}$ can now be written in a neighborhood of y_0 as $\hat{v} = v(y)$, with

$$J(y) \equiv \frac{\partial v}{\partial y'} = -\left(\frac{\partial h}{\partial v'}\right)^{-1} \frac{\partial h}{\partial y'}. \tag{A.26}$$

Hence, if (A.25) holds, it follows that

$$\sqrt{N}(\hat{v} - v_0) \xrightarrow{d} \mathcal{N}\big(0, J(y_0)AJ(y_0)'\big),$$

where J is defined in (A.26).

A.8 Bibliographical notes

A.1 Lancaster and Tismenetsky (1985) is an excellent book on the mathematical theory of matrices. A book that contains many results on matrix algebra relevant to statistics is Harville (1997). Kronecker products and the vec operator have been discussed in Graham (1981) and Henderson and Searle (1979, 1981b). The generalization of the Kronecker product and the vec operator to the block Kronecker product and the vecb operator, which is useful for partitioned matrices, has been discussed by Koning, Neudecker, and Wansbeek (1991). A complete theory of matrix differentiation is given by Magnus and Neudecker (1985, 1988) and Nel (1980). Many results on inverses and determinants are given by Harville (1997) and Henderson and Searle (1981a). The Frisch-Waugh theorem is due to Frisch and Waugh (1933).

A.2 Theorem A.8 is due to Bekker et al. (1987). Generalized inverses of matrices have been treated extensively by Rao and Mitra (1971).

A.3 On definite matrices, see Bekker (1988) and Bekker and Neudecker (1989). The Cauchy-Schwarz inequality exists under several names, although usually at least one of the names of Cauchy and Schwarz is used. Similarly, it has several forms, varying from very specific results for vectors or integrals to very general results for arbitrary inner products, see, e.g., Apostol (1967, 1969) or Dunford and Schwartz (1958, pp. 372–373).

A.4 A large number of definitions and properties of special matrices of the type discussed in this section can be found in Henderson and Searle (1981b), Magnus (1983, 1988), Magnus and Neudecker (1979, 1980, 1986, 1988), Neudecker and Wansbeek (1983), and Wansbeek (1989). Note that Browne (1974) defined a matrix K_p of order $p^2 \times p(p+1)/2$, which is similar to the matrix $(D_p^+)'$, except that the nonduplicated elements are ordered as $(1,1)$, $(2,1)$, $(2,2)$, $(3,1)$, $(3,3)$, etc., which differs from the ordering in the duplication matrix as given here, which is taken from Magnus and Neudecker (1988). Note that the ordering of the p^2 elements in the symmetrization matrix is unique, and hence $K_p K_p^- = K_p(K_p' K_p)^{-1} K_p' = Q_p$.

A.5 The method of repeated conditioning is from Merckens and Wansbeek (1989). The argument as to the expectation of the inverse of a Wishart matrix is from Schaafsma (1982), who ascribes it to M.L. Eaton.

A.6 The name Slutsky theorem is with reference to Slutsky (1925), although he only discussed convergence in probability to random variables or constants. General results were obtained by Mann and Wald (1943). Our usage of the term Slutsky theorem follows that of Ferguson (1996). For the delta method see, e.g., Rao (1973, p. 388).

A.7 For the implicit function theorem see, e.g., Rudin (1964, p. 196), or Apostol (1969, pp. 237–239). Several versions of the mean value theorem are given in Apostol (1967).

Appendix B

The chi-square distribution

Testing a hypothesis is often based on a statistic of the form $T = N\hat{h}'\hat{W}\hat{h}$, where $\sqrt{N}\hat{h}$ converges in distribution to a normal vector and $\hat{W}$ converges in probability to a symmetric positive semidefinite matrix. Hence, by Slutsky's theorem, T converges in distribution to a quadratic function in a normal vector variable. Therefore, the asymptotic distribution of T is the distribution of such a quadratic function, which is the chi-square distribution or a generalization thereof.

In section B.1, we derive the mean and the variance of a quadratic function in a normal vector variable. In section B.2, we derive the distribution in general. A major special case is described in section B.3. The solutions to a number of matrix equations connected to the chi-square distribution are derived in section B.4.

B.1 Mean and variance

We consider a p-dimensional normal variable x with mean μ and symmetric positive semidefinite covariance matrix Σ of rank $q \leq p$. We need the distribution of $x'Ax$, where A is a nonrandom symmetric positive semidefinite matrix. In typical applications, Σ is not of full rank, whereas A is of full rank, but we will allow the possibility that A is not of full rank.

Let us first derive the mean and variance of $x'Ax$.

$$
\begin{aligned}
\mathrm{E}(x'Ax) &= \mathrm{E}(\mathrm{tr}(Axx')) \\
&= \mathrm{tr}(A\ \mathrm{E}(xx')) \\
&= \mathrm{tr}\Big(A\left(\mathrm{E}(x-\mu)(x-\mu)' + \mu\mu'\right)\Big) \\
&= \mathrm{tr}(A\Sigma) + \mu' A\mu .
\end{aligned}
$$

For the variance, we use the method of repeated conditioning from section A.5:

$$
\begin{aligned}
\operatorname{Var}(x'Ax) &\equiv \mathrm{E}\big((x'Ax)^2\big) - \big(\mathrm{E}(x'Ax)\big)^2 \\
&= \mathrm{E}(x_1'Ax_2x_3'Ax_4) - \big(\operatorname{tr}(A\Sigma) + \mu'A\mu\big)^2 \\
&= (\mathrm{E}_{12}\,\mathrm{E}_{34} + \mathrm{E}_{13}\,\mathrm{E}_{24} + \mathrm{E}_{14}\,\mathrm{E}_{23})(x_1'Ax_2x_3'Ax_4) - \big(\operatorname{tr}(A\Sigma) + \mu'A\mu\big)^2 \\
&= \big(\operatorname{tr}(A\Sigma) + \mu'A\mu\big)^2 + \mathrm{E}_{13}\,\mathrm{E}_{24}(x_1'Ax_2x_4'Ax_3) \\
&\quad + \operatorname{tr}\big(A(\Sigma + \mu\mu')A(\Sigma + \mu\mu')\big) - \big(\operatorname{tr}(A\Sigma) + \mu'A\mu\big)^2 \\
&= 2\operatorname{tr}\big(A(\Sigma + \mu\mu')A(\Sigma + \mu\mu')\big) \\
&= 2\operatorname{tr}(A\Sigma A\Sigma + A\mu\mu'A\Sigma + A\Sigma A\mu\mu' + A\mu\mu'A\mu\mu') \\
&= 2\operatorname{tr}(A\Sigma A\Sigma) + 4\mu'A\Sigma A\mu + 2(\mu'A\mu)^2.
\end{aligned}
$$

B.2 The distribution of quadratic forms in general

We will now study the distribution of $x'Ax$ in more detail. We will first derive a number of auxiliary results.

Let the eigenvalue decomposition of Σ be $\Sigma = K\Delta K'$, where $K'K = I_q$ and Δ is a $q \times q$ diagonal matrix with positive diagonal elements. Furthermore, let L be an orthogonal complement of K, i.e., $L'K = 0$ and $L'L = I_{p-q}$. Then $L'x = L'\mu$ with probability 1, and $LL' = I_p - \Sigma\Sigma^+ = I_p - \Sigma^+\Sigma$. Let

$$\Upsilon \equiv \Delta^{1/2}K'AK\Delta^{1/2}, \tag{B.1}$$

with eigenvalue decomposition

$$\Upsilon = \Delta^{1/2}K'AK\Delta^{1/2} = U\Lambda U', \tag{B.2}$$

where $U'U = I_r$ and Λ is an $r \times r$ diagonal matrix with positive diagonal elements. Because UU' projects onto the space spanned by the columns of Υ,

$$UU'\Delta^{1/2}K'A = \Delta^{1/2}K'A. \tag{B.3}$$

Next, let $R \equiv K\Delta^{-1/2}U + LL'AK\Delta^{1/2}U\Lambda^{-1}$. Then

$$
\begin{aligned}
R\Lambda R' &= K\Delta^{-1/2}U\Lambda U'\Delta^{-1/2}K' + LL'AK\Delta^{1/2}U\Lambda^{-1}U'\Delta^{1/2}K'ALL' \\
&\quad + K\Delta^{-1/2}UU'\Delta^{1/2}K'ALL' + LL'AK\Delta^{1/2}UU'\Delta^{-1/2}K' \\
&= KK'AKK' + LL'AK\Delta^{1/2}(\Delta^{1/2}K'AK\Delta^{1/2})^+\Delta^{1/2}K'ALL' \\
&\quad + KK'ALL' + LL'AKK' \\
&= (KK' + LL')A(KK' + LL') - LL'(A - AK(K'AK)^+K'A)LL' \\
&= A - (I_p - \Sigma^+\Sigma)(A - A\Sigma(\Sigma A\Sigma)^+\Sigma A)(I_p - \Sigma\Sigma^+).
\end{aligned}
$$

Likewise,

$$R'\Sigma R = U'\Delta^{-1/2}K'K\Delta K'K\Delta^{-1/2}U = I_r.$$

The last result provides the connection with the chi-square distribution.

Let $z \equiv R'x$, then this result implies that $z \sim \mathcal{N}_r(R'\mu, I_r)$, i.e., z is a vector of independent normal variables with unit variance, and on using $L'x = L'\mu$, it follows that $z'\Lambda z = x'R\Lambda R'x = x'Ax - \delta$, where

$$\delta \equiv \mu'(I_p - \Sigma^+\Sigma)(A - A\Sigma(\Sigma A\Sigma)^+\Sigma A)(I_p - \Sigma\Sigma^+)\mu.$$

On rearrangement, we obtain

$$x'Ax = z'\Lambda z + \delta.$$

This leads to the main result on the distribution of $x'Ax$ when $x \sim \mathcal{N}_p(\mu, \Sigma)$, with $A \geq 0$ and $\Sigma \geq 0$. The distribution of $x'Ax$ consists of a random term, $z'\Lambda z$, and a constant term, δ. As to the first term, we note that it can be written as

$$z'\Lambda z = \sum_{j=1}^{r} \lambda_j z_j^2,$$

where z_j is the j-th element of z and the λ_j's, $j = 1, \ldots, r$ are the positive diagonal elements of Λ, i.e., the positive eigenvalues of Υ as defined in (B.1). Because in general the matrices BC and CB have the same nonzero eigenvalues, the λ_j's are also the positive eigenvalues of $A\Sigma$. It was derived above that z is a vector of independently normally distributed variables, each having unit variance and having means $\gamma_j \equiv e_j'\gamma \equiv e_j'R'\mu$, with e_j the j-th unit vector. Hence, $z'\Lambda z$ is a weighted sum of independent noncentral chi-squared distributed variables with noncentrality parameters γ_j^2 and weights λ_j. Adding the constant term δ to the random term $z'\Lambda z$ provides the distribution of $x'Ax$.

As to the constant term, note that $\delta = 0$ if $\Sigma > 0$ because then $\Sigma^+ = \Sigma^{-1}$ and hence $I_p - \Sigma\Sigma^+ = 0$. If on the other hand Σ is of deficient rank, but $A > 0$, then $\delta = 0$ is equivalent with $(I_p - \Sigma\Sigma^+)\mu = 0$. This can be seen as follows. Note that $\Sigma\Sigma^+ = KK'$ and $I_p - \Sigma\Sigma^+ = LL'$. Furthermore, when $A > 0$,

$$A - A\Sigma(\Sigma A\Sigma)^+\Sigma A = A - AK(K'AK)^{-1}K'A = L(L'A^{-1}L)^{-1}L',$$

where the last equality follows from theorem A.7. Hence, $\delta = 0$ if and only if $L'\mu = 0$ and the stated result follows.

A leading example in which this condition is satisfied is when $x = Py$, where P is a matrix of (possibly) deficient rank and y is a normally distributed vector (not necessarily of dimension p) with mean η and positive definite covariance matrix Π. Then $\Sigma = P\Pi P'$ and $\mu = P\eta$. By defining $Q \equiv P\Pi^{1/2}$ and $\xi \equiv \Pi^{-1/2}\eta$, it follows that $\Sigma = QQ'$, $\mu = Q\xi$, and

$$(I_p - \Sigma\Sigma^+)\mu = \left(I_p - Q(Q'Q)^+Q'\right)Q\xi = 0.$$

Of course, in any case, $(I_p - \Sigma\Sigma^+)\mu = 0$ is sufficient for $\delta = 0$, but if both A and Σ are of deficient rank this is not a necessary condition.

B.3 The idempotent case

As we just saw, the distribution of $x'Ax$ is fairly complicated. Note, however, that the random variable $z'\Lambda z$ follows a noncentral chi-square distribution with r degrees of freedom if and only if $\Lambda = I_r$. So a major simplification is obtained if A is chosen such that $\Lambda = I_r$.

The discussion of the distribution of $x'Ax$ was motivated by its use in the context of hypothesis testing. Then, the null hypothesis typically is $\mu = 0$, which implies $\gamma = 0$ and $\delta = 0$, so that $z'\Lambda z = x'Ax$ follows a central chi-square distribution with r degrees of freedom. Hence, the null hypothesis is rejected at level α if $x'Ax$ exceeds the $(1 - \alpha)$-th quantile of the chi-square distribution, which can be easily verified in practice.

To see what the relation between A and Σ is in the idempotent case, note that then (B.2) becomes

$$\Upsilon = UU' = \Delta^{1/2}K'AK\Delta^{1/2}.$$

Evidently, UU' is idempotent, and hence $\Delta^{1/2}K'AK\Delta^{1/2}$ is idempotent, so that

$$\Delta^{1/2}K'AK\Delta^{1/2} = \Delta^{1/2}K'AK\Delta K'AK\Delta^{1/2},$$

or, equivalently,

$$\Sigma A\Sigma A\Sigma = \Sigma A\Sigma. \tag{B.4}$$

We call this the idempotent case and we call (B.4) the idempotency condition. It is the necessary and sufficient condition under which $z'\Lambda z$ follows a noncentral chi-square distribution. If Σ is of full rank, the idempotency condition is equivalent to $\Sigma = A^-$ for some generalized inverse of A, whereas if A is of full rank, it is equivalent to $A = \Sigma^-$ for some generalized inverse of Σ. The former follows from pre- and postmultiplying (B.4) by Σ^{-1}, whereas the latter follows from writing (B.4) as

$$K\Delta K'AK\Delta K'AK\Delta K' = K\Delta K'AK\Delta K',$$

which is equivalent to $K'AK\Delta = I_q$, because A is of full rank $p > q$ and K and Δ are of rank q. Hence, $K'AK = \Delta^{-1}$. It follows that

$$\Sigma A \Sigma = K\Delta K'AK\Delta K' = K\Delta K' = \Sigma,$$

or $A = \Sigma^-$. Clearly, if either $\Sigma = A^-$ or $A = \Sigma^-$, (B.4) is satisfied, regardless of the ranks of A and Σ.

We now derive the noncentrality parameter for the idempotent case. In this case, R becomes $\tilde{R}$, say, with

$$\tilde{R} \equiv K\Delta^{-1/2}U + LL'AK\Delta^{1/2}U.$$

Hence, using (B.2) and (B.3),

$$\begin{aligned} U\tilde{R}' &= UU'\Delta^{-1/2}K' + UU'\Delta^{1/2}K'ALL' \\ &= \Delta^{1/2}K'AK\Delta^{1/2}\Delta^{-1/2}K' + \Delta^{1/2}K'ALL' \\ &= \Delta^{1/2}K'A, \end{aligned}$$

so that $\tilde{R}\tilde{R}' = \tilde{R}U'U\tilde{R}' = A\Sigma A$. The noncentrality parameter in the idempotent case is $\mu'A\Sigma A\mu$, because $z \sim \mathcal{N}_r(\tilde{R}'\mu, I_r)$. If $\Sigma = A^-$, this reduces evidently to $\mu'A\mu$.

The number of degrees of freedom r is the number of unit eigenvalues of Υ, which is also the rank of Υ and the trace of Υ, because Υ is symmetric and idempotent. This can be computed more conveniently as

$$r = \mathrm{tr}(\Upsilon) = \mathrm{tr}\big(\Delta^{1/2}K'AK\Delta^{1/2}\big) = \mathrm{tr}(AK\Delta K') = \mathrm{tr}(A\Sigma).$$

The expectation of a noncentral chi-squared distributed variable is equal to its number of degrees of freedom plus its noncentrality parameter, $r + \mu'A\Sigma A\mu$ in this case. Using $r = \mathrm{tr}(A\Sigma)$, $\mathrm{E}(x'Ax) = \mathrm{tr}(A\Sigma) + \mu'A\mu$ and $\mathrm{E}(x'Ax) = \mathrm{E}(z'z) + \delta$, we find that δ can be computed conveniently as

$$\begin{aligned} \delta &= \mathrm{tr}(A\Sigma) + \mu'A\mu - (r + \mu'A\Sigma A\mu) \\ &= \mu'A\mu - \mu'A\Sigma A\mu. \end{aligned}$$

Note that $\delta \geq 0$ and thus apparently $A \geq A\Sigma A$. Clearly, in the cases where $\mu'A\Sigma A\mu = \mu'A\mu$, we also have $\delta = 0$. As this is the case that is most frequently encountered, we see that typically, if A is chosen to satisfy (B.4), $x'Ax$ is distributed as a noncentral chi-squared distributed variable with degrees of freedom $r = \mathrm{tr}(A\Sigma)$ and noncentrality parameter $\mu'A\mu$.

B.4 Robustness characterizations

In this section we present a few theorems that play a role in the discussion of the robustness of a variety of results, in particular relating to the chi-square distribution. The first of these characterizes the condition under which the Cauchy-Schwarz inequality is an equality.

Theorem B.1. Let $A > 0$, $B > 0$, and X of full column rank. Then

$$(X'AX)^{-1}X'ABAX(X'AX)^{-1} = (X'B^{-1}X)^{-1} \tag{B.5}$$

is equivalent to

$$BAX = XD, \tag{B.6}$$

for some nonsingular matrix D, or, equivalently,

$$A^{-1} = \alpha B + XPX' + BYQY'B, \tag{B.7}$$

where Y is such that (X, Y) is nonsingular and $Y'X = 0$, α is an arbitrary constant, and P and Q are arbitrary symmetric matrices, provided that the resulting A^{-1} is positive definite, i.e., $\alpha(Y'BY)^{-1} + Q > 0$ and $\alpha(X'B^{-1}X)^{-1} + P > 0$.

Proof. Let $C > 0$ be such that $C^2 = B^{-1}$, and let

$$\begin{aligned} \bar{A} &\equiv C^{-1}AC^{-1} \\ \bar{X} &\equiv CX(X'C^2X)^{-1/2}, \end{aligned}$$

so that $\bar{X}'\bar{X} = I$,

$$\begin{aligned} \bar{X}'\bar{A}\bar{X} &= (X'B^{-1}X)^{-1/2}X'AX(X'B^{-1}X)^{-1/2} \\ \bar{X}'\bar{A}^2\bar{X} &= (X'B^{-1}X)^{-1/2}X'ABAX(X'B^{-1}X)^{-1/2}. \end{aligned}$$

Hence, (B.5) is equivalent to $(\bar{X}'\bar{A}\bar{X})^{-1}\bar{X}'\bar{A}^2\bar{X}(\bar{X}'\bar{A}\bar{X})^{-1} = I$, or

$$\bar{X}'\bar{A}^2\bar{X} = (\bar{X}'\bar{A}\bar{X})^2. \tag{B.8}$$

Let $\bar{A} = (\bar{X}, \bar{Y})U(\bar{X}, \bar{Y})'$, with $U > 0$ partitioned as

$$U = \begin{bmatrix} U_{11} & U_{12} \\ U_{21} & U_{22} \end{bmatrix},$$

and $\bar{Y}$ a matrix with $\bar{Y}'\bar{X} = 0$ and $\bar{Y}'\bar{Y} = I$ such that $(\bar{X}, \bar{Y})$ is nonsingular. Note that $\bar{Y}'\bar{X} = 0$ implies that $\bar{Y} = C^{-1}Y$. Then, (B.8) becomes

$$U_{11}^2 + U_{12}U_{21} = U_{11}^2.$$

Hence, $U_{12} = U'_{21} = 0$, and thus $\bar{A} = \bar{X}U_{11}\bar{X}' + \bar{Y}U_{22}\bar{Y}'$ and $\bar{A}^{-1} = \bar{X}U_{11}^{-1}\bar{X}' + \bar{Y}U_{22}^{-1}\bar{Y}'$. The latter expression can be rewritten as

$$\bar{A}^{-1} = \alpha I + \bar{X}(U_{11}^{-1} - \alpha I)\bar{X}' + \bar{Y}(U_{22}^{-1} - \alpha I)\bar{Y}'.$$

Using the formulas for $\bar{A}$, $\bar{X}$, and $\bar{Y}$, this expression reduces to

$$\begin{aligned} CA^{-1}C = \alpha I &+ CX(X'C^2X)^{-1/2}(U_{11}^{-1} - \alpha I)(X'C^2X)^{-1/2}X'C' \\ &+ C^{-1}Y(U_{22}^{-1} - \alpha I)Y'C^{-1}, \end{aligned}$$

which implies (B.7). Now, postmultiply (B.7) by $B^{-1}X$ to obtain

$$A^{-1}B^{-1}X = \alpha X + XPX'B^{-1}X = X(\alpha I + PX'B^{-1}X),$$

or $BAX = X(\alpha I + PX'B^{-1}X)^{-1}$, which implies (B.6). Finally, from (B.6),

$$\begin{aligned} (X'AX)^{-1}X'ABAX(X'AX)^{-1} &= (X'AX)^{-1}X'AXD(X'AX)^{-1} \\ &= D(X'B^{-1}BAX)^{-1} \\ &= D(X'B^{-1}XD)^{-1} \\ &= (X'B^{-1}X)^{-1}, \end{aligned}$$

which is (B.5). Therefore, (B.5) is equivalent with (B.6) and (B.7).

That $\alpha(Y'BY)^{-1} + Q > 0$ and $\alpha(X'B^{-1}X)^{-1} + P > 0$ are necessary and sufficient for positive definiteness of the right-hand side of (B.7) can be seen by postmultiplication with the nonsingular matrix $(B^{-1}X, Y)$ and premultiplication with its transpose. □

The second robustness result, which is important in a number of situations, is the condition that $X'ABAX = X'AX$, where A and B are symmetric positive definite matrices and X is of full column rank. It denotes situations under which the chi-square difference test is asymptotically chi-squared distributed, situations under which the formula of the LM test reduces to a much more concise form, and situations under which the estimator of the asymptotic covariance matrix of GMM estimators is consistent under nonoptimal weighting.

Theorem B.2. Let $A > 0$, $B > 0$, and X of full column rank. Then the equation

$$X'ABAX = X'AX \qquad \text{(B.9)}$$

has solution

$$A^{-1} = B + XPX' + XR'Y'B + BYRX' + BYQY'B', \qquad \text{(B.10)}$$

where Y is a matrix of full column rank such that $Y'X = 0$ and (X, Y) is nonsingular, Q is an arbitrary symmetric matrix, provided that $\tilde{Q} \equiv (Y'BY)^{-1} + Q > 0$, R is an arbitrary matrix, and

$$P = R'\tilde{Q}^{-1}\big(\tilde{Q} + (Y'BY)^{-1}\big)\tilde{Q}^{-1}R. \tag{B.11}$$

Proof. Because $Z \equiv (X, BY)$ is nonsingular, the form (B.10) does not restrict A^{-1}. This form can also be written as

$$A^{-1} = B + (X, BY)\begin{bmatrix} P & R' \\ R & Q \end{bmatrix}(X, BY)' = B + ZSZ',$$

with S implicitly defined. First, note that

$$Y'A^{-1}Y = Y'BY + (Y'BY)Q(Y'BY) = (Y'BY)\big((Y'BY)^{-1} + Q\big)(Y'BY).$$

Because Y is of full column rank and $A > 0$, the left-hand side of this equation is positive definite. Hence, $\tilde{Q} > 0$.

Second, it can now be straightforwardly checked that A can be written as

$$A = B^{-1} - B^{-1}ZS(I + Z'B^{-1}ZS)^{-1}Z'B^{-1}.$$

Note that S is not necessarily nonsingular, but nonsingularity of A implies nonsingularity of $I + Z'B^{-1}ZS$, which follows from the determinantal formulas in section A.1. The condition (B.9) only contains A in the form AX, which is now seen equivalent to

$$AX = B^{-1}X - B^{-1}ZS(I + Z'B^{-1}ZS)^{-1}Z'B^{-1}X.$$

Because $Z'B^{-1}X = (X'B^{-1}X, 0)'$, we only need the left blocks in the partitioned matrix $(I + Z'B^{-1}ZS)^{-1}$. Furthermore,

$$Z'B^{-1}Z = \begin{bmatrix} X'B^{-1}X & 0 \\ 0 & Y'BY \end{bmatrix}$$

$$I + Z'B^{-1}ZS = \begin{bmatrix} I + X'B^{-1}XP & X'B^{-1}XR' \\ Y'BYR & Y'BY\tilde{Q} \end{bmatrix}$$

$$(I + Z'B^{-1}ZS)^{-1} = \begin{bmatrix} T_1 & T_3 \\ T_2 & T_4 \end{bmatrix},$$

with

$$T_1 \equiv \big(I + X'B^{-1}XP - X'B^{-1}XR'\tilde{Q}^{-1}R\big)^{-1}$$
$$T_2 \equiv -\tilde{Q}^{-1}RT_1.$$

Now, define $\tilde{P} \equiv P - R'\tilde{Q}^{-1}R$ and $\tilde{R} \equiv (Y'BY)^{-1}\tilde{Q}^{-1}R$. Next, partition $B^{-1}ZS(I + Z'B^{-1}ZS)^{-1}$ as (V_1, V_2), say, with $V_1 \equiv B^{-1}X\tilde{P}T_1 + Y\tilde{R}T_1$. Hence,

$$\begin{aligned} AX &= B^{-1}X - V_1 X'B^{-1}X \\ &= B^{-1}X - B^{-1}X\tilde{P}T_1X'B^{-1}X - Y\tilde{R}T_1X'B^{-1}X \end{aligned} \tag{B.12}$$

or

$$X'ABAX - X'AX = -X'AX\tilde{P}T_1X'B^{-1}X - X'ABY\tilde{R}T_1X'B^{-1}X, \tag{B.13}$$

the left-hand side of which should be zero because of (B.9). Inserting the transpose of the right-hand side of (B.12) for $X'A$ in the right-hand side of (B.13), premultiplication by $(T_1^{-1})'(X'B^{-1}X)^{-1}$ and postmultiplication by $(X'B^{-1}X)^{-1}T_1^{-1}$ leads to the equivalent condition

$$-(T_1^{-1})'\tilde{P} + \tilde{P}X'B^{-1}X\tilde{P} + \tilde{R}'Y'BY\tilde{R} = 0.$$

Using the definitions of T_1, $\tilde{P}$, and $\tilde{R}$ and cleaning up the result gives (B.11). It is simple to see that, under the stated conditions, $A^{-1} > 0$. □

Theorem B.3. Let $A > 0$, $B > 0$, and X of full column rank. Then (B.5) and (B.9) both hold if and only if

$$BAX = X, \tag{B.14}$$

or, equivalently,

$$A^{-1} = B + BYQY'B, \tag{B.15}$$

where Y is a matrix such that $Y'X = 0$ and (X, Y) is nonsingular, and Q is an arbitrary symmetric matrix, provided that $Q + (Y'BY)^{-1} > 0$.

Proof. As we have seen in theorem B.1, (B.5) is equivalent with $BAX = XD$, with D a nonsingular matrix. By inserting this in (B.9) and noting that it follows from the assumptions that $X'AX$ is nonsingular, it follows immediately that $D = I$, which gives (B.14). Starting from (B.14), we obtain $X = A^{-1}B^{-1}X$, or, equivalently, $(A^{-1} - B)B^{-1}X = 0$, from which it follows that $A^{-1} - B = Q^*Y'B$, for some matrix Q^*. From the symmetry of A and B, it follows that $Q^* = BYQ$ for some symmetric matrix Q, which gives (B.15). Conversely, from (B.15), it follows that $(A^{-1} - B)B^{-1}X = 0$, or $BAX = X$, which implies (B.9) and (B.5). □

The third result on robustness gives the conditions under which the chi-square statistic is (noncentrally) chi-squared distributed.

Theorem B.4. Let $A > 0$, $B > 0$, let X be of full column rank, let $P \equiv X(X'AX)^{-1}X'A$, and let $V \equiv (I-P)B(I-P)'$. Then the solution of

$$VAVAV = VAV \tag{B.16}$$

is given by

$$A^{-1} = B + XC' + CX', \tag{B.17}$$

where C is arbitrary provided that $B + XC' + CX' > 0$.

Proof. Let Y be a matrix with $Y'X = 0$ and (X, Y) nonsingular. Let

$$\begin{aligned} Q &\equiv (I-P)'A(I-P) \\ &= A - AX(X'AX)^{-1}X'A \\ &= Y(Y'A^{-1}Y)^{-1}Y'. \end{aligned}$$

The last step follows from theorem A.7. Note that

$$QA^{-1}Q = Q. \tag{B.18}$$

Using the definition of Q, it follows that (B.16) is equivalent with

$$(I-P)BQBQB(I-P)' = (I-P)BQB(I-P)'.$$

Premultiplication by the nonsingular matrix (AX, Y) and postmultiplication by its transpose shows that this is equivalent with $Y'BQBQBY = Y'BQBY$. Using (B.18) shows that this is again equivalent with $Y'BQ(A^{-1} - B)QBY = 0$, or, using the nonsingularity of $Y'BY$ and $(Y'A^{-1}Y)^{-1}$, with $Y'(A^{-1} - B)Y = 0$, which has solution (B.17). □

Theorem B.5. Let $A > 0$, $B > 0$, and X of full column rank. Then (B.5) and (B.17) are both satisfied if and only if A^{-1} can be written as

$$A^{-1} = B + XPX', \tag{B.19}$$

where P is an arbitrary symmetric matrix provided $B + XPX' > 0$.

Proof. Using (B.7), it follows immediately that (B.19) is sufficient. Let Y be as before. Necessity follows by premultiplying (B.17) by Y' and postmultiplying the result by AX. This gives the condition

$$Y'X = Y'BAX + Y'XC'AX + Y'CX'AX.$$

By using (B.6), $Y'X = 0$, and the nonsingularity of $X'AX$, it follows that $Y'C = 0$, which is equivalent with $C = XE$ for some matrix E. Inserting this into (B.17) gives (B.19), with $P = E + E'$. □

Theorem B.6. Let $A > 0$, $B > 0$, and X of full column rank. Then (B.9) and (B.17) are both satisfied if and only if A^{-1} can be written as

$$A^{-1} = B + XR'Y'B + BYRX' + 2XR'Y'BYRX', \tag{B.20}$$

where R is an arbitrary matrix, and Y is a matrix such that $Y'X = 0$ and (X, Y) is nonsingular.

Proof. It follows immediately by comparing (B.17) with (B.10) that $Q = 0$ in the latter condition is a necessary and sufficient condition. Inserting $Q = 0$ in (B.11) leads straightforwardly to (B.20). □

Theorem B.7. Let $A > 0$, $B > 0$, and X of full column rank. Then (B.5), (B.9), and (B.17) are all satisfied if and only if $A^{-1} = B$.

Proof. This follows immediately by comparing (B.15) and (B.19). □

B.5 Bibliographical notes

B.1 The formulas derived in this section have been utilized by Satorra and Bentler (1988, 1994) to define two test statistics that may be used to test (in the current notation) $\mu = 0$ with GMM estimation under nonoptimal weighting. The first, called the scaled test statistic, uses a consistent estimator for the mean with $\mu = 0$ to scale the quadratic form such that its asymptotic mean becomes equal to its number of degrees of freedom under the null hypothesis, which corresponds with the chi-square distribution under optimal weighting. The second, called the adjusted test statistic, uses consistent estimators for the mean and the variance with $\mu = 0$ to scale the quadratic form such that its asymptotic variance is twice its asymptotic mean, which implies that the first two moments are equal to the first two moments of a chi-square distribution with number of degrees of freedom equal to the asymptotic mean of the resulting test statistic. The resulting number of degrees of freedom may not be an integer. See also section 10.3 for a discussion of the first of these test statistics.

For $\mu = 0$, Box (1954, theorem 2.2) gave the formula for the cumulants,

$$\kappa_s(x'Ax) = 2^{s-1}(s-1)!\,\mathrm{tr}\big((A\Sigma)^s\big),$$

of which the given formulas for the mean and variance are special cases. Corresponding formulas for the higher cumulants if $\mu \neq 0$ can be easily derived from this formula.

B.2 Results similar to those derived in this section have been presented for $\mu = 0$ by Box (1954, theorem 2.1) and Satorra and Bentler (1988, 1994). See, Davies (1980) for the computation of the quantiles of the general distribution.

B.3 Subsets and extensions of the conditions presented in this section have been given by numerous authors, see, e.g., Graybill (1961, chapter 4) or Rao and Mitra (1971, chapter 9). Extensive discussions of the properties of the central and noncentral chi-square distributions have been given by Lancaster (1969), Johnson and Kotz (1970a, chapter 17), and Johnson and Kotz (1970b, chapter 28). Note that the noncentrality parameter is sometimes defined differently. Our definition is taken from Johnson and Kotz (1970b, p. 130): if $y \sim \mathcal{N}_\nu(\mu, I_\nu)$, then $y'y$ is a noncentral chi-squared distributed variate with ν degrees of freedom and noncentrality parameter $\mu'\mu$. For the same case, Graybill (1961, p. 74) defined the noncentrality parameter as $\frac{1}{2}\mu'\mu$.

B.4 Most results derived in this section have also been given by Shapiro (1986, 1987). The conditions under which the Cauchy-Schwarz inequality reduces to an equality have been studied extensively by Rao and Mitra (1971, chapter 8) in the context of efficiency of OLS and GLS linear regression estimators.

References

Aasness, J., Biørn, E., and Skjerpen, T. (1993). Engle functions, panel data, and latent variables. *Econometrica*, *61*, 1395–1422.

Aigner, D. J. (1973). Regression with a binary independent variable subject to errors of observation. *Journal of Econometrics*, *1*, 49–59.

Aigner, D. J. (1974). MSE dominance of least squares with errors of observation. *Journal of Econometrics*, *2*, 365–372.

Aigner, D. J., and Goldberger, A. S. (Eds.). (1977). *Latent variables in socio-economic models*. Amsterdam: North-Holland.

Aigner, D. J., Hsiao, C., Kapteyn, A., and Wansbeek, T. J. (1984). Latent variable models in econometrics. In Z. Griliches and M. D. Intriligator (Eds.), *Handbook of econometrics* (Vol. II, pp. 1321–1393). Amsterdam: North-Holland.

Aitchison, J., and Silvey, S. D. (1958). Maximum-likelihood estimation of parameters subject to restraints. *The Annals of Mathematical Statistics*, *29*, 813–828.

Akaike, H. (1987). Factor analysis and AIC. *Psychometrika*, *52*, 317–332.

Albæk, K., Arai, M., Asplund, R., Barth, E., and Strøjer Madsen, E. (1998). Measuring wage effects of plant size. *Labour Economics*, *5*, 425–448.

Aldrich, J. (1994). Haavelmo's identification theory. *Econometric Theory*, *10*, 198–219.

Allison, P. D. (1987). Estimation of linear models with incomplete data. In C. C. Clogg (Ed.), *Sociological methodology 1987* (pp. 71–103). San Francisco: Jossey-Bass.

Alonso-Borrego, C., and Arellano, M. (1999). Symmetrically normalized instrumental-variable estimation using panel data. *Journal of Business & Economic Statistics*, *17*, 36–49.

Altonji, J. G., and Segal, L. M. (1996). Small-sample bias in GMM estimation of covariance structures. *Journal of Business & Economic Statistics*, *14*, 353–366.

Amemiya, T. (1966). On the use of principal components of independent variables in two-stage least-squares estimation. *International Economic Review*, *7*, 282–303.

Amemiya, Y. (1985). Instrumental variable estimator for the nonlinear errors-in-variables model. *Journal of Econometrics*, *28*, 273–289.

Amemiya, Y. (1990). Two-stage instrumental variable estimators for the nonlinear errors-in-variables model. *Journal of Econometrics*, *44*, 311–332.

Amemiya, Y. (1993). Instrumental variable estimation for nonlinear factor analysis. In

C. M. Cuadras and C. R. Rao (Eds.), *Multivariate analysis: Future directions 2* (pp. 113–129). Amsterdam: North-Holland.

Amemiya, Y., and Anderson, T. W. (1990). Asymptotic chi-square tests for a large class of factor analysis models. *The Annals of Statistics*, *18*, 1453–1463.

Amemiya, Y., and Fuller, W. A. (1988). Estimation for the nonlinear functional relationship. *The Annals of Statistics*, *16*, 147–160.

Anderson, J. C., and Gerbing, D. W. (1984). The effect of sampling error on convergence, improper solutions, and goodness-of-fit indices for maximum likelihood confirmatory factor analysis. *Psychometrika*, *49*, 155–173.

Anderson, T. W. (1984a). Estimating linear statistical relationships. *The Annals of Statistics*, *12*, 1–45.

Anderson, T. W. (1984b). *An introduction to multivariate statistical analysis* (2nd ed.). New York: Wiley.

Anderson, T. W., and Amemiya, Y. (1988). The asymptotic normal distribution of estimators in factor analysis under general conditions. *The Annals of Statistics*, *16*, 759–771.

Anderson, T. W., and Rubin, H. (1949). Estimation of the parameters of a single equation in a complete system of stochastic equations. *The Annals of Mathematical Statistics*, *20*, 46–63.

Anderson, T. W., and Rubin, H. (1950). The asymptotic properties of estimates of the parameters of a single equation in a complete system of stochastic equations. *The Annals of Mathematical Statistics*, *21*, 570–582.

Anderson, T. W., and Rubin, H. (1956). Statistical inference in factor analysis. In J. Neyman (Ed.), *Proceedings of the third Berkeley symposium on mathematical statistics and probability V* (pp. 111–150). Berkeley: University of California Press.

Andrews, D. W. K. (1991). Heteroskedasticity and autocorrelation consistent covariance matrix estimation. *Econometrica*, *59*, 817–858.

Andrews, D. W. K., and Monahan, J. C. (1992). An improved heteroskedasticity and autocorrelation consistent covariance matrix estimator. *Econometrica*, *60*, 953–966.

Aneuryn-Evans, G., and Deaton, A. (1980). Testing linear *versus* logarithmic regression models. *Review of Economic Studies*, *47*, 275–291.

Angrist, J. D., Imbens, G. W., and Krueger, A. B. (1999). Jackknife instrumental variables estimation. *Journal of Applied Econometrics*, *14*, 57–67.

Angrist, J. D., and Krueger, A. B. (1992). The effect of age at school entry on educational attainment: An application of instrumental variables with moments from two samples. *Journal of the American Statistical Association*, *87*, 328–336.

Angrist, J. D., and Krueger, A. B. (1995). Split-sample instrumental variables estimators and the return to education. *Journal of Business & Economic Statistics*, *13*, 225–235.

Apostol, T. M. (1967). *Calculus* (Vol. I, 2nd ed.). New York: Wiley.

Apostol, T. M. (1969). *Calculus* (Vol. II, 2nd ed.). New York: Wiley.

Arbuckle, J. L. (1996). Full information estimation in the presence of incomplete data.

In G. A. Marcoulides and R. E. Schumacker (Eds.), *Advanced structural equation modeling: Issues and techniques* (pp. 243–277). Mahwah, NJ: Erlbaum.

Arbuckle, J. L. (1997). *Amos user's guide. Version 3.6.* Chicago: Smallwaters.

Arellano, M., and Meghir, C. (1992). Female labour supply and on-the-job search: An empirical model estimated using complementary data sets. *Review of Economic Studies*, *59*, 537–559.

Arminger, G., and Küsters, U. L. (1988). Latent trait models with indicators of mixed measurement level. In R. Langeheine and J. Rost (Eds.), *Latent trait and latent class models* (pp. 51–73). New York: Plenum Press.

Arminger, G., and Muthén, B. O. (1998). A Bayesian approach to nonlinear latent variable models using the Gibbs sampler and the Metropolis-Hastings algorithm. *Psychometrika*, *63*, 271–300.

Arminger, G., Wittenberg, J., and Schepers, A. (1996). *MECOSA 3: Mean and covariance structure analysis.* Friedrichsdorf, Germany: Additive.

Attfield, C. L. F. (1977). Estimation of a model containing unobservable variables using grouped observations: An application to the permanent income hypothesis. *Journal of Econometrics*, *6*, 51–63.

Banks, J., Blundell, R., and Lewbel, A. (1997). Quadratic Engel curves and consumer demand. *The Review of Economics and Statistics*, *79*, 527–539.

Barankin, E., and Gurland, J. (1951). On asymptotically normal efficient estimators: I. *University of California Publications in Statistics*, *1*, 86–130.

Barnett, V. D. (1967). A note on linear structural relationships when both residual variances are known. *Biometrika*, *54*, 670–672.

Barnett, V. D. (1970). Fitting straight lines. the linear functional relationship with replicated observations. *Applied Statistics*, *19*, 135–144.

Bartholomew, D. J. (1980). Factor analysis for categorical data. *Journal of the Royal Statistical Society B*, *42*, 293–321. (with discussion)

Bartholomew, D. J., and Knott, M. (1999). *Latent variable models and factor analysis* (2nd ed.). London: Arnold.

Bartlett, M. S. (1937). The statistical conception of mental factors. *British Journal of Psychology*, *28*, 97–104.

Bartlett, M. S. (1949). Fitting a straight line when both variables are subject to error. *Biometrics*, *5*, 207–212.

Basilevsky, A. (1994). *Statistical factor analysis and related methods: Theory and applications.* New York: Wiley.

Bates, C., and White, H. L. (1985). A unified theory of consistent estimation. *Econometric Theory*, *1*, 151–178.

Bekker, P. A. (1986). Comment on identification in the linear errors in variables model. *Econometrica*, *54*, 215–217.

Bekker, P. A. (1988). The positive semidefiniteness of partitioned matrices. *Linear Algebra and Its Applications*, *111*, 261–278.

Bekker, P. A. (1989). Identification in restricted factor models and the evaluation of rank conditions. *Journal of Econometrics*, *41*, 5–16.

Bekker, P. A. (1994). Alternative approximations to the distributions of instrumental variable estimators. *Econometrica*, *62*, 657–681.

Bekker, P. A., Dobbelstein, P., and Wansbeek, T. J. (1996). The APT model as reduced rank regression. *Journal of Business & Economic Statistics*, *14*, 199–202.

Bekker, P. A., Kapteyn, A., and Wansbeek, T. J. (1984). Measurement error and endogeneity in regression: bounds for ML and 2SLS estimates. In T. K. Dijkstra (Ed.), *Misspecification analysis* (pp. 85–103). Berlin: Springer.

Bekker, P. A., Kapteyn, A., and Wansbeek, T. J. (1987). Consistent sets of estimates for regressions with correlated or uncorrelated measurement errors in arbitrary subsets of all variables. *Econometrica*, *55*, 1223–1230.

Bekker, P. A., Merckens, A., and Wansbeek, T. J. (1994). *Identification, equivalent models, and computer algebra.* Boston: Academic Press.

Bekker, P. A., and Neudecker, H. (1989). Albert's theorem applied to problems of efficiency and MSE superiority. *Statistica Neerlandica*, *43*, 157–167.

Bekker, P. A., and Ten Berge, J. M. F. (1997). Generic global identification in factor analysis. *Linear Algebra and its Applications*, *264*, 255–263.

Bekker, P. A., Van Montfort, K., and Mooijaart, A. (1991). Regression analysis with dichotomous regressors and misclassification. *Statistica Neerlandica*, *45*, 107–120.

Bekker, P. A., and Wansbeek, T. J. (1996). Proxies versus omitted variables in regression analysis. *Linear Algebra and its Applications*, *237/238*, 301–312.

Bekker, P. A., Wansbeek, T. J., and Kapteyn, A. (1985). Errors in variables in econometrics: New developments and recurrent themes. *Statistica Neerlandica*, *39*, 129–141.

Bentler, P. M. (1982). Linear systems with multiple levels and types of latent variables. In K. G. Jöreskog and H. Wold (Eds.), *Systems under indirect observation: Causality, structure, prediction. Part I* (pp. 101–130). Amsterdam: North-Holland.

Bentler, P. M. (1983a). Simultaneous equation systems as moment structure models, with an introduction to latent variable models. *Journal of Econometrics*, *22*, 13–42.

Bentler, P. M. (1983b). Some contributions to efficient statistics in structural models: Specification and estimation of moment structures. *Psychometrika*, *48*, 493–517.

Bentler, P. M. (1989). *EQS structural equations program manual.* Los Angeles: BMDP.

Bentler, P. M. (1990). Comparative fit indexes in structural models. *Psychological Bulletin*, *107*, 238–246.

Bentler, P. M. (1995). *EQS structural equations program manual.* Encino, CA: Multivariate Software.

Bentler, P. M., and Bonett, D. G. (1980). Significance tests and goodness of fit in the analysis of covariance structures. *Psychological Bulletin*, *88*, 588–606.

Bentler, P. M., and Dijkstra, T. K. (1985). Efficient estimation via linearization in structural models. In P. R. Krishnaiah (Ed.), *Multivariate analysis — VI* (pp. 9–42). Amsterdam: Elsevier Science.

Bentler, P. M., and Dudgeon, P. (1996). Covariance structure analysis: Statistical practice, theory, and directions. *Annual Review of Psychology*, *47*, 563–592.

Bentler, P. M., Lee, S.-Y., and Weng, L.-J. (1997). Multiple population covariance structure analysis under arbitrary distribution theory. *Communications in Statistics — Theory and Methods*, *16*, 1951–1964.

Bentler, P. M., and Mooijaart, A. (1989). Choice of structural model via parsimony: A rationale based on precision. *Psychological Bulletin*, *106*, 315–317.

Bentler, P. M., and Weeks, D. G. (1980). Linear structural equations with latent variables. *Psychometrika*, *45*, 289–308.

Bentler, P. M., and Yuan, K.-H. (1999). Structural equation modeling with small samples: Test statistics. *Multivariate Behavioral Research*, *34*, 181–197.

Beran, R., and Srivastava, M. S. (1985). Bootstrap tests and confidence regions for functions of a covariance matrix. *The Annals of Statistics*, *13*, 95–115.

Berkson, J. (1950). Are there two regressions? *Journal of the American Statistical Association*, *45*, 164–180.

Berkson, J. (1980). Minimum chi-square, not maximum likelihood! *The Annals of Statistics*, *8*, 457–487. (with discussion)

Bickel, P. J., and Ritov, Y. (1987). Efficient estimation in the errors in variables model. *The Annals of Statistics*, *15*, 513–540.

Biemer, P. P., Groves, R. M., Lyberg, L. E., Mathiowetz, N. A., and Sudman, S. (1991). *Measurement error in surveys*. New York: Wiley.

Bijleveld, C. C. J. H., Mooijaart, A., Van der Kamp, L. J. T., and Van der Kloot, W. A. (1998). Structural equation models for logitudinal data. In C. C. J. H. Bijleveld and L. J. T. Van der Kamp (Eds.), *Longitudinal data analysis: Designs, models and methods* (pp. 207–268). London: Sage.

Biørn, E. (1992a). The bias of some estimators for panel data models with measurement errors. *Empirical Economics*, *17*, 51–66.

Biørn, E. (1992b). Panel data with measurement errors. In L. Mátyás and P. Sevestre (Eds.), *The econometrics of panel data* (pp. 152–195). Dordrecht: Kluwer.

Birch, M. W. (1964). A note on the maximum likelihood estimation of a linear structural relationship. *Journal of the American Statistical Assocation*, *59*, 1175–1178.

Blomquist, S., and Dahlberg, M. (1999). Small sample properties of LIML and jackknife IV estimators: Experiments with weak instruments. *Journal of Applied Econometrics*, *14*, 68–88.

Blundell, R., Bond, S., Devereux, M., and Schiantarelli, F. (1992). Investment and Tobin's *Q*: Evidence from company panel data. *Journal of Econometrics*, *51*, 233–257.

Bock, R. D., and Aitkin, M. (1981). Marginal maximum likelihood estimation of item parameters: Application of an EM algorithm. *Psychometrika*, *46*, 443–459.

Bock, R. D., Gibbons, R., and Muraki, E. (1988). Full-information item factor analysis. *Applied Psychological Measurement*, *12*, 261–280.

Bock, R. D., and Lieberman, M. (1970). Fitting a response model for n dichotomously scored items. *Psychometrika*, *35*, 179–197.

Boggs, P. T., Donaldson, J. R., Schnabel, R. B., and Spiegelman, C. H. (1988). A computational examination of orthogonal distance regression. *Journal of Econometrics*, *38*, 169–201.

Bollen, K. A. (1989). *Structural equations with latent variables*. New York: Wiley.

Bollen, K. A., and Jöreskog, K. G. (1985). Uniqueness does not imply identification. a note on confirmatory factor analysis. *Sociological Methods & Research*, *14*, 155-163.

Bollen, K. A., and Long, J. S. (Eds.). (1993). *Testing structural equation models.* Newbury Park, CA: Sage.

Bollen, K. A., and Stine, R. A. (1992). Bootstrapping goodness-of-fit measures in structural equation models. *Sociological Methods & Research*, *21*, 205–229.

Bollinger, C. R. (1996). Bounding mean regressions when a binary regressor is mismeasured. *Journal of Econometrics*, *73*, 387–399.

Boomsma, A. (1983). *On the robustness of LISREL (maximum likelihood estimation) against small sample size and nonnormality.* Unpublished Ph.D. Thesis, University of Groningen, Groningen, The Netherlands.

Boomsma, A. (1985). Nonconvergence, improper solutions, and starting values in LISREL maximum likelihood estimation. *Psychometrika*, *50*, 229–242.

Booth, J. R., and Smith, R. L. (1985). The application of errors-in-variables methodology to capital market research: Evidence on the small-firm effect. *Journal of Financial and Quantitative Analysis*, *20*, 501–515.

Bound, J., Brown, C., Duncan, G. J., and Rodgers, W. L. (1990). Measurement error in cross-sectional and longitudinal labor market surveys: Validation survey evidence. In J. Hartog, G. Ridder, and J. Theeuwes (Eds.), *Panel data and labor market studies* (pp. 1–19). Amsterdam: North-Holland.

Bound, J., Brown, C., Duncan, G. J., and Rodgers, W. L. (1994). Evidence on the validity of cross-sectional and longitudinal labor market data. *Journal of Labor Economics*, *12*, 345–368.

Bound, J., Jaeger, D. A., and Baker, R. M. (1995). Problems with instrumental variables estimation when the correlation between the instruments and the endogenous explanatory variable is weak. *Journal of the American Statistical Association*, *90*, 443–450.

Bound, J., and Krueger, A. B. (1991). The extent of measurement error in longitudianl earnings data: Do two wrongs make a right? *Journal of Labor Economics*, *9*, 1–24.

Bowden, R. J. (1973). The theory of parametric identification. *Econometrica*, *41*, 1069–1074.

Bowden, R. J., and Turkington, D. A. (1984). *Instrumental variables.* Cambridge, UK: Cambridge University Press.

Box, G. E. P. (1954). Some theorems on quadratic forms applied in the study of analysis of variance problems, I. effect of inequality of variance in the one-way classification. *The Annals of Mathematical Statistics*, *25*, 290–302.

Bozdogan, H. (1987). Model selection and Akaike's Information Criterion (AIC): The general theory and its analytical extensions. *Psychometrika*, *52*, 345–370.

Bozdogan, H. (1988). ICOMP: A new model selection criterion. In H. H. Bock (Ed.), *Classification and related methods of data analysis* (pp. 599–608). Amsterdam: North-Holland.

Breckler, S. J. (1990). Applications of covariance structure modeling in psychology:

Cause for concern? *Psychological Bulletin*, *107*, 260–273.

Breusch, T. S., Qian, H., Schmidt, P., and Wyhowski, D. (1999). Redundancy of moment conditions. *Journal of Econometrics*, *91*, 89–111.

Breusch, T. S., and Schmidt, P. (1988). Alternative forms of the Wald test: How long is a piece of string? *Communications in Statistics — Theory and Methods*, *17*, 2789–2795.

Brown, P. J., and Fuller, W. A. (Eds.). (1990). *Statistical analysis of measurement error models and applications.* Providence, RI: American Mathematical Society.

Brown, R. L. (1957). Bivariate structural relation. *Biometrika*, *44*, 84–96.

Browne, M. W. (1974). Generalized least squares estimators in the analysis of covariance structures. *South African Statistical Journal*, *8*, 1–24. (Reprinted in D. J. Aigner and A. S. Goldberger, Eds., 1977, *Latent Variables in Socio-Economic Models*, pp. 205–226, Amsterdam: North-Holland.)

Browne, M. W. (1982). Covariance structures. In D. M. Hawkins (Ed.), *Topics in applied multivariate analysis* (pp. 72–141). London: Cambridge University Press.

Browne, M. W. (1984). Asymptotically distribution-free methods for the analysis of covariance structures. *British Journal of Mathematical and Statistical Psychology*, *37*, 62–83.

Browne, M. W. (1987). Robustness of statistical inference in factor analysis and related models. *Biometrika*, *74*, 375–384.

Browne, M. W., and Cudeck, R. (1992). Alternative ways of assessing model fit. *Sociological Methods & Research*, *21*, 230–258.

Browne, M. W., Mels, G., and Coward, M. (1994). Path analysis: RAMONA. In *SYSTAT for DOS: Advanced applications, version 6* (pp. 163–224). Evanston, IL: Systat.

Browne, M. W., and Shapiro, A. (1988). Robustness of normal theory methods in the analysis of linear latent variate models. *British Journal of Mathematical and Statistical Psychology*, *41*, 193–208.

Buonaccorsi, J. P. (1989). Errors-in-variables with systematic biases. *Communications in Statistics – Theory and Methods*, *18*, 1001–1021.

Burr, D. (1988). On errors-in-variables in binary regression—Berkson case. *Journal of the American Statistical Association*, *83*, 739–743.

Byrne, B. M. (1994). *Structural equation modeling with EQS and EQS/Windows.* Thousand Oaks, CA: Sage.

Cadima, J., and Jolliffe, I. (1997). Some comments on ten Berge, j. m. f. & kiers, h. a. l. (1996). optimality criteria for principal component analysis and generalizations. *British Journal of Mathematical and Statistical Psychology*, *50*, 365–366.

Cameron, A. C., and Windmeijer, F. A. G. (1997). An *r*-squared measure of goodness of fit for some common nonlinear regression models. *Journal of Econometrics*, *77*, 329–342.

Carroll, R. J., Ruppert, D., and Stefanski, L. A. (1995). *Measurement error in nonlinear models.* London: Chapman & Hall.

Carroll, R. J., Spiegelman, C. H., Lan, K. K. G., Bailey, K. T., and Abbott, R. D. (1984). On errors-in-variables for binary regression models. *Biometrika*, *71*, 19–25.

Carroll, R. J., Wu, C. F. J., and Ruppert, D. (1988). The effect of estimating weights in weighted least squares. *Journal of the American Statistical Association*, *83*, 1045–1054.

Casella, G., and George, E. I. (1992). Explaining the Gibbs sampler. *The American Statistician*, *46*, 167–174.

Casson, M. C. (1974). Generalized errors in variables regression. *Review of Economic Studies*, *41*, 347–352.

Chamberlain, G. (1977). An instrumental variable interpretation of identification in variance-components and MIMIC models. In P. Taubman (Ed.), *Kinometrics: The determinants of socio-economic success within and between families*. Amsterdam: North-Holland.

Chamberlain, G. (1982). Multivariate regression models for panel data. *Journal of Econometrics*, *18*, 5–46.

Chamberlain, G. (1987). Asymptotic efficiency in estimation with conditional moment restrictions. *Journal of Econometrics*, *34*, 305–335.

Chamberlain, G. (1990). Distinguished fellow – Arthur S. Goldberger and latent variables in econometrics. *Journal of Economic Perspectives*, *4*, 125–152.

Chamberlain, G., and Griliches, Z. (1975). Unobservables with a variance-components structure: Ability, schooling and the economic success of brothers. *International Economic Review*, *16*, 422–449.

Chan, L. K., and Mak, T. K. (1979a). Maximum likelihood estimation of a linear structural relationship with replication. *Journal of the Royal Statistical Society B*, *41*, 263–268.

Chan, L. K., and Mak, T. K. (1979b). On the maximum likelihood estimation of a linear structural relationship when the intercept is known. *Journal of Multivariate Analysis*, *9*, 304–313.

Chan, L. K., and Mak, T. K. (1984). Maximum likelihood estimation in multivariate structural relationships. *Scandinavian Journal of Statistics*, *11*, 45–50.

Chan, L. K., and Mak, T. K. (1985). On the polynomial functional relationship. *Journal of the Royal Statistical Society B*, *47*, 510–518.

Chan, N. N., and Mak, T. K. (1983). Estimation of multivariate linear functional relationships. *Biometrika*, *70*, 263–267.

Chan, N. N., and Mak, T. K. (1984). Heteroscedastic errors in a linear functional relationship. *Biometrika*, *71*, 212–215.

Chan, W., Yung, Y.-F., and Bentler, P. M. (1995). A note on using an unbiased weight matrix in the ADF test statistic. *Multivariate Behavioral Research*, *30*, 453–460.

Chatterjee, S., and Hadi, A. S. (1988). *Sensitivity analysis in linear regression.* New York: Wiley.

Chen, C.-F. (1981). The EM approach to the multiple indicators and multiple causes model via the estimation of the latent variable. *Journal of the American Statistical Association*, *76*, 704–708.

Cheng, C.-L., and Van Ness, J. W. (1999). *Statistical regression with measurement error.* London: Arnold.

Chesher, A. (1991). The effect of measurement error. *Biometrika*, *78*, 451–462.

Chiang, C. L. (1956). On regular best asymptotically normal estimates. *The Annals of Mathematical Statistics*, *27*, 336–351.

Christoffersson, A. (1975). Factor analysis of dichotomized variables. *Psychometrika*, *40*, 5–32.

Christoffersson, A., and Gunsjö, A. (1996). A short note on the estimation of the asymptotic covariance matrix for polychoric correlations. *Psychometrika*, *61*, 173–175.

Cochran, W. G. (1968). Errors of measurement in statistics. *Technometrics*, *10*, 637–666.

Conway, D. A., and Roberts, H. V. (1983). Reverse regression, fairness, and employment discrimination. *Journal of Business & Economic Statistics*, *1*, 75–85.

Copas, J. B. (1972). The likelihood surface in the linear functional relationship problem. *Journal of the Royal Statistical Society B*, *34*, 274–278.

Cragg, J. G. (1994). Making good inferences from bad data. *Canadian Journal of Economics*, *27*, 776–800.

Cragg, J. G., and Donald, S. G. (1997). Inferring the rank of a matrix. *Journal of Econometrics*, *76*, 223–250.

Cramér, H. (1946). *Mathematical methods of statistics.* Princeton: Princeton University Press.

Creasy, M. (1956). Confidence limits for the gradient in the linear functional relationship. *Journal of the Royal Statistical Society B*, *18*, 65–69.

Cudeck, R. (1989). Analysis of correlation matrices using covariance structure models. *Psychological Bulletin*, *105*, 317–327.

Cudeck, R., and Browne, M. W. (1983). Cross-validation of covariance structures. *Multivariate Behavioral Research*, *18*, 147–167.

Cumby, R. E., Huizinga, J., and Obstfeld, M. (1983). Two-step two-stage least squares estimation in models with rational expectations. *Journal of Econometrics*, *21*, 333–355.

Cummins, J. G., Hassett, K. A., and Hubbard, R. G. (1994). A reconsideration of investment behavior using tax reforms as natural experiments. *Brookings Papers on Economic Activity*, *2*, 1–74.

Dagenais, M. G. (1994). Parameter estimation in regression models with errors in the variables and autocorrelated disturbances. *Journal of Econometrics*, *64*, 145–163.

Dagenais, M. G., and Dagenais, D. L. (1997). Higher moment estimators for linear regression models with errors in the variables. *Journal of Econometrics*, *76*, 193–221.

Dagenais, M. G., and Dufour, J.-M. (1991). Invariance, nonlinear models, and asymptotic tests. *Econometrica*, *59*, 1601–1615.

Davidson, R., and MacKinnon, J. G. (1993). *Estimation and inference in econometrics.* Oxford: Oxford University Press.

Davies, R. B. (1980). The distribution of a linear combination of χ^2 random variables. *Applied Statistics*, *29*, 323–333.

Davison, A. C., and Hinkley, D. V. (1997). *Bootstrap methods and their application.* Cambridge, UK: Cambridge University Press.

DeGracie, J. S., and Fuller, W. A. (1972). Estimation of the slope and analysis of covariance when the concomitant variable is measured with error. *Journal of the American Statistical Association*, *67*, 930–937.

De Haan, J., and Kooi, W. (1997). What really matters: Conservativeness or independence? *Banca Nazionale del Lavoro Quarterly Review*, *50*, 23–38.

Deistler, M., and Anderson, B. D. O. (1989). Linear dynamic errors-in-variables models: Some structure theory. *Journal of Econometrics*, *41*, 39–63.

De Jong, R. M., and Davidson, J. (2000). Consistency of kernel estimators of heteroscedastic and autocorrelated covariance matrices. *Econometrica*, *68*, 407–423.

De Leeuw, J. (1988). Model selection in multinomial experiments. In T. K. Dijkstra (Ed.), *On model uncertainty and its statistical implications* (pp. 118–138). Berlin: Springer.

Del Pino, G. (1989). The unifying role of iterative generalized least squares in statistical algorithms. *Statistical Science*, *4*, 394–408.

Dempster, A. (1988). Employment discrimination and statistical science. *Statistical Science*, *3*, 149–161.

Dijkstra, T. K. (1992). On statistical inference with parameter estimates on the boundary of the parameter space. *British Journal of Mathematical and Statistical Psychology*, *45*, 289–309.

Dijkstra, T. K., and Wansbeek, T. J. (1990). Comment on 'instrumental variables and maximum likelihood'. *Annales d'Économie et de Statistique*, *17*, 205–209.

Divgi, D. R. (1979). Calculation of the tetrachoric correlation coefficient. *Psychometrika*, *44*, 169–172.

Dolby, G. R. (1972). Generalized least squares and maximum likelihood estimation of nonlinear functional relationships. *Journal of the Royal Statistical Society B*, *34*, 393–400.

Dolby, G. R. (1976a). The connection between methods of estimation in implicit and explicit nonlinear models. *Applied Statistics*, *25*, 157–162.

Dolby, G. R. (1976b). A note on the linear structural relation when both residual variances are known. *Journal of the American Statistical Association*, *71*, 352–353.

Dolby, G. R. (1976c). The ultrastructural relation: A synthesis of the functional and structural relations. *Biometrika*, *63*, 39–50.

Dolby, G. R., and Freeman, T. G. (1975). Functional relationships having many independent variables and errors with multivariate normal distribution. *Journal of Multivariate Analysis*, *5*, 466–479.

Dolby, G. R., and Lipton, S. (1972). Maximum likelihood estimation of the general nonlinear relationship with replicated observations and correlated errors. *Biometrika*, *59*, 121–129.

Dorff, M., and Gurland, J. (1961a). Estimation of the parameters of a linear functional relation. *Journal of the Royal Statistical Society B*, *23*, 160–170.

Dorff, M., and Gurland, J. (1961b). Small sample behavior of slope estimators in a linear functional relation. *Biometrics*, *17*, 283–298.

Dunford, N., and Schwartz, J. T. (1958). *Linear operators. part I: General theory.* New

York: Interscience.

Dunn, G., Everitt, B., and Pickles, A. (1993). *Modelling covariances and latent variables using EQS.* London: Chapman & Hall.

Durbin, J. (1954). Errors in variables. *International Statistical Review, 22*, 23–32.

Eckart, C., and Young, G. (1936). The approximation of one matrix by another of lower rank. *Psychometrika, 1*, 211–218.

Efron, B. (1979). Bootstrap methods: Another look at the jackknife. *The Annals of Statistics, 7*, 1–26.

Efron, B., and Tibshirani, R. J. (1993). *An introduction to the bootstrap.* New York: Chapman and Hall.

Egerton, M. F., and Laycock, P. J. (1979). Maximum likelihood estimation of multivariate non-linear functional relationships. *Mathematische Operationsforschung und Statistik, 10*, 273–280.

Eicker, F. (1963). Asymptotic normality and consistency of the least squares estimators for families of linear regressions. *The Annals of Mathematical Statistics, 34*, 447–456.

Eicker, F. (1967). Limit theorems for regressions with unequal and dependent errors. In L. Le Cam and J. Neyman (Eds.), *Proceedings of the Fifth Berkeley Symposium on Mathematical Statistics and Probability* (Vol. I, pp. 59–82). Berkeley: University of California Press.

Elffers, H., Bethlehem, J. G., and Gill, R. D. (1978). Indeterminacy problems and the interpretation of factor analysis results. *Statistica Neerlandica, 32*, 181–199.

Elrod, T., and Keane, M. P. (1995). A factor-analytic probit model for representing the market structure in panel data. *Journal of Marketing Research, 32*, 1–16.

Engle, R. F. (1984). Wald, likelihood ratio, and Lagrange Multiplier tests in econometrics. In Z. Griliches and M. D. Intriligator (Eds.), *Handbook of econometrics* (Vol. II, pp. 775–826). Amsterdam: North-Holland.

Engle, R. F., Lilien, D. M., and Watson, M. (1985). A DYMIMIC model of housing price determination. *Journal of Econometrics, 28*, 307–326.

Erickson, T. (1989). Proper posteriors from improper priors for an unidentified errors-in-variables model. *Econometrica, 57*, 1299–1316.

Fan, J., and Truong, Y. K. (1993). Nonparametric regression with errors in variables. *The Annals of Statistics, 21*, 1900–1925.

Fazzari, S. M., and Petersen, B. C. (1993). Working capital and fixed investment: New evidence on financing constraints. *Rand Journal of Economics, 24*, 328–342.

Ferguson, T. S. (1958). A method of generating best asymptotically normal estimates with application to the estimation of bacterial densities. *The Annals of Mathematical Statistics, 29*, 1046–1062.

Ferguson, T. S. (1967). *Mathematical statistics: A decision theoretic approach.* San Diego: Academic Press.

Ferguson, T. S. (1996). *A course in large sample theory.* London: Chapman & Hall.

Feuerverger, A., and Mureika, R. A. (1977). The empirical characteristic function and its applications. *The Annals of Statistics, 5*, 88–97.

Fienberg, S. E. (Ed.). (1988). *The evolving role of statistical assessments as evidence in the courts.* New York: Springer.

Fisher, F. M. (1966). *The identification problem in econometrics.* New York: McGraw-Hill.

Fisher, R. A. (1921). On the mathematical foundations of theoretical statistics. *Philosophical Transactions of the Royal Society of London, Series A*, *222*, 309–368.

Florens, J.-P., Mouchart, M., and Richard, J.-F. (1974). Bayesian inference in error-in-variables models. *Journal of Multivariate Analysis*, *4*, 419–452.

Freedman, D. A. (1987). As others see us: A case study in path analysis. *Journal of Educational Statistics*, *12*, 101–223. (with discussion)

Freeman, R. B. (1984). Longitudinal analyses of effects of trade unions. *Journal of Labor Economics*, *2*, 1–26.

Friedman, M. (1957). *A theory of the consumption function.* Princeton, NJ: Princeton University Press.

Frisch, R. (1934). *Statistical confluence analysis by means of complete regression systems.* Oslo: University Institute of Economics.

Frisch, R., and Waugh, F. V. (1933). Partial time regressions as compared with individual trends. *Econometrica*, *1*, 387–401.

Fuller, W. A. (1980). Properties of some estimators for the errors-in-variables model. *The Annals of Statistics*, *8*, 407–422.

Fuller, W. A. (1987). *Measurement error models.* New York: Wiley.

Fuller, W. A., and Hidiroglou, M. A. (1978). Regression estimation after correcting for attenuation. *Journal of the American Statistical Association*, *73*, 99–104.

Garber, S., and Klepper, S. (1980). Extending the classical normal errors-in-variables model. *Econometrica*, *48*, 1541–1546.

Geman, S., and Geman, D. (1984). Stochastic relaxation, Gibbs distributions, and the Bayesian restoration of images. *IEEE Transactions on Pattern Analysis and Machine Intelligence*, *6*, 721–741.

Geraci, V. J. (1976). Identification of simultaneous equation models with measurement error. *Journal of Econometrics*, *4*, 263–283.

Geraci, V. J. (1977). Estimation of simultaneous equation models with measurement error. *Econometrica*, *45*, 1243–1255.

Geraci, V. J. (1983). Errors in variables and the individual structural equation. *International Economic Review*, *24*, 217–236.

Geraci, V. J. (1987). Errors in variables. In J. Eatwell, M. Milgate, and P. Newman (Eds.), *The new Palgrave: A dictionary of economics* (Vol. 2, pp. 189–192). London: Macmillan.

Gerbing, D. W., and Anderson, J. C. (1985). The effects of sampling error and model characteristics on parameter estimation for maximum likelihood confirmatory factor analysis. *Multivariate Behavioral Research*, *20*, 255–271.

Geweke, J. F., and Singleton, K. J. (1981a). Latent variable models for time series: A frequency domain approach with an application to the permanent income hypothesis. *Journal of Econometrics*, *17*, 287–304.

Geweke, J. F., and Singleton, K. J. (1981b). Maximum likelihood "confirmatory" factor analysis of economic time series. *International Economic Review*, *22*, 37–54.

Gibson, W. M., and Jowett, G. H. (1957a). Three-group regression analysis. Part I: Simple regression analysis. *Applied Statistics*, *6*, 114–122.

Gibson, W. M., and Jowett, G. H. (1957b). Three-group regression analysis. Part II: Multiple regression analysis. *Applied Statistics*, *6*, 189–197.

Gill, P. E., Murray, W., and Wright, M. H. (1981). *Practical optimization.* London: Academic Press.

Gleser, L. J. (1985). A note on G. R. Dolby's unreplicated ultrastructural model. *Biometrika*, *72*, 117–124.

Godambe, V. P. (Ed.). (1991). *Estimating functions.* Oxford: Clarendon Press.

Goldberger, A. S. (1971). Econometrics and psychometrics: A survey of communalities. *Psychometrika*, *36*, 83–107.

Goldberger, A. S. (1972a). Maximum-likelihood estimation of regressions containing unobservable independent variables. *International Economic Review*, *13*, 1–15.

Goldberger, A. S. (1972b). Structural equation methods in the social sciences. *Econometrica*, *40*, 979–1001.

Goldberger, A. S. (1974). Unobservable variables in econometrics. In P. Zarembka (Ed.), *Frontiers in econometrics* (pp. 193–213). New York: Academic Press.

Goldberger, A. S. (1984a). Redirecting reverse regression. *Journal of Business & Economic Statistics*, *2*, 114–116.

Goldberger, A. S. (1984b). Reverse regression and salary discrimination. *The Journal of Human Resources*, *19*, 293–319.

Goldberger, A. S., and Duncan, O. D. (Eds.). (1973). *Structural equation models in the social sciences.* New York: Seminar Press.

Goldstein, H. (1995). *Multilevel statistical models.* London: Edward Arnold.

Golub, G. H., and Van Loan, C. F. (1980). An analysis of the total least squares problem. *SIAM Journal on Numerical Analysis*, *17*, 883–893.

Golub, G. H., and Van Loan, C. F. (1996). *Matrix computations* (3rd ed.). Baltimore: The Johns Hopkins University Press.

Gorsuch, S. A. (1974). *Factor analysis.* Philadelphia: Saunders.

Gouriéroux, C., Holly, A., and Monfort, A. (1982). Likelihood ratio test, Wald test, and Kuhn-Tucker test in linear models with inequality constraints on the regression parameters. *Econometrica*, *50*, 63–80.

Gouriéroux, C., and Monfort, A. (1989). A general framework for testing a null hypothesis in a "mixed" form. *Econometric Theory*, *5*, 63–82.

Gouriéroux, C., and Monfort, A. (1991). Simulation based inference in models with heterogeneity. *Annales d'Économie et de Statistique*, *20/21*, 69–107.

Gouriéroux, C., and Monfort, A. (1993). Simulation-based inference. A survey with special reference to panel data models. *Journal of Econometrics*, *59*, 5–33.

Gouriéroux, C., and Monfort, A. (1994). Testing non-nested hypotheses. In R. F. Engle and D. L. McFadden (Eds.), *Handbook of econometrics* (Vol. IV, pp. 2583–2637). Amsterdam: Elsevier Science.

Gouriéroux, C., and Monfort, A. (1995). *Statistics and econometric models.* Cambridge, UK: Cambridge University Press.

Gouriéroux, C., and Monfort, A. (1996). *Simulation-based econometric methods.* Oxford: Oxford University Press.

Gouriéroux, C., Monfort, A., and Trognon, A. (1985). Moindres carrés asymptotiques [Asymptotic least squares]. *Annales de l'INSEE*, *58*, 91–120.

Graham, A. (1981). *Kronecker products and matrix calculus: with applications.* New York: Ellis Horwood.

Graybill, F. A. (1961). *An introduction to linear statistical models* (Vol. I). New York: McGraw-Hill.

Gregory, A. W., and Veall, M. R. (1985). Formulating Wald tests of nonlinear restrictions. *Econometrica*, *53*, 1465–1468.

Griliches, Z. (1974). Errors in variables and other unobservables. *Econometrica*, *42*, 971–998.

Griliches, Z. (1986). Economic data issues. In Z. Griliches and M. D. Intriligator (Eds.), *Handbook of econometrics* (Vol. III). Amsterdam: North-Holland.

Griliches, Z., and Hausman, J. A. (1986). Errors in variables in panel data. *Journal of Econometrics*, *32*, 93–118.

Griliches, Z., and Ringstad, V. (1970). Error-in-the-variables bias in nonlinear contexts. *Econometrica*, *38*, 368–370.

Haavelmo, T. (1944). The probability approach in econometrics. *Econometrica*, *12*. (supplement)

Hägglund, G. (1982). Factor analysis by instrumental variables methods. *Psychometrika*, *47*, 209–221.

Haitovsky, Y. (1972). On errors of measurement in regression analysis in economics. *International Statistical Review*, *40*, 23–35.

Hajivassiliou, V. A. (1993). Simulation estimation methods for limited dependent variable models. In G. S. Maddala, C. R. Rao, and H. D. Vinod (Eds.), *Handbook of statistics, vol. 11: Econometrics* (pp. 519–543). Amsterdam: North-Holland.

Hajivassiliou, V. A., and Ruud, P. A. (1994). Classical estimation methods for LDV models using simulation. In R. F. Engle and D. L. McFadden (Eds.), *Handbook of econometrics* (Vol. IV, pp. 2383–2441). Amsterdam: Elsevier Science.

Hall, P. (1992). *The bootstrap and Edgeworth expansion.* New York: Springer.

Halton, J. H. (1970). A retrospective and prospective survey of the Monte Carlo method. *SIAM Review*, *12*, 1–63.

Hamilton, J. D. (1994). *Time series analysis.* Princeton: Princeton University Press.

Hammersley, J. M., and Handscomb, D. C. (1964). *Monte Carlo methods.* London: Methuen.

Hampel, F. R., Ronchetti, E. M., Rousseeuw, P. J., and Stahel, W. A. (1986). *Robust statistics: The approach based on influence functions.* New York: Wiley.

Hansen, L. P. (1982). Large sample properties of generalized method of moments estimators. *Econometrica*, *50*, 1029–1054.

Hansen, L. P., Heaton, J., and Yaron, A. (1996). Finite-sample properties of some alternative GMM estimators. *Journal of Business & Economic Statistics*, *14*, 262–280.

Hansen, L. P., and Singleton, K. J. (1982). Generalized instrumental variables estimation of nonlinear rational expectations models. *Econometrica*, *50*, 1269–1286.

Harman, H. H. (1976). *Modern factor analysis* (3rd ed.). Chicago: The University of Chicago Press.

Harville, D. A. (1997). *Matrix algebra from a statistician's perspective.* New York: Springer.

Hashimoto, M., and Kochin, L. (1980). A bias in the statistical estimation of the effects of discrimination. *Economic Inquiry*, *18*, 478–486.

Hauser, R. M., and Goldberger, A. S. (1971). The treatment of unobservable variables in path analysis. In H. L. Costner (Ed.), *Sociological methodology 1971* (pp. 81–117). San Francisco: Jossey-Bass.

Hausman, J. A. (1977). Errors in variables in simultaneous equation models. *Journal of Econometrics*, *5*, 389–401.

Hausman, J. A. (1978). Specification tests in econometrics. *Econometrica*, *46*, 1251–1271.

Hausman, J. A., Newey, W. K., Ichimura, H., and Powell, J. L. (1991). Identification and estimation of polynomial errors-in-variables models. *Journal of Econometrics*, *50*, 273–295.

Hausman, J. A., Newey, W. K., and Powell, J. L. (1995). Nonlinear errors in variables estimation of some Engel curves. *Journal of Econometrics*, *65*, 205–233.

Hayduk, L. A. (1987). *Structural equation modeling with LISREL. essentials and advances.* Baltimore: The Johns Hopkins University Press.

Henderson, H. V., and Searle, S. R. (1979). Vec and vech operators for matrices, with some uses in Jacobians and multivariate statistics. *The Canadian Journal of Statistics*, *7*, 65–81.

Henderson, H. V., and Searle, S. R. (1981a). On deriving the inverse of a sum of matrices. *SIAM Review*, *23*, 53–60.

Henderson, H. V., and Searle, S. R. (1981b). The vec-permutation matrix, the vec operator and Kronecker products: A review. *Linear and Multilinear Algebra*, *9*, 271–288.

Hendry, D. F., and Morgan, M. S. (1989). A re-analysis of confluence analysis. *Oxford Economic Papers*, *41*, 35–52.

Hershberger, S. L. (1994). The specification of equivalent models before the collection of data. In A. Von Eye and C. C. Clogg (Eds.), *Latent variables analysis. applications for developmental research* (pp. 68–105). Thousand Oaks, CA: Sage.

Heywood, H. B. (1931). On finite sequences of real numbers. *Proceedings of the Royal Society, Series A*, *134*, 486–510.

Himmelberg, C. P., and Petersen, B. C. (1994). R&D and internal finance: A panel study of small firms in high-tech industries. *The Review of Economics and Statistics*, *76*, 38–51.

Holly, A., and Magnus, J. R. (1988). A note on instrumental variables and maximum likelihood. *Annales d'Économie et de Statistique*, *10*, 121–138.

Hoogland, J. J., and Boomsma, A. (1998). Robustness studies in covariance structure modeling: An overview and meta-analysis. *Sociological Methods & Research, 26*, 329–367.

Hooper, J. W., and Theil, H. (1958). The extension of Wald's method of fitting straight lines to multiple regression. *Review of the International Statistical Institute, 26*, 37–47.

Höschel, H.-P. (1978). Generalized least squares estimators of linear functional relations with known error-covariance. *Mathematische Operationsforschung und Statistik, 9*, 9–26.

Hotelling, H. (1933). Analysis of a complex of statistical variables into principal components. *Journal of Educational Statistics, 24*, 417–441.

Hoyle, R. H. (Ed.). (1995). *Structural equation modeling: Concepts, issues, and applications.* Thousand Oaks, CA: Sage.

Hsiao, C. (1976). Identification and estimation of simultaneous equation models with measurement error. *International Economic Review, 17*, 319–339.

Hsiao, C. (1983). Identification. In Z. Griliches and M. D. Intriligator (Eds.), *Handbook of econometrics* (Vol. I, pp. 223–283). Amsterdam: North-Holland.

Hsiao, C. (1987). Identification. In J. Eatwell, M. Milgate, and P. Newman (Eds.), *The new Palgrave: A dictionary of economics* (Vol. 2, pp. 714–716). London: Macmillan.

Hsiao, C. (1989). Consistent estimation for some nonlinear errors-in-variables models. *Journal of Econometrics, 41*, 159–185.

Hsiao, C. (1992). Nonlinear latent variable models. In L. Mátyás and P. Sevestre (Eds.), *The econometrics of panel data* (pp. 242–261). Dordrecht: Kluwer.

Hsiao, C., and Taylor, G. (1991). Some remarks on measurement errors and the identification of panel data models. *Statistica Neerlandica, 45*, 187–194.

Hsiao, C., and Wang, Q. K. (2000). Estimation of structural nonlinear errors-in-variables models by simulated least squares method. *International Economic Review, 41*, 523–542.

Hu, L.-t., and Bentler, P. M. (1995). Evaluating model fit. In R. H. Hoyle (Ed.), *Structural equation modeling: Concepts, issues, and applications* (pp. 76–99). Thousand Oaks, CA: Sage.

Hu, L.-t., Bentler, P. M., and Kano, Y. (1992). Can test statistics in covariance structure analysis be trusted? *Psychological Bulletin, 112*, 351–362.

Humak, K. M. S. (1983). *Statistische Methoden der Modellbildung II* [Statistical methods of model building II]. Berlin: Akademie-Verlag.

Hwang, J. T. (1986). Multiplicative errors-in-variables models with applications to recent data released by the U.S. Department of Energy. *Journal of the American Statistical Association, 81*, 680–688.

Imbens, G. W. (1997). One-step estimators for over-identified generalized method of moments models. *Review of Economic Studies, 64*, 359–383.

Isogawa, Y. (1984). Exact and approximate distributions of slope estimator in a linear functional relationship. *Journal of the Japan Statistical Society, 14*, 43–48.

Iwata, S. (1992). Instrumental variables estimation in errors-in-variables models when instruments are correlated with errors. *Journal of Econometrics*, *53*, 297–322.

Izenman, A. J. (1975). Reduced-rank regression for the multivariate linear model. *Journal of Multivariate Analysis*, *5*, 248–264.

Jennrich, R. I. (1978). Rotational equivalence of factor loading matrices with specified values. *Psychometrika*, *43*, 421–426.

Jennrich, R. I., and Sampson, P. F. (1966). Rotation for simple loadings. *Psychometrika*, *31*, 313–323.

Johnson, N. L., and Kotz, S. (1970a). *Distributions in statistics: Continuous univariate distributions-1.* Boston: Houghton Mifflin.

Johnson, N. L., and Kotz, S. (1970b). *Distributions in statistics: Continuous univariate distributions-2.* Boston: Houghton Mifflin.

Jöreskog, K. G. (1967). Some contributions to maximum likelihood factor analysis. *Psychometrika*, *32*, 443–482.

Jöreskog, K. G. (1969). A general approach to confirmatory maximum likelihood factor analysis. *Psychometrika*, *34*, 183–202.

Jöreskog, K. G. (1970). A general method for analysis of covariance structures. *Biometrika*, *57*, 239–251.

Jöreskog, K. G. (1971). Simultaneous factor analysis in several populations. *Psychometrika*, *36*, 409–426.

Jöreskog, K. G. (1977). Structural equation models in the social sciences: Specification, estimation and testing. In P. R. Krishnaiah (Ed.), *Applications of statistics* (pp. 265–287). Amsterdam: North-Holland.

Jöreskog, K. G. (1978). Structural analysis of covariance and correlation matrices. *Psychometrika*, *43*, 443–477.

Jöreskog, K. G. (1990). New developments in LISREL: Analysis of ordinal variables using polychoric correlations and weighted least squares. *Quality and Quantity*, *24*, 387–404.

Jöreskog, K. G. (1994). On the estimation of polychoric correlations and their asymptotic covariance matrix. *Psychometrika*, *59*, 381–389.

Jöreskog, K. G., and Goldberger, A. S. (1972). Factor analysis by generalized least squares. *Psychometrika*, *37*, 243–260.

Jöreskog, K. G., and Goldberger, A. S. (1975). Estimation of a model with multiple indicators and multiple causes of a single latent variable. *Journal of the American Statistical Association*, *70*, 631–639.

Jöreskog, K. G., and Sörbom, D. (1981). *LISREL V user's guide.* Chicago: International Educational Services.

Jöreskog, K. G., and Sörbom, D. (1993). *LISREL 8 user's reference guide.* Chicago: Scientific Software International.

Jöreskog, K. G., and Yang, F. (1996). Nonlinear structural equation models: The Kenny-Judd model with interaction effects. In G. A. Marcoulides and R. E. Schumacker (Eds.), *Advanced structural equation modeling: Issues and techniques* (pp. 57–88). Mahwah, NJ: Erlbaum.

Kaiser, H. F. (1958). The varimax criterion for analytic rotation in factor analysis. *Psy-*

chometrika, 23, 187–200.

Kalman, R. E. (1982). System identification from noisy data. In A. Bednarek and L. Cesari (Eds.), *Proceedings of the International Symposium on Dynamical Systems*. New York: Academic Press.

Kamalich, R. F., and Polachek, S. W. (1982). Discrimination: Fact or fiction? An examination using an alternative approach. *Southern Economic Journal, 49*, 450–461.

Kano, Y., Bentler, P. M., and Mooijaart, A. (1993). Additional information and precision of estimators in multivariate structural models. In K. Matusita, M. L. Puri, and T. Hayakawa (Eds.), *Statistical sciences and data analysis. Proceedings of the third Pacific Area Statistical Conference* (pp. 187–196). Utrecht, The Netherlands: VSP.

Kapsalis, C. (1982). A new measure of wage discrimination. *Economics Letters, 9*, 287–293.

Kapteyn, A., and Wansbeek, T. J. (1984). Errors in variables: Consistent Adjusted Least Squares (CALS) estimation. *Communications in Statistics — Theory and Methods, 13*, 1811–1837.

Keller, W. J. (1975). A new class of limited-information estimators for simultaneous equation systems. *Journal of Econometrics, 3*, 71–92.

Keller, W. J., and Wansbeek, T. J. (1983). Multivariate methods for quantitative and qualitative data. *Journal of Econometrics, 22*, 91–111.

Kelly, G. (1984). The influence function in the errors in variables problem. *The Annals of Statistics, 12*, 87–100.

Kemp, G. C. R. (1992). The potential for efficiency gains in estimation from the use of additional moment restrictions. *Journal of Econometrics, 53*, 387–399.

Kendall, M. G., and Stuart, A. (1973). *The advanced theory of statistics* (Vol. 2, 3rd ed.). London: Griffin.

Kenny, D. A., and Judd, C. M. (1984). Estimating the nonlinear and interactive effects of latent variables. *Psychological Bulletin, 96*, 201–210.

Ketellapper, R. H. (1981). On estimating a consumption function when incomes are subject to measurement errors. *Economics Letters, 7*, 343–348.

Ketellapper, R. H. (1982). Two-stage least squares estimation in the simultaneous equation model with errors in the variables. *The Review of Economics and Statistics, 64*, 696–701.

Kim, J.-O., and Ferree, G. D., Jr. (1981). Standardization in causal analysis. *Sociological Methods & Research, 10*, 187–210.

Kim, J.-O., and Mueller, C. W. (1976). Standardized and unstandardized coefficients in causal analysis: An expository note. *Sociological Methods & Research, 4*, 428–438.

Klepper, S. (1988a). Bounding the effects of measurement error in regressions involving dichotomous variables. *Journal of Econometrics, 37*, 343–359.

Klepper, S. (1988b). Regressor diagnostics for the classical errors in variables model. *Journal of Econometrics, 37*, 225–250.

Klepper, S., and Leamer, E. E. (1984). Consistent sets of estimates for regressions with errors in all variables. *Econometrica, 52*, 163–183.

Kloek, T., and Mennes, L. B. M. (1960). Simultaneous equations estimation based on principal components of predetermined variables. *Econometrica*, *28*, 45–61.

Kmenta, J. (1991). Latent variables in econometrics. *Statistica Neerlandica*, *45*, 73–84.

Koning, R. H., Neudecker, H., and Wansbeek, T. J. (1991). Block Kronecker products and the vecb operator. *Linear Algebra and its Applications*, *149*, 165–184.

Koning, R. H., Neudecker, H., and Wansbeek, T. J. (1992). Unbiased estimation of fourth-order matrix moments. *Linear Algebra and its Applications*, *160*, 163–174.

Koning, R. H., Neudecker, H., and Wansbeek, T. J. (1993). Imposed quasi-normality in covariance structure analysis. In K. Haagen, D. J. Bartholomew, and M. Deistler (Eds.), *Statistical modelling and latent variables* (pp. 191–202). Amsterdam: North-Holland.

Koopmans, T. C. (1937). *Linear regression analysis of economic time series*. Haarlem: Bohn.

Koopmans, T. C., and Reiersøl, O. (1950). The identification of structural characteristics. *The Annals of Matrematical Statistics*, *21*, 165–181.

Kooreman, P. (2000). The labeling effect of a child benefit system. *The American Economic Review*, *90*, 571–583.

Krane, W. R., and McDonald, R. P. (1978). Scale invariance and the factor analysis of correlation matrices. *British Journal of Mathematical and Statistical Psychology*, *31*, 218–228.

Krasker, W. S., and Pratt, J. W. (1986). Bounding the effects of proxy variables on regression coefficients. *Econometrica*, *54*, 641–655.

Krasker, W. S., and Pratt, J. W. (1987). Bounding the effects of proxy variables on instrumental-variables coefficients. *Journal of Econometrics*, *35*, 233–252.

Krijnen, W. P., Wansbeek, T. J., and Ten Berge, J. M. F. (1996). Best linear predictors for factor scores. *Communications in Statistics — Theory and Methods*, *25*, 3013–3025.

Kroch, E. (1988). Bounds on specification error arising from data proxies. *Journal of Econometrics*, *37*, 171–192.

Krueger, A. B., and Summers, L. H. (1988). Efficiency wages and the inter-industry wage structure. *Econometrica*, *56*, 259–293.

Lakshminarayanan, M. Y., and Gunst, R. F. (1984). Estimation of parameters in linear structural relationships: Sensitivity to the choice of the ratio of error variances. *Biometrika*, *71*, 569–573.

Lancaster, H. O. (1969). *The chi-squared distribution*. New York: Wiley.

Lancaster, P., and Tismenetsky, M. (1985). *The theory of matrices* (2nd ed.). Orlando, FL: Academic Press.

Lancaster, T. (2000). The incidental parameter problem since 1948. *Journal of Econometrics*, *95*, 391–413.

Lawley, D. N., and Maxwell, A. E. (1971). *Factor analysis as a statistical method* (2nd ed.). New York: American Elsevier.

Leamer, E. E. (1978). *Specification searches: Ad hoc inference with nonexperimental data*. New York: Wiley.

Leamer, E. E. (1982). Sets of posterior means with bounded variance priors. *Econometrica, 50*, 725–763.

Leamer, E. E. (1987). Errors in variables in linear systems. *Econometrica, 55*, 893–909.

Ledermann, W. (1937). On the rank of the reduced correlational matrix in multiple factor analysis. *Psychometrika, 2*, 85–93.

Lee, S., and Hershberger, S. L. (1990). A simple rule for generating equivalent models in covariance structure modeling. *Multivariate Behavioral Research, 25*, 313–334.

Lee, S.-H., and Yum, B.-J. (1989). Large-sample comparisons of calibration procedures when both measurements are subject to error: The unreplicated case. *Communications in Statistics — Theory and Methods, 18*, 3821–3840.

Lee, S.-Y. (1980). Estimation of covariance structure models with parameters subject to functional restraints. *Psychometrika, 45*, 309–324.

Lee, S.-Y. (1986). Estimation for structural equation models with missing data. *Psychometrika, 51*, 93–99.

Lee, S.-Y. (1987). A distribution-free method for structural equation models with incomplete data. *Communications in Statistics — Theory and Methods, 16*, 1133–1151.

Lee, S.-Y., and Bentler, P. M. (1980). Some asymptotic properties of constrained generalized least squares estimation in covariance structure models. *South African Statistical Journal, 14*, 121–136.

Lee, S.-Y., and Jennrich, R. I. (1979). A study of algorithms for covariance structure analysis with specific comparisons using factor analysis. *Psychometrika, 44*, 99–113.

Lee, S.-Y., and Poon, W.-Y. (1986). Maximum likelihood estimation of polyserial correlations. *Psychometrika, 51*, 113–121.

Lee, S.-Y., and Poon, W.-Y. (1987). Two-step estimation of multivariate polychoric correlation. *Communications in Statistics—Theory and Methods, 16*, 307–320.

Lee, S.-Y., Poon, W.-Y., and Bentler, P. M. (1989). Simultaneous analysis of multivariate polytomous variates in several groups. *Psychometrika, 54*, 63–73.

Lee, S.-Y., Poon, W.-Y., and Bentler, P. M. (1990a). Full maximum likelihood analysis of structural equation models with polytomous variables. *Statistics & Probability Letters, 9*, 91–97.

Lee, S.-Y., Poon, W.-Y., and Bentler, P. M. (1990b). A three-stage estimation procedure for structural equation models with polytomous variables. *Psychometrika, 55*, 45–51.

Lee, S.-Y., Poon, W.-Y., and Bentler, P. M. (1992). Structural equation models with continuous and polytomous variables. *Psychometrika, 57*, 89–105.

Lee, S.-Y., Poon, W.-Y., and Bentler, P. M. (1995). A two-stage estimation of structural equation models with continuous and polytomous variables. *British Journal of Mathematical and Statistical Psychology, 48*, 339–358.

Lehmann, E. L. (1983). *Theory of point estimation.* New York: Chapman & Hall. (Originally published by Wiley, New York)

Lerman, S., and Manski, C. F. (1981). On the use of simulated frequencies to approximate choice probabilities. In C. F. Manski and D. L. McFadden (Eds.), *Structural analysis of discrete data with econometric applications* (pp. 305–319). Cambridge,

MA: MIT Press.

Levi, M. D. (1973). Errors in the variables bias in the presence of correctly measured variables. *Econometrica*, *41*, 985–986.

Levi, M. D. (1977). Measurement error and bounded OLS estimates. *Journal of Econometrics*, *6*, 165–171.

Levine, D. (1985). The sensitivity of the MLE to measurement error. *Journal of Econometrics*, *28*, 223–230.

Lewbel, A. (1997). Constructing instruments for regressions with measurement error when no additional data are available, with an application to patents and R & D. *Econometrica*, *65*, 1201–1213.

Lewbel, A. (1998). Semiparametric latent variable model estimation with endogenous or mismeasured regressors. *Econometrica*, *66*, 105–121.

Lewis-Beck, M. S. (Ed.). (1994). *Factor analysis & related techniques.* London: Sage/Toppan.

Li, T. (2000). Estimation of nonlinear errors-in-variables models: A simulated minimum distance estimator. *Statistics & Probability Letters*, *47*, 243–248.

Lindley, D. V., and El-Sayyad, G. M. (1968). The Bayesian estimation of a linear functional relationship. *Journal of the Royal Statistical Society B*, *30*, 198–202.

Linssen, H. N. (1977). Nonlinear regression with nuisance parameters: An efficient algorithm to estimate the parameters. In J. R. B. Barra (Ed.), *Recent developments in statistics* (pp. 531–533). Amsterdam: North-Holland.

Liviatan, N. (1961). Errors in variables and Engel curve analysis. *Econometrica*, *29*, 336–362.

Liviatan, N. (1963). Tests of the permanent-income hypothesis based on a reinterview savings survey. In C. F. Christ, M. Friedman, L. A. Goodman, Z. Griliches, A. C. Harberger, N. Liviatan, J. Mincer, Y. Mundlak, M. Nerlove, D. Patinkin, L. G. Telser, and H. Theil (Eds.), *Measurement in economics* (pp. 29–66). Stanford, CA: Stanford University Press. (with discussion)

Loehlin, J. C. (1987). *Latent variable models. An introduction to factor, path, and structural analysis.* Hillsdale, NJ: Erlbaum.

Löwner, K. (1934). Über monotone Matrixfunktionen [On monotone matrix functions]. *Mathematische Zeitschrift*, *38*, 177–216.

Luijben, T. C. W. (1991). Equivalent models in covariance structure analysis. *Psychometrika*, *56*, 653–665.

MacCallum, R. C. (1986). Specification searches in covariance structure modeling. *Psychological Bulletin*, *100*, 107–120.

MacCallum, R. C., Wegener, D. T., Uchino, B. N., and Fabrigar, L. R. (1993). The problem of equivalent models in covariance structure analysis. *Psychological Bulletin*, *114*, 185–199.

Madansky, A. (1959). The fitting of straight lines when both variables are subject to error. *Journal of the American Statistical Association*, *54*, 173–205.

Madansky, A. (1976). *Foundations of econometrics.* Amsterdam: North-Holland.

Magnus, J. R. (1983). L-structured matrices and linear matrix equations. *Linear and*

Multilinear Algebra, *14*, 67–88.

Magnus, J. R. (1988). *Linear structures.* London: Griffin.

Magnus, J. R., and Neudecker, H. (1979). The commutation matrix: Some properties and applications. *The Annals of Statistics*, *7*, 381–394.

Magnus, J. R., and Neudecker, H. (1980). The elimination matrix: Some lemmas and applications. *SIAM Journal on Algebra and Discrete Mathematics*, *1*, 422–449.

Magnus, J. R., and Neudecker, H. (1985). Matrix differential calculus with applications to simple, Hadamard and Kronecker products. *Journal of Mathematical Psychology*, *29*, 474–492.

Magnus, J. R., and Neudecker, H. (1986). Symmetry, 0–1 matrices and Jacobians: A review. *Econometric Theory*, *2*, 157–190.

Magnus, J. R., and Neudecker, H. (1988). *Matrix differential calculus with applications in statistics and econometrics.* Chichester: Wiley.

Malinvaud, E. (1970). *Statistical methods of econometrics* (2nd ed.). Amsterdam: North-Holland.

Mann, H. B., and Wald, A. (1943). On stochastic limit and order relationships. *The Annals of Mathematical Statistics*, *14*, 217–226.

Manski, C. F. (1983). Closest empirical distribution estimation. *Econometrica*, *51*, 305–319.

Manski, C. F. (1988). *Analog estimation methods in econometrics.* New York: Chapman & Hall.

Manski, C. F. (1989). Anatomy of the selection problem. *The Journal of Human Resources*, *24*, 343–360.

Manski, C. F. (1995). *Identification problems in the social sciences.* Cambridge, MA: Harvard University Press.

Marcoulides, G. A., and Schumacker, R. E. (Eds.). (1996). *Advanced structural equation modeling: Issues and techniques.* Mahwah, NJ: Erlbaum.

Mariano, R. S., and Brown, B. W. (1993). Stochastic simulations for inference in nonlinear errors-in-variables models. In G. S. Maddala, C. R. Rao, and H. D. Vinod (Eds.), *Handbook of statistics, vol. 11: Econometrics* (pp. 611–627). Amsterdam: North-Holland.

Marsh, H. W., Balla, J. R., and Hau, K.-T. (1996). An evaluation of incremental fit indices: A clarification of mathematical and empirical properties. In G. A. Marcoulides and R. E. Schumacker (Eds.), *Advanced structural equation modeling: Issues and techniques* (pp. 315–353). Mahwah, NJ: Erlbaum.

Marsh, H. W., Balla, J. R., and McDonald, R. P. (1988). Goodness-of-fit indexes in confirmatory factor analysis: The effect of sample size. *Psychological Bulletin*, *103*, 391–410.

McArdle, J. J., and McDonald, R. P. (1984). Some algebraic properties of the Reticular Action Model for moment structures. *British Journal of Mathematical and Statistical Psychology*, *37*, 234–251.

McCallum, B. T. (1972). Relative asymptotic bias from error of omission and measurement. *Econometrica*, *40*, 757–758.

McCullagh, P., and Nelder, J. A. (1989). *Generalized linear models* (2nd ed.). London: Chapman & Hall.

McDonald, R. P. (1962). A general approach to nonlinear factor analysis. *Psychometrika*, *27*, 397–415.

McDonald, R. P. (1965). Difficulty factors and non-linear factor analysis. *British Journal of Mathematical and Statistical Psychology*, *18*, 11-23.

McDonald, R. P. (1967). Numerical methods for polynomial models in nonlinear factor analysis. *Psychometrika*, *32*, 77–112.

McDonald, R. P. (1985). *Factor analysis and related methods.* Hillsdale, NJ: Erlbaum.

McDonald, R. P., and Burr, E. J. (1967). A comparison of four methods of constructing factor scores. *Psychometrika*, *32*, 381–401.

McDonald, R. P., and Marsh, H. W. (1990). Choosing a multivariate model: Noncentrality and goodness of fit. *Psychological Bulletin*, *107*, 247–255.

McFadden, D. L. (1974). Conditional logit analysis of qualitative choice behavior. In P. Zarembka (Ed.), *Frontiers in econometrics* (pp. 105–142). New York: Academic Press.

McFadden, D. L. (1989). A method of simulated moments for estimation of discrete response models without numerical integration. *Econometrica*, *57*, 995–1026.

McFadden, D. L., and Ruud, P. A. (1994). Estimation by simulation. *The Review of Economics and Statistics*, *76*, 591–608.

McManus, D. A. (1992). How common is identification in parametric models? *Journal of Econometrics*, *53*, 5–23.

Meijer, E. (1998). *Structural equation models for nonnormal data.* Leiden: DSWO Press.

Meijer, E., and Mooijaart, A. (1996). Factor analysis with heteroscedastic errors. *British Journal of Mathematical and Statistical Psychology*, *49*, 189–202.

Meijer, E., and Wansbeek, T. J. (1999). Quadratic prediction of factor scores. *Psychometrika*, *64*, 495–507.

Meijer, E., and Wansbeek, T. J. (2000). Measurement error in a single regressor. *Economics Letters*, *69*, 277–284.

Meijerink, F. (1996). *A nonlinear structural relations model.* Leiden, The Netherlands: DSWO Press.

Merckens, A., and Wansbeek, T. J. (1989). Formula manipulation in statistics on the computer: Evaluating the expectation of higher-degree functions of normally distributed matrices. *Computational Statistics & Data Analysis*, *8*, 189–200.

Mislevy, R. J. (1986). Recent developments in the factor analysis of categorical variables. *Journal of Educational Statistics*, *11*, 3–31.

Moberg, L., and Sundberg, R. (1978). Maximum likelihood estimation of a linear functional relationship when one of the departure variances is known. *Scandinavian Journal of Statistics*, *5*, 61–64.

Mooijaart, A. (1983). Two kinds of factor analysis for ordered categorical variables. *Multivariate Behavioral Research*, *18*, 423–441.

Mooijaart, A. (1985). Factor analysis for non-normal variables. *Psychometrika*, *50*, 323–342.

Mooijaart, A., and Bentler, P. M. (1985). The weight matrix in asymptotic distribution-free methods. *British Journal of Mathematical and Statistical Psychology, 38*, 190–196.

Mooijaart, A., and Bentler, P. M. (1986). Random polynomial factor analysis. In E. Diday, Y. Escoufier, L. Lebart, J. P. Pagès, Y. Schektman, and R. Tomassone (Eds.), *Data analysis and informatics, IV* (pp. 241–250). Amsterdam: North-Holland.

Mooijaart, A., and Bentler, P. M. (1991). Robustness of normal theory statistics in structural equation models. *Statistica Neerlandica, 45*, 159–171.

Moran, P. A. P. (1971). Estimating structural and functional relationships. *Journal of Multivariate Analysis, 1*, 232–255.

Morgenstern, O. (1963). *On the accuracy of economic observations* (2nd ed.). Princeton, NJ: Princeton University Press.

Morrison, D. F. (1990). *Multivariate statistical methods* (3rd ed.). New York: McGraw-Hill.

Mouchart, M. (1977). A regression model with an explanatory variable which is both binary and subject to errors. In D. J. Aigner and A. S. Goldberger (Eds.), *Latent variables in socio-economic models* (pp. 48–66). Amsterdam: North-Holland.

Mueller, R. O. (1996). *Basic principles of structural equation modeling: An introduction to LISREL and EQS.* New York: Springer.

Mulaik, S. A. (1972). *The foundations of factor analysis.* New York: McGraw-Hill.

Muthén, B. O. (1978). Contributions to factor analysis of dichotomous variables. *Psychometrika, 43*, 551–560.

Muthén, B. O. (1979). A structural probit model with latent variables. *Journal of the American Statistical Association, 74*, 807–811.

Muthén, B. O. (1982). Some categorical response models with continuous latent variables. In K. G. Jöreskog and H. Wold (Eds.), *Systems under indirect observation: Causality, structure, prediction. Part I* (pp. 65–79). Amsterdam: North Holland.

Muthén, B. O. (1983). Latent variable structural equation modeling with categorical data. *Journal of Econometrics, 22*, 43–65.

Muthén, B. O. (1984). A general structural equation model with dichotomous, ordered categorical, and continuous latent variable indicators. *Psychometrika, 49*, 115–132.

Muthén, B. O. (1987). *LISCOMP. analysis of linear structural equations with a comprehensive measurement model. theoretical integration and user's guide.* Mooresville, IN: Scientific Software.

Muthén, B. O. (1989a). Latent variable modeling in heterogeneous populations. *Psychometrika, 54*, 557–585.

Muthén, B. O. (1989b). Multiple-group structural modelling with non-normal continuous variables. *British Journal of Mathematical and Statistical Psychology, 42*, 55–62.

Muthén, B. O. (1989c). Tobit factor analysis. *British Journal of Mathematical and Statistical Psychology, 42*, 241–250.

Muthén, B. O. (1990). Moments of the censored and truncated bivariate normal distribution. *British Journal of Mathematical and Statistical Psychology, 43*, 131–143.

Muthén, B. O., and Christoffersson, A. (1981). Simultaneous factor analysis of dichotomous variables in several groups. *Psychometrika, 46*, 407–419.

Muthén, B. O., and Hofacker, C. (1988). Testing the assumptions underlying tetrachoric correlations. *Psychometrika*, *53*, 563–578.

Muthén, B. O., and Kaplan, D. (1985). A comparison of some methodologies for the factor analysis of non-normal Likert variables. *British Journal of Mathematical and Statistical Psychology*, *38*, 171–189.

Muthén, B. O., and Kaplan, D. (1992). A comparison of some methodologies for the factor analysis of non-normal Likert variables: A note on the size of the model. *British Journal of Mathematical and Statistical Psychology*, *45*, 19–30.

Muthén, B. O., Kaplan, D., and Hollis, M. (1987). On structural equation modeling with data that are not missing completely at random. *Psychometrika*, *52*, 431–462.

Muthén, B. O., and Satorra, A. (1989). Multilevel aspects of varying parameters in structural models. In R. D. Bock (Ed.), *Multilevel analysis of educational data* (pp. 87–99). San Diego: Academic Press.

Muthén, B. O., and Satorra, A. (1995). Technical aspects of Muthén's LISCOMP approach to estimation of latent variable relations with a comprehensive measurement model. *Psychometrika*, *60*, 489–503.

Muthén, L. K., and Muthén, B. O. (1998). *Mplus: The comprehensive modeling program for applied researchers.* Los Angeles: Muthén & Muthén.

Neale, M. C., Boker, S. M., Xie, G., and Maes, H. H. (1999). MX*: Statistical modeling* (5th ed.). Richmond, VA: Virginia Commonwealth University, Department of Psychiatry.

Nel, D. G. (1980). On matrix differentiation in statistics. *South African Statistical Journal*, *14*, 137–193.

Nelson, C. R., and Startz, R. (1990a). The distribution of the instrumental variables estimator and its t-ratio when the instrument is a poor one. *Journal of Business*, *63*, S125–S140.

Nelson, C. R., and Startz, R. (1990b). Some further results on the exact small sample properties of the instrumental variable estimator. *Econometrica*, *58*, 967–976.

Neudecker, H., and Wansbeek, T. J. (1983). Some results on commutation matrices, with statistical applications. *The Canadian Journal of Statistics*, *11*, 221–231.

Neudecker, H., and Wesselman, A. M. (1990). The asymptotic variance matrix of the sample correlation matrix. *Linear Algebra and its Applications*, *127*, 598–599.

Nevels, K. (1986). A direct solution for pairwise rotations in Kaiser's varimax rotation. *Psychometrika*, *51*, 327–329.

Newey, W. K. (1985). Generalized method of moments specification testing. *Journal of Econometrics*, *29*, 229–256.

Newey, W. K. (1988). Asymptotic equivalence of closest moments and GMM estimators. *Econometric Theory*, *4*, 336–340.

Newey, W. K. (1990). Semiparametric efficiency bounds. *Journal of Applied Econometrics*, *5*, 99–135.

Newey, W. K. (1993). Efficient estimation of models with conditional moment restrictions. In G. S. Maddala, C. R. Rao, and H. D. Vinod (Eds.), *Handbook of statistics, vol. 11: Econometrics* (pp. 419–454). Amsterdam: North-Holland.

Newey, W. K., and McFadden, D. L. (1994). Large sample estimation and hypothesis testing. In R. F. Engle and D. L. McFadden (Eds.), *Handbook of econometrics* (Vol. IV, pp. 2111–2245). Amsterdam: Elsevier Science.

Newey, W. K., and West, K. D. (1987). A simple, positive semi-definite, heteroskedasticity and autocorrelation consistent covariance matrix. *Econometrica*, *55*, 703–708.

Newey, W. K., and West, K. D. (1994). Automatic lag selection in covariance matrix estimation. *Review of Economic Studies*, *61*, 631–653.

Neyman, J., and Pearson, E. S. (1928). On the use and interpretation of certain test criteria for purposes of statistical inference. *Biometrika*, *20A*, 175–240, 263–295.

Neyman, J., and Pearson, E. S. (1933). On the problem of the most efficient tests of statistical hypotheses. *Philosophical Transactions of the Royal Society of London, Series A*, *231*, 289–337.

Neyman, J., and Scott, E. L. (1948). Consistent estimates based on partially consistent observations. *Econometrica*, *16*, 1–32.

Nowak, E. (1993). The identification of multivariate linear dynamic errors-in-variables models. *Journal of Economterics*, *59*, 213–227.

Nussbaum, M. (1977). Asymptotic optimality of estimators of a linear functional relation if the ratio of the error variances is known. *Mathematische Operationsforschung und Statistik*, *8*, 173–198.

Nyquist, H. (1988). Least orthogonal absolute deviations. *Computational Statistics & Data Analysis*, *6*, 361–367.

Ogasawara, H. (2000). Some relationships between factors and components. *Psychometrika*, *65*, 167–185.

Olsson, U. (1979a). Maximum likelihood estimation of the polychoric correlation coefficient. *Psychometrika*, *44*, 443–460.

Olsson, U. (1979b). On the robustness of factor analysis against crude classification of the observations. *Multivariate Behavioral Research*, *14*, 485–500.

Olsson, U., Drasgow, F., and Dorans, N. J. (1982). The polyserial correlation coefficient. *Psychometrika*, *47*, 337–347.

Pakes, A. (1982). On the asymptotic bias of Wald-type estimators of a straight line when both variables are subject to error. *International Economic Review*, *23*, 491–497.

Pakes, A., and Pollard, D. (1989). Simulation and the asymptotics of optimization estimators. *Econometrica*, *57*, 1027–1057.

Pal, M. (1980). Consistent moment estimators of regression coefficients in the presence of errors in variables. *Journal of Econometrics*, *14*, 349–364.

Pal, M., and Bhaumik, M. (1981). A note on Bartlett's method of grouping in regression analysis. *Sankhyā*, *43*, 399–404.

Patefield, W. M. (1978). The unreplicated ultrastructural relation: Large sample properties. *Biometrika*, *65*, 535–540.

Patefield, W. M. (1981). Multivariate linear relationships: Maximum likelihood estimation and regression bounds. *Journal of the Royal Statistical Society B*, *43*, 342–352.

Pearson, K. (1894). Contributions to the mathematical theory of evolution. *Philosophical Transactions of the Royal Society of London, Series A*, *185*, 71–110.

Pearson, K. (1901a). Mathematical contributions to the theory of evolution.—VII. On the correlation of characters not quantitatively measurable. *Philosophical Transactions of the Royal Society of London, Series A*, *195*, 1–47.

Pearson, K. (1901b). On lines and planes of closest fit to systems of points in space. *The London, Edinburgh, and Dublin Philosophical Magazine and Journal of Science, Sixth Series*, *2*, 559–572.

Pearson, K., and Heron, D. (1913). On theories of association. *Biometrika*, *9*, 159–315.

Phillips, P. C. B., and Park, J. Y. (1988). On the formulation of Wald tests of nonlinear restrictions. *Econometrica*, *56*, 1065–1083.

Poirier, D. J. (1998). Revising beliefs in nonidentified models. *Econometric Theory*, *14*, 483–509.

Poon, W.-Y., and Lee, S.-Y. (1987). Maximum likelihood estimation of multivariate polyserial and polychoric correlation coefficients. *Psychometrika*, *52*, 409–430. (Errata, *Psychometrika*, 1988, *53*, 301)

Poon, W.-Y., and Lee, S.-Y. (1992). Statistical analysis of continuous and polytomous variables in several populations. *British Journal of Mathematical and Statistical Psychology*, *45*, 139–149.

Poon, W.-Y., and Lee, S.-Y. (1999). Two practical issues in using LISCOMP for analysing of continuous and ordered categorical variables. *British Journal of Mathematical and Statistical Psychology*, *52*, 195–211.

Poon, W.-Y., Lee, S.-Y., and Bentler, P. M. (1990). Pseudo maximum likelihood estimation of multivariate polychoric and polyserial correlations. *Computational Statistics Quarterly*, *1*, 41–53.

Poon, W.-Y., Lee, S.-Y., and Tang, M.-L. (1997). Analysis of structural equation models with censored data. *British Journal of Mathematical and Statistical Psychology*, *50*, 227–241.

Poon, W.-Y., and Leung, Y.-P. (1993). Analysis of structural equation models with interval and polytomous data. *Statistics & Probability Letters*, *17*, 127–137.

Prais, S. J., and Aitchison, J. (1954). The grouping of observations in regression analysis. *Review of the International Statistical Institute*, *22*, 1–22.

Rao, C. R. (1948). Large sample tests of statistical hypotheses concerning several parameters with application to problems of estimation. *Proceedings of the Cambridge Philosophical Society*, *44*, 50–57.

Rao, C. R. (1973). *Linear statistical inference and its applications* (2nd ed.). New York: Wiley.

Rao, C. R., and Mitra, S. K. (1971). *Generalized inverse of matrices and its applications.* New York: Wiley.

Raykov, T., and Penev, S. (1999). On structural model equivalence. *Multivariate Behavioral Research*, *34*, 199–244.

Reboussin, B. A., and Liang, K.-Y. (1998). An estimating equations approach for the LISCOMP model. *Psychometrika*, *63*, 165–182.

Reiersøl, O. (1941). Confluence analysis by means of lag moments and other methods of confluence analysis. *Econometrica*, *9*, 1–24.

Reiersøl, O. (1945). Confluence analysis by means of instrumental sets of variables. *Arkiv för Mathematik, Astronomi och Fysik, 32A*, 1–119.

Reiersøl, O. (1950). Identifiability of a linear relation between variables which are subject to error. *Econometrica, 18*, 375–389.

Reilly, P. M., and Patino-Leal, H. (1985). A Bayesian study of the error-in-variables model. *Technometrics, 23*, 221–231.

Reinsel, G. C., and Velu, R. P. (1998). *Multivariate reduced rank regression: Theory and applications.* New York: Springer.

Reynolds, R. A. (1982). Posterior odds for the hypothesis of independence between stochastic regressors and disturbances. *International Economic Review, 23*, 479–490.

Richardson, D. H., and Wu, D.-M. (1970). Least squares and grouping method estimators in the errors in variables model. *Journal of the American Statistical Association, 65*, 724–748.

Richmond, J. (1974). Identifiability in linear models. *Econometrica, 42*, 731–736.

Rindskopf, D. (1983). Parameterizing inequality constraints on unique variances in linear structural models. *Psychometrika, 48*, 73–83.

Rindskopf, D. (1984a). Structural equation models: Empirical identification, Heywood cases, and related problems. *Sociological Methods & Research, 13*, 109–119.

Rindskopf, D. (1984b). Using phantom and imaginary latent variables to parameterize constraints in linear structural models. *Psychometrika, 49*, 37–47.

Robertson, C. A. (1974). Large sample theory for the linear structural relation. *Biometrika, 61*, 353–359.

Ronner, A. E., and Steerneman, A. G. M. (1985). The occurrence of outliers in the explanatory variable considered in an errors-in-variables framework. *Metrika, 32*, 97–107.

Ronner, A. E., Steerneman, A. G. M., and Kuper, G. (1985). On the performance of moment estimators in a structural regression model with outliers in the explanatory variable. *Methods of Operations Research, 55*, 253–262.

Rothenberg, T. J. (1971). Identification in parametric models. *Econometrica, 39*, 577–592.

Rudin, W. (1964). *Principles of mathematical analysis.* New York: McGraw-Hill.

Sargan, J. D. (1958). The estimation of economic relationships using instrumental variables. *Econometrica, 26*, 393–415.

Sargan, J. D. (1964). Wages and prices in the United Kingdom: A study in econometric methodology. In P. E. Hart, G. Mills, and J. K. Whitaker (Eds.), *Econometric analysis for national economic planning* (pp. 25–63). London: Butterworths. (with discussion)

SAS Institute. (1990). *SAS/STAT user's guide* (Vol. 1). Cary, NC: SAS Institute.

Satorra, A. (1989). Alternative test criteria in covariance structure analysis: A unified approach. *Psychometrika, 54*, 131–151.

Satorra, A., and Bentler, P. M. (1988). Scaling corrections for chi-square statistics in covariance structure analysis. In *1988 Proceedings of the Business and Economic Statistics Section of the American Statistical Association* (pp. 308–313).

Satorra, A., and Bentler, P. M. (1990). Model conditions for asymptotic robustness in the analysis of linear relations. *Computational Statistics & Data Analysis*, *10*, 235–249.

Satorra, A., and Bentler, P. M. (1994). Corrections to test statistics and standard errors in covariance structure analysis. In A. Von Eye and C. C. Clogg (Eds.), *Latent variables analysis. applications for developmental research* (pp. 399–419). Thousand Oaks, CA: Sage.

Schaafsma, W. (1982). Selecting variables in discriminant analysis for improving upon classical procedures. In P. R. Krishnaiah and L. N. Kanal (Eds.), *Handbook of statistics* (Vol. 2, pp. 857–881). Amsterdam: North-Holland.

Schafer, D. W. (1987a). Covariate measurement error in generalized linear models. *Biometrika*, *74*, 385–391.

Schafer, D. W. (1987b). Measurement-error diagnostics and the sex discrimination problem. *Journal of Business & Economic Statistics*, *5*, 529–537.

Schepers, A., Arminger, G., and Küsters, U. L. (1992). The analysis of non-metric endogenous variables in latent variable models: The MECOSA approach. In J. Gruber (Ed.), *Econometric decision models: New methods of modeling and applications* (pp. 459–472). Heidelberg: Springer.

Schneeweiss, H. (1976). Consistent estimation of a regression with errors in the variables. *Metrika*, *23*, 101–115.

Schneeweiss, H. (1982). Note on Creasy's confidence limits for the gradient in the linear functional relationship. *Journal of Multivariate Analysis*, *12*, 155–158.

Schneeweiss, H., and Mathes, H. (1995). Factor analysis and principal components. *Journal of Multivariate Analysis*, *55*, 105–124.

Schneeweiss, H., and Mittag, H.-J. (1986). *Lineare Modellen mit fehlerbehafteten Daten* [Linear models with errors in variables]. Heidelberg: Physika.

Schoenberg, R., and Arminger, G. (1990). *LINCS: A user's guide.* Kent, WA: Aptech.

Schumacker, R. E., and Marcoulides, G. A. (Eds.). (1998). *Interaction and nonlinear effects in structural equation modeling.* Mahwah, NJ: Erlbaum.

Serrecchia, A. (1980). On the conditions under which the method of moments and the method of maximum likelihood coincide. *Metron*, *38*, 107–119.

Shapiro, A. (1983). Asymptotic distribution theory in the analysis of covariance structures (a unified approach). *South African Statistical Journal*, *17*, 33–81.

Shapiro, A. (1984). A note on the consistency of estimators in the analysis of moment structures. *British Journal of Mathematical and Statistical Psychology*, *37*, 84–88.

Shapiro, A. (1985a). Asymptotic distribution of test statistics in the analysis of moment structures under inequality constraints. *Biometrika*, *72*, 133–144.

Shapiro, A. (1985b). Asymptotic equivalence of minimum discrepancy function estimators to G.L.S. estimators. *South African Statistical Journal*, *19*, 73–81.

Shapiro, A. (1985c). Identifiability of factor analysis: Some results and open problems. *Linear Algebra and its Applications*, *70*, 1–7. (Erratum, 1989, 125–149)

Shapiro, A. (1986). Asymptotic theory of overparameterized structural models. *Journal of the American Statistical Association*, *81*, 142–149.

Shapiro, A. (1987). Robustness properties of the MDF analysis of moment structures. *South African Statistical Journal*, *21*, 39–62.

Shapiro, A., and Browne, M. W. (1983). On the investigation of local identifiability: A counterexample. *Psychometrika*, *48*, 303–304.

Shapiro, A., and Browne, M. W. (1990). On the treatment of correlation structures as covariance structures. *Linear Algebra and its Applications*, *127*, 567–587.

Silvey, S. D. (1959). The Lagrangian multiplier test. *The Annals of Mathematical Statistics*, *30*, 389–407.

Singleton, K. J. (1980). A latent time series model of the cyclical behavior of interest rates. *International Economic Review*, *21*, 559–576.

Slutsky, E. (1925). Ueber stochastische Asymptoten und Grenzwerte [On stochastic asymptotes and limit values]. *Metron*, *5*(3), 3–89.

Smith, R. J. (1992). Non-nested tests for competing models estimated by generalized method of moments. *Econometrica*, *60*, 973–980.

Solari, M. E. (1969). The 'maximum likelihood solution' to the problem of estimating a linear functional relationship. *Journal of the Royal Statistical Society B*, *31*, 372–375.

Solon, G. (1983). Errors in variables and reverse regression in the measurement of wage discriminations. *Economics Letters*, *13*, 393–396.

Soong, T. T. (1969). An extension of the moment method in statistical estimation. *SIAM Journal of Applied Mathematics*, *17*, 560–568.

Sörbom, D. (1974). A general method for studying differences in factor means and factor structure between groups. *British Journal of Mathematical and Statistical Psychology*, *17*, 560–568.

Sörbom, D. (1982). Structural equation models with structured means. In K. G. Jöreskog and H. Wold (Eds.), *Systems under indirect observation: Causality, structure, prediction. Part I* (pp. 183–195). Amsterdam: North-Holland.

Sörbom, D. (1989). Model modification. *Psychometrika*, *54*, 371–384.

Spearman, C. (1904). "General intelligence," objectively determined and measured. *American Journal of Psychology*, *15*, 201–293.

Sprent, P. (1966). A generalized least-squares approach to linear functional relationships. *Journal of the Royal Statistical Society B*, *28*, 278–297.

Sprent, P. (1970). The saddle point of the likelihood surface for a linear functional relationship. *Journal of the Royal Statistical Society B*, *32*, 432–434.

Staiger, D., and Stock, J. H. (1997). Instrumental variables regression with weak instruments. *Econometrica*, *65*, 557–586.

Stapleton, D. C., and Young, D. J. (1984). Censored regression with measurement error on the dependent variable. *Econometrica*, *52*, 737–760.

Stefanski, L. A., and Carroll, R. J. (1985). Covariate measurement error in logistic regression. *The Annals of Statistics*, *13*, 1335–1351.

Stefanski, L. A., and Carroll, R. J. (1987). Conditional scores and optimal scores for generalized linear measurement-error models. *Biometrika*, *74*, 703–716.

Steiger, J. H. (1990). Structural model evaluation and modification: An interval estimation approach. *Multivariate Behavioral Research, 25*, 173–180.

Stelzl, I. (1986). Changing a causal hypothesis without changing the fit: Dome rules for generating equivalent path models. *Multivariate Behavioral Research, 21*, 309–331.

Stern, S. (1997). Simulation-based estimation. *Journal of Economic Literature, 35*, 2006–2039.

Stine, R. A. (1990). An introduction to bootstrap methods. Examples and ideas. In J. Fox and J. S. Long (Eds.), *Modern methods of data analysis* (pp. 325–373). Newbury Park, CA: Sage.

Stroud, T. W. F. (1971). On obtaining large-sample tests from asymptotically normal estimators. *The Annals of Mathematical Statistics, 42*, 1412–1424.

Sullivan, J. L., and Feldman, S. (1979). *Multiple indicators, an introduction.* Beverly Hills, CA: Sage.

Swain, A. J. (1975). A class of factor analysis estimation procedures with common asymptotic sampling properties. *Psychometrika, 40*, 315–335.

Swaminathan, H., and Algina, J. (1978). Scale freeness in factor analysis. *Psychometrika, 43*, 581–583.

Takayama, A. (1985). *Mathematical economics* (2nd ed.). Cambridge, UK: Cambridge University Press.

Tanaka, J. S., and Huba, G. J. (1985). A fit index for covariance structure models under arbitrary GLS estimation. *British Journal of Mathematical and Statistical Psychology, 38*, 197–201.

Tang, M.-L., and Bentler, P. M. (1997). Maximum likelihood estimation in covariance structure analysis with truncated data. *British Journal of Mathematical and Statistical Psychology, 50*, 339–349.

Ten Berge, J. M. F. (1993). *Least squares optimization in multivariate analysis.* Leiden: DSWO Press.

Ten Berge, J. M. F., and Kiers, H. A. L. (1996). Optimality criteria for principal component analysis and generalizations. *British Journal of Mathematical and Statistical Psychology, 49*, 335–345.

Ten Berge, J. M. F., and Kiers, H. A. L. (1997). Are all varieties of PCA the same? A reply to Cadima & Jolliffe. *British Journal of Mathematical and Statistical Psychology, 50*, 367–368.

Ten Berge, J. M. F., Krijnen, W. P., Wansbeek, T. J., and Shapiro, A. (1999). Some new results on correlation preserving factor scores prediction methods. *Linear Algebra and its Applications, 289*, 311–318.

Terceiro Lomba, J. (1990). *Estimation of dynamic econometric models with errors in variables.* Berlin: Springer.

Theil, H. (1971). *Principles of econometrics.* Amsterdam: North-Holland.

Theil, H., and Van IJzeren, J. (1956). On the efficiency of Wald's method of fitting straight lines. *Review of the International Statistical Institute, 24*, 17–26.

Thurstone, L. L. (1935). *The vectors of mind.* Chicago: University of Chicago Press.

Thurstone, L. L. (1947). *Multiple factor analysis.* Chicago: University of Chicago Press.

Train, K. E., McFadden, D. L., and Goett, A. A. (1987). Consumer attitudes and voluntary rate schedules for public utilities. *The Review of Economics and Statistics, 69,* 383–391.

Tso, M. K.-S. (1981). Reduced-rank regression and canonical analysis. *Journal of the Royal Statistical Society B, 43,* 183–189.

Tucker, L. R., and Lewis, C. (1973). A reliability coefficient for maximum likelihood factor analysis. *Psychometrika, 38,* 1–10.

Van de Stadt, H., Kapteyn, A., and Van de Geer, S. (1985). The relativity of utility: Evidence from panel data. *The Review of Economics and Statistics, 67,* 179–187.

Van der Leeden, R. (1990). *Reduced rank regression with structured residuals.* Leiden, The Netherlands: DSWO Press.

Van Casteren, P. H. F. M. (1994). *Statistical model selection rules.* Unpublished Ph.D. Thesis, Free University, Amsterdam.

Van Driel, O. P. (1978). On various causes of improper solutions in maximum likelihood factor analysis. *Psychometrika, 43,* 225–243.

Van Huffel, S., and Vandewalle, J. (1991). *The total least squares problem: Computational aspects and analysis.* Philadelphia: SIAM.

Van Montfort, K. (1989). *Estimating in structural models with non-normal distributed variables: Some alternative approaches.* Leiden, The Netherlands: DSWO Press.

Van Montfort, K., Mooijaart, A., and De Leeuw, J. (1987). Regression with errors in variables: Estimators based on third order moments. *Statistica Neerlandica, 41,* 223–239.

Van Montfort, K., Mooijaart, A., and De Leeuw, J. (1989). Estimation of regression coefficients with the help of characteristic functions. *Journal of Econometrics, 41,* 267–278.

Van Schaaijk, M. (1987). Verdienen vrouwen meer dan mannen? [Do women earn more than men?]. *Economisch Statistische Berichten, 72,* 315–317.

Van Uven, M. J. (1930). Adjustment of n points (in n-dimensional space) to the best linear $(n - 1)$-dimensional space. *Proceedings of the Section of Sciences, Koninklijke Nederlandse Akademie van Wetenschappen te Amsterdam, 33,* 143–158, 307–326.

Velicer, W. F., and Jackson, D. N. (1990). Component analysis versus common factor analysis: Some issues in selecting an appropriate procedure. *Multivariate Behavioral Research, 25,* 1–114. (with discussion)

Wald, A. (1940). The fitting of straight lines if both variables are subject to error. *The Annals of Mathematical Statistics, 11,* 284–300.

Wald, A. (1943). Tests of statistical hypotheses concerning several parameters when the number of observations is large. *Transactions of the American Mathematical Society, 54,* 426–482.

Wald, A. (1948). Estimation of a parameter when the number of unknown parameters increases indefinitely with the number of observations. *The Annals of Mathematical Statistics, 19,* 220–227.

Wang, L. (1998). Estimation of censored linear errors-in-variables models. *Journal of*

Econometrics, *84*, 383–400.

Wansbeek, T. J. (1989). Permutation matrix — II. In S. Kotz and N. L. Johnson (Eds.), *Encyclopedia of statistical sciences, supplement volume* (pp. 121–122). New York: Wiley.

Wansbeek, T. J., and Koning, R. H. (1991). Measurement error and panel data. *Statistica Neerlandica*, *45*, 85–92.

Ware, J. H. (1972). The fitting of straight lines when both variables are subject to error and the ranks of the means are known. *Journal of the American Statistical Association*, *67*, 891–897.

Weiss, A. A. (1993). Some aspects of measurement-error in a censored regression model. *Journal of Econometrics*, *56*, 169–188.

White, H. L. (1980). A heteroskedasticity-consistent covariance matrix estimator and a direct test for heteroskedasticity. *Econometrica*, *48*, 817–838.

White, H. L. (1982). Instrumental variables regression with independent observations. *Econometrica*, *50*, 483–499.

White, H. L. (1984). *Asymptotic theory for econometricians*. New York: Academic Press.

White, H. L., and Domowitz, I. (1984). Nonlinear regression with dependent observations. *Econometrica*, *52*, 143–161.

Wickens, M. R. (1972). A note on the use of proxy variables. *Econometrica*, *40*, 759–761.

Wilks, S. S. (1938). The large-sample distribution of the likelihood ratio for testing composite hypotheses. *The Annals of Mathematical Statistics*, *9*, 60–62.

Willassen, Y. (1984). Testing hypotheses on the unidentifiable structural parameters in the classical 'errors-in-variables' model with applications to Friedman's permanent income model. *Economics Letters*, *14*, 221–228.

Willassen, Y. (1987). A simple alternative derivation of a useful theorem in linear "errors-in-variables" regression models together with some clarifications. *Journal of Multivariate Analysis*, *21*, 296–311.

Williams, L. J., Bozdogan, H., and Aiman-Smith, L. (1996). Inference problems with equivalent models. In G. A. Marcoulides and R. E. Schumacker (Eds.), *Advanced structural equation modeling: Issues and techniques* (pp. 279–314). Mahwah, NJ: Erlbaum.

Wolak, F. A. (1989a). Local and global testing of linear and nonlinear inequality constraints in nonlinear econometric models. *Econometric Theory*, *5*, 1–35.

Wolak, F. A. (1989b). Testing inequality constraints in linear econometric models. *Journal of Econometrics*, *41*, 205–235.

Wolter, K. M., and Fuller, W. A. (1982a). Estimation of nonlinear errors-in-variables models. *The Annals of Statistics*, *10*, 539–548.

Wolter, K. M., and Fuller, W. A. (1982b). Estimation of the quadratic errors-in-variables model. *Biometrika*, *96*, 175–182.

Wong, M. Y. (1989). Likelihood estimation of a simple linear regression model when both variables have error. *Biometrika*, *76*, 141–148.

Wright, S. (1918). On the nature of size factors. *Genetics*, *3*, 367–374.

Wright, S. (1920). The relative importance of heredity and environment in determining the piebald pattern of guinea pigs. *Proceedings of the National Academy of Sciences, 6*, 320–332.

Wright, S. (1921). Correlation and causation. *Journal of Agricultural Research, 20*, 557–585.

Wright, S. (1934). The method of path coefficients. *The Annals of Mathematical Statistics, 5*, 161–215.

Wu, D.-M. (1973). Alternative tests of independence between stochastic regressors and disturbances. *Econometrica, 41*, 733–750.

Yatchew, A., and Griliches, Z. (1985). Specification error in probit models. *Review of Economics and Statistics, 67*, 134–139.

Yuan, K.-H., and Bentler, P. M. (1997a). Improving parameter tests in covariance structure analysis. *Computational Statistics & Data Analysis, 26*, 177–198.

Yuan, K.-H., and Bentler, P. M. (1997b). Mean and covariance structure analysis: Theoretical and practical improvements. *Journal of the American Statistical Association, 92*, 767–774.

Yuan, K.-H., and Bentler, P. M. (1998a). Normal theory based test statistics in structural equation modelling. *British Journal of Mathematical and Statistical Psychology, 51*, 289–309.

Yuan, K.-H., and Bentler, P. M. (1998b). Robust mean and covariance structure analysis. *British Journal of Mathematical and Statistical Psychology, 51*, 63–88.

Yuan, K.-H., and Bentler, P. M. (1999). f-tests for mean and covariance structure analysis. *Journal of Educational and Behavioral Statistics, 24*, 225–244.

Yule, G. U. (1912). On the methods of measuring association between two attributes. *Journal of the Royal Statistical Society, 75*, 579–652. (with discussion)

Zellner, A. (1970). Estimation of regression relationships containing unobservable independent variables. *International Economic Review, 11*, 441–454.

Author Index

A

Aasness, J., 145, 387
Abbott, R. D., 344, 393
Aigner, D. J., 4, 7, 8, 32, 145, 387
Aiman-Smith, L., 225, 419
Aitchison, J., 32, 311, 387, 413
Aitkin, M., 345, 391
Akaike, H., 316, 387
Albæk, K., 31, 387
Aldrich, J., 88, 387
Algina, J., 224, 417
Allison, P. D., 225, 387
Alonso-Borrego, C., 144, 387
Altonji, J. G., 274, 387
Amemiya, T., 183, 387
Amemiya, Y., 276, 313, 347, 387, 388
Anderson, B. D. O., 8, 396
Anderson, J. C., 313, 388, 398
Anderson, T. W., 7, 87, 143, 183, 184, 222, 276, 313, 388
Andrews, D. W. K., 275, 388
Aneuryn-Evans, G., 311, 388
Angrist, J. D., 143, 144, 274, 388
Apostol, T. M., 372, 374, 388
Arai, M., 31, 387
Arbuckle, J. L., 223, 225, 313, 388, 389
Arellano, M., 143, 144, 387, 389
Arminger, G., 224, 344, 345, 389, 415
Asplund, R., 31, 387
Attfield, C. L. F., 223, 389

B

Bailey, K. T., 344, 393
Baker, R. M., 144, 392
Balla, J. R., 313, 316, 408
Banks, J., 343, 389
Barankin, E., 277, 389
Barnett, V. D., 56, 146, 389
Barth, E., 31, 387
Bartholomew, D. J., 183, 345, 389
Bartlett, M. S., 144, 165, 183, 389
Basilevsky, A., 183, 389
Bates, C., 273, 274, 389
Bekker, P. A., 7, 31, 32, 57, 58, 87, 88, 131, 143–145, 183, 191, 201, 223–225, 273, 374, 389, 390
Bentler, P. M., 4, 223–225, 273–276, 300, 312, 313, 315, 316, 343, 345, 346, 385, 386, 390, 391, 394, 402, 404, 406, 410, 413–415, 417, 420
Beran, R., 313, 391
Berkson, J., 30, 32, 277, 391
Bethlehem, J. G., 184, 397
Bhaumik, M., 144, 412
Bickel, P. J., 107, 391
Biemer, P. P., 7, 391
Bijleveld, C. C. J. H., 224, 391
Biørn, E., 145, 387, 391
Birch, M. W., 56, 391
Blomquist, S., 144, 391
Blundell, R., 145, 343, 389, 391

Bock, R. D., 345, 391
Boggs, P. T., 108, 391
Boker, S. M., 224, 411
Bollen, K. A., 223, 273, 311, 313, 391, 392
Bollinger, C. R., 145, 392
Bond, S., 145, 391
Bonett, D. G., 315, 316, 390
Boomsma, A., 182, 313, 345, 392, 402
Booth, J. R., 56, 392
Bound, J., 30, 31, 144, 392
Bowden, R. J., 87, 88, 143, 392
Box, G. E. P., 385, 386, 392
Bozdogan, H., 225, 316, 392, 419
Breckler, S. J., 224, 392
Breusch, T. S., 277, 312, 393
Brown, B. W., 277, 408
Brown, C., 30, 31, 392
Brown, P. J., 7, 393
Brown, R. L., 56, 393
Browne, M. W., 223, 224, 273, 275, 300, 312, 313, 315, 316, 374, 393, 395, 416
Buonaccorsi, J. P., 31, 393
Burr, D., 345, 393
Burr, E. J., 183, 409
Byrne, B. M., 223, 393

C

Cadima, J., 182, 393
Cameron, A. C., 315, 393
Carroll, R. J., 274, 344, 347, 393, 394, 416
Casella, G., 277, 394
Casson, M. C., 107, 394
Chamberlain, G., 3, 7, 146, 223, 274, 277, 394
Chan, L. K., 87, 107, 342, 394
Chan, N. N., 107, 394
Chan, W., 275, 394
Chatterjee, S., 31, 394
Chen, C.-F., 223, 394
Cheng, C.-L., 7, 107, 342, 394
Chesher, A., 344, 395
Chiang, C. L., 274, 395
Christoffersson, A., 345, 346, 395, 410
Cochran, W. G., 7, 395
Conway, D. A., 56, 57, 395
Copas, J. B., 87, 107, 395
Coward, M., 224, 393
Cragg, J. G., 30, 223, 395
Cramér, H., 277, 395
Creasy, M., 56, 395
Cudeck, R., 224, 313, 315, 316, 393, 395
Cumby, R. E., 275, 395
Cummins, J. G., 145, 395

D

Dagenais, D. L., 144, 395
Dagenais, M. G., 144, 145, 312, 395
Dahlberg, M., 144, 391
Davidson, J., 275, 396
Davidson, R., 143, 273, 395
Davies, R. B., 386, 395
Davison, A. C., 277, 312, 395
De Haan, J., 223, 396
De Jong, R. M., 275, 396
De Leeuw, J., 144, 315, 396, 418
Deaton, A., 311, 388
DeGracie, J. S., 107, 396
Deistler, M., 8, 396
Del Pino, G., 276, 396
Dempster, A., 57, 396
Devereux, M., 145, 391
Dijkstra, T. K., 143, 182, 273, 274, 276, 311, 390, 396
Divgi, D. R., 346, 396
Dobbelstein, P., 223, 390
Dolby, G. R., 56, 87, 107, 347, 396
Domowitz, I., 275, 419
Donald, S. G., 223, 395
Donaldson, J. R., 108, 391
Dorans, N. J., 346, 412
Dorff, M., 144, 396
Drasgow, F., 346, 412
Dudgeon, P., 223, 390
Dufour, J.-M., 312, 395

Duncan, G. J., 30, 31, 392
Duncan, O. D., 224, 399
Dunford, N., 374, 396
Dunn, G., 223, 397
Durbin, J., 7, 397

E
Eckart, C., 182, 397
Efron, B., 277, 312, 397
Egerton, M. F., 347, 397
Eicker, F., 143, 275, 397
El-Sayyad, G. M., 88, 407
Elffers, H., 184, 397
Elrod, T., 345, 397
Engle, R. F., 8, 311, 397
Erickson, T., 88, 397
Everitt, B., 223, 397

F
Fabrigar, L. R., 225, 407
Fan, J., 347, 397
Fazzari, S. M., 145, 397
Feldman, S., 182, 417
Ferguson, T. S., 273, 274, 312, 374, 397
Ferree, G. D., Jr., 225, 404
Feuerverger, A., 144, 397
Fienberg, S. E., 57, 398
Fisher, F. M., 87, 398
Fisher, R. A., 277, 398
Florens, J.-P., 88, 398
Freedman, D. A., 224, 398
Freeman, R. B., 145, 398
Freeman, T. G., 87, 396
Friedman, M., 7, 398
Frisch, R., 7, 56, 374, 398
Fuller, W. A., 7, 107, 342, 347, 388, 393, 396, 398, 419

G
Garber, S., 32, 398
Geman, D., 277, 398
Geman, S., 277, 398
George, E. I., 277, 394
Geraci, V. J., 7, 224, 398
Gerbing, D. W., 313, 388, 398
Geweke, J. F., 8, 398, 399
Gibbons, R., 345, 391
Gibson, W. M., 144, 399
Gill, P. E., 182, 399
Gill, R. D., 184, 397
Gleser, L. J., 87, 399
Godambe, V. P., 273, 399
Goett, A. A., 344, 418
Goldberger, A. S., 7, 56, 57, 143, 182, 223, 224, 273, 387, 399, 401, 403
Goldstein, H., 146, 399
Golub, G. H., 108, 183, 399
Gorsuch, S. A., 183, 399
Gouriéroux, C., 273, 274, 277, 311, 399, 400
Graham, A., 374, 400
Graybill, F. A., 386, 400
Gregory, A. W., 311, 400
Griliches, Z., 2, 4, 7, 145, 146, 342, 345, 394, 400, 420
Groves, R. M., 7, 391
Gunsjö, A., 346, 395
Gunst, R. F., 56, 405
Gurland, J., 144, 277, 389, 396

H
Haavelmo, T., 88, 400
Hadi, A. S., 31, 394
Hägglund, G., 183, 400
Haitovsky, Y., 30, 400
Hajivassiliou, V. A., 277, 400
Hall, P., 277, 312, 400
Halton, J. H., 277, 400
Hamilton, J. D., 273, 400
Hammersley, J. M., 277, 400
Hampel, F. R., 315, 400
Handscomb, D. C., 277, 400
Hansen, L. P., 273–275, 277, 312, 400, 401
Harman, H. H., 183, 401
Harville, D. A., 374, 401
Hashimoto, M., 56, 401

Hassett, K. A., 145, 395
Hau, K.-T., 316, 408
Hauser, R. M., 224, 401
Hausman, J. A., 143, 145, 224, 311, 342, 400, 401
Hayduk, L. A., 343, 401
Heaton, J., 275, 401
Henderson, H. V., 374, 401
Hendry, D. F., 7, 401
Heron, D., 346, 413
Hershberger, S. L., 225, 401, 406
Heywood, H. B., 182, 401
Hidiroglou, M. A., 107, 398
Himmelberg, C. P., 145, 401
Hinkley, D. V., 277, 312, 395
Hofacker, C., 346, 411
Hollis, M., 225, 411
Holly, A., 143, 311, 399, 401
Hoogland, J. J., 313, 402
Hooper, J. W., 144, 402
Höschel, H.-P., 107, 402
Hotelling, H., 182, 402
Hoyle, R. H., 223, 402
Hsiao, C., 4, 87, 145, 224, 346, 387, 402
Hu, L.-t., 313, 316, 402
Huba, G. J., 315, 417
Hubbard, R. G., 145, 395
Huizinga, J., 275, 395
Humak, K. M. S., 7, 402
Hwang, J. T., 7, 31, 402

I

Ichimura, H., 342, 401
Imbens, G. W., 144, 275, 388, 402
Isogawa, Y., 56, 402
Iwata, S., 58, 402
Izenman, A. J., 223, 403

J

Jackson, D. N., 183, 418
Jaeger, D. A., 144, 392
Jennrich, R. I., 184, 223, 276, 403, 406
Johnson, N. L., 386, 403
Jolliffe, I., 182, 393
Jöreskog, K. G., 182, 183, 222–225, 273, 276, 315, 343, 345, 346, 392, 403
Jowett, G. H., 144, 399
Judd, C. M., 324, 343, 404

K

Kaiser, H. F., 184, 403
Kalman, R. E., 57, 404
Kamalich, R. F., 56, 404
Kano, Y., 276, 313, 402, 404
Kaplan, D., 225, 313, 345, 411
Kapsalis, C., 56, 404
Kapteyn, A., 4, 7, 31, 50, 58, 88, 107, 387, 390, 404, 418
Keane, M. P., 345, 397
Keller, W. J., 184, 404
Kelly, G., 56, 404
Kemp, G. C. R., 276, 404
Kendall, M. G., 7, 87, 144, 277, 404
Kenny, D. A., 324, 343, 404
Ketellapper, R. H., 32, 144, 224, 404
Kiers, H. A. L., 182, 183, 417
Kim, J.-O., 225, 404
Klepper, S., 32, 57, 58, 145, 398, 404
Kloek, T., 183, 405
Kmenta, J., 7, 405
Knott, M., 183, 389
Kochin, L., 56, 401
Koning, R. H., 145, 275, 276, 374, 405, 419
Kooi, W., 223, 396
Koopmans, T. C., 43, 88, 405
Kooreman, P., 31, 405
Kotz, S., 386, 403
Krane, W. R., 224, 405
Krasker, W. S., 58, 405
Krijnen, W. P., 183, 184, 405, 417
Kroch, E., 107, 405
Krueger, A. B., 31, 143–145, 388, 392, 405
Kuper, G., 145, 414
Küsters, U. L., 345, 389, 415

L
Lakshminarayanan, M. Y., 56, 405
Lan, K. K. G., 344, 393
Lancaster, H. O., 386, 405
Lancaster, P., 373, 405
Lancaster, T., 31, 405
Lawley, D. N., 183, 184, 405
Laycock, P. J., 347, 397
Leamer, E. E., 57, 58, 87, 315, 404–406
Ledermann, W., 170, 406
Lee, S., 225, 406
Lee, S.-H., 56, 406
Lee, S.-Y., 225, 274, 276, 345, 346, 390, 406, 413
Lehmann, E. L., 315, 406
Lerman, S., 277, 406
Leung, Y.-P., 345, 413
Levi, M. D., 31, 56, 347, 407
Levine, D., 347, 407
Lewbel, A., 144, 343, 347, 389, 407
Lewis, C., 308, 316, 418
Lewis-Beck, M. S., 183, 407
Li, T., 346, 407
Liang, K.-Y., 345, 413
Lieberman, M., 345, 391
Lilien, D. M., 8, 397
Lindley, D. V., 88, 407
Linssen, H. N., 347, 407
Lipton, S., 347, 396
Liviatan, N., 143, 407
Loehlin, J. C., 183, 184, 407
Long, J. S., 311, 392
Löwner, K., 356, 407
Luijben, T. C. W., 225, 407
Lyberg, L. E., 7, 391

M
MacCallum, R. C., 225, 315, 407
MacKinnon, J. G., 143, 273, 395
Madansky, A., 7, 107, 407
Maes, H. H., 224, 411
Magnus, J. R., 143, 374, 401, 407, 408
Mak, T. K., 87, 107, 342, 394
Malinvaud, E., 107, 108, 408
Mann, H. B., 374, 408
Manski, C. F., 58, 273, 274, 277, 406, 408
Marcoulides, G. A., 223, 343, 408, 415
Mariano, R. S., 277, 408
Marsh, H. W., 313, 315, 316, 408, 409
Mathes, H., 183, 415
Mathiowetz, N. A., 7, 391
Maxwell, A. E., 183, 184, 405
McArdle, J. J., 224, 408
McCallum, B. T., 31, 408
McCullagh, P., 276, 409
McDonald, R. P., 183, 224, 313, 315, 343, 405, 408, 409
McFadden, D. L., 273, 274, 277, 311, 315, 344, 409, 412, 418
McManus, D. A., 342, 409
Meghir, C., 143, 389
Meijer, E., 107, 183, 225, 273, 276, 313, 315, 342–344, 409
Meijerink, F., 346, 409
Mels, G., 224, 393
Mennes, L. B. M., 183, 405
Merckens, A., 88, 374, 390, 409
Mislevy, R. J., 345, 409
Mitra, S. K., 374, 386, 413
Mittag, H.-J., 7, 415
Moberg, L., 107, 409
Monahan, J. C., 275, 388
Monfort, A., 273, 274, 277, 311, 399, 400
Mooijaart, A., 144, 145, 183, 224, 225, 276, 313, 315, 343, 345, 390, 391, 404, 409, 410, 418
Moran, P. A. P., 7, 32, 410
Morgan, M. S., 7, 401
Morgenstern, O., 7, 410
Morrison, D. F., 183, 184, 410
Mouchart, M., 88, 145, 398, 410
Mueller, C. W., 225, 404
Mueller, R. O., 223, 410
Mulaik, S. A., 183, 410
Muraki, E., 345, 391
Mureika, R. A., 144, 397

Murray, W., 182, 399
Muthén, B. O., 146, 224, 225, 313, 344–346, 389, 410, 411
Muthén, L. K., 224, 345, 411

N
Neale, M. C., 223, 345, 411
Nel, D. G., 374, 411
Nelder, J. A., 276, 409
Nelson, C. R., 144, 411
Neudecker, H., 224, 275, 276, 374, 390, 405, 408, 411
Nevels, K., 184, 411
Newey, W. K., 273–275, 277, 311, 342, 401, 411, 412
Neyman, J., 31, 311, 412
Nowak, E., 8, 412
Nussbaum, M., 107, 412
Nyquist, H., 108, 412

O
Obstfeld, M., 275, 395
Ogasawara, H., 183, 412
Olsson, U., 345, 346, 412

P
Pakes, A., 144, 277, 412
Pal, M., 144, 412
Park, J. Y., 312, 413
Patefield, W. M., 57, 87, 412
Patino-Leal, H., 88, 414
Pearson, E. S., 311, 412
Pearson, K., 108, 182, 273, 346, 412, 413
Penev, S., 225, 413
Petersen, B. C., 145, 397, 401
Phillips, P. C. B., 312, 413
Pickles, A., 223, 397
Poirier, D. J., 88, 413
Polachek, S. W., 56, 404
Pollard, D., 277, 412
Poon, W.-Y., 345, 346, 406, 413
Powell, J. L., 342, 401
Prais, S. J., 32, 413
Pratt, J. W., 58, 405

Q
Qian, H., 277, 393

R
Rao, C. R., 311, 374, 386, 413
Raykov, T., 225, 413
Reboussin, B. A., 345, 413
Reiersøl, O., 88, 143, 405, 413, 414
Reilly, P. M., 88, 414
Reinsel, G. C., 223, 414
Reynolds, R. A., 143, 414
Richard, J.-F., 88, 398
Richardson, D. H., 56, 144, 414
Richmond, J., 87, 414
Rindskopf, D., 182, 224, 343, 414
Ringstad, V., 342, 400
Ritov, Y., 107, 391
Roberts, H. V., 56, 57, 395
Robertson, C. A., 107, 414
Rodgers, W. L., 30, 31, 392
Ronchetti, E. M., 315, 400
Ronner, A. E., 144, 145, 414
Rothenberg, T. J., 87, 88, 414
Rousseeuw, P. J., 315, 400
Rubin, H., 87, 143, 222, 388
Rudin, W., 374, 414
Ruppert, D., 274, 347, 393, 394
Ruud, P. A., 277, 400, 409

S
Sampson, P. F., 184, 403
Sargan, J. D., 143, 414
SAS Institute, 224, 414
Satorra, A., 146, 300, 311–313, 345, 385, 386, 411, 414, 415
Schaafsma, W., 374, 415
Schafer, D. W., 57, 344, 415
Schepers, A., 224, 345, 389, 415
Schiantarelli, F., 145, 391
Schmidt, P., 277, 312, 393
Schnabel, R. B., 108, 391
Schneeweiss, H., 7, 56, 107, 183, 415
Schoenberg, R., 224, 415

Schumacker, R. E., 223, 343, 408, 415
Schwartz, J. T., 374, 396
Scott, E. L., 31, 412
Searle, S. R., 374, 401
Segal, L. M., 274, 387
Serrecchia, A., 277, 415
Shapiro, A., 183, 184, 223, 224, 273, 274, 311, 313, 315, 386, 393, 415–417
Silvey, S. D., 311, 387, 416
Singleton, K. J., 8, 277, 398, 399, 401, 416
Skjerpen, T., 145, 387
Slutsky, E., 374, 416
Smith, R. J., 311, 416
Smith, R. L., 56, 392
Solari, M. E., 87, 416
Solon, G., 57, 416
Soong, T. T., 277, 416
Sörbom, D., 223, 225, 276, 315, 345, 403, 416
Spearman, C., 182, 416
Spiegelman, C. H., 108, 344, 391, 393
Sprent, P., 87, 107, 416
Srivastava, M. S., 313, 391
Stahel, W. A., 315, 400
Staiger, D., 144, 416
Stapleton, D. C., 345, 416
Startz, R., 144, 411
Steerneman, A. G. M., 145, 414
Stefanski, L. A., 344, 347, 393, 416
Steiger, J. H., 316, 417
Stelzl, I., 225, 417
Stern, S., 277, 417
Stine, R. A., 277, 313, 392, 417
Stock, J. H., 144, 416
Strøjer Madsen, E., 31, 387
Stroud, T. W. F., 311, 417
Stuart, A., 7, 87, 144, 277, 404
Sudman, S., 7, 391
Sullivan, J. L., 182, 417
Summers, L. H., 145, 405
Sundberg, R., 107, 409
Swain, A. J., 274, 417
Swaminathan, H., 224, 417

T
Takayama, A., 57, 417
Tanaka, J. S., 315, 417
Tang, M.-L., 345, 413, 417
Taylor, G., 145, 402
Ten Berge, J. M. F., 182–184, 223, 390, 405, 417
Terceiro Lomba, J., 8, 417
Theil, H., 144, 402, 417
Thurstone, L. L., 183, 184, 417, 418
Tibshirani, R. J., 277, 312, 397
Tismenetsky, M., 373, 405
Train, K. E., 344, 418
Trognon, A., 274, 400
Truong, Y. K., 347, 397
Tso, M. K.-S., 223, 418
Tucker, L. R., 308, 316, 418
Turkington, D. A., 143, 392

U
Uchino, B. N., 225, 407

V
Van Casteren, P. H. F. M., 316, 418
Van de Geer, S., 50, 418
Van de Stadt, H., 50, 418
Van der Kamp, L. J. T., 224, 391
Van der Kloot, W. A., 224, 391
Van der Leeden, R., 223, 418
Van Driel, O. P., 182, 418
Van Huffel, S., 108, 418
Van IJzeren, J., 144, 417
Van Loan, C. F., 108, 183, 399
Van Montfort, K., 144, 145, 342, 390, 418
Van Ness, J. W., 7, 107, 342, 394
Van Schaaijk, M., 37, 418
Van Uven, M. J., 107, 418
Vandewalle, J., 108, 418
Veall, M. R., 312, 400
Velicer, W. F., 183, 418

Velu, R. P., 223, 414

W
Wald, A., 88, 144, 311, 374, 408, 418
Wang, L., 344, 418
Wang, Q. K., 346, 402
Wansbeek, T. J., 4, 7, 31, 32, 58, 88, 107, 143, 145, 183, 184, 223, 275, 276, 374, 387, 390, 396, 404, 405, 409, 411, 417, 419
Ware, J. H., 56, 144, 419
Watson, M., 8, 397
Waugh, F. V., 374, 398
Weeks, D. G., 224, 391
Wegener, D. T., 225, 407
Weiss, A. A., 344, 419
Weng, L.-J., 225, 390
Wesselman, A. M., 224, 411
West, K. D., 275, 412
White, H. L., 143, 273–275, 389, 419
Wickens, M. R., 31, 419
Wilks, S. S., 311, 419
Willassen, Y., 57, 58, 419
Williams, L. J., 225, 419
Windmeijer, F. A. G., 315, 393
Wittenberg, J., 224, 389
Wolak, F. A., 311, 419
Wolter, K. M., 342, 346, 419
Wong, M. Y., 56, 419
Wright, M. H., 182, 399
Wright, S., 182, 419, 420
Wu, C. F. J., 274, 394
Wu, D.-M., 56, 143, 144, 414, 420
Wyhowski, D., 277, 393

X
Xie, G., 224, 411

Y
Yang, F., 343, 403
Yaron, A., 275, 401
Yatchew, A., 345, 420
Young, D. J., 345, 416
Young, G., 182, 397
Yuan, K.-H., 275, 300, 312, 313, 315, 391, 420
Yule, G. U., 346, 420
Yum, B.-J., 56, 406
Yung, Y.-F., 275, 394

Z
Zellner, A., 193, 223, 420

Subject Index

Symbols
0–1 matrices, 361–364, *see also* commutation matrix; diagonalization matrix; duplication matrix; symmetrization matrix
2SIV, 120–123, 143
 in LISREL, 217–218
2SLS, 112, 113, 123, 144, 345

A
additional moment conditions, 257–262, 276, 299, 340
ADF, 253, 274–276, 313, 343, *see also* residual-based ADF test statistic
adjusted R^2, *see* R^2, adjusted
admissible values for β, 20–22
AGFI, 315
AGLS, 275
AIC, 309–310, 316
Akaike's information criterion, *see* AIC
alternative asymptotics, 130, 131
AMOS, 223, 313
analysis of covariance structures, 201, *see also* covariance structures; structural equation model
antithetic sampling, 265
AR(1), 27, 140, 199
arbitrage pricing theory, 223
asymptotic equivalence, 241, 247, 256, 270, 272–274, 290–292
asymptotic least squares, 274
asymptotically distribution free, *see* ADF
attenuation, 17–22, 330
augmented moment matrix, 343, 344
autocorrelation, 27, 140, 145, 249–252, 275

B
Bartlett predictor, *see* predictor, Bartlett
Bartlett weights, 251
Bayesian approach, 58, 88, 145, 277, 344
Bentler-Weeks model, 202–204, 206–207, 224, *see also* EQS; structural equation model
Berkson model, 29–30, 32, 61, 144
 probit, 330, 345
 with limited-dependent variables, 330
BGLS, 144
bias, 96, 108, 129, 134, 135, 140, 141, 144, 145, 165, 166, 241, 253, 274–276, 301, 306, 307, 309, 319, 320, 366, *see also* inconsistency; omitted variables bias
binary choice models, 326–327, *see also* logit model; probit model
biserial correlation, 346

bootstrap, 241, 243, 274, 276, 277, 301, 312, 313
boundary value, 289, 290, 311
bounds
  multiple regression, 43–46
  on linear combinations of parameters, 49
  on measurement error variance, 46–58
  usefulness, 58
  when IV's are correlated with measurement error, 58
  with uncorrelated measurement error, 52–56
Box-Cox transformation, 346

C

CAIC, 310, 316
CALIS, *see* PROC CALIS
CALS, 89–108, 344
  asymptotic distribution, 91–94
canonical correlation, 179, 181
canonical parameter, 76, 77
canonical regression, 179, 181
categorical variable, 184, 334, 338, 339, 345, *see also* ordered categorical variable; qualitative variables
categorized variables, 29–30
Cauchy-Schwarz inequality, 112, 120, 242, 359–360, 374, 380
  equality, 380, 386
censored least absolute deviations, 344
censored regression model, 329, 331, 334, 339, 344–347, *see also* limited-dependent variables
centering matrix, 40, 139, 364, 366
central bank independence, 187–189, 212, 223
central limit theorem, 67, 87, 122, 234, 335
CFA, 160–161, 186–191, 196, 208, 209, 213, 214, 222, 302–303, 313, 314, *see also* FA; identification in CFA
CFI, 307, 310, 315, 316
characteristic function, 83–86, 145, *see also* empirical characteristic function
chi-square difference test, 241, 286–288, 290–298, 306, 311
chi-square distribution, 369–370, 375, 377–379, 385, 386
  idempotent case, 378–379
  noncentral, 377–379, 386
chi-square statistic, 298–303, 305, 307–310, 312–314
chi-square test, 296–301, 304, 312, 313
classification error, *see* misclassification
common variance, 150
communality, 150, 171, 172, 188
commutation matrix, 69, 161, 361, 374
comparative fit index, *see* CFI
computer algebra, 191, 201
conditional moments, 261–262, 266, 277, 340–342
confidence interval, 56, 241, 275, 294–295, 312, 316
confidence set, 294–295, 312
confirmatory factor analysis, *see* CFA
conservativeness of a test, 299, 312
consistency, *see* GMM, consistency; identification; IV, consistency; root-N consistency
consistent adjusted least squares, *see* CALS
consistent AIC, *see* CAIC
consistent estimation
  and identification, 80
  error variance known, 107
  error variance ratio known, 36, 56
  existence of consistent estimator, 80
  functional model, 80–82
  nonlinear model, 319
  quadratic model, 321
  structural model, 80–82

constraint, 283, *see also* equality restriction; inequality restriction; nonlinear constraints
contingency tables, 312
continuous updating, 246–248, 256, 275, 276
control variates, 266
convergence, 313
correlation matrix
  asymptotic variance, 224
covariance equations, 148
covariance preserving predictor, *see* predictor, covariance preserving
covariance structures, 201, 202, 220, 223, 232, 252–256, 273–276, 311, *see also* LISREL, covariance structure; LISCOMP, covariance structure
Cramér-Rao lower bound, 273
cumulants, 321, 342, 385
  fourth-order, 314
  higher order, 144

D

Davidon-Fletcher-Powell method, 182
deconvolution, 347
definite matrices, 356–358, 374
degrees of freedom, 117, 170, 289, 290, 292, 297, 304, 306, 308–310, 312, 313, 315, 369, 370, 378, 379, 385, 386
delta method, 69, 91, 239, 282, 336, 337, 370, 373, 374
diagonalization matrix, 303, 363–364, 374
dichotomous regressor, 145
differential equation, 75
direct oblimin, *see* oblimin
direct regression, 34, 218
discrepancy function, 273
discrete choice model, 344
discrimination, 36, 42, 56–57
distance function, 234–236, 273, 274, 337
distance metric (DM) test, 288
duplication matrix, 77, 254, 303, 362–363, 374
dynamic model, 8, *see also* panel data, dynamic

E

EFA, 160–161, 170, 171, 186, 207, 208, 211, 214, 316, 322
  on the correlation matrix, 214
efficiency, *see* GMM, asymptotic efficiency; optimal weighting; restricted estimator, efficiency
eigenvalue, 101, 102, 105, 106, 126, 151, 153–158, 162, 163, 170–172, 175–178, 182, 250, 276, 357–359, 376, 377, 379
eigenvector, 101, 102, 106, 153, 154, 157, 158, 162, 163, 177–178, 357
elementary regressions, 45, 219
ellipsoid bound, 48
  for β, 20–22
  for κ, 18–20
EM algorithm, 223
empirical characteristic function, 144
empirical likelihood, 275
Engel curves, 144, 191, 342
EQS, 202–204, 206–207, 212, 216, 223, 224, 274–276, 312, 313, 345, *see also* Bentler-Weeks model
equality restriction, 280, 283, *see also* constraint
  binding, 281
equivalent models, 218–222, 225
errors-in-variables, 11
estimating equations, 229–231, 273, 336, 337
estimating functions, 273
experimental data, 61
exploratory factor analysis, *see* EFA
exponential family, 76–78, 266–273

F

F-distribution, 312
F-statistic, 16
F-test, 16, 304, 312
FA, 8, 147–184, 195, 200, 201, 206, 207, 209, 232, 237, 256, 273, 324, 327, 331, 341, 342, 344, 345, *see also* CFA; EFA; measurement model; structural equation model
  categorical data, 345
  global identification, 183
  likelihood with fixed factors, 87
  local identification, 183
  maximum likelihood estimation, 151–155, 161–163, 182, 183
  multiple factors, 159–170
  nonlinear, 339
  number of factors, 170
  on the correlation matrix, 159
  one factor, 150–159, 182
  polynomial, 323, 343
  quadratic, 321–323
factor analysis, *see* FA
factor loadings, 150, 152–154, 160, 167–169, 171–173, 189, 195, 200, 208, 212, 213, 215, 232, 237, 327, 331, 341
factor score predictor, *see also* predictor
factor scores, 150, 158, 174
fairness, 57
feasible GLS, 119, 120
filter function, 317, 318
filter matrix, 203–206
fit, *see* model fit
fit index, *see* CFI; GFI; NFI; NTLI; RMSEA; RNI; TLI
fit indexes, 304–311, 313
fixed-x option, *see* LISREL, fixed x
Frisch-Waugh theorem, *see* theorem, Frisch-Waugh
functional model, 11, 60–65, 92, 93, 186
  consistent estimation, 80–82
  identification, 79
  likelihood, 64–65
  ML estimation, 70–73
  nonlinear, 347
  polynomial, 342
  versus structural model, 60–65

G

gamma distribution, 229, 267
Gaussian quadrature, 328
generalized inverse (g-inverse), *see* matrix, generalized inverse
generalized least squares, *see* GLS
generalized linear model, 344, 347
generalized method of moments, *see* GMM
GFI, 305, 315, 316
Gibbs sampler, 277, 344
global identification, 74
GLS, 255, 256, 273, 314
GMM, 227–277, 280, 287, 288, 296, 299, 304, 305, 309, 311, 312, 314, 315, 325, 327, 328, 343, 344, 385, *see also* minimum distance estimator
  asymptotic distribution, 238–239
  asymptotic efficiency, 241–242, 257–261, 266, 277, 301–303, 313, 314
  compared with ML, 230–231, 266–273, 277
  consistency, 237–238
  covariance matrix estimation, 243–252
  criterion function, 233, 237, 240, 245, 246, 248, 254–256, 266, 275, 276, 283, 287, 297–299, 305, 307, 337
  goodness of fit, *see* model fit
  iteratively reweighted, 246–248, 255, 256, 275
  linearized, *see* LGMM
  simulated, 262–266, 277, 328–329, 333, 340

small-sample properties, *see* small-sample properties of GMM estimator
two-step estimator, 246–248, 275
GMM bound, 262
goodness of fit, *see* model fit
gradient, 238
grouping, 131–135, 144

H

Hadamard product, 137, 364
Hausman test, 311
Hessian matrix, 238
heteroskedasticity, 107, 118–121, 143, 223, 225, 243, 249–252, 275, 283, 301, 303, 310, 313, 316
heteroskedasticity and autocorrelation consistent (HAC), 249–252, 275
Heywood case, 182, *see also* improper solution
homoskedasticity, 118–120, 142, 262, 283, 301, 304
hypothesis test, 275, 280–301, 310–313, *see also* chi-square difference test; LM test; measurement error, testing for; test of close fit; Wald test
conservativeness, 299, 312

I

ICOMP, 225
idempotency condition, 378
idempotent case, *see* chi-square distribution, idempotent case
idempotent matrix, 118, 177, 298, 359, 364, 369, 378, 379
identification, 74–88, *see also* just identification; overidentification; rotation
and consistent estimation, 80
in binary choice model, 326
in CFA, 189–191, 222, 289
in GMM, 237–238, 276, 277
nonlinear model, 319, 321–323, 342
structural model, 82–88
IDFAC, 191
IDLIS, 201
IGLS, 255, 256, 276
IGMM, *see* GMM, iteratively reweighted
imaginary variables, 224
implicit function theorem, 239, 293, 296, 336, 371, 373, 374
importance sampling, 265
improper solution, 313
incidental parameters, 12, 31, 80
inclusive form, 233, 236, 239, 245–246, 248, 266, 274, 298
inconsistency
of b, 12–15, 18, 115
of s_ε^2, 15
sign, 23–24
independence model, 305
indicator function, 268, 329
indicators, 150, 156, 159–161, 167, 168, 174, 182, 188, 189, 191, 192, 208, 212, 213, 215, 324, 325, 327, 341, 344, 345, *see also* product indicators
binary, 330, 335
indirect utility, *see* utility
individual effect, 138–141
inequality restriction, 311
inequality restrictions, 289, *see also* LISREL, inequality constraints
influence function, 56, 315
information criteria, 307–311, 316, *see also* AIC; CAIC; ICOMP; Kullback-Leibler information
information matrix, 66, 74–77, 79, 88, 201, 237, 270
information matrix criterion, 238
instrumental variables, *see* IV
interaction, 324–325, 343, 344, *see also* Kenny-Judd model
intercept, 214–216, 304, 319

interior point, 238, 239
intermediate parameters, 333–337
invariance under reparameterization, 292–295, 311, 312
inverse GLS, 256
iterative reweighting, *see* GMM, iteratively reweighted; IGLS
IV, 109–146, 148, 179, 181–182, 231, 261–262, 274, 344, *see also* 2SIV; 2SLS; conditional moments; JIVE; LIML; panel data model, IV estimation; SSIV; symmetrically normalized IV; weak instruments
    and factor analysis, 183
    and measurement error, 114–116
    consistency, 111
    correlated with error term, 58
    error variance estimation, 113
    in LISREL, 196–198
    inconsistency, 130
    nonlinear model, 347
    using nonnormality, 135–138

J

jackknife, 241, 243, 274
jackknife IV estimator, *see* JIVE
Jacobian matrix, 76–79, 86, 190
Jacobian matrix criterion, 76–78, 225, 238
JIVE, 144
just identification, 299

K

Kaiser normalization, 168
Kenny-Judd model, 324–325, 343, 344, *see also* interaction
kernel, 347
Kronecker product, 350, 374
    block, 374
Kullback-Leibler divergence, 315
Kullback-Leibler information, 309
kurtosis, 135, *see also* moments, fourth-order

L

lag truncation parameter, 250, 251, 275
Lagrange function, 104, 105, 126, 157, 176, 178, 283
Lagrange multiplier, 105, 157, 176, 178, 283, 284, 286
Lagrange multiplier test, *see* LM test
latent response variable, 329–332, 334, 338, 346
latent variable, on definition of, 4
law of large numbers, 237, 263
Ledermann bound, 169–170, 183
LGMM, 239–241, 274
likelihood ratio test, 286, 288, 311, *see also* chi-square difference test
limited information maximum likelihood, *see* LIML
limited-dependent variables, 266, 325–331, 346, *see also* Berkson model with limited-dependent variables; binary choice models; categorical variable; censored regression model; LISCOMP; logit model; ordered categorical variable; probit model; qualitative variables
LIML, 123–131, 143, 144, 179, 181–182, 184, 231, 273, *see also* IV; ML
    in LISREL, 198
LINCS, 224
linear regression vs. loglinear regression, 289, 311
linearized GMM, *see* LGMM
LISCOMP, 331–339, 342, 345–346
    covariance structure, 332, 338
    estimation, 332–339, 345
    extensions, 345
    intermediate parameters, 333–337
    program, 331

specification, 331–332
structural parameters, 333, 334, 337–338
LISREL, 194–207, 212, 216, 218, 220, 223, 275, 313, 314, 331, 338, 343, 345, *see also* structural equation model
covariance structure, 200–202
fixed x, 196, 198
inequality constraints, 224
mean structure, 216
polynomial constraints, 224
program, 182, 196, 202, 223
LM test, 241, 283–286, 288, 290–295, 306, 310, 311
local alternative, 291, 292, 306, 315
local identification, 74–76, 88, 225
logistic distribution, 326
logit model, 315, 327–329, 339, 340, 344, *see also* binary choice models; categorical variable; qualitative variables
loglinear model, *see* linear regression vs. loglinear regression
lognormal distribution, 228, 229, 243, 267
longitudinal data, 138
Löwner ordering, 112, 165, 241, 356
LR test, *see* chi-square difference test; likelihood ratio test

M

matrix
differentiation, 350, 374
expectation of random matrix, 350
generalized inverse, 117, 118, 254, 300, 344, 351–352, 356, 374, 378
Moore-Penrose inverse, 66, 178, 254, 351–352, 362
partitioned, 351, 368, 374
maximum likelihood, *see* ML
mean square prediction error, 309
mean structures, 215–217, 220, 225, 325
mean value theorem, 75, 239, 240, 272, 284, 291, 370, 372–374
measurement error
as IV model, 114–116
correlated with dependent variable, 57
correlated with true value, 30
grouping, 132–135
in a single regressor, 22–25, 31, 347
in the dependent variable, 25–27, 345
logit model, 327–329, 339
multiplicative, 31, 318
nonparametric regression, 347
polynomial model, 342–343
quadratic model, 320–321, 342
single regressor, 94–100
testing for, 116–118, 143
measurement model, 195, 200, 206, 215, 220, 329, 339, 344, *see also* FA
MECOSA, 224, 345
method of moments, *see* MM
method of simulated moments, 277, *see also* GMM, simulated
MFA, 159–170, 176, 186, 187, 189, 192, *see also* CFA; EFA; FA
MIMIC, 191–193, 196, 200, 223
minimum distance estimator, 232, 234, 274, 277, 312, 337
misclassification, 145
missing data, 217–218, 225
ML, 127, 149, 159, 198, 201, 229, 230, 233, 237, 255, 256, 276, 286, 309, 311, 313–315, 327, 330, 332, 345–347, 366, *see also* LIML; SML
compared with GMM, 230–231, 266–273, 277
pseudo, 334
MM, 228–231, 259, 260, 273, 275, 277, 299

model fit, 303–311, 315–316, *see also* fit indexes; chi-square test; R^2; RNI; TLI
model selection, 170, 303–311, 313, 315–316, *see also* AIC; CAIC
modification index, 304, 315
moment conditions, 137, 189, 207, 229–232, 237, 244, 261, 263, 270, 275–277, 296, 297, 299, 302, 303, 309, 327, 328, 339, 340, 342, 344
moment equations, 148, 149, *see also* moment conditions
moment structures, 214–215, 273, 276, *see also* covariance structures; mean structures
moments
  fourth-order, 136, 211, 214, 215, 253, 343, 344, *see also* kurtosis
  higher order, 78, 144, 183, 201, 214–215, 225, 321, 340, 342, 343
  third-order, 137, 225, 230, 276, 322, 343, *see also* skewness
Moore-Penrose inverse, *see* matrix, Moore-Penrose inverse
moving average, 251
M*plus*, 224, 345
multicollinearity, 343
multilevel model, 146
multinomial probit model, *see* probit model, multinomial
multiple factor analysis, *see* MFA
multiple groups, 216–218, 220, 225
multiple indicators multiple causes, *see* MIMIC
multiplicative measurement error, *see* measurement error, multiplicative
Mx, 204, 223, 295, 345

N
nearest neighbor, 277
NFI, 305–307, 315, 316
noise-to-signal ratio, 13, 31
noncentral chi-square distribution, *see* chi-square distribution, noncentral
noncentrality parameter, 292, 306, 307, 377, 379, 386
nonduplicated elements, 169, 232, 254, 303, 305, 374
nonidentification, 260, 289, 296, 311, 319
nonlinear constraints, 200, 210, 338, 343, *see also* equality restrictions; inequality restrictions
nonlinear latent variable model, 264, 266, 277, 317–347
nonlinear models, 107
nonlinear regression, 283, 339–342, 346–347
nonnested test, 289, 311
nonnormality, 135, 144
  and IV, 135–138
  in FA, 183, 302–303
  robustness to, 302–303
nonnormed fit index, 308, 316, *see also* TLI
nonoptimal weighting, 244, 245, 259, 260, 274, 285, 288, 290, 292, 299–301, 385, *see also* optimal weighting
nonparametric regression, 262, 277, 342, 347, *see also* series approximation
normal distribution, 364–369
  conditional, 134, 367–368
  Jacobian matrix criterion, 77–78
  loglikelihood, 364–366
  mean of quadratic form, 375
  variance of quadratic form, 376
  variance of sample variance, 366–367
normal equations, 353
normal-theory GLS, *see* GLS
normed fit index, *see* NFI

normed Tucker-Lewis index, *see* NTLI
NTLI, 308, 316
nuisance parameters, 258–259, 276
null model, 304–308

O

oblimin, 169, 172, 175, 184, 187, 213
oblique rotation, 168–169, 175
observational equivalence, 74, 75, 219, 237
OLS, 96, 115, 118, 119, 132, 135, 140, 141, 145, 179, 180, 301, 318, 320, 330, 342, 352
omitted variables bias, 24, 330
optimal weighting, 242, 243, 253, 255, 257, 259, 260, 264, 266, 267, 271, 274, 275, 285, 296, 298, 300, 325, 337, 344, 385, *see also* nonoptimal weighting
order condition, 77, 79
ordered categorical variable, 329, 331–339, 346
ordered probit, 329
ordinary least squares, *see* OLS
orthogonal complement, 376
orthogonal regression, 104–108, 179–180, 182, 347
  compared with weighted regression, 106
orthonormal matrix, 112, 167, 168, 178, 322, 323, 368
outliers, 315
overidentification, 299

P

panel data, 138–143, 145, 215, 224
  comparison of estimators, 140
  consistent estimation, 141–143
  dynamic, 199–200, 211, 231
  in LISREL, 198–200
  inconsistency, 140
  IV estimation, 143
parsimony, 160, 307–311, 315
partial likelihood, 334
path diagram, 150, 151, 182, 187, 188, 192, 207, 220–222
PCA, 156–159, 166, 170, 179–180, 182–183, 194, 207, 214
  on the correlation matrix, 214
permanent income, 193, 223
permutation matrix, 361
perturbation, 31
phantom variables, 224, 343
polychoric correlation, 346
polyhedral bounds, 55
polynomial factor analysis, *see* FA, polynomial
polynomial model, 319–325, *see also* measurement error, polynomial model
polynomial regression, 339, 342
polyserial correlation, 346
positive definite matrix, *see* definite matrices
prediction
  factor scores, 158, 163–166, 223
  in the normal structural model, 28
  with error variances known, 56
predictor
  Bartlett, 165, 166, 183
  correlation preserving, 184
  covariance preserving, 184
  factor scores, 155–156, 183
  quadratic, 183
  regression, 164, 165, 183
preference formation, 50
prewhitening, 275
principal component, 158, 159, 207
principal components analysis, *see* PCA
principal factors, 175–182, 184, 194
  maximum likelihood estimation, 176–178
principal relations, 175–182, 184, 194
  maximum likelihood estimation, 176–178, 180
privacy, 2
probit model, 329, 330, 339, 345, *see*

also binary choice models; categorical variable; LISCOMP; ordered categorical variable; qualitative variables
multinomial, 265, 345
omitted variables, 330, 345
PROC CALIS, 204, 224
product indicators, 343, 344
productivity, 36–39
projection matrix, 124, 369, 376
proxy variable, 10
omission, 24–25, 31
pseudo R^2, *see* R^2, pseudo
pseudo score, 233, 286

Q

quadratic factor analysis, *see* FA, quadratic
quadratic forms, 376–379
quadratic model, *see* measurement error, quadratic model
quadratic regression model, 343
qualitative variables, 266, 325–330, *see also* categorical variable
quasi-experimental data, 61

R

R^2, 15–16, 34, 150, 218, 304, 305, 307, 308
adjusted, 308
pseudo, 315
RAM, 204–207, 212, 216, 224, *see also* structural equation model
RAMONA, 224
random coefficients, 266, 290
random polynomial factor analysis, *see* FA, polynomial
rank condition, 77
reduced form, 123, 186, 192, 193, 200, 201, 212, 213, 332, 338
reduced rank regression, *see* RRR
reflection, 173, 323
regression predictor, *see* predictor, regression
regular point, 74–76
reliability, 13, 31, 344
reparameterization, 149, 189, 200, 213, *see also* invariance under reparameterization
repeated conditioning, 366, 374, 376
replication, 108, 146, 347
residual plots, 304
residual-based ADF test statistic, 300, 312
residual-based F-statistic, 312, 313
restricted estimator, 274, 280, 283, 287, 290, 294, 297, *see also* CALS
efficiency, 285
restricted factor analysis, 186
restriction, *see* equality restriction; inequality restriction
reticular action model, *see* RAM
reverse regression, 34–42, 56, 218, 219
RMSEA, 309, 316
RNI, 307, 310, 315, 316
robust statistics, 314, 315
robustness, 301–303, 313–315, 380–385
to misspecification, 230, 231, 244, 245
to model misspecification, 313
to nonnormality, 302–303
root mean square error of approximation, *see* RMSEA
root-N consistency, 240, 241
rotation, 167–169, 184, 194, 322, 323, *see also* oblimin; varimax
angle, 323
in CFA, 223
oblique, 168–169
RRR, 193–194, 196, 223

S

saddlepoint, 72
SAS PROC CALIS, *see* PROC CALIS
Satorra-Bentler adjusted test statistic, 312, 385

Satorra-Bentler scaled test statistic, 300, 301, 312, 385
saturated model, 219, 225, 296
scale invariance, 159, 208–214, 224
scaling, 159
 in structural equation model, 207–214
Schur complement, 351
score test, 286, 311, *see also* LM test
score vector, 233, 269, 270, *see also* pseudo score
scree plot, 170–172
SEM, *see* structural equation model
semiparametric regression, 342, 347
sensitivity analysis, 347
separated form, 233, 234, 236, 238, 244–248, 252, 262, 266, 273, 274, 283, 297, 305, 337, 339, 340
series approximation, 277, 319, 342
shrinkage, 165–166
signal-to-noise ratio, 31
simple structure, 167–168, 184
simulated GMM (SGMM), *see* GMM, simulated
simulated maximum likelihood, *see* SML
simulation study, 144, 275, 294, 313, 316
simultaneous equations model, 112, 123–124, 183, 195, 196, 206, 224
singular value decomposition, 157–158, 182
skewness, 135, *see also* moments, third-order
Slutsky's theorem, *see* theorem, Slutsky
small σ asymptotics, 344, 347
small-sample properties
 of GMM estimators, 248, 274–276, 313
 of tests, 292–295, 299, 300, 311, 313
SML, 328–329, 333
specification search, 315, *see also* model selection
specification test, *see* hypothesis test
spline transformation, 346
split-sample IV, *see* SSIV
SSIV, 144
standard errors, 210–211, 214, 275, 294, 295, 303, 313
standardized solution, 212–214, 224
step function, 346
structural equation model, 141, 185–225, 232, 252, 273, 287, 288, 295, 299, 300, 302–305, 309, 311, 313, 315, 316, 324, 325, 338, 343, 345, 346, *see also* CFA; FA; measurement model; MIMIC; simultaneous equations model
 for correlation matrix, 209–211, 224
 pitfalls, 224
 software, 207, 215, 223–224, 345
 structural model, 195, 200, 220, 331, 338
structural model, 11, 60–70, 92, 93, 107, 186
 consistent estimation, 80–82
 identification, 78, 82–88
 likelihood, 62–65
 ML estimation, 65–66
 ML under functional assumptions, 67–70
 nonlinear, 320
 two meanings, 186
 under normality, 27–29
 versus functional model, 60–65
structural parameters, 70, 76, 80, 81, 83
 in LISCOMP, 333, 334, 337–338
 in PF/PR, 184
 in simultaneous equations model, 123
sufficient statistic, 266–270, 273, 277, 315
SVD, *see* singular value decomposition

symmetrically normalized IV, 144
symmetrization matrix, 66, 69, 77, 92, 161, 254, 314, 361–362, 374

T

t-statistic, 98, 99
t-test, 16
t-value, 98–100, 310
target model, 296, 304–308, 310
test of close fit, 316
test of overidentifying restrictions, *see* chi-square test
test statistic, *see* chi-square difference test; chi-square statistic; chi-square test; LM test; residual-based ADF statistic; Satorra-Bentler adjusted test statistic; Satorra-Bentler scaled test statistic; Wald test; Yuan-Bentler residual-based test statistic
tetrachoric correlation, 346
theorem
  Bekker, 84, 88
  Frisch-Waugh, 41, 352–353, 374
  Gauss-Markov, 165
  Koopmans, 43, 57–58
  Perron-Frobenius, 57
  Reiersøl, 83, 88
  Rothenberg, 74
  Slutsky, 122, 128, 229, 239, 240, 272, 282, 285, 288, 298, 369–370, 373–375
threshold, 329, 331–337
time series, 61, 243, 249, 290, 309, *see also* autocorrelation; dynamic model
TLI, 308, 315, 316
Tobin's *q*, 95, 145
triangle inequality, 273
true score, 31
truncated variable, 334, 339, *see also* limited-dependent variables
Tucker-Lewis index, *see* TLI
TV network viewership, 171–175, 184, 186–190, 213
two-sample instrumental variables, *see* 2SIV
two-stage least squares, *see* 2SLS

U

ultrastructural model, 87
unique variance, 150
unit root, 211, 290
unit vector, 152, 377
utility, 326

V

varimax, 168, 172, 173, 184
vec operator, 349, 350, 374
  vecb operator, 374
violation of assumptions, 156, 301

W

wage discrimination, *see* discrimination
Wald test, 282, 288, 290–295, 306, 310, 311
weak instruments, 128–131, 144
weight matrix, 121, 232, 236, 241–244, 246–248, 253, 254, 259, 260, 266, 270, 271, 275, 276, 283, 287, 298, 337, 344
weighted least squares, *see* WLS
weighted regression, 101–103, 179, 180
  compared with orthogonal regression, 106
Wishart distribution, 368–369, 374
WLS, 275

Y

Yuan-Bentler residual-based test statistic, 312, 313

Z

Zellner model, 193, 223